Systems Analysis and Design

Systems Analysis and Design

An Object-Oriented Approach with UML

Seventh Edition

David P. Tegarden
Virginia Tech

Binny M. Samuel
University of Cincinnati

Roman Lukyanenko
University of Virginia

Alan R. Dennis
Indiana University

Barbara Haley Wixom
Massachusetts Institute of Technology

GROUP VP	Amanda Miller
EDITORIAL DIRECTOR	Justin Vaughan
EDITOR	Jennifer Manias
MARKETING MANAGER	Veronica Alvarez
MANAGING EDITOR	Pascal Raj Francois
PRODUCTION EDITOR	Dimple Philip
COVER PHOTO	© Solveig/stock.adobe.com

This book was set in 10/12 Minion pro by Straive.

Wiley is a global leader in research and education, unlocking human potential by enabling discovery, powering education, and shaping work-forces. For over 200 years, Wiley has fueled the world's knowledge ecosystem. Today, our high-impact content, platforms, and services help researchers, learners, institutions, and corporations achieve their goals in an ever-changing world. Visit us at Wiley.com.

The manufacturer's authorized representative according to the EU General Product Safety Regulation is Wiley-VCH GmbH, Boschstr. 12, 69469 Weinheim, Germany, e-mail: Product_Safety@wiley.com.

Readers should be aware that websites listed in this work may have changed or disappeared between when this work was written and when it is read. Neither the publisher nor authors shall be liable for any loss of profit or any other commercial damages, including but not limited to special, incidental, consequential, or other damages.

Evaluation copies are provided to qualified academics and professionals for review purposes only, for use in their courses during the next academic year. These copies are licensed and may not be sold or transferred to a third party. Upon completion of the review period, please return the evaluation copy to Wiley. Return instructions and a free of charge return shipping label are available at www.wiley.com/go/returnlabel. If you have chosen to adopt this textbook for use in your course, please accept this book as your complimentary desk copy. Outside of the United States, please contact your local representative.

Library of Congress Cataloging-in-Publication Data applied for

Print ISBN: 978-1-394-33176-5 (PAPERBACK)
Epub ISBN: 978-1-394-33172-7
Epdf ISBN: 978-1-394-33175-8

The inside back cover will contain printing identification and country of origin if omitted from this page. In addition, if the ISBN on the back cover differs from the ISBN on this page, the one on the back cover is correct.

 MWEP402666011025

PREFACE

PURPOSE OF THIS BOOK

Systems Analysis and Design (SAD) is an exciting, active field in which analysts continually learn new techniques and approaches to develop systems more effectively and efficiently. However, there is a core set of skills that all analysts need to know—no matter what approach or methodology is used. All information systems projects require analysts to gather requirements, model the business needs, and create blueprints for how the system should be built; and all projects require an understanding of organizational behavior concepts like change management and team building. Today, the cost of developing modern software is composed primarily of the cost associated with the developers themselves and not the computers.

Today, object-oriented approaches, which view a system as a collection of self-contained objects that have both data and processes, are the preferred approaches to SAD. This has occurred primarily to the adoption of the Unified Modeling Language (UML). UML provides a common vocabulary of object-oriented terms and diagramming techniques that is rich enough to model any systems development project from analysis through implementation.

This book captures the dynamic aspects of the field by keeping students focused on doing SAD while presenting the core set of skills that we feel every systems analyst needs to know today and in the future. This book also builds on our professional experience as systems analysts and on our experience in teaching SAD in the classroom.

This book will be of particular interest to instructors who have students do a major project as part of their course. Each chapter describes one part of the process, provides clear explanations on how to do it, gives a detailed example, and then has exercises for the students to practice. In this way, students can leave the course with experience that will form a rich foundation for further work as a systems analyst.

OUTSTANDING FEATURES

A Focus on Doing SAD

The goal of this book is to enable students to do SAD—not just read about it, but understand the issues so that they can actually analyze and design systems. The book introduces each major technique, explains what it is, explains how to do it, presents a set of running examples, and provides Your Turn opportunities through each chapter for students to practice each new technique before they do it for real in a project. After reading each chapter, the student will be able to perform that step in the system development process.

Rich Examples of Success and Failure

This book has a set of running examples including a library management system and a "Your Turn" exercise that deals with a campus housing system that aids students in finding an appropriate residence at college. Each chapter demonstrates how the chapter concepts are applied in situations in the examples. In this way, the examples can serve as a template that students can apply to their own work.

Real World Focus

The skills that students learn in a systems analysis and design course should mirror the work that they ultimately will do in real organizations. We have tried to make this book as "real" as possible by building extensively on our experience as professional systems analysts for organizations. Many students who use this book will eventually use the skills on the job in a business environment, and we believe they will have a competitive edge in understanding what successful practitioners feel is relevant in the real world.

Project Approach

We have presented the topics in this book in the order in which an analyst encounters them in a typical project. Although the presentation is necessarily linear (because students have to learn concepts in the way in which they build on each other), we emphasize the iterative, complex nature of SAD as the book unfolds. The presentation of the material should align well with courses that encourage students to work on projects because it presents topics as students need to apply them.

WHAT'S NEW IN THIS EDITION

- Throughout the book, a greater weight has been placed on developing information systems using an incremental and iterative approach. Also, we have put much more emphasis on verifying, validating, and testing.
- Based on the experience of using both the fifth and sixth edition in our classes, the book has gone through a reorganization. This includes streamlining the Analysis and Design sections to place greater emphasis on the engineering workflows of the Unified Process and the addition of a separate section that focuses on the managerial aspects of systems development with the supporting workflows of the Unified Process.
- Throughout the book, the library management system example has been greatly expanded. We have added many examples of the development team interacting with the library staff to better capture the requirements, develop the design, and to verify and validate everything. We also have converted the campus housing service example to an interactive Your Turn exercise where the students can practice developing solutions on a problem in which they are familiar. Suggested solutions to each Your Turn exercise are included with instructor's material.
- In Chapter 1: Introduction to Systems Analysis and Design, we streamline much of the historical material on systems development methodologies by removing the structured design, rapid application development and the extreme programming sections. We shrunk the coverage of the agile, DevOps and custom methodologies in this chapter. But we have added a new chapter (Chapter 13) that focuses on these newer approaches. Finally, we have added a new section that introduces the sequence, decision, and looping/repeating programming structures to the appendix.
- We have moved the Project Management chapter from Chapter 2 to Chapter 11.
- In Chapter 2: Business Modeling & Requirements Determination, we have added project identification and the system request to a new section that covers business

modeling. We have expanded the description on text analysis and added a new section on storytelling. Finally, we moved the agile based user stories from this chapter to the new chapter an agile development.

- In Chapter 3: Business Process and Functional Modeling, to improve the flow of material some minor reorganization was performed. We also, modified the approach we have taken to the use case descriptions that focused on using the alternate/exceptional flows instead of nested if statements in the normal flow of events.

- In Chapter 4: Structural Modeling, we added a small section on the use of common object lists, and we have added a section on using activity diagrams with swimlanes as a way to assign the activities to the responsibilities/operations of the structural model.

- In Chapter 5: Behavioral Modeling, we moved the section on activity diagrams back to the previous chapter, and explicitly tied the messages on the sequence diagrams back to the collaborators with the CRC cards.

- In Chapter 6: Moving on to Design, we moved the adding specifications, identifying opportunities for reuse, and restructuring the design sections of the object design activities in the Class and Method design chapter to this chapter.

- In Chapter 7: Class and Method Design, we moved the adding specifications, identifying opportunities for reuse, and restructuring the design sections of the object design activities to the previous chapter, and we expanded the coverage of constraints by splitting out the use of CRC cards and invariants and the use of contracts with pre- and post-conditions. To place greater emphasis on verification and validation, we moved and updated the software testing material from the old construction chapter to this chapter.

- In Chapter 8: Data Management Layer Design, we expanded the coverage of NoSQL data stores and we have added a new section on data distribution.

- In Chapter 9: Human-Computer Interaction Layer Design, we updated the use scenarios and real use cases to match the use cases in Chapter 3.

- In Chapter 10, we have added a section on peer-to-peer architectures and moved the cloud computing section into the Elements of the Application Architecture Layer section, and we have added a Level of Data Distribution section to the "Selecting an Application Architecture" section. We also moved the Green IT coverage to the Ethical Considerations section in Chapter 11.

- In Chapter 11: Project Management (the old Chapter 2), we did a very large reorganization by moving sections within the chapter around, moving some content to other chapters, and by bringing in content from other chapters. Specifically, we moved the agile content to the new chapter (Chapter 13) that deals with agile development, the content regarding the Environment and Infrastructure Management workflows and the Configuration and Change Management workflow to Chapter 12, and the Project Identification content to Chapter 2. We also brought in content on managing programming teams from the old Chapter 12 and project assessment from the old Chapter 13. This allows for the description of the project management workflow to be all in one place.

- Chapter 12: Other Unified Process Workflows brings together the non-project management managerial aspects of developing information systems in to a single place. The material came throughout the previous edition chapters and has been organized around the Environment and Infrastructure Management, Configuration and Change Management, Implementation, Deployment, and Operations and Support workflows.

- Chapter 13: Agile Methodologies and Modeling for Information Systems is a new chapter. It overviews agile approaches to information systems development.

ORGANIZATION OF THIS BOOK

This book is loosely organized around the phases and workflows of the enhanced Unified Process. Each chapter has been written to teach students specific tasks that analysts need to accomplish over the course of a project, and the deliverables that will be produced from the tasks. As students complete the chapters, they will realize the iterative and incremental nature of the tasks in object-oriented systems development.

Chapter 1 introduces the roles and skills needed for a systems analyst, SDLC, object-oriented systems analysis and design, the Unified Process, the UML, and the use of UML and the Unified Process as an agile development technique. The Chapter 1 appendix covers the basic characteristics of object-oriented systems.

Part One focuses on creating analysis models. Chapter 2 introduces students to business modeling including project identification creating a system request, an assortment of requirements analysis strategies and a variety of requirements-gathering techniques that are used to determine the functional and nonfunctional requirements of the system, and to the creation of a system proposal. Chapter 3 focuses on constructing business process and functional models using use-case diagrams, activity diagrams, and use-case descriptions. Chapter 4 addresses producing structural models using CRC cards, class diagrams, and object diagrams. It also uses covers the use of activity diagrams with swimlanes to document the results of role playing the CRC cards to assign the activities to the responsibilities. Chapter 5 tackles creating behavioral models using sequence diagrams, CRUDE analysis and matrices, and behavioral state machines. Chapters 3 through 5 also cover the verification and validation of the models described in each chapter.

Part Two addresses design modeling. In Chapter 6, students learn to evolve the analysis models into design models via the use of factoring, partitions, and layers and to use package diagrams to support the design models. The students also learn about the design criteria, some object design activities, and to create an alternative matrix that can be used to compare custom, packaged, and outsourcing alternatives. Chapter 7 concentrates on designing the individual classes and their respective methods. Specifically, the students learn about some optimization approaches, how to map the design to different types of implementation languages, how to model constraints using OCL, CRC cards, and contracts, to design methods with method specifications, and software testing is introduced. Chapter 8 presents the issues involved in designing persistence for objects. These issues include the different storage formats that can be used for object persistence, how to map an object-oriented design into the chosen storage format, and how to design a set of data access and manipulation classes that act as a translator between the classes in the application and the object persistence. This chapter also focuses on the nonfunctional requirements that impact the data management layer and the necessary verification and validation activities associate with the data management layer. The appendices to this chapter include how to optimize a relational data base management system and how to convert a class diagram to an entity-relationship diagram. Chapter 9 presents the design of the human–computer interaction layer, where students learn how to design user interfaces using use scenarios, windows navigation diagrams, storyboards, wireframe diagrams, user interface prototypes, real use cases, interface standards, and user interface templates; to perform user interface evaluations using heuristic evaluation, walkthrough evaluation, interactive evaluation, and formal usability testing; and to address nonfunctional requirements such as user interface layout, content awareness, aesthetics, user experience, and consistency. This chapter also addresses issues related to mobile computing, social media, games, multidimensional information visualizations, immersive environments, and international and cultural issues with regard to user interface design. Chapter 10 focuses on the application architecture and infrastructure design, which includes deployment diagrams and hardware/software specification. In today's world, this also includes issues related to cloud computing, ubiquitous computing, and the Internet of things. This chapter, like the previous design chapters, covers the impact that nonfunctional requirements can have on the application architecture layer and the required activities to verify and validate the design of the layer.

Part Three provides material that is related to supporting workflows of the Unified Process. Consequently, it focuses on the managerial aspects of information systems development. Chapter 11 presents topics related to the project management workflow of the Unified Process, including feasibility analysis, project selection, staffing the project, meeting management, team management, project assessment, traditional project management tools (including work breakdown structures, network diagrams, and PERT analysis), project effort estimation using use-case points, evolutionary work breakdown structures, and iterative workplans. Chapter 12 focuses on managerial issues related to the Environment and Infrastructure Management workflows, the Configuration and Change Management workflow, the Implementation workflow, the Deployment workflow, and the Operations and Support Workflow of the Unified Process.

Part Four focuses on future directions of SAD. Specifically, Chapter 13 overviews the agile approach to systems development. This includes coverage of the foundations of agile approaches, a set of common agile frameworks, effective agile practices and tools, agile modeling, and some limitations of the agile approaches.

SUPPLEMENTS

Systems Analysis and Design: An Object-Oriented Approach with UML, Seventh Edition is accompanied by a comprehensive set of instructor and student resources.

Instructor Book Companion Website

www.wiley.com/go/dennis/systemsanalysisuml7e

- **Instructor's Manual:** Provides resources to support the instructor both inside and out of the classroom. The manual includes short experiential exercises that instructors can use to help students experience and understand key topics in each chapter. Short stories have been provided by people working in both corporate and consulting environments for instructors to insert into lectures to make concepts more colorful and real. Additional minicases for every chapter allow students to perform some of the key concepts that were learned in the chapter. Solutions to the end of chapter questions and exercises are provided.
- **Test Bank:** Includes a variety of questions ranging from multiple-choice, true/false, and short answer questions. A *Computerized Test Bank*, powered by Respondus, is also available.
- **PowerPoint Presentations:** Slides highlight key figures from the text as well as many additional lecture outlines and concepts. These provide a versatile opportunity to add high-quality visual support to lectures.
- **Image Gallery:** Instructors can create slides and teaching visuals using the Image Gallery, a complete set of text figures and art included in the book.
- **Casebook:** A running case study about a fictitious company called Patterson Superstore that includes a small health care clinic. Each chapter of the case study demonstrates how the concepts are applied in situations at Patterson Superstore. In this way, the running case serves as a template that students can apply to their own work.

Student Book Companion Website

www.wiley.com/go/dennis/systemsanalysisuml7e/stu

- **Casebook:** A running case study about a fictitious company called Patterson Superstore that includes a small health care clinic. Each chapter of the case study demonstrates how the concepts are applied in situations at Patterson Superstore. In this way, the running case serves as a template that students can apply to their own work.
- **PowerPoint Presentations:** Slides highlight key figures from the text as well as many additional lecture outlines and concepts. These provide an additional study tool post lecture.

ACKNOWLEDGMENTS

We would like to thank the students who have taken ACIS 3515: Information Systems Development 1, ACIS 3516: Information Systems Development II, BIT 3514 Systems Analysis, and BIT 4524: Systems Development at Virginia Tech for giving many suggestions over the various editions that has driven most of the changes throughout the text. Also, we would like to acknowledge the conversations that we have had with Gerhard Fischer, Brian Henderson-Sellers, Clayton Lewis, and David Monarchi regarding object-oriented modeling over the years. We also would like to welcome Binny Samuel and Roman Lukyanenko onto the author team. We are looking forward to their insight into the development of future editions. Lastly, we would like to thank our dedicated team at Wiley.

CONTENTS

Chapter 3
Business Process and Functional Modeling   79

Chapter 4
Structural Modeling   117

Chapter 8
Data Management Layer Design 279

Appendices

Chapter 9
Human–Computer Interaction Layer Design 326

Chapter 10
Application Architecture Layer Design 380

■ PART THREE
SUPPORTING UNIFIED
PROCESS WORKFLOWS 419

Chapter 11
Project Management 420

Chapter 12
Finishing Touches: Final Unified Process Workflows 469

Chapter 13
Agile Methodologies and Modeling for Information Systems 502

CHAPTER 1

INTRODUCTION TO SYSTEMS ANALYSIS AND DESIGN

Chapter 1 introduces the *systems development life cycle (SDLC)*, the fundamental four-phase model (planning, analysis, design, and implementation) common to all information systems development projects. It describes the evolution of system development methodologies and discusses the roles and skills required of a systems analyst. The chapter then provides an overview of the basic characteristics of object-oriented systems and the fundamentals of object-oriented systems analysis and design. The chapter closes with a description of the Unified Process, and its extensions, and the Unified Modeling Language.

OBJECTIVES

- Be familiar with the different roles played by and the skills of a systems analyst.
- Understand the fundamental systems development life cycle.
- Understand the fundamental principles of modern systems development approaches.
- Be familiar with the agile, DevOps, and custom methodologies.
- Be familiar with the Unified Process, its extensions, and the Unified Modeling Language.
- Be familiar with how the Unified Process and the Unified Modeling Language can be used as an agile or DevOps methodology.
- Be familiar with the basic characteristics of object-oriented systems.

INTRODUCTION

We live in the age of digital information, ubiquitous computing, and mind-blowing artificial intelligence. One of the most rewarding careers of the modern age involves creating and managing information systems (IS) so people can accomplish their work, order groceries, take courses, travel to exotic destinations, vote in elections, capture life's special moments, and connect with family and friends. Yet, despite the growing reliance on IS and information technology (IT)—that is the knowledge and tools of building IS—IS projects continue to fail, causing losses, frustration, and hardship.

It is common to underestimate just how difficult it is to build successful information systems. If you have taken a programming class or have programmed on your own, building IS could sound simple. Just open a coding tool, ask ChatGPT for help, and post your app for people to use. Simple, right? Unfortunately, it is not. Building information systems involves not only coding, but also the considerations of how individuals and organizations will use these systems, and how these systems interact with other systems. Failure to consider not only the technical (e.g., the programming code), but also the psychological, managerial, legal, financial, ethical, environmental, and cultural complexities of IS can lead to costly and even deadly consequences.

The Standish Group found that 42 percent of all corporate IS projects were abandoned before completion, and a similar study conducted by the General Accounting Office found 53 percent of all U.S. government IS projects were scrapped. Unfortunately, many of the systems that are not abandoned are delivered to the users significantly late, cost far more than planned, and have fewer features than originally planned. As examples, IAG Consulting reports that 80 percent of the projects were over time, 72 percent were over budget, and 55 percent contained less than the promised functionality; Panorama Consulting Solutions reports that 54 percent of Enterprise Resource Planning (ERP) projects took longer than planned, 56 percent were over budget, and 48 percent delivered less than 50 percent of the initial benefits; and an IBM study reports that 59 percent of the projects missed one or more of on time, within budget, and quality constraints.[1] Clearly, in a world so dependent on IS we must do better. This is why we wrote this book.

Although we would like to promote this book as a silver bullet that will keep you from IS failures, we readily admit that a silver bullet that guarantees IS development success simply does not exist. Instead, this book provides you with several fundamental concepts and many practical techniques that you can use to increase the probability of success.

The key person in developing a system is the systems analyst, who analyzes the business situation, identifies opportunities for improvements, and designs an information system to implement them. Being a systems analyst is one of the most interesting, exciting, and challenging jobs around. Systems analysts work with a variety of people and learn how they conduct business. Specifically, they work with a team of systems analysts, programmers, and others on a common mission. Systems analysts feel the satisfaction of seeing systems that they designed and developed make a significant business impact, knowing that they contributed unique skills to make that happen.

However, the primary objective of a systems analyst is not to create a wonderful system; instead, it is to create value for the organization, which typically means increasing profits (government agencies and not-for-profit organizations measure value differently). Many failed systems have been abandoned because systems analysts tried to build a wonderful system without clearly understanding how it fits with an organization's goals, current business processes, and other information systems to provide value. An investment in an information system is like any other investment. The goal should never be to acquire a new tool because the tool is only a means to an end; the goal should be to enable the organization to perform work better so that it can earn greater profits or serve its constituents more effectively.

This book introduces the fundamental skills a systems analyst needs in a pragmatic manner as well as best practices for systems development. Systems analysts often follow a systems development life cycle (SDLC) as a roadmap for understanding how an IS can support business needs. This book does not present a general survey of systems development that covers everything about the topic. By definition, systems analysts do things and challenge the current way that organizations work. To get the most out of this book, you will need to actively apply its ideas and concepts to your own systems development project. This book guides you through all the steps for delivering a successful information system. By the time you finish the book, you won't be an expert analyst, but you will be ready to start building systems for real.

---

[1] For more information on the problem, see Capers Jones, *Patterns of Software System Failure and Success* (London: International Thompson Computer Press, 1996); Keith Ellis, *Business Analysis Benchmark: The Impact of Business Requirements on the Success of Technology Projects* (2008). Retrieved May 2014 from IAG Consulting, www.iag.biz; H. H. Jorgensen, L. Owen, and A. Neus, *Making Change Work* (2008). Retrieved May 2014 from IBM, www.ibm.com; Panorama Consulting Solutions, *2012 ERP Report* (2012). Retrieved May 2014 from Panorama-Consulting.com.

TYPICAL SYSTEMS ANALYST ROLES AND SKILLS

It is clear during systems development that the project team needs a variety of skills. Project members are *change agents* who identify ways to improve an organization, build an information system to support them, and train and motivate others to use the system. Understanding what to change and how to change it—and convincing others of the need for change—requires a wide range of skills. These skills can be broken down into six major categories: technical, business, analytical, interpersonal, management, and ethical.

Analysts must have the technical skills to understand the organization's existing technical environment, the technology that will make up the new system, and the way both can fit into an integrated technical solution. Business skills are required to understand how information technology (IT) can be applied to business situations and to ensure that the IT delivers real business value. Analysts are continuous problem solvers at both the project and the organizational level, and they put their analytical skills to the test regularly.

Analysts often need to communicate effectively one-on-one with users and business managers (who often have little experience with technology) and with programmers (who often have more technical expertise than the analyst). They must be able to give presentations to large and small groups and write reports. Not only do they need to have strong interpersonal abilities, but they also need to manage people with whom they work and they need to manage the pressure and risks associated with unclear situations.

Finally, analysts must deal fairly, honestly, and ethically with other project team members, managers, and system users. Analysts often deal with confidential information or information that, if shared with others, could cause harm (e.g., dissent among employees); it is important to maintain confidence and trust with all people.

In addition to these six general skill sets, analysts require many specific skills associated with roles performed on a project. In the early days of systems development, most organizations expected one person, the analyst, to have all the specific skills needed to conduct a systems development project. Some small organizations still expect one person to perform many roles, but because organizations and technology have become more complex, most large organizations now build project teams containing several individuals with clearly defined responsibilities. Different organizations divide the roles differently. Most IS teams include many other individuals, such as the *programmers*, who actually write the programs that make up the system, and *technical writers*, who prepare the help screens and other documentation (e.g., users manuals and systems manuals).

Business Analyst

A *business analyst* focuses on the business issues surrounding the system. These issues include identifying the business value that the system will create, developing ideas and suggestions for how the business processes can be improved, and designing the new processes and policies in conjunction with the systems analyst. This individual likely has business experience and some type of professional training. He or she represents the interests of the project sponsor and the ultimate users of the system. A business analyst assists in the planning and design phases but is most active in the analysis phase.

Systems Analyst

A *systems analyst* focuses on the intersection of the information, technology and business issues surrounding the information system (IS). This person develops ideas and suggestions for how information technology can improve business processes, designs the new business processes with help from the business analyst, designs the new information system, and ensures that all IS standards are maintained. A systems analyst likely has significant training and experience in analysis and design, programming, and even areas of the business. He or she represents the interests of the IS department and works intensively through the project but perhaps less so during the implementation phase.

Infrastructure Analyst

An *infrastructure analyst* focuses on the technical issues surrounding how the system will interact with the organization's technical infrastructure (e.g., hardware, software, networks, and databases). An infrastructure analyst's tasks include ensuring that the new information system conforms to organizational standards and identifying infrastructure changes needed to support the system. This individual probably has significant training and experience in networking, database administration, and various hardware and software products. He or she represents the interests of the organization and IS group that will ultimately have to operate and support the new system once it has been installed. An infrastructure analyst works throughout the project but perhaps less so during planning and analysis phases.

Change Management Analyst

A *change management analyst* focuses on the people and management issues surrounding the system installation. The roles of this person include ensuring that the adequate documentation and support are available to users, providing user training on the new system, and developing strategies to overcome resistance to change. This individual should have significant training and experience in organizational behavior in general and change management in particular. He or she represents the interests of the project sponsor and users for whom the system is being designed. A change management analyst works most actively during the implementation phase but begins laying the groundwork for change during the analysis and design phases.

Project Manager

A *project manager* is responsible for ensuring that the project is completed on time and within budget and that the system delivers all benefits intended by the project sponsor. The role of the project manager includes managing the team members, developing the project plan, assigning resources, and being the primary point of contact when people outside the team have questions about the project. This individual likely has significant experience in project management and has probably worked for many years as a systems analyst beforehand. He or she represents the interests of the IS department and the project sponsor. The project manager works intensely during all phases of the project.

THE SYSTEMS DEVELOPMENT LIFE CYCLE

In many ways, building an information system is similar to building a house. First, the house (or the information system) starts with a basic idea. Second, this idea is transformed into a simple drawing that is shown to the customer and refined (often through several drawings, each improving on the last) until the customer agrees that the picture depicts what he or she wants. Third, a set of blueprints is designed that presents much more detailed information about the house (e.g., the type of water faucets or where the telephone jacks will be placed). Finally, the house is built following the blueprints, often with some changes directed by the customer as the house is erected.

The systems development life cycle (SDLC) is a popular roadmap for understanding how an IS can support organizational or personal needs by designing a system, building it, and delivering it to users. The SDLC has a similar set of four fundamental *phases* to those of constructing a house: planning, analysis, design, and implementation. Different projects might emphasize different parts of the SDLC or approach the SDLC phases in different ways, but all projects have elements of these four phases. Each *phase* is itself composed of a series of *steps*, which rely upon *techniques* that produce *deliverables* (specific documents and files that provide understanding about the project).

For example, in applying for admission to a university, all students go through the same phases: information gathering, applying, and accepting. Each of these phases has steps; for example, information gathering includes steps such as searching for schools, requesting information, and reading brochures. Students then use techniques (e.g., Internet searching) that can be applied to steps (e.g., requesting information) to create *deliverables* (e.g., lists of pros and cons of different universities).

In many projects, the SDLC phases and steps proceed in a logical path from start to finish. In other projects, the project teams move through the steps consecutively, incrementally, iteratively, or in other patterns. In this section, we describe the phases, the actions, and some of the techniques that are used to accomplish the steps at a very high level.

For now, there are two important points to understand about the SDLC. First, you should get a general sense of the phases and steps through which IS projects move and some of the techniques that produce certain deliverables. Second, it is important to understand that the SDLC is a process of *gradual refinement*. The deliverables produced in the analysis phase provide a general idea of the shape of the new system. These deliverables are used as input to the design phase, which then refines them to produce a set of deliverables that describes in much more detailed terms exactly how the system will be built. These deliverables, in turn, are used in the implementation phase to produce the actual system. Each phase refines and elaborates on the work done previously.

Planning

The *planning phase* is the fundamental process of understanding why an information system should be built and determining how the project team will go about building it. It has two elements:

1. During *project initiation*, the system's business value to the organization is identified: How will it lower costs or increase revenues? Most ideas for new systems come from outside the IS area (e.g., from the marketing department and accounting department) in the form of a *system request*. A system request presents a brief summary of a business need, and it explains how a system that supports the need will create business value. The IS department works together with the person or department that generated the request (called the *project sponsor*) to conduct a *feasibility analysis*.

   The system request and feasibility analysis are presented to an information systems *approval committee* (sometimes called a steering committee), which decides whether the project should be undertaken.

2. Once the project is approved, it enters *project management*. During project management, the *project manager* creates a *workplan*, staffs the project, and puts techniques in place to help the project team control and direct the project through the entire SDLC. The deliverable for project management is a *project plan*, which describes how the project team will go about developing the system.

Analysis

The *analysis phase* answers the questions of who will use the system, what the system will do, and where and when it will be used. During this phase, the project team investigates any current system(s), identifies opportunities for improvement, and develops a concept for the new system.

This phase has three steps:

1. An *analysis strategy* is developed to guide the project team's efforts. Such a strategy usually includes an analysis of the current system (called the *as-is system*) and its problems and then ways to design a new system (called the *to-be system*).

2. The next step is *requirements gathering* (e.g., through interviews or questionnaires). The analysis of this information—in conjunction with input from the project sponsor and many other people—leads to the development of a concept for a new system. The system concept is then used as a basis to develop a set of business *analysis models*, which describe how the business will operate if the new system is developed.

3. The analyses, system concept, and models are combined into a document called the *system proposal*, which is presented to the project sponsor and other key decision makers (e.g., members of the approval committee) who decide whether the project should continue to move forward.

The system proposal is the initial deliverable that describes what business requirements the new system should meet. Because it is really the first step in the design of the new system, some experts argue that it is inappropriate to use the term "analysis" as the name for this phase; some argue a better name would be "analysis and initial design." Most organizations continue to use the name analysis for this phase, however, so we use it in this book as well. Just keep in mind that the deliverable from the analysis phase is both an analysis and a high-level initial design for the new system.

Design

The *design phase* decides how the system will operate, in terms of the hardware, software, and network infrastructure; the user interface, forms, and reports; and the specific programs, databases, and files that will be needed. Although most of the strategic decisions about the system were made in the development of the system concept during the analysis phase, the steps in the design phase determine exactly how the system will operate. The design phase has four components:

1. The *design strategy* is first developed. It clarifies whether the system will be developed by the company's own programmers, whether the system will be outsourced to another firm (usually a consulting firm), or whether the company will buy an existing software package.

2. This leads to the development of the basic *architecture design* for the system, which describes the hardware, software, and network infrastructure to be used. In most cases, the system will add or change the infrastructure that already exists in the organization. The *interface design* specifies how the users will move through the system (e.g., navigation methods such as menus and on-screen buttons) and the forms and reports that the system will use.

3. The *database and file specifications* are developed. These define exactly what data will be stored, how they will be stored (the type of database technology and the specification of database structures), and where they will be stored.

4. The analyst team develops the *program design*, which defines the modules or components that need to be written and exactly what each program will do.

This collection of deliverables (architecture design, interface design, database and file specifications, and program design) is the *system specification* that is handed to the programming team for implementation. At the end of the design phase, the feasibility analysis and project plan are reexamined and revised, and another decision is made by the project sponsor and approval committee about whether to terminate the project or continue.

Implementation

The final phase in the SDLC is the *implementation phase*, during which the system is actually built (or purchased, in the case of a packaged software). This is the phase that usually gets the most attention, because for most systems it is the longest and most expensive single part of the development process. This phase has three steps:

1. System *construction* is the first step. The system is built and tested to ensure that it performs as designed. Because the cost of bugs can be immense, testing is one of the most critical steps in implementation. Most organizations give more time and attention to testing than to writing the programs in the first place.

2. The system is installed. *Installation* is the process by which the old system is turned off and the new one is turned on. One of the most important aspects of conversion is the development of a *training plan* to teach users how to use the new system and help manage the changes caused by the new system.

3. The analyst team establishes a *support plan* for the system. This plan usually includes a formal or informal post-implementation review, a systematic way for identifying major and minor changes needed for the system, as well as ongoing maintenance that may be needed (software patches and updates).

SYSTEMS DEVELOPMENT METHODOLOGIES

A *methodology* is a formalized approach to implementing the SDLC (i.e., it is a list of steps and deliverables). There are many different systems development methodologies, and each one is unique, based on the order and focus it places on each SDLC phase. Some methodologies are formal standards used by government agencies, whereas others have been developed by consulting firms to sell to clients. Many organizations have internal methodologies that have been honed over the years, and they explain exactly how each phase of the SDLC is to be performed in that company.

There are many ways to categorize methodologies. One way is by looking at whether they focus on business processes or the data that support the business. A *process-centered methodology* emphasizes process models as the core of the system concept. In Figure 1-1, for example, process-centered methodologies would focus first on defining the processes (e.g., assemble sandwich ingredients). *Data-centered methodologies* emphasize data models as the core of the system concept. In Figure 1-1, data-centered methodologies would focus first on defining the contents of the storage areas (e.g., refrigerator) and how the contents were organized.[2] By contrast, *object-oriented methodologies* attempt to balance the focus between process and data by incorporating both into one model. In Figure 1-1, these methodologies would focus first on defining the major elements of the system (e.g., sandwiches and lunches) and look at the processes and data involved with each element.

---

[2] The classic modern process-centered methodology is that by Edward Yourdon, *Modern Structured Analysis* (Englewood Cliffs, NJ: Yourdon Press, 1989). An example of a data-centered methodology is information engineering; see James Martin, *Information Engineering*, vols. 1–3 (Englewood Cliffs, NJ: Prentice Hall, 1989). A widely accepted standardized non–object-oriented methodology that balances processes and data is IDEF; see FIPS 183, *Integration Definition for Function Modeling*, Federal Information Processing Standards Publications, U.S. Department of Commerce, 1993.

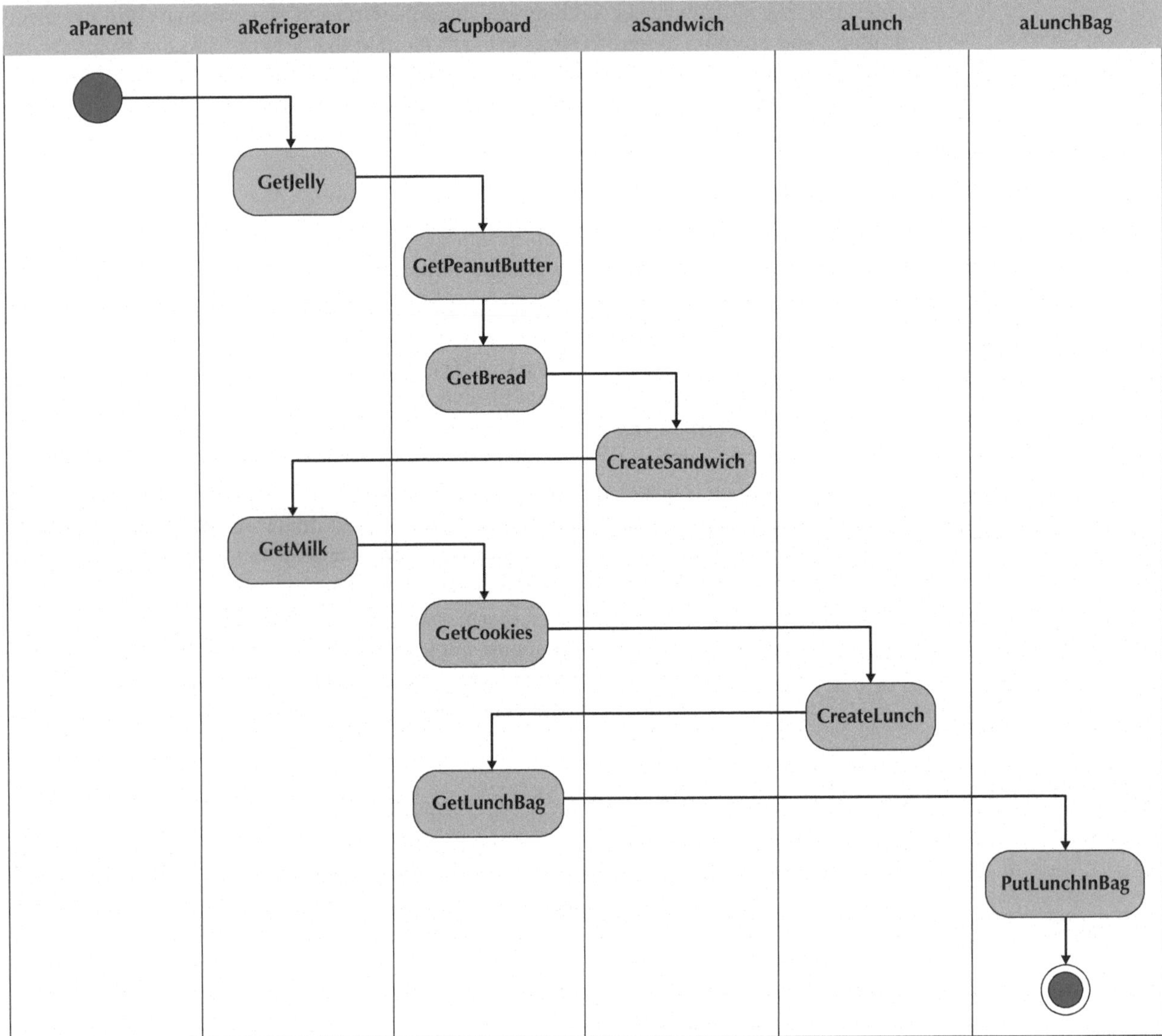

FIGURE 1-1   A Simple Behavioral Model for Making a Simple Lunch

Another important factor in categorizing methodologies is the sequencing of the SDLC phases and the amount of time and effort devoted to each.[3] In the early days of computing, programmers did not understand the need for formal and well-planned life-cycle methodologies. They tended to move directly from a very simple planning phase right into the construction step of the implementation phase—in other words, from a very fuzzy, not-well-thought-out system request into writing code. This is the same approach that you sometimes use when writing programs for a programming class. It can work for small programs that require only one programmer, but if the requirements are complex or unclear, you might miss important aspects of the problem and have to start all over again, throwing away part of

[3] A good reference for comparing systems development methodologies is Steve McConnell, *Rapid Development* (Redmond, WA: Microsoft Press, 1996).

the program (and the time and effort spent writing it). This approach also makes teamwork difficult because members have little idea about what needs to be accomplished and how to work together to produce a final product. In this section, we describe a set of modern system development methodologies: object-oriented, agile, DevOps, and custom.

Object-Oriented Systems Analysis and Design (OOSAD)

Object-oriented approaches balance the emphasis between the *functional, structural,* and *behavioral views* of a system by using a decomposition of problems perspective on objects that contain both data and processes. According to the creators of the Unified Modeling Language (UML) and the Unified Process (UP), Grady Booch, Ivar Jacobson, and James Rumbaugh,[4] any modern approach to developing information systems must be use-case driven, architecture-centric, and iterative and incremental.

Use-Case Driven *Use-case driven* means that *use cases* are the primary modeling tools defining the behavior of the system. A use case describes how the user interacts with the system to perform some activity, such as placing an order, making a reservation, or searching for information. The use cases are used to identify and to communicate the requirements for the system to the programmers who must write the system. Use cases are inherently simple because they focus on only one business process at a time. In contrast, the process model diagrams used by traditional structured and RAD methodologies are far more complex because they require the systems analyst and user to develop models of the entire system. With traditional methodologies, each system is decomposed into a set of subsystems, which are, in turn, decomposed into further subsystems, and so on. This goes on until no further process decomposition makes sense, and it often requires dozens of pages of interlocking diagrams. In contrast, a use case focuses on only one business process at a time, so developing models is much simpler.[5]

Architecture-Centric Any modern approach to systems analysis and design should be architecture-centric. *Architecture-centric* means that the underlying software architecture of the evolving system specification drives the specification, construction, and documentation of the system. Modern object-oriented systems analysis and design approaches should support at least three separate but interrelated architectural views of a system: functional, structural, and behavioral. The *functional,* or *external, view* describes the behavior of the system from the perspective of the user. The *structural,* or *static, view* describes the system in terms of attributes, methods, classes, and relationships. The *behavioral,* or *dynamic, view* describes the behavior of the system in terms of messages passed among objects and state changes within an object.

Iterative and Incremental Modern object-oriented systems analysis and design approaches emphasize *iterative* and *incremental* development that undergoes continuous testing and refinement throughout the life of the project. This implies that the systems analysts develop their understanding of a user's problem by building up the three architectural views little by little. The systems analyst does this by working with the user to create a functional representation of the system under study. Next, the analyst attempts to build a structural representation

---

[4] Grady Booch, Ivar Jacobson, and James Rumbaugh, *The Unified Modeling Language User Guide* (Reading, MA: Addison-Wesley, 1999); Ivar Jacobson, Grady Booch, and James Rumbaugh, *The Unified Software Development Process* (Reading, MA: Addison-Wesley, 1999).

[5] For those of you who have experience with traditional structured analysis and design, this is one of the most unusual aspects of object-oriented analysis and design using UML. Unlike structured approaches, object-oriented approaches stress focusing on just one use case at a time and distributing that single use case over a set of collaborating objects.

of the evolving system. Using the structural representation of the system, the analyst distributes the functionality of the system over the evolving structure to create a behavioral representation of the evolving system. As an analyst works with the user in developing the three architectural views of the evolving system, the analyst iterates over each of and among the views. That is, as the analyst better understands the structural and behavioral views, the analyst uncovers missing requirements or misrepresentations in the *functional view*. This, in turn, can cause changes to be cascaded back through the structural and behavioral views. All three architectural views of the system are interlinked and dependent on each other (see Figure 1-2). As each increment and iteration is completed, a more-complete representation of the user's real functional requirements is uncovered.

Benefits of Object-Oriented Systems Analysis and Design Concepts in the object-oriented approach enable analysts to break a complex system into smaller, more-manageable modules, work on the modules individually, and easily piece the modules back together to form an information system. This modularity makes systems development easier to grasp, easier to share among members of a project team, and easier to communicate to users, who are needed to provide requirements and confirm how well the system meets the requirements throughout the systems development process. By modularizing systems development, the project team actually is creating reusable pieces that can be plugged into other systems efforts or used as starting points for other projects. Ultimately, this can save time because new projects don't have to start completely from scratch.

Agile

Agile development methodologies are based on the agile manifesto.[6] The emphasis of the manifesto is to focus the developers on the working conditions of the developers, the working software, the customers, and addressing changing requirements instead of focusing on detailed systems development processes, tools, all-inclusive documentation, legal contracts, and detailed plans. Agile approaches urge developers to follow the KISS principle.[7] Projects emphasize simple, iterative application development.[8] We discuss this methodology more in Chapter 13.

FIGURE 1-2
Object-Oriented
Iterative and
Incremental
Development

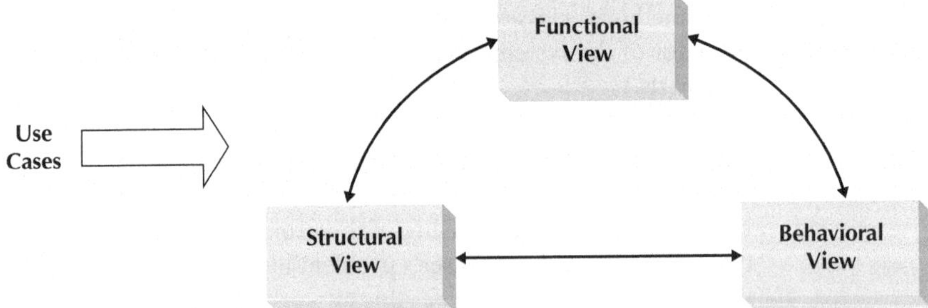

---

[6] Three good sources of information on agile development and object-oriented systems are, S. W. Ambler, *Agile Modeling: Effective Practices for Extreme Programming and the Unified Process* (New York, NY: Wiley, 2002); C. Larman, *Agile & Iterative Development: A Manager's Guide* (Boston: Addison-Wesley, 2004); R. C. Martin, *Agile Software Development: Principles, Patterns, and Practices* (Upper Saddle River, NJ: Prentice Hall, 2003).

[7] Keep it simple, stupid.

[8] See Agile Alliance, www.agilealliance.com.

While the idea of being agile is attractive to many organizations, the agile methodology is not without criticism. One of the major criticisms deals with today's business environment, where much of the actual information systems development is offshored, outsourced, and/or subcontracted. Given agile development methodologies requiring co-location of the development team, this seems to be a very unrealistic assumption. A second major criticism is that if agile development is not carefully managed, and by definition it is not, the development process can devolve into a prototyping approach that essentially becomes a "programmers gone wild" environment where programmers attempt to hack together solutions. A third major criticism, based on the lack of actual documentation created during the development of the software, raises issues regarding the auditability of the systems being created. Without sufficient documentation, neither the system nor the systems-development process can be assured. A fourth major criticism is based on whether agile approaches can deliver large mission-critical systems.

DevOps

Another category of systems development methodologies is DevOps.[9] *DevOps* approaches incorporate ideas from both object-oriented approaches to systems development and lean manufacturing into the agile approaches. The primary extensions that DevOps approaches support are the inclusion of operations personnel with the development team and continuous deployment.

In earlier approaches, end users were identified as very important stakeholders that should be included in the development team. However, increasing the developers realize that including end users, even though necessary, is not sufficient to deliver high quality systems. For example, with cloud technologies concerns related to deployment of the system should be addressed before the development team "throws the system over the wall" to the operations personnel. Consequently, DevOps approaches include operations personnel as members of the development team. In this way, non-functional requirements, such as maintenance and security, can be addressed during the design of the system to be deployed.

With both object-oriented and agile approaches, deployment was only performed after a version of the system was completed. In other words, the operations personnel took over the system and deployed it. With DevOps approaches, deployment is completed when a new chunk of software has passed a set of relevant tests. Consequently, deployment of a new version of the system is not performed all at once. Instead, the new version is deployed in pieces over time; this is also referred to as a rolling upgrade. This approach requires quite a bit of automation of the actual deployment pipeline.[10]

Custom Methodologies

This last category of systems development methodologies supports the idea of applying both agile and object-oriented ideas to the system development methodology itself. The idea behind these approaches is to support the development team in a way that is customized to their specific systems development project. In this case, only a high-level framework is used to create the project specific method. Two of the approaches that have made progress in this

---

[9] For more information, see Gene Kim, Jez Humble, Patrick Debois, and John Willis, *The DevOps Handbook: How to Create World-Class Agility, Reliability, & Security in Technology Organizations* (Portland, OR: IT Revolution Press, 2016); Nicole Forsgren, Jex Humble, and Gene Kim, *The Science Behind* DevOps, *Accelerate: Building and Scaling High Performing Technology Organizations* (Portland, OR: IT Revolution Press, 2018).

[10] A good overview of these approaches is described in Len Bass, Ingo Weber, and Liming Zhu, *DevOps: A Software Architect's Perspective* (Upper Saddle River, NJ: Pearson Education, 2015).

area are based on the work of Brian Henderson-Sellers[11] and of Ivar Jacobson.[12] Both of these groups allow the team to pick and choose different components of a methodology from a component repository to create a custom methodology. Care must be taken to ensure that each component is plug compatible. By that we mean, the inputs into a component are compatible with the outputs of the preceding component in the methodology.

THE UNIFIED PROCESS

The Unified Process is a specific methodology that maps out when and how to use the various Unified Modeling Language (UML) techniques for object-oriented analysis and design. The primary contributors were Grady Booch, Ivar Jacobsen, and James Rumbaugh. Whereas the UML provides structural support for developing the structure and behavior of an information system, the Unified Process provides the behavioral support. The Unified Process, of course, is use-case driven, architecture-centric, and iterative and incremental. Furthermore, the Unified Process is a two-dimensional systems development process described by a set of phases and workflows. The phases are inception, elaboration, construction, and transition. The workflows include business modeling, requirements, analysis, design, implementation, test, deployment, configuration and change management, project management, and environment.[13] Figure 1-3 depicts the Unified Process.

Phases

The phases of the Unified Process support an analyst in developing information systems in an iterative and incremental manner. The phases describe how an information system evolves through time. Depending on which development phase the evolving system is currently in, the level of activity varies over the *workflows*. The curve in Figure 1-3 associated with each workflow approximates the amount of activity that takes place during the specific phase. For example, the inception phase primarily involves the business modeling and requirements workflows, while practically ignoring the test and deployment workflows. Each phase contains a set of iterations, and each iteration uses the various workflows to create an incremental version of the evolving system. As the system evolves through the phases, it improves and becomes more complete. Each phase has objectives, a focus of activity over the workflows, and incremental deliverables. Each of the phases is described next.

---

[11] For more information, see Ian Graham, Brian Henderson-Sellers, and Houman Younessi, *The OPEN Process Specification* (New York, NY: ACM Press, 1997); Brian Henderson-Sellers, Anthony Simons, and Houman Younessi, *The OPEN Toolbox of Techniques* (New York, NY: ACM Press, 1998); Donald G. Firesmith and Brian Henderson-Sellers, *The OPEN Process Framework* (London: Addison-Wesley, 2002); Brian Henderson-Seller, Jolita Ralyte, Par J. Agerfalk, and Matti Rossi, *Situational Method Engineering* (Berlin: Springer, 2014).

[12] For more information, see Ivar Jaconson, Pan-Wei Ng, Paul E. McMahon, Ian Spence, and Svante Lidman, *The ESSENCE of Software Engineering: Applying the SEMAT Kernel* (Upper Saddle River, NJ: Addison-Wesley, 2013); Ivar Jacobson, Harold, "Bud" Lawson, Pan-Wei Ng, Paul E. McMahon, Michael Goedicke, *The Essentials of Modern Software Engineering: Free the Practices from the Method Prisons!* (ACM Books, 2019).

[13] The material in this section is based on Khawar Zaman Ahmed and Cary E. Umrysh, *Developing Enterprise Java Applications with J2EE and UML* (Boston, MA: Addison-Wesley, 2002); Jim Arlow and Ila Neustadt, *UML and The Unified Process: Practical Object-Oriented Analysis & Design* (Boston, MA: Addison-Wesley, 2002); Peter Eeles, Kelli Houston, and Wojtek Kozacynski, *Building J2EE Applications with the Rational Unified Process* (Boston, MA: Addison-Wesley, 2003); Ivar Jacobson, Grady Booch, and James Rumbaugh, *The Unified Software Development Process* (Reading, MA: Addison-Wesley, 1999); Phillipe Krutchten, *The Rational Unified Process: An Introduction*, 2nd Ed. (Boston, MA: Addison-Wesley, 2000); "Rational Unified Process: Best Practices for Software Development Teams," Rational Software White Paper, TP026B, Rev 11/01.

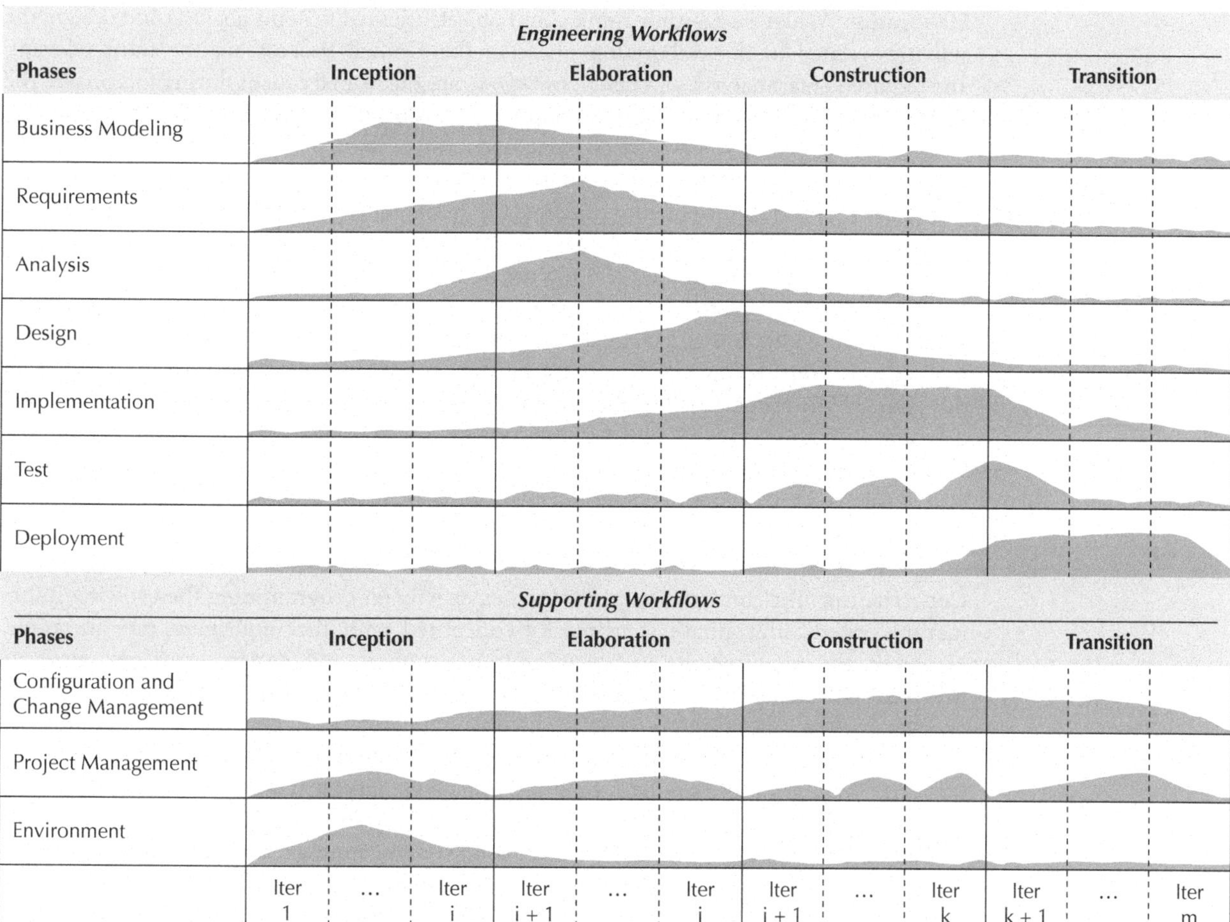

FIGURE 1-3 The Unified Process

Inception In many ways, the *inception phase* is very similar to the planning phase of a traditional SDLC approach. In this phase, a business case is made for the proposed system. This includes feasibility analysis that should answer questions such as the following:

Do we have the technical capability to build it (technical feasibility)?

If we build it, will it provide business value (economic feasibility)?

If we build it, will it be used by the organization (organizational feasibility)?

To answer these questions, the development team performs work related primarily to the business modeling, requirements, and analysis workflows. In some cases, depending on the technical difficulties that could be encountered during the development of the system, a throwaway prototype is developed. This implies that the design, implementation, and test workflows could also be involved. The project management and environment supporting workflows are very relevant to this phase. The primary deliverables from the inception phase are a vision document that sets the scope of the project; identifies the primary requirements and constraints; sets up an initial project plan; and describes the feasibility of and risks associated with the project, the adoption of the necessary environment to develop the system, and some aspects of the problem domain classes being implemented and tested.

Elaboration When we typically think about object-oriented systems analysis and design, the activities related to the elaboration phase of the Unified Process are the most relevant. The requirements, analysis, and *design workflows* are the primary focus during this phase. The elaboration phase continues with developing the vision document, including finalizing the business case, revising the risk assessment, and completing a project plan in sufficient detail to allow the stakeholders to be able to agree with constructing the actual final system. It deals with gathering the requirements, building the UML functional, structural, and behavioral models of the problem domain, and detailing how the problem domain models fit into the evolving system architecture. Developers are involved with all but the deployment engineering workflow in this phase. As the developers iterate over the workflows, the importance of addressing configuration and change management becomes apparent. Also, the development tools acquired during the inception phase become critical to the success of the project during this phase.[14] The primary deliverables of this phase include the UML structure and behavioral diagrams and an executable of a baseline version of the evolving information system. The baseline version serves as the foundation for all later iterations. By providing a solid foundation at this point, the developers have a basis for completing the system in the construction and transition phases.

Construction The *construction phase* focuses heavily on programming the evolving information system. This phase is primarily concerned with the *implementation workflow*. However, the *requirements workflow* and the *analysis* and *design* workflows also are involved with this phase. It is during this phase that missing requirements are identified and the analysis and design models are finally completed. Typically, there are iterations of the workflows during this phase, and during the last iteration, the deployment workflow kicks into high gear. The *configuration and change management workflow*, with its version-control activities, becomes extremely important during the construction phase. At times, an iteration has to be rolled back. Without good version controls, rolling back to a previous version (incremental implementation) of the system is nearly impossible. The primary deliverable of this phase is an implementation of the system that can be released for beta and acceptance testing.

Transition Like the construction phase, the *transition phase* addresses aspects typically associated with the implementation phase of a traditional SDLC approach. Its primary focus is on the testing and deployment workflows. Essentially, the business modeling, requirements, and analysis workflows should have been completed in earlier iterations of the evolving information system. Furthermore, the testing workflow will have been executing during the earlier phases of the evolving system. Depending on the results from the testing workflow, some redesign and programming activities on the design and implementation workflows could be necessary, but they should be minimal at this point. From a managerial perspective, the project management, configuration and change management, and environment are involved. Some of the activities that take place are beta and acceptance testing, fine-tuning the design and implementation, user training, and rolling out the final product onto a production platform. Obviously, the primary deliverable is the actual executable information system. The other deliverables include user manuals, a plan to support the users, and a plan for upgrading the information system in the future.

---

[14] With UML comprising fifteen different, related diagramming techniques, keeping the diagrams coordinated and the different versions of the evolving system synchronized is typically beyond the capabilities of a mere mortal systems developer. These tools typically include project management and CASE tools.

Workflows

The workflows describe the tasks or activities that a developer performs to evolve an information system over time. The workflows of the Unified Process are grouped into two broad categories: engineering and supporting.

Engineering Workflows *Engineering workflows* include business-modeling, requirements, analysis, design, implementation, test, and deployment workflows. The engineering workflows deal with the activities that produce the technical product (i.e., the information system).

Business Modeling Workflow The *business-modeling workflow* uncovers problems and identifies potential projects within a user organization. This workflow aids management in understanding the scope of the projects that can improve the efficiency and effectiveness of a user organization. The primary purpose of business modeling is to ensure that both developer and user organizations understand where and how the to-be-developed information system fits into the business processes of the user organization. This workflow is primarily executed during the inception phase to ensure that we develop information systems that make business sense. The activities that take place on this workflow are most closely associated with the planning phase of the traditional SDLC; however, requirements gathering, and use-case and business process modeling techniques also help us to understand the business situation.

Requirements Workflow In the Unified Process, the requirements workflow includes eliciting both functional and nonfunctional requirements. Typically, requirements are gathered from project stakeholders, such as end users, managers within the end user organization, and even customers. The requirements workflow is used the most during the inception and elaboration phases. The identified requirements are very helpful for developing the vision document and the use cases used throughout the development process. Additional requirements tend to be discovered throughout the development process. In fact, only the transition phase tends to have few, if any, additional requirements identified.

Analysis Workflow The *analysis workflow* primarily addresses the creation of an analysis model of the problem domain. In the Unified Process, the analyst begins designing the architecture associated with the problem domain; using the UML, the analyst creates functional, structural, and behavioral diagrams that depict a description of the problem domain classes and their interactions. The primary purpose of the analysis workflow is to ensure that both the developer and user organizations understand the underlying problem and its domain without over analyzing. If they are not careful, analysts can create *analysis paralysis*, which occurs when the project becomes so bogged down with analysis that the system is never actually designed or implemented. A second purpose of the analysis workflow is to identify useful reusable classes for class libraries. By reusing predefined classes, the analyst can avoid reinventing the wheel when creating the structural and behavioral diagrams. The analysis workflow is predominantly associated with the elaboration phase, but like the requirements workflow, it is possible that additional analysis will be required throughout the development process.

Design Workflow The design workflow transitions the analysis model into a form that can be used to implement the system: the *design model*. Whereas the analysis workflow concentrated on understanding the problem domain, the design workflow focuses on developing a solution that will execute in a specific environment. Basically, the design workflow simply enhances the description of the evolving system by adding classes that address the environment of the system to the evolving analysis model. The design workflow uses activities such as detailed problem domain class design, optimization of the evolving information system, database design, user-interface design, and application architecture design. The design workflow is associated primarily with the elaboration and construction phases of the Unified Process.

Implementation Workflow The primary purpose of the implementation workflow is to create an executable solution based on the design model (i.e., programming). This includes not only writing new classes but also incorporating reusable classes from executable class libraries into the evolving solution. As with any programming activity, the new classes and their interactions with the incorporated reusable classes must be tested. Finally, in the case of multiple groups performing the implementation of the information system, the implementers also must integrate the separate, individually tested modules to create an executable version of the system. The implementation workflow is associated primarily with the elaboration and construction phases.

Testing Workflow The primary purpose of the *testing workflow* is to increase the quality of the evolving system. Testing goes beyond the simple unit testing associated with the implementation workflow. In this case, testing also includes testing the integration of all modules used to implement the system, user acceptance testing, and the actual alpha testing of the software. Practically speaking, testing should go on throughout the development of the system; testing of the analysis and design models occurs during the elaboration and construction phases, whereas implementation testing is performed primarily during the construction and, to some degree, transition phases. Basically, at the end of each iteration during the development of the information system, some type of test should be performed.

Deployment Workflow The deployment workflow is most associated with the transition phase of the Unified Process. The *deployment workflow* includes activities such as software packaging, distribution, installation, and beta testing. When actually deploying the new system into a user organization, the developers might have to convert the current data, interface the new software with the existing software, and train the end user to use the new system.

Supporting Workflows The supporting workflows include the project management, configuration and change management, and environment workflows. The supporting workflows focus on the managerial aspects of information systems development.

Project Management Workflow Whereas the other workflows associated with the Unified Process are technically active during all four phases, the *project management workflow* is the only truly cross-phase workflow. The development process supports incremental and iterative development, so information systems tend to grow or evolve over time. At the end of each iteration, a new incremental version of the system is ready for delivery. The project management workflow is quite important owing to the complexity of the two-dimensional development model of the Unified Process (workflows and phases). This workflow's activities include identifying and managing risks, managing scope, estimating the time to complete each iteration and the entire project, estimating the cost of the individual iteration and the whole project, and tracking the progress being made toward the final version of the evolving information system.

Configuration and Change Management Workflow The primary purpose of the configuration and change management workflow is to keep track of the state of the evolving system. In a nutshell, the evolving information system comprises a set of artifacts (e.g., diagrams, source code, and executables). During the development process, these artifacts are modified.

A substantial amount of work—and, hence, money—is involved in developing the artifacts. The artifacts themselves should be handled as any expensive asset would be handled—access controls must be put into place to safeguard the artifacts from being stolen or destroyed. Furthermore, because the artifacts are modified on a regular, if not continuous, basis, good version control mechanisms should be established. Finally, a good deal of project management information needs to be captured (e.g., author, time, and location of each modification). The configuration and change management workflow is associated mostly with the construction and transition phases.

Environment Workflow During the development of an information system, the development team needs to use different tools and processes. The *environment workflow* addresses these needs. For example, a CASE tool that supports the development of an object-oriented information system via the UML could be required. Other tools necessary include programming environments, project management tools, and configuration management tools. The environment workflow involves acquiring and installing these tools. Even though this workflow can be active during all of the phases of the Unified Process, it should be involved primarily with the inception phase.

Extensions to the Unified Process

As large and as complex as the Unified Process is, many authors have pointed out a set of critical weaknesses. First, the Unified Process does not address staffing, budgeting, or contract management issues. These activities were explicitly left out of the Unified Process. Second, the Unified Process does not address issues relating to maintenance, operations, or support of the product once it has been delivered. Thus, it is not a complete software process; it is only a development process. Third, the Unified Process does not address cross- or inter-project issues. Considering the importance of reuse in object-oriented systems development and the fact that in many organizations employees work on many different projects at the same time, leaving out inter-project issues is a major omission.

To address these omissions, Ambler and Constantine suggest adding a production phase and two workflows: the operations and support workflow and the infrastructure management workflow (see Figure 1-4).[15] In addition to these new workflows, the test, deployment, and environment workflows are modified, and the project management and the configuration and change management workflows are extended into the production phase. These extensions are based on alternative object-oriented software processes: the OPEN process (Object-oriented Process, Environment, and Notation) and the Object-Oriented Software Process.[16]

Production Phase The *production phase* is concerned primarily with issues related to the software product after it has been successfully deployed. This phase focuses on issues related to updating, maintaining, and operating the software. Unlike the previous phases, there are

---

[15] S. W. Ambler and L. L. Constantine, *The Unified Process Inception Phase: Best Practices in Implementing the UP* (Lawrence, KS: CMP Books, 2000); S. W. Ambler and L. L. Constantine, *The Unified Process Elaboration Phase: Best Practices in Implementing the UP* (Lawrence, KS: CMP Books, 2000); S. W. Ambler and L. L. Constantine, *The Unified Process Construction Phase: Best Practices in Implementing the UP* (Lawrence, KS: CMP Books, 2000); S. W. Ambler and L. L. Constantine, *The Unified Process Transition and Production Phases: Best Practices in Implementing the UP* (Lawrence, KS: CMP Books, 2002).

[16] S. W. Ambler, *Process Patterns—Building Large-Scale Systems Using Object Technology* (Cambridge, UK: SIGS Books/Cambridge University Press, 1998); S. W. Ambler, *More Process Patterns—Delivering Large-Scale Systems Using Object Technology* (Cambridge, UK: SIGS Books/Cambridge University Press, 1999); I. Graham, B. Henderson-Sellers, and H. Younessi, *The OPEN Process Specification* (Harlow, UK: Addison-Wesley, 1997); B. Henderson-Sellers and B. Unhelkar, *OPEN Modeling with UML* (Harlow, UK: Addison-Wesley, 2000).

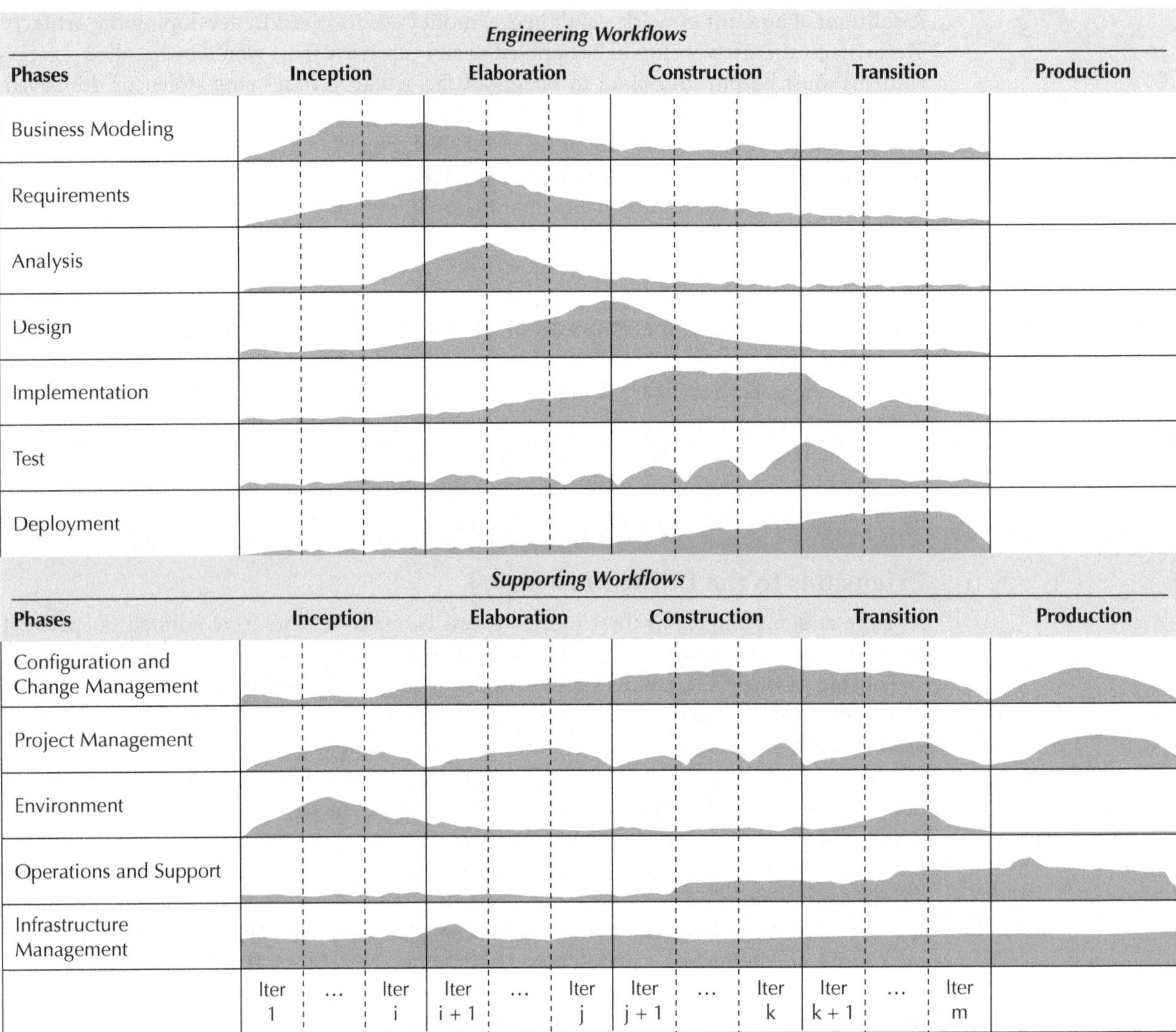

FIGURE 1-4   The Enhanced Unified Process

no iterations or incremental deliverables. If a new release of the software is to be developed, then the developers must begin a new run through the first four phases. Based on the activities that take place during this phase, no engineering workflows are relevant. The supporting workflows that are active during this phase include the configuration and change management workflow, the project management workflow, the new operations and support workflow, and the infrastructure management workflow.

Operations and Support Workflow The *operations and support workflow*, as you might guess, addresses issues related to supporting the current version of the software and operating the software on a daily basis. Activities include creating plans for the operation and support of the software product once it has been deployed, creating training and user documentation, putting into place necessary backup procedures, monitoring and optimizing the performance of the software, and performing corrective maintenance on the software. This workflow becomes active during the construction phase; its level of activity increases throughout the transition and, finally, the production phase. The workflow finally drops off when the current version of the software is replaced by a new version. Many developers are under the false impression that once the software has been delivered to the customer, their work is finished. In most cases, the work of supporting the software product is much more costly and time consuming than the original development. At that point, the developer's work may have just begun. When considering the newer DevOps approaches, it is obvious that operations personnel should be actively involved with this workflow.

Infrastructure Management Workflow The *infrastructure management workflow*'s primary purpose is to support the development of the infrastructure necessary to develop object-oriented systems. Activities such as development and modification of libraries, standards, and enterprise models are very important. When the development and maintenance of a problem-domain architecture model goes beyond the scope of a single project and reuse is going to occur, the infrastructure management workflow is essential. Another very important set of cross-project activities is the improvement of the software development process. Because the activities on this workflow tend to affect many projects and the Unified Process focuses only on a specific project, the Unified Process tends to ignore these activities (i.e., they are simply beyond the scope and purpose of the Unified Process).

Existing Workflow Modifications and Extensions In addition to the workflows that were added to address deficiencies contained in the Unified Process, existing workflows had to be modified and/or extended into the production phase. These workflows include the test, deployment, environment, project management, and configuration and change management workflows.

Test Workflow For high-quality information systems to be developed, testing should be done on every deliverable, including those created during the inception phase. Otherwise, less than high-quality systems will be delivered to the customer.

Deployment Workflow Legacy systems exist in most corporations today, and these systems have databases associated with them that must be converted to interact with the new systems. Owing to the complexity of deploying new systems, the conversion requires significant planning. Therefore, the activities on the deployment workflow need to begin in the inception phase instead of waiting until the end of the construction phase, as suggested by the Unified Process.

Environment Workflow The environment workflow needs to be modified to include activities related to setting up the operations and production environment. The actual work performed is similar to the work related to setting up the development environment that was performed during the inception phase. In this case, the additional work is performed during the transition phase.

Project Management Workflow Even though the project management workflow does not include staffing the project, managing the contracts among the customers and vendors, and managing the project's budget, these activities are crucial to the success of any software development project. We suggest extending project management to include these activities. This workflow should additionally occur in the production phase to address issues such as training, staff management, and client relationship management.

Configuration and Change Management Workflow The configuration and change management workflow is extended into the new production phase. Activities performed during the production phase include identifying potential improvements to the operational system and assessing the potential impact of the proposed changes. Once developers have identified these changes and understood their impact, they can schedule the changes to be made and deployed with future releases.

Figure 1-5 shows the chapters in which the Enhanced Unified Process's phases and workflows are covered. Given the offshore outsourcing and automation of information technology[17] in this textbook, we focus primarily on the inception and elaboration phases and the business modeling, requirements, analysis, design, test, and project management workflows of the Enhanced Unified Process. However, as Figure 1-5 shows, the other phases and workflows are covered. In many object-oriented systems development environments today, code generation is supported. Thus, from a business perspective, we believe the activities associated with these workflows are the most important.

Enhanced UP Phases	Chapters
Inception	2, 3, 11
Elaboration	2–10
Construction	7, 12
Transition	12
Production	12
Enhanced UP Engineering Workflows	**Chapters**
Business Modeling	2, 3
Requirements	2–5, 9
Analysis	3–5
Design	6–10
Implementation	7, 12
Test	3–10
Deployment	10, 12
Enhanced UP Supporting Workflows	**Chapters**
Project Management	11
Configuration and Change Management	12
Environment	12
Operations and Support	12
Infrastructure Management	12

FIGURE 1-5 The Enhanced Unified Process and the Textbook Organization

[17] See Thomas L. Friedman, *The World Is Flat: A Brief History of the Twenty-First Century, Updated and Expanded Edition* (New York, NY: Farrar, Straus, and Giroux, 2006); Daniel H. Pink, *A Whole New Mind: Why Right-Brainers Will Rule the Future* (New York, NY: Riverhead Books, 2006).

THE UNIFIED MODELING LANGUAGE

Until 1995, object concepts were popular but implemented in many different ways by different developers. Each developer had his or her own methodology and notation (e.g., Booch, Coad, Moses, OMT, OOSE, and SOMA).[18] Then in 1995, Rational Software brought three industry leaders together to create a single approach to object-oriented systems development. Grady Booch, Ivar Jacobson, and James Rumbaugh worked with others to create a standard set of diagramming techniques known as the *Unified Modeling Language (UML)*. The objective of UML was to provide a common vocabulary of object-oriented terms and diagramming techniques rich enough to model any systems development project from analysis through implementation. In November 1997, the *Object Management Group (OMG)* formally accepted UML as the standard for all object developers. During the following years, the UML has gone through multiple minor revisions. The current version of UML is Version 2.5.

Version 2.5 of the UML defines a set of fifteen diagramming techniques used to model a system. The diagrams are broken into two major groupings: one for modeling the structure of a system and one for modeling behavior. *Structure diagrams* provide a way to represent the data and static relationships in an information system. The structure diagrams include class, object, package, deployment, component, composite structure, and profile diagrams. *Behavioral diagrams* provide the analyst with a way to depict the dynamic relationships among the instances or objects that represent the business information system. They also allow modeling of the dynamic behavior of individual objects throughout their lifetime. The behavioral diagrams support the analyst in modeling the functional requirements of an evolving information system. The behavioral diagrams include activity, sequence, communication, interaction overview, timing, behavior state machine, protocol state machine, and use-case diagrams.[19] Figure 1-6 provides an overview of these diagrams.

Depending on where in the development process the system is, different diagrams play a more important role. In some cases, the same diagramming technique is used throughout the development process. In that case, the diagrams start off very conceptual and abstract. As the system is developed, the diagrams evolve to include details that ultimately lead to generating and developing code. In other words, the diagrams move from documenting the requirements to laying out the design. Overall, the consistent notation, integration among the diagramming techniques, and application of the diagrams across the entire development process make the UML a powerful and flexible language for analysts and developers. Later chapters provide more detail on using a subset of the UML in object-oriented systems analysis and design. In particular, these chapters describe use case, activity, class, sequence, package, and deployment

---

[18] See Grady Booch, *Object-Oriented Analysis and Design with Applications*, 2nd Ed. (Redwood City, CA: Benjamin/Cummings, 1994); Peter Coad and Edward Yourdon, *Object-Oriented Analysis*, 2nd Ed. (Englewood Cliffs, NJ: Yourdon Press, 1991); Peter Coad and Edward Yourdon, *Object-Oriented Design* (Englewood Cliffs, NJ: Yourdon Press, 1991); Brian Henderson-Sellers and Julian Edwards, *Book Two of Object-Oriented Knowledge: The Working Object* (Sydney, Australia: Prentice Hall, 1994); James Rumbaugh, Michael Blaha, William Premerlani, Frederick Eddy, and William Lorensen, *Object-Oriented Modeling and Design* (Englewood Cliffs, NJ: Prentice Hall, 1991); Ivar Jacobson, Magnus Christerson, Patrik Jonsson, and Gunnar Overgaard, *Object-Oriented Software Engineering: A Use Case Approach* (Wokingham, England: Addison-Wesley, 1992); Ian Graham, *Migrating to Object Technology* (Wokingham, England: Addison-Wesley, 1994).

[19] The material contained in this section is based on the OMG *Unified Modeling Language Version 2.5.1, December 2017* (www.uml.org). Additional useful references include Michael Jesse Chonoles and James A. Schardt, *UML 2 for Dummies* (Indianapolis, IN: Wiley, 2003); Hans-Erik Eriksson, Magnus Penker, Brian Lyons, and David Fado, *UML 2 Toolkit* (Indianapolis, IN: Wiley, 2004); Ian Graham, *Fast Track UML 2.0* (Berkeley, CA: Apress, 2004). For a complete description of all diagrams, see www.uml.org.

Diagram Name	Used to...	Primary Phase
Structure Diagrams		
Class	illustrate the relationships between classes modeled in the system.	Analysis, Design
Object	illustrate the relationships between objects modeled in the system. Used when actual instances of the classes will better communicate the model.	Analysis, Design
Package	group other UML elements together to form higher level constructs	Analysis, Design, Implementation
Deployment	show the physical architecture of the system. Can also be used to show software components being deployed onto the physical architecture.	Physical Design, Implementation
Component	illustrate the physical relationships among the software components.	Physical Design, Implementation
Composite Structure	illustrate the internal structure of a class, i.e., the relationships among the parts of a class.	Analysis, Design
Profile	develop extensions to the UML itself.	None
Behavioral Diagrams		
Activity	illustrate business workflows independent of classes, the flow of activities in a use case, or detailed design of a method.	Analysis, Design
Sequence	model the behavior of objects within a use case. Focuses on the time-based ordering of an activity.	Analysis, Design
Communication	model the behavior of objects within a use case. Focuses on the communication among a set of collaborating objects of an activity.	Analysis, Design
Interaction Overview	illustrate an overview of the flow of control of a process.	Analysis, Design
Timing	illustrate the interaction that takes place among a set of objects and the state changes in which they go through along a time axis.	Analysis, Design
Behavioral State Machine	examine the behavior of one class.	Analysis, Design
Protocol State Machine	illustrate the dependencies among the different interfaces of a class.	Analysis, Design
Use-Case	capture business requirements for the system and to illustrate the interaction between the system and its environment.	Analysis

FIGURE 1-6   UML 2.5 Diagram Summary

diagrams and the behavior state machines. We also introduce an optional UML diagram, the windows navigation diagram, that is an extension to the behavioral state machine that is used to design user navigation through an information system's user interfaces.

THE UNIFIED PROCESS, UML, AND AGILE DEVELOPMENT

Given that the Unified Process (and its extensions) is a highly iterative process, the key to using it as an agile software development approach is the amount of emphasis that is placed on the different workflows and the number of iterations performed for each phase. One of the primary advantages of the Unified Process is its scalability.[20] Depending on the criticality of

[20] See Craig Larman, *Agile & Iterative Development: A Manager's Guide* (Boston, MA: Addison-Wesley, 2004).

the project, more or less emphasis can be placed on the phases and workflows. For example, a small project can quickly move through the Inception and Elaboration phases. This would allow the developer to have more tightly defined timeboxes (or iterations) within the Construction and Transition phases which focus more on the Requirements, Analysis, Design, Implementation, and Test workflows. Furthermore, the extensions to the Unified Process described previously allow the Unified Process to support DevOps approaches. Finally, the Unified Process is flexible enough to support the creation of a custom methodology.

With regard to the UML and agile development, a subset of the diagrams can be useful in communicating the current understanding of the problem requirements with the users. Obviously, from an agile perspective, using the full power of the UML is not necessary. Some of the more useful diagrams in an agile approach include the use case, activity, class, and sequence diagrams. In later chapters, we provide more detail on these diagrams.

APPLYING THE CHAPTER CONCEPTS

This book introduces many new concepts regarding object-oriented analysis and design. To make these concepts more relevant and understandable, we apply the concepts introduced in each chapter to a set of independent examples.

The first example describes a typical college library management system. In this example, the system must support resource procurement, borrowing and returning different resources, reserving different resources, and retiring different resources. Also, the system must support different types of borrowers (e.g., faculty, students, and visitors) and different types of resources (e.g., books, DVDs, and CDs). This example is used to demonstrate the various concepts throughout the book.

The second example is the familiar problem that all students face when trying to find a place to live while at their university. The campus housing service is a small university department that matches students with rental units. The service keeps track of rental unit information, information regarding how to visit rental units, and the service acts as a liaison for the student to sign a lease with the rental unit management. The service also supports the owners/managers of the rental units by making sure that all information about the available units is up to date. This example is included as a set of "Your Turn" exercises throughout the book.

CHAPTER REVIEW

After reading and studying this chapter, you should be able to:

- ☐ Explain the different roles played by a systems analyst in the process of developing information systems.
- ☐ Describe the four primary phases of the Systems Development Life Cycle (SDLC).
- ☐ Discuss the three basic characteristics of all object-oriented systems analysis and design approach: use-case driven, architecture-centric, and iterative and incremental development.
- ☐ Describe agile, DevOps, and custom methodologies.
- ☐ Describe the Unified Process and its extensions.
- ☐ List and categorize, as to their primary purpose, the different diagrams associated with the Unified Modeling Language (UML).

KEY TERMS

Agile development
Analysis model
Analysis paralysis
Analysis phase
Analysis strategy
Analysis workflow
Approval committee
Architecture-centric
Architecture design
As-is system
Behavioral diagrams
Behavioral view
Business analyst
Business modeling workflow
Change agent
Change management analyst
Configuration and change
  management workflow
Construction
Construction phase
Database and file specification
Data-centered methodology

Deliverable
Deployment workflow
Design model
Design phase
Design strategy
Design workflow
DevOps
Dynamic view
Elaboration phase
Engineering workflow
Environment workflow
External view
Feasibility analysis
Functional view
Gradual refinement
Implementation phase
Implementation workflow
Inception phase
Incremental
Infrastructure analyst
Infrastructure management
  workflow

Interface design
Iterative
Methodology
Object Management
  Group (OMG)
Object-oriented
  methodologies
Operations and support
  workflow
Phases
Planning phase
Process-centered
  methodology
Production phase
Program design
Programmer
Project initiation
Project management
Project management workflow
Project manager
Project plan
Project sponsor

Requirements gathering
Requirements workflow
Static view
Structure diagrams
Support plan
System proposal
System request
System specification
Systems analyst
Systems development life
  cycle (SDLC)
Technical writer
Testing workflow
To-be system
Training plan
Transition phase
Unified Modeling
  Language (UML)
Use case
Use-case driven
Workflows
Workplan

QUESTIONS

1. What are the major roles played by a systems analyst on a project team?
2. Compare and contrast the role of a systems analyst, business analyst, and infrastructure analyst.
3. Compare and contrast phases, steps, techniques, and deliverables.
4. Describe the major phases in the SDLC.
5. Which phase in the SDLC is most important? Why?
6. Describe the principal steps in the planning phase. What are the major deliverables?
7. Describe the principal steps in the analysis phase. What are the major deliverables?
8. Describe the principal steps in the design phase. What are the major deliverables?
9. Describe the principal steps in the implementation phase. What are the major deliverables?
10. What are the roles of a project sponsor and the approval committee?
11. What does *gradual refinement* mean in the context of SDLC?
12. What is a use case?
13. What is meant by use-case driven?
14. Why is it important for an OOSAD approach to be architecture-centric?
15. What does it mean for an OOSAD approach to be incremental and iterative?
16. Describe the major elements and issues with an object-oriented approach to developing information systems.
17. What are the phases and workflows of the Unified Process?
18. Compare the phases of the Unified Process with the phases of the waterfall model.
19. Who is the Object Management Group?
20. What is the Unified Modeling Language?
21. What is the primary purpose of structure diagrams? Give some examples of structure diagrams.
22. For what are behavioral diagrams used? Give some examples of behavioral diagrams.

EXERCISES

A. Look on the Web for different kinds of job opportunities that are available for people who want analyst positions? Compare and contrast the skills that the ads ask for to the skills that we presented in this chapter.

B. Think about your ideal analyst position. Write an ad to hire someone for that position. What requirements would the job have? What skills and experience would be required? How would an applicant be able to demonstrate having the appropriate skills and experience?

C. Investigate IBM's Rational Unified Process (RUP) on the Web. RUP is a commercial version that extends aspects of the Unified Process. Write a brief memo describing how it is related to the Unified Process as described in this chapter.

D. Suppose you are a project manager who typically has been using the Unified Process methodology on a large and complex project. Your manager has just read the latest article in Computerworld that advocates replacing this methodology with an agile methodology and comes to you requesting you to switch. What do you say?

E. Suppose you are an analyst working for a small company to develop an accounting system. Would you use the Unified Process to develop the system, or would you prefer to use an agile process? Why?

F. Suppose you are an analyst developing a new information system to automate the sales transactions and manage inventory for each retail store in a large chain. The system would be installed at each store and exchange data with a mainframe computer at the company's head office. Would you use the Unified Process to develop the system, or would you prefer to use an agile process? Why?

G. Investigate the Unified Modeling Language on the Web. Write a paragraph news brief describing the current state of the UML.

H. Investigate the Object Management Group (OMG) on the Web. Write a report describing the purpose of the OMG and what it is involved with besides the UML.

I. Using the Web, find a set of CASE tools that support the UML. A couple of examples include Poseidon, IBM Rational UML, and Visual Paradigm. Find at least two more. Write a short report describing how well they support the UML, and make a recommendation as to which one you believe would be best for a project team to use in developing an object-oriented information system using the UML.

MINICASES

1. Barbara Singleton, manager of western regional sales at the WAMAP Company, requested that the IS department develop a sales force management and tracking system that would enable her to better monitor the performance of her sales staff. Unfortunately, owing to the massive backlog of work facing the IS department, her request was given a low priority. After six months of inaction by the IS department, Barbara decided to take matters into her own hands. Based on the advice of friends, Barbara purchased simple database software and constructed a sales force management and tracking system on her own.

Although Barbara's system has been "completed" for about six weeks, it still has many features that do not work correctly, and some functions are full of errors. Barbara's assistant is so mistrustful of the system that she has secretly gone back to using her old paper-based system, because it is much more reliable.

Over dinner one evening, Barbara complained to a systems analyst friend, "I don't know what went wrong with this project. It seemed pretty simple to me. Those IS guys wanted me to follow this elaborate set of steps and tasks, but I didn't think all that really applied to a PC-based system. I just thought I could build this system and tweak it around until I got what I wanted without all the fuss and bother of the methodology the IS guys were pushing. I mean, doesn't that just apply to their big, expensive systems?"

Assuming you are Barbara's systems analyst friend, how would you respond to her complaint?

2. Marcus Weber, IS project manager at ICAN Mutual Insurance Co., is reviewing the staffing arrangements for his next major project, the development of an expert system-based underwriter's assistant. This new system will involve a whole new way for the underwriters to perform their tasks. The underwriter's assistant system will function as sort of an underwriting supervisor, reviewing key elements of each application, checking for consistency in the underwriter's decisions, and ensuring that no critical factors have been overlooked. The goal of the new system is to improve the quality of the underwriters' decisions and to improve underwriters' productivity. It is expected that the new system will substantially change the way the underwriting staff do their jobs.

Marcus is dismayed to learn that because of budget constraints, he must choose between one of two available staff members. Barry Filmore has had considerable experience and training in individual and organizational behavior. Barry has worked on several other projects in which the end users had to make significant adjustments to the new system, and Barry seems to have a knack for anticipating problems and smoothing the transition to a new work environment. Marcus had hoped to have Barry's involvement in this project.

Marcus's other potential staff member is Kim Danville. Prior to joining ICAN Mutual, Kim had considerable work experience with the expert system technologies that ICAN has chosen for this expert system project. Marcus was counting on Kim to help integrate the new expert system technology into ICAN's systems environment, and also to provide on-the-job training and insights to the other developers on this team.

Given that Marcus's budget will only permit him to add Barry or Kim to this project team, but not both, what choice do you recommend for him? Justify your answer.

3. Joe Brown, the president of Roanoke Manufacturing, requested that Jack Jones, the MIS department manager, investigate the viability of selling their products

over the Web. Currently, the MIS department is still using an IBM mainframe as their primary deployment environment. As a first step, Jack contacted his friends at IBM to see if they had any suggestions as to how Roanoke Manufacturing could move toward supporting sales in an electronic commerce environment while keeping their mainframe as their main system. His friends explained that IBM (www.ibm.com) now supports Java and Linux on their mainframes. Jack has also learned that IBM owns Rational (www-01.ibm.com/software/rational/), the creator of the UML and the Unified Process. Jack's friends suggested that Jack investigate using object-oriented systems as a basis for developing the new system. They also suggested that using the Rational Unified Process (RUP), Java, and virtual Linux machines on his current mainframe as a way to support the move toward a distributed electronic commerce system would protect his current investment in his legacy systems while allowing the new system to be developed in a more modern manner. Even though Jack's IBM friends were very persuasive, Jack is still a little wary about moving his operation from a structured systems approach to this new object-oriented approach. Assuming that you are one of Jack's IBM friends, how would you convince him to move toward using an object-oriented systems development method, such as RUP, and using Java and Linux as a basis for developing and deploying the new system on Roanoke Manufacturing's current mainframe?

Basic Characteristics of Object-Oriented Systems

Object-oriented systems can be traced back to Simula and Smalltalk programming languages. However, until the increase in processor power and the decrease in processor cost that occurred in the 1980s, object-oriented approaches were not practical. Many of the specific details concerning the basic characteristics of object-orientation are language dependent; that is, each object-oriented programming language tends to implement some of the object-oriented basics in a different way. Consequently, we need to know which programming language is going to be used to implement the different aspects of the solution. Otherwise, the system could behave in a manner different than the analyst, designer, and client expect. Today, the Python, C/C++, Java, and C#, programming languages tend to be the more predominant languages used.[1] In this appendix, we describe the basic characteristics of object-oriented systems, which include classes, objects, methods, messages, encapsulation, information hiding, inheritance, polymorphism, and dynamic binding.

CLASSES AND OBJECTS

A *class* is the general template we use to define and create specific instances, or objects. Every object is associated with a class. For example, all the objects that capture information about patients could fall into a class called Patient, because there are attributes (e.g., name, address, birth date, phone, and insurance carrier) and methods (e.g., make appointment, calculate last visit, change status, and provide medical history) that all patients share (see Figure A1-1).

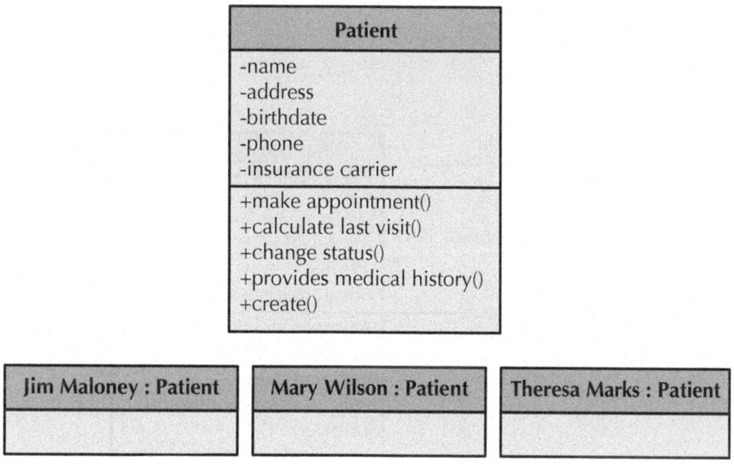

Patient

-name
-address
-birthdate
-phone
-insurance carrier

+make appointment()
+calculate last visit()
+change status()
+provides medical history()
+create()

Jim Maloney : Patient | Mary Wilson : Patient | Theresa Marks : Patient

FIGURE A1-1
Classes and Objects

[1] See www.tiobe.com/tiobe-index/ (retrieved May 29, 2024).

An *object* is a specific instance of a class (often referred to as an instantiation of a class). In other words, an object is a specific person, place, or thing about which we want to capture information. If we were building an appointment system for a doctor's office, classes might include Doctor, Patient, and Appointment. Specific patients, such as Jim Maloney, Mary Wilson, and Theresa Marks, are considered *instances*, or objects, of the patient class (see Figure A1-1).

Each object has *attributes* that describe information about the object, such as a patient's name, birth date, address, and phone number. Attributes are also used to represent relationships between objects; for example, there could be a department attribute in an employee object with a value of a department object that captures in which department the employee object works. Objects also have *states*, which are defined by the value of their attributes and their relationships with other objects at a particular point in time. For example, a patient might have a state of new or current or former.

Each object also has *behaviors*. The behaviors specify what the object can do. For example, an appointment object can probably schedule a new appointment, delete an appointment, and locate the next available appointment. In object-oriented programming, behaviors are implemented as methods (see the next section).

One of the more confusing aspects of object-oriented systems development is the fact that in most object-oriented programming languages, both classes and instances of classes can have attributes and methods. Class attributes and methods tend to be used to model attributes (or methods) that deal with issues related to all instances of the class. For example, to create a new patient object, a message is sent to the Patient class to create a new instance of itself. However, in this book, we focus primarily on attributes and methods of objects and not of classes.

METHODS AND MESSAGES

Methods implement an object's behavior. A method is an action that an object can perform. *Messages* are information sent to objects to trigger methods. A message is essentially a function or *procedure call* from one object to another object. For example, if a patient is new to the doctor's office, the receptionist sends a create message to the application. The patient class receives the create message and executes its create() method which then creates a new object: aPatient (see Figure A1-2).

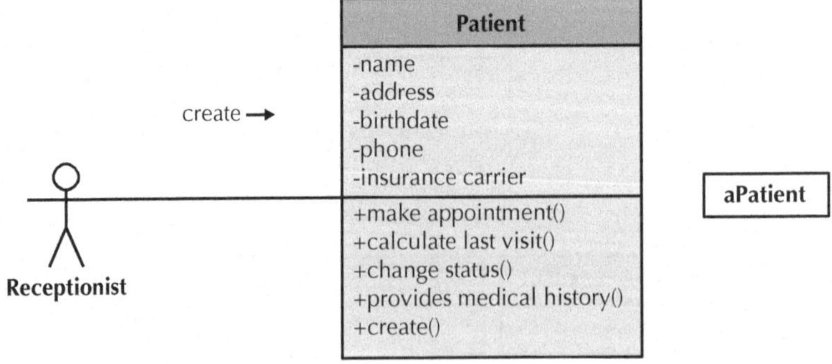

FIGURE A1-2
Messages and
Methods

ENCAPSULATION AND INFORMATION HIDING

The ideas of *encapsulation* and *information hiding* are interrelated in object-oriented systems. However, neither of the terms is new. And, they are different. For example, Python supports encapsulation but does not support information hiding, while C supports information hiding (to a degree) but does not support encapsulation. Encapsulation is the combination of process and data into a single object. *Information hiding* suggests that only the information required to use an object should be available outside the object; that is, information hiding is related to the *visibility* of the methods and attributes. Typically, this implies that the information required to be passed to the object and the information returned from the object are published. Exactly how the object implements the required functionality is not relevant as long as the object functions correctly. All that is required to use an object are the set of methods and the messages needed to be sent to trigger them. The only communication between objects should be through an object's methods.

The fact that we can use an object by calling methods is the key to reusability because it shields the internal workings of the object from changes in the outside system, and it keeps the system from being affected when changes are made to an object. In Figure A1-2, notice how a message (create) is sent to an object, yet the internal algorithms needed to respond to the message are hidden from other parts of the system. The only information that an object needs to know is the set of operations, or methods, that other objects can perform and what messages need to be sent to trigger them. In object-oriented systems, combining encapsulation with the information-hiding principle supports treating objects as black boxes.

POLYMORPHISM AND DYNAMIC BINDING

Polymorphism means having the ability to take several forms. By supporting polymorphism, object-oriented systems can send the same message to a set of objects, which can be interpreted differently by different classes of objects. For example, inserting a patient means something different than inserting an appointment. Therefore, different pieces of information need to be collected and stored. Based on encapsulation and information hiding, an object does not have to be concerned with *how* something is done when using other objects. We can simply send a message to an object, and that object will be responsible for interpreting the message appropriately. For example, if an artist sent the message 'Draw yourself' to a square object, a circle object, and a triangle object, the results would be very different, even though the message is the same. Notice in Figure A1-3 how each object responds appropriately (and differently) even though the messages are identical.

Polymorphism is made possible through *dynamic binding*. Dynamic, or late, binding is a technique that delays typing the object until run-time. The specific method that is actually called is not chosen by the object-oriented system until the system is running. However, the specific level of support for polymorphism and dynamic binding is language specific. Most object-oriented programming languages support dynamic binding of methods, and some support dynamic binding of attributes. Dynamic binding is in contrast to *static binding*. In a statically bound system, the type of object is determined at compile-time. Therefore, the developer has to choose which method should be called instead of allowing the system to do it. This is why most traditional programming languages have complicated decision logic based on the different types of objects in a system. For example, in a traditional programming language, instead of sending the message 'Draw yourself' to the different types of graphical objects in Figure A1-3, we would have to write decision logic using a case statement or a set

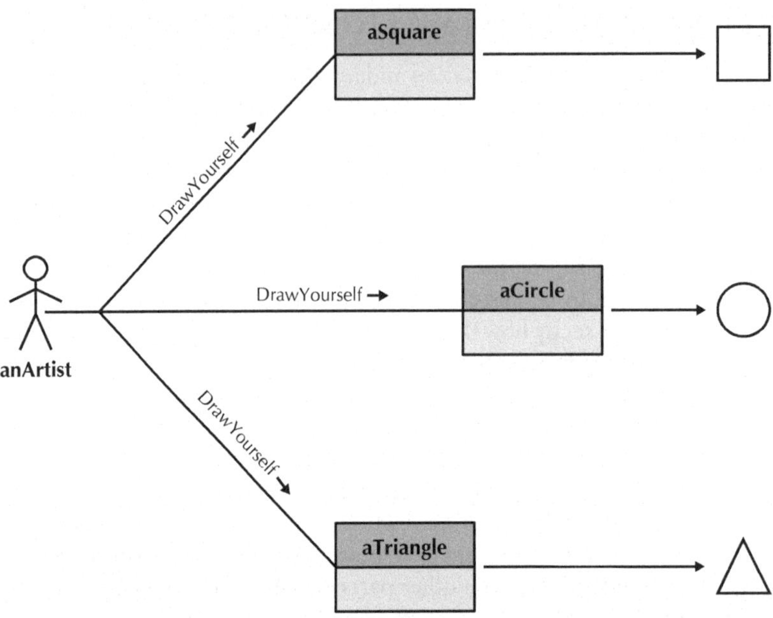

FIGURE A1-3
Polymorphism

of if statements to determine what kind of graphical object we wanted to draw, and we would have to name each draw function differently (e.g., draw square, draw circle, or draw triangle). This obviously makes the system much more complicated and difficult to understand.

But polymorphism can be a double-edged sword. Through the use of dynamic binding, there is no way to know before run time which specific object will be asked to execute its method. In effect, there is a decision made by the system that is not coded anywhere.[2] Because all these decisions are made at run time, it is possible to send a message to an object that it does not understand (i.e., the object does not have a corresponding method). This can cause a run-time error that, if the system is not programmed to handle it correctly, can cause the system to abort.[3]

Finally, if the methods are not semantically consistent, the developer cannot assume that all methods with the same name will perform the same generic operation. For example, imagine that you have an array of type person that contains instances of employees and customers (see Figure A1-4). These both implement a compute pay method. An object can send the message to each instance contained in the array to execute the compute pay method for that individual instance. In the case of an instance of employee, the compute pay method computes the amount that the employee is owed by the firm, whereas the compute pay method associated with an instance of a customer computes the amount owed the firm by the customer. Depending on whether the instance is an employee or a customer, a different meaning is associated with the method. Therefore, the semantics of each method must be determined individually. This substantially increases the difficulty of understanding individual objects. The key to controlling the difficulty of understanding object-oriented systems when using polymorphism is to ensure that all methods with the same name implement that same generic operation (i.e., they are semantically consistent).

---

[2] From a practical perspective, there is an implied case statement. The system chooses the method based on the type of object being asked to execute it and the parameters passed as arguments to the method. This is typically done through message dispatch tables that are hidden from the programmer.

[3] In most object-oriented programming languages, these errors are referred to as exceptions that the system "throws" and must "catch." In other words, the programmer must correctly program the throw and catch or the systems will abort. Again, each programming language can handle these situations in a unique manner.

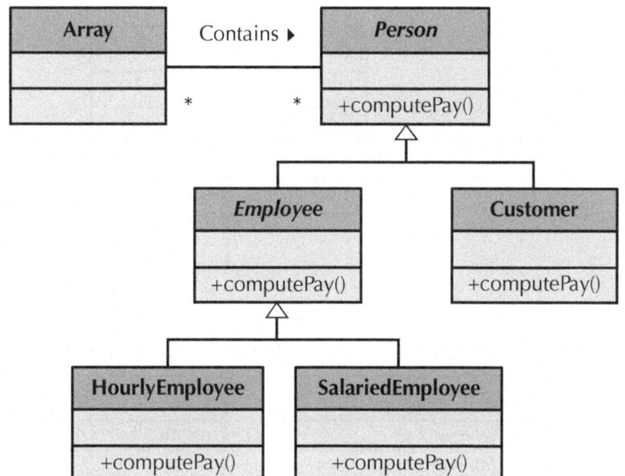

FIGURE A1-4
Example of Polymor-
phism Misuse

INHERITANCE

Inheritance allows developers to define classes incrementally by reusing classes defined previously as the basis for new classes. Inheritance, as an information systems development characteristic, was first proposed in data modeling in the late 1970s and the early 1980s. The data modeling literature suggests using inheritance to identify higher-level, or more general, classes of objects. Common sets of attributes and methods can be organized into *superclasses*. Typically, classes are arranged in a hierarchy whereby the superclasses, or general classes, are at the top and the *subclasses,* or specific classes, are at the bottom. In Figure A1-5, Person is a superclass to the classes Doctor and Patient. Doctor, in turn, is a superclass to General Practitioner and Specialist. Notice how a class (e.g., Doctor) can serve as a superclass and subclass concurrently. The relationship between the class and its superclass is known as the *a-kind-of* relationship. For example in Figure A1-5, a General Practitioner is a-kind-of Doctor, which is a-kind-of Person.

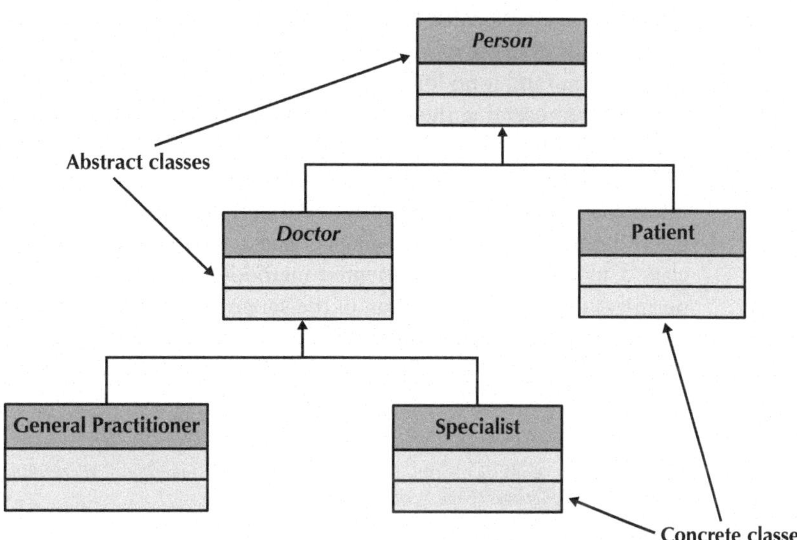

FIGURE A1-5
Class Hierarchy
with Abstract and
Concrete Classes

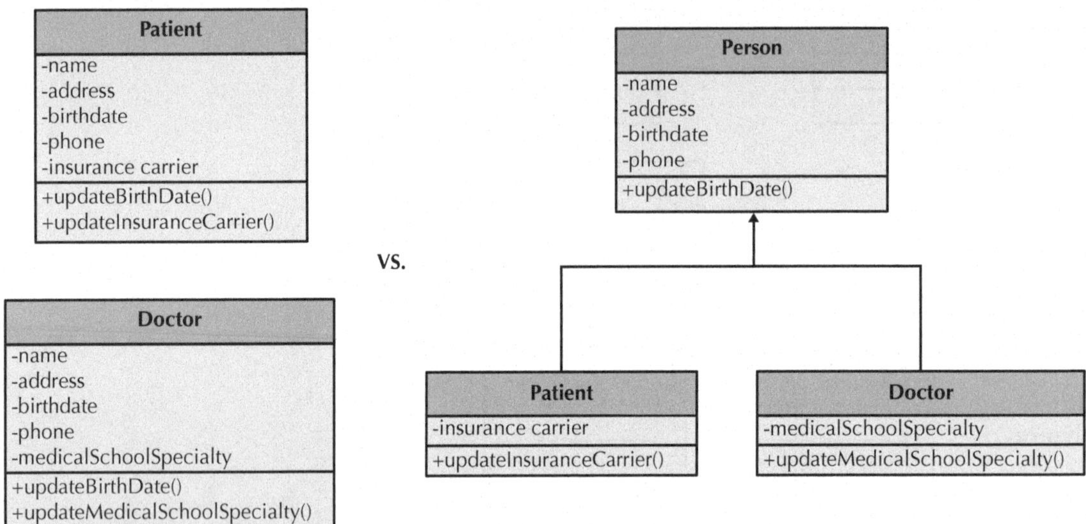

FIGURE A1-6   Inheritance Advantage

Subclasses *inherit* the appropriate attributes and methods from the superclasses above them. That is, each subclass contains attributes and methods from its parent superclass. For example, Figure A1-5 shows that both Doctor and Patient are subclasses of Person and therefore inherit the attributes and methods of the Person class. Inheritance makes it simpler to define classes. Instead of repeating the attributes and methods in the Doctor and Patient classes separately, the attributes and methods that are common to both are placed in the Person class and inherited by the classes below it. Notice how much more efficient inheritance hierarchies of object classes are than the same objects without an inheritance hierarchy (see Figure A1-6).

Most classes throughout a hierarchy lead to instances; any class that has instances is called a *concrete class*. For example, if Mary Wilson and Jim Maloney are instances of the Patient class, Patient would be considered a concrete class (see Figure A1-1). Some classes do not produce instances because they are used merely as templates for other, more-specific classes (especially classes located high up in a hierarchy). The classes are referred to as *abstract classes*. Person is an example of an abstract class. While it is technically possible to create an object from Person (and it no longer be an abstract class), it is more practical and efficient to create instances representing the more-specific classes of Specialist and Patient, both types of Person (see Figure A1-5).

There have been many different types of inheritance mechanisms associated with object-oriented systems.[4] The most common inheritance mechanisms include different forms of single and multiple inheritance. *Single inheritance* allows a subclass to have only a single parent class. Currently, all object-oriented methodologies, databases, and programming languages permit extending the definition of the superclass through single inheritance.

Some object-oriented methodologies, databases, and programming languages allow a subclass to redefine some or all the attributes and/or methods of its superclass. With *redefinition*

---

[4] See, for example, M. Lenzerini, D. Nardi, and M. Simi, *Inheritance Hierarchies in Knowledge Representation and Programming Languages* (New York: Wiley, 1991).

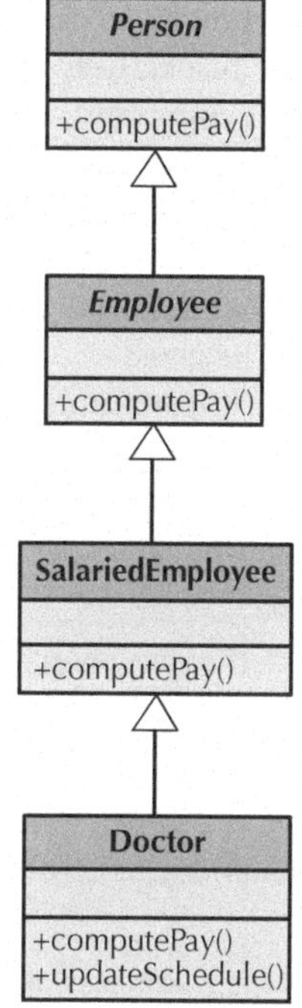

FIGURE A1-7
Example of Redefinition and Inheritance Conflict

capabilities, it is possible to introduce an *inheritance conflict* [i.e., an attribute (or method) of a subclass with the same name as an attribute (or method) of a super-class]. For example, in Figure A1-7, Doctor is a subclass of Employee. Both have methods named ComputePay(). This causes an inheritance conflict. Furthermore, when the definition of a superclass is modified, all its subclasses are affected. This can introduce additional inheritance conflicts in one (or more) of the superclass's subclasses. For example in Figure A1-7, Employee could be modified to include an additional method, UpdateSchedule(). This would add another inheritance conflict between Employee and Doctor. Therefore, developers must be aware of the effects of the modification not only in the superclass but also in each subclass that inherits the modification.

Finally, through redefinition capabilities, it is possible for a programmer to arbitrarily cancel the inheritance of methods by placing stubs[5] in the subclass that will override the definition of the inherited method. If the cancellation of methods is necessary for the correct definition of the subclass, then it is likely that the subclass has been misclassified (i.e., it is inheriting from the wrong superclass).

As you can see, from a design perspective, inheritance conflicts and redefinition can cause all kinds of problems with interpreting the final design and implementation.[6] However, most inheritance conflicts are due to poor classification of the subclass in the inheritance hierarchy (the generalization a-kind-of semantics are violated), or the actual inheritance mechanism violates the encapsulation and information hiding principle (i.e., subclasses are capable of directly addressing the attributes or methods of a superclass). To address these issues, Jim Rumbaugh and his colleagues suggested the following guidelines:[7]

- Do not redefine query operations.
- Methods that redefine inherited ones should restrict only the semantics of the inherited ones.
- The underlying semantics of the inherited method should never be changed.
- The signature (argument list) of the inherited method should never be changed.

However, many existing object-oriented programming languages violate these guidelines. When it comes to implementing the design, different object-oriented programming languages address inheritance conflicts differently. Therefore, it is important at this point in the development of the system to know what the chosen programming language supports. We must be sure that the design can be implemented as intended. Otherwise, the design needs to be modified before it is turned over to remotely located programmers.

When considering the interaction of inheritance with polymorphism and dynamic binding, object-oriented systems provide the developer with a very powerful, but dangerous, set of tools. Depending on the object-oriented programming language used, this interaction can allow the same object to be associated with different classes at different times. For example, an

---

[5] In this case, a stub is simply the minimal definition of a method to prevent syntax errors from occurring.

[6] For more information, see Ronald J. Brachman, "I Lied about the Trees Or, Defaults and Definitions in Knowledge Representation," *AI Magazine* 5, no. 3 (Fall 1985): 80–93.

[7] J. Rumbaugh, M. Blaha, W. Premerlani, F. Eddy, and W. Lorensen, *Object-Oriented Modeling and Design* (Englewood Cliffs, NJ: Prentice Hall, 1991).

instance of Doctor can be treated as an instance of Employee or any of its direct and indirect superclasses, such as Salaried Employee and Person, respectively (see Figure A1-7). Therefore, depending on whether static or dynamic binding is supported, the same object may execute different implementations of the same method at different times. Or, if the method is defined only with the Salaried Employee class and it is currently treated as an instance of the Employee class, the instance could cause a run-time error to occur.[8] It is important to know what object-oriented programming language is going to be used so that these kinds of issues can be solved with the design, instead of the implementation, of the class.

With *multiple inheritance*, a subclass may inherit from more than one superclass. In this situation, the types of inheritance conflicts are multiplied. In addition to the possibility of having an inheritance conflict between the subclass and one (or more) of its superclasses, it is now possible to have conflicts between two (or more) superclasses. In this latter case, three different types of additional inheritance conflicts can occur:

- Two inherited attributes (or methods) have the same name (spelling) and semantics.
- Two inherited attributes (or methods) have different names but identical semantics (i.e., they are *synonyms*).
- Two inherited attributes (or methods) have the same name but different semantics (i.e., they are *heteronyms, homographs,* or *homonyms*). This also violates the proper use of polymorphism.

For example, in Figure A1-8, Robot-Employee is a subclass of both Employee and Robot. In this case, Employee and Robot conflict with the attribute name. Which one should Robot-Employee inherit? Because they are the same, semantically speaking, does it really matter? It is also possible that Employee and Robot could have a semantic conflict on the classification and type attributes if they have the same semantics. Practically speaking, the only way to prevent this situation is for the developer to catch it during the design of the subclass. Finally, what if the running Time attributes have different semantics? In the case of Employee objects, the running Time attribute stores the employee's time running a mile, whereas the running Time attribute for Robot objects stores the average time between checkups. Should Robot-Employee inherit both of them? It really depends on whether the robot employees can run the mile or not. With the potential for these additional types of conflicts, there is a risk of decreasing the understandability in an object-oriented system instead of increasing it through the use of multiple inheritance. Our advice is to use great care when using multiple inheritance.

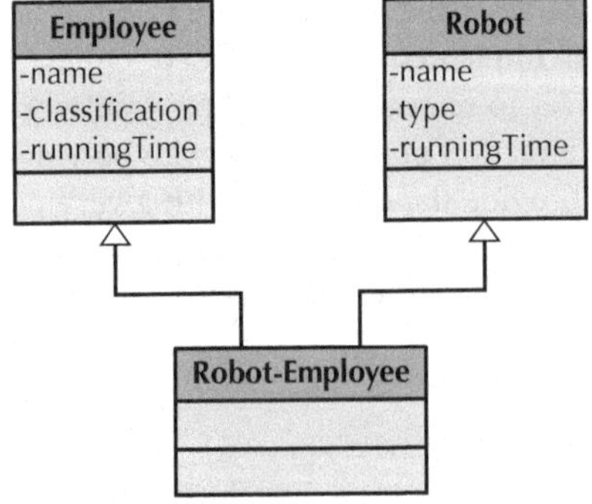

FIGURE A1-8
Additional Inheritance Conflicts with Multiple Inheritance

---

[8] This happens with novices quite regularly when using C++.

PROGRAMMING STRUCTURES

Essentially there are three high-level programming structures: sequence, decision, and looping/repeating. These are programming language independent. From an object-oriented perspective, they are associated with the detailed design of processes and methods. We describe each below.

The sequence construct simply means that the code is executed in a linear or sequential manner. For example, in Figure A1-9, Step 1 is executed first, Step 2 is executed second, and Step 3 is executed last. Obviously, this is the most simple of the structures.

There are two basic decision structures: binary and multiway. A binary decision structure is typically implemented using an If, Then, Else, End-If structure. This is shown on the left side of Figure A1-10. The diamond at the top represents the decision test. The labels represent the values of the tests. In this case either True or False. If the result value is True, then execute Step 1a, else if it is False, then execute Step 1b. The diamond at the bottom represents the End-If idea that closes off the decision block. The multiway structure is typically supported by a case statement that supports multiple branches coming out of a decision test. For example, in Figure A1-10, there are three separate branches coming out of the test. If the result is equal to A, then Routine A will be executed. If the result is equal to B, then Routine B will be executed. And finally, if the result is equal to C, then Routine C is executed. Regardless, all three routines flow to the diamond that closes off the decision block. In this case, the bottom diamond represents the idea of an End-Case statement. Even though closing off decisions may be implicit in specific programming languages, it is always better to explicitly show the complete structure.

There are three different approaches that programming languages can support looping over or repeating chunks of code: Do-While, Do-Until, and Recursion. All three are shown in Figure A1-11. Different programming languages support the constructs differently. In fact, some even use the incorrect name for the construct. Here we present the three constructs in a programming language independent manner. The Do-While loop is shown on the left side of

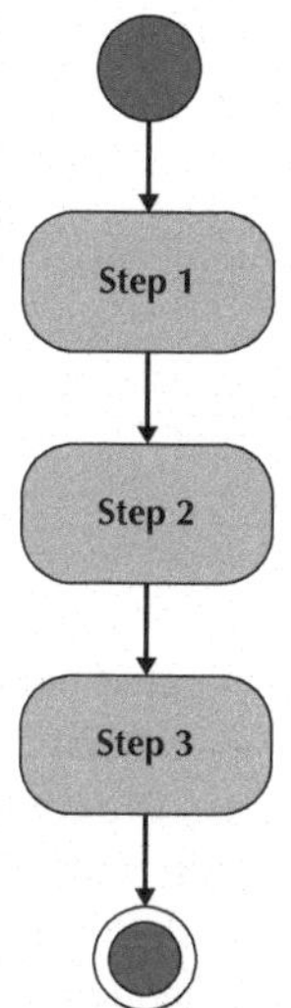

Figure A1-9
Sequence Programming Construct

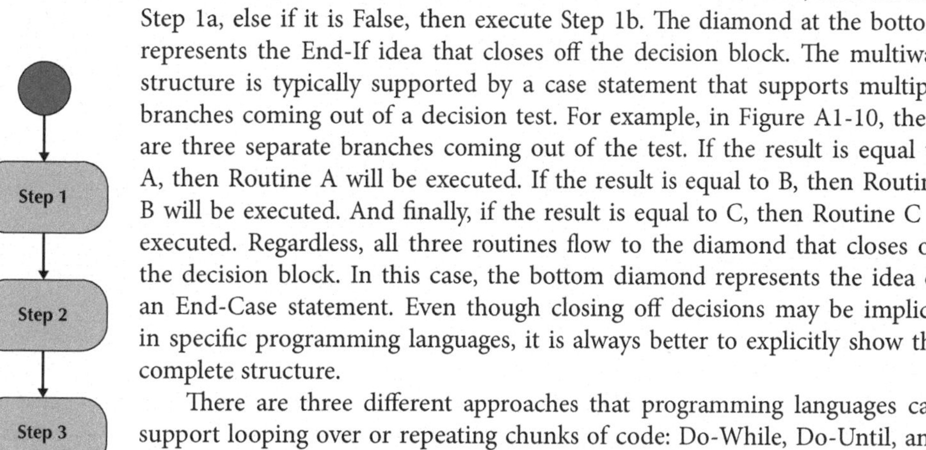

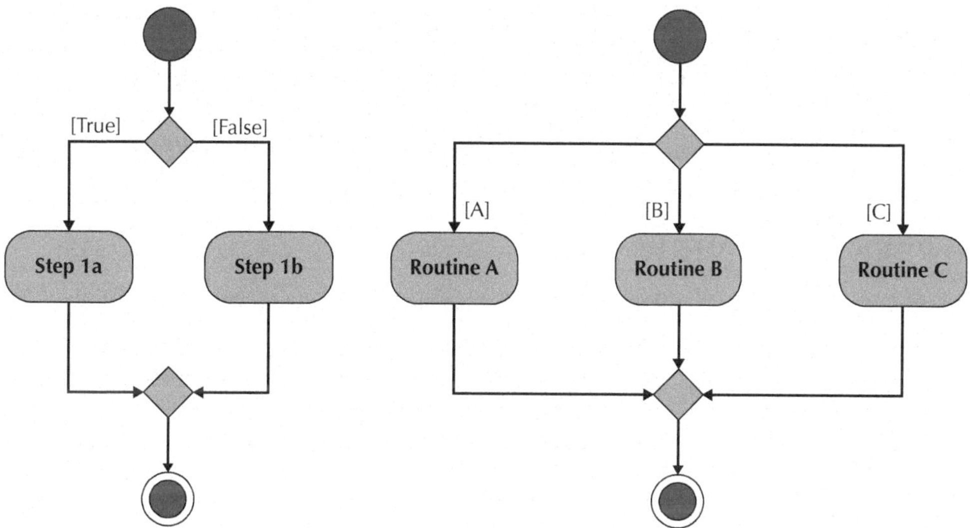

Figure A1-10
Decision Programming Constructs

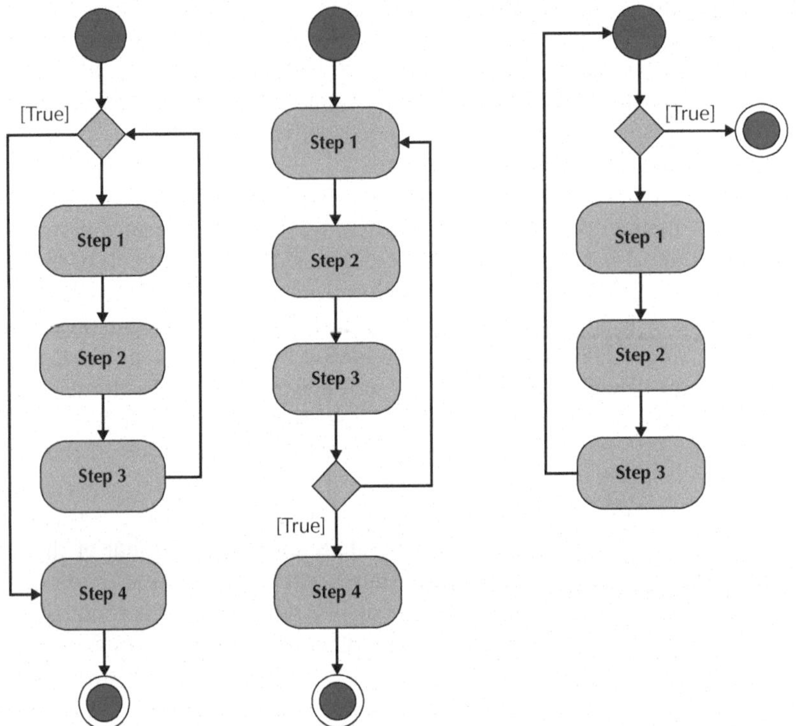

Figure A1-11
Looping/Repeating
Programming
Constructs

the figure. Its primary characteristic is that a test is performed before the steps in the body of the loop are executed. As such, it is possible that the loop itself may never be executed. For example, in this case once the result of the test is True, then the control flows from the decision down to Step 4. The Do-Until loop is shown in the middle of the figure. Its primary characteristic is that the steps in the body of the loop are executed at least one time. For example, in this case Step 1, Step 2, and Step 3 are all executed in sequence before the test is executed. Once the result of the test is True, then the control flows from the decision down to Step 4. If the test result of the test is not True, then Steps 1 through 3 are executed again. Finally, recursion is shown on the right side of the figure. Given that most modern programming languages support recursion, we include it here. Recursive routines call or execute themselves. We portray this in Figure A1-11 by having Step 3 flow to the top of the entire diagram of the recursion example. However, recursive processes are typically not required to support business processes; the Do-While and Do-Until constructs are typically sufficient.

APPENDIX REVIEW

After reading and studying this appendix, you should be able to:

- Describe the basic characteristics of object-oriented systems: objects, attributes, methods, messages, encapsulation, information hiding, polymorphism, dynamic binding, and inheritance.
- Describe the basic programming structures: sequence, decision, and looping/repeating.

KEY TERMS

Abstract classes	DoUntil	Instance	Recursion
Attribute	DoWhile	Iteration	Repeating
Behavior	Dynamic binding	Looping	Sequence
Case	Encapsulation	Message	State
Class	Information hiding	Method	Static binding
Concrete classes	Inherit	Object	Subclass
Decision	Inheritance	Polymorphism	Superclass

QUESTIONS

1. What is the difference between classes and objects?
2. What are methods and messages?
3. Why are encapsulation and information hiding important characteristics of object-oriented systems?
4. What is meant by polymorphism when applied to object-oriented systems?
5. Compare and contrast dynamic and static binding.
6. What are the different decision structures?
7. What is the difference between DoWhile and DoUntil programming structures?
8. What is recursion?

EXERCISES

A. Using your favorite Web search engine, find alternative descriptions of the basic characteristics of object-oriented systems.

B. Look up object-oriented programming in Wikipedia. Write a short report based on its entry.

C. Choose an object-oriented programming language, such as C++, Java, Objective-C, Smalltalk, or VB.Net, and use the Web to find out how the language supports the basic characteristics of object-oriented systems.

D. Assume that you have been assigned the task of creating an object-oriented system that could be used to support students in finding an appropriate apartment to live in next semester. What are the different types of objects (i.e., classes) you would want to include in your system? What attributes or methods would you want to include in their definition? Is it possible to arrange them into an inheritance hierarchy? If so, do it. If not, why not?

E. Create an inheritance hierarchy that could be used to represent the following classes: accountant, customer, department, employee, manager, organization, and salesperson.

PART ONE

ANALYSIS MODELING

Analysis modeling answers the questions of *who* will use the system, *what* the system will do, and *where* and *when* it will be used. During analysis, a system request is created, detailed requirements are identified, and a system proposal is created. The team then produces the functional model (use-case diagram, activity diagrams, and use-case descriptions), structural model (CRC cards and class diagram, and object diagrams), and behavioral models (sequence diagrams, a CRUDE matrix, and behavioral state machines).

CHAPTER 2 Business Modeling & Requirements Determination

Business Modeling & Project Identification

Requirements Determination

Requirements Analysis Approaches

Requirements-Gathering Techniques

Text Analysis

Requirements Definition

Storytelling

The System Proposal

CHAPTER 3 Business Process and Functional Modeling

Business Process Identification with Use Cases and Use-Case Diagrams

Business Process Modeling with Activity Diagrams

Business Process Documentation with Use-Case Descriptions

Verifying and Validating the Business Processes and Functional Models

CHAPTER 4 Structural Modeling

Structural Models

Object Identification

CRC Cards

Class Diagrams

Creating Structural Models Using CRC Cards and Class Diagrams

Verifying and Validating the Structural Model

CHAPTER 5 Behavioral Modeling

Behavioral Models

Interaction Diagrams

CRUDE Analysis

Behavioral State Machines

Verifying and Validating the Behavioral Model

CHAPTER 2

BUSINESS MODELING & REQUIREMENTS DETERMINATION

One of the first activities of an analyst, along with their client, is to identify business needs which a new system could address. Based on the identified need, the business requirements for a new system must be identified. This chapter begins by describing how business needs are identified and they are documented with a system request. Next, the chapter presents how to analyze requirements using requirements analysis approaches and how to gather requirements using interviews, questionnaires, observation, and document analysis. The chapter next describes a set of approaches to perform text analysis on all of the material gathered. It then describes the requirements definition as a way to document the new system's requirements. Finally, the chapter describes the system proposal document that pulls everything together.

OBJECTIVES

- Understand how a project is identified.
- Be able to create a system request.
- Become familiar with requirements-analysis approaches.
- Understand when to use each requirements-analysis approach.
- Understand how to gather requirements using interviews, questionnaires, observation, and document analysis.
- Understand how sentence diagramming and ethnographic analysis can be used to uncover the actual system requirements.
- Understand how to create a requirements definition.
- Understand how storytelling can be used as an alternative to the traditional requirements definition.
- Be able to begin creating a system proposal.

INTRODUCTION

The systems development process aids an organization in moving from the current system (often called the *as-is system*) to the new system (often called the *to-be system*). New systems development projects should start from a business need or opportunity. Typically, based on a business need, a system request kicks off the development of a new system. Usually, a manager, staff member, sales representative, or systems analyst identifies some business value that can be gained from using information technology. Many ideas for new systems or improvements to existing ones arise from the application of a new technology, but an understanding of technology is usually secondary to a solid understanding of the business and its objectives. For example, the *consumerization of IT* refers to how business people often find inspiration from technology use in the personal lives and see how it can be applied in an organization context.

This does not mean that technical people should not recommend new systems projects. In fact, the ideal situation is for both IT people (i.e., the experts in systems) and business people (i.e., the experts in business) to work closely to find ways for technology to support business needs. A *system request* documents the business need for building a new system. It typically includes a project sponsor, business need, business requirements, and the expected business value that the system will provide. The process of creating a system request is usually performed during the inception phase as part of the business modeling workflow. In this way, organizations can leverage the exciting innovative technologies that are available while ensuring that projects are based upon real business objectives, such as increasing sales, improving customer service, and decreasing operating expenses. Ultimately, information systems need to affect the organization's bottom line (in a positive way!). To ensure that a real business need is being addressed, the affected business organization (called the *project sponsor*), proposes the new systems development project using a *system request*. The system request effectively kicks off the inception phase for the new systems development project. The request is forwarded to an *approval committee* for consideration. The approval committee reviews the request and makes an initial determination of whether to investigate the proposal or not. If the committee initially approves the request, the systems development team gathers more information to determine the feasibility of the project.

Once the system request is approved, analysis takes the general ideas in the system request and refines them into a detailed requirements definition, functional models (Chapter 3), structural models (Chapter 4), and behavioral models (Chapter 5) that together form the *system proposal*. The system proposal also includes revised project management deliverables (Chapter 11). The output of analysis, the system proposal, is presented to the approval committee, who decides if the project is to continue. If approved, the system proposal moves into design, and its elements (requirements definition and functional, structural, and behavioral models) are used as inputs to the steps in design. This further refines them and defines in much more detail how the system will be built.

The line between analysis and design is very blurry. This is because the deliverables created during analysis are really the first step in the design of the new system. Many of the major design decisions for the new system are found in the analysis deliverables. It is important to remember that the deliverables from analysis are really the first step in the design of the new system.

In many ways, because it is here that the major elements of the system first emerge, the requirements determination step is the single most critical step of the entire system development process. During requirements determination, the system is easy to change because little work has been done. As the system moves through the system development process, it becomes harder and harder to return to requirements determination and to make major changes because of all of the rework that is involved. Several studies have shown that more than half of all system failures are due to problems with the requirements.[1] This is why the iterative approaches of object-oriented methodologies can be effective—small batches of requirements can be identified and implemented in incremental stages, allowing the overall system to evolve over time. However, every technology decision and implementation in an organization always has future implications (constraints) for the next iterations of technology that may be built.

BUSINESS MODELING & PROJECT IDENTIFICATION

A project is identified when someone in the organization identifies a *business need* to build a system. This could occur within a business unit or IT, come from a steering committee

---

[1] For example, see *The Scope of Software Development Project Failures* (Dennis, MA: The Standish Group, 1995).

charged with identifying business opportunities, or evolve from a recommendation made by external consultants. Examples of business needs include supporting a new marketing campaign, reaching out to a new type of customer, or improving interactions with suppliers. Sometimes, needs arise from some kind of "pain" within the organization, such as a drop in market share, poor customer service levels, or increased competition. Other times, new business initiatives and strategies are created, and a system is required to enable them.

Business needs also can surface when the organization identifies unique and competitive ways of using IT. Many organizations keep an eye on *emerging technologies*, which are technologies that are still being developed and are not yet viable for widespread business use. For example, if companies stay abreast of technology such as the augmented reality, artificial intelligence, and quantum computers, they can develop business strategies that leverage the capabilities of these technologies and introduce them into the marketplace as a *first mover*. Ideally, they can then enjoy the first-mover advantage by making money and continuing to innovate while competitors trail behind.

The project sponsor is someone who recognizes the strong business need for a system and has an interest in seeing the system succeed. He or she will work throughout the development process to make sure that the project is moving in the right direction from the perspective of the business. The project sponsor serves as the primary point of contact for the system. Usually, the sponsor of the project is from a business function, such as marketing, accounting, or finance; however, members of the IT area also can sponsor or cosponsor a project.

The size or scope of a project determines the kind of sponsor needed. A small departmental system might require sponsorship from only a single manager, whereas a large organizational initiative might need support from the entire senior management team and even the CEO. If a project is purely technical in nature (e.g., improvements to the existing IT infrastructure or research into the viability of an emerging technology), then sponsorship from IT is appropriate. When projects have great importance to the business yet are technically complex, joint sponsorship by both the business and IT may be necessary.

The business need drives the high-level *business requirements* for the system. Requirements are what the information system will do or the *functionality* it will contain. They need to be explained at a high level so that the approval committee and, ultimately, the project team understand what the business expects from the final product. Business requirements are the features and capabilities the information system will have to include, such as the ability to collect customer orders online or the ability for suppliers to receive inventory information as orders are placed and sales are made.

The project sponsor also should have an idea of the *business value* to be gained from the system, both in tangible and intangible ways. *Tangible value* can be quantified and measured easily (e.g., 2 percent reduction in operating costs). An *intangible value* results from an intuitive belief that the system provides important, but hard-to-measure, benefits to the organization (e.g., improved customer service or a better competitive position).

Once the project sponsor identifies a project that meets an important business need and he or she can identify the system's business requirements and value, it is time to formally initiate the project. In most organizations, project initiation begins with a document called a *system request*.

System Request

A system request is a document that describes the business reasons for building a system and the value that the system is expected to provide. The project sponsor usually completes this form as part of a formal system project selection process within the organization. Most system requests include five elements: project sponsor, business need, business requirements,

System Request–Name of Project	
Project sponsor:	Name of Project Sponsor
Business Need:	Short description of business need
Business Requirements:	Description of business requirements
Business Value:	Expected value that the system will provide
Special Issues or Constraints:	Any additional information that may be relevant to the stakeholders

FIGURE 2-1
System Request
Template

business value, and *special issues*. The sponsor describes the person who will serve as the primary contact for the project, and the business need presents the reasons prompting the project. The business requirements of the project refer to the business capabilities that the system will need to have, and the business value describes the benefits that the organization should expect from the system. Special issues are included on the document as a catch-all for other information that should be considered in assessing the project. For example, the project may need to be completed by a specific deadline. Project teams need to be aware of any special circumstances that could affect the outcome of the system. Figure 2-1 shows a template for a system request.

The completed system request is submitted to the approval committee for consideration. This approval committee could be a company steering committee that meets regularly to make information systems decisions, a senior executive who has control of organizational resources, or any other decision-making body that governs the use of business investments. The committee reviews the system request and makes an initial determination, based on the information provided, of whether to investigate the proposal or not.

REQUIREMENTS DETERMINATION

The purpose of requirements determination is to turn the very high-level explanation of the business requirements stated in the system request into a more precise list of requirements that can be used as inputs to the rest of analysis. This expansion of the requirements ultimately leads to the design of the system. However, the most difficult aspect of determining the actual requirements is analogous to the story of the blind men and the elephant (see Figure 2-2). In this story, depending on which part of the elephant each blind man touches, each perceives the elephant differently. In many ways, the analyst is like one of the blind men. Depending on which part of the proverbial elephant the analyst touches, the analyst will perceive the requirements differently. Also, like the blind men, the analyst may only be able to perceive the individual part in a biased manner. Therefore, the analyst must be on guard to prevent the poor elephant (requirements) from being misrepresented.

Another way to look at this is to realize that the systems analyst must be able to separate simple symptoms of a problem and be able to identify the actual problem. A useful metaphor is for the analyst to visualize the problem domain as an iceberg that has cracks in it. Using this metaphor, the job of the analyst is to understand which of the cracks are critical and which ones are simply annoying. Also, the analyst must realize that from the perspective of a specific user, by definition, their problem (or their crack in the iceberg) is the most critical. However, since the user typically only has a limited view of the system, a specific user is only capable of seeing symptoms of the underlying problem. Consequently, without understanding the actual problem, the user may identify a "major" crack in the iceberg that does not pose any danger to the existence of the iceberg. On the other hand, the user may ignore a "small" crack that

It was six men of Indostan
To learning much inclined,
Who went to see the Elephant
(Though all of them were blind),
That each by observation
Might satisfy his mind

The First approached the Elephant,
And happening to fall
Against his broad and sturdy side,
At once began to bawl:
God bless me! but the Elephant
Is very like a wall!

The Second, feeling of the tusk,
Cried, Ho! what have we here
So very round and smooth and sharp?
To me tis mighty clear
This wonder of an Elephant
Is very like a spear!

The Third approached the animal,
And happening to take
The squirming trunk within his hands,
Thus boldly up and spake:
I see, quoth he, the Elephant
Is very like a snake!

The Fourth reached out an eager hand,
And felt about the knee.
What most this wondrous beast is like
Is mighty plain, quoth he;
'Tis clear enough the Elephant
Is very like a tree!

The Fifth, who chanced to touch the ear,
Said: Even the blindest man
Can tell what this resembles most;
Deny the fact who can
This marvel of an Elephant
Is very like a fan!?

The Sixth no sooner had begun
About the beast to grope,
Than, seizing on the swinging tail
That fell within his scope,
I see, quothhe, the Elephant
Is very like a rope!

And so these men of Indostan
Disputed loud and long,
Each in his own opinion
Exceeding stiff and strong,
Though each was partly in the right,
And all were in the wrong!

Moral:
So oft in theologic wars,
The disputants, I ween,
Rail on in utter ignorance
Of what each other mean,
And prate about an Elephant
Not one of them has seen!

—John Godfrey Saxe

FIGURE 2-2 The Blind Men and
the Elephant

happens to be right above a major void in the iceberg such that if this small "inconsequential" crack would deepen, the iceberg could actually be cleaved into multiple pieces. Or in other words, the analyst must uncover the objective reality of the problem while realizing that users can only see a subjective reality. Figure 2-3 portrays this by showing that real-world objects (and concepts) have real-world properties.[2] But neither any user nor an analyst can provide a complete description of the real objects. As humans, we only have our perceptions of a subjective reality. That is, we can only observe the reality through our experiences and biases. Consequently, our understanding (and misunderstanding) of a problem is flawed. Therefore, we need to capture the requirements from many different stakeholders and multiple inter-related perspectives. In fact, one of the goals of requirements determination is to surface our (the systems analyst) misunderstandings so that the different stakeholders can correct our misunderstandings of the problem. This can build and foster trust in the ideal ongoing partnership between IT personnel and business people suggested earlier; both are part of the same organization. In this book, we suggest using different requirements analysis approaches and requirements gathering techniques with the different stakeholders. Furthermore, we model the problem using three different architectural views: functional, structural, and behavioral. Looking at the requirements through these three interrelated views supports the expansion of the requirements that ultimately leads to the design of the system.

Defining a Requirement

A *requirement* is simply a statement of what the system must do or what characteristic it must have. During analysis, requirements are written from the perspective of the businessperson, and they focus on the "what" of the system. Because they focus on the needs of the business user, they are usually called *business requirements* (and sometimes user requirements).

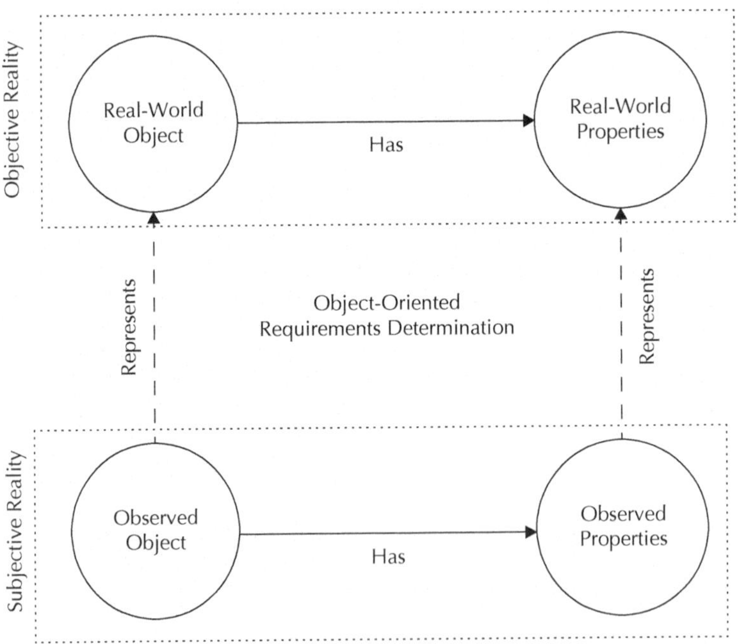

FIGURE 2-3
Requirements Determination Purpose

2 For a more detailed description of this philosophical position, see Graham Harman, *Object-Oriented Ontology: A New Theory of Everything* (United Kingdom: Pelican, 2018).

Later in design, business requirements evolve to become more technical, and they describe how the system will be implemented. Requirements in design are written from the developer's perspective, and they are usually called *system requirements.*

We want to stress that there is no clear-cut line dividing a business requirement and a system requirement—and some companies use the terms interchangeably. The important thing to remember is that a requirement is a statement of what the system must do, and requirements will change over time as the project moves from inception to elaboration to construction. Requirements evolve from detailed statements of the business capabilities that a system should have to detailed statements of the technical way the capabilities will be implemented in the new system.

Requirements can be either functional or nonfunctional in nature. A *functional requirement* relates directly to a process a system has to perform or information it needs to contain. For example, requirements stating that a system must have the ability to search for available inventory or to report actual and budgeted expenses are functional requirements. Functional requirements flow directly into the creation of functional, structural, and behavioral models that represent the functionality of the evolving system (see Chapters 3, 4, and 5). Functional requirements are essentially the business requirements uncovered as part of modeling the problem domain.

Nonfunctional requirements refer to behavioral properties that the system must have, such as performance and usability. The ability to access the system using a Web browser is considered a nonfunctional requirement. Nonfunctional requirements can influence the rest of analysis (functional, structural, and behavioral models) but often do so only indirectly; nonfunctional requirements are used primarily in design when decisions are made about the database, the user interface, the hardware and software, and the system's underlying application architecture.

Nonfunctional requirements describe a variety of characteristics regarding the system: operational, performance, security, and cultural and political. Operational requirements address issues related to the physical and technical requirements in which the system will operate. Performance requirements address issues related to the speed, capacity, and reliability of the system. Security requirements deal with issues with regard to who has access to the system, what type of access, and under what specific circumstances. In today's world of cyberwar, denial of service attacks, malware, phishing, ransomware, social engineering, spyware, Trojan horses, and many other types of security threats, the security requirements have become the most important of the nonfunctional requirements. Cultural and political requirements deal with issues related to the cultural and political factors and legal requirements that affect the system. Given that nonfunctional requirements do not describe business processes or information, in many cases, they have been ignored. However, if a system is to be deployed successfully, all of these requirements must be addressed. For pedagogical purposes, we delay addressing these requirements in detail until later in the book when we discuss design (see Chapters 6, 7, 8, 9, and 10).

One area of information systems development that focused on differentiating functional and nonfunctional requirements is *software quality*. There have been many different models proposed to measure the quality of software. However, virtually all of them differentiate functional and nonfunctional requirements. From a quality perspective, *functional* quality is related to the degree that the software meets the functional requirements, i.e., how much of the actual problem is solved by the software solution provided. Whereas, the nonfunctional requirements are associated with the efficiency, maintainability, portability, reliability, reusability, testability, and usability quality dimensions.

When considering ISO 9000 compliance, quality dimensions are further decomposed into those that the user can see (*external*) and those that the user cannot see (*internal*).

The external nonfunctional dimensions include efficiency, reliability, and usability, whereas the internal nonfunctional dimensions include maintainability, portability, reusability, and testability. From a user's perspective, the external dimensions are more important. If the system is too difficult to use, regardless of how well the system solves the problem, the user will simply not use the system. In other words, from a user's perspective, for an information system to be successful, the system must not only meet the functional specification, but it must also meet the external nonfunctional specifications. From a developer's perspective, the internal dimensions are also important. For example, given that successful systems tend to be long-lived and multiplatform, both the maintainability and portability dimensions can have strategic implications for the system being developed. Also, given the *agile* development approaches being used in industry today, the development of reusable and testable software is crucial.

Three additional topics that have influenced information system requirements are the Sarbanes–Oxley Act, COBIT (Control OBjectives for Information and related Technology) compliance, and Capability Maturity Model compliance. Depending on the system being considered, these three topics could affect the definition of a system's functional requirements, nonfunctional requirements, or both. The Sarbanes–Oxley Act, for example, mandates additional functional and nonfunctional requirements. These include additional security concerns (nonfunctional) and specific information requirements that management must now provide (functional). When developing financial information systems, information system developers should be sure to include Sarbanes–Oxley expertise in the development team. Moreover, a client could insist on COBIT compliance or that a specific Capability Maturity Model level had been reached in order for the firm to be considered as a possible vendor to supply the system under consideration. Obviously, these types of requirements add to the nonfunctional requirements. Further discussion of these topics is beyond the scope of this book.[3]

Another recent topic that influences requirements for some systems is globalization. For example, a global information supply chain generates a large number of additional nonfunctional requirements. If the necessary operational environments do not exist for a mobile solution to be developed, it is important to adapt the solution to the local environment. Or, it may not be reasonable to expect to deploy a high-technology-based solution in an area that does not have the necessary power and communications infrastructure. In some cases, we may need to consider supporting some parts of the global information supply chain with manual—rather than automated—systems.

Manual systems have an entirely different set of nonfunctional requirements that create different performance expectations and additional security concerns. Furthermore, cultural and political concerns are potentially paramount. A simple example that affects the design of user interfaces is the proper use of color on forms (on a screen or paper). Different cultures interpret different colors differently. In other words, in a global, multicultural business environment, addressing cultural concerns goes well beyond simply having a multilingual user interface. We must be able to adapt the global solution to the local realities. Friedman refers to these concerns as glocalization.[4] Otherwise, we will simply create another example of a failed information system development project.

---

[3] A concise discussion of the Sarbanes–Oxley Act is presented in G. P. Lander, *What Is Sarbanes–Oxley?* (New York: McGraw-Hill, 2004). A good reference for Sarbanes-Oxley Act-based security requirements is D. C. Brewer, *Security Controls for Sarbanes–Oxley Section 404 IT Compliance: Authorization, Authentication, and Access* (Indianapolis, IN: Wiley, 2006). For detailed information on COBIT, see www.isaca.org/resources/cobit; for ISO 9000, see www.iso.org/standards/popular/iso-9000-family; and for details on the Capability Maturity Model, see cmmiinstitute.com/

[4] T. L. Friedman, *The World Is Flat: A Brief History of the Twenty-First Century, Updated and Expanded Edition.* (New York: Farrar, Straus, and Giroux, 2006.)

REQUIREMENTS ANALYSIS APPROACHES

Before the project team can determine what requirements are appropriate for a given system, there needs to be a clear vision of the kind of system that will be created and the level of change that it will bring to the organization. The basic process of *analysis* is divided into three steps: understanding the as-is system, identifying improvements, and developing requirements for the to-be system.

Sometimes the first step (i.e., understanding the as-is system) is skipped or is performed in a cursory manner. This happens when no current system exists, if the existing system and processes are irrelevant to the future system, or if the project team is using an agile development methodology in which the as-is system is not emphasized. Newer agile and object-oriented methodologies focus almost exclusively on improvements and the to-be system requirements, and they spend little time investigating the current as-is system.

Requirements analysis approaches help the analyst lead users through the analysis steps so that the vision of the system can be developed. Requirements analysis approaches and requirements-gathering techniques go hand in hand. Analysts use requirements-gathering techniques to collect information; requirements analysis approaches drive the kind of information that is gathered and how it is ultimately analyzed. The requirements analysis approaches and requirements gathering happen concurrently and are complementary activities.

To move the users from the as-is system to the to-be system, an analyst needs strong *critical thinking skills*. Critical thinking is the ability to recognize strengths and weaknesses and recast an idea in an improved form, and critical thinking skills are needed to really understand issues and develop new business processes. Furthermore, critical thinking requires the ability to identify not just the primary effects of a requirement, but also the secondary and tertiary effects, i.e., a thorough understanding of causality is required. Analysts must also have strong *systems thinking skills*. One major misunderstanding is that all IT personnel will have systems thinking skills. But this is not so. Systems thinking skills have to do with the ability to see the whole from the different parts of the "system" where a system could be a biological system; not simply an IT system. Furthermore, it refers to the ability to see across different systems to find possible metaphors and analogies that could be useful in the understanding of the current systems development project. These skills are also needed to thoroughly examine the results of requirements gathering, to identify business requirements, and to translate those requirements into a concept for the new system. Both critical and systems thinking skills are so-called twenty-first century skills that are very difficult to automate.[5]

Problem Analysis

The most straightforward (and probably the most commonly used) requirements-analysis approach is *problem analysis*. Problem analysis means asking the users and managers to identify problems with the as-is system and to describe how to solve them in the to-be system. Most users have a very good idea of the changes they would like to see, and most are quite vocal about suggesting them. Most changes tend to solve problems rather than capitalize on opportunities, but the latter is possible as well. Improvements from problem analysis tend to be small and incremental (e.g., provide more space in which to type the customer's name and address; provide a new report that currently does not exist).

---

[5] For more information see Joseph E. *Aoun, Robot-Proof: Higher Education in the Age of Artificial Intelligence* (Cambridge, MA: MIT Press, 2017); Cathy N. Davidson, *The New Education: How to Revolutionize The University to Prepare Students for a World in Flux* (New York, NY: Basic Books, 2017); James Bellanca, Ron Brandt (Eds.), *21st century skills: Rethinking How Students Learn* (Bloomington, IN: Solution Tree Press, 2010).

This type of improvement often is very effective at improving a system's efficiency or ease of use. However, it often provides only minor improvements in business value—the new system is better than the old, but it may be hard to identify significant monetary benefits from the new system.

Root Cause Analysis

The ideas produced by problem analysis tend to be solutions to problems. All solutions make assumptions about the nature of the problem, assumptions that might or might not be valid. In our experience, users (and most people in general) tend to quickly jump to solutions without fully considering the nature of the problem. Sometimes the solutions are appropriate, but many times they address a *symptom* of the problem, not the true problem or *root cause* itself.[6]

For example, suppose a firm notices that its users report inventory stock-outs. The cost of inventory stock-outs can be quite significant. In this case, since they happen frequently, customers could find another source for the items that they are purchasing from the firm. It is in the firm's interest to determine the underlying cause and not simply provide a knee-jerk reaction such as arbitrarily increasing the amount of inventory kept on hand. In the business world, the challenge lies in identifying the root cause—few real-world problems are simple. The users typically propose a set of causes for the problem under consideration. The solutions that users propose can address either symptoms or root causes, but without a careful analysis, it is difficult to tell which one is addressed.

Root cause analysis, therefore, focuses on problems, not solutions. The analyst starts by having the users generate a list of problems with the current system and then prioritize the problems in order of importance. Starting with the most important, the users and/or the analysts then generate all the possible root causes for the problems. Each possible root cause is investigated (starting with the most likely or easiest to check) until the true root causes are identified. If any possible root causes are identified for several problems, those should be investigated first, because there is a good chance they are the real root causes influencing the symptom problems. In our example, there are several possible root causes:

- The firm's supplier might not be delivering orders to the firm in a timely manner.
- There could be a problem with the firm's inventory controls.
- The reorder level and quantities could be set wrong.

Sometimes, using a *fishbone diagram* to represent the causal relationships helps with the analysis. Fishbone diagrams were developed in the quality control area.[7] The causes are shown as "bones" off of the "spine" of the fish while the effect is shown as the "head" of the fish on the far-right side of the diagram. As Figure 2-4 shows, there are many possible root causes that underlie the higher-level causes identified. The key point in root cause analysis is always to challenge the obvious.

Duration Analysis

Duration analysis requires a detailed examination of the amount of time it takes to perform each process in the current as-is system. The analysts begin by determining the total amount of time it takes, on average, to perform a set of business processes for a typical input. They then time each of the individual steps (or subprocesses) in the business process. The time to

---

[6] Two good books that discuss the difficulty in finding the root causes to problems are: E. M. Goldratt and J. Cox, *The Goal* (Croton-on-Hudson, NY: North River Press, 1986); E. M. Goldratt, *The Haystack Syndrome* (Croton-on-Hudson, NY: North River Press, 1990).

[7] Kaoru Ishikawa, *Guide to Quality Control* (Tokyo: Asian Productivity Organization, 1982).

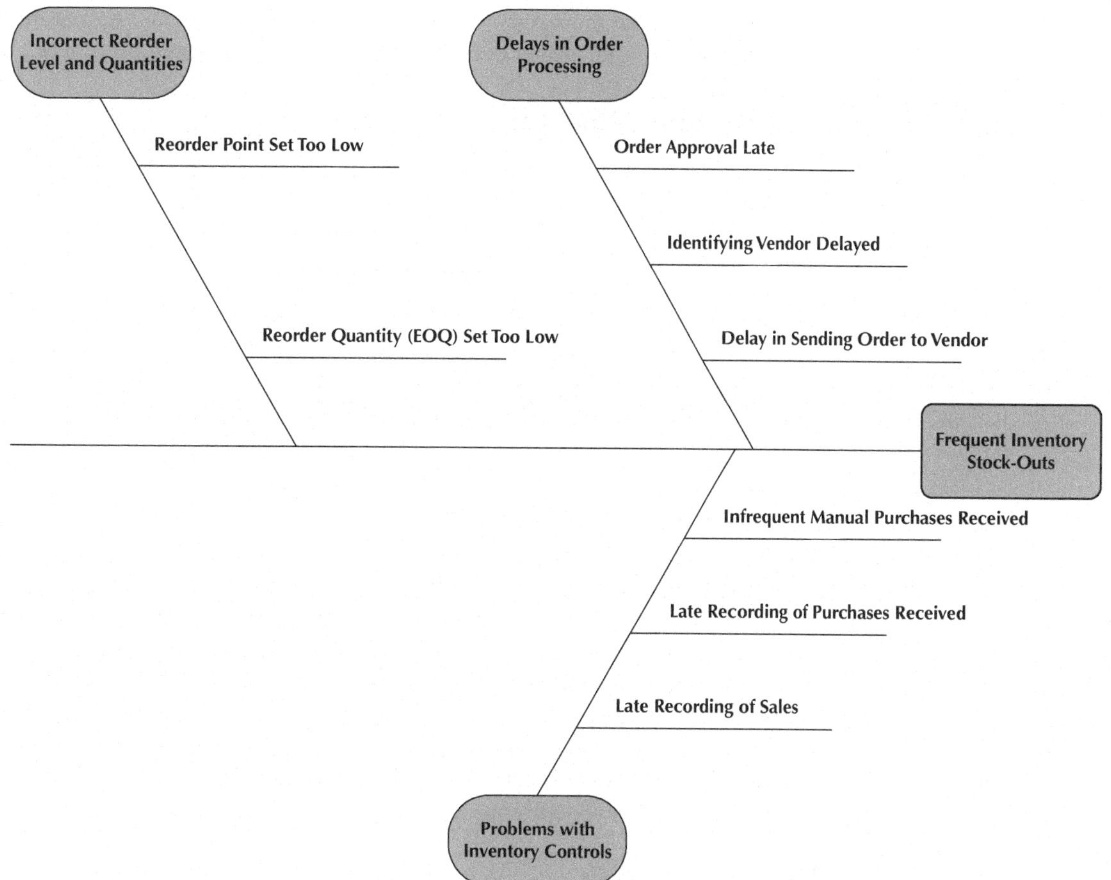

FIGURE 2-4   Root Cause Analysis for Inventory Stock-Outs

complete the basic step is then totaled and compared to the total for the overall process. A significant difference between the two—and in our experience the total time often can be 10 or even 100 times longer than the sum of the parts—indicates that this part of the process is badly in need of a major overhaul.

For example, suppose that the analysts are working on a home mortgage system and discover that on average, it takes thirty days for the bank to approve a mortgage. They then look at each of the basic steps in the process (e.g., data entry, credit check, title search, and appraisal) and find that the total amount of time actually spent on each mortgage is about eight hours. This is a strong indication that the overall process is badly broken, because it takes thirty days to perform one day's work.

These problems probably occur because the process is badly fragmented. Many different people must perform different activities before the process finishes. In the mortgage example, the application probably sits on many people's desks for long periods of time before it is processed.

Processes in which many different people work on small parts of the inputs are prime candidates for *process integration* or *parallelization*. Process integration means changing the fundamental process so that fewer people work on the input, which often requires changing the processes and retraining staff to perform a wider range of duties. Process parallelization means changing the process so that all the individual steps are performed at the same time.

For example, in the mortgage application case, there is probably no reason that the credit check cannot be performed at the same time as the appraisal and title check.

Activity-Based Costing

Activity-based costing is a similar analysis; it examines the cost of each major process or step in a business process rather than the time taken.[8] The analysts identify the costs associated with each of the basic functional steps or processes, identify the most costly processes, and focus their improvement efforts on them.

Assigning costs is conceptually simple. Analysts simply examine the direct cost of labor and materials for each input. Materials costs are easily assigned in a manufacturing process, whereas labor costs are usually calculated based on the amount of time spent on the input and the hourly cost of the staff. However, as you may recall from a managerial accounting course, there are indirect costs, such as rent, depreciation, and so on, that also can be included in activity costs.

Informal Benchmarking

Benchmarking refers to studying how other organizations perform a business process in order to learn how your organization can do something better. Benchmarking helps the organization by introducing ideas that employees may never have considered but that have the potential to add value. Consultants can also be hired to suggest best practices.

Informal benchmarking is fairly common for customer-facing business processes (i.e., processes that interact with the customer). With informal benchmarking, the managers and analysts think about other organizations or visit them as customers to watch how the business process is performed. In many cases, the business studied may be a known leader in the industry or simply a related firm.

Outcome Analysis

Outcome analysis focuses on understanding the fundamental outcomes that provide value to customers. Although these outcomes sound as though they should be obvious, they often are not. For example, consider an insurance company. One of its customers has just had a car accident. What is the fundamental outcome from the *customer's* perspective? Traditionally, insurance companies have answered this question by assuming the customer wants to receive the insurance payment quickly. To the customer, however, the payment is only a *means* to the real outcome: a repaired car. The insurance company might benefit by extending its view of the business process past its traditional boundaries to include not paying for repairs but performing the repairs or contracting with an authorized body shop to do them.

With this approach, system analysts encourage the managers and project sponsor to pretend they are customers and to think carefully about what the organization's products and services enable the customers to do—and what they *could* enable the customer to do.

A variation of outcome analysis is *givens-means-ends (GME) analysis*.[9] The primary difference between regular outcome analysis and GME analysis is that GME also considers the givens that the analyst must consider. Effectively, a given is a constraint that cannot be changed to affect the outcome (end). Only the means can be modified to effect any change in the outcome. For example, if the leadership of an organization cannot change, then the

---

8 Many books have been written on activity-based costing. Useful ones include K. B. Burk and D. W. Webster, *Activity-Based Costing* (Fairfax, VA: American Management Systems, 1994); D. T. Hicks, *Activity-Based Costing: Making It Work for Small and Mid-sized Companies* (New York: Wiley, 1998). The two books by Eli Goldratt mentioned previously (*The Goal* and *The Haystack Syndrome*) also offer unique insights into costing.

9 GME analysis has been developed in organizational research with regard to analyzing cognitive maps and in cognitive psychology with research dealing with problem solving and more recently with cognitive load theory.

current leadership will either be a positive or negative driver on possible means that can be used to reach the desired goal or end, i.e., the leadership is a constraint. Knowing the actual constraints that can affect a solution is useful.

Technology Analysis

Many major changes in business since the turn of the century have been enabled by new technologies. *Technology analysis* starts by having the analysts and managers develop a list of important and interesting technologies. Then the group systematically identifies how every technology could be applied to the business process and identifies how the business would benefit. It is important to note that the technology analysis in no way implies adopting technology for technology's sake. Rather the focus is on using new technologies to meet the goals of the organization.

Activity Elimination

Activity elimination is exactly what it sounds. The analysts and managers work together to identify how the organization could eliminate each activity in the business process, how the function could operate without it, and what effects are likely to occur. Initially, managers are reluctant to conclude that processes can be eliminated, but this is a force-fit exercise in that they must eliminate each activity. In some cases, the results are silly; nonetheless, participants must address every activity in the business process. It could be that prior activities in a business process were implemented due to constraints that are no longer true in information technology (e.g., desktop vs. mobile).

REQUIREMENTS-GATHERING TECHNIQUES

An analyst is very much like a detective (and business users are sometimes like elusive suspects). He or she knows that there is a problem to be solved and therefore must look for clues that uncover the solution. Unfortunately, the clues are not always obvious (and are often missed), so the analyst needs to notice details, talk with witnesses, and follow leads just as Sherlock Holmes would have done. The best analysts thoroughly gather requirements using a variety of techniques and make sure that the current business processes and the needs for the new system are well understood before moving into design. Analysts don't want to discover later that they have key requirements wrong—such surprises late in the development process can cause all kinds of problems.

The requirements-gathering process is used for building political support for the project and establishing trust and rapport between the project team building the system and the users who ultimately will choose to use or not use the system. Involving someone in the process implies that the project teams view that person as an important resource and value his or her opinions. All the key stakeholders (the people who can affect the system or who will be affected by the system) must be included in the requirements-gathering process. The stakeholders might include managers, employees, staff members, operations personnel, and even some customers and suppliers. If a key person is not involved, that individual might feel slighted, which can cause problems during implementation (e.g., How could they have developed the system without my input?).

The second challenge of requirements gathering is choosing the way(s) information is collected. There are many techniques for gathering requirements that vary from asking people questions to watching them work. Some other very useful requirements-gathering and documentation techniques include use cases and role-playing CRC cards with use-case-based scenarios. Use cases, as described in Chapter 1, are the fundamental approach that the

Unified Process and Unified Modeling Language (UML) use to document and gather functional requirements. We describe them in Chapter 3. Role-playing CRC cards with use-case-based scenarios are very useful when creating structural (see Chapter 4) and behavioral (see Chapter 5) models. We describe role-playing in Chapter 4.

In this section, we focus on the four most commonly used techniques: interviews, questionnaires, observation, and document analysis. Each technique has its own strengths and weaknesses, many of which are complementary, so most projects use a combination of techniques.[10]

Interviews

An interview is the most commonly used requirements-gathering technique. After all, it is natural—if you need to know something, you usually ask someone. In general, interviews are conducted one-on-one (one interviewer and one interviewee), but sometimes, owing to time constraints, several people are interviewed at the same time. There are five basic steps to the interview process: selecting interviewees, designing interview questions, preparing for the interview, conducting the interview, and post-interview follow-up.[11]

1. Select Interviewees

The first step in interviewing is to create an *interview schedule* listing who will be interviewed, when, and for what purpose (see Figure 2-5). The schedule can be an informal list that is used to help set up meeting times or a formal list that is incorporated into the workplan. The people who appear on the interview schedule are selected based on the analyst's information needs. The project sponsor, key business users, and other members of the project team can help the analyst determine who in the organization can best provide important information about requirements. These people are listed on the interview schedule in the order in which they should be interviewed.

People at different levels of the organization have varying perspectives on the system, so it is important to include both managers who manage the processes and staff who actually perform the processes to gain both high-level and low-level perspectives on an issue. Also, the kinds of interview subjects needed can change over time. For example, at the start of the project, the analyst has a limited understanding of the as-is business process. It is common to begin by interviewing one or two senior managers to get a strategic view and then to move to midlevel managers who can provide broad, overarching information about the business process and the expected role of the system being developed. Once the analyst has a good understanding of the big picture, lower-level managers and staff members can fill in the exact details of how the process works. Like most other things about systems analysis, this is an iterative process—starting with senior managers, moving to midlevel managers, then staff members, back to midlevel managers, and so on, depending upon what information is needed along the way.

It is quite common for the list of interviewees to grow, often by 50 to 75 percent. As people are interviewed, more information that is needed and additional people who can provide the information will probably be identified.

---

[10] Some excellent books that address the importance of gathering requirements and various techniques include Alan M. Davis, *Software Requirements: Objects, Functions, & States, Revision* (Englewood Cliffs, NJ: Prentice Hall, 1993); Gerald Kotonya and Ian Sommerville, *Requirements Engineering* (Chichester, England: Wiley, 1998); Dean Leffingwell and Don Widrig, *Managing Software Requirements: A Unified Approach* (Reading, MA: Addison-Wesley, 2000).

[11] A good book on interviewing is that by Brian James, *The Systems Analysis Interview* (Manchester, England: NCC Blackwell, 1989).

Name	Position	Purpose of Interview	Meeting
Andria McClellan	Director, Accounting	Strategic vision for new accounting system	Mon., March 1 8:00–10:00 AM
Jennifer Draper	Manager, Accounts Receivable	Current problems with accounts receivable process; future goals	Mon., March 1 2:00–3:15 PM
Mark Goodin	Manager, Accounts Payable	Current problems with accounts payable process; future goals	Mon., March 1 4:00–5:15 PM
Anne Asher	Supervisor, Data Entry	Accounts receivable and payable processes	Wed., March 3 10:00–11:00 AM
Fernando Merce	Data Entry Clerk	Accounts receivable and payable processes	Wed., March 3 1:00–3:00 PM

FIGURE 2-5
Sample Interview
Schedule

2. Design Interview Questions

There are three types of interview questions: closed-ended questions, open-ended questions, and probing questions. *Closed-ended questions* are those that require a specific answer. They are similar to multiple-choice or arithmetic questions on an exam (see Figure 2-6). Closed-ended questions are used when an analyst is looking for specific, precise information (e.g., how many credit card requests are received per day). In general, precise questions are best. For example, rather than asking, Do you handle a lot of requests? it is better to ask, How many requests do you process per day? Closed-ended questions enable analysts to control the interview and obtain the information they need. However, these types of questions don't uncover *why* the answer is the way it is, nor do they uncover information that the interviewer does not think to ask for ahead of time.

Open-ended questions are those that leave room for elaboration on the part of the interviewee. They are similar in many ways to essay questions that you might find on an exam (see Figure 2-6). Open-ended questions are designed to gather rich information and give the interviewee more control over the information that is revealed during the interview. Sometimes the information that the interviewee chooses to discuss uncovers information that is just as important as the answer (e.g., if the interviewee talks only about other departments when asked for problems, it may suggest that he or she is reluctant to admit his or her own problems).

The third type of question is the probing question. Probing questions follow up on what has just been discussed in order to learn more, and they often are used when the interviewer is unclear about an interviewee's answer. They encourage the interviewee to expand on or to confirm information from a previous response, and they signal that the interviewer is listening and is interested in the topic under discussion. Many beginning analysts are reluctant to use probing questions because they are afraid that the interviewee might be offended at being challenged or because they believe it shows that they didn't understand what the interviewee said. When done politely, probing questions can be a powerful tool in requirements gathering.

In general, an interviewer should not ask questions about information that is readily available from other sources. For example, rather than asking what information is used to perform a task, it is simpler to show the interviewee a form or report (see the section on document analysis) and ask what information on it is used. This helps focus the interviewee on the task and saves time, because the interviewee does not need to describe the information detail—he or she just needs to point it out on the form or report.

No type of question is better than another, and a combination of questions is usually used during an interview. At the initial stage of an IS development project, the as-is process can be unclear, so the interview process begins with *unstructured interviews,* interviews that seek broad and roughly defined information. In this case, the interviewer has a general sense of the information needed but has few closed-ended questions to ask. These are the most challenging interviews to conduct because they require the interviewer to ask open-ended questions and probe for important information on the fly.

As the project progresses, the analyst comes to understand the business process much better and needs very specific information about how business processes are performed (e.g., exactly how a customer credit card is approved). At this time, the analyst conducts *structured interviews,* in which specific sets of questions are developed before the interviews. There usually are more closed-ended questions in a structured interview than in the unstructured approach.

No matter what kind of interview is being conducted, interview questions must be organized into a logical sequence so that the interview flows well. For example, when trying to gather information about the current business process, it can be useful to move in logical order through the process or from the most important issues to the least important.

There are two fundamental approaches to organizing the interview questions: top down or bottom up (see Figure 2-7). With the *top-down interview,* the interviewer starts with broad, general issues and gradually works toward more-specific ones. With the *bottom-up interview,* the interviewer starts with very specific questions and moves to broad questions. In practice, analysts mix the two approaches, starting with broad, general issues, moving to specific questions, and then returning to general issues.

The top-down approach is an appropriate strategy for most interviews (it is certainly the most common approach). The top-down approach enables the interviewee to become accustomed to the topic before he or she needs to provide specifics. It also enables the interviewer to understand the issues before moving to the details because the interviewer might not have sufficient information at the start of the interview to ask very specific questions. Perhaps most importantly, the top-down approach enables the interviewee to raise a set of big-picture issues before becoming enmeshed in details, so the interviewer is less likely to miss important issues.

One case in which the bottom-up strategy may be preferred is when the analyst already has gathered a lot of information about issues and just needs to fill in some holes with details. Bottom-up interviewing may be appropriate if lower-level staff members feel threatened or unable to answer high-level questions. For example, How can we improve customer service? might be too broad a question for a customer service clerk, whereas a specific question is readily answerable (e.g., How can we speed up customer returns?). In any event, all interviews should begin with noncontroversial questions and then gradually move into more contentious issues after the interviewer has developed some rapport with the interviewee.

Types of Questions	Examples
Closed-ended questions	• How many telephone orders are received per day? • How do customers place orders? • What information is missing from the monthly sales report?
Open-ended questions	• What do you think about the current system? • What are some of the problems you face on a daily basis? • What are some of the improvements you would like to see in a new system?
Probing questions	• Why? • Can you give me an example? • Can you explain that in a bit more detail?

FIGURE 2-6 Three Types of Questions

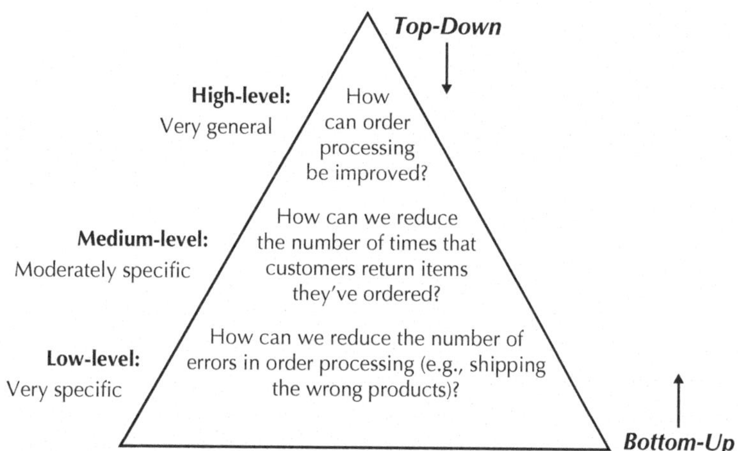

FIGURE 2-7
Top-Down and
Bottom-Up
Questioning
Strategies

3. Prepare for the Interview

It is important to prepare for the interview in the same way that you would prepare to give a presentation. The interviewer should have a general interview plan listing the questions to be asked in the appropriate order, should anticipate possible answers and provide follow-up with them, and should identify segues between related topics. The interviewer should confirm the areas in which the interviewee has knowledge so as not to ask questions that the interviewee cannot answer. Review the topic areas, the questions, and the interview plan, and clearly decide which have the greatest priority in case time runs short.

In general, structured interviews with closed-ended questions take more time to prepare than unstructured interviews. Some beginning analysts prefer unstructured interviews, thinking that they can wing it. This is very dangerous and often counterproductive, because any information not gathered in the first interview will require follow-up efforts, and most users do not like to be interviewed repeatedly about the same issues. Furthermore, the old adage "Time is money" applies here. So, asking for the same information from the same user can be a waste of time and money.

The interviewer should be sure to prepare the interviewee as well. When the interview is scheduled, the interviewee should be told the reason for the interview and the areas that will be discussed far enough in advance so that he or she has time to think about the issues and organize his or her thoughts. This is particularly important when the interviewer is an outsider to the organization and for lower-level employees, who often are not asked for their opinions and who may be uncertain about why they are being interviewed.

4. Conduct the Interview

The first goal is to build rapport with the interviewee, so that he or she trusts the interviewer and is willing to tell the whole truth, not just give the answers that he or she thinks are wanted. The interviewer should appear to be a professional and unbiased, independent seeker of information. The interview should start with an explanation of why the interviewer is there and why he or she has chosen to interview the person; then the interviewer should move into the planned interview questions.

It is critical to carefully record all the information that the interviewee provides. In our experience, the best approach is to take careful notes—write down *everything* the interviewee says, even if it does not appear immediately relevant. The interviewer shouldn't be afraid to ask the person to slow down or to pause while writing, because this is a clear indication that the interviewee's information is important. One potentially controversial issue is whether or not to audio-record an interview. Recording ensures that the interviewer does not miss important points, but it can be intimidating for the interviewee. Most organizations have policies or generally accepted practices about the recording of interviews, so they should be determined before an interview. If the interviewer is worried about missing information and cannot tape the interview, then he or she can bring along a second person to take detailed notes. Another alternative and potential complement to audio-recording is to invite another analyst to join you to act as a scribe to jot down their key learning from the interviews so that you can compare their notes with yours.

As the interview progresses, it is important to understand the issues that are discussed. If the interviewer does not understand something, he or she should ask for clarification. The interviewer should not be afraid to ask dumb questions, because the only thing worse than appearing dumb is to be dumb by not understanding something. If the interviewer doesn't understand something during the interview, he or she certainly won't understand it afterward. Jargon should be recognized and defined; any jargon not understood should be clarified. One good strategy to increase understanding during an interview is to periodically summarize the key points that the interviewee is communicating. This avoids misunderstandings and also demonstrates that the interviewer is listening. Again, this is where having another analyst present with you during the interview can be helpful; one can focus on taking notes and the other can focus on the bigger picture issues, and both can ask questions when they do not understand something.

Finally, facts should be separated from opinion. The interviewee may say, for example, We process too many credit card requests. This is an opinion, and it is useful to follow this up with a probing question requesting support for the statement (e.g., Oh, how many do you process in a day?). It is helpful to check the facts because any differences between the facts and the interviewee's opinions can point out key areas for improvement. Suppose the interviewee complains about a high or increasing number of errors, but the logs show that errors have been decreasing. This suggests that errors are viewed as a very important problem that should be addressed by the new system, even if they are declining.

As the interview draws to a close, the interviewee should have time to ask questions or provide information that he or she thinks is important but was not part of the interview plan. In most cases, the interviewee has no additional concerns or information, but in some cases, this leads to unanticipated, but important, information. Likewise, it can be useful to ask the interviewee if there are other people who should be interviewed. The interview should end on time (if necessary, some topics can be omitted or another interview can be scheduled).

As a last step in the interview, the interviewer should briefly explain what will happen. The interviewer shouldn't prematurely promise certain features in the new system or a specific delivery date, but he or she should reassure the interviewee that his or her time was well spent and very helpful to the project. It would also be wise to ask the interviewee if it would be possible to contact them again in the future for a short follow-up in case you need clarification of one of their points.

One last thing that the interviewer should realize. An interview is essentially a type of meeting. Consequently, the meeting management issues described in Chapter 11 are relevant.

After the interview is over, the analyst needs to prepare an *interview report* that describes the information from the interview (Figure 2-8). The report contains *interview notes*, information that was collected over the course of the interview and is summarized in a useful format. In general, the interview report should be written within forty-eight hours of the interview, because the longer the interviewer waits, the more likely he or she is to forget information.

Often, the interview report is sent to the interviewee with a request to read it and inform the analyst of clarifications or updates. The interviewee needs to be convinced that the interviewer genuinely wants his or her corrections to the report. Usually there are few changes, but the need for any significant changes suggests that a second interview will be required. Never distribute someone's information without prior approval.

<table>
<tr><td colspan="2" align="center">Interview Notes Approved by: Linda Estey</td></tr>
<tr><td colspan="2">

Person Interviewed: Linda Estey, Director, Human Resources

Interviewer: Barbara Wixom

Purpose of Interview:
- Understand reports produced for Human Resources by the current system.
- Determine information requirements for future system.

Summary of Interview:
- Sample reports of all current HR reports are attached to this report. The information that is not used and missing information are noted on the reports.
- Two biggest problems with the current system are:
  1. The data are too old (the HR Department needs information within two days of month end; currently, information is provided to them after a three-week delay).
  2. The data are of poor quality (often reports must be reconciled with departmental HR database).
- The most common data errors found in the current system include incorrect job level information and missing salary information.

Open Items:
- Get current employee roster report from Mary Skudrna (extension 4355).
- Verify calculations used to determine vacation time with Mary Skudrna.
- Schedule interview with Jim Wack (extension 2337) regarding the reasons for data quality problems.

Detailed Notes: See attached transcript.

</td></tr>
</table>

FIGURE 2-8   Interview Report

PRACTICAL	**2-1 Developing Interpersonal Skills**
TIP	

Interpersonal skills are skills that enable you to develop rapport with others, and they are very important for interviewing. They help you to communicate with others effectively. Some people develop good interpersonal skills at an early age; they simply seem to know how to communicate and interact with others. Other people are less lucky and need to work hard to develop their skills.

Interpersonal skills, like most skills, can be learned. Here are some tips:

- **Don't worry, be happy.** Happy people radiate confidence and project their feelings on others. Try interviewing someone while smiling and then interviewing someone else while frowning and see what happens.

- **Pay attention.** Pay attention to what the other person is saying (which is harder than you might think). See how many times you catch yourself with your mind on something other than the conversation at hand.

- **Summarize key points.** At the end of each major theme or idea that someone explains, repeat the key points back to the speaker (e.g., Let me make sure I understand. The key issues are. . . ."). This demonstrates that you consider the information important, and it also forces you to pay attention (you can't repeat what you didn't hear).

- **Be succinct.** When you speak, be succinct. The goal in interviewing (and in much of life) is to learn, not to impress. The more you speak, the less time you give to others.

- **Be honest.** Answer all questions truthfully, and if you don't know the answer, say so.

- **Watch body language (yours and theirs).** The way a person sits or stands conveys much information. In general, a person who is interested in what you are saying sits or leans forward, makes eye contact, and often touches his or her face. A person leaning away from you or with an arm over the back of a chair is uninterested. Crossed arms indicate defensiveness or uncertainty, and steepling (sitting with hands raised in front of the body with fingertips touching) indicates a feeling of superiority.

Questionnaires

A questionnaire is a set of written questions used to obtain information from individuals. Questionnaires are often used when there is a large number of people from whom information and opinions are needed. In our experience, questionnaires are a common technique with systems intended for use outside the organization (e.g., by customers or vendors) or for systems with business users spread across many geographic locations. Most people automatically think of paper when they think of questionnaires, but today more questionnaires are being distributed in electronic form, either via e-mail or on the Web. Electronic distribution can save a significant amount of money as compared to distributing paper questionnaires. A good process to use when using questionnaires follows four steps.

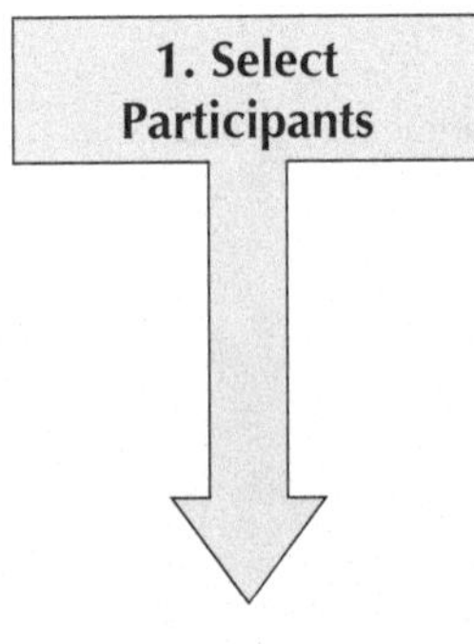

As with interviews, the first step is to identify the individuals to whom the questionnaire will be sent. However, it is not usual to select every person who could provide useful information. The standard approach is to select a *sample,* or subset, of people who are representative of an entire group. Sampling guidelines are discussed in most statistics books, and most business schools include courses that cover the topic, so we do not discuss it here. The important point in selecting a sample, however, is to realize that not everyone who receives a questionnaire will actually complete it. On average, only 30 to 50 percent of paper and e-mail questionnaires are returned. Response rates for Web-based questionnaires tend to be significantly lower (often only 5 to 30 percent), and multiple reminders or prompts to fill out the questionnaires are often needed.

Because the information on a questionnaire cannot be immediately clarified for a confused respondent, developing good questions is critical for questionnaires. Questions on questionnaires must be very clearly written and leave little room for misunderstanding. Given that questionnaires effectively are surveys, issues related to the reliability and validity of the questionnaire must be taken into consideration. For example, if the answers provided by the participants vary widely, then the reliability of the questionnaire is in doubt. Therefore, the results could be useless. Or worse, if the questionnaire has no validity, the results could be misleading. To ensure validity, the questions should be well balanced in that they cover the entire domain of possible answers and the questions are measuring what they intended to measure. For example, does a multiple-choice exam measure the level of knowledge that a student has attained, or does it actually measure how fast a student can read. If it is the latter, then the multiple-choice exam does not measure the knowledge level attained by the student. If that is the case, it might be wise to have a different type of question (e.g., essay) and/or include a variety of types of questions. Finally, given the low response rates stated above, non-response bias should be addressed. Depending on the cause of the non-response, the results of the questionnaire could again be misleading.

Questions must clearly enable the analyst to separate facts from opinions. Opinion questions often ask respondents the extent to which they agree or disagree (e.g., Are network problems common?), whereas factual questions seek more precise values (e.g., How often does a network problem occur: once an hour, once a day, once a week?). See Figure 2-9 for guidelines on questionnaire design.

Perhaps the most obvious issue—but one that is sometimes overlooked—is to have a clear understanding of how the information collected from the questionnaire will be analyzed and used. This issue must be addressed before the questionnaire is distributed, because it is too late afterward. If a variety of types of questions were asked, each may need to be analyzed with different techniques. Survey items that use Likert scales will be interpreted differently than essay ques-

---

[12] A good source for questionnaire design is Floyd J. Fowler, Jr., *Survey Research Methods, 5th Ed.* (Thousand Oaks, CA: Sage Publications, 2014).

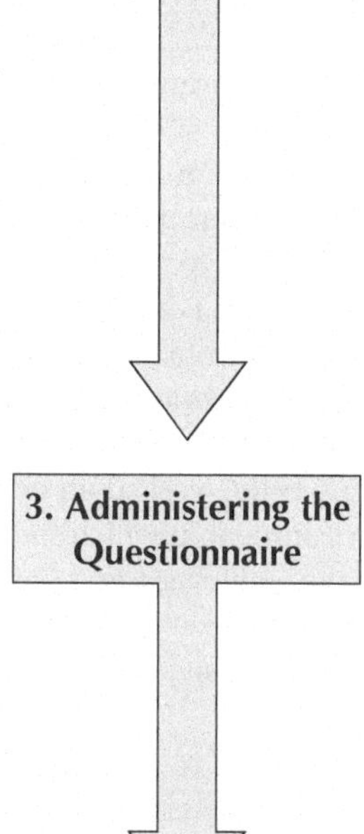

FIGURE 2-9
Good Questionnaire
Design

- Begin with nonthreatening and interesting questions.
- Group items into logically coherent sections.
- Do not put important items at the very end of the questionnaire.
- Do not crowd a page with too many items.
- Avoid abbreviations.
- Avoid biased or suggestive items or terms.
- Number questions to avoid confusion.
- Pretest the questionnaire to identify confusing questions.
- Provide anonymity to respondents.

tions in an open text-box response. The former might use quantitative aggregation techniques whereas the latter tends to include some form of natural language processing (NLP) such as LDA or LSA (techniques used to uncover topics and common patterns in text).

Questions should be relatively consistent in style, so that the respondent does not have to read instructions for each question before answering it. It is generally good practice to group related questions together to make them simpler to answer. Some experts suggest that questionnaires should start with questions important to respondents, so that the questionnaire immediately grabs their interest and induces them to answer it. Perhaps the most important step is to have several colleagues review the questionnaire and then pretest it with a few people drawn from the groups to whom it will be sent. It is surprising how often seemingly simple questions can be misunderstood.

3. Administering the Questionnaire

The key issue in administering the questionnaire is getting participants to complete the questionnaire and send it back. Dozens of marketing research books have been written about ways to improve response rates. Commonly used techniques include clearly explaining why the questionnaire is being conducted and why the respondent has been selected, stating a date by which the questionnaire is to be returned, offering an incentive to complete the questionnaire (e.g., a free pen and free food), and offering to supply a summary of the questionnaire responses. Systems analysts have additional techniques to improve response rates inside the organization, such as personally handing out the questionnaire and personally contacting those who have not returned them after a week or two, as well as requesting the respondents' supervisors to administer the questionnaires in a group meeting.

4. Questionnaire Follow-up

It is helpful to process the returned questionnaires and develop a questionnaire report soon after the questionnaire deadline. This ensures that the analysis process proceeds in a timely fashion and that respondents who requested copies of the results receive them promptly.

Observation

Observation, the act of watching processes being performed, is a powerful tool for gathering information about the as-is system because it enables the analyst to see the reality of a situation, rather than listening to others describe it in interviews. Several research studies have shown that many managers really do not remember how they work and how they allocate their time. (Quick, how many hours did you spend last week on each of your courses?) Observation is a good way to check the validity of information gathered from indirect sources such as interviews and questionnaires.

In many ways, the analyst becomes an anthropologist as he or she walks through the organization and observes the business system as it functions. The goal is to keep a low profile, to not interrupt those working, and to not influence those being observed, i.e., to become a

Fly on the Wall.[13] This implies that the analyst, in many ways, should strive to become simply a part of the environment having no more effect that a new piece of furniture. Nonetheless, it is important to understand that what analysts observe may not be the normal day-to-day routine because people tend to be extremely careful in their behavior when they are being watched. Even though normal practice may be to break formal organizational rules, the observer is unlikely to see this. (Remember how you drove the last time a police car followed you?) Thus, what you see might *not* be what you get.

Observation is often used to supplement interview information. The location of a person's office and its furnishings give clues to the person's power and influence in the organization and can be used to support or refute information given in an interview. For example, an analyst might become skeptical of someone who claims to use the existing computer system extensively if the computer is never turned on while the analyst visits. In most cases, observation supports the information that users provide in interviews. When it does not, it is an important signal that extra care must be taken in analyzing the business system.

When doing an observation, it is critical that good field notes are written immediately after the observation session. Otherwise, the memory of what was observed will begin to fade. In ethnographic research, there are different types of observations that can be made. For example, grand and mini tour, focused, and selected observations can be performed. The purpose of the grand and mini tour observations is to simply allow the observer to get a "feel" for the location. Focused observations narrow the scope of the observation task. For example, where a tour-based observation may only deal with issues such as layout of the office and the overall interrelationships among the individuals being observed, a focused observation uses the categories that the tour-based observations uncovered that need to be investigated in a more detailed manner. These categories could include the objects that are being worked on by the employees, the employees themselves, objects that make up the environment in which the employees work, e.g., furniture or machines, tasks being performed by the employees, and the processes in which the tasks make up. Finally, a selected observation drills down even further into what is being observed. For example, attempting to observe the individual steps in a task being performed by a specific employee.[14]

Document Analysis

Project teams often use document analysis to understand the as-is system. Under ideal circumstances, the project team that developed the existing system will have produced documentation that was then updated by all subsequent projects. In this case, the project team can start by reviewing the documentation and examining the system itself.

Unfortunately, many systems are not well documented because project teams fail to document their projects along the way, and when the projects are over, there is no time to go back and document. Therefore, there might not be much technical documentation about the current systems available, or it might not contain updated information about recent system changes. However, many helpful documents do exist in an organization: paper reports, memorandums, policy manuals, user-training manuals, organization charts, forms, and, of course, the user interface with the existing system.

---

[13] This term was originally applied by journalists, and later by directors in documentaries, to mean that they needed to be able to get to the truth in a manner that did not affect the ones being watched. Given the Hawthorne effect, this is obviously very difficult to attain.

[14] For more information see James P. Spradley, *Participant Observation* (New York, NY: Hold, Rinehart and Winston, 1980); Dennis Wixon and Judith Ramey, Eds., *Field Methods Casebook for Software Design* (New York, NY: John Wiley & Sons, 1996).

But these documents tell only part of the story. They represent the *formal system* that the organization uses. Quite often, the real, or *informal, system* differs from the formal one, and these differences, particularly large ones, give strong indications of what needs to be changed. For example, forms or reports that are never used should probably be eliminated. Likewise, boxes or questions on forms that are never filled in (or are used for other purposes) should be rethought. See Figure 2-10 for an example of how a document can be interpreted.

The most powerful indication that the system needs to be changed is when users create their own forms or add additional information to existing ones. It can sometimes be difficult to predict what users will do in advance. Such changes clearly demonstrate the need for improvements to existing systems. Thus, it is useful to review both blank and completed forms to identify these deviations. Likewise, when users access multiple reports to satisfy their information needs, it is a clear sign that new information or new information formats are needed.

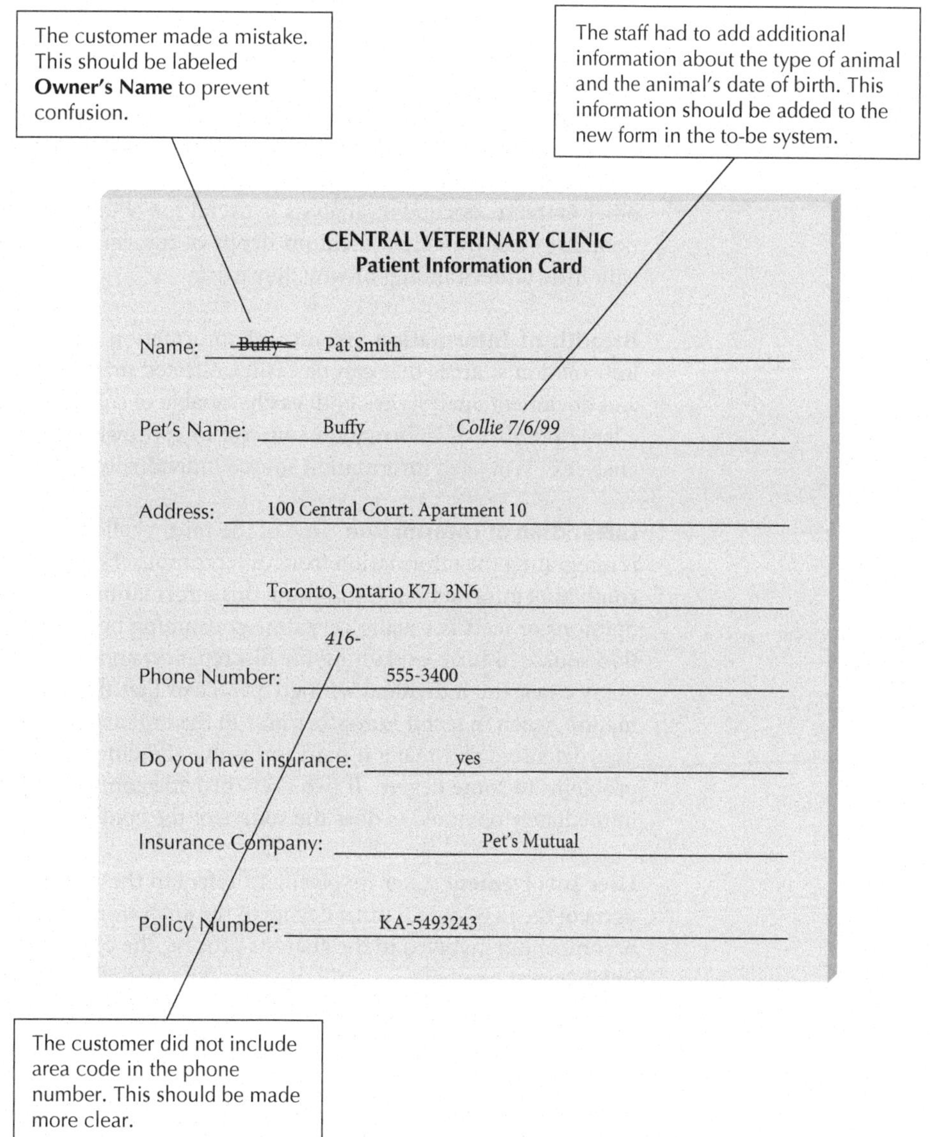

FIGURE 2-10
Performing a Document Analysis

Selecting the Appropriate Techniques

Each of the requirements-gathering techniques discussed earlier has strengths and weaknesses. No one technique is always better than the others, and in practice most projects use a combination of techniques. One issue not discussed is that of the analysts' experience. In general, document analysis requires the least amount of training, whereas interviewing, questionnaire development, and observation requires extensive training to be effective.

Type of Information The first characteristic is the type of information. Some techniques are more suited for use at different stages of the analysis process, whether understanding the as-is system, identifying improvements, or developing the to-be system. Interviews are commonly used in all three stages. In contrast, document analysis and observation usually are most helpful for understanding the as-is system, although occasionally they provide information about current problems that need to be improved. Questionnaires are often used to gather information about the as-is system as well as general information about improvements.

Depth of Information The depth of information refers to how rich and detailed the information is that the technique usually produces and the extent to which the technique is useful for obtaining not only facts and opinions but also an understanding of *why* those facts and opinions exist. Interviews and observations are very useful for providing a good depth of rich and detailed information and helping the analyst to understand the reasons behind them. At the other extreme, document analysis is useful for obtaining facts, but little beyond that. Questionnaires can provide a medium depth of information, soliciting both facts and opinions with little understanding of why they exist.

Breadth of Information Breadth of information refers to the range of information and information sources that can be easily collected using the chosen technique. Questionnaires and document analysis are both easily capable of soliciting a wide range of information from a large number of information sources. In contrast, interviews and observation require the analyst to visit each information source individually and, therefore, take more time.

Integration of Information One of the most challenging aspects of requirements gathering is integrating the information from different sources. Simply put, different people can provide conflicting information. Combining this information and attempting to resolve differences in opinions or facts is usually very time consuming because it means contacting each information source in turn, explaining the discrepancy, and attempting to refine the information. In many cases, the individual wrongly perceives that the analyst is challenging his or her information, when in fact it is another user in the organization who is doing so. This can make the user defensive and make it hard to resolve the differences. All techniques suffer integration problems to some degree. If two users provide conflicting information, the conflict becomes immediately obvious, as does the source of the conflict.

User Involvement User involvement refers to the amount of time and energy the intended users of the new system must devote to the analysis process. It is generally agreed that as users become more involved in the analysis process, the chance of success increases. However, user involvement can have a significant cost, and not all users are willing to contribute valuable time and energy. Questionnaires, document analysis, and observation place the least burden on users, whereas interviews require the greatest effort.

Cost Cost is always an important consideration. In general, questionnaires, document analysis, and observation are low-cost techniques (although observation can be quite consuming). The low cost does not imply that they are more or less effective than the other techniques. Interviews generally have moderate costs.

Combining Techniques   In practice, requirements gathering combines a series of different techniques. Most analysts start by using interviews with senior manager(s) to gain an understanding of the project and the big-picture issues. From these interviews, it becomes clear whether large or small changes are anticipated. These interviews are often followed with analysis of documents and policies to gain some understanding of the as-is system. Usually interviews come next to gather the rest of the information needed for the as-is picture.

TEXT ANALYSIS

Given that virtually all of the requirements gathering techniques produce text, performing some type of text analysis could be worthwhile. A very useful, but old tool, that can be used to perform some simple text analysis is *sentence diagraming*.[15] This tool was originally designed to aid students to learn English grammar. The tool forces the student to "draw" a sentence using a set of lines that represent the different parts of speech. For example, Figure 2-11 portrays the following sentences as sentence diagrams:

- The patient contacts the office regarding an appointment.
- The receptionist asks the patient for possible appointment times.

By drawing the sentence diagrams, it is easy to identify the different parts of speech and therefore the primary objects of interest. In this case, the objects of interest are patient, office, appointment, and receptionist.

Text analysis also has been used in the past to design programs and databases. Once the different parts of speech have been identified, one can follow the guidelines in Figure 2-12 to identify different functional requirements. For example, referring to Figure 2-11, the objects

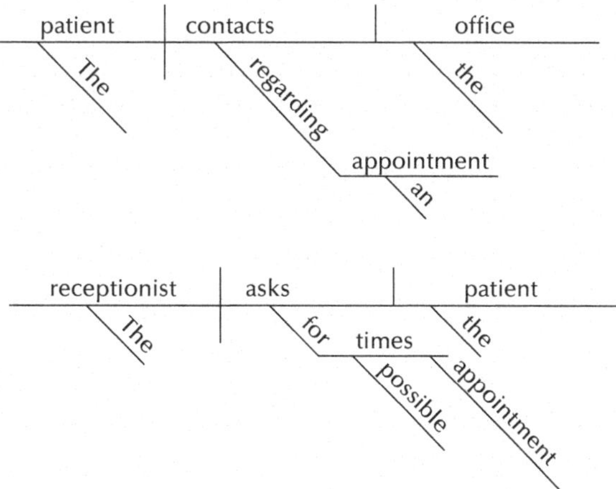

FIGURE 2-11
Sample Sentence
Diagrams

---

[15] A good reference sentence diagraming is Cindy L. Vitto, *Grammar by Diagram: Understanding English Grammar Through Traditional Sentence Diagraming* (Peterborough, Ontario: Broadview Press, 2003).

> - A common or improper noun implies an actor or a class of objects.
> - A proper noun or direct reference implies a specific actor or instance of a class.
> - A collective noun implies a class of objects made up of groups of instances of another class.
> - A doing verb implies a functional requirement, activity, or operation.
> - A being verb implies a classification relationship between use cases or between an object and its class.
> - A having verb implies a relationship between use cases and/or between classes.
>
> Adapted from: Russell J. Abbott, "Program Design by Informal English Descriptions," *Communications of the ACM*, 26(11), 1983, pp. 882–94; Peter P-S Chen, "English Sentence Structure and Entity-Relationship Diagrams," *Information Sciences: An International Journal,* 29(2–3), 1983, pp. 127–149; and Ian Graham, *Migrating to Object Technology* (Reading, MA: Addison Wesley Longman, 1995).

FIGURE 2-12 Text Analysis Guidelines

of interest could refer to actors and classes while the verbs provide a basis for use cases. Furthermore, the other noun, appointment, could refer to another useful problem domain class. Using text analysis to identify requirements has been criticized as being too simple, but because its primary purpose is to create an initial rough-cut structural model, its simplicity is a major advantage.

Another useful tool for text analysis is an ethnographic analysis.[16] Specifically, performing domain, taxonomic, componential, and theme analysis. The purpose of *domain analysis* is to uncover the objects of interest in the problem domain. Unlike sentence diagramming, which only focuses on the grammar of the text, domain analysis concentrates on the meaning or semantics, and possibly pragmatics, of the objects of interest. Domain analysis begins by trying to identify the semantic relationships among the objects. In most cases, a standard or universal set of semantic relationships is sufficient. Figure 2-13 lists a set of useful universal semantic relationships that can be used as a starting point. However, in some cases these relationships may need to be extended to include problem-domain-specific relationships, e.g., in some problem domains it may be more useful to use a set-theoretic based relationship instead of the more generic Part-Whole relationship.

Taxonomic analysis builds up a node and arc type of graph by using the semantic relationships to connect the different objects of interest in the problem domain. Figure 2-14 portrays a partial taxonomy for an appointment system where a doctor is a kind of employee, an appointment is located at the office, the medical history is an attribute of a patient, etc. By modeling the objects of interest using the semantic relationships, a taxonomy of the problem domain is created.

Where taxonomic analysis focuses on the creation of a taxonomy, *componential analysis* specifically focuses on the attribution semantic relationship. For example, a doctor may have a set of attributes that include first name, last name, home address, office address, and a specialty, among others. Finally, *theme analysis* attempts to identify any underlying themes that were uncovered during the requirements gathering process. Here automated NLP techniques of LDA or LSA can be especially useful. A theme represents any assumptions that are tacit or explicit in the problem domain. In many cases, by reviewing all of the objects of interest and semantic relationships in the taxonomy, themes can be identified by simply reading the various combinations of nodes and arcs in the taxonomy.

---

[16] A good reference for this type of analysis is James P. Spradley, *The Ethnographic Interview* (New York, NY: Holt, Rinehart and Winston, 1979).

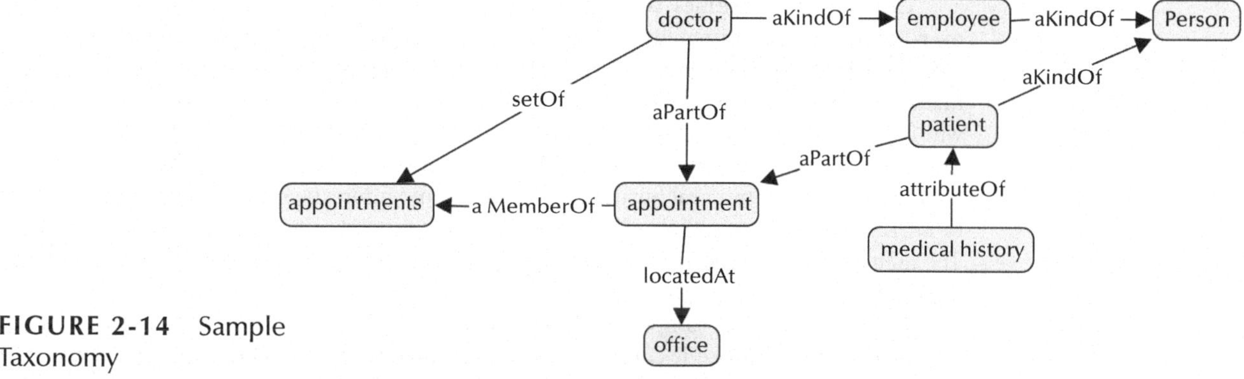

• Attribution	X is an attribute of Y.
• Cause-effect	X is a cause of Y.
• Class Inclusion	X is a kind of Y.
• Contrasts	X is the opposite of Y.
• Means-ends	X is a way to do Y.
• Part-Whole	X is a part of Y.
• Rationale	X is a reason for doing Y.
• Sequence	X is a step in Y.
• Similars	X is similar to Y.
• Spatial	X is located at Y.

James P. Spradley, *The Ethnographic Interview* (New York, NY: Holt, Rinehart and Winston, 1979); Keng Siau, "Relationship Construct in Modeling Information Systems: Identifying Relationships Based on Relation Element Theory," *Journal of Database Management* (Jul–Sep, 2004).

FIGURE 2-13
Sample Universal Semantic Relationships

FIGURE 2-14   Sample Taxonomy

REQUIREMENTS DEFINITION

The requirements definition report—usually just called the *requirements definition*—is a straightforward report that simply lists the functional and nonfunctional requirements in an outline format. Determining requirements for the requirements definition is both a business task and an information technology task. In the early days of computing, there was a presumption that the systems analysts, as experts with computer systems, were in the best position to define how a computer system should operate. Many systems failed because they did not adequately address the true business needs of the users. Gradually, the presumption changed so that the users, as the business experts, were seen as being the best position to define how a computer system should operate. However, many systems failed to deliver performance benefits because users simply automated an existing inefficient system, and they failed to incorporate new opportunities offered by technology.

Therefore, the most effective approach is to have both users and analysts working together to determine business requirements. Sometimes, however, users don't know exactly what they want, and analysts need to help them discover their needs. By using the requirements analysis approaches described earlier in the chapter, analysts can guide the users in explaining what is wanted from a system. Thus, analysts can help users critically examine the current state of systems and processes (the as-is system), identify exactly what needs to change, and develop a concept for a new system (the to-be system).

Creating a Requirements Definition

Creating a requirements definition is an iterative and ongoing process whereby the analyst collects information with requirements-gathering techniques (e.g., interviews, document analysis, etc.), critically analyzes the information to identify appropriate business requirements for the system and adds the requirements to the requirements definition report. The requirements definition is kept up to date so that the project team and business users can refer to it and get a clear understanding of the new system.

To create a requirements definition, the project team first determines the kinds of functional and nonfunctional requirements that they will collect about the system (of course, these may change over time). These become the main sections of the document. Next, the analysts use a variety of requirements-gathering techniques described earlier to collect information, and they list the business requirements that were identified from that information. Finally, the analysts work with the entire project team and the business users to verify, change, and complete the list and to help prioritize the importance of the requirements that were identified.

This process continues throughout analysis, and the requirements definition evolves over time as new requirements are identified and as the project moves into later phases of the Unified Process. Beware: The evolution of the requirements definition must be carefully managed. The project team cannot keep adding to the requirements definition, or the system will keep growing and growing and never get finished. Instead, the project team carefully identifies requirements and evaluates which ones fit within the scope of the system. When a requirement reflects a real business need but is not within the scope of the current system or current release, it is either added to a list of future requirements or given a low priority. The management of requirements (and system scope) is one of the hardest parts of managing a project.

Figure 2-15 shows a sample requirements definition for an appointment system in a typical doctor's office. Notice it contains both functional and nonfunctional requirements. The functional requirements include managing appointments, producing schedules, and recording the availability of the individual doctors. The nonfunctional requirements include items such as the expected amount of time that it takes to store a new appointment, the need to support wireless printing, and which types of employees have access to the different parts of the system.

The requirements are numbered in a legal or outline format so that each requirement is clearly identified. The requirements are first grouped into functional and nonfunctional requirements; within each of those headings, they are further grouped by the type of nonfunctional requirement or by function.

Sometimes business requirements are prioritized on the requirements definition. They can be ranked as having high, medium, or low importance in the new system, or they can be labeled with the version of the system that will address the requirement (e.g., release 1, release 2, and release 3). This practice is particularly important when using object-oriented or agile methodologies since they deliver systems in an incremental manner.

The most obvious purpose of the requirements definition is to provide the information needed by the other deliverables in analysis, which include functional, structural, and behavioral models, and to support activities in design. The most important purpose of the requirements definition, however, is to define the scope of the system. The document describes to the analysts exactly what the system needs to end up doing. When discrepancies arise, the document serves as the place to go for clarification.

Functional Requirements
1. **Manage Appointments**
    1.1.   Patient makes new appointment.
    1.2.   Patient changes appointment.
    1.3.   Patient cancels appointment.
2. **Produce Schedule**
    2.1.   Office Manager checks daily schedule.
3. **Record Doctor Availability**
    3.1.   Doctor updates schedule.

Nonfunctional Requirements
1. **Operational Requirements**
    1.1.   The system will operate in Windows environment.
    1.2.   The system should be able to connect to printers wirelessly.
    1.3.   The system should automatically back up at the end of each day.
2. **Performance Requirements**
    2.1.   The system will store a new appointment in 2 seconds or less.
    2.2.   The system will retrieve the daily appointment schedule in 2 seconds or less.
3. **Security Requirements**
    3.1.   Only doctors can set their availability.
    3.2.   Only a manager can produce a schedule.
4. **Cultural and Political Requirements**
    4.1.   No special cultural and political requirements are anticipated.

FIGURE 2-15
Sample
Requirements
Definition

In object-oriented and agile approaches there are two alternatives to the traditional functional requirements definition as described above. With object-oriented approaches, use cases are the primary approach used to identify and document the functional requirements. These are covered in Chapter 3.

STORYTELLING[17]

One new approach to represent requirements that has shown promise is the idea of telling stories that describe the situation that the system will be created to solve. Storytelling should not be confused with the user stories associated with agile approaches. In this case, *storytelling* involves the creation of narratives that describe the user needs that should be met by the new system. In comparison to the traditional requirements definition, stories are easier for the different stakeholders of a new system to relate. Furthermore, stories can support the development team's shared understanding of the problem that the new system will solve in a manner that is less threatening and more humanizing which, in turn, can enhance communication and build empathy among the different stakeholders. Obviously, before a story can be created, a good deal of work must be completed so that the writer can create a relevant narrative. For example, we need to know who the players are and the tasks that they perform. Thus, all of the requirements gathering techniques described can be used as a way to gather information

[17] A couple of good references regarding stories are Stefan Hofer and Henning Schwentner, *Domain* Storytelling: *A Collaborative, Visual, and Agile Way to Build Domain-Driven Software* (Boston, MA: Addison-Wesley, 2022) and Ben Rinzler, *Telling Stories: A Short Path to Writing Better Software Requirements* (Indianapolis, IN: Wiley Publishing, 2009).

FIGURE 2-16
Sample Story

> Upon arriving at the office, the office manager reviews today's appointments for each of the doctors in the practice. After reviewing the appointment schedule, the office manager releases the schedule to each doctor and their staff. Once the office opens, patients call in to schedule a new appointment, change an existing appointment, or to delete an existing appointment. Consequently, the appointment schedule for each doctor is continuously updated during the day. Finally, the doctors update their individual future schedules by blocking out times to review and update patient records, vacations, breaks, and to provide time for each doctor to review new medical information that is pertinent for their practice.

to create the narratives. Storytelling can also be a useful manner to verify and validate the evolving requirements with the user. Figure 2-16 shows a sample story that is equivalent to the traditional requirements definition in Figure 2-15. Some research has even suggested that these kinds of stories in the form of narratives can be especially effective when they include real people, places, and things.[18]

THE SYSTEM PROPOSAL

A system proposal brings together into a single comprehensive document the material created during the business modeling, requirements and analysis workflows. The system proposal typically includes an executive summary, the system request, the workplan, the feasibility analysis, the requirements definition, and the evolving models that describe the new system. The evolving models include functional models (see Chapter 3), structural models (see Chapter 4), and behavioral models (see Chapter 5).[19]

The executive summary provides all critical information in a very concise form. It can be thought of as a summary of the complete proposal. Its purpose is to allow a busy executive to quickly read through it and determine which parts of the proposal he or she needs to go through more thoroughly. The executive summary normally contains a statement of the problem that the project will address, any background information that is necessary to understand the problem and to understand the proposed solution, a description of any alternative solutions that have been considered and ruled out, and the major points of the proposed solution. The executive summary is typically no more than a single page long. Figure 2-17 provides a template for a system proposal and references to where the other sections of the proposal are described.

---

[18] See M. Hvalshagen, *Harnessing the Power or Narratives to Understand User Requirements. ProQuest Dissertations and Theses, Indiana University*, 2011. ProQuest Dissertations & Theses Global, Accessed 31 May 2024 and M. Hvalshagen, R. Lukyanenko, and B. M. Samuel, Empowering Users with Narratives: Examining the Efficacy of Narratives for Understanding Data-Oriented Conceptual Models. *Information Systems Research* 34, no. 3 (2022):890–909.

[19] Depending on the client, much more detailed specifications may be required; for example the Department of Defense, NASA, IEEE/ANSI, and the Naval Research Laboratory all have very specific formats that must be followed. For more information on these more detailed specifications, see A. M Davis, *Software Requirements, Revision* (Upper Saddle River, NJ: Prentice Hall, 1993); G. Kotonya and I. Sommerville, *Requirements Engineering* (Chichester, England: Wiley, 1998); R. H. Thayer and M. Dorfman (Eds.), *Software Requirements Engineering*, 2nd Ed. (Los Alamitos, CA: IEEE Computer Society Press, 1997).

1. **Table of Contents**

2. **Executive Summary**

   A summary of all the essential information in the proposal so a busy executive can read it quickly and decide what parts of the proposal to read in more depth.

3. **System Request**

   The revised system request form (this chapter).

4. **Workplan**

   The original workplan, revised after having completed analysis (see Chapter 11).

5. **Feasibility Analysis**

   A revised feasibility analysis, using the information from analysis (see Chapter 11).

6. **Requirements Definition**

   A list of the functional and nonfunctional business requirements for the system (this chapter).

7. **Functional Model**

   A use-case diagram, a set of activity diagrams, and a set of use case descriptions that illustrate the basic processes or external functionality that the system needs to support (see Chapter 3).

8. **Structural Models**

   A set of CRC cards, class diagram, and object diagrams that describe the structural aspects of the to-be system (see Chapter 4). This may also include structural models of the current as-is system that will be replaced.

9. **Behavioral Models**

   A set of activity diagrams with swimlanes, a set of sequence diagrams, a CRUDE matrix, and a set of behavioral-state machines that describe the internal behavior of the to-be system (see Chapter 5). This may include behavioral models of the as-is system that will be replaced.

10. **Appendices**

    These contain additional material relevant to the proposal, often used to support the recommended system. This might include results of a questionnaire survey or interviews, industry reports and statistics, and so on.

FIGURE 2-17
System Proposal
Template

APPLYING THE CHAPTER CONCEPTS

Chapter 2 introduced requirements determination for object-oriented systems development projects. Determining the system's requirements is the most important activity in the systems development process. A requirement is WHAT the system must do or WHAT characteristics it must have. If the requirements are not fully or correctly defined, the system developed is unlikely to meet the needs of the user. In other words, if the requirements are wrong, the system will be wrong. In this chapter's installment of the Library Management example and the Campus Housing Service "Your Turn," we see the requirements analysis and requirement-gathering techniques that the analysts used to determine requirements for each. We also see the functional and nonfunctional requirements that were developed and an initial draft of the developing systems proposal for the project. This systems proposal will be finalized after the functional (Chapter 3), structural (Chapter 4), and behavioral (Chapter 5) modeling of the system has been completed.

Library Management System Example Susan (our systems analyst) met with John (the head librarian) to develop a system request for the library to update its resource management system. Based on the meeting, they created the system request shown in Figure 2-18.

In this installment of the Library Management System, we deal with the process of borrowing from and returning to the library different resources. The following is a transcript of an interview that took place with our systems analyst (Susan) and one of the librarians (Joe).

System Request–Library Management System	
Project sponsor:	John
Business Need:	Increase the efficiency of the library and its patrons.
Business Requirements:	Need to better support the procurement, retiring, reserving, borrowing, and returning resources for the library.
Business Value:	Increase the use and satisfaction of the library's patrons.
Special Issues or Constraints:	None.

FIGURE 2-18 The Library Management System System Request

SUSAN: Joe, it's great that you can take the time to sit down with me and provide me with information so that we can improve the Library Management system.

JOE: Susan, we are excited that you and your firm are working with us to improve the experience of our patrons. So, where would you like to start.

SUSAN: We're interested in working through a set of tasks that the current system doesn't support very well. But, to begin with, we would like to focus our attention on the aspect of the Library Management System that mostly impacts your patrons; the process of borrowing and returning of different types of resources. Obviously, this particular process may affect the other processes that you have previously mentioned: resource procurement, retiring resources, and reserving resources. However, for now, we only want to focus on the borrowing and returning process.

JOE: That's sounds good. But I want to make sure that we don't ignore those other related processes. So, where do you want to begin?

SUSAN: Tell me about the process of borrowing and returning books.

JOE: Okay, let me describe the process of checking out a book first. To begin with, there are three types of borrowers: students, faculty or staff, and guests. Regardless of the type of borrower, the borrower must have a valid ID card. If the borrower is a student, the system checks with the registrar's office to validate the ID card. On the other hand, if the borrower is a faculty or staff member, the system checks with the personnel office to validate the card. Finally, if the borrower is a guest, the card is checked against the library's own system. If the card is valid, the system then checks to determine whether the borrower has any overdue books or unpaid fines. But, if the card is invalid, the borrower has overdue books, or the borrower has unpaid fines, the system rejects the borrower's request to check out a book, otherwise the request is honored. Once the request is honored, the system updates the library's collection to reflect the book's new status.

SUSAN: How does the patron find the book in which they are interested?

JOE: Well. They use the system's search capability.

SUSAN: I assume that the search process is a fairly detailed process. So, let's delay that description for a little while. Instead, could you describe what's involved in returning a book?

JOE: Well, in this case, it is very straight forward. The patron simply brings the book back to the library and places it in the return box.

SUSAN: That's okay, but what happens behind the scenes?

JOE: Once we get the book out of the return box, we make sure that the book hasn't been damaged. If it has not been damaged, then the book is simply reshelved. On the other hand, if the book is damaged, then we inspect it to see whether it can be repaired or whether we need to remove it from the collection. In either case, the patron is fined for an appropriate amount. Obviously, this process is more involved than I have described. Do you want me to go into more detail at this point?

SUSAN: No, for now your description is sufficient to get us started. So, let's stop for today. In the near future, we'll return to this and talk about the other types of resources that the library makes available to its patrons. Thank you for your time today.

JOE: You are welcome. We are looking forward to your suggested improvements.

Obviously, the above transcript not only does not address all of the process of borrowing and returning books, it also does not address resource procurement, reserving different resources, and retiring different resources. However, for our purposes, this is sufficient. For the purposes of this example, Susan simply applies some of the text analysis rules to identify a few of the functional requirements associated with the above interview. To begin with, the above interview describes the requirements for borrowing from and returning books to the library. The functional requirements are shown in Figure 2-19:

Based on the description in Chapter 1, there are quite a few other requirements that need to be addressed beyond the borrow books and return books requirements. For example, what about borrowing and returning other resources such as DVDs and CDs? What about online resources? How about requesting to borrow something from another library, i.e., Inter Library Loan? Also, how does the library procure, retire, and reserve resources?

Campus Housing Service "Your Turn" In this installation of the Campus Housing Service (CHS) "Your Turn" exercise, we see Jane (a university student) interacting with Emma (a CHS employee). Jane would like to find an apartment to lease for the next academic year and has come to the CHS for help. Here is a portion of the interaction between Jane and Emma.

JANE: Emma, I am moving out of the dorms next year and need to find a place to live. I was hoping that CHS could help me.

EMMA: Jane, that's why we are here. So, let's get down to finding you a great place to live next year. To begin with, I need some general information. Could you tell me what you are looking for?

JANE: Well, I think I would like an apartment that is either in walking distance of campus or on a bus route. I noticed last year how difficult it was for some of my friends to find parking on campus. So, I would prefer to not have to deal with parking.

---

1. Borrow Books.
   a. Search for book and take it to checkout.
   b. Give librarian book and ID card.
   c. Librarian checks card validity based on borrower type: If student, check registrar's system, if faculty or staff, check personnel
      system, if guest, check library system.
   d. If card is valid, librarian checks library system to determine whether borrower has any overdue books or unpaid fines.
      i. If no overdue books or unpaid fees, then process checkout.
      ii. If there is either overdue books or unpaid fees, then deny checkout.
   e. If card is invalid, deny overdue books or unpaid fees, then deny checkout.
2. Return Books.
   a. Patron places book in return box.
   b. Librarian retrieves books from return box.
   c. Librarian checks the book for damage.
   d. If the book is not damaged, then the book is reshelved.
   e. If the book is damaged, the book is carefully examined to determine whether it can be repaired.
      i. If the book can be repaired, then it is sent off to be fixed, else it is removed from the collection.
      ii. The patron is assessed an appropriate fine for the amount of damage.
3. . . .

FIGURE 2-19 The Library Management System Identified Functional Requirements

EMMA: Meeting that criterion is not going to be a problem. The majority of the apartments in which students live are at least on a bus route. Also, do you have any roommate considerations? Having roommates can dramatically lower the cost of an apartment.

JANE: I would prefer to not have any roommates. But, my total budget for a place is about $1000 a month. So, if I can't get an acceptable place for that amount, then I would consider having roommates. But, since I prefer living by myself, I feel that I would need to meet any potential roommates before I would agree to live with them.

EMMA: Okay, what types of amenities would you have to have?

JANE: Since I do have a car, I definitely would need a parking place. Given the nature of the courses that we all take today, a very dependable, high-speed internet capability is a must. Otherwise, I won't be able to complete the assignments at the apartment. I would have to do everything on campus instead. Also, having an on-site laundry would definitively be a requirement.

EMMA: Does the laundry need to be within the apartment or is having one that is available in the complex sufficient?

JANE: Having one in the complex would work.

EMMA: Are there other things that you would like? For example, having access to a gym or pool on site.

JANE: Now that you mention it, I would like to have access to cable. But, since the university has both good gym and pool facilities, I wouldn't be opposed to a complex that has them but neither one would be a requirement.

EMMA: Great, I have a general idea as to what are your requirements and financial constraints. A couple of other things that I need to know are does the apartment need to furnished, what sources of income do you have, e.g., do you have a job, are your parents helping you financially, etc., and when do you plan on moving in. Also, I need your contact information so that once I find a set of potential apartments, I can contact you to take the next step.

JANE: To begin with, the apartment does not need to be furnished. From a financial perspective, I do have a part-time job on campus but my parents will be providing the support for me to live off campus. As to when I want to move in, as long as I can get moved in and settled before classes begin, I'm very flexible. My phone number is 012-345-6789 and my email is jane123@myUniversity.edu.

EMMA: Perfect. I'll get started on finding you a great place to live next year. As soon as I find a set of potential options, I'll contact you and we can set up the next steps.

JANE: Thank you so much for being so helpful. I was nervous about starting this search. But, now that we have met, I'm very comfortable that you will be able to help me.

EMMA: Your very welcome. We at CHS do our best to help our students. I'll be in touch soon.

JANE: Goodbye.

There are other requirements (see Chapter 1) that also need to be addressed. These include keeping track of rental unit information, information regarding how to visit rental units, and CHS also acts as a liaison for the student to sign a lease with the rental unit management. CHS also supports the owners/managers of the rental units by making sure that all information about the available units is up to date. However, in this case, we are only dealing with identifying the functional requirements based on the above situation. To identify the nonfunctional requirements (operational, performance, security, and cultural and political), we would need to go back to CHS and interview the different employees. So, we need to identify the requirements for a system that supports CHS in finding places to live for students. Remember, this is only one interaction between one student and one user. In this "Your Turn" exercise, you should create a system request (see Figure 2-1) and a requirements definition (see Figure 2-15).

CHAPTER REVIEW

After reading and studying this chapter, you should be able to:

- ☐ Differentiate between a functional and a nonfunctional requirement.
- ☐ Discuss the problem analysis requirements approaches.
- ☐ Discuss the root cause analysis requirements approach.
- ☐ Discuss the duration analysis requirements approach.
- ☐ Discuss the activity-based costing analysis requirements approach.
- ☐ Discuss the informal benchmarking analysis requirements approach.
- ☐ Discuss the outcome analysis requirements approach.
- ☐ Discuss the technology analysis requirements approach.
- ☐ Discuss the activity elimination requirements approach.
- ☐ Discuss how to use interviews to gather requirements.
- ☐ Discuss how to use questionnaires to gather requirements.
- ☐ Discuss how to use observation to gather requirements.
- ☐ Discuss how to use document analysis to gather requirements.
- ☐ Discuss how to use text analysis to understand the requirements gathered.
- ☐ Create a requirements definition.
- ☐ Describe the use of storytelling as an alternative to the traditional requirements definition.
- ☐ Describe the purpose and contents of system proposal.

KEY TERMS

Activity elimination
Activity-based costing
Analysis
Approval committee
As-is system
Benchmarking
Bottom-up interview
Breadth of analysis
Business need
Business requirements
Closed-ended question
Componential analysis
Consumerization of IT
Critical thinking skills
Emerging technology
Document analysis
Domain analysis
Duration analysis

Facilitator
Fishbone diagram
Fly on the wall
Formal system
Functional requirements
Givens-Means-Ends
  (GME) analysis
Ground rules
Informal benchmarking
Informal system
Interpersonal skills
Interview
Interview notes
Interview report
Interview schedule
Means
Nonfunctional requirements
Observation

Open-ended question
Outcome analysis
Parallelization
Process Integration
Post-session report
Potential business value
Probing question
Problem analysis
Project cost
Project sponsor
Questionnaire
Requirement
Requirements definition
Requirements determination
Risk
Root cause
Root cause analysis
Sample

Scribe
Sentence diagram
Software quality
Storytelling
Structured interview
System proposal
System request
System requirements
Systems thinking skills
Taxonomic analysis
Technology analysis
Text analysis
Theme analysis
To-be system
Top-down interview
Unstructured interview
Walkthrough

QUESTIONS

1. What are the key deliverables that are created during analysis? What is the final deliverable from analysis, and what does it contain?
2. What is the difference between an as-is system and a to-be system?
3. What are the three basic steps of the analysis process? Which step is sometimes skipped or done in a cursory fashion? Why?
4. Compare and contrast problem analysis and root cause analysis. Under what conditions would you use problem analysis? Under what conditions would you use root cause analysis?
5. Compare and contrast duration analysis and activity-based costing.
6. Describe the five major steps in conducting interviews.
7. Explain the differences among a closed-ended question, an open-ended question, and a probing question. When would you use each?
8. Explain the differences between unstructured interviews and structured interviews. When would you use each approach?
9. Explain the difference between a top-down and bottom-up interview approach. When would you use each approach?
10. How can you differentiate between facts and opinions? Why can both be useful?
11. How does designing questions for questionnaires differ from designing questions for interviews?
12. What are typical response rates for questionnaires, and how can you improve them?
13. What are the key aspects of using observation in the information-gathering process?
14. What is document analysis?
15. How does the formal system differ from the informal system? How does document analysis help you understand both?
16. Explain factors that can be used to select information-gathering techniques.
17. Describe the different approaches for text analysis.
18. What is the purpose of the requirements definition?
19. Describe why storytelling can be useful in gathering requirements.
20. What information is typically included in a system proposal?
21. What is the purpose of the executive summary of the system proposal?

EXERCISES

A. Review the Amazon.com website. Develop the requirements definition for the site. Create a list of functional business requirements that the system meets. What different kinds of nonfunctional business requirements does the system meet? Provide examples for each kind.

B. Suppose you are going to build a new system that automates or improves the interview process for the career services department of your school. Develop a requirements definition for the new system. Include both functional and nonfunctional system requirements. Pretend you will release the system in three different versions. Prioritize the requirements accordingly.

C. Describe in very general terms the as-is business process for registering for classes at your university. Collaborate with another student in your class, and evaluate the process using problem analysis and root cause analysis. Based on your work, list some improvements that you have identified.

D. Describe in very general terms the as-is business process for applying for admission at your university. Collaborate with another student in your class, and evaluate the process using informal benchmarking. Based on your work, list some improvements that you have identified.

E. Describe in very general terms the as-is business process for registering for classes at your university. Collaborate with another student in your class, and evaluate the process using activity elimination. Based on your work, list some improvements that you have identified.

F. Suppose your university is having a dramatic increase in enrollment and is having difficulty finding enough seats in courses for students. Perform a technology analysis to identify new ways to help students complete their studies and graduate.

G. Suppose you are the analyst charged with developing a new system for the university bookstore so that students can order books online and have them delivered to their dorms or off-campus housing. What requirements-gathering techniques will you use? Describe in detail how you would apply the techniques.

H. Suppose you are the analyst charged with developing a new system to help senior managers make better strategic decisions. What requirements-gathering techniques will you use? Describe in detail how you would apply the techniques.

I. Find a partner and interview each other about what tasks each did in the last job you held (full-time, part-time, past, or current). If you haven't worked before, then assume your job is being a student. Before you do this, develop a brief interview plan. After your partner interviews you, identify the type of interview, interview approach, and types of questions used.

J. Find a questionnaire on the Web that has been created to capture customer information. Describe the purpose of the survey, the way questions are worded, and how the questions have been organized. How can it be improved? How will the responses be analyzed?

K. Develop a questionnaire that will help gather information regarding processes at a popular restaurant or the college cafeteria (e.g., ordering and customer service). Give the questionnaire to ten to fifteen students, analyze the responses, and write a brief report that describes the results.

L. Contact the career services department at your university, and find all the pertinent documents designed to help students find permanent and/or part-time jobs. Analyze the documents and write a brief report.

M. Consider your university's class scheduling system. Create a story that describes how you go about signing up for classes using the system.

MINICASES

1. The State Firefighter's Association has a membership of 15,000. The purpose of the organization is to provide some financial support to the families of deceased member firefighters and to organize a conference each year bringing together firefighters from all over the state. Members are billed dues and calls annually. Calls are additional funds required to take care of payments made to the families of deceased members. The bookkeeping work for the association is handled by the elected treasurer, Bob Smith, although it is widely known that his wife, Laura, does all the work. Bob runs unopposed each year at the election, because no one wants to take over the tedious and time-consuming job of tracking memberships. Bob is paid a stipend of $8,000 per year, but his wife spends well over twenty hours per week on the job. The organization, however, is not happy with their performance.

A computer system is used to track the billing and receipt of funds. This system was developed in 2004 by a computer science student and his father. The system is a simple MS Access application. The most immediate problem facing the treasurer and his wife is the fact that no one around knows how to maintain the system. One query, in particular, takes seventeen hours to run. Over the years, they have just avoided running this query, although the information in it would be quite useful. Questions from members concerning their statements cannot easily be answered. Usually, Bob or Laura just jots down the inquiry and returns a call with the answer. Sometimes it takes three to five hours to find the information needed to answer the question. Often, they have to perform calculations manually because the system was not programmed to handle certain types of queries. When member information is entered into the system, each field is presented one at a time, which makes it very difficult to return to a field and correct a value that was entered. Sometimes a new member is entered but disappears from the records. The report of membership used in the conference materials does not alphabetize members by city. Only cities are listed in the correct order.

What requirements analysis approach or approaches would you recommend for this situation? Explain your answer.

2. Brian Callahan, IS project manager, is just about ready to depart for an urgent meeting called by Joe Campbell, manager of manufacturing operations. A major project sponsored by Joe recently cleared the approval hurdle, and Brian helped bring the project through project initiation. Now that the approval committee has given the go-ahead, Brian has been working on the project's analysis plan.

One evening, while playing golf with a friend who works in the manufacturing operations department, Brian learned that Joe wants to push the project's time frame up from Brian's original estimate of thirteen months. Brian's friend overheard Joe say, "I can't see why that IS project team needs to spend all that time analyzing things. They've got two weeks scheduled just to look at the existing system! That seems like a real waste. I want that team to get going on building my system."

Because Brian has a little inside knowledge about Joe's agenda for this meeting, he has been considering how to handle Joe. What do you suggest Brian tell Joe?

3. Barry has recently been assigned to a project team that will be developing a new retail store management system for a chain of submarine sandwich shops. Barry has several years of experience in programming, but he has not done much analysis in his career. He was a little nervous about the new work he would be doing, but he was confident he could handle any assignment he was given.

One of Barry's first assignments was to visit one of the submarine sandwich shops and prepare an observation report on how the store operates. Barry planned to arrive at the store around noon, but he chose a store in an area of town he was unfamiliar with, and due to traffic delays and difficulty in finding the store, he did not arrive until 1:30. The store manager was not expecting him and refused to let a stranger behind the counter until Barry had her contact the project sponsor (the director of store management) at company headquarters to verify who he was and what his purpose was.

After finally securing permission to observe, Barry stationed himself prominently in the work area behind the counter so that he could see everything. The staff had to maneuver around him as they went about their tasks, but there were only minor occasional collisions. Barry noticed that the store staff seemed to be going about their work very slowly and deliberately, but he supposed that was because the store wasn't very busy. At first, Barry questioned each worker about what he or she was doing, but the store manager eventually asked him not to interrupt their work so much—he was interfering with their service to the customers.

By 3:30, Barry was a little bored. He decided to leave, figuring he could get back to the office and prepare his report before 5:00 that day. He was sure his team leader would be pleased with his quick completion of his assignment. As he drove, he reflected, "There really won't be much to say in this report. All they do is take the order, make the sandwich, collect the payment, and hand over the order. It's really simple!" Barry's confidence in his analytical skills soared as he anticipated his team leader's praise.

Back at the store, the store manager shook her head, commenting to her staff, "He comes here at the slowest time of day on the slowest day of the week. He never even looked at all the work I was doing in the back room while he was here—summarizing yesterday's sales, checking inventory on hand, making up resupply orders for the weekend . . . plus he never even considered our store-opening and -closing procedures. I hate to think that the new store management system is going to be built by someone like that. I'd better contact Chuck [the director of store management] and let him know what went on here today."

Evaluate Barry's conduct of the observation assignment.

4. Anne has been given the task of conducting a survey of sales clerks who will be using a new order-entry system being developed for a household products catalog company. The goal of the survey is to identify the clerks' opinions on the strengths and weaknesses of the current system. There are about 50 clerks who work in three different cities, so a survey seemed like an ideal way of gathering the needed information from the clerks.

Anne developed the questionnaire carefully and pretested it on several sales supervisors who were available at corporate headquarters. After revising it based on their suggestions, she sent a paper version of the questionnaire to each clerk, asking that it be returned within one week. After one week, she had only three completed questionnaires returned. After another week, Anne received just two more completed questionnaires. Feeling somewhat desperate, Anne then sent out an e-mail version of the questionnaire, again to all the clerks, asking them to respond to the questionnaire by e-mail as soon as possible. She received two e-mail questionnaires and three messages from clerks who had completed the paper version expressing annoyance at being bothered with the same questionnaire a second time. At this point, Anne has just a 14 percent response rate, which she is sure will not please her team leader. What suggestions do you have that could have improved Anne's response rate to the questionnaire?

CHAPTER 3

BUSINESS PROCESS AND FUNCTIONAL MODELING

Functional models describe business processes and the interaction of an information system with its environment. In object-oriented systems development, use-case diagrams, activity diagrams, and use-case descriptions are used to describe the functionality of an information system. Use-case diagrams provide an overview of the functions of the information system. Activity diagrams support the logical modeling of business processes and workflows. Both use case and activity diagrams can be used to describe the current as-is system and the to-be system being developed. Use-case descriptions provide a text-based model that combines and extends the information contained within the use case and activity diagrams. This chapter describes business process and functional modeling as a means to document and understand requirements and to understand the functional or external behavior of the system.

OBJECTIVES

- Understand the process used to identify business processes and use cases.
- Understand the process used to create use-case diagrams.
- Understand the process used to model business processes with activity diagrams.
- Understand the rules and style guidelines for activity diagrams.
- Understand the process used to create use-case descriptions.
- Understand the rules and style guidelines for use-case descriptions.
- Be able to create functional models of business processes using use-case diagrams, activity diagrams, and use-case descriptions.

INTRODUCTION

The previous chapter discussed popular requirements-gathering techniques, such as interviewing, questionnaires, observation, and document analysis. Using these techniques, along with text analysis, the analyst determined the requirements and created a requirements definition. The requirements definition defined what the system is to do. In this chapter, we focus our attention on use-case driven development. Given that the Unified Modeling Language (UML) has been accepted as the standard notation by the Object Management Group (OMG), almost all object-oriented development projects today use UML to document and organize the requirements that are obtained during the analysis workflow.[1] In this chapter, we discuss how the information that is gathered using these techniques is organized and presented in the

---

[1] Other, similar techniques that are commonly used in non-UML projects are task modeling and scenario-based design. For task modeling, see Ian Graham, *Migrating to Object Technology* (Reading, MA: Addison-Wesley, 1995); Ian Graham, Brian Henderson-Sellers, and Houman Younessi, *The OPEN Process Specification* (Reading, MA: Addison-Wesley, 1997). For scenario-based design, see John M. Carroll, *Scenario-Based Design: Envisioning Work and Technology in System Development* (New York: Wiley, 1995).

form of use cases that are modeled and documented using use-case and activity diagrams and use-case descriptions.

As pointed out in Chapter 1, all object-oriented systems development approaches are use-case driven, architecture-centric, and iterative and incremental. A *use case* is a formal way of representing the way a business system interacts with its environment. Essentially, a use case is a high-level overview of the business processes in a business information system. From a practical perspective, use cases represent the entire basis for an object-oriented system. Use cases can document the current system (i.e., as-is system) or the new system being developed (i.e., to-be system). Given that object-oriented systems are use-case driven, use cases also form the foundation for software testing (see Chapter 7) and user-interface design (see Chapter 9). Two forms of use-case driven testing are walkthroughs (described later in this chapter) and role-playing (described in Chapter 4).

From an architecture-centric perspective, use-case modeling supports the creation of an external or functional view of a business process in that it shows how the users view the process rather than the internal mechanisms by which the process and supporting systems operate. The structural and behavioral architecture-based views are described in Chapters 4 and 5, respectively. Finally, all object-oriented systems development approaches are developed in an incremental and iterative manner. Even though we present the three architectural views in a sequential manner, this is done primarily for pedagogical reasons. You will find that you will need to not only iterate across the business process and functional models (described in this chapter), you will also have to iterate across all three architectural views to fully capture and represent the requirements for a business information system.

Activity diagrams are typically used to augment our understanding of the business processes and our use-case model. Technically, an activity diagram can be used for any type of process modeling.[2] In this chapter, we describe their use in the context of business process modeling. *Process models* depict how a business system operates. They illustrate the processes or activities that are performed and how objects (data) move among them. A process model can be used to document a current system (i.e., as-is system) or a new system being developed (i.e., to-be system), whether computerized or not. Many different process-modeling techniques are in use today.[3]

Activity diagrams and use cases are *logical models*—models that describe the business domain's activities without suggesting how they are conducted. Logical models are sometimes referred to as *problem domain models*. Reading a use-case or activity diagram, in principle, should not indicate if an activity is computerized or manual, for example, if a piece of information is collected by paper form or via the Web, or if information is placed in a filing cabinet or a large database. These physical details are defined during design when the logical models are refined into *physical models*. These models provide information that is needed to ultimately build the system. By focusing on logical activities first, analysts can focus on how the business should run without being distracted with implementation details.

As a first step, the project team gathers requirements from the users. Using the gathered requirements, the project team then identifies the business processes and their environment using use cases and *use-case diagrams*. Next, users work closely with the team to model the

---

[2] We actually used an activity diagram to describe a simple process in Chapter 1 (see Figure 1-1).

[3] From an object-oriented perspective, a good book that uses the UML to address business process modeling is Hans-Erik Eriksson and Magnus Penker, *Business Modeling with UML* (New York: Wiley, 2000). Also, a new process modeling technique is BPMN (Business Process Modeling Notation). A good book that compares the notation and use of BPMN to UML's activity diagram is Martin Schedlbauer, *The Art of Business Process Modeling: The Business Analysts Guide to Process Modeling with UML & BPMN* (Sudbury, MA: The Cathris Group, 2010).

business processes in the form of activity diagrams, and the team documents the business processes described in the use-case and activity diagrams by creating a *use-case description* for each use case. Finally, the team verifies and validates the business processes by ensuring that all three models (use-case diagram, activity diagram(s), and use-case descriptions) agree with one another. Once the current understanding of the business processes is documented in the functional models, the team is ready to move on to structural modeling (see Chapter 4).

In this chapter, we first describe business process identification using use cases and use-case diagrams. Second, we describe business process modeling with activity diagrams. Third, we describe use-case descriptions, their elements, and a set of guidelines for creating them. Fourth, we describe the process of verification and validation of the business process and functional models.

BUSINESS PROCESS IDENTIFICATION WITH USE CASES AND USE-CASE DIAGRAMS

In the previous chapter, we learned about approaches and techniques that are useful in identifying the different business processes of a system so that a requirements definition could be created. In this section, we learn how to begin modeling business processes with use cases and the use-case diagram. An analyst can employ use cases to better understand the functionality of the system at a very high level. Typically, a use-case diagram provides a simple, straightforward way of communicating to the users exactly what the system will do. Consequently, a use-case diagram is drawn when gathering and defining requirements for the system and can encourage the users to provide additional high-level requirements. A use-case diagram illustrates in a very simple way the main functions of the system and the different kinds of users that will interact with it. Figure 3-1 describes the basic syntax rules for a use-case diagram. Figure 3-2 presents a use-case diagram for the doctor's office appointment system introduced in the previous chapter. We can see from the diagram that patients, doctors, and management personnel will use the appointment system to manage appointments, record availability, and produce schedules, respectively.

Use cases are the primary drivers for all the UML diagramming techniques. A use case communicates at a high level what the system needs to do, and all the UML diagramming techniques build on this by presenting the use-case functionality in a different way for a different purpose. Use cases are the building blocks by which the system is designed and built.

Use cases capture the typical interaction of the system with the system's users (end users and other systems). These interactions represent the external, or functional, view of the system from the perspective of the user. Each use case describes one and only one function in which users interact with the system. Although a use case may contain several paths that a user can take while interacting with the system, each possible execution path through the use case is referred to as a *scenario*. Another way to look at a scenario is as if a scenario is an instantiation of a specific use case. Scenarios are used extensively in behavioral modeling (see Chapter 5). Finally, by identifying all scenarios and trying to execute them through role-playing CRC cards (see Chapter 4), you will be testing the clarity and completeness of your evolving understanding of the system being developed.

Elements of Use-Case Diagrams

The elements of a use-case diagram include actors, use cases, subject boundaries, and a set of relationships among actors, actors and use cases, and use cases. Each of these elements is described next.

An actor: ■ is a person or system that derives benefit from and is external to the subject. ■ is depicted as either a stick figure (default) or, if a nonhuman actor is involved, a rectangle with <<actor>> in it (alternative). ■ is labeled with its role. ■ can be associated with other actors using a specialization/superclass association, denoted by an arrow with a hollow arrowhead. ■ is placed outside the subject boundary.	**Actor/Role** **<<actor>>** **Actor/Role**
A use case: ■ represents a major piece of system functionality. ■ can extend another use case. ■ can include another use case. ■ is placed inside the system boundary. ■ is labeled with a descriptive verb–noun phrase.	**Use Case**
A subject boundary: ■ includes the name of the subject inside or on top. ■ represents the scope of the subject, e.g., a system or an individual business process.	**Subject**
An association relationship: ■ links an actor with the use case(s) with which it interacts.	* *
An include relationship: ■ represents the inclusion of the functionality of one use case within another. ■ has an arrow drawn from the base use case to the used use case.	<<include>>
An extend relationship: ■ represents the extension of the use case to include optional behavior. ■ has an arrow drawn from the extension use case to the base use case.	<<extend>>
A generalization relationship: ■ represents a specialized use case to a more generalized one. ■ has an arrow drawn from the specialized use case to the base use case.	

FIGURE 3-1 Syntax for Use-Case Diagram

Actors The stick figures on the diagram represent actors (see Figure 3-1). An *actor* is not a specific user but instead is a role (think class) that a user (think object) can play while interacting with the system. An actor can also represent another system in which the current system interacts. In this case, the actor optionally can be represented by a rectangle containing <<actor>> and the name of the system. Basically, actors represent the principal elements in the environment in which the system operates. Actors can provide input to the system, receive output from the system, or both. The diagram in Figure 3-2 shows that three actors will interact with the appointment system (a patient, a doctor, and management).

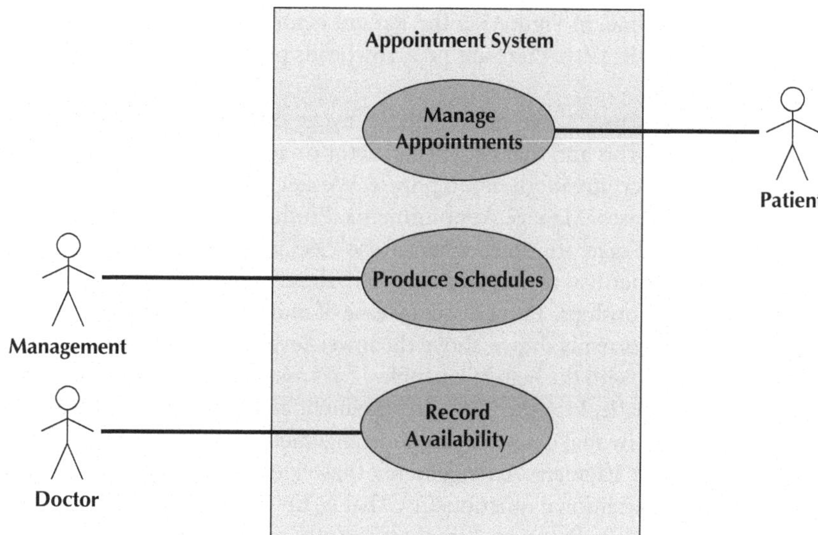

FIGURE 3-2
Use-Case Diagram
for the Appointment
System

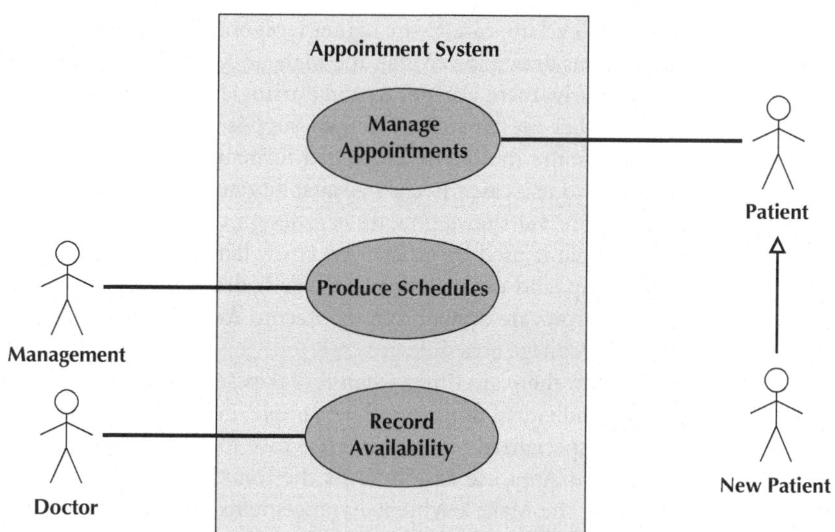

FIGURE 3-3
Use-Case Diagram
with a Specialized
Actor

Sometimes an actor plays a specialized role of a more general type of actor. For example, there may be times when a new patient interacts with the system in a way that is somewhat different from a general patient. In this case, a *specialized actor* (i.e., new patient) can be placed on the model, shown using a line with a hollow triangle at the end of the more-general actor (i.e., patient). The specialized actor inherits the behavior of the more general actor and extends it in some way (see Figure 3-3).

Association Use cases are connected to actors through association relationships; these relationships show with which use cases the actors interact (see Figure 3-1). A line drawn from an actor to a use case depicts an association. The association typically represents two-way communication between the use case and the actor. If the communication is only one way, then a solid arrowhead can be used to designate the direction of the flow of information. For example, in Figure 3-2 the Patient actor communicates with the Manage Appointments use case. Because there are no arrowheads on the association, the communication is two-way.

Use Case A use case, depicted by an oval in the UML, is a major process that the system performs and that benefits an actor or actors in some way (see Figure 3-1); it is labeled using a descriptive verb–noun phrase. We can tell from Figure 3-2 that the system has three primary use cases: Manage Appointments, Produce Schedule, and Record Availability.

There are times when a use case includes, extends, or generalizes the functionality of another use case in the diagram. These are shown using include, extend, and generalization relationships. To increase the ease of understanding a use-case diagram, higher-level use cases are normally drawn above the lower-level ones. It may be easier to understand these relationships with the help of examples. Let's assume that every time a patient makes an appointment, the patient is asked to verify payment arrangements. However, it is occasionally necessary to actually make new payment arrangements. Therefore, we may want to have a use case called Make Payment Arrangements that extends the Manage Appointments use case to include this additional functionality. That is, the Manage Appointments optionally can call or execute the Make Payment Arrangements use case. In Figure 3-4, an arrow labeled with extend was drawn from the Make Payment Arrangements use case to the Manage Appointment use case to denote this special use-case relationship, i.e., the extend relationship is drawn from the lower-level use case to the higher level one. In this case, the Make Payment Arrangements use case was drawn lower than the Manage Appointments use case.

Similarly, there are times when a single use case contains common functions that are used by other use cases. For example, suppose there is a use case called Manage Schedule that performs some routine tasks needed to maintain the doctor's office appointment schedule, and the two use cases Record Availability and Produce Schedule both perform the routine tasks. Figure 3-4 shows how we can design the system so that Manage Schedule is a shared use case that is used by others. An arrow labeled with include is used to denote the include relationship, and the included use case is drawn below the use cases that contain it. Notice that the arrows are drawn from the Record Availability and Produce Schedule use cases to the common Manage Schedule use case.

Finally, there are times when it makes sense to use a generalization relationship to simplify the individual use cases. For example, in Figure 3-4, the Manage Appointments use case has been specialized to include a use case for an Old Patient and a New Patient. The Make Old Patient Appt use case inherits the functionality of the Manage Appointments use case (including the Make Payment Arrangements use-case extension) and extends its own functionality with the Update Patient Information use case. The Make New Patient Appt use case also inherits all the functionality of the generic Manage Appointments use case and calls the Create New Patient use case, which includes the functionality necessary to create the new patient. The generalization relationship is represented as an unlabeled hollow arrow with the more general use case being higher than the lower use cases. Also, notice that we have added a second specialized actor, Old Patient, and that the Patient actor is now simply a generalization of the Old and New Patient actors.

Subject Boundary The use cases are enclosed within a *subject boundary,* which is a box that defines the scope of the system and clearly delineates what parts of the diagram are external or internal to it (see Figure 3-1). One of the more difficult decisions to make is where to draw the subject boundary. A subject boundary can be used to separate a software system from its environment, a subsystem from other subsystems within the software system, or an individual process in a software system. They also can be used to separate an information system, including both software and internal actors, from its environment.

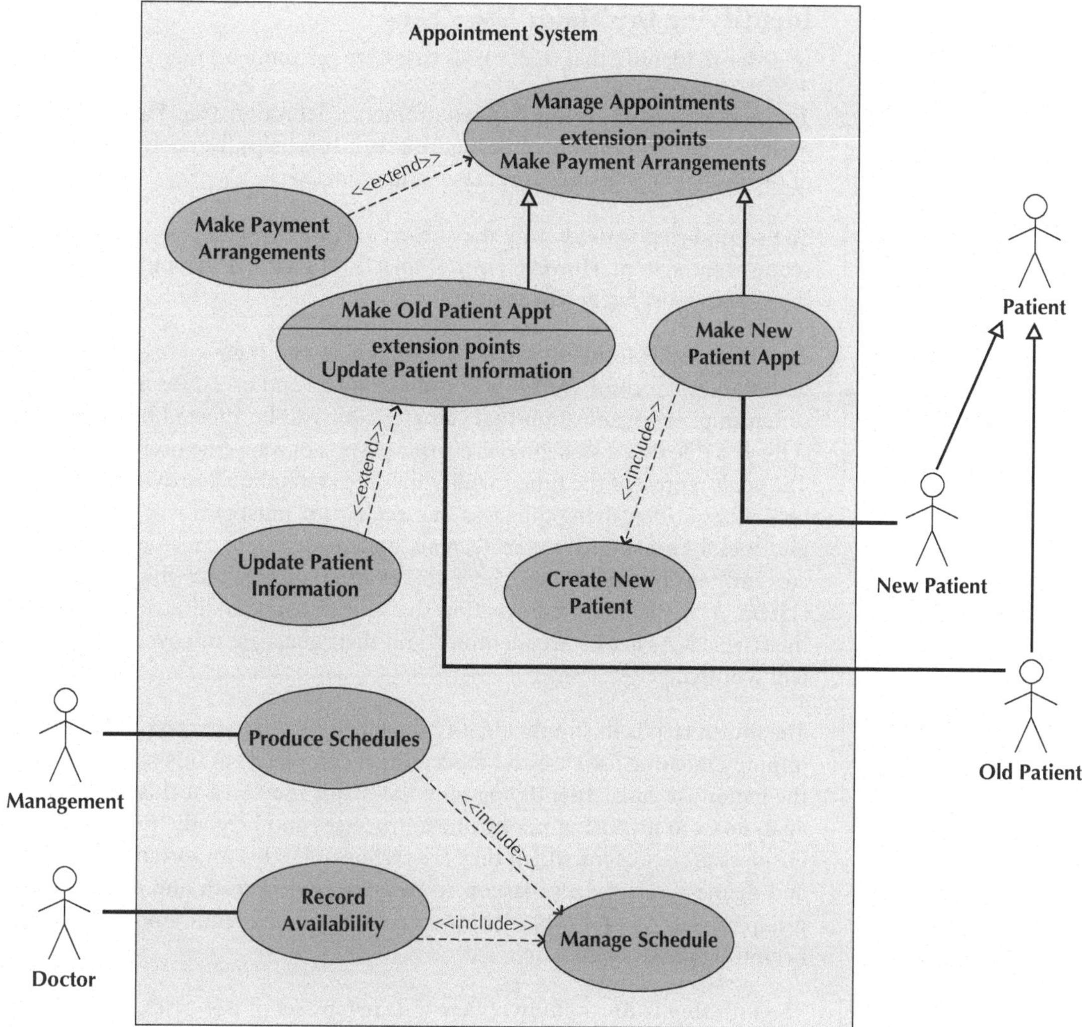

FIGURE 3-4 Extend and Include Relationships

The name of the subject can appear either inside or on top of the box. The subject boundary is drawn based on the scope of the information system. In the appointment system, we assumed that the Management and Doctor actors are outside of the scope of the system; that is, they use the system. However, we could have added an internal actor (Receptionist) that captures the interaction between the patients and the respective make appt use cases. If we did this, we would add another boundary inside of the current boundary in which the internal actor would reside. Given that including the internal actor starts to include implementation decisions, we have decided not to include the receptionist on the diagram.[4] Care should be taken to decide the scope of the information system.

[4] In other non-UML approaches to object-oriented systems development, it is possible to represent external actors along with internal actors. In this example, the receptionist would be considered an internal actor (see Graham, *Migrating to Object Technology*, and Graham, Henderson-Sellers, and Younessi, *The OPEN Process Specification*).

Identifying the Major Use Cases

In order to identify that major uses cases, we recommend that you use the following steps.

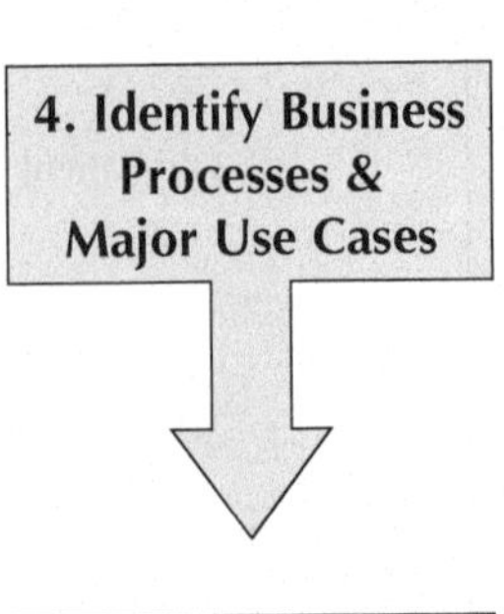

The first step is to review the requirements definition (see Figure 2-15) or the story that describes the requirements (see Figure 2-16). This helps the analyst to get a complete overview of the underlying business process being modeled.

The second step is to identify the subject's boundaries. This helps the analyst to identify the scope of the system. However, as we work through the development process, the boundary of the system most likely will change.

The third step is to identify the primary actors and their goals. The primary actors involved with the system come from a list of stakeholders and users. Recall that a stakeholder is a person, group, or organization that can affect (or will be affected by) a new system, whereas an actor is a role that a stakeholder or user plays, not a specific user (e.g., doctor, not Dr. Jones). The goals represent the functionality that the system must provide the actor for the system to be a success. Identifying the tasks that each actor must perform can facilitate this. For example, does the actor need to create, read, update, delete, or execute (CRUDE)[5] any information currently in the system, are there any external changes of which an actor must inform the system, or is there any information that the system should give the actor? Steps 2 and 3 are intertwined. As actors are identified and their goals are uncovered, the boundary of the system will change.

The fourth step is to simply identify the business processes and major use cases. Rather than jumping into one use case and describing it completely at this point, we only want to identify the major use cases. Identifying only the major use cases at this time prevents the users and analysts from forgetting key business processes and helps the users explain the overall set of business processes for which they are responsible. It is important at this point to understand and define acronyms and jargon so that the project team and others from outside the user group can clearly understand the use cases. Again, the requirements definition is a very useful beginning point for this step.

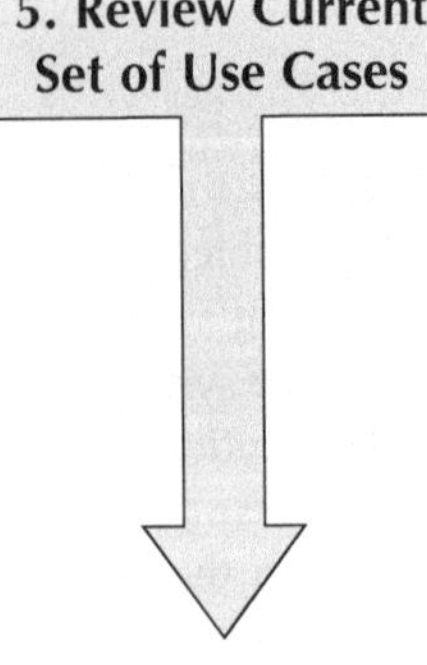

The fifth step is to carefully review the current set of use cases. It may be necessary to split some of them into multiple use cases or merge some of them into a single use case. Also, based on the current set, a new use case may be identified. You should remember that identifying use cases is an iterative process, with users often changing their minds about what a use case is and what it includes. It is very easy to get trapped in the details at this point, so you need to remember that the goal at this step is to only identify the *major* use cases. For example, in the doctor's office example in Figure 3-2, we defined one use case as Manage Appointments. This use case included the cases for both new patients and existing patients, as well as for when a patient changes or cancels an appointment. We could have defined each of these activities (makes an appointment, changes an appointment, or cancels an appointment) as separate use cases, but this would have created a huge set of small use cases.

The trick is to select the right size and number of use cases such that the problem domain is represented in a semantically sound manner. However, too many use cases may suggest that the use cases are too small or that the system boundary is too large, while too few use cases may imply that the size and complexity of the individual use cases are simply too large. Too large use cases will increase the complexity of the activity diagrams that we use to model the

---

[5] We describe the use of CRUDE analysis and matrices in Chapter 5.

use case details (see later in this chapter). Consequently, the right number of use cases is really a function of the complexity of the problem domain. In other words, from a semantic modeling perspective, we will have to trade off the complexity of the problem domain by shifting it between the number of use cases on the use-case diagram and the detailed modeling of the business process with the activity diagrams. In some situations, the use cases could be grouped together into *packages* (i.e., logical groups of use cases) to make the use-case diagrams easier to read and to keep the activity diagrams at a reasonable level of complexity.[6] This challenge is often referred to as keeping all use cases of the same use-case diagram on the same level of abstraction, and it is not an easy thing to master. One can always decompose the major use cases into more detailed ones that are on the same level of abstraction later (e.g., have a use-case diagram for each package).

Creating a Use-Case Diagram

Basically, drawing the use-case diagram is straightforward once use cases have been detailed. The actual use-case diagram encourages the use of information hiding. The only parts drawn on the use-case diagram are the system boundary, the use cases themselves, the actors, and the various associations between these components. The major strength of the use-case diagram is that it provides the user with an overview of the business processes. However, remember that any time a use case changes, it could affect the use-case diagram. There are four major steps in drawing a use-case diagram.

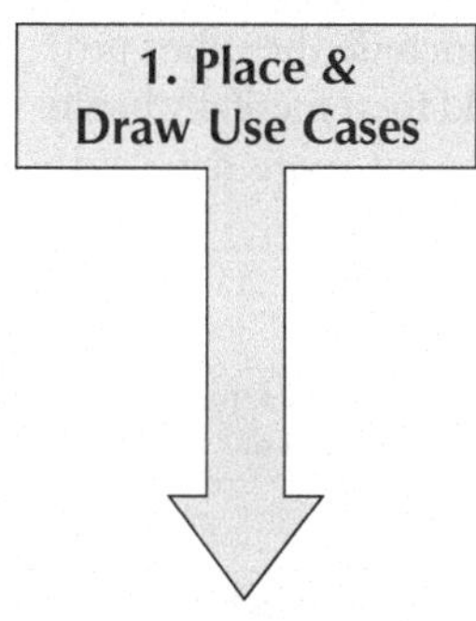

First, we place and draw the use cases on the diagram. These are taken directly from the major use cases previously identified. Special use-case associations (include, extend, or generalization) are also added to the model at this point. Be careful in laying out the diagram. There is no formal order to the use cases, so they can be placed in whatever fashion is needed to make the diagram easy to read and to minimize the number of lines that cross. It often is necessary to redraw the diagram several times with use cases in different places to make the diagram easy to read. Also, for understandability purposes, the number of use cases on the diagram should be balanced with the complexity of the individual activity diagram for each use case. Consequently, there are many possible "correct" use-case diagrams for the same problem domain. Correctness of the use-case diagram is dependent on the associated activity diagrams.

Second, the actors are placed and drawn on the diagram. To minimize the number of lines that cross on the diagram, the actors should be placed near the use cases with which they are associated.

Third, the subject boundary is drawn. This forms the border of the subject, separating use cases (i.e., the subject's functionality) from actors (i.e., the roles of the external users).

The fourth and last step is to add associations by drawing lines to connect the actors to the use cases with which they interact. No order is implied by the diagram, and the items added along the way do not have to be placed in a particular order; therefore, it might help to rearrange the symbols a bit to minimize the number of lines that cross, making the diagram less confusing.

---

[6] For those familiar with structured analysis and design, packages serve a similar purpose as the leveling and balancing processes used in data flow diagramming. Packages are described in Chapter 6.

APPLYING THE CHAPTER CONCEPTS

Library Management System Example In the previous installation of the Library Management System (LMS) example, Susan identified the functional requirements for borrowing from and returning books to the library (see Figure 2-19). She also identified, at a high level, additional functional requirements that included reserving resources, procuring and retiring resources, borrowing and returning other resources such as DVDs and CDs, borrowing and returning resources from other libraries, and dealing with online resources. Also, in this example, using the process described above, Susan created a use-case diagram that provides a high-level description of the relevant business processes.

To begin with, Susan identified the primary external actors: patron and librarian. The goal of the primary external actors is to complete a borrow resource transaction. Next, Susan carefully reviewed the functional requirements to identify the major business processes and use cases. In this case, they are borrow books and return books. Given that Susan also has identified business processes for reserving resources, procuring and retiring resources, borrowing and returning other resources such as DVDs and CDs, borrowing and returning resources from other libraries, and dealing with online resources, she has decided to generalize the borrow books and return books processes to borrow resources and return resources. This required her to go back and get additional information regarding other resources from Joe. We'll cover those with the activity diagram installation in the next section of the chapter. Even though she has only captured detailed specifications of the borrow books and return books processes, she also decided to include the other processes at this time in the use-case diagram. She realized that this would incrementally begin the development process and that she will need to go back to Joe to get more details on

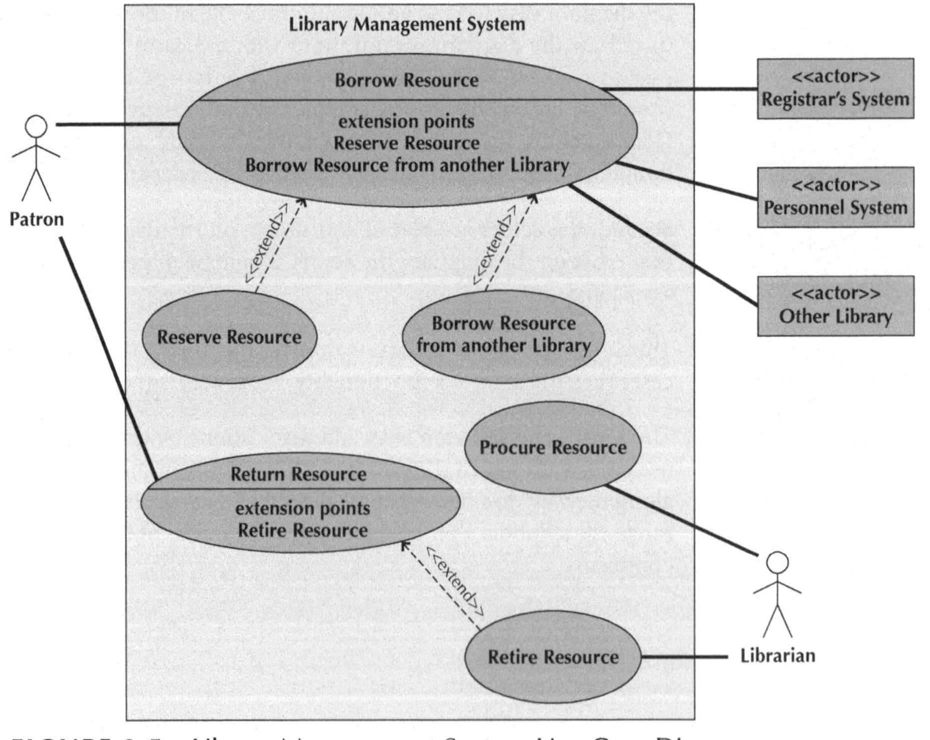

FIGURE 3-5 Library Management System Use-Case Diagram

these other processes. Using the identified actors and use cases and following the process described above, the use-case diagram in Figure 3-5 was created. Notice that the diagram includes two human external actors, three external system actors, and six use cases. Based on the diagram, a patron can borrow and return resources. If the requested resource isn't available, the patron can either request to reserve the resource or request the library find it at another library. We will return to LMS in the next section of the chapter.

Campus Housing Service "Your Turn"   In the previous installation of the Campus Housing Service (CHS) "Your Turn" exercise, you were to identify the functional requirements. In this installment of the Campus Housing Service (CHS) example, you should review the functional requirements developed to identify the actors and use cases so that you can create a use-case diagram. We will return to CHS in the next section of the chapter.

BUSINESS PROCESS MODELING WITH ACTIVITY DIAGRAMS

Business process models describe the different activities that, when combined, support a business process. Business processes typically cut across functional departments (e.g., the creation of a new product involves many different activities that combine the efforts of many employees in many departments). From an object-oriented perspective, these processes cut across multiple objects. Many of the earlier object-oriented systems development approaches tended to ignore business process modeling. However, today we realize that modeling business processes themselves is a very constructive activity that can be used to make sense of the gathered requirements (see Chapter 2). The one potential problem of building business process models, from an object-oriented systems development perspective, is that they tend to reinforce a functional decomposition mindset. However, as long as they are used properly, business process models are very powerful tools for communicating the analyst's current understanding of the requirements to the user.

Martin Schedlbauer provides a set of best practices to follow when modeling business processes.[7]

- Be realistic, because it is virtually impossible to identify everything that is included in a business process at this point in the evolution of the system. Even if we could identify everything, everything is not equally important.
- Be agile because even though we might not identify every single feature of a business process, the features that we do identify should be identified in a rigorous manner.
- All modeling is a collaborative/social activity. Therefore, business process modeling must be performed with teams, not by individuals. When an individual creates a model, the chance of mixing up or omitting important tasks is greatly increased.
- Do not use a CASE tool (that is, computer software) to do the modeling but use whiteboards instead. However, once the process is understood, it is a good idea to use a CASE tool to formally document the process.
- Process modeling should be done in an iterative manner. As you better understand a business process, you will need to return to the documented version of the process and revise it.

[7] Martin Schedlbauer, *The Art of Business Process Modeling: The Business Analysts Guide to Process Modeling with UML & BPMN* (Sudbury, MA: The Cathris Group, 2010).

- When modeling a business process, stay focused on that specific process. If tasks associated with other business processes are identified, simply record them on a to-do list and get back to the business process that you are currently modeling.

- Remember that a business process model is an abstraction of reality. By that, we mean that you should not include every minor task in the current description of the business process. Remember, you cannot afford to lose sight of the proverbial forest for the sake of detailed understanding of a single tree. Too many details at this point in the evolution of the system can cause confusion and actually prevent you from solving the underlying problem being addressed by the new system.

In this chapter, activity diagrams are used to model the behavior in a business process independent of objects. Activity diagrams can be used to model everything from a high-level business workflow that involves many different use cases, to the details of an individual use case, all the way down to the specific details of an individual method. In a nutshell, activity diagrams can be used to model any type of process.[8] However, in this chapter, we restrict our coverage of activity diagrams to documenting and modeling high-level business processes, i.e., we limit the modeling to detail, essential use cases. Consequently, the activity diagrams in this chapter provide a graphical model of the detail use-case description described and discussed later in this chapter.

Elements of an Activity Diagram

Activity diagrams portray the primary activities and the relationships among the activities in a process. Figure 3-6 shows the syntax of an activity diagram. Figure 3-7 presents a simple activity diagram that represents the Manage Appointments use case of the appointment system for the doctor's office example.[9]

Actions and Activities *Actions* and *activities* are performed for some specific business reason. Actions and activities can represent manual or digitized behavior. They are depicted in an activity diagram as a rounded rectangle (see Figure 3-6). They should have a name that begins with a verb and ends with a noun (e.g., Get Patient Information or Make Payment Arrangements). Names should be short, yet contain enough information so that the reader can easily understand exactly what they do. The only difference between an action and an activity is that an activity can be decomposed further into a set of activities and/or actions, whereas an action represents a simple non-decomposable piece of the overall behavior being modeled. Typically, only activities are used for business process or workflow modeling. In most cases, each activity is associated with a use case. The activity diagram in Figure 3-7 shows a set of separate but related activities for the Manage Appointments use case (see Figure 3-2): Request Appointment, Get Patient Information, Update Patient Information, Create New Patient, Make Payment Arrangements, Create New Appointment, Change Appointment, and Cancel Appointment. Notice that the Make Payment Arrangements and

---

[8] Technically speaking, activity diagrams combine process-modeling ideas from many different techniques, including event models, statecharts, and Petri nets. However, UML 2.0's activity diagram has more in common with Petri nets than the other process-modeling techniques. For a good description of using Petri nets to model business workflows, see Wil van der Aalst and Kees van Hee, *Workflow* Management: *Models, Methods, and Systems* (Cambridge, MA: MIT Press, 2002).

[9] Owing to the actual complexity of the syntax of activity diagrams, we follow a minimalist philosophy in our coverage [see John M. Carrol, *The Nurnberg Funnel: Designing Minimalist Instruction for Practical Computer Skill* (Cambridge, MA: MIT Press, 1990)]. However, the material contained in this section is based on the *OMG Unified Modeling Language: Version 2.5.1, formal/2017-12-05* (www.uml.org). Additional useful references include Michael Jesse Chonoles and James A. Schardt, *UML 2 for Dummies* (Indianapolis, IN: Wiley, 2003); Hans-Erik Eriksson, Magnus Penker, Brian Lyons, and David Fado, *UML 2 Toolkit* (Indianapolis: Wiley, 2004); Kendall Scott, *Fast Track UML 2.0* (Berkeley, CA: Apress, 2004). For a complete description of all diagrams, see www.uml.org.

An action: ■ is a simple, nondecomposable piece of behavior. ■ is labeled by its name.	Action
An activity: ■ is used to represent a set of actions. ■ is labeled by its name.	Activity
An object node: ■ is used to represent an object that is connected to a set of object flows. ■ is labeled by its class name.	Class Name
A control flow: ■ shows the sequence of execution.	⟶
An object flow: ■ shows the flow of an object from one activity (or action) to another activity (or action).	- - - - - ⟶
An initial node: ■ portrays the beginning of a set of actions or activities.	●
A final-activity node: ■ is used to stop all control flows and object flows in an activity (or action).	◉
A final-flow node: ■ is used to stop a specific control flow or object flow.	⊗
A decision node: ■ is used to represent a test condition to ensure that the control flow or object flow only goes down one path. ■ is labeled with the decision criteria to continue down the specific path.	[Decision Criteria] ◇ [Decision Criteria]
A merge node: ■ is used to bring back together different decision paths that were created using a decision node.	◇
A fork node: ■ is used to split behavior into a set of parallel or concurrent flows of activities (or actions)	
A join node: ■ is used to bring back together a set of parallel or concurrent flows of activities (or actions)	
A swimlane: ■ is used to break up an activity diagram into rows and columns to assign the individual activities (or actions) to the individuals or objects that are responsible for executing the activity (or action) ■ is labeled with the name of the individual or object responsible	Swimlane

FIGURE 3-6   Syntax for an Activity Diagram

Create Appointment activities appear twice in the diagram: once for an "old" patient scenario and once for a "new" patient scenario. This is preferred to better portray the decision structure of this use case. When this use case is actually implemented, these activities could simply be realized as a function once or as an extended use case that would be called for the different separate scenarios.

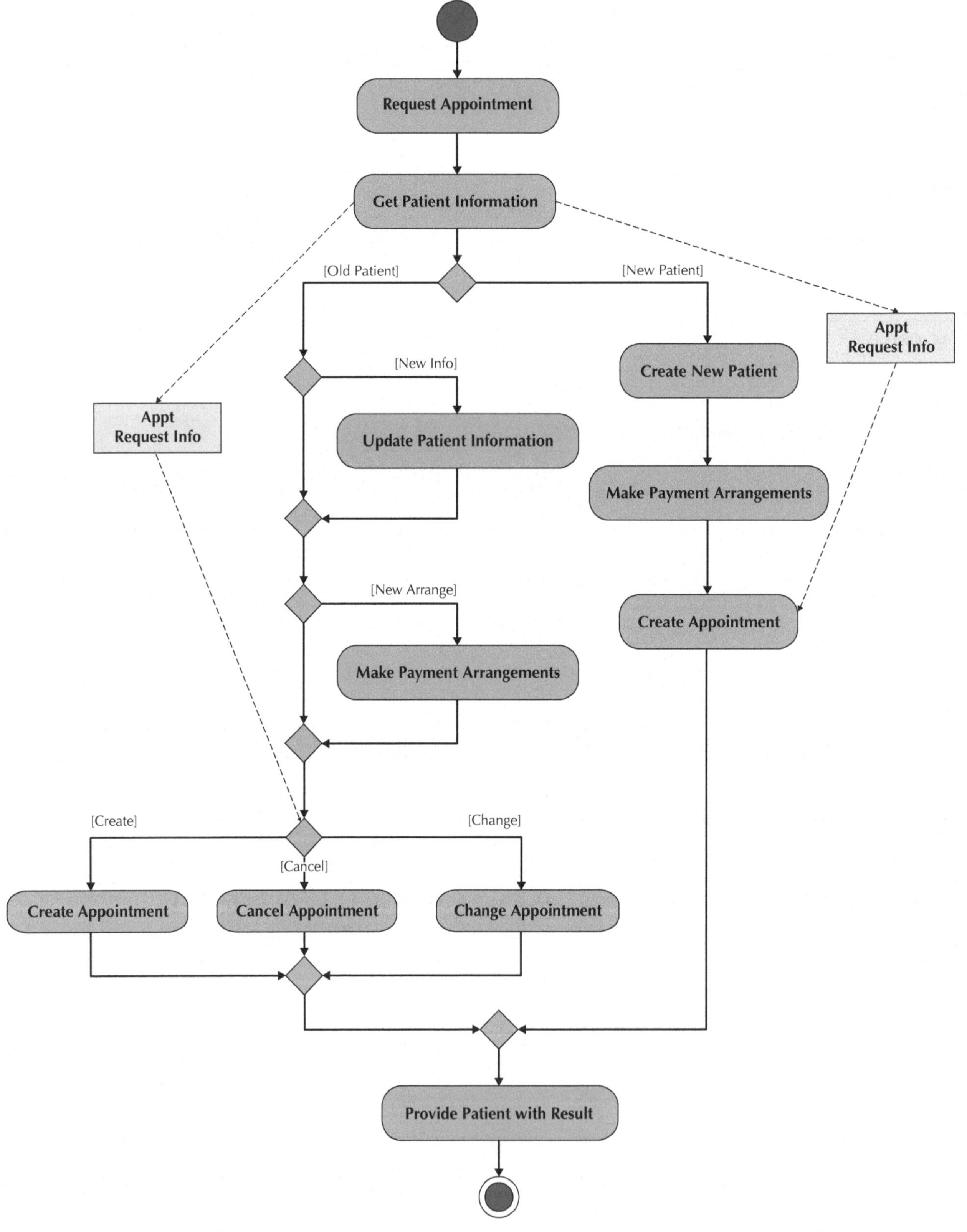

FIGURE 3-7 Activity Diagram for the Manage Appointments Use Case

Object Nodes Activities and actions typically modify or transform objects. *Object nodes* model these objects in an activity diagram. Object nodes are portrayed in an activity diagram as rectangles (see Figure 3-6). The name of the class of the object is written inside the rectangle. Essentially, object nodes represent the flow of information from one activity to another activity. The simple appointment system portrayed in Figure 3-7 shows object nodes flowing from Get Patient Information activity. In most business process-based activity diagrams, object nodes are not included. We have included them in Figure 3-7 for demonstration purposes only.

Control Flows and Object Flows There are two different types of flows in activity diagrams: control and object (see Figure 3-6). *Control flows* model the paths of execution through a business process. A control flow is portrayed as a solid line with an arrowhead on it showing the direction of flow. Control flows can be attached only to actions or activities. Figure 3-7 portrays a set of control flows through the doctor's office's appointment system. *Object flows* model the flow of objects through a business process. Because activities and actions modify or transform objects, object flows are necessary to show the actual objects that flow into and out of the actions or activities. An object flow is depicted as a dashed line with an arrowhead on it showing the direction of flow. An individual object flow must be attached to an action or activity on one end and an object node on the other end. Figure 3-7 portrays a set of control and object flows through the appointment system of a doctor's office. Like with object nodes, in most business process-based activity diagrams, object flows are not included. We have included them in Figure 3-7 for demonstration purposes only.

Control Nodes There are seven different types of *control nodes* in an activity diagram: initial, final-activity, final-flow, decision, merge, fork, and join (see Figure 3-6). An *initial node* portrays the beginning of a set of actions or activities. An initial node is shown as a small filled-in circle. A *final-activity node* is used to stop the process being modeled. Any time a final-activity node is reached, all actions and activities are ended immediately, regardless of whether they are completed. A final-activity node is represented as a circle surrounding a small, filled-in circle, making it resemble a bull's-eye. A *final-flow* node is similar to a final-activity node, except that it stops a specific path of execution through the business process but allows the other concurrent or parallel paths to continue. A final-flow node is shown as a small circle with an X in it. In most business process-based activity diagrams, it is better to not include them. It is much more difficult to understand a business process that has multiple exit points. Consequently, it is better to always attempt to limit the exit from the business process with a single unifying final-activity node.

The decision and merge nodes support modeling the decision structure of a business process. The *decision node* is used to represent the actual test condition that determines which of the paths exiting the decision node is to be traversed. In this case, each exiting path must be labeled with a guard condition. A *guard condition* represents the value of the test for that particular path to be executed. For example, in Figure 3-7, the decision node immediately below the Get Patient Information activity has two mutually exclusive paths that could be executed: one for old, or previous, patients and the other for new patients. The *merge node* is used to bring back together multiple mutually exclusive paths that have been split based on an earlier decision (e.g., the old- and new-patient paths in Figure 3-7 are brought back together near the bottom of the diagram). However, sometimes, for clarity, it is better not to use a merge node. From a business process modeling perspective, a good deal of common sense can go a long way.

The fork and join nodes allow parallel and concurrent processes to be modeled (see Figure 3-6). The *fork node* is used to split the behavior of the business process into multiple parallel or concurrent flows. Unlike the decision node, the paths are not mutually exclusive (i.e., both paths are executed concurrently). For example, in Figure 3-8, the fork node is used to show a set of parallel processes that are to be executed concurrently to process an order. The purpose of the join node is similar to that of the merge node. The *join node* simply brings back together the separate parallel or concurrent flows in the business process into a single flow.

Swimlanes Activity diagrams can model a business process independent of any object implementation. However, there are times when it helps to break up an activity diagram in such a way that it can be used to assign responsibility to objects or individuals who would actually perform the activity. This is especially useful when modeling a business workflow and is accomplished through the use of *swimlanes*. Swimlanes can be drawn in a vertical manner or horizontally. In an actual business workflow, there would be activities that should be associated with roles of individuals involved in the business workflow (e.g., employees or customers) and the activities to be accomplished by the information system being created. This association of activities with external roles, internal roles, and the system is very useful when creating the use-case descriptions described later in this chapter. We will return to the use of swimlanes with activity diagrams when we attempt to assign individual activities to actors (both external and internal) and the classes/objects that we identify with the structural models (see Chapter 4).

Guidelines for Creating Activity Diagrams

Scott Ambler suggests the following guidelines when creating activity diagrams:[10]

- Because an activity diagram can be used to model any kind of process, you should set the context or scope of the activity being modeled. Once you have determined the scope, you should give the diagram an appropriate title.
- You must identify the activities, control flows, and object flows that occur between the activities.
- You should identify any decisions that are part of the process being modeled.
- You should attempt to identify any prospects for parallelism in the process.
- You should draw the activity diagram.

When drawing an activity diagram, the diagram should be limited to a single initial node that starts the process being modeled. This node should be placed at the top or top left of the

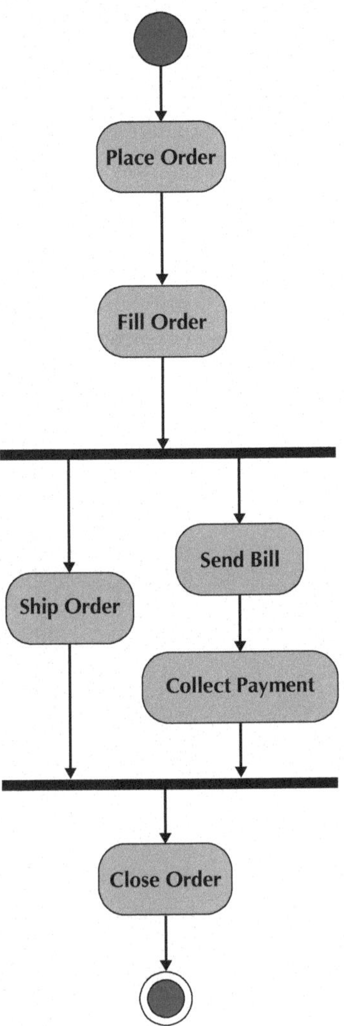

FIGURE 3-8
Activity Diagram for Order Processing

<hr>

10 The guidelines presented here are based on work done by Scott Ambler. For more details, see Scott W. Ambler, *The Object Primer: The Application Developer's Guide to Object Orientation and the UML*, 2nd Ed. (Cambridge, England: Cambridge University Press/SIGS Books, 2001); Scott W. Ambler, *The Elements of UML Style* (Cambridge, England: Cambridge University Press, 2003).

diagram, depending on the complexity of the diagram. For most business processes, there should only be a single final-activity node. This node should be placed at the bottom or bottom right of the diagram (see Figures 3-7 and 3-8). Because most high-level business processes are sequential, not parallel, the use of a final-flow node should be limited.

When modeling high-level business processes or workflows, only the more important decisions should be included in the activity diagrams. In those cases, the guard conditions associated with the outflows of the decision nodes should be mutually exclusive. The outflows and guard conditions should form a complete set (i.e., all potential values of the decision are associated with one of the flows). Furthermore, in decision modeling, forks and joins should be included only to represent the more important parallel activities in the process.

When laying out the activity diagram, line crossings should be minimized to enhance the readability of the diagram. The activities on the diagram should also be laid out in a left-to-right and/or top-to-bottom order based on the order in which the activities are executed.

Finally, any activity that does not have any outflows or any inflows should be challenged. Activities with no outflows are referred to as *black-hole activities*. If the activity is truly an end point in the diagram, the activity should have a control flow from it to a final-activity or final-flow node. An activity that does not have any inflow is known as a *miracle activity*. In this case, the activity is missing an inflow either from the initial node of the diagram or from another activity.

Creating Activity Diagrams

We recommend that you use the following steps to create an Activity Diagram. There are five steps in creating an activity diagram to document and model a business process.

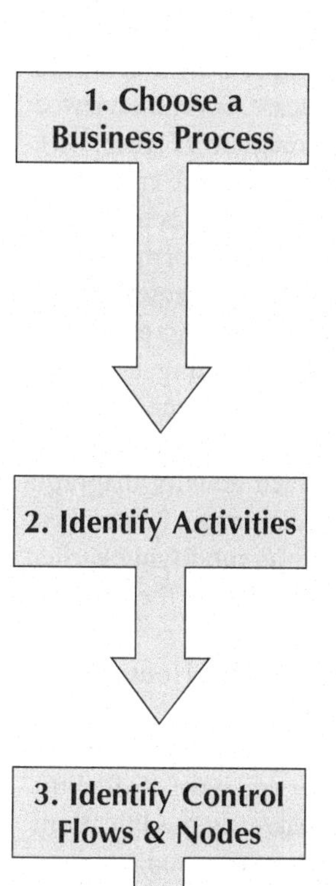

First, you must choose a business process that was previously identified to model. To do this, you should review the requirements definition (see Figure 2-15) or the story that describes the requirements (see Figure 2-16) and the use-case diagram (see Figures 3-2, 3-3, and 3-4) created to represent the requirements. You should also review all of the documentation created during the requirements-gathering process (see Chapter 2), e.g., interviews, observations, questionnaires, and document analysis along with the associated text analysis. In most cases, the use cases on the use-case diagram will be the best place to start. For example, in the appointment system, we had identified three primary use cases: Manage Appointments, Produce Schedule, and Record Doctor Availability. We also identified a whole set of minor use cases (these will be useful in identifying the elements of the activity diagram).

Second, identify the set of activities necessary to support the business process. For example, in Figure 2-15, three processes are identified as being part of the Manage Appointments business process. Also, by reviewing the use-case diagram (see Figure 3-4), we see that five minor use cases are associated with the Manage Appointments major use case. Based on this information, we can identify a set of activities. In this case, the activities are Request Appointment, Get Patient Information, Update Patient Information, Make Payment Arrangements, Create New Patient, Create Appointment, Cancel Appointment, and Change Appointment.

Third, identify the control flows and nodes necessary to document the logic of the business process. For example, in Figure 3-4, the Make Payment Arrangements and Update Patient Information use cases are extensions to the Manage Appointments and Make Old Patient Appt use cases. We know that these use cases are executed only in certain circumstances. From this we can infer that the activity diagram must include some decision and merge nodes. Based on the requirements definition (see Figure 2-15), we can infer another set of decision and merge nodes based on the Create Appointment, Cancel Appointment, and Change Appointment activities identified in the previous step.

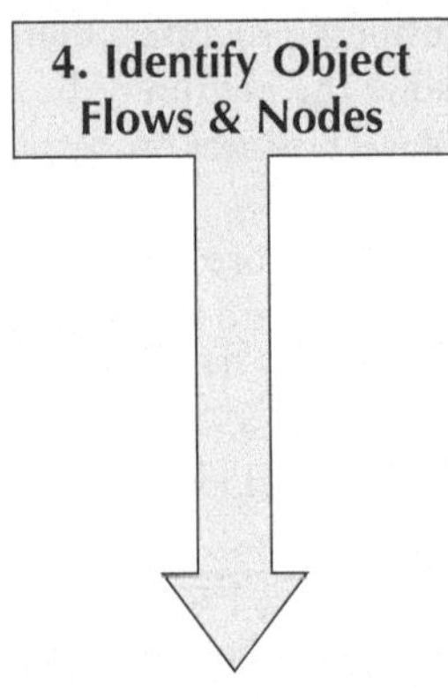

Fourth, identify the object flows and nodes necessary to support the logic of the business process. Typically, object nodes and flows are not shown on many activity diagrams used to model a business process. The primary exception is if information captured by the system in one activity is used in an activity that is performed later, but *not* immediately after the activity that captured the information. In the appointment example, it is obvious that we need to be able to determine whether the patient is an old or new patient and the type of action that the patient would like to have performed (create, cancel, or change an appointment). It is obvious that a new patient cannot cancel or change an appointment because the patient is by definition a new patient. Obviously, we need to capture this type of information at the beginning of the business process and use it when required. For example, in the appointment problem, we need to have a Get Patient Information activity that captures the appropriate information and makes it available at the appropriate time in the process.

Fifth, lay out and draw the activity diagram to document the business process. For esthetic and understandability reasons, just as when drawing a use-case diagram, you should attempt to minimize potential line crossings. Based on the previous steps and carefully laying out the diagram, the activity diagram in Figure 3-7 was created to document the Manage Appointments business process.

APPLYING THE CHAPTER CONCEPTS

Library Management System Example In this installation of the Library Management System, Susan must first choose one of the use cases to detail using an activity diagram to model. In this case, she chose to start with the Borrow Resource use case. So, she reviewed both the functional requirements (Figure 2-15) and the use-case diagram (Figure 3-5). Based on her review and the additional information that she got from Joe, she created an activity diagram for the Borrow Resource use case (Figure 3-9). Based on this activity diagram, Susan realized that she would need to go back and slightly modify the Borrow Books functional requirements to become the Borrow Resource functional requirements (Figure 3-10). Now that Susan has the first activity diagram completed, she incrementally continues the modeling by creating an activity diagram for each remaining use case: Reserve Resource, Borrow Resource from Another Library, Return Resource, Procure Resource, and Retire Resource. As she worked through each use case, she typically had to iterate back and modify the functional requirements that drove each activity diagram. Furthermore, in some cases, she had to modify existing activity diagrams. Remember, systems development tends to be iterative and incremental. Therefore, modifying earlier representations is very common. We will return to LMS in the next section of the chapter.

Campus Housing Service "Your Turn" In this installation of the Campus Housing Service example, you must first choose one of the use cases to detail using an activity diagram. So, you should review both the functional requirements created with the last chapter and the use case diagram you created with the previous installation. After you have created the activity diagram for the first use case, you should iterate back and make any modifications to the functional requirements that drove the activity diagram. Next, you need to incrementally create activity diagrams for each remaining use case. Also, you need to iterate back over the functional requirements and the other activity diagrams to make sure that they are still valid representations of each use case. We will return to the CHS "Your Turn" exercise in the next section of the chapter.

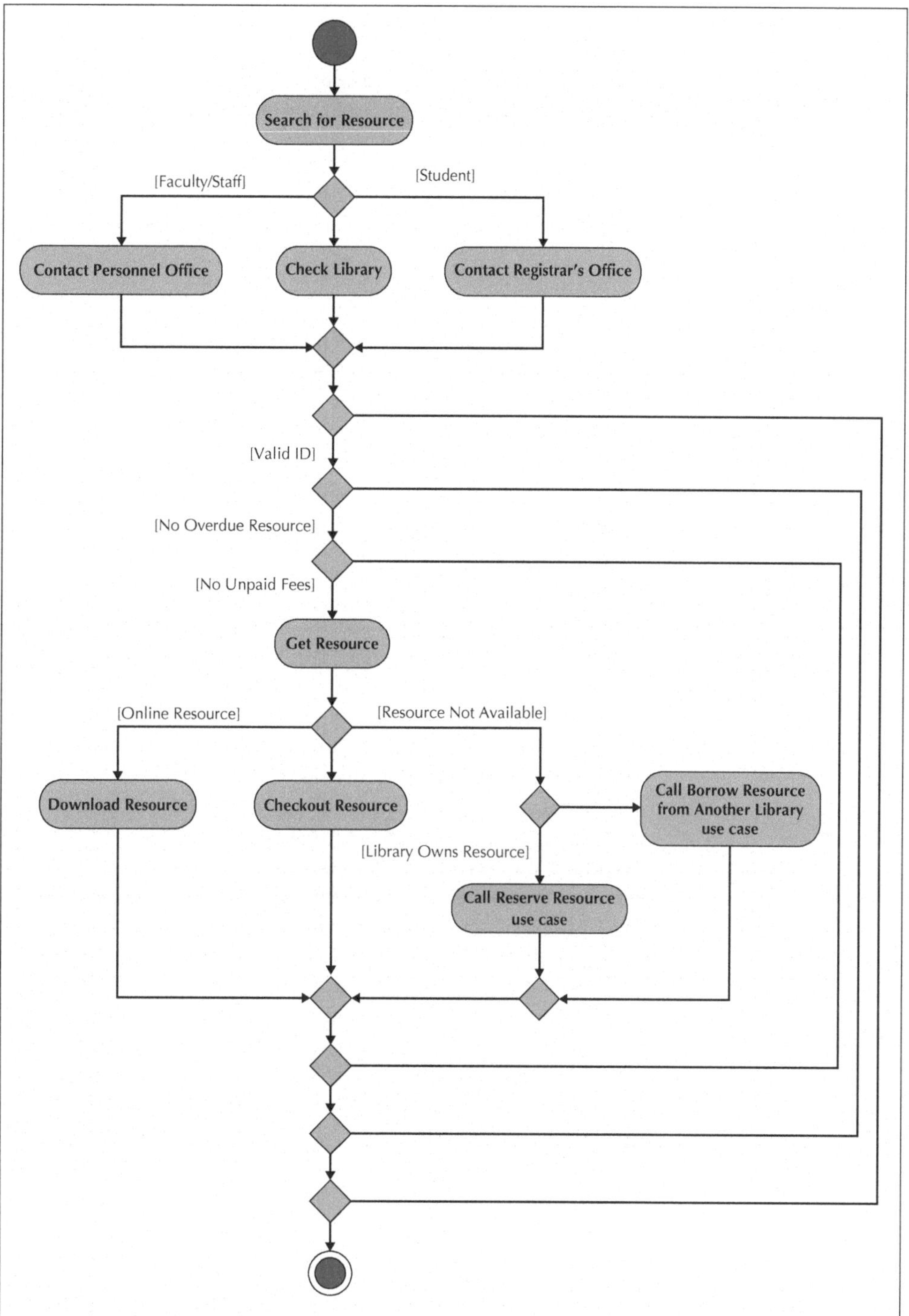

FIGURE 3-9 Library Management System Borrow Resource Use-Case Activity Diagram

1. **Borrow Resource.**
   a. Search for resource and take it to checkout.
   b. Give librarian resource and ID card.
   c. Librarian checks card validity based on borrower type: If student, check registrar's system, if faculty or staff, check personnel system, if guest, check library system.
      i. If card is invalid, then deny checkout.
   d. If card is valid, Librarian checks library system to determine whether borrower has any overdue resources or unpaid fines.
      i. If overdue resources, then deny checkout.
      ii. If unpaid fees, then deny checkout.
   e. If card is valid, no overdue resources, and no unpaid fees, then get resource to borrow.
      i. If online resource, then download resource.
      ii. If resource not available and library owns resource, then reserve resource.
      iii. If resource not available and library does not own resource, then borrow from another library.
      iv. If resource is physical and available, then checkout resource.

FIGURE 3-10   Library Management System updated Borrow Resource Functional Requirements

BUSINESS PROCESS DOCUMENTATION WITH USE-CASE DESCRIPTIONS

Use-case diagrams provided a bird's-eye view of the basic functionality of the business processes contained in the evolving system. Activity diagrams, in a sense, open up the black box of each business process by providing a more-detailed graphical view of the underlying activities that support each business process. Use-case descriptions provide a means to more fully document the different aspects of each individual use case.[11] The use-case descriptions are based on the identified functional requirements, use-case diagram, and the activity diagram descriptions of the business processes. Use-case descriptions contain all the information needed to document the functionality of the business processes.[12]

When creating use-case descriptions, the project team must work closely with the users to fully document the functional requirements. Organizing the functional requirements and documenting them in a use-case description are a relatively simple process, but it takes considerable practice to ensure that the descriptions are complete enough to use in structural (Chapter 4) and behavioral (Chapter 5) modeling. The best place to begin is to review the use-case and activity diagrams. The key thing to remember is that each use case is associated with a primary *actor* that represents one and only one *role* that users have in the system. For example, a receptionist in a doctor's office may play multiple roles—he or she can make appointments, answer the telephone, file medical records, welcome patients, and so on. It is possible that multiple users will play the same role. Therefore, use cases should be associated with the roles played by the users and not with the users themselves.

---

[11] For a more detailed description of use-case modeling, see Alistair Cockburn, *Writing Effective Use Cases* (Reading, MA: Addison-Wesley, 2001).

[12] Nonfunctional requirements, such as reliability requirements and performance requirements, are often documented outside of the use case through more traditional requirements documents. See Gerald Kotonya and Ian Sommerville, *Requirements Engineering* (Chichester, England: Wiley, 1998); Benjamin L. Kovitz, *Practical Software Requirements: A Manual of Content & Style* (Greenwich, CT: Manning, 1999); Dean Leffingwell and Don Widrig, *Managing Software Requirements: A Unified Approach* (Reading, MA: Addison-Wesley, 2000); Richard H. Thayer, M. Dorfman, and Sidney C. Bailin (Eds.), *Software Requirements Engineering*, 2nd Ed. (Los Alamitos, CA: IEEE Computer Society, 1997).

Types of Use Cases

There are many different types of use cases. We suggest two separate dimensions on which to classify a use case based on the purpose of the use case and the amount of information that the use case contains: overview versus detail and essential versus real.

An *overview use case* is used to enable the analyst and user to agree on a high-level overview of the requirements. Typically, overview use cases are created very early in the process of understanding the system requirements, and they document only basic information about the use case, such as its name; ID number; primary actor; type; a brief description; and the relationships among the actors, actors and use cases, and use cases. These can easily be created immediately after the creation of the use-case diagram.

Once the user and the analyst agree upon a high-level overview of the requirements, the overview use cases are converted to detail use cases. A *detail use case* typically documents, as far as possible, all the information needed for the use case. These can be based on the activities and control flows contained in the activity diagrams.

An *essential use case* is one that describes only the minimum essential issues necessary to understand the required functionality. A *real use case* goes farther and describes a specific set of steps. For example, an essential use case in a doctor office might say that the receptionist should attempt to match the patient's desired appointment times with the available times, whereas a real use case might say that the receptionist should look up the available dates on the calendar using Google Calendar to determine if the requested appointment times were available. The primary difference is that essential use cases are implementation independent, whereas real use cases are detailed descriptions of how to use the system once it is implemented. Thus, real use cases tend to be used only in the design, implementation, and testing.

In this chapter, we limit our discussion to essential use cases; overview and detail. We model and document overview, essential use cases using use-case diagrams and overview use-case descriptions; while we model and document detail, essential use cases with activity diagrams and detail use-case descriptions.

Elements of a Use-Case Description

A use-case description contains all the information needed to build the structural (Chapter 4) and behavioral (Chapter 5) diagrams that follow, but it expresses the information in a less-formal way that is usually simpler for users to understand. Figure 3-11 portrays an updated use-case diagram for the appointment system. Based on the updated use-case diagram, an updated activity diagram for the Management Appointments use case (see Figure 3-12) was created. Figure 3-13 shows a sample use-case description for the Manage Appointments use case.[13]

Overview Use-Case Section The overview use case identifies the use case and provides basic background information about the use case. This section of the use-case description is associated with the use-case diagram. The *use-case name* should be a verb–noun phrase (e.g., Manage Appointments). The *use-case ID number* provides a unique way to find every use case and also enables the team to trace design decisions back to a specific requirement. The *use-case type* is either overview or detail, and essential or real. The *primary actor* is usually the trigger of the use case—the person or thing that starts the execution of the use case. The primary

---

[13] Currently there is no standard set of elements for a use case. The elements described in this section are based on recommendations contained in Alistair Cockburn, *Writing Effective Use Cases* (Reading, MA: Addison-Wesley, 2001); Craig Larman, *Applying UML and Patterns: An Introduction to Object-Oriented Analysis and Design and the Unified Process*, 2nd Ed. (Upper Saddle River, NJ: Prentice Hall, 2002); Brian Henderson-Sellers and Bhuvan Unhelkar, *OPEN Modeling with UML* (Reading, MA: Addison-Wesley, 2000). Also see Graham, *Migrating to Object Technology*.

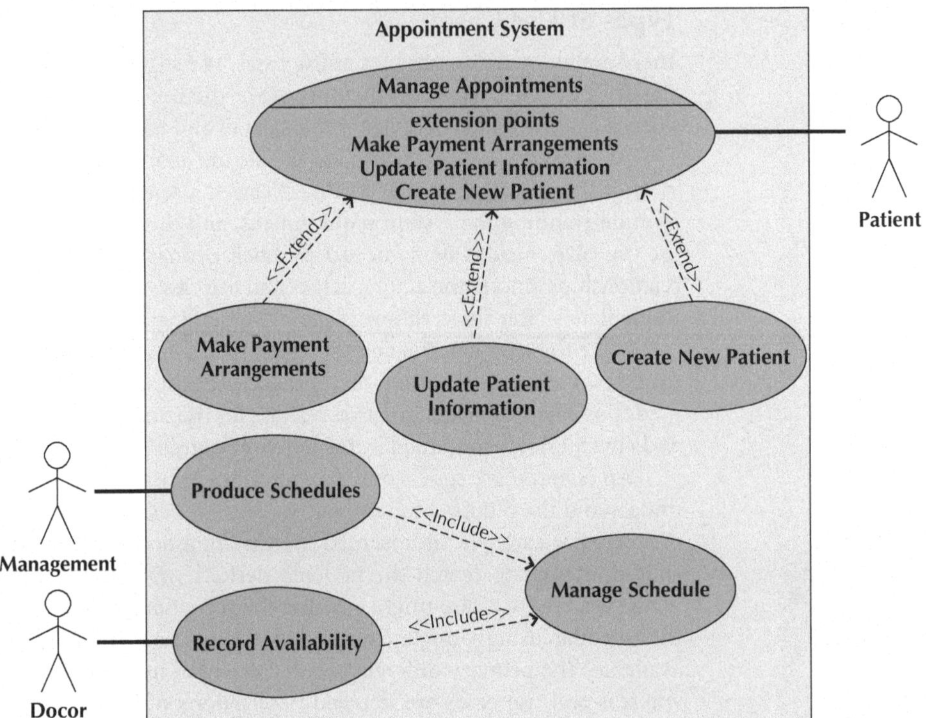

FIGURE 3-11
Updated Use-Case Diagram for the Appointment System

purpose of the use case is to meet the goal of the primary actor. The identification of the primary actor, along with the stakeholders, also provides information that will be useful in addressing role-based access controls that support the security nonfunctional requirements covered in the design chapters later in the book. The *brief description* is typically a single sentence that describes the essence of the use case.

The *importance level* can be used to prioritize the use cases. The importance level enables the users to explicitly prioritize which business functions are most important and need to be part of the first version of the system and which are less important and can wait until later versions if necessary. The importance level can use a fuzzy scale, such as high, medium, and low (e.g., in Figure 3-13 we have assigned an importance level of high to the Manage Appointments use case). It can also be done more formally using a weighted average of a set of criteria. For example, Craig Larman[14] suggests rating each use case over the following criteria using a scale from zero to five:

- The use case represents an important business process.
- The use case supports revenue generation or cost reduction.
- Technology needed to support the use case is new or risky and therefore requires considerable research.
- Functionality described in the use case is complex, risky, and/or time critical. Depending on a use case's complexity, it may be useful to consider splitting its implementation over several different versions.
- The use case could increase understanding of the evolving design relative to the effort expended.

[14] Craig Larman, *Applying UML and Patterns: An Introduction to Object-Oriented Analysis and Design and the Unified Process*, 2nd Ed. (Upper Saddle River, NJ: Prentice Hall, 2002).

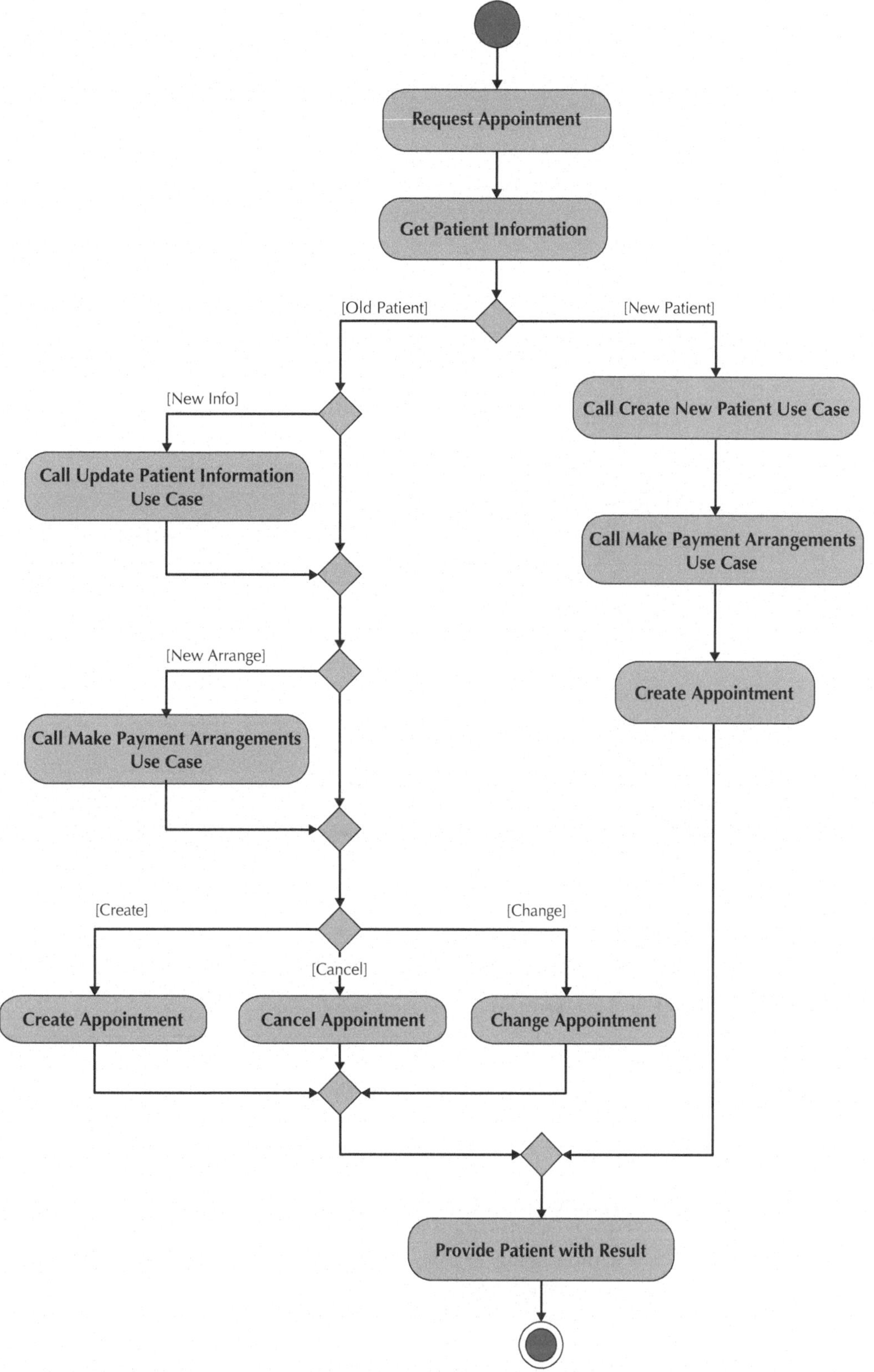

FIGURE 3-12 Updated Activity Diagram for the Manage Appointment Use Case

Use-Case Name: Manage Appointments	ID: 2	Importance Level: High

Primary Actor: Patient	Use-Case Type: Detail, Essential

Stakeholders and Interests:
Patient – wants to make, change, or cancel an appointment
Doctor – wants to ensure patient's needs are met in a timely manner

Brief Description: This use case describes how we make appointment as well as changing or canceling an appointment for a patient.

Trigger: Patient calls and asks to make a new appointment, change an existing appointment, or to cancel an existing appointment

Type: External

Relationships:
Association: Patient
Include:
Extend: Create New Patient, Make Payment Arrangements, Update Patient Information
Generalization:

Normal Flow of Events:
1. The Patient contacts the office regarding an appointment.
2. The Patient provides the receptionist with their information.
3. Call S-1: Create New Patient Subflow.
4. Receptionist provides Patient with the result.

SubFlows:
S-1: Create New Patient Subflow
    1. Call Create New Patient use case.
    2. Call Make Payment Arrangements use case.
    3. Create Appointment.
S-2: Old Patient Subflow
    1. Call Update Patient Information use case.
    2. Call Make Payment Arrangements use case.
    3. Create Appointment.

Alternate/Exceptional Flows:
3a. Call S-2: Old Patient Subflow.
S-2, 1a. Pass.
S-2, 2a. Pass.
S-2, 3a. Cancel appointment.
S-2, 3b. Change appointment.

FIGURE 3-13 Sample Use-Case Description

A use case may have multiple *stakeholders* that have an interest in the use case. Each use case lists each of the stakeholders with each one's interest in the use case (e.g., Patient and Doctor). The stakeholders' list always includes the primary actor (e.g., Patient).

Each use case typically has a *trigger*—the event that causes the use case to begin (e.g., Patient calls and asks for a new appointment or asks to cancel or change an existing appointment). A trigger can be an *external trigger*, such as a customer placing an order or the fire alarm ringing, or it can be a *temporal trigger*, such as a book being overdue at the library or the need to pay the rent.

Use-case relationships explain how the use case is related to other use cases and users. There are four basic types of *relationships*: association, extend, include, and generalization. An *association relationship* documents the communication that takes place between the use case and the actors that use the use case. An actor is the UML representation for the role that a user plays in the use case. For example, in Figure 3-13, the Manage Appointments use case is associated with the actor Patient (see Figure 3-11). All actors involved in the use case are documented with the association relationship.

An *include relationship* represents the mandatory inclusion of another use case. The include relationship enables *functional decomposition*—the breaking up of a complex use case into several simpler ones. For example, in Figure 3-11, the Manage Schedule use case was considered to be complex and complete enough to be factored out as a separate use case that could be executed by the Produce Schedules and Record Availability use cases. The include relationship also enables parts of use cases to be reused by creating them as separate use cases.

An *extend relationship* represents the extension of the functionality of the use case to incorporate optional behavior. In Figure 3-11, the Manage Appointments use case condition-ally uses the Update Patient Information, Make Payment Arrangements, and Create New Patient use cases. These use cases are executed only if a specific set of conditions is met. The specific conditions are specified in the activity diagram for the use case.

The *generalization relationship* allows use cases to support *inheritance*. For example, in Figure 3-4, the Manage Appointments use case, was specialized so that a new patient would be associated with the Make New Patient Appt and an old patient could be associated with a Make Old Patient Appt. The common, or generalized, behavior that both the Make New Patient Appointment and Make Old Patient Appointment use cases contain would be placed in the gen-eralized Manage Appointments use case. In other words, the Make New Patient Appointment and Make Old Patient Appointment use cases would inherit the common functionality from the Manage Appointments use case. The specialized behavior would be placed in the appropriate specialized use case. For example, the extend relationship to the Update Patient Information use case would be placed with the specialized Make Old Patient Appointment use case. However, we decided to simplify the use-case diagram for the appointment system and collapsed the two specialized use cases back into the generalized use case (see Figures 3-4 and 3-11). For the pur-poses of the remaining discussion, we focus on the use-case diagram in Figure 3-11.

Detail Use-Case Section Finally, for detail use cases, individual steps within the business process are described. These steps are associated with the activity diagrams. Three different categories of steps, or *flows of events,* can be documented: normal flow of events, subflows, and alternative, or exceptional, flows:

- The *normal flow of events* includes only steps that normally are executed in a use case. The steps are listed in the order in which they are performed. In Figure 3-13, the patient contacts the office and has a conversation with the receptionist regarding the patient's name, address, and action to be performed.

- In some cases, the normal flow of events should be decomposed into a set of *subflows* to keep the normal flow of events as simple as possible. In Figure 3-13, we have iden-tified two subflows: one for old patients and another one for new patients. Each of the steps of the subflows is listed. These subflows are based on the control flow logic in the activity diagram representation of the business process (see Figure 3-12). Alternatively, we could replace a subflow with a separate use case that could be incorporated via the include relationships (see the earlier discussion). However, this should be done only if the newly created use case makes sense by itself. For example, in Figure 3-11, we previously factored out three extended use cases: Make Payment Arrangements, Update Patient Information, and Create New Patient. These use cases are called by the individual subflows in our example (see Figure 3-12).

■ *Alternative or exceptional flows* are ones that do happen but are not considered to be the norm. These must be documented. For example, in Figure 3-13, we have identified a set of alternative or exceptional flows. The first one simply models the decision of whether the patient calling is a new or old patient. It was decided to model the creation of a new patient as the normal event and the old patient process as the exceptional or alternate flow. The decision of being the normal step or the alternate step is somewhat arbitrary. In this case, event 3 in the Normal Flow of events and the Alternate/Exceptional flow event 3a can be swapped without any change to the underlying structure of the use case. The second Alternate/Exceptional Flow simply models the decision that is made regarding whether an old patient needs to update their patient information or not. In this case, the "normal" flow of the Old Patient Subflow was to call the Update Patient Information use case while the Alternate/Exceptional subflow was to do nothing, hence the word Pass. Like the subflows, the primary purpose of separating out alternate or exceptional flows is to keep the normal flow of events as simple as possible. Again, as with the subflows, it is possible to replace the alternate or exceptional flows with separate use cases that could be integrated via the extend relationship (see the earlier discussion).

When should events be factored out from the normal flow of events into subflows? When should subflows and/or alternative or exceptional flows be factored out into separate use cases? Or when should things simply be left alone? The primary criteria should be based on the level of complexity that the use case entails. The more difficult it is to understand the use case, the more likely events should be factored out into subflows, or subflows and/or alternative or exceptional flows should be factored out into separate use cases that are called by the current use case. This, of course, creates more use cases. Therefore, the use-case diagram will become more cluttered. In other words, the choice that the analyst must make is to have a more complex use-case diagram with simpler use cases or have a simpler use-case diagram with more complex use-case descriptions. Practically speaking, we must decide which makes more sense. This varies greatly, depending on the problem and the client. Remember, we are trying to represent, in a manner as *complete* and *concise* as possible, our understanding of the business processes that we are investigating so that the client can validate the requirements that we are modeling. That is, the client can point out our misunderstandings. Therefore, there really is no single right answer. It really depends on the analyst, the client, and the problem.

Optional Characteristics Other characteristics of use cases can be documented by use-case descriptions. These include the level of complexity of the use case; the estimated amount of time it takes to execute the use case; the system with which the use case is associated; specific data flows between the primary actor and the use case; any specific attribute, constraint, or operation associated with the use case; any preconditions that must be satisfied for the use case to execute; or any postconditions that guarantee an acceptable result of the use case. As we noted at the beginning of this section, there is no standard set of characteristics of a use case that must be captured. We suggest that the information contained in Figure 3-13 is the minimal amount to be captured.

Guidelines for Creating Use-Case Descriptions[15]

The essence of a use case is the flow of events. Writing the flow of events in a manner that is useful for later stages of development generally comes with experience.

---

[15] These guidelines are based on Cockburn, *Writing Effective Use Cases*, and Graham, *Migrating to Object Technology*.

First, write each individual step in the form subject–verb–direct object and, optionally, preposition–indirect object. This form is relatively easy to diagram (see sentence diagramming in Chapter 2) and has become known as *SVDPI* sentences. This form of sentence has proved to be useful in identifying classes and operations (see Chapter 4). For example, in Figure 3-13, the first step in the normal flow of events, the Patient contacts the office regarding an appointment, suggests the possibility of three classes of objects: Patient, Office, and Appointment. This approach simplifies the process of identifying the classes in the structural model (see Chapter 4). SVDPI sentences cannot be used for all steps, but they should be used whenever possible.

Second, make clear who or what is the initiator of the action and who or what is the receiver of the action in each step. Normally, the initiator should be the subject of the sentence and the receiver should be the direct object of the sentence. For example, in Figure 3-13, the second step, Patient provides the Receptionist with his or her name and address, clearly portrays the Patient as the initiator and the Receptionist as the receiver.

Third, write the step from the perspective of an independent observer. To accomplish this, each step might have to be written first from the perspective of both the initiator and the receiver. Based on the two points of view, the bird's-eye view version can then be written. For example, in Figure 3-13, when the Patient provides the Receptionist with his or her name and address, neither the patient's nor the receptionist's perspective is explicitly represented.

Fourth, write each step at the same level of abstraction. Each step should make about the same amount of progress toward completing the use case as each of the other steps. On high-level use cases, the amount of progress could be very substantial, whereas in a low-level use case, each step could represent only incremental progress.

Fifth, ensure that the use case contains a sensible set of actions. Each use case should represent a transaction. Therefore, each use case should comprise four parts:

1. The primary actor initiates the execution of the use case by sending a request (and possibly data) to the system.
2. The system ensures that the request (and data) is valid.
3. The system processes the request (and data) and possibly changes its own internal state.
4. The system sends the primary actor the result of the processing.

For example, in Figure 3-13, an old patient requests an appointment (steps 1 and 2), the receptionist determines whether any of the patient's information has changed (steps S-2, 1 and S2, 1a), the receptionist determines whether the patient's payments arrangements have changed (steps S-2, 2 and S-2, 2a), the receptionist sets up the appointment transaction (step S-2,3; S-2, 3a; and S-2, 3b), and the receptionist provides the results of the transaction to the patient (step 4).

The sixth guideline is the KISS principle. If the use case becomes too complex and/or too long, the use case should be decomposed into a set of use cases. Furthermore, if the normal flow of events of the use case becomes too complex, subflows should be used. For example, in Figure 3-13, the fifth step in the normal flow of events was sufficiently complex to decompose it into separate subflows. However, care must be taken to avoid the possibility of decomposing too much. Most decomposition should be done with classes (see Chapter 4).

The seventh guideline deals with repeating steps. Normally, in a programming language, we put loop definition and controls at the beginning of the loop. However, because the use-case steps are written in simple English, it is normally better to simply write Repeat steps A through E until some condition is met after step E. This approach makes the use case more readable to people unfamiliar with programming.

Creating Use-Case Descriptions

Use cases provide a bird's-eye view of the business processes contained in the evolving system. The use-case diagram depicts the communication path between the actors and the system, while the activity diagram portrays the underlying logic structure of the use case. Use-case description documentation tends to be used to model both the contexts of the system and the detailed requirements for the system. Even though the primary purpose of use cases is to document the functional requirements of the system, they also are used as a basis for testing the evolving system and as a foundation of the user interface design. In this section, we provide a set of steps that can be used to guide the actual creation of a use-case description for each use case in the use-case diagram based on the requirements definition and the use-case and activity diagrams.[16] These steps are performed in order, but of course the analyst often cycles among them in an iterative fashion as he or she moves from one use case to another use case.

1. Choose a Use Case The first step is to choose one of the use cases to document with a use-case description. Using the importance level of the use case can help do this. For example, in Figure 3-13, the Manage Appointments use case has an importance level of high. As such, it should be one of the earlier use cases to be expanded. The criteria suggested by Larman[17] can also be used to set the prioritization of the use cases, as noted earlier. An alternative approach suggests that each use case should be voted on by each member of the development team. In this approach, each team member is given a set of "dots" that they can use to vote on the use cases. They can use all of their dots to vote for a single use case, or they can spread them over a set of use cases. The use cases can then be ranked based on the number of dots received. Use-case descriptions are created for the individual use cases based on the rank order.[18]

2. Create Overview Description The second step is to create an overview description of the use case; that is, name the primary actor, set the type for the use case, list all of the identified stakeholders and their interests in the use case, identify the level of importance of the use case, give a brief description of the use case, give the trigger information for the use case, and list the relationships in which the use case participates. This can be done immediately after the use-case diagram has been created.

3. Describe the Normal Flow of Events The third step is to fill in the steps of the normal flow of events required to describe each use case. The steps focus on what the business process does to complete the use case, as opposed to what actions the users or other external entities do. In general, the steps should be listed in the order in which they are performed, from first to last. Remember to write the steps in an SVDPI form whenever possible. In writing the use case, remember the seven guidelines described earlier. The goal at this point is to describe how the chosen use case operates. One of the best ways to begin to understand how an actor works through a use case is to visualize performing the steps in the use case—i.e., role play. The techniques of visualizing how to interact with the system and of thinking about how other systems work (informal benchmarking) are important techniques that help analysts and users understand how systems work and how to write a use case. Both techniques (visualization and informal benchmarking) are common in practice. It is important to remember that at this point in the development of a use case, we are interested only in the typical successful execu-

---

[16] The approach in this section is based on the work of Cockburn, *Writing Effective Use Cases*; Graham, *Migrating to Object Technology*; George Marakas and Joyce Elam, "Semantic Structuring in Analyst Acquisition and Representation of Facts in Requirements Analysis," *Information Systems Research* 9, no. 1 (1998): 37–63; Alan Dennis, Glenda Hayes, and Robert Daniels, "Business Process Modeling with Group Support Systems," *Journal of Management Information Systems* 15, no. 4 (1999): 115–142.

[17] C. Larman, *Applying UML and Patterns: An Introduction to Object-Oriented Analysis and Design.*

[18] C. Larman, *Agile & Iterative Development: A Manager's Guide* (Boston, MA: Addison-Wesley, 2004).

tion of the use case. If we try to think of all of the possible combinations of activities that could go on, we will never get anything written. Focus only on performing the typical process that the use case represents. If the activity diagram has been completed, then the activities will serve as a basis for the events. Furthermore, the most likely path through the activity diagram should be the basis for the normal flow of events.

4. Check the Normal Flow of Events The fourth step is to ensure that the steps listed in the normal flow of events are not too complex or too long. Each step should be about the same size as the others. For example, if we were writing steps for preparing a meal, steps such as take fork out of drawer and put fork on table are much smaller than prepare cake using mix. If we end up with steps that vary greatly in size, we should go back and review each step carefully and possibly rewrite the steps.

One good approach to produce the steps for a use case is to have the users visualize themselves actually performing the use case and to have them write down the steps as if they were writing a recipe for a cookbook. In most cases, the users will be able to quickly define what they do in the as-is model. Defining the steps for to-be use cases might take a bit more coaching. In our experience, the descriptions of the steps change greatly as users work through a use case. Our advice is to use a blackboard or whiteboard (or paper with pencil) that can be easily erased to develop the list of steps and then write the list on the use-case form. It should be written on the use-case form only after the set of steps is fairly well defined. As stated above, these steps should be associated with the activities in the activity diagram.

5. Identify Alternative or Exceptional Flows The fifth step focuses on identifying and writing the alternative or exceptional flows. Alternative or exceptional flows are flows of success that represent optional or exceptional behavior. They tend to occur infrequently or as a result of a normal flow failing. They should be labeled so that there is no doubt as to which normal flow of events it is related. For example, in Figure 3-13, alternative/exceptional flow 3a executes when step 3 of the normal flow fails (i.e., the patient was an old patient, not a new one). Like the normal flows and subflows, alternative or exceptional flows should be written in the SVDPI form whenever possible.

6. Review the Use-Case Description The sixth step is to carefully review the use-case description and confirm that the use case is correct as written, which means reviewing the use case with the users to make sure each step is correct. The review should look for opportunities to simplify a use case by decomposing it into a set of smaller use cases, merging it with others, looking for common aspects in both the semantics and syntax of the use cases, and identifying new use cases. This is also the time to look into adding the include, extend, and/or generalization relationships between use cases. The most powerful way to confirm a use case is to ask the user to role-play, or execute the process, using the written steps in the use case.[19] The analyst hands the user pieces of paper labeled with the major inputs to the use case and has the user follow the written steps like a recipe to make sure that those steps really can produce the outputs defined for the use case using its inputs.

7. Repeat Until Done The seventh and final step is to *iterate* the entire set of steps again. Users often change their minds about what is a use case and what it includes. It is very easy to get trapped in the details at this point, so remember that the goal is to just address the major use cases. Therefore, the analyst should continue to iterate these steps until he or she and the users believe that a sufficient number of use cases have been documented to begin identifying candidate classes for the structural model (see Chapter 4). As candidate classes are identified, it is likely that additional use cases will be uncovered.

---

[19] This process is related to role-playing, which is discussed in Chapter 4.

APPLYING THE CHAPTER CONCEPTS

Library Management System Example After Susan had created an activity diagram for each use case, she created a use-case description for each. So, as with the activity diagrams, she chose to begin the creation of the use-case descriptions with the Borrow Resource use case. This required her to review the use-case diagram (Figure 3-5), the activity diagram for the Borrow Resources use case (Figure 3-9) and the updated functional requirements for the Borrow Resources use case (Figure 3-10).

After reviewing the use-case diagram, Susan was able to begin filling out the use-case description form for the Borrow Resources use case. First, Susan fills in the name and primary actor of the use case. The name is Borrow Resources and the primary actor is Patron. She also adds the primary actor to the stakeholder's section and to the association relationships. Next, she added the two extended use cases to the extends relationship section: Reserve Resource and Borrow Resource from Another Library. All of this information came directly from the use-case diagram. Next, she assigns a value of 1 to the ID and given the use case's relevance and importance to LMS, she assigns a high value to the importance level characteristic. Once this has been done, Susan identifies an additional stakeholder (Librarian) and documents both the Librarian's and Patron's interests in this use case. To complete the overview section of the use-case description, Susan writes a high-level, brief description of the use case and identifies the trigger and its type. These results are shown in the top half of Figure 3-14.

Now that Susan has completed the overview section of the use-case description, she carefully reviews both the functional requirements and the activity diagram for the Borrow Resource use case to develop the flow of event sections of the use-case description. Given the complexity of the decision logic in the Borrow Resource use case, Susan very carefully writes the different subflows and alternate/exceptional flows by focusing on the different scenarios. Remember, a scenario is a single path through a use case. In this case, there are 21 unique scenarios. In this way, she was able to minimize the complexity so that she could correctly document the control flows through the use case. Figure 3-14 portrays the use-case description for the Borrow Resource use case. Next, Susan worked her way through the remaining use cases by developing a use-case description for each one. In some cases, Susan discovered that she had to iterate back and modify some of the earlier representations. We will return to this example in the next chapter when we begin to create a structural model for the Library Management System.

Campus Housing Service "Your Turn" After reviewing the use case and the activity diagrams that you created, you need to create a use-case description for each of the use cases. The name and the primary actor of the use case comes directly from the use-case diagram. Also, the primary actor is assigned to the association relationship. Given that you have already created a use-case diagram and an activity diagram for the use case, the type of use case is Detail, Essential. Next, you should assign a number to the ID and a value to the importance level of the use case. Next, you should identify all interested stakeholders and their interests. The first stakeholder should be the primary actor. Be sure to include any other interested stakeholder. You should also create a brief description of the use case and identify the trigger that causes the use case to execute. Next, using the functional requirements and activity diagram of the use case, develop the flow of events sections. Obviously, you should be very thorough in this exercise. You will be using the results in the next chapter.

Use-Case Name: Borrow Resource		ID: ___1___	Importance Level: ___High___
Primary Actor: Patron		Use-Case Type: Detail, Essential	

Stakeholders and Interests:
Patron – Would like to be able to borrow a resource
Librarian – Would like to provide resources to patrons

Brief Description: Describes how resources are borrowed from the library.

Trigger: Patron desires to borrow a resource from the library.

Type: External

Relationships:
Association: Patron
Include:
Extend: Reserve Resource, Borrow Resource from Another Library
Generalization:

Normal Flow of Events:
1. Patron searches for the desired resource.
2. Librarian contacts Personnel Office to validate faculty/staff ID.
3. Call S-1: Process Request.

SubFlows:
S-1: Process Request
 1. Get Resource.
 2. Call S-2: Checkout Resource.
S-2: Checkout Resource
 1. Patron gets a physical Resource.
 2. Patron checks out the Resource.
S-3: Download Resource
 1. Patron gets a downloadable Resource.
 2. Patron checks out the Resource.
S-4: Resource not Available
 1. Call Reserve Resource use case.

Alternate/Exceptional Flows:
2a. Librarian contacts Registrar's Office to validate student ID.
2b. Librarian checks the library system to validate guest ID.
3a. Pass.
S-1, 2a. Call S-3: Download Resource.
S-1, 2b. Call S-4: Resource not Available.
S-4, 1a. Call Borrow Resource from Another Library use case.

FIGURE 3-14 Use-Case Description for the Borrow Resource Use Case

VERIFYING AND VALIDATING THE BUSINESS PROCESSES AND FUNCTIONAL MODELS[20]

Before we move on to structural (Chapter 4) and behavioral (Chapter 5) modeling, we need to verify and validate the current set of functional models to ensure that they faithfully represent the business processes under consideration. This includes testing the fidelity of each

[20] The material in this section has been adapted from E. Yourdon, *Modern Structured Analysis* (Englewood Cliffs, NJ: Prentice Hall, 1989). Verifying and validating are types of testing.

model; for example, we must be sure that the activity diagram(s), use-case descriptions, use-case diagrams all describe the same functional requirements. Before we describe the specific tests to consider, we describe walkthroughs, a manual approach that supports verifying and validating the evolving models.[21]

Verification and Validation through Walkthroughs

A *walkthrough* is essentially a peer review of a product. In the case of the functional models, a walkthrough is a review of the different models and diagrams created during functional modeling. This review typically is completed by a team whose members come from the development team and the client. The purpose of a walkthrough is to thoroughly *test* the fidelity of the functional models to the functional requirements and to ensure that the models are consistent. That is, a walkthrough uncovers *errors* or *faults* in the evolving specification. However, a walkthrough does not correct errors—it simply identifies them. Error correction is to be accomplished by the team after the walkthrough is completed.

Walkthroughs are very interactive. As the presenter walks through the representation (a model or diagram), members of the walkthrough team should ask questions regarding the representation. For example, if the presenter is walking through an activity diagram, another member of the team could ask why certain activities or objects were not included. The actual process of simply presenting the representation to a new set of eyes can uncover obvious misunderstandings and omissions. In many cases, the representation creator can get lost in the proverbial trees and not see the forest.[22] In fact, many times the act of walking through the representation causes a presenter to see the error himself or herself. For psychological reasons, hearing the representation helps the analyst to see the representation more completely. Therefore, the representation creators should regularly do a walkthrough of the models themselves by reading the representations out loud to themselves, regardless of how they think it might make them look.

There are specified roles that different members of the walkthrough team can play. The first is the *presenter* role. This should be played by the person who is primarily responsible for the specific representation being reviewed. This individual presents the representation to the walkthrough team. The second role is *recorder*, or *scribe*. The recorder should be a member of the analysis team. This individual carefully takes the minutes of the meeting by recording all significant events that occur during the walkthrough. In particular, all errors that are uncovered must be documented so that the analysis team can address them. Another important role is to have someone who raises issues regarding maintenance of the representation. Yourdon refers to this individual as a *maintenance oracle*.[23] Owing to the emphasis on reusability in object-oriented development, this role becomes particularly crucial. Finally, someone must be responsible for calling, setting up, and running the walkthrough meetings.

For a walkthrough to be successful, the members of the walkthrough team must be fully prepared. All materials to be reviewed must be distributed with sufficient time for the team members to review them before the actual meeting. All team members should be expected to mark up the representations so that during the walkthrough meeting, all relevant issues can be discussed. Otherwise, the walkthrough will be inefficient and ineffective. During the actual meeting, as the presenter is walking through the representation, the team members

---

[21] Even though many modern CASE tools can automate much of the verifying and validating of the analysis models, we feel that it is paramount that systems analysts understand the principles of verification and validation. Furthermore, some tools, such as Visio, that support UML diagramming are only diagramming tools. Regardless, the analyst is expected to perform all diagramming correctly.

[22] In many cases, developers can get lost in all of the nitty-gritty detail.

[23] See Appendix D of Yourdon, *Modern Structured Analysis*.

should point out any potential errors or misunderstandings. In many cases, the errors and misunderstandings are caused by invalid assumptions that would not be uncovered without the walkthrough.

One potential danger of walkthroughs is when management decides the results of uncovering errors in the representation reflect an analyst's capability. This must be avoided at all costs. Otherwise, the underlying purpose of the walkthrough—to improve the fidelity of the representation—will be thwarted. Depending on the organization, it may be necessary to omit management from the walkthrough process. If not, the walkthrough process could break down into a slugfest to make some team members look good by destroying the presenter. To say the least, this is obviously counterproductive.

Functional Model Verification and Validation

We have suggested three different representations for the functional model: activity diagrams, use-case descriptions, and use-case diagrams. In this section, we describe a set of rules to ensure that these three representations are consistent among themselves.

First, when comparing an activity diagram to a use-case description, there should be at least one event recorded in the normal flow of events, subflows, or alternative/exceptional flows of the use-case description for each activity or action that is included on an activity diagram, and each event should be associated with an activity or action. For example, in Figure 3-12, there is an activity labeled Get Patient Information that is associated with the second event contained in the normal flow of events of the use-case description shown in Figure 3-13.

Second, all objects portrayed as an object node in an activity diagram must be mentioned in an event in the normal flow of events, subflows, or alternative/exceptional flows of the use-case description. In this case, to simplify the activity diagram, we have already removed the object node and flows (compare Figures 3-7 and 3-12).

Third, the sequential order of events in a use-case description should match the order of activities in an activity diagram. For example, in Figures 3-12 and 3-13, the events associated with the Get Patient Information activity (event 2) should occur before the Provide Patient with Result activity (event 4).

Fourth, when comparing a use-case description to a use-case diagram, there must be one and only one use-case description for each use case, and vice versa. For example, Figure 3-13 portrays the use-case description of the Manage Appointments use case. The use-case diagram shown in Figure 3-11 shows that given the extends relationships the Make Payment Arrangements, Update Patient Information, and the Create New Patient use cases should only be called optionally. When we review the use-case description, we see that indeed these use cases are called only within a decision structure. So, they are only called optionally.

Fifth, all actors listed in a use-case description must be portrayed on the use-case diagram. Each actor must have an association link that connects it to the use case and must be listed with the association relationships in the use-case description. For example, the Patient actor is listed in the use-case description of the Manage Appointments use case (see Figure 3-13) as an association and it is connected to the use case in the use-case diagram (see Figure 3-11).

Sixth, in some organizations, we should also include the stakeholders listed in the use-case description as actors in the use-case diagram. For example, there could have been an association between the Doctor actor and the Manage Appointment use case (see Figures 3-13 and 3-11). However, in this case it was decided not to include this association because the Doctor never participates in the Manage Appointment use case.[24]

---

[24] Another possibility, as described earlier in the chapter, could have been to include a Receptionist actor. However, we had previously decided that the Receptionist was in fact part of the Appointment System and not simply a user of the system.

Seventh, all other relationships listed in a use-case description (include, extend, and generalization) must be portrayed on a use-case diagram. For example, in Figure 3-13, there is an extend relationship listed with the Update Patient Information use case, and in Figure 3-11, we see that it appears on the diagram between the two use cases.

Finally, there are many diagram-specific requirements that must be enforced. For example, in an activity diagram a decision node can be connected to activity or action nodes only with a control flow, and for every decision node there should be a matching merge node. Every type of node and flow has different restrictions. However, the complete restrictions for all the UML diagrams are beyond the scope of this text.[25]

CHAPTER REVIEW

After reading and studying this chapter, you should be able to:

- ☐ Explain the purpose of a use case in business process and functional modeling.
- ☐ Describe the different elements of a use-case diagram.
- ☐ Create use-case diagrams that portray how business information systems interact with their environment.
- ☐ Explain how to model a specific use case with an activity diagram.
- ☐ Describe the different elements of an activity diagram.
- ☐ Create an activity diagram that represents a specific use case.
- ☐ Document a business process with a use-case description.
- ☐ Describe the different types of use cases.
- ☐ Describe the different elements of a use-case description.
- ☐ Create a use-case description that represents a specific use case.
- ☐ Verify and validate the evolving functional model using walkthroughs.
- ☐ Verify and validate the functional model by ensuring the consistency of the three functional representations: use-case diagrams, activity diagrams, and use-case descriptions.

KEY TERMS

Action	Faults	Miracle activity	Stakeholders
Activity	Final-activity node	Normal flow of events	Subflows
Activity diagram	Final-flow node	Object flow	Subject boundary
Actor	Flow of events	Object node	SVDPI
Alternative flows	Fork node	Overview use cases	Swimlanes
Association relationship	Functional decomposition	Packages	Temporal trigger
Black-hole activities	Generalization relationship	Physical model	Test
Brief description	Guard condition	Presenter	Trigger
Control flow	Importance level	Primary actor	Use case
Control node	Include relationship	Process models	Use-case description
Decision node	Inheritance	Real use case	Use-case diagram
Detail use case	Initial node	Recorder	Use-case ID number
Errors	Iterate	Relationships	Use-case name
Essential use case	Join node	Role	Use-case type
Exceptional flows	Logical model	Scenario	Validation
Extend relationship	Maintenance oracle	Scribe	Verification
External trigger	Merge node	Specialized actor	Walkthrough

[25] A good reference for these types of restrictions is S.W. Ambler, *The Elements of UML 2.0 Style* (Cambridge, UK: Cambridge University Press, 2005).

QUESTIONS

1. Why is business process modeling important?
2. How do you create use cases?
3. Why do we strive to have about three to nine major use cases in a business process?
4. How do you create use-case diagrams?
5. How is use-case diagramming related to functional modeling?
6. Explain the following terms: actor, use case, system boundary, relationship. Use layperson's language, as though you were describing them to a user.
7. Every association must be connected to at least one __________ and one __________. Why?
8. What are some heuristics for creating a use-case diagram?
9. Why is iteration important in creating use cases?
10. What is the purpose of an activity diagram?
11. What is the difference between an activity and an action?
12. What is the purpose of a fork node?
13. What are the different types of control nodes?
14. What is the difference between a control flow and an object flow?
15. What is an object node?
16. Explain how a detail use case differs from an overview use case. When are each used?
17. How does an essential use case differ from a real use case?
18. What are the major elements of an overview use case?
19. What are the major elements of a detail use case?
20. What is the viewpoint of a use case, and why is it important?
21. What are some guidelines for designing a set of use cases? Give two examples of the extend associations on a use-case diagram. Give two examples for the include associations.
22. Which of the following could be an actor found on a use-case diagram? Why?
23. Ms. Mary Smith
24. Supplier
25. Customer
26. Internet customer
27. Mr. John Seals
28. Data entry clerk
29. Database administrator
30. What is a walkthrough? How does it relate to verification and validation?
31. What are the different roles played during a walkthrough? What are their purposes?
32. How are the different functional models related, and how does this affect the verification and validation of the models?

EXERCISES

A. Investigate the UML website at the Object Management Group (www.uml.org). Write a paragraph news brief on the current state of UML (e.g., the current version and when it will be released, future improvements).

B. Investigate the Object Management Group. Write a brief memo describing what it is, its purpose, and its influence on UML and the object approach to systems development. (*Hint:* A good resource is www.omg.org.)

C. Draw a use-case diagram and a set of activity diagrams for the process of buying glasses from the viewpoint of the patient. The first step is to see an eye doctor who will give you a prescription. Once you have a prescription, you go to an optical dispensary, where you select your frames and place the order for your glasses. Once the glasses have been made, you return to the store for a fitting and pay for the glasses.

D. Create a set of detailed use-case descriptions for the process of buying glasses in exercise C.

E. Draw a use-case diagram and a set of activity diagrams for the following doctor's office system. Whenever new patients are seen for the first time, they complete a patient information form that asks their name, address, phone number, and brief medical history, which are stored in the patient information file. When a patient calls to schedule a new appointment or change an existing appointment, the receptionist checks the appointment file for an available time. Once a good time is found for the patient, the appointment is scheduled. If the patient is a new patient, an incomplete entry is made in the patient's file; the full information will be collected when the patient arrives for the appointment. Because appointments are often made far in advance, the receptionist usually mails a reminder postcard to each patient two weeks before the appointment.

F. Create a set of detail use-case descriptions for the dentist's office system in exercise E.

G. Draw a use-case diagram and a set of activity diagrams for an online university registration system. The system should enable the staff of each academic department to examine the courses offered by their department, add and remove courses, and change the information about them (e.g., the maximum number of students permitted). It should permit students to examine currently available courses, add and drop courses to and from their schedules, and examine the courses for which they are enrolled. Department staff should be able to print a variety of reports about the courses and the students enrolled in them. The system should ensure that no student takes too many courses and that students who have any unpaid fees are not permitted to register (assume that fees data are maintained by the university's financial office, which the registration system accesses but does not change).

H. Create a set of detailed use-case descriptions for the online university registration system in exercise G.

I. Draw a use-case diagram and a set of activity diagrams for the following system. A Real Estate Inc. (AREI) sells houses. People who want to sell their houses sign a contract with AREI and provide information on their house. This information is kept in a database by AREI, and a subset of this information is sent to the citywide multiple-listing service used by all real estate agents. AREI works with two types of potential buyers. Some buyers have an interest in one specific house. In this case, AREI prints information from its database, which the real estate agent uses to help show the house to the buyer (a process beyond the scope of the system to be modeled). Other buyers seek AREI's advice in finding a house that meets their needs. In this case, the buyer completes a buyer information form that is entered into a buyer database, and AREI real estate agents use its information to search AREI's database and the multiple-listing service for houses that meet their needs. The results of these searches are printed and used to help the real estate agent show houses to the buyer.

J. Create a set of detailed use-case descriptions for the real estate system in exercise I.

K. Perform a verification and validation walkthrough of the functional models of the real estate system described in exercises I and J.

L. Draw a use-case diagram and a set of activity diagrams for the following system. A Video Store (AVS) runs a series of fairly standard video stores. Before a video can be put on the shelf, it must be cataloged and entered into the video database. Every customer must have a valid AVS customer card in order to rent a video. Customers rent videos for three days at a time. Every time a customer rents a video, the system must ensure that he or she does not have any overdue videos. If so, the overdue videos must be returned and an overdue fee paid before customer can rent more videos. Likewise, if the customer has returned overdue videos but has not paid the overdue fee, the fee must be paid before new videos can be rented. Every morning, the store manager prints a report that lists overdue videos. If a video is two or more days overdue, the manager calls the customer to remind him or her to return the video. If a video is returned in damaged condition, the manager removes it from the video database and may sometimes charge the customer.

M. Create a set of detailed use-case descriptions for the video system in exercise L.

N. Perform a verification and validation walkthrough of the functional models of the video store system described in exercises L and M.

O. Draw a use-case diagram and a set of activity diagrams for a gym membership system. When members join the gym, they pay a fee for a certain length of time. Most memberships are for one year, but memberships as short as two months are available. Throughout the year, the gym offers a variety of discounts on their regular membership prices (e.g., two memberships for the price of one for Valentine's day). It is common for members to pay different amounts for the same length of membership. The gym wants to mail out reminder letters to members asking them to renew their memberships one month before their memberships expire. Some members have become angry when asked to renew at a much higher rate than their original membership contract, so the club wants to track the prices paid so that the manager can override the regular prices with special prices when members are asked to renew. The system must track these new prices so that renewals can be processed accurately. One of the problems in the industry is the high turnover rate of members. Although some members remain active for many years, about half of the members do not renew their memberships. This is a major problem, because the gym spends a lot in advertising to attract each new member. The manager wants the system to track each time a member comes into the gym. The system will then identify the heavy users and generate a report so that the manager can ask them to renew their memberships early, perhaps offering them a reduced rate for early renewal. Likewise, the system should identify members who have not visited the gym in more than a month, so the manager can call them and attempt to reinterest them in the gym.

P. Create a set of detailed use-case for the system in exercise O.

Q. Perform a verification and validation walkthrough of the functional models of the gym membership system described in exercises O and P.

R. Draw a use-case diagram and a set of activity diagrams for the following system. Picnics R Us (PRU) is a small catering firm with five employees. During a typical summer weekend, PRU caters fifteen picnics with twenty to fifty people each. The business has grown rapidly over the past year, and the owner wants to install a new computer system for managing the ordering and buying process. PRU has a set of ten standard menus. When potential customers call, the receptionist describes the menus to them. If the customer decides to book a picnic, the receptionist records the customer information (e.g., name, address, and phone number) and the information about the picnic (e.g., place, date, time, which one of the standard menus, and total price) on a contract. The customer is then faxed a copy of the contract and must sign and return it along with a deposit (often a credit card or by debit card) before the picnic is officially booked. The remaining money is collected when the picnic is delivered. Sometimes, the customer wants something special (e.g., birthday cake). In this case, the receptionist takes the information and gives it to the owner, who determines the cost; the receptionist then calls the customer back with the price information. Sometimes the customer accepts the price; other times, the customer requests some changes that have to go back to the owner for a new cost estimate. Each week, the owner looks through the picnics scheduled for that weekend and orders the supplies (e.g., plates) and food (e.g., bread and chicken) needed to make them. The owner would like to use the system for marketing as well. It should be able to track how customers learned about PRU and identify repeat customers, so that PRU can mail special offers to them. The owner also wants to track the picnics for which PRU sent a contract, but the customer never signed the contract and actually booked a picnic.

S. Create a set of detailed use-case descriptions the system in exercise R.

T. Perform a verification and validation walkthrough of the functional models of the catering system described in exercises R and S.

U. Draw a use-case diagram and a set of activity diagrams for the following system. Of-the-Month Club (OTMC) is an innovative young firm that sells memberships to people who have an interest in certain products. People pay membership fees for one year and each month receive a product by mail. For example, OTMC has a coffee-of-the-month club that sends members one pound of special coffee each month. OTMC currently has six memberships (coffee, wine, beer, cigars, flowers, and computer games), each of which costs a different amount. Customers usually belong to just one, but some belong to two or more. When people join OTMC, the telephone operator records the name, mailing address, phone number, e-mail address, credit-card information, start date, and membership service(s) (e.g., coffee). Some customers request a double or triple membership (e.g., two pounds of coffee and three cases of beer). The computer game membership operates a bit differently from the others. In this case, the member must also select the type of game (action, arcade, fantasy/science fiction, educational, etc.) and age level. OTMC is planning to greatly expand the number of memberships it offers (e.g., video games, movies, toys, cheese, fruit, and vegetables), so the system needs to accommodate this future expansion. OTMC is also planning to offer three-month and six-month memberships.

V. Create a set of detailed use-case descriptions for the system in exercise U.

W. Perform a verification and validation walkthrough of the functional models of the Of-the-Month Club system described in exercises U and V.

MINICASES

1. Williams Specialty Company is a small printing and engraving organization. When Pat Williams, the owner, brought computers into the business office five years ago, the business was very small and very simple. Pat was able to use an inexpensive PC-based accounting system to handle the basic information-processing needs of the firm. As time has gone on, however, the business has grown and the work being performed has become significantly more complex. The simple accounting software still in use is no longer adequate to keep track of many of the company's sophisticated deals and arrangements with its customers.

Pat has a staff of four people in the business office who are familiar with the intricacies of the company's record-keeping requirements. Pat recently met with her staff to discuss her plan to hire an IS consulting firm to evaluate the organization's information system needs and recommend a strategy for upgrading its computer system. The staff are excited about the prospect of a new system, because the current system causes them much annoyance. No one on the staff has ever done anything like this before, however, and they are a little wary of the consultants who will be conducting the project.

Assume that you are a systems analyst on the consulting team assigned to the Williams Specialty Co. engagement. At your first meeting with the Williams staff, you want to be sure that they understand the work that your team will be performing and how they will participate in that work.

a. Explain, in clear, nontechnical terms, the goals of the analysis of the project.

b. Explain, in clear, nontechnical terms, how functional models will be used by the project team to model the identified business processes. Explain what these models are, what they represent in the system, and how they will be used by the team.

2. Professional and Scientific Staff Management (PSSM) is a unique type of temporary staffing agency. Many organizations today hire highly skilled technical employees on a short-term, temporary basis to assist with special projects or to provide a needed technical skill. PSSM negotiates contracts with its client companies in which it agrees to provide temporary staff in specific job categories for a specified cost. For example, PSSM has a contract with an oil and gas exploration company in which it agrees to supply geologists with at least a master's degree for $5,000 per week. PSSM has contracts with a wide range of companies and can place almost any type of professional or scientific staff members, from computer programmers to geologists to astrophysicists.

When a PSSM client company determines that it will need a temporary professional or scientific employee, it issues a staffing request against the contract it had previously negotiated with PSSM. When PSSM's contract manager receives a staffing request, the contract number referenced on the staffing request is entered into the contract database. Using information from the database, the contract manager reviews the terms and conditions of the contract and determines whether the staffing request is valid. The staffing request is valid if the contract has not expired, the type of professional or scientific employee requested is listed on the original contract, and the requested fee falls within the negotiated fee range. If the staffing request is not valid, the contract manager sends the staffing request back to the client with a letter stating why the staffing request cannot be filled, and a copy of the letter is filed. If the staffing request is valid, the contract manager enters the staffing request into the staffing request database as an outstanding staffing request. The staffing request is then sent to the PSSM placement department.

In the placement department, the type of staff member, experience, and qualifications requested on the staffing request are checked against the database of available professional and scientific staff. If a qualified individual is found, he or she is marked "reserved" in the staff database. If a qualified individual cannot be found in the database or is not immediately available, the placement department creates a memo that explains the inability to meet the staffing request and attaches it to the staffing request. All staffing requests are then sent to the arrangements department.

In the arrangements department, the prospective temporary employee is contacted and asked to agree to the placement. After the placement details have been worked out and agreed to, the staff member is marked "placed" in the staff database. A copy of the staffing request and a bill for the placement fee is sent to the client. Finally, the staffing request, the "unable-to-fill" memo (if any), and a copy of the placement fee bill are sent to the contract manager. If the staffing request was filled, the contract manager closes the open staffing request in the staffing request database. If the staffing request could not be filled, the client is notified. The staffing request, placement fee bill, and unable-to-fill memo are then filed in the contract office.

a. Create a use-case diagram for the system described here.

b. Create a set of activity diagrams for the uses cases identified.

c. For each major use case identified in the use-case diagram, develop both an overview and a detail use-case description.

d. Verify and validate the functional models.

CHAPTER 4

STRUCTURAL MODELING

$\mathbf{A}$ structural, or conceptual, model describes the structure of the objects that support the business processes in an organization. During analysis, the structural model presents the logical organization of the objects without indicating how they are stored, created, or manipulated so that analysts can focus on the business, without being distracted by technical details. Later during design, the structural model is updated to reflect exactly how the objects will be stored in databases and files. This chapter describes CRC cards, class diagrams, and object diagrams.

OBJECTIVES

- Understand the rules and style guidelines for creating CRC cards, class diagrams, and object diagrams.
- Understand how to use activity diagrams to assign activities to actors and classes.
- Understand the processes used to create CRC cards, class diagrams, and object diagrams.
- Be able to create CRC cards, class diagrams, and object diagrams.
- Understand how to verify and validate the structural models.
- Understand how to balance the structural models with the functional models.

INTRODUCTION

During analysis, analysts create business process and functional models to represent how the business system will behave. At the same time, analysts need to understand the information that is used and created by the business system (e.g., customer information and order information). In this chapter, we discuss how the objects underlying the behavior modeled in the business process and functional models are organized and presented.

As *pointed* out in Chapter 1, all object-oriented systems development approaches are use-case driven, architecture-centric, and iterative and incremental. Use cases, described in Chapter 3, form the foundation on which the information system is created. From an architecture-centric perspective, structural modeling supports the creation of an internal structural or static view of an information system in that it shows how the system is structured to support the underlying business processes. Finally, as with business process and functional modeling, you will find that you will need to not only iterate across the structural models (described in this chapter), but you will also have to iterate across all three architectural views (functional, structural, and behavioral) to fully capture and represent the requirements for an information system.

A *structural model* is a formal way of representing the objects that are used and created by an information system. It illustrates people, places, or things about which information is captured and how they are related to one another. The structural model is drawn using an iterative process in which the model becomes more detailed and less conceptual over time. In analysis, analysts draw a *conceptual model,* which shows the logical organization of the objects without indicating how the objects are stored, created, or manipulated. Because this model is free from any implementation or technical details, the analysts can focus more easily on matching the model to the real business requirements of the system.

In *design*, analysts evolve the conceptual structural model into a design model that reflects how the objects will be organized in databases and software. At this point, the model is checked for redundancy, and the analysts investigate ways to make the objects easy to retrieve. The specifics of the design model are discussed in detail in the design chapters.

STRUCTURAL MODELS

Every time a systems analyst encounters a new problem to solve, the analyst must learn the underlying problem domain. The goal of the analyst is to discover the key objects contained in the problem domain and to build a structural model. Object-oriented modeling allows the analyst to reduce the semantic gap between the underlying problem domain and the evolving structural model. However, the real world and the world of software are very different. The real world tends to be messy, whereas the world of software must be neat and logical. Recall, in Chapter 2 we discussed the idea of an objective and a subjective reality. From a structural modeling perspective, the problem domain is equivalent to the objective reality while the structural model is equivalent to the subjective reality as portrayed in Figure 2-3. Thus, an exact mapping between the structural model and the problem domain may not be possible.

One of the *primary* purposes of the structural model is to build out a vocabulary from the uses cases that can be used by the analyst and the users. Structural models represent the things, ideas, or concepts contained in the domain of the problem. They also allow the representation of the relationships among the things, ideas, or concepts. By creating a structural model of the problem domain, the analyst creates the vocabulary necessary for the analyst and users to communicate effectively.

It is *important* to remember that at this stage of development, the structural model does not represent software components or classes in an object-oriented programming language, even though the structural model does contain analysis classes, attributes, operations, and the relationships among the analysis classes. The refinement of these initial classes into programming-level objects comes later. Nonetheless, the structural model at this point should represent the responsibilities of each class and the collaborations among the classes. Typically, structural models are depicted using CRC cards, class diagrams, and object diagrams. However, before describing CRC cards, class diagrams, and object diagrams, we describe the basic elements of structural models: classes, attributes, operations, and relationships.

Classes, Attributes, and Operations

A *class* is a general template that we use to create specific instances, or *objects,* in the problem domain (for more details please see Chapter 1 Appendix). All objects of a given class are identical in structure and behavior but contain different data values in their attributes. There are two general kinds of classes of interest during analysis: concrete and abstract. Normally, when an analyst describes the application domain classes, he or she is referring to concrete classes; that is, *concrete classes* are used to create objects. *Abstract classes* do not actually exist in the real world; they are simply useful abstractions. For example, from an employee class and a customer class, we may identify a generalization of the two classes and name the abstract class *person*. We might not actually instantiate the person class in the system itself, instead creating and using only employees and customers.[1]

A second classification of classes is the type of real-world thing that a class represents. There are domain classes, user-interface classes, data structure classes, file structure classes, operating environment classes, document classes, and various types of multimedia classes. At this point in the development of our evolving system, we are interested only in domain classes. *Domain classes* represent objects in the problem domain, i.e., they are used to represent objects that meet the functional, not non-functional requirements. Later in design and implementation, the other types of classes, which represent the non-functional requirements, become relevant.

An *attribute* of an analysis class represents a piece of information that is relevant to the description of the class within the application domain of the problem being investigated. An attribute contains information the analyst or user feels the system should keep track of. In other words, it is associated with the attribution semantic relationship (see Figure 2-13). For example, a possible relevant attribute of an employee class is employee name, whereas one that might not be as relevant is hair color. Both describe something about an employee, but hair color is probably not all that useful for most business applications. Only attributes that are important to the task should be included in the class. Finally, only attributes that are primitive or atomic types (i.e., integers, strings, doubles, date, time, and Boolean) should be added. Most complex or compound attributes are really placeholders for relationships between classes. Therefore, they should be modeled as relationships, not as attributes (see the next section).

The behavior of an analysis class is defined in an *operation* or service. During design, the analyst will convert the operations to *methods*. However, because methods are more related to implementation, at this point in the development we use the term *operation* to describe the actions to which the *instances* of the class (i.e., actual objects in the real-world) are capable of responding. Like attributes, only problem domain–specific operations that are relevant to the functional requirements should be considered. For example, it is normally required that classes provide means of creating instances, deleting instances, accessing individual attribute values, setting individual attribute values, accessing individual relationship values, and removing individual relationship values.

Relationships

There are many different types of relationships that can be defined, but all can be classified into three basic categories of data abstraction mechanisms: generalization relationships, aggregation relationships, and association relationships. These data-abstraction mechanisms allow the analyst to focus on the important dimensions while ignoring nonessential dimensions. As with attributes, the analyst must be careful to include only relationships that address the functional requirements.

Generalization Relationships The generalization relationship is the same relationship as the class inclusion semantic relationship that was used in domain and taxonomic analysis (see Chapter 2). The generalization abstraction enables the analyst to create classes that inherit attributes and operations of other classes. The analyst creates a *superclass* that contains basic attributes and operations that will be used in several *subclasses*. The subclasses inherit the attributes and operations of their superclass and can also contain attributes and operations that are unique just to them. For example, a customer class and an employee class can

---

[1] Because abstract classes are essentially not necessary and are not instantiated, arguments have been made that it would be better not to include any of them in the description of the evolving system at this stage of development (see J. Evermann and Y. Wand, "Towards Ontologically Based Semantics for UML Constructs," in H. S. Junii, S. Jajodia, and A. Solvberg (eds.) *ER 2001, Lecture Notes in Computer Science 2224* (Berlin: Springer-Verlag, 2001: 354–367). However, because abstract classes traditionally have been included at this stage of development, we also include them.

be generalized into a person class by extracting the attributes and operations both have in common and placing them into the new superclass, *person*. In this way, the analyst can reduce the redundancy in the class definitions so that the common elements are defined once and then reused in the subclasses. Generalization is represented with the *a-kind-of* relationship, so that we say that an employee is a-kind-of person.[2]

The analyst also can use the opposite of generalization. *Specialization* uncovers additional classes by allowing new subclasses to be created from an existing class. For example, an employee class can be specialized into a secretary class and an engineer class. Furthermore, generalization relationships between classes can be combined to form generalization hierarchies. Based on the previous examples, a secretary class and an engineer class can be subclasses of an employee class, which in turn could be a subclass of a person class. This would be read as a secretary and an engineer are a-kind-of employee and a customer and an employee are a-kind-of person.

The generalization data abstraction is a very powerful mechanism that encourages the analyst to focus on the properties that make each class unique by allowing the similarities to be factored into superclasses. However, to ensure that the semantics of the subclasses are maintained, the analyst should apply the principle of *substitutability*. By this we mean that the subclass should be technically capable of substituting for the superclass anywhere that uses the superclass (e.g., anywhere we use the employee superclass, we could also logically use its secretary subclass although it might cause confusion to use a secretary class for all employees). By focusing on the a-kind-of interpretation of the generalization relationship, the principle of substitutability is supported.

Aggregation Relationships The aggregation relationship is the same relationship as the part whole semantic relationship that was used in domain and taxonomic analysis (see Chapter 2). Generally speaking, all aggregation relationships relate *parts* to *wholes* or *assemblies*. For our purposes, we use the *a-part-of* or *has-parts* semantic relationship to represent the aggregation abstraction. For example, a door is a-part-of a car, an employee is a-part-of a department, or a department is a-part-of an organization. Like the generalization relationship, aggregation relationships can be combined into aggregation hierarchies. For example, a piston is a-part-of an engine, and an engine is a-part-of a car.

Aggregation relationships are bidirectional. The flip side of aggregation is *decomposition*. The analyst can use decomposition to uncover parts of a class that should be modeled separately. For example, if a door and an engine are a-part-of a car, then a car has-parts door and engine. The analyst can bounce around between the various parts to uncover new parts. For example, the analyst can ask, What other parts are there to a car? or To which other assemblies can a door belong?

Association Relationships There are other types of relationships that do not fit neatly into a generalization (a-kind-of) or aggregation (a-part-of) framework. Technically speaking, these relationships are usually a weaker form of the aggregation relationship. For example, a patient schedules an appointment. It could be argued that a patient is a-part-of an appointment. However, there is a clear semantic difference between this type of relationship and one that models the relationship between doors and cars or even workers and unions. Thus, they are simply considered to be *associations* between instances of classes.

OBJECT IDENTIFICATION

Different approaches have been suggested to aid the analyst in identifying a set of candidate objects for the structural model. The most common approaches are text analysis, brainstorming, common object lists, and patterns. Most analysts use a combination of these techniques to make sure that no important objects and object attributes, operations, and relationships have been overlooked.

---

[2] See Footnote 1.

Text Analysis

The analyst performs *text analysis* by reviewing the artifacts created so far. These include the functional requirements (Chapter 2), use-case and activity diagrams, and examining the text in the use-case descriptions (Chapter 3) to identify potential objects, attributes, operations, and relationships. The nouns in the use case suggest candidate classes, and the verbs suggest possible operations. Figure 4-1 presents a summary of useful guidelines. These guidelines are based on those described in Chapter 2 (see Figure 2-12). In addition to these guidelines, the other text analysis approaches described in Chapter 2 are helpful. Textual analysis of use-case descriptions, as with the identification of requirements, has been criticized as being too simple. However, since its primary purpose is to create an initial rough-cut structural model, its simplicity is a major advantage. For example, if we applied these rules to the Manage Appointments use case described in Chapter 3 (see Figure 3-13), we can easily identify potential objects for a patient, doctor, appointment, office, receptionist, name, and address. We also can easily identify potential operations that can be associated with the identified objects. For example, patient contacts office, patient provides name and address, create a new appointment, cancels an existing appointment, and changes an existing appointment. Furthermore, given the extended use cases that it calls, there must be operations that deal with creating a new patient, making payment arrangements, and updating existing patient information. So, as you can see, using text analysis on the use-case descriptions is a good place to start.

Brainstorming

Brainstorming is a discovery technique that has been used successfully in identifying candidate classes. Essentially, in this context, brainstorming is a process that a set of individuals sitting around a table suggest candidate classes that could be useful for the problem under consideration, i.e., that meet the functional requirements. Typically, a brainstorming session is kicked off by a facilitator who asks the set of individuals to address a specific question or statement that frames the session. For example, using the appointment problem described previously, the facilitator could ask the development team and users to think about their experiences of making appointments and to identify candidate classes based on their past experiences. Notice that this approach does not use the functional models developed earlier. It simply asks the participants to identify the objects with which they have interacted. For example, a potential set of objects that come to mind are doctors, nurses, receptionists, appointment, illness, treatment, prescriptions, insurance card, and medical records. However, if textual analysis has been done previously, the identified candidate classes can be used to

---

- A common or improper noun implies a class of objects.
- A proper noun or direct reference implies an instance of a class.
- A collective noun implies a class of objects made up of groups of instances of another class.
- An adjective implies an attribute of an object.
- A doing verb implies an operation.
- A being verb implies a classification relationship between an object and its class.
- A having verb implies an aggregation or association relationship.
- A transitive verb implies an operation.
- An intransitive verb implies an exception.
- A predicate or descriptive verb phrase implies an operation.
- An adverb implies an attribute of a relationship or an operation.

Adapted from: These guidelines are based on Russell J. Abbott, "Program Design by Informal English Descriptions," *Communications of the ACM* 26, no. 11 (1983): 882–894; Peter P-S Chen, "English Sentence Structure and Entity-Relationship Diagrams," *Information Sciences: An International Journal* 29, no. 2–3 (1983): 127–149; and Ian Graham, *Migrating to Object Technology* (Reading, MA: Addison Wesley Longman, 1995).

FIGURE 4-1 Text Analysis Guidelines

seed the brainstorming session. Once a sufficient number of candidate objects have been identified, the participants should discuss and select which of the candidate objects should be considered further. Once these have been identified, further brainstorming can take place to identify potential attributes, operations, and relationships for each of the identified objects.

Bellin and Simone[3] have suggested a set of useful principles to guide a brainstorming session. First, all suggestions should be taken seriously. At this point in the development of the system, it is much better to have to delete something later than to accidentally leave something critical out. Second, all participants should begin thinking fast and furiously. After all ideas are out on the proverbial table, then the participants can be encouraged to ponder the candidate classes they have identified. Third, the facilitator must manage the fast and furious thinking process. Otherwise, the process will be chaotic. Furthermore, the facilitator should ensure that all participants are involved and that a few participants do not dominate the process. To get the most complete view of the problem, we suggest using a round-robin approach wherein participants take turns suggesting candidate classes. Another approach is to use a digital form of brainstorming such as a Microsoft Word or Google Doc to allow everyone to contribute ideas rapidly and anonymously.[4] Fourth, the facilitator can use humor to break the ice so that all participants can feel comfortable in making suggestions.

Common Object Lists

As its name implies, a *common object list* is simply a list of objects common to the business domain of the system. Several categories of objects have been found to help the analyst in creating the list, such as physical or tangible things, incidents, roles, and interactions.[5] Analysts should first look for physical, or *tangible, things* in the business domain. These could include books, desks, chairs, and office equipment. Normally, these types of objects are the easiest to identify. *Incidents* are events that occur in the business domain, such as meetings, flights, performances, or accidents. Reviewing the use cases can readily identify the *roles* that the people play in the problem, such as doctor, nurse, patient, or receptionist. Typically, an *interaction* is a transaction that takes place in the business domain, such as a sales transaction. Other types of objects that can be identified include places, containers, organizations, business records, catalogs, and policies. In rare cases, processes themselves may need information stored about them. In these cases, processes may need an object, in addition to a use case, to represent them. Finally, there are libraries of reusable objects that have been created for different business domains. For example, with regard to the appointment problem, the Common Open Source Medical Objects[6] could be useful to investigate for potential objects that should be included.

Patterns

The idea of using patterns in object-oriented systems development has been around a while as a way to encourage reuse.[7] While there are many definitions of pattern, from our perspective,

<hr>

[3] D. Bellin and S. S. Simone, *The CRC Card Book* (Reading, MA: Addison-Wesley, 1997).

[4] A.R. Dennis, J.S. Valacich, T. Connolly, and B.E. Wynne, "Process Structuring in Electronic Brainstorming," *Information Systems Research* 7, no. 2 (June 1996): 268–277.

[5] For example, see C. Larman, *Applying UML and Patterns: An Introduction to Object-Oriented Analysis and Design* (Englewood Cliffs, NJ: Prentice Hall, 1998); S. Shlaer and S. J. Mellor, *Object-Oriented Systems Analysis: Modeling the World in Data* (Englewood Cliffs, NJ: Yourdon Press, 1988).

[6] See Common Open Source Medical Objects, Sourceforge, sourceforge.net/projects/cosmos/.

[7] Many books have been devoted to this topic. For example, see P. Coad, D. North, and M. Mayfield, *Object Models: Strategies, Patterns, & Applications*, 2nd Ed. (Englewood Cliffs, NJ: Prentice Hall, 1997); H.-E. Eriksson and M. Penker, *Business Modeling with UML: Business Patterns at Work* (New York: Wiley, 2000); M. Fowler, *Analysis Patterns: Reusable Object Models* (Reading, MA: Addison-Wesley, 1997); E. Gamma, R. Helm, R. Johnson, and J. Vlissides, *Design Patterns: Elements of Reusable Object-Oriented Software* (Reading, MA: Addison-Wesley, 1995); David C. Hay, *Data Model Patterns: Conventions of Thought* (New York: Dorset House, 1996); L. Silverston, *The Data Model Resource Book: A Library of Universal Data Models for All Enterprises, Volume 1, Revised Ed.* (New York, NY; Wiley, 2001).

a *pattern* is simply a useful group of collaborating classes that provide a solution to a commonly occurring problem. Because patterns provide a solution to commonly occurring problems, they are reusable.

An architect, Christopher Alexander, has inspired much of the work associated with using patterns in object-oriented systems development. According to Alexander and his colleagues,[8] it is possible to make very sophisticated buildings by stringing together commonly found patterns, rather than creating entirely new concepts and designs. In a similar manner, it is possible to put together commonly found object-oriented patterns to form elegant object-oriented information systems. For example, many business transactions involve the same types of objects and interactions. Virtually all transactions would require a transaction class, a transaction line item class, an item class, a location class, and a participant class. By reusing these existing patterns of classes, we can more quickly and more completely define the system than if we start with a blank piece of paper.

Many types of patterns have been proposed, ranging from high-level business-oriented patterns to more low-level detailed design patterns. For example, Figure 4-2 depicts a set of useful analysis patterns.[9] Figure 4-3 portrays a class diagram that we created by merging the patterns contained in Figure 4-2 into a single reusable pattern. In this case, we merged the Transaction–Entry–Account pattern (located at the bottom left of Figure 4-2) with the Place–Transaction–Participant–Transaction Line Item–Item pattern (located at the top left of Figure 4-2) on the common Transaction class. Next, we merged the

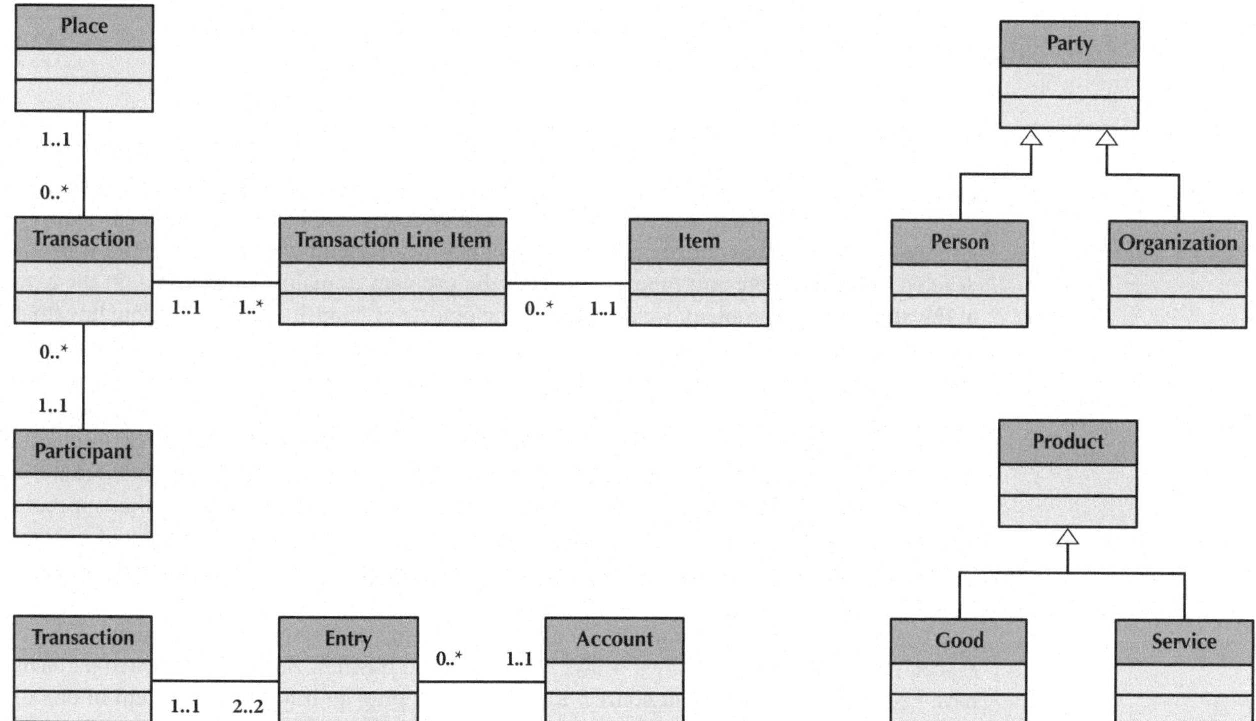

FIGURE 4-2 Sample Patterns

[8] C. Alexander, S. Ishikawa, M. Silverstein, M. Jacobson, I. Fiksdahl-King, and S. Angel, *A Pattern Language* (New York: Oxford University Press, 1977).

[9] The patterns are portrayed using UML Class Diagrams. We describe the syntax of the diagrams later in this chapter. The specific patterns shown have been adapted from patterns described in P. Coad, D. North, and M. Mayfield, *Object Models: Strategies, Patterns, & Applications,* 2nd Ed.; M. Fowler, *Analysis Patterns: Reusable Object Models;* L. Silverston, *The Data Model Resource Book: A Library of Universal Data Models for All Enterprises, Volume 1, Revised Edition.*

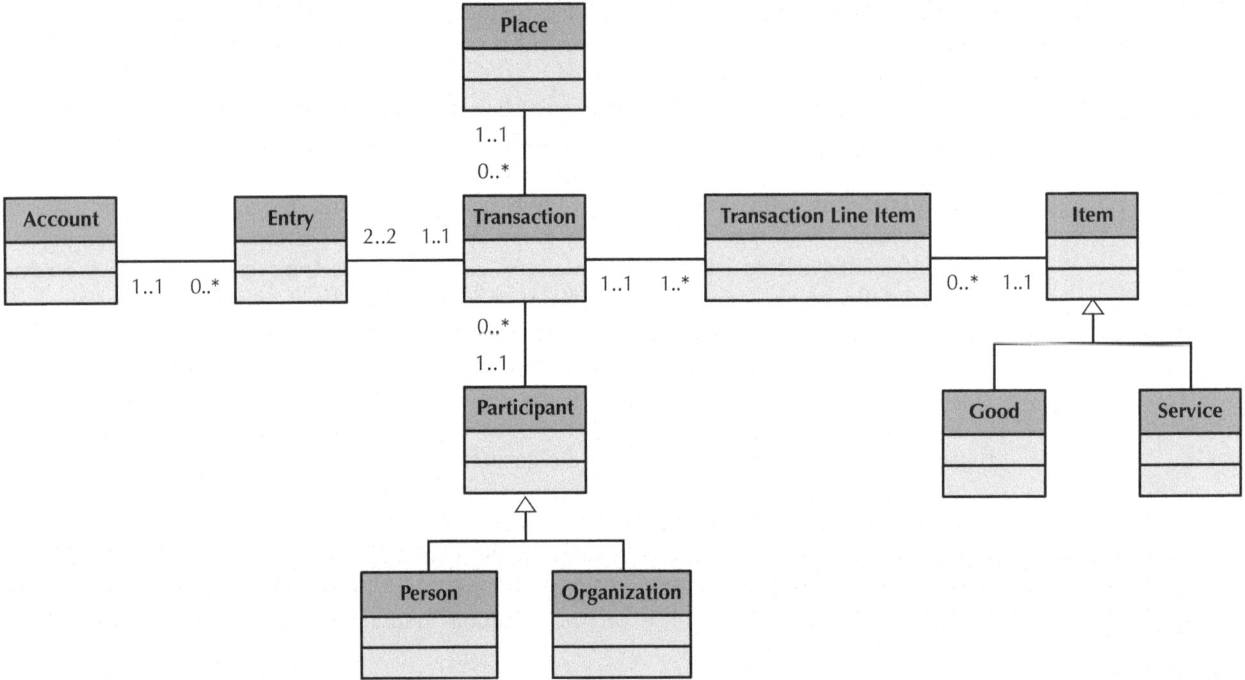

FIGURE 4-3 Sample Integration of Sample Patterns

Party–Person–Organization (located at the top right of Figure 4-2) by merging the Participant and Party classes. Finally, we extended the Item class by merging the Item class with the Product class of the Product–Good–Service pattern (located at the bottom right of Figure 4-2).

In this manner, using patterns from different sources enables the development team to leverage knowledge beyond that of the immediate team members and allows the team to develop more complete and robust models of the problem domain. For example, in the case of the appointment problem, we can look at the objects previously identified through textual analysis and brainstorming and see if it makes sense to map any of them into any predefined reusable patterns. In this specific case, we can look at an appointment as a type of transaction in which a doctor's office participates. By looking at an appointment as a type of transaction, we can apply the pattern we created in Figure 4-3 and discover a set of previously unidentified objects, such as Place, Patient as a type of Participant, and Transaction Line Items that are associated with different types of Items (Goods and/or Services). Discovering these specific additional objects could be useful in developing the billing side of the appointment system. Even though these additional objects could be applicable, they were not uncovered using the other techniques.

Based on this simple example, it is obvious that using patterns to develop structural models can be advantageous. Figure 4-4 lists some common business domains for which patterns have been developed and their source. If we are developing an information system in one of these business domains, then the patterns developed for that domain may be a very useful starting point in identifying needed classes and their attributes, operations, and relationships.

Business Domains	Sources of Patterns
Accounting	3, 4
Actor-Role	2
Assembly-Part	1
Container-Content	1
Contract	2, 4
Document	2, 4
Employment	2, 4
Financial Derivative Contracts	3
Geographic Location	2, 4
Group-Member	1
Interaction	1
Material Requirements Planning	4
Organization and Party	2, 3
Plan	1, 3
Process Manufacturing	4
Trading	3
Transactions	1, 4

1. Peter Coad, David North, and Mark Mayfield, *Object Models: Strategies, Patterns, and Applications*, 2nd Ed. (Englewood Cliffs, NJ: Prentice Hall, 1997).
2. Hans-Erik Eriksson and Magnus Penker, *Business Modeling with UML: Business Patterns at Work* (New York: Wiley, 2000).
3. Martin Fowler, *Analysis Patterns: Reusable Object Models* (Reading, MA: Addison-Wesley, 1997).
4. David C. Hay, *Data Model Patterns: Conventions of Thought* (New York, NY: Dorset House, 1996).

FIGURE 4-4
Useful Patterns

CRC CARDS

CRC (Class–Responsibility–Collaboration) cards are used to document the responsibilities and collaborations of a class. In some object-oriented and agile systems development methodologies, CRC cards are seen to be an alternative competitor to the Unified Process employment of use cases and class diagrams. However, we see them as a useful, low-tech approach that can complement a typical high-tech Unified Process approach that uses CASE tools. We use an extended form of the CRC card to capture all relevant information associated with a class.[10] We describe the elements of our CRC cards later, after we explain responsibilities and collaborations.

Responsibilities and Collaborations

Responsibilities of a class can be broken into two separate types: knowing and doing. *Knowing responsibilities* are those things that an instance of a class must be capable of knowing. An instance of a class typically knows the values of its attributes and its relationships. *Doing responsibilities* are those things that an instance of a class must be capable of doing. In this case, an instance of a class can execute its operations or it can request a second instance (a collaborator), which it knows about, to execute one of its operations on behalf of the first instance.

[10] Our CRC cards are based on the work of D. Bellin and S. S. Simone, *The CRC Card Book* (Reading, MA: Addison-Wesley, 1997); I. Graham, *Migrating to Object Technology* (Wokingham, England: Addison-Wesley, 1995); B. Henderson-Sellers and B. Unhelkar, *OPEN modeling with UML* (Harlow, England: Addison-Wesley, 2000).

The structural model describes the objects necessary to support the business processes modeled by the use cases. Most use cases involve a set of several classes, not just one class. These classes form *collaborations*. Collaborations allow the analyst to think in terms of clients, servers, and contracts.[11] A *client* object is an instance of a class that sends a request (message) to an instance of another class for an operation to be executed. A *server* object is the instance that receives the request (message) from the client object. Practically speaking, the server object is a collaborator of the client object's operation that sent the request. A *contract* formalizes the interactions between the client and server objects. Chapter 7 provides a more-detailed explanation of contracts and examples of their use.

An analyst can use the idea of class responsibilities and client–server–contract collaborations to help identify the classes, along with the attributes, operations, and relationships, involved with a use case. One of the easiest ways to use CRC cards in developing a structural model is through anthropomorphism—pretending that the classes have human characteristics. Members of the development team can either ask questions of themselves or be asked questions by other members of the team. Typically, the questions asked are of the form:

> Who or what are you?
> What do you know?
> What can you do?

The answers to the questions are then used to add detail to the evolving CRC cards. For example, in the appointment problem, a member of the team can pretend that he or she is an appointment. In this case, the appointment would answer that he or she knows about the doctor and patient who participate in the appointment and they would know the date and time of the appointment. Furthermore, an appointment would have to know how to create itself, delete itself, and to possibly change different aspects of itself. In some cases, this approach will uncover additional objects that have to be added to the evolving structural model.

Elements of a CRC Card

The set of CRC cards contains all the information necessary to build a logical structural model of the problem under investigation. Figure 4-5 shows a sample CRC card. Each CRC card captures and describes the essential elements of a class. The front of the card contains the class's name, ID, type, description, associated use cases, the class's responsibilities, and the responsibility's collaborators. The name of a class should be a noun (but not a proper noun, such as the name of a specific person or thing). Just like the use cases, in later stages of development, it is important to be able to trace back design decisions to specific requirements. In conjunction with the list of associated use cases, the ID number for each class can be used to accomplish this. Also, by associating the use cases with the individual classes allows the analyst to be able to track back to determine the primary actor and stakeholders. This provides the information required to limit the access to the instances of the class to the individuals who play the roles identified by the primary actors and stakeholders. This can be very useful when considering the access controls used to address the security nonfunctional requirements.[12] The description is simply a brief statement that can be used as a textual definition for the class. The responsibilities of the class represent the operations that the class must contain (i.e., the doing responsibilities).

---

[11] For more information, see K. Beck and W. Cunningham, "A Laboratory for Teaching Object-Oriented Thinking," *Proceedings of OOPSLA, SIGPLAN Notices,* 24, no. 10 (1989): 1–6; B. Henderson-Sellers and B. Unhelkar, *OPEN Modeling with UML* (Harlow, England: Addison-Wesley, 2000); C. Larman, *Applying UML and Patterns: An Introduction to Object-Oriented Analysis and Design* (Englewood Cliffs, NJ: Prentice Hall, 1998); B. Meyer, *Object-Oriented Software Construction* (Englewood Cliffs, NJ: Prentice Hall, 1994); R. Wirfs-Brock, B. Wilkerson, and L. Wiener, *Designing Object-Oriented Software* (Englewood Cliffs, NJ, Prentice Hall, 1990).

[12] We cover this in more detail in the design portion of the textbook.

Front:

Class Name: Patient	**ID:** 3	**Type:** Concrete, Domain
Description: An individual that needs to receive or has received medical attention		**Associated Use Cases:** 2

Responsibilities	Collaborators
Make appointment	Appointment
Calculate last visit	
Change status	
Provide medical history	Medical history

Back:

Attributes:
Amount
Insurance carrier

Relationships:

Generalization (a-kind-of): Person

Aggregation (has-parts): Medical history

Other Associations: Appointment

FIGURE 4-5
Sample CRC Card

Collaborators are those server objects to which a message is sent by the responsibility of the client object. For example, the Patient Make appointment responsibility sends a request to an Appointment object, the Patient Provide medical history responsibility sends a request to a Medical history object, while the remaining responsibilities of a Patient object are self-sufficient, i.e., they have no collaborators. If the responsibility requires multiple collaborators, then a list of the collaborators for that specific responsibility is used to portray all of the server objects. Furthermore, if multiple responsibilities use the same collaborator, then the collaborator is listed multiple times; once for each responsibility that uses it.

The back of a CRC card contains the attributes and relationships of the class. The attributes of the class represent the knowing responsibilities that each instance of the class has to meet. Three types of relationships typically are captured at this point: generalization, aggregation, and other associations. In Figure 4-5, we see that a Patient is a-kind-of Person and that a Patient is associated with Appointments.

APPLYING THE CHAPTER CONCEPTS

Library Management System Example In the previous chapter, Susan identified a set of use cases for the Library Management System (Figure 3-5). She also updated the functional requirements (Figure 3-10) and developed an activity diagram (Figure 3-9) and use-case description (Figure 3-14) for the Borrow Resource use case. In this example, she uses the Borrow Resource use-case description as a basis for identifying the candidate classes.

To identify the candidate classes, Susan carefully reviews the Borrow Resource use-case description. By simply looking for the nouns, she identifies patron, librarian, resource, library, Personnel Office, faculty/staff, ID, physical resource, downloadable resource, Registrar's Office, and library system. Next, she reviewed the functional requirements and use case diagram. In this case, she identified another library as an additional actor-based class. Next, based on these candidate classes, she brainstormed and identified student and

<table>
<tr><td colspan="3">Front:</td></tr>
<tr><td>Class Name: Patron</td><td>ID: 25</td><td>Type: Abstract, Domain</td></tr>
<tr><td colspan="2">Description: Describes the common properties of the Faculty/Staff, Student, and Guest subclasses</td><td>Associated Use Cases: 1</td></tr>
<tr><td colspan="2" align="center">Responsibilities
Checkout Resource</td><td align="center">Collaborators</td></tr>
</table>

Back:

Attributes:
- Name
- ID number
- Address

Relationships:

Generalization (a-kind-of): ____________

Aggregation (has-parts): ____________

Other Associations: Resource

FIGURE 4-6   Sample CRC Cards for the Library Management System

guest as additional types of patrons and she identified different types of resources including books, DVDs, and CDs. Before attempting to identify any more, she decided that it would be a good idea to challenge the need for some of these. Her first challenge was to review the actor-based classes: patron, librarian, Personnel Office, Registrar's Office, and another library. To challenge them, she asked what information that the system would need to be kept track of for each instance of the class for this problem. Upon doing this, she decided to keep only patron. The other actor-based classes seemed only to be actors. Next, given that the library was just the client, and that the library system was the system being developed, she removed both candidate classes from her list. Based on the remaining candidate classes, Susan created a CRC card for each. (A sample of the CRC cards are shown in Figure 4-6.)

Front:

Class Name: Resource	**ID:** 26	**Type:** Abstract, Domain
Description: Describes the common properties of the Physical and Downloadable classes		**Associated Use Cases:** 1,2

Responsibilities	**Collaborators**
Checkout	Patron

Back:

Attributes:
Title
ID number
Publisher

Relationships:
Generalization (a-kind-of):

Aggregation (has-parts):

Other Associations: Patron, Location

FIGURE 4-6   *Continued*

Front:

Class Name: Collection	**ID:** 28	**Type:** Concrete, Domain
Description: Describes a container class that holds different collections, e.g., books, DVDs, Podcasts, etc.		**Associated Use Cases:** 1,2

Responsibilities	**Collaborators**
Add Resource	
Delete Resource	

Back:

Attributes:
Name
ID number

Relationships:
Generalization (a-kind-of):

Aggregation (has-parts): Resource

Other Associations:

FIGURE 4-6 *Continued*

Campus Housing Service "Your Turn" Exercise In the previous chapter, you were supposed to create a set of use-case descriptions for each use case. By reviewing these descriptions, you should easily identify a set of candidate classes. Next, you should play devil's advocate with each candidate class to determine whether it should be kept or not. Once you are comfortable with your candidate classes, you should create a set of CRC cards to represent the classes.

CRC cards are used to document the essential properties of a class. However, once the cards are filled out, the analyst can use the cards and anthropomorphisms in role-playing (described in the next section) to uncover missing properties by executing the different scenarios associated with the use cases (see Chapter 3). Role-playing also can be used as a basis to test the clarity and completeness of the evolving representation of the system.

Role-Playing CRC Cards with Use Cases[13]

In addition to the object identification approaches described earlier (textual analysis, brainstorming, common object lists, and patterns), CRC cards can be used in a *role-playing* exercise that has been shown to be useful in discovering additional objects, attributes, relationships, and operations. Furthermore, in addition to walkthroughs, described later in this chapter, role-playing is very useful in testing the fidelity of the evolving structural model. In general, members of the team perform roles associated with the actors and objects previously identified with the different use cases. Technically speaking, the members of the team perform the different steps associated with a specific scenario of a use case. Remember, a scenario is a single, unique execution path through a use case. A useful place to look for the different scenarios of a use case is the activity diagrams (e.g., see Figure 3-12). A different scenario exists for each time a decision node causes a split in the execution path of the use case. Also, scenarios can be identified from the alternative/exceptional flows in a use-case description (e.g., see Figure 3-13). Considering the incremental and iterative nature and that activity diagrams and use-case descriptions should contain the same information, reviewing both representations will ensure that relevant scenarios are not missed.

1. Review Use Cases

The first step is to review the activity diagrams and use-case descriptions (see Figures 3-12 and 3-13). This allows the team to pick a specific use case to role-play. Even though it is tempting to try to complete as many use cases as possible in a short time, the team should not choose the easiest use cases first. Instead, at this point in the development of the system, the team should choose the use case that is the most important, the most complex, or the least understood.

2. Identify Relevant Actors and Objects

The second step is to identify the relevant roles that are to be played. Each role is associated with either an actor or an object. To choose the relevant objects, the team reviews each of the CRC cards and picks the ones that are associated with the chosen use case. For example, in Figure 4-5, we see that the CRC card that represents the Patient class is associated with Use-case number 2. So, if we were going to role-play the Manage Appointments use case (see Figures 3-12 and 3-13), we would need to include the Patient CRC card. By reviewing the use-case description, we can easily identify the Patient and Doctor actors (see Primary Actor and Stakeholders section of the use case description in Figure 3-13). By reading the event section of the use-case description, we identify the internal actor role of Receptionist. After identifying all of the relevant roles, we assign each one to a different member of the team.

3. Role-Play Scenarios

The third step is to role-play scenarios of the use case by having the team members perform each one. To do this, each team member must pretend that he or she is an instance of the role assigned to him or her. Furthermore, each event or activity must be assigned to either an actor or to a class (CRC card's responsibility). For example, if a team member was assigned the role of the Receptionist, then he or she would have to be able to perform the different steps in the scenario associated with the Receptionist. In the case of the scenario in which an old patient wants to change their appointment but not update their patient information or to make new payment arrangements, this would include steps 1, 2, 3a, S-2, S-2 1a, S-2 2a, and S-2 3b (see Figure 3-13). However, when this scenario is performed (role-played), it would be discovered that the second activity was somewhat convoluted. For example, what actually occurs in the second event: The Patient provides the receptionist with their information? What specific information is provided by the patient? There seems to be a lot of information contained in this event that is only identified in an implicit, not explicit, manner. When the information is not identified explicitly, there is a lot of room for interpretation, which requires the team members to make assumptions. It is much better to remove the need to make an assumption by making each step explicit. In this case, Step 2 of the Normal Flow of Events should be modified. For example, what type of appointment is being requested, when would the patient like to schedule the appointment, and are they a new or old patient. Once the step has been fixed, the scenario is

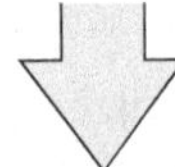

4. Repeat Steps 1 through 3

5. Document the Results of Role-Playing

tried again. This process is repeated until the scenario can be executed to a successful conclusion. Once the scenario has successfully concluded, the next scenario is performed. This is repeated until all of the scenarios of the use case can be performed successfully.[14]

The fourth step is to simply repeat steps 1 through 3 for the remaining use cases.

In addition to updating the CRC cards, a couple of useful ways to document the results of role-playing is to update the events in the use-case description and to add *swimlanes* to the use case's activity diagram (see Figures 3-12 and 3-13). In this case, we will add the swimlanes to the activity diagram first and then modify the Flow of Events section of the use-case description based on those changes.

As shown in Chapter 3, activity diagrams can model a business process independent of any actors or objects. However, there are times when it helps to break up an activity diagram in such a way that it can be used to assign the activities to objects or actors that would actually perform the activity. In fact, the responsibilities with the CRC cards should be related to the activities in the activity diagrams and the events in the use-case descriptions. Developers use activity diagrams with swimlanes to associate the activities with the external roles, the internal roles, and the classes (objects) contained in the structural model. Swimlanes can be laid out in either a horizontal or a vertical manner. In this section, we demonstrate how to "spread" the *activities* contained in a business process or workflow over the actors and objects using the Manage Appointments use case of the appointment system example.

Only a subset of the entire set of classes in the problem domain will be relevant to the Manage Appointments Use Case (Figures 3-12 and 3-13). By looking at the use-case diagram, it is obvious that the Patient actor will be involved in the use case. Also, by looking at the activity diagram and the CRC cards, we identify that the Patient and Appointment classes are necessary to support the Manage Appointments use case. Therefore, as a first step in assigning activities to the relevant actors and classes, we should set up three swimlanes; one for the actor and one each for the two classes. For example, given that in object-oriented systems, creating, reading, updating, and deleting operations can **only** be performed by the object itself, we quickly assign the Create New Patient, Update Patient Information, and Make Payment Arrangements activities to the Patient class. However, each of these processes are actually handled in separate "extended" use cases that are called from the Manage Appointments use case. Consequently, the Patient class is not required in this activity diagram. Furthermore, it is obvious that the Create Appointment, Cancel Appointment, and Change Appointment activities should be assigned to the Appointment class. This leaves us with only trying to assign the Request Appointment and Get Patient Information activities to something. Based on the diagram, we cannot determine who or what should implement these activities. To figure this out, we need to review the use case description. When we do such, we discover that there is another actor involved in the process: Receptionist. The Receptionist actor is an internal actor that is a human part of the system. This is why it does not appear in the use-case diagram. Consequently, we need to add another swimlane to our diagram. Furthermore, based on the role-playing of the CRC cards, we realize that the Get Patient Information activity actually is a dialogue between the two actors. Therefore, the Get Patient Information activity is decomposed into different aspects of the overall Get Patient Information activity, e.g., Determine Appointment Type and Get Appointment Times. Based on all of the above, the activity diagram for the Manage Appointments use case is portrayed in Figure 4-7. This figure shows that some of the activities will be performed by actors while others will need to be implemented as responsibilities on CRC cards. We also have updated the use-case description for the Manage Appointments use case (see Figure 4-8).

---

[14] In some cases, some scenarios are only executed in very rare circumstances. So, from a practical perspective, each scenario could be prioritized individually and only "important" scenarios would have to be implemented for the first release of the system. Only those scenarios would have to be tested at this point in the evolution of the system.

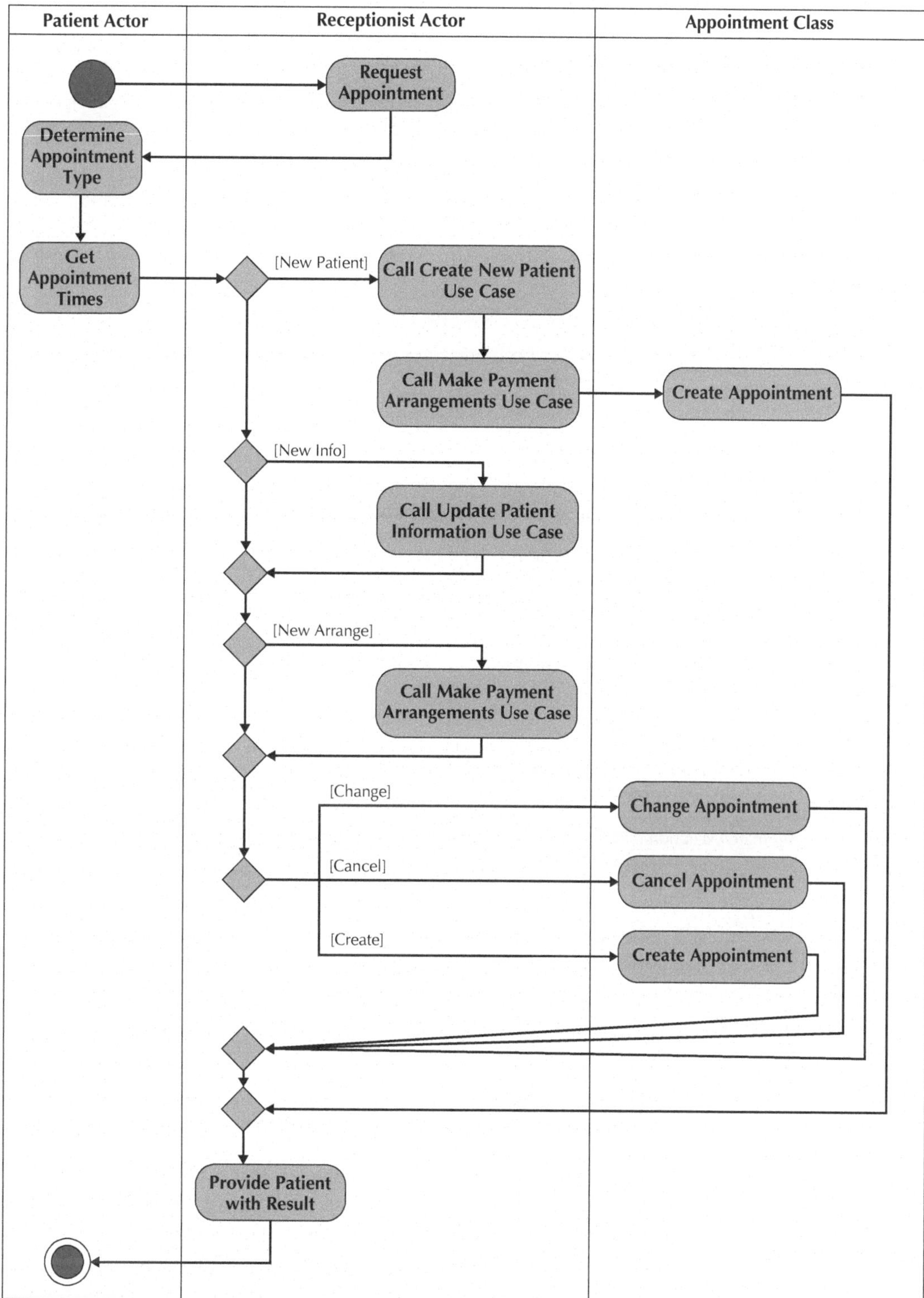

FIGURE 4-7 Manage Appointments Use-Case Activity Diagram with relevant swimlanes

Use Case Name: Manage Appointments		ID: 2	Importance Level: High
Primary Actor: Patient	Use Case Type: Detail, Essential		

Stakeholders and Interests:
Patient – wants to make, change, or cancel an appointment
Doctor – wants to ensure patient's needs are met in a timely manner

Brief Description: This use case describes how we make appointment as well as changing or canceling an appointment for a patient.

Trigger: Patient calls and asks to make a new appointment, change an existing appointment, or to cancel an existing appointment

Type: External

Relationships:
    Association: Patient
    Include:
    Extend: Create New Patient, Make Payment Arrangements, Update Patient Information
    Generalization:

Normal Flow of Events:
    1. The Patient contacts the office regarding an appointment.
    2. The Patient provides the receptionist with the appointment type.
    3. The Patient provides the receptionist with their preferred appointment times.
    4. Call S-1: Create New Patient Subflow.
    5. Receptionist provides Patient with the result.

SubFlows:
    S-1: Create New Patient Subflow
        1. Call Create New Patient use case.
        2. Call Make Payment Arrangements use case.
        3. Create Appointment.
    S-2: Old Patient Subflow
        1. Call Update Patient Information use case.
        2. Call Make Payment Arrangements use case.
        3. Create Appointment.

Alternate/Exceptional Flows:
    4a. Call S-2: Old Patient Subflow.
    S-2, 1a. Pass.
    S-2, 2a. Pass.
    S-2, 3a. Cancel appointment.
    S-2, 3b. Change appointment.

FIGURE 4-8   Manage Appointments Use-Case Description

APPLYING THE CHAPTER CONCEPTS

Library Management System Example In this installation, armed with the CRC cards, Susan went back to the library to talk with Joe to determine whether any other classes should be identified. Below is part of their conversation.

JOE: Glad to see that you are making progress on the project. How can I help you?

SUSAN: I would like you to go through this set of index cards with me to see if there is anything important that I have left out. Here we have a card for each class that I have

JOE: identified. First, we have a set of cards that represent the patrons of the library: patron, faculty/staff, student, and guest. Are there any other types of patrons?

JOE: Yes. Since we participate in an interlibrary loan system where we allow patrons of other libraries to check out resources, we have other libraries as a type of patron. So, we need to keep track of which library has borrowed one of our resources for one of their patrons.

SUSAN: That's an important omission. I'm glad that you caught that. Next, we have a set of cards that describe different types of resources including resource, physical resource, downloadable resource, books, DVDs, and CDs. Are there any other types of resources?

JOE: Let me think. From a physical resource stand point, we also need to keep track of journals. And, from a downloadable resource perspective, we need to keep track of books, journals, podcasts, movies, and music. All of these are subscription-based. Consequently, we need to know which ones are actually being used.

SUSAN: That only leaves me with one card for you to review: ID. Do we need to keep track of information regarding a patron's ID or is ID essentially the same thing as patron?

JOE: From our perspective, the ID represents the patron. So, I guess they represent the same thing.

SUSAN: Great, is there anything that we have left out?

JOE: It's important for us to be able to know the location of a resource that a patron wants to borrow. So, I think you need to keep track of the location of the resources. Currently, we need to know whether a resource is in the library, in storage, or is something that we need to borrow from another library. Also, I think we should consider some way to keep track of the different resources as a set of collections. For example, a book collection or a DVD collection. That way it will be easier for the patron or us to find a resource.

SUSAN: Thanks for all of this. I'll go back and modify the cards and create a class diagram that portrays all of this. Once I have this done, I'll come back and we can role-play the activity diagrams to see whether we need to do more development of the CRC cards.

Once Susan got back to the team, she and her team role-played each of the use cases to make sure that everything worked as expected. Finally, she created an activity diagram with swimlanes for each use case. Figure 4-9 portrays the diagram for the Borrow Resource use case. Notice there are a few additional activities that were required when comparing to the original diagram (Figure 3-9).

Campus Housing Service "Your Turn" Exercise Using the CRC cards created in the previous "Your Turn" exercise, you should role play the use cases. As you role play the use cases, make sure that you assign the different events/activities to either one of the actors or to one of the classes. Once you are satisfied with the results, document each use case using an activity diagram with swimlanes.

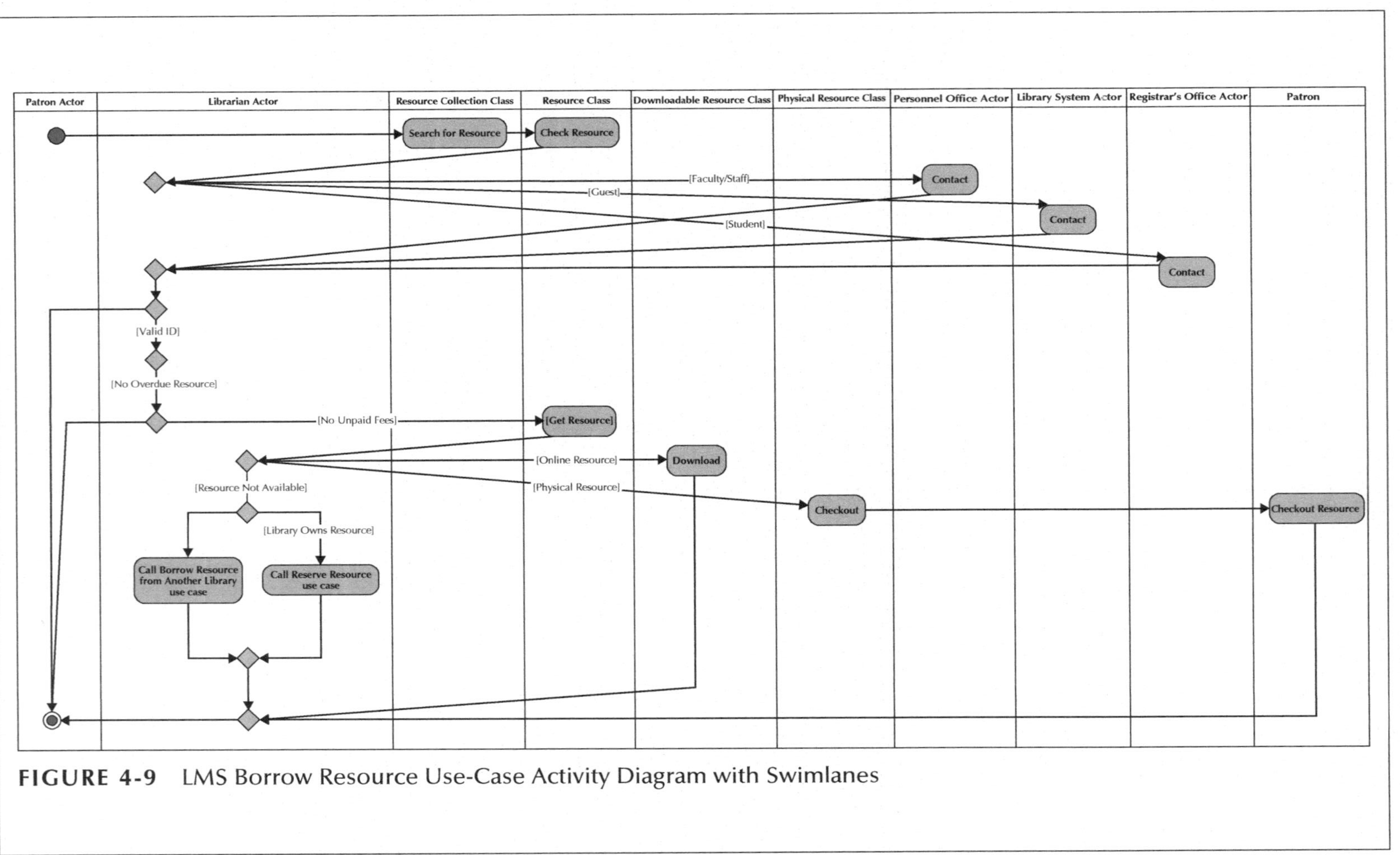

FIGURE 4-9   LMS Borrow Resource Use-Case Activity Diagram with Swimlanes

136

CLASS DIAGRAMS

A *class diagram* is a *static model* that shows the classes and the relationships among classes that remain constant in the system over time. The class diagram depicts classes, which include both behaviors and states, with the relationships between the classes. The following sections present the elements of the class diagram, different approaches that can be used to simplify a class diagram, and an alternative structure diagram: the object diagram.

Elements of a Class Diagram

Figure 4-11 shows a class diagram that was created to reflect the classes and relationships associated with the appointment system. This diagram is based on the classes uncovered through the object identification techniques and the role-playing of the CRC cards described earlier.

Class The main building block of a class diagram is the class, which stores and manages information in the system (see Figure 4-10). Classes support encapsulation by capturing both the attributes and operations in a single construct. During analysis, classes refer to the people, places, and things about which the system will capture information. Later, during design and implementation, classes can refer to implementation-specific artifacts such as windows, forms, and other objects used to build the system. Each class is drawn using a three-part rectangle, with the class's name at the top, attributes in the middle, and operations at the bottom. We can see that the classes identified earlier, such as Participant, Doctor, Patient, Receptionist, Medical History, Appointment, and Symptom, are included in Figure 4-11. The value of an object's attributes define the *state* of the object and the behavior of an object is represented by the operations that are defined with the object's class.

Attributes are properties of the class about which we want to capture information (see Figure 4-10). Notice that the Participant class in Figure 4-11 contains the attributes: lastname, firstname, address, phone, and birthdate. At times, you might want to store *derived attributes*, which are attributes that can be calculated or derived; these special attributes are denoted by placing a slash (/) before the attribute's name. Notice how the person class contains a derived attribute called/age, which can be derived by subtracting the patient's birth date from the current date. It is also possible to show the *visibility* of the attribute on the diagram. Visibility relates to the level of *information hiding* to be enforced for the attribute. The visibility of an attribute can be public (+), protected (#), or private (−). A *public attribute* is one that is not hidden from any other object. As such, other objects can modify its value. A *protected attribute* is one that is hidden from all other classes except its immediate subclasses. A *private attribute* is one that is hidden from all other classes. The default visibility for an attribute is normally private.

Operations are actions or functions that a class can perform (see Figure 4-10). The functions that are available to all classes (e.g., create a new instance, return a value for a particular attribute, set a value for a particular attribute, and delete an instance) are not explicitly shown within the class rectangle. Instead, only operations unique to the class and aligned with the use cases are included, such as the cancel without notice operation in the Appointment class and the calculate last visit operation in the Patient class in Figure 4-11. Notice that both the operations are followed by parentheses, which contain the parameter(s) needed by the operation. If an operation has no parameters, the parentheses are still shown but are empty. As with attributes, the visibility of an operation can be designated public, protected, or private. The default visibility for an operation is normally public.

Term	Symbol
A class: • represents a kind of person, place, or thing about which the system will need to capture and store information. • has a name typed in bold and centered in its top compartment. • has a list of attributes in its middle compartment. • has a list of operations in its bottom compartment. • does not explicitly show operations that are available to all classes.	**Class1** -Attribute-1 +Operation-1()
An attribute: • represents properties that describe the state of an object. • can be derived from other attributes, shown by placing a slash before the attribute's name.	attribute name /derived attribute name
An operation: • represents the actions or functions that a class can perform. • can be classified as a constructor, query, update, or destructor operation. • includes parentheses that may contain parameters or information needed to perform the operation.	operation name ()
An association: • represents a relationship between multiple classes or a class and itself. • is labeled using a verb phrase or a role name, whichever better represents the relationship. • can exist between one or more classes. • contains multiplicity symbols, which represent the minimum and maximum times a class instance can be associated with the related class instance.	AssociatedWith 0..* 1
A generalization: • represents a-kind-of relationship between multiple classes.	
An aggregation: • represents a logical a-part-of relationship between multiple classes or a class and itself. • is a special form of an association.	0..* IsPartOf ▸ 1
A composition: • represents a physical a-part-of relationship between multiple classes or a class and itself • is a special form of an association.	1..* IsPartOf ▸ 1

FIGURE 4-10 Class Diagram Syntax

There are four types of operations that all classes should contain: constructor, query, update, and destructor (similar to the CRUDE acronym we introduced in an earlier chapter). A *constructor operation* creates a new instance of a class. For example, the patient class may have a method called insert (), which creates a new patient instance as patients are entered into the system. If an operation simply implements one of the basic functions (e.g., create a new instance), it can be omitted from the class diagram.

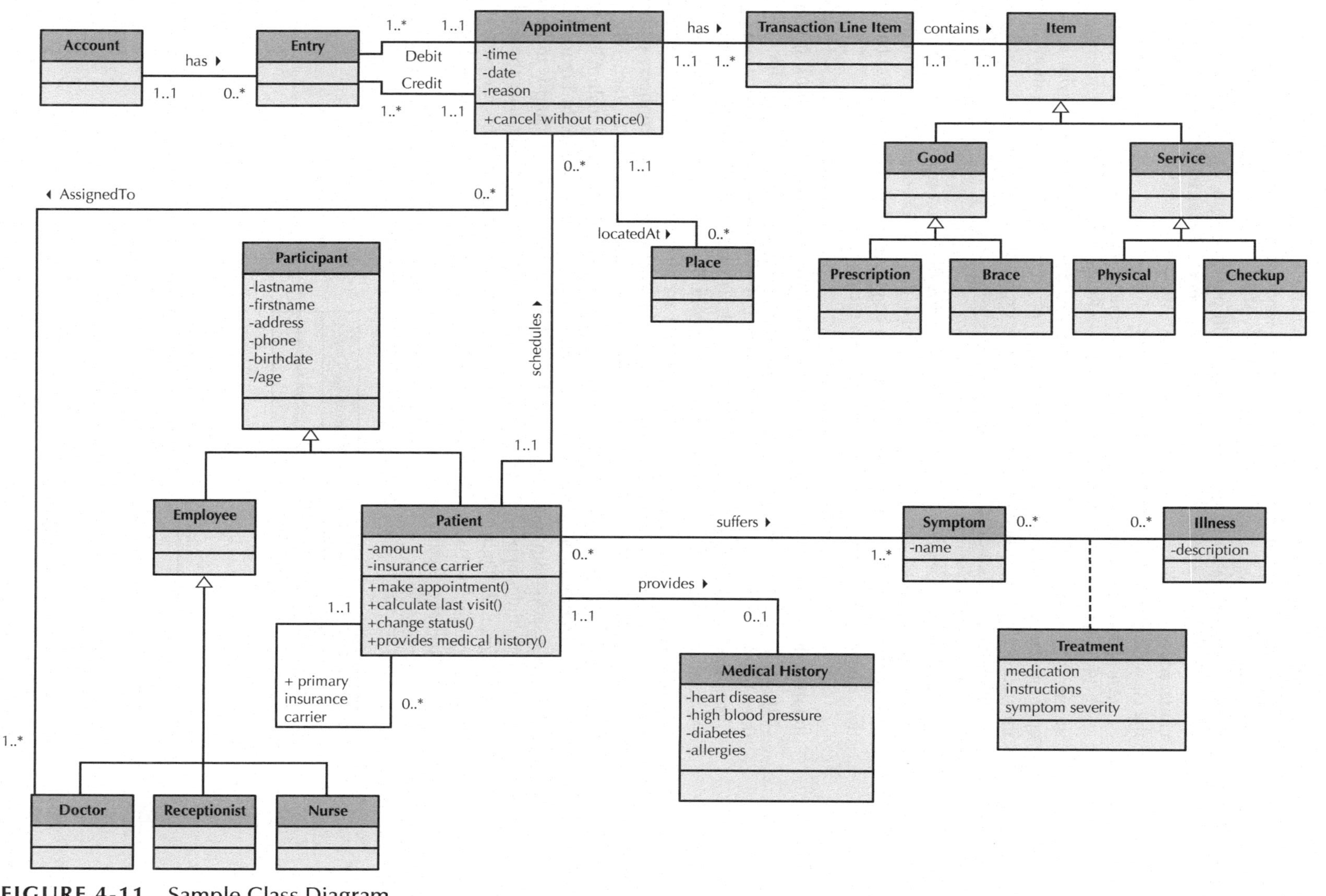

FIGURE 4-11   Sample Class Diagram

A *query operation* makes information about the state of an object available to other objects, but it does not alter the object in any way. For instance, the calculate last visit () operation that determines when a patient last visited the doctor's office will result in the object's being accessed by the system, but it will not make any change to its information. If a query method merely asks for information from attributes in the class (e.g., a patient's name, address, and phone), then like a simple constructor operation, it can be omitted from the class diagram.

An *update operation* changes the value of some or all the object's attributes, which may result in a change in the object's state. Consider changing the status of a patient from new to current with a method called change status() or associating a patient with a particular appointment with make appointment (appointment). If the result of the operation can change the state of the object, then the operation must be explicitly included on the class diagram. On the other hand, if the update operation is a simple assignment operation, it too can be omitted from the diagram.

A *destructor operation* simply deletes or removes the object from the system. For example, if an employee object no longer represents an actual employee associated with the firm, a destructor operation would be used to delete the employee object. Like the other basic operations, destructor operations can be omitted from the diagram.

Relationships A primary purpose of a class diagram is to show the relationships, or associations, that classes have with one another. These are depicted on the diagram by drawing lines between classes (see Figure 4-10). When multiple classes share a relationship (or a class shares a relationship with itself), a line is drawn and labeled with either the name of the relationship or the roles that the classes play in the relationship. For example, in Figure 4-11 the two classes patient and appointment are associated with one another whenever a patient schedules an appointment. Thus, a line labeled schedules connects patient and appointment, representing exactly how the two classes are related to each other. Also, notice that there is a small solid triangle beside the name of the relationship. The triangle allows a direction to be associated with the name of the relationship. In Figure 4-11, the schedules relationship includes a triangle, indicating that the relationship is to be read as "patient schedules appointment." Inclusion of the triangle simply increases the readability of the diagram. In Figure 4-12, three additional examples of associations are portrayed: An Invoice is AssociatedWith a Purchase Order (and vice versa), a Pilot Flies an Aircraft, and a Spare Tire IsLocatedIn a Trunk.

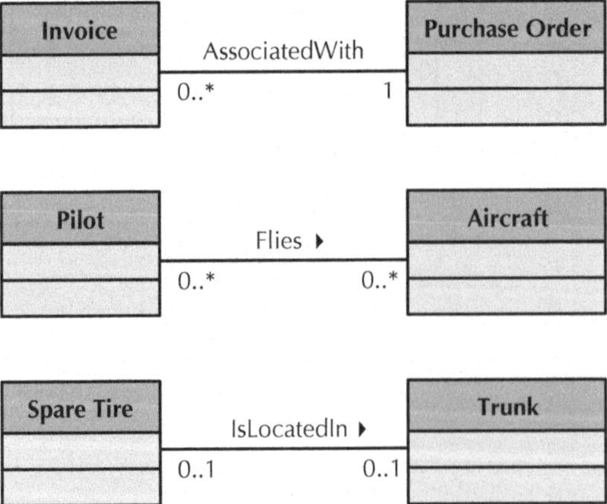

FIGURE 4-12
Sample
Association

Sometimes a class is related to itself, as in the case of a patient being the primary insurance carrier for other patients (e.g., spouse and children). In Figure 4-11, notice that a line was drawn between the patient class and itself and called *primary insurance carrier* to depict the role that the class plays in the relationship. Notice that a plus (+) sign is placed before the label to communicate that it is a role as opposed to the name of the relationship. When labeling an association, we use either a relationship name or a role name (not both), whichever communicates a more thorough understanding of the model.

Relationships also have *multiplicity*, which documents how an instance of an object can be associated with other instances. Numbers are placed on the association path to denote the minimum and maximum instances that can be related through the association in the format minimum number..maximum number (see Figure 4-13). The numbers specify the relationship from the class at the far end of the relationship line to the end with the number. One approach is to depict multiplicity as a range from zero or one (minimum), up to one or "many" (maximum). For example, in Figure 4-11, there is a 0..* on the appointment end of the patient schedules appointment relationship. This means that a patient can be associated with zero to many different appointments. At the patient end of this same relationship, there is a 1..1, meaning that an appointment must be associated with one and only one patient. In Figure 4-12, we see that an instance of the Invoice class must be AssociatedWith one instance of the Purchase Order class and that an instance of the Purchase Order class may be AssociatedWith zero or more instances of the Invoice class, that an instance of the Pilot class Flies zero or more instances of the Aircraft class, and that an instance of the Aircraft class may be flown by zero or more instances of the Pilot class. Finally, we see that an instance of the Spare Tire class IsLocatedIn zero or one instance of the Trunk class, whereas an instance of the Trunk class can contain zero or one instance of the Spare Tire class. As shown in Figure 4-13, specific or precise ranges of number and/or multiple, disjoint ranges are also permitted.

There are times when a relationship itself has associated properties, especially when its classes share a many-to-many relationship. In these cases, a class called an *association class* is formed, which has its own attributes and operations.[15] It is shown as a rectangle attached by a dashed line to the association path, and the rectangle's name matches the label of the association. Think about the case of capturing information about illnesses and symptoms. An illness (e.g., the flu) can be associated with many symptoms (e.g., sore throat and fever), and a symptom (e.g., sore throat) can be associated with many illnesses (e.g., the flu, strep throat, the common cold). Figure 4-11 shows how an association class can capture information about remedies that change depending on the various combinations. For example, a sore throat caused by strep throat requires antibiotics, whereas treatment for a sore throat from the flu or a cold could be throat lozenges or hot tea. Another way to decide when to use an association class is when attributes that belong to the intersection of the two classes involved in the association must be captured. We can visually think about an association class as a Venn diagram. For example, in Figure 4-14, the Grade idea is really an intersection of the Student and Course classes, because a grade exists only at the intersection of these two ideas. Another example shown in Figure 4-14 is that a job may be viewed as the intersection between a Person and a Company. Most often, classes are related through a normal association; however, there are two special cases of an association that you will see appear quite often: generalization and aggregation.

---

[15] For those familiar with data modeling, associative classes serve a purpose similar to the one the associative entity serves in ER diagramming.

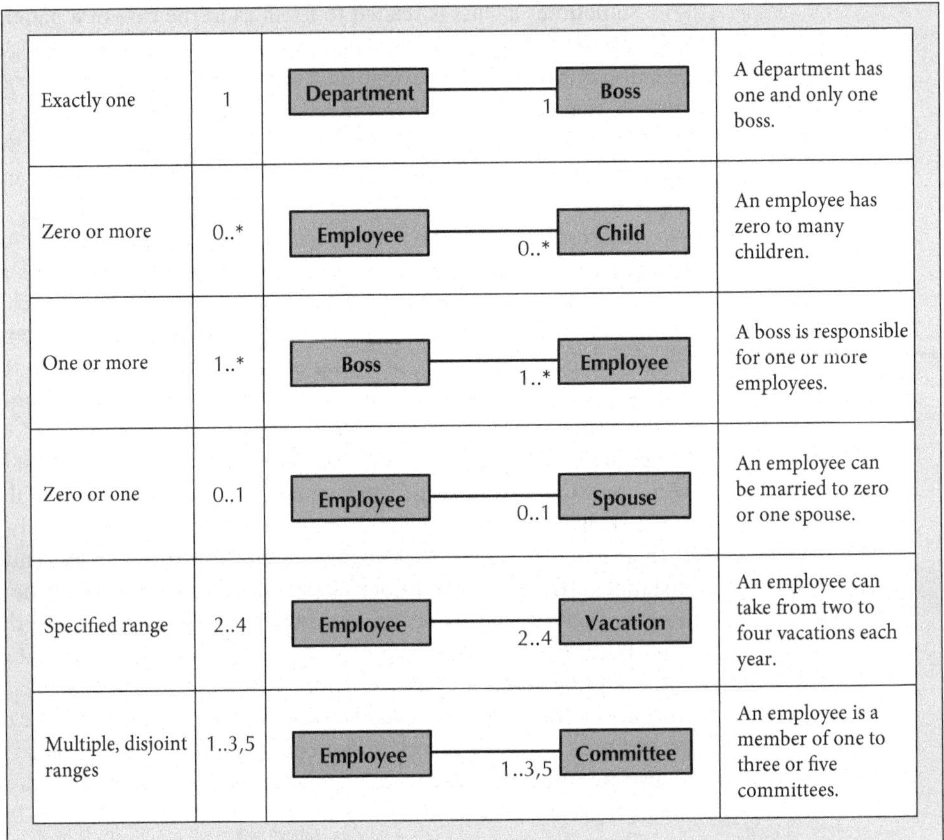

FIGURE 4-13
Multiplicity

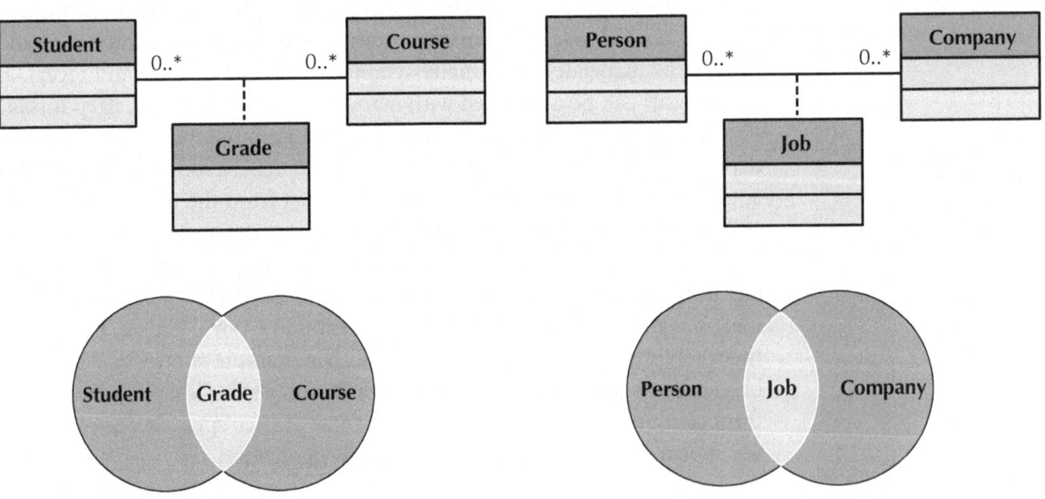

FIGURE 4-14 Sample Association Classes

Generalization and Aggregation Associations A *generalization association* shows that one class (subclass) inherits from another class (superclass), meaning that the properties and operations of the superclass are also valid for objects of the subclass, i.e., the generalization association supports the generalization and class inclusion relationships. The generalization path is shown with a solid line from the subclass to the superclass and a hollow arrow pointing at the superclass (see Figure 4-10). For example, Figure 4-11 communicates that doctors, nurses, and receptionists are all kinds of employees and those employees and patients are kinds of participants. Remember that the generalization relationship occurs when you need to use words like "is a kind of" to describe the relationship. Some additional examples of generalization are given in Figure 4-15. For example, Cardinal is a-kind-of Bird, which is a-kind-of Animal; a General Practitioner is a-kind-of Physician, which is a-kind-of Person; and a Truck is a-kind-of Land Vehicle, which is a-kind-of Vehicle.

An *aggregation association* is used when classes comprise other classes. The aggregation association supports the aggregation and part-whole relationships. For example, think about a doctor's office that has decided to create health care teams that include doctors, nurses, and administrative personnel. As patients enter the office, they are assigned to a health care team, which cares for their needs during their visits. We could include this new knowledge in Figure 4-11 by adding two new classes (Administrative Personnel and Health Team) and aggregation relationships from the Doctor, the Nurse, and the new Administrative Personnel classes to the new Health Team class. A diamond is placed nearest the class representing the aggregation (health care team), and lines are drawn from the diamond to connect the classes that serve as its parts (doctors, nurses, and administrative personnel). Typically, you can identify these kinds of associations when you need to use words like "is a part of" or "is made up of" to describe the relationship. However, from a UML perspective, there are two types of aggregation associations: aggregation and composition (see Figure 4-10).

Aggregation is used to portray logical a-part-of relationships and is depicted on a UML class diagram by a hollow or white diamond. For example, in Figure 4-16 three logical aggregations are shown. Logical implies that it is possible for a part to be associated with multiple wholes or that is relatively simple for the part to be removed from the whole. For example, an instance of the Employee class IsPartOf an instance of at least one instance of the Department class, an instance of the Wheel class IsPartOf an instance of the Vehicle class, and an instance of the Desk class IsPartOf an instance of the Office class. Obviously, in many cases an employee can be associated with more than one department, and it is relatively easy to remove a wheel from a vehicle or move a desk from an office.

Composition is used to portray a physical part of relationships and is shown by a black diamond. Physical implies that the part can be associated with only a single whole. For example in Figure 4-17, three physical compositions are illustrated: an instance of a door can be a part of only a single instance of a car, an instance of a room can be a part of an instance only of a single building, and an instance of a button can be a part of only a single mouse. However, in many cases, the distinction that you can achieve by including aggregation (white diamonds) and composition (black diamonds) in a class diagram might not be worth the price of adding additional graphical notation for the client to learn. Therefore, many UML experts view the inclusion of aggregation and composition notation to the UML class diagram as simply "syntactic sugar" and not necessary because the same information can always be portrayed by simply using the correct multiplicities with the association relationship syntax (see Figure 4-10).

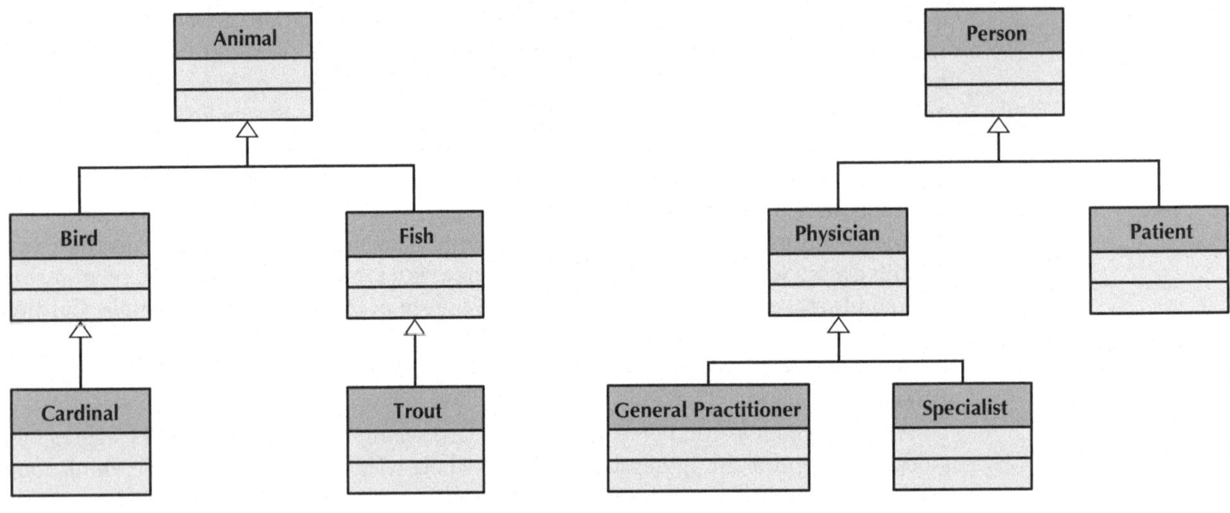

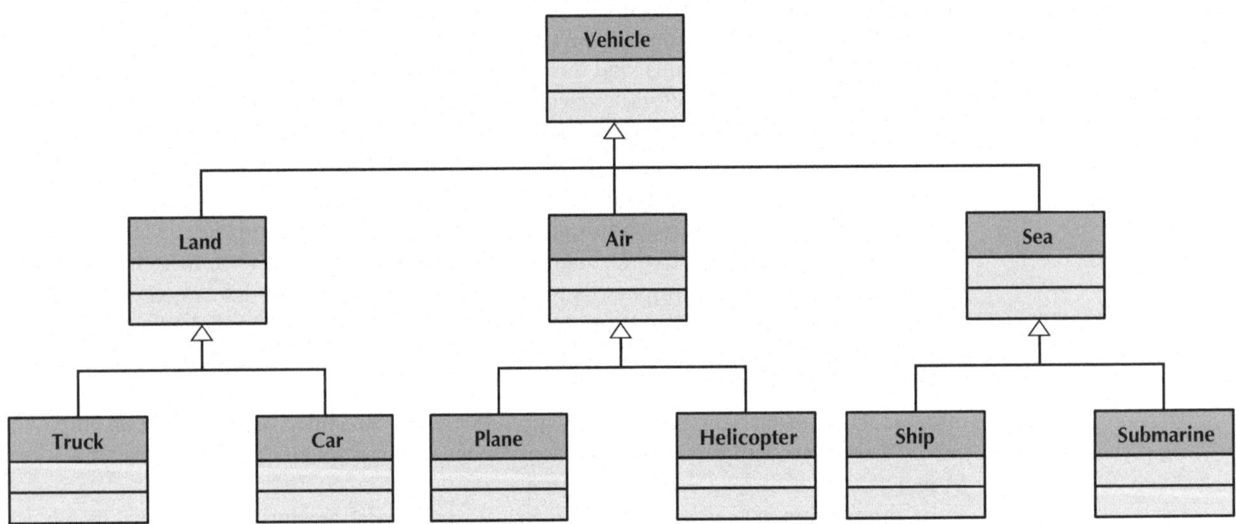

FIGURE 4-15   Sample Generalizations

Simplifying Class Diagrams

When a class diagram is fully populated with all the classes and relationships for a real-world system, the class diagram can become very difficult to interpret (i.e., can be very complex). For example, a typical real-world system could have hundreds of classes. Therefore, it is sometimes necessary to simplify the diagram. One way to simplify the class diagram is to show only concrete classes.[16] However, depending on the number of associations that are connected to abstract classes—and thus inherited down to the concrete classes—this particular suggestion could make the diagram more difficult to comprehend.

A second way to simplify the class diagram is through the use of a *view* mechanism. Views were developed originally with relational database management systems to show only

[16] See footnote 1.

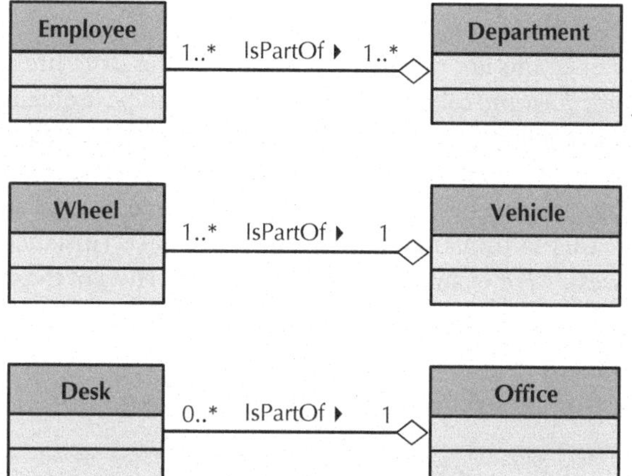

FIGURE 4-16
Sample Aggregation
Associations

a subset of the information contained in the database. In this case, the view would be a useful subset of the class diagram, such as a use-case view that shows only the classes and relationships relevant to a particular use case. A second view could be to show only a particular type of relationship: aggregation, association, or generalization. A third type of view is to restrict the information shown with each class, for example, show only the name of the class, the name and attributes, or the name and operations. These view mechanisms can be combined to further simplify the diagram.

A third approach to simplifying a class diagram is through the use of *packages* (i.e., logical groups of classes). To make the diagrams easier to read and keep the models at a reasonable level of complexity, the classes can be grouped together into packages. Packages are general constructs that can be applied to any of the elements in UML models. In Chapter 3, we introduced the package idea to simplify use-case diagrams. In the case of class diagrams, it is simple to sort the classes into groups based on the relationships that they share.[17] We describe packages in more detail in Chapter 6.

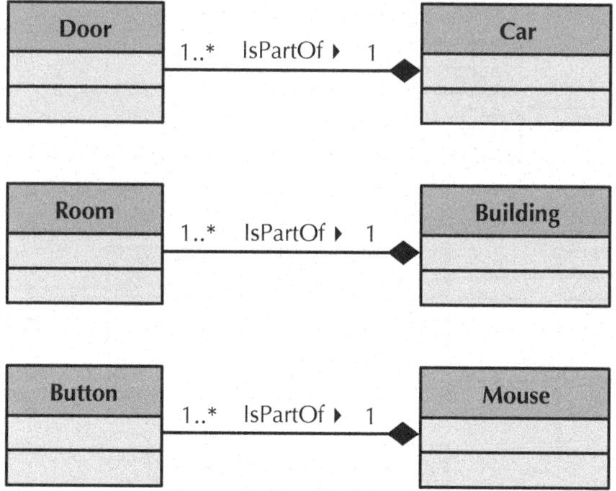

FIGURE 4-17
Sample Composition
Associations

---

[17] For those familiar with structured analysis and design, packages serve a purpose similar to the leveling and balancing processes used in data flow diagramming. Packages and package diagrams are described in more detail in Chapter 6.

Object Diagrams

Although class diagrams are necessary to document the structure of the classes, a second type of *static structure diagram*, called an object diagram, can be useful in revealing additional information. An *object diagram* is essentially an instantiation of all or part of a class diagram. *Instantiation* means to create an instance of the class with a set of appropriate attribute values.

Object diagrams can be very useful when trying to uncover details of a class. Generally speaking, it is easier to think in terms of concrete objects (instances) rather than abstractions of objects (classes).[18] For example, in Figure 4-18, a portion of the class diagram in Figure 4-11

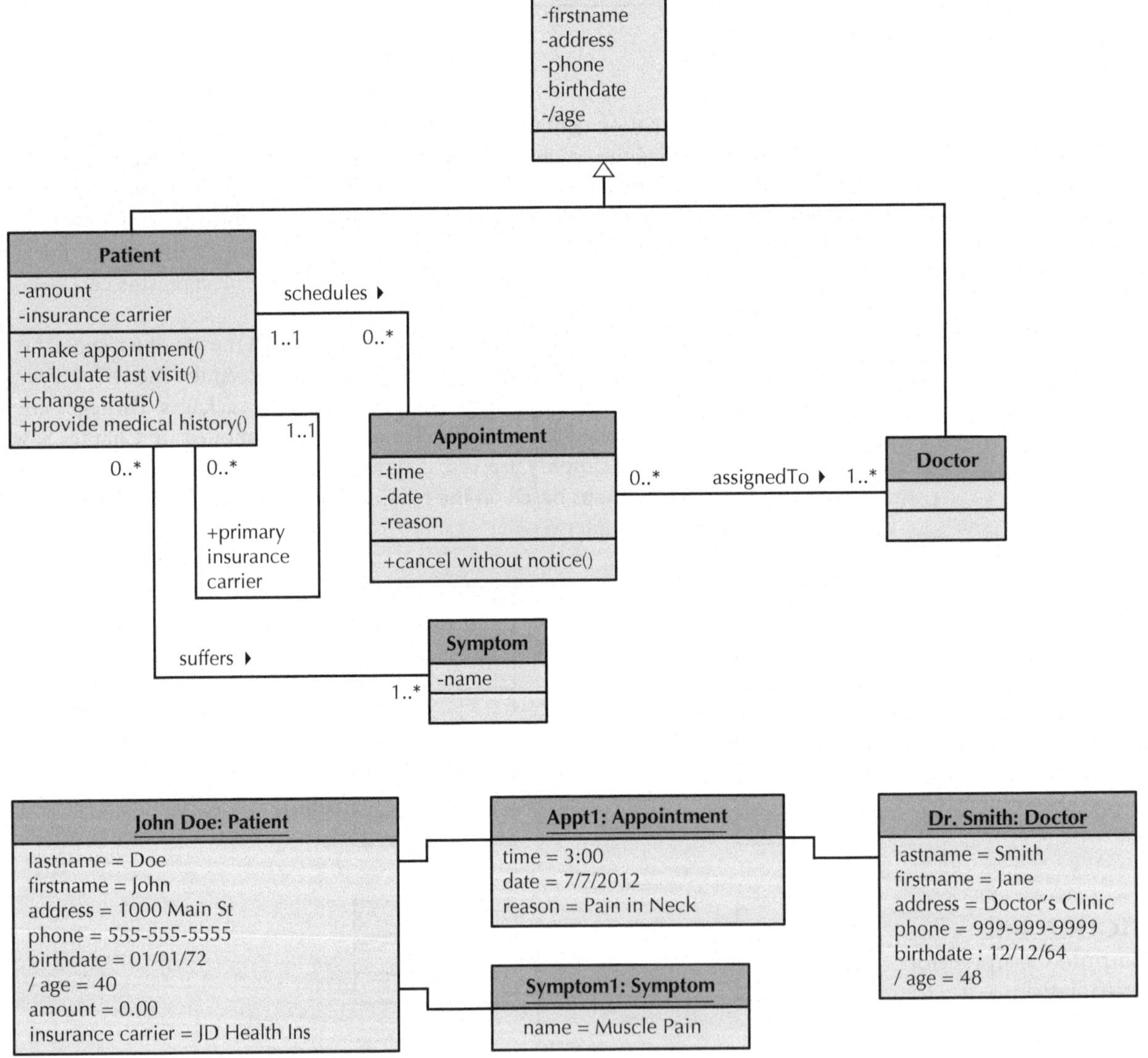

FIGURE 4-18   Sample Object Diagram

[18] See M. Hvalshagen, R. Lukyanenko, B. M. Samuel. "Empowering Users with Narratives: Examining the Efficacy of Narratives for Understanding Data-Oriented Conceptual Models," *Information Systems Research* 34, No. 3 (2022): 890–909, and B. Samuel, V. Khatri, and R. Venkataraman. "Exploring the Effects of Extensional Versus Intentional Representations on Domain Understanding," *MIS Quarterly* 42, No. 4, (2018): 1187–1209.

has been copied and instantiated. The top part of the figure simply is a copy of a small view of the overall class diagram. The lower portion is the object diagram that instantiates that subset of classes. By reviewing the actual instances involved, John Doe, Appt1, Symptom1, and Dr. Smith, we may discover additional relevant attributes, relationships, and/or operations or possibly misplaced attributes, relationships, and/or operations. For example, an appointment has a reason attribute. Upon closer examination, the reason attribute might have been better modeled as an association with the Symptom class. Currently, the Symptom class is associated with the Patient class. After reviewing the object diagram, this seems to be in error. Therefore, we should modify the class diagram to reflect this new understanding of the problem.

CREATING STRUCTURAL MODELS USING CRC CARDS AND CLASS DIAGRAMS

Creating a structural model is an incremental and iterative process whereby the analyst makes a rough cut of the model and then refines it over time. Structural models can become quite complex—in fact, there are systems that have hundreds of classes. It is important to remember that CRC cards and class diagrams can be used to describe both the as-is and to-be structural models of the evolving system, but they are most often used for the to-be model. There are many different ways to identify a set of candidate objects and to create CRC cards and class diagrams. Today most object identification begins with the use cases identified for the problem (see Chapter 3). In this section, we describe a use-case–driven process that can be used to create the structural model of a problem domain.

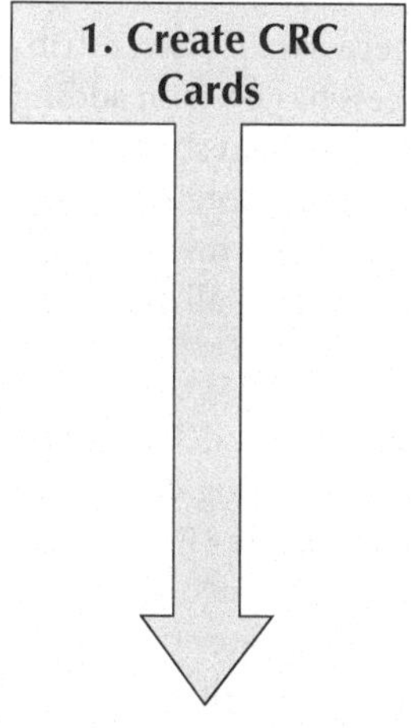

We could begin creating the structural model with a class diagram instead of CRC cards. However, owing to the low-tech nature and the ease of role-playing use-case scenarios with CRC cards, we prefer to create the CRC cards first and then transfer the information from the CRC cards into a class diagram later. As a result, the first step of our recommended process is to create CRC cards. Performing textual analysis on the use-case descriptions does this. If you recall, the normal flow of events, subflows, and alternative/exceptional flows of the use-case description were written in a special form called Subject–Verb–Direct-Object–Preposition–Indirect object (*SVDPI*). By writing the use-case events in this form, it is easier to use the guidelines for textual analysis in Figure 4-1 and the text analysis approaches described in Chapter 3 to identify the objects. Reviewing the primary actors, stakeholders and interests, and brief descriptions of each use case allows additional candidate classes to be identified. It is useful to go back and review the original requirements to look for information that was not included in the text of the use cases. Record all the uncovered information for each candidate object on a CRC card.

The second step is to review the CRC cards to determine if additional candidate classes, attributes, operations, and relationships are missing. In conjunction with this review, using the brainstorming and common object list approaches described earlier can aid the team in identifying missing classes, attributes, operations, and relationships. For example, the team could start a brainstorming session with a set of questions such as:

- What are the tangible things associated with the problem?
- What are the roles played by the people in the problem domain?
- What incidents and interactions take place in the problem domain?

As you can readily see, by beginning with the use-case descriptions, many of these questions already have partial answers. For example, the primary actors and stakeholders are the roles

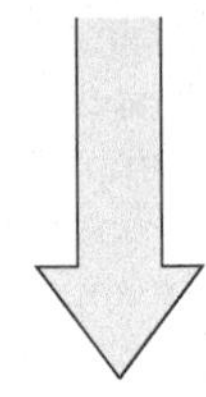

that are played by the people in the problem domain. However, it is possible to uncover additional roles not thought of previously. This obviously would cause the use-case descriptions, and possibly the use-case diagram, to be modified and possibly expanded. As in the previous step, be sure to record all the uncovered information onto the CRC cards. This includes any modifications uncovered for any previously identified candidate classes and any information regarding any new candidate classes identified.

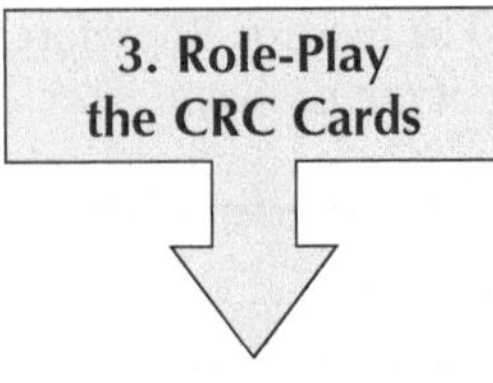
3. Role-Play the CRC Cards

The third step is to role-play each use-case scenario using the CRC cards. Each CRC card should be assigned to an individual who will perform the operations for the class on the CRC card. As the performers act out their roles, the system tends to break down. When this occurs, additional classes, attributes, operations, or relationships will be identified. Again, as in the previous steps, any time any new information is discovered, new CRC cards are created or modifications to existing CRC cards are made.

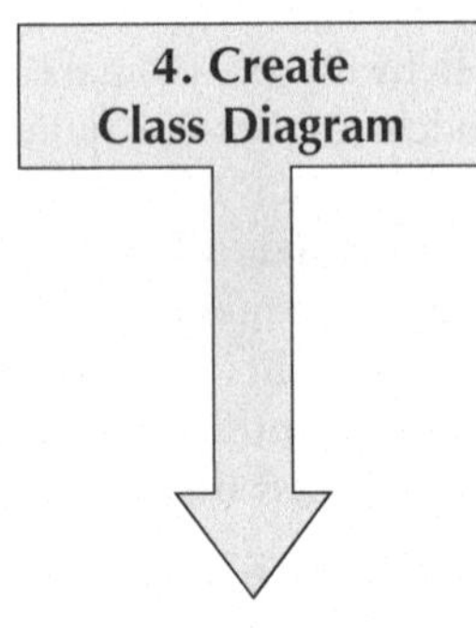
4. Create Class Diagram

The fourth step is to create the class diagram based on the CRC cards. Information contained on the CRC cards is transferred to the class diagrams. The responsibilities are transferred as operations; the attributes are drawn as attributes; and the relationships are drawn as generalization, aggregation, or association relationships. However, the class diagram also requires that the visibility of the attributes and operations be known. As a general rule, attributes are private and operations are public. Therefore, unless the analyst has a good reason to change the default visibility of these properties, then the defaults should be accepted. Finally, the analyst should examine the model for additional opportunities to use aggregation or generalization relationships. These types of relationships can simplify the individual class descriptions. As in the previous steps, all changes must be recorded on the CRC cards.

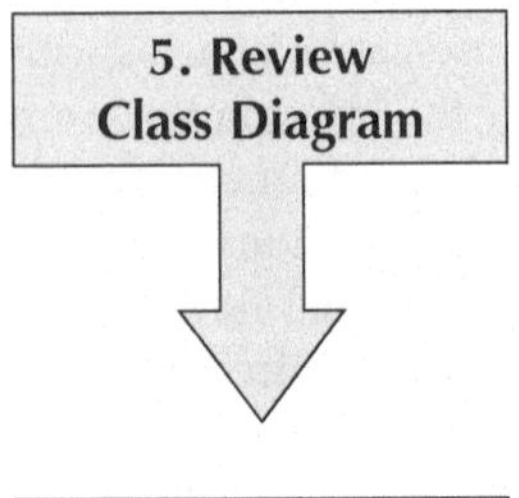
5. Review Class Diagram

The fifth step is to review the structural model for missing and/or unnecessary classes, attributes, operations, and relationships. Until this step, the focus of the process has been on adding information to the evolving model. At this point, the focus begins to switch from simply adding information to also challenging the reasons for including the information contained in the model. One very useful approach here is to play devil's advocate, where a team member, just for the sake of being a pain in the neck, challenges the reasoning for including all aspects of the model.

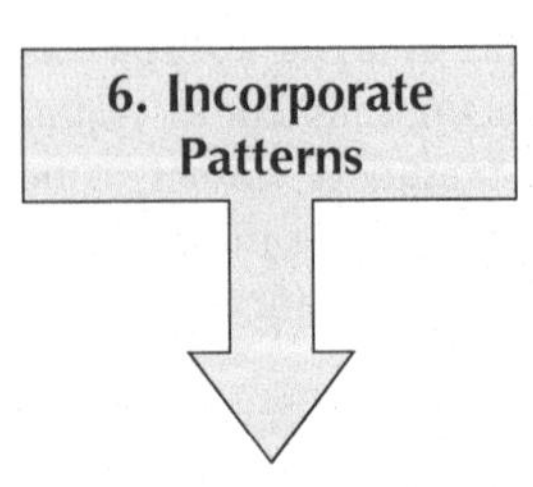
6. Incorporate Patterns

The sixth step is to incorporate useful patterns into the evolving structural model. A useful pattern is one that would allow the analyst to more fully describe the underlying domain of the problem being investigated. Looking at the collection of patterns available (Figures 4-2 and 4-4) and comparing the classes contained in the patterns with those in the evolving class diagram enable this. After identifying the useful patterns, the analyst incorporates the identified patterns into the class diagram and modifies the affected CRC cards. This includes adding and removing classes, attributes, operations, and/or relationships.

7. Review the Model

The seventh and final step is to validate the structural model, including both the CRC cards and the class diagram. We discuss this content in the next section of the chapter and in Chapter 5.

APPLYING THE CHAPTER CONCEPTS

Library Management System Example Based on the results of role-playing the CRC cards, Susan and her team creates and reviews the equivalent class diagram. Based on the modifications that were identified, Susan created a high-level class diagram (Figure 4-19).

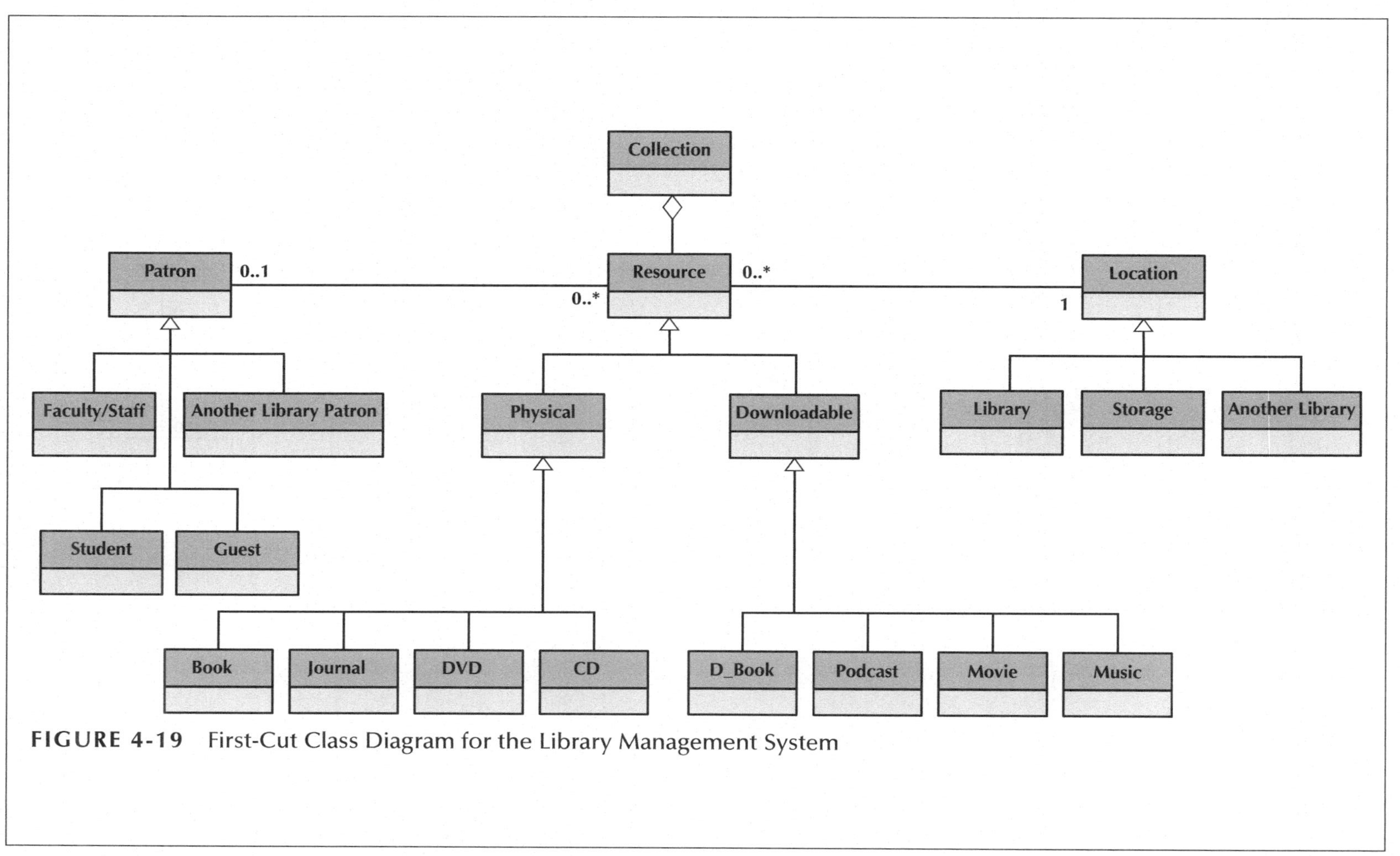

FIGURE 4-19   First-Cut Class Diagram for the Library Management System

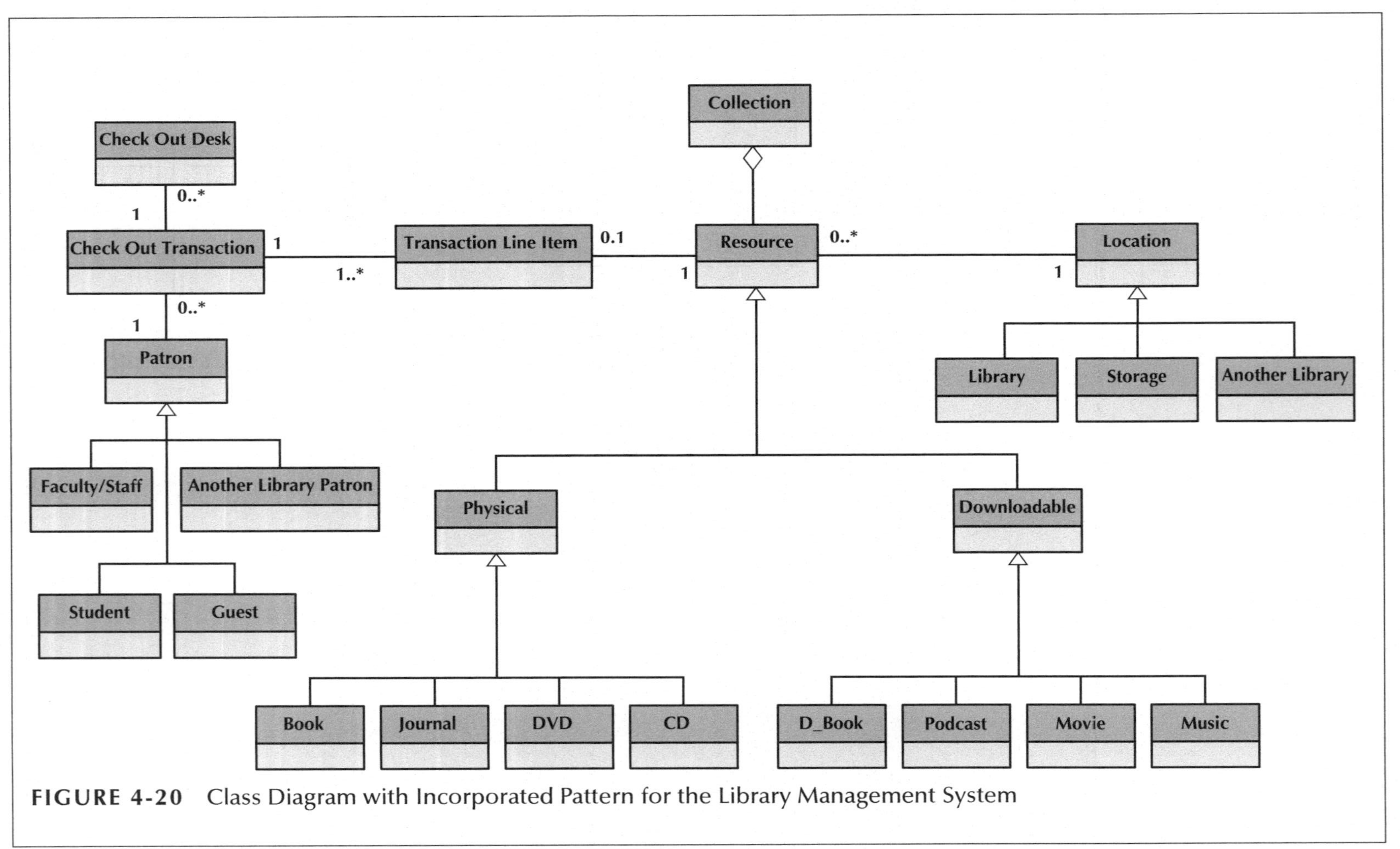

FIGURE 4-20 Class Diagram with Incorporated Pattern for the Library Management System

Once she completed the high-level diagram, she then decided to determine whether any pattern (Figures 4-2 and 4-4) could be applicable. Upon carefully reviewing the patterns, she realized that the transaction pattern (upper left corner of Figure 4-2) was applicable. Consequently, she updated the CRC cards and class diagram (Figure 4-20) to include this useful pattern. Finally, she carefully reviews the model.

Upon updating the CRC cards and class diagram, Susan set up another meeting with Joe so that they could add the details to both the CRC cards and class diagram. Based on the class diagram, Susan realizes that she needs to go back and ask Joe a few more questions. For example, does the system really need the Book, Journal, DVD, CD, D_Book, Podcast, Movie, and Music subclasses? If so, the Get Resource activity probably needs to be specialized into separate activities for each subtype of resource. Also, the current use case does not take into consideration the pattern-based classes that she added: Check-Out Desk, Transaction, and Transaction Line Item. Therefore, she should modify the use case to incorporate them. Finally, Susan wonders whether the extended use cases should be collapsed back into a single use case. Regardless, she realizes that the class diagram in Figure 4-20 and the activity diagram in Figure 4-9 will probably need to be modified again. As she pointed out to Joe in an earlier meeting, developing system is a very iterative and incremental process. So, Susan calls Joe to set up the next meeting.

Campus Housing Service "Your Turn" Exercise Based on the modified CRC cards created in the previous "Your Turn" exercise, create an equivalent class diagram. Don't worry about including any patterns at this time.

VERIFYING AND VALIDATING THE STRUCTURAL MODEL[19]

Before we move on to creating behavioral models (see Chapter 5) of the problem domain, we need to verify and validate the structural model. In the previous chapter, we introduced the notion of walkthroughs as a way to verify and validate business processes and functional models. In this chapter, we combine walkthroughs with the power of role-playing as a way to more completely verify and validate the structural model that will underlie the business processes and functional models. In fact, all of the object identification approaches described in this chapter can be viewed as a way to test the fidelity of the structural model. Because we have already introduced the idea of role-playing the CRC cards and object identification, in this section we focus on performing walkthroughs.

In this case, the verification and validation of the structural model are accomplished during a formal review meeting using a walkthrough approach in which an analyst presents the model to a team of developers and users. The analyst walks through the model, explaining each part of the model and all the reasoning behind the decision to include each of the classes in the structural model. This explanation includes justifications for the attributes, operations, and relationships associated with the classes. Each class should be linked back to at least one use case; otherwise, the purpose of including the class in the structural model will not be understood. Also including people outside the development team who produced the model can bring a fresh perspective to the model and uncover missing objects.

Previously, we suggested three representations that could be used for structural modeling: CRC cards, class diagrams, and object diagrams. Because an object diagram is simply

---

[19] The material in this section has been adapted from E. Yourdon, *Modern Structured Analysis* (Englewood Cliffs, NJ: Prentice Hall, 1989).

an instantiation of some part of a class diagram, we limit our discussion to CRC cards and class diagrams. Similar to how we verified and validated the business process and functional models in the last chapter, we provide a set of rules that will test the consistency within the structural models. For example, we use the appointment problem described in Chapter 3 and in this chapter. An example of the CRC card for the patient class is shown in Figure 4-5, and the associated class diagram is portrayed in Figure 4-11.

First, every CRC card should be associated with a class on the class diagram, and vice versa. In the appointment example, the Patient class represented by the CRC card and on the class diagram (see Figures 4-5 and 4-11) represent the same thing.

Second, the responsibilities listed on the front of the CRC card must be included as operations in a class on a class diagram, and vice versa. The make appointment responsibility on the Patient CRC card also appears as the make appointment() operation in the Patient class on the class diagram. Every responsibility and operation must be checked.

Third, collaborators on the front of the CRC card imply some type of relationship on the back of the CRC card and some type of association that is connected to the associated class on the class diagram. The appointment collaborator on the front of the Patient CRC card also appears as an other association on the back of the CRC card and as an association on the class diagram that connects the Patient class with the Appointment class.

Fourth, attributes listed on the back of the CRC card must be included as attributes in a class on a class diagram, and vice versa. For example, the amount attribute on the Patient CRC card is included in the attribute list of the Patient class on the class diagram.

Fifth, the relationships included on the back of the CRC card must be portrayed using the appropriate notation on the class diagram. For example, in Figure 4-5, instances of the Patient class are *a-kind-of* Person, it has instances of the Medical History class as part of it, and it has an association with instances of the Appointment class. Thus, the association from the Patient class to the Person class should indicate that the Person class is a generalization of its subclasses, including the Patient class; the association from the Patient class to the Medical History class should be in the form of an aggregation association (a white diamond); and the association between instances of the Patient class and instances of the Appointment class should be a simple association. However, when we review the class diagram in Figure 4-11, this is not what we find. If you recall, we included in the class diagram the transaction pattern portrayed in Figure 4-3. When we did this, many changes were made to the classes contained in the class diagram. All of these changes should have been cascaded back through all of the CRC cards. In this case, the CRC card for the Patient class should show that a Patient is a-kind-of Participant (not Person) and that the relationship from Patient to Medical History should be a simple association (see Figure 4-21).

Sixth, an association class, such as the Treatment class in Figure 4-11, should be created only if there is indeed some unique characteristic (attribute, operation, or relationship) about the intersection of the connecting classes. If no unique characteristic exists, then the association class should be removed and only an association between the two connecting classes should be displayed.

Finally, as in the functional models, specific representation rules must be enforced. For example, a class cannot be a subclass of itself. The Patient CRC card cannot list Patient with the generalization relationships on the back of the CRC card, nor can a generalization relationship be drawn from the Patient class to itself. Again, all the detailed restrictions for each representation are beyond the scope of this book.[20]

---

[20] A good reference for these types of restrictions is S.W. Ambler, *The Elements of UML 2.0 Style* (Cambridge, UK: Cambridge University Press, 2005).

Front:

Class Name: Patient	**ID:** 3	**Type:** Concrete, Domain
Description: An individual who needs to receive or has received medical attention.		**Associated Use Cases:** 2

Responsibilities	**Collaborators**
Make appointment	Appointment
Calculate last visit	
Change status	
Provide medical history	Medical history

Back:

Attributes:
Amount
Insurance carrier

Relationships:
Generalization (a-kind-of): Participant

Aggregation (has-parts):

Other Associations: Appointment, Medical History

FIGURE 4-21
Patient CRC Card

Balancing Functional and Structural Models

To balance the functional and structural models, we must ensure that the two sets of models are consistent with each other. That is, the activity diagrams, use-case descriptions, and use-case diagrams must agree with the CRC cards and class diagrams that represent the evolving model of the problem domain. In this case, there are four sets of associations between the models. This gives us a place to begin balancing the functional and structural models.[21]

First, every class on a class diagram and every CRC card must be associated with at least one use case, and vice versa. For example, the CRC card portrayed in Figure 4-21 and its related class contained in the class diagram (see Figure 4-11) are associated with the Manage Appointments use case described in Figure 4-8.

---

[21] Role-playing the CRC cards also can be very useful in verifying and validating the relationships among the functional and structural models.

Front:

Class Name: Appointment	ID: 5	Type: Concrete, Domain
Description: A scheduled appointment between a patient and a doctor		Associated Use Cases: 5

Responsibilities	Collaborators
Cancel without notice	
Create appointment	
Cancel appointment	
Change appointment	

Back:

Attributes:

time
date
reason

Relationships:

Generalization (a-kind-of): _______________

Aggregation (has-parts): _______________

Other Associations: Entry, Transaction Line Item, Place, Patient, Doctor

FIGURE 4-22
Appointment CRC
Card

Second, every activity or action contained in a class-based swimlane of an activity diagram (see Figure 4-7) and every event contained in a use-case description (see Figure 4-8) should be related to a single responsibility on a CRC card and a single operation in a class on a class diagram and vice versa. For example, the Create Appointment activity on the example activity diagram (see Figure 4-7) and the create appointment events (S-1 3 and S-2 3) on the use-case description (see Figure 4-8) should be associated with a create appointment responsibility on the CRC card (see Figure 4-22) and a create() operation in the Appointment class on the class diagram (see Figure 4-11). However, with regards to the class diagram, there is no create operation. In this case, to keep the complexity of the diagram under control, we did not show the simple create, read, update, or delete operations.

Third, every object node on an activity diagram must be associated with an instance of a class on a class diagram (i.e., an object) and a CRC card or an attribute contained in a class and on a CRC card.

Fourth, every attribute and association/aggregation relationships contained on a CRC card (and connected to a class on a class diagram) should be related to the subject or object of an event in a use-case description. For example, in Figure 4-8, the third event states: The Patient provides the Receptionist with preferred appointment times. By reviewing the CRC card in Figure 4-22 and the class diagram in Figure 4-11, we see that the Appointment class includes attributes for time and date.

CHAPTER REVIEW

After reading and studying this chapter, you should be able to:

- [ ] Describe the purpose of a structural model.
- [ ] Describe the different elements of a structural model.
- [ ] Explain the difference between abstract and concrete classes.
- [ ] Describe the three general types of relationships typically used in a structural model.
- [ ] Create a structural model using textual analysis of use-case descriptions, brainstorming, common object lists, and patterns.
- [ ] Explain the purpose of a CRC card in structural modeling.
- [ ] Create a structural model using CRC cards.
- [ ] Describe the different elements of a CRC card.
- [ ] Describe how to role-play CRC cards using use-case scenarios.
- [ ] Describe how to document role playing CRC cards with activity diagrams with swimlanes.
- [ ] Describe the different elements of a class diagram.
- [ ] Describe the four basic operations that can be represented on a class diagram.
- [ ] Explain the differences between the types of relationships supported on a class diagram.
- [ ] Create a class diagram that represents a structural model.
- [ ] Describe the different elements of an object diagram.
- [ ] Create an object diagram that represents an instantiation of a portion of a class diagram.
- [ ] Verify and validate the evolving structural model using role-playing and walkthroughs.
- [ ] Verify and validate the structural model by ensuring the consistency of the CRC cards and class diagram.
- [ ] Verify and validate both the structural and functional models by balancing the two sets of models.

KEY TERMS

A-kind-of	Constructor operation	Multiplicity	Static model
A-part-of	Contract	Object	Static structure diagram
Abstract class	Class–Responsibility–	Object diagram	Structural model
Activity diagram	Collaboration (CRC)	Operation	Subclass
Aggregation association	CRC cards	Package	Substitutability
Assemblies	Decomposition	Parts	Superclass
Association	Derived attribute	Pattern	SVDPI
Association class	Doing responsibility	Private attribute	Swimlanes
Attribute	Destructor operation	Protected attribute	Tangible things
Brainstorming	Domain classes	Public attribute	Text analysis
Class	Generalization association	Query operation	Update operation
Class diagram	Has-parts	Responsibility	View
Client	Information hiding	Role-playing	Visibility
Collaboration	Instance	Roles	Wholes
Common object list	Instantiation	Server	
Conceptual model	Knowing responsibility	Specialization	
Concrete class	Method	State	

QUESTIONS

1. Describe to a businessperson the multiplicity of a relationship between two classes.
2. Describe how the use of activity diagrams with swimlanes are helpful in behavioral modeling.
3. How does a use case relate to an activity diagram?
4. How does a use case scenario relate to an activity diagram?
5. Why are assumptions important to a structural model?
6. What is an association class?
7. Contrast the following sets of terms: object, class, method, attribute, superclass, subclass, concrete class, abstract class.
8. Give three examples of derived attributes that may exist on a class diagram. How would they be denoted on the class diagram?
9. What are the different types of visibility? How would they be denoted on a class diagram?
10. Draw the relationships that are described by the following business rules. Include the multiplicities for each relationship.

   A patient must be assigned to only one doctor, and a doctor can have one or many patients.

   An employee has one phone extension, and a unique phone extension is assigned to an employee.

   A movie theater shows at least one movie, and a movie can be shown at up to four other movie theaters around town.

   A movie either has one star, two costars, or more than ten people starring together. A star must be in at least one movie.

11. How do you designate the reading direction of a relationship on a class diagram?
12. For what is an association class used in a class diagram? Give an example of an association class that may be found in a class diagram that captures students and the courses that they have taken.
13. Give two examples of aggregation, generalization, and association relationships. How is each type of association depicted on a class diagram?
14. Identify the following operations as constructor, query, or update. Which operations would not need to be shown in the class rectangle?

   Calculate employee raise (raise percent)
   Calculate sick days ()
   Increment number of employee vacation days ()
   Locate employee name ()
   Place request for vacation (vacation day)
   Find employee address ()
   Insert employee ()
   Change employee address ()
   Insert spouse ()

15. How are the different structural models related, and how does this affect verification and validation of the model?
16. How are the different structural models related to the different functional models, and how does this affect verification and validation of the models?

EXERCISES

A. Create a CRC card for each of the following classes: Movie (title, producer, length, director, and genre) Ticket (price, adult or child, showtime, and movie) Patron (name, adult or child, and age)
B. Create a class diagram based on the CRC cards you created for exercise A.
C. Create a CRC card for each of the following classes. Consider that the entities represent a system for a patient billing system. Include only the attributes that would be appropriate for this context. Patient (age, name, hobbies, blood type, occupation, insurance carrier, address, phone) Insurance carrier (name, number of patients on plan, address, contact name, phone) Doctor (specialty, provider identification number, golf handicap, age, phone, name)
D. Create a class diagram based on the CRC cards you created for exercise C.
E. Draw a class diagram for each of the following situations:
   1. Whenever new patients are seen for the first time, they complete a patient information form that asks their name, address, phone number, and insurance carrier, which are stored in the patient

information file. Patients can be signed up with only one carrier, but they must be signed up to be seen by the doctor. Each time a patient visits the doctor, an insurance claim is sent to the carrier for payment. The claim must contain information about the visit, such as the date, purpose, and cost. It would be possible for a patient to submit two claims on the same day.

2. The state of Georgia is interested in designing a system that will track its researchers. Information of interest includes researcher name, title, position, researcher's university name, university location, university enrollment, and researcher's research interests. Researchers are associated with one institution, and each researcher has several research interests.

3. A department store has a wedding registry. This registry keeps information about the customer (usually the bride), the products that the store carries, and the products for which each customer registers. Customers typically register for a large number of products, and many customers register for the same products.

4. Jim Smith's dealership sells Fords, Hondas, and Toyotas. In order to get in touch with these manufacturers easily, the dealership keeps information about each of them. The dealership keeps information about the models of cars from each manufacturer, including dealer price, model name, and series (e.g., Honda, Civic, LX). Additionally, the dealership also keeps all sales information, including buyer's name, address and phone number, car purchased, and amount paid.

F. Examine the class diagrams that you created for exercise E. How would the models change (if at all) based on these new assumptions?

1. Two patients have the same first and last names.
2. Researchers can be associated with more than one institution.
3. The store would like to keep track of purchase items.
4. Many buyers have purchased multiple cars from Jim over time because he is such a good dealer.

G. Visit a website that allows customers to order a product over the Web (e.g., Amazon.com). Create a structural model (CRC cards and class diagram) that the site must need to support its business process. Include classes to show what they need information about. Be sure to include the attributes and operations to represent the type of information they use and create. Finally, draw relationships, making assumptions about how the classes are related.

H. Using the seven-step process described in this chapter, create a structural model (CRC cards and class diagram) for exercise C in Chapter 3.

I. Perform a verification and validation walkthrough for the structural model created for exercise H.

J. Using the seven-step process described in this chapter, create a structural model for exercise E in Chapter 3.

K. Perform a verification and validation walkthrough for the structural model created for exercise J.

L. Using the seven-step process described in this chapter, create a structural model for exercise G in Chapter 3.

M. Perform a verification and validation walkthrough for the structural model created for exercise L.

N. Using the seven-step process described in this chapter, create a structural model for A Real Estate Inc. problem in exercise I in Chapter 3.

O. Perform a verification and validation walkthrough for the structural model created for exercise N.

P. Using the seven-step process described in this chapter, create a structural model for the A Video Store problem in exercise L in Chapter 3.

Q. Perform a verification and validation walkthrough for the structural model created for exercise P.

R. Using the seven-step process described in this chapter, create a structural model for the gym membership problem in exercise O in Chapter 3.

S. Perform a verification and validation walkthrough for the structural model created for exercise R.

T. Using the seven-step process described in this chapter, create a structural model for the Picnics R Us problem in exercise R in Chapter 3.

U. Perform a verification and validation walkthrough for the structural model created for exercise T.

V. Using the seven-step process described in this chapter, create a structural model for Of-the-Month-Club problem in exercise U in Chapter 3.

W. Perform a verification and validation walkthrough for the structural model created for exercise V.

MINICASES

1. West Star Marinas is a chain of twelve marinas that offer lakeside service to boaters; service and repair of boats, motors, and marine equipment; and sales of boats, motors, and other marine accessories. The systems development project team at West Star Marinas has been hard at work on a project that eventually will link all the marina's facilities into one unified, networked system.

   The project team has developed a use-case diagram of the current system. This model has been carefully checked. Last week, the team invited a number of system users to role-play the various use cases, and the use cases were refined to the users' satisfaction. Right now, the project manager feels confident that the as-is system has been adequately represented in the use-case diagram.

   The director of operations for West Star is the sponsor of this project. He sat in on the role-playing of the use cases and was very pleased by the thorough job the team had done in developing the model. He made it clear to you, the project manager, that he was anxious to see your team begin work on the use cases for the to-be system. He was a little skeptical that it was necessary for your team to spend any time modeling the current system in the first place but grudgingly admitted that the team really seemed to understand the business after going through that work.

   The methodology you are following, however, specifies that the team should now turn its attention to developing the structural models for the as-is system. When you stated this to the project sponsor, he seemed confused and a little irritated. "You are going to spend even more time looking at the current system? I thought you were done with that! Why is this necessary? I want to see some progress on the way things will work in the future!"

   What is your response to the director of operations? Why do we perform structural modeling? Is there any benefit to developing a structural model of the current system at all? How do the use cases and use-case diagram help us develop the structural model?

2. Holiday Travel Vehicles sells new recreational vehicles and travel trailers. When new vehicles arrive at Holiday Travel Vehicles, a new vehicle record is created. Included in the new vehicle record are a vehicle serial number, name, model, year, manufacturer, and base cost.

   When a customer arrives at Holiday Travel Vehicles, he or she works with a salesperson to negotiate a vehicle purchase. When a purchase has been agreed upon, a sales invoice is completed by the salesperson.

The invoice summarizes the purchase, including full customer information, information on the trade-in vehicle (if any), the trade-in allowance, and information on the purchased vehicle. If the customer requests dealer-installed options, they are listed on the invoice as well. The invoice also summarizes the final negotiated price, plus any applicable taxes and license fees. The transaction concludes with a customer signature on the sales invoice.

   a. Identify the classes described in the preceding scenario (you should find six). Create CRC cards for each class.

   Customers are assigned a customer ID when they make their first purchase from Holiday Travel Vehicles. Name, address, and phone number are recorded for the customer. The trade-in vehicle is described by a serial number, make, model, and year. Dealer-installed options are described by an option code, description, and price.

   b. Develop a list of attributes for each class. Place the attributes onto the CRC cards.

   Each invoice lists just one customer. A person does not become a customer until he or she purchases a vehicle. Over time, a customer may purchase a number of vehicles from Holiday Travel Vehicles.

   Every invoice must be filled out by only one salesperson. A new salesperson might not have sold any vehicles, but experienced salespeople have probably sold many vehicles.

   Each invoice only lists one new vehicle. If a new vehicle in inventory has not been sold, there will be no invoice for it. Once the vehicle sells, there will be just one invoice for it.

   A customer may decide to have no options added to the vehicle or may choose to add many options. An option may be listed on no invoices, or it may be listed on many invoices.

   A customer may trade in no more than one vehicle on a purchase of a new vehicle. The trade-in vehicle may be sold to another customer who later trades it in on another Holiday Travel vehicle.

   c. Based on the preceding business rules in force at Holiday Travel Vehicles and CRC cards, draw a class diagram and document the relationships with the appropriate multiplicities. Remember to update the CRC cards.

CHAPTER 5

BEHAVIORAL MODELING

Behavioral models describe the internal dynamic aspects of an information system that supports the business processes in an organization. During analysis, behavioral models describe what the internal logic of the processes is without specifying how the processes are to be implemented. Later, in the design and implementation phases, the detailed design of the operations contained in the object is fully specified. In this chapter, we describe two Unified Modeling Language (UML) diagrams that are used in behavioral modeling (sequence diagrams and behavioral state machines) and CRUDE (create, read, update, delete, execute) matrices.

OBJECTIVES

- Understand the rules and style guidelines for sequence diagrams and behavioral state machines.
- Understand the processes used to create sequence diagrams, CRUDE matrices, and behavioral state machines.
- Understand how to verify and validate the behavioral models.
- Understand how to balance the behavioral models with the functional and structural models.

INTRODUCTION

The previous two chapters discussed how analysts create both business process and functional models and structural models. Systems analysts use business process and functional models to describe the functional or external behavioral view of an information system. And, they use structural models to depict the internal structural or static view of an information system. In this chapter, we discuss how analysts use *behavioral models* to represent the internal behavior or dynamic view of an information system.

By supporting all three views (functional, structural, and behavioral), object-oriented systems analysis and design supports an architecture-centric approach to developing information systems. Furthermore, the behavioral view is driven by the original use cases uncovered during business process and functional modeling. As such, behavioral modeling is also use case driven. Finally, as with business process and functional modeling and structural modeling, you will find that you will need to not only iterate across the behavioral models (described in this chapter), but you will also have to iterate across all three architectural views (functional, structural, and behavioral) to capture and represent the requirements for a business information system.

There are two types of behavioral models. First, there are behavioral models used to represent the underlying details of a business process portrayed by a use-case model. In UML, activity (see Chapters 3 and 4) and sequence diagrams are used for this type of behavioral model. Practically speaking, these interaction diagrams allow the analyst to model the distribution of the behavior of the system over the actors and objects in the system. In this way, we can easily see how actors and objects collaborate to provide the functionality defined in a use case. Second, a behavioral model is used to represent the changes that occur in the underlying data. UML uses behavioral state machines for this.

During analysis, analysts use behavioral models to capture a basic understanding of the dynamic aspects of the underlying business process. Traditionally, behavioral models have been used primarily during design, where analysts refine the behavioral models to include implementation details (see Chapter 7). For now, our focus is on *what* the dynamic view of the evolving system is and not on *how* the dynamic aspect of the system will be implemented.

In this chapter, we concentrate on creating behavioral models of the underlying business process. Using the sequence diagrams and behavioral state machines, it is possible to give a complete view of the dynamic aspects of the evolving business information system. We first describe behavioral models and their components. We then describe each of the diagrams, how they are created, and how they are related to the functional and structural models described in Chapters 3 and 4. Finally, we describe CRUDE analysis and the process to verify and validate the behavioral models.

BEHAVIORAL MODELS

When an analyst is attempting to understand the underlying application domain of a problem, he or she must consider both structural and behavioral aspects of the problem. Unlike other approaches to the development of information systems, object-oriented approaches attempt to view the underlying application domain in a holistic manner. By viewing the problem domain as a set of *use cases* that are supported by a set of collaborating objects, object-oriented approaches allow an analyst to minimize the semantic gap between the real-world set of objects and the evolving object-oriented model of the problem domain. However, as we pointed out in the previous chapter, the real world tends to be messy; since software must be logical to work, perfect modeling of the application domain is nearly impossible.

One of the primary purposes of *behavioral models* is to show how the underlying objects in a problem domain will work together to form a *collaboration* to support each of the *use cases*. Whereas structural models represent the objects and the relationships between them, behavioral models depict the internal view of the business process that a use case describes. The process can be shown by the interaction that takes place between the objects that collaborate to support a use case through the use of activity (see Chapters 3 and 4) and sequence diagrams. It is also possible to show the effect that the set of use cases that make up the system has on the objects in the system through the use of behavioral state machines.

Creating behavioral models is an iterative process that iterates not only over the individual behavioral models, but also over the functional (see Chapter 3) and structural (see Chapter 4) models. As the behavioral models are created, it is not unusual to make changes to the functional and structural models. In this chapter, we describe behavioral modeling using sequence diagrams, CRUDE analysis, and behavioral state machines.

INTERACTION DIAGRAMS

One of the primary differences between class diagrams and interaction diagrams, besides the obvious difference that one describes structure and the other behavior, is that the modeling focus on a class diagram is at the class level, whereas the interaction diagrams focus on the object level. In this section, we review objects, operations, and messages and we cover the sequence diagrams that can be used to model the interactions that take place between the objects in an information system.

Objects, Operations, and Messages

An object is an instantiation of a *class,* i.e., an actual person, place, or thing about which we want to capture information. If we were building an appointment system for a doctor's office, classes might include doctor, patient, and appointment. The specific patients, such as Jim Maloney, Vijay Sarkar, and Theresa Marks, are considered objects—i.e., *instances* of the patient class.

Each object has *attributes* that describe information about the object, such as a patient's name, birth date, address, and phone number. Each object also has *behaviors*. At this point in the development of the evolving system, the behaviors are described by *operations*. An operation is an action that an object can perform. For example, an appointment object can probably schedule a new appointment, delete an appointment, and locate the next available appointment. Later during the development of the evolving system, the operations will be implemented as *methods*.

Each object also can send and receive messages. *Messages* are information sent to objects to tell an object to execute one of its operations. Essentially, a message is a function or procedure call from one object to another object. For example, if a patient is new to the doctor's office, the system sends an insert message to the application. The patient object receives the instruction (the message) and does what it needs to do to insert the new patient into the system (the behavior).

Sequence Diagrams

Like an activity diagram with swimlanes, *sequence diagrams* illustrate the actors and objects that collaborate in a use case and the messages that pass between them over time for *one* use case. A *sequence diagram* is a *dynamic model* that shows the explicit sequence of messages that are passed between objects in a defined interaction.

The sequence diagram can be a *generic sequence diagram* that shows all possible scenarios[1] for a use case, but usually each analyst develops a set of *instance sequence diagrams*, each of which depicts a single *scenario* within the use case. The diagrams are used throughout the analysis and design phases. However, the design diagrams are very implementation specific, often including database objects or specific user interface components as the objects.

Elements of a Sequence Diagram Figure 5-1 shows an instance sequence diagram that depicts the objects and messages for the Manage Appointments use case. This diagram describes the scenario where an existing patient creates a new appointment for the doctor's office appointment system. This scenario is based on the activity diagram in Figure 4-6.

Actors and *objects* that participate in the sequence are placed across the top of the diagram using actor symbols and object symbols (see Figure 5-2). Notice that the *actors* and objects in Figure 5-1 are aPatient, aReceptionist, and Appointment.[2] For each of the objects, the name of the class of which they are an instance is given after the object's name, e.g., anAppointment means that anApointment is an instance of the Appointment class (see Figure 5-3).

---

[1] Remember that a scenario is a single executable path through a use case. Or, it is an instance of the use case.

[2] In some versions of the sequence diagram, object symbols are used as surrogates for the actors. However, for clarity, we recommend using actor symbols for actors instead.

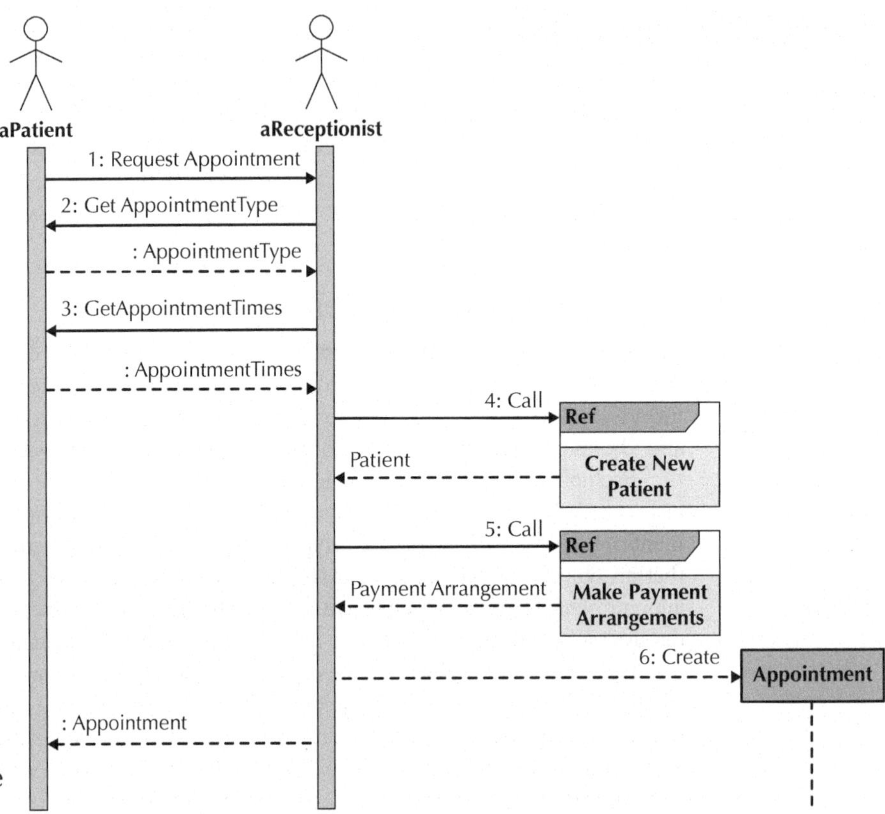

FIGURE 5-1 Example Sequence Diagram

A dotted line runs vertically below each actor and object to denote the *lifeline* of the actors and objects over time (see Figure 5-1).[3] Sometimes an object creates a *temporary object*; in this case, an X is placed at the end of the lifeline at the point where the object is destroyed (not shown). For example, think about a shopping cart object for a Web commerce application. The shopping cart is used for temporarily capturing line items for an order, but once the order is confirmed, the shopping cart is no longer needed. In this case, an X would be located at the point at which the shopping cart object is destroyed. When objects continue to exist in the system after they are used in the sequence diagram, then the lifeline continues to the bottom of the diagram (this is the case with all of the objects in Figure 5-1).

A thin rectangular box, called the *execution occurrence*, is overlaid onto the lifeline to show when the classes are sending and receiving messages (see Figure 5-2). A *message* is a communication between objects that conveys information with the expectation that activity will ensue. Many different types of messages can be portrayed on a sequence diagram. However, in the case of using sequence diagrams to model use cases, two types of messages are typically used: operation call and return. *Operation call messages* passed between objects are shown using solid lines connecting two objects with an arrow on the line showing which way the message is being passed. Argument values for the message are placed in parentheses next to the message's name. The order of messages goes from the top to the bottom of the page, so messages located higher on the diagram represent messages that occur earlier on in the sequence, versus the lower messages that occur later. A *return message* is depicted as a dashed line with an arrow on the end of the line portraying the direction of the return.

---

[3] Technically speaking, in UML 2.0 the lifeline actually refers to both the object (actor) and the dashed line drawn vertically underneath the object (actor). However, we prefer to use the older terminology because it is more descriptive of what is actually being represented.

Term and Definition	Symbol
An actor: ■ is a person or system that derives benefit from and is external to the system. ■ participates in a sequence by sending and/or receiving messages. ■ is placed across the top of the diagram. ■ is depicted either as a stick figure (default) or, if a nonhuman actor is involved, as a rectangle with <<actor>> in it (alternative).	**anActor** **<<actor>>** **anActor**
An object: ■ participates in a sequence by sending and/or receiving messages. ■ is placed across the top of the diagram.	**anObject : aClass**
A lifeline: ■ denotes the life of an object during a sequence. ■ contains an X at the point at which the class no longer interacts.	
An execution occurrence: ■ is a long narrow rectangle placed atop a lifeline. ■ denotes when an object is sending or receiving messages.	
A message: ■ conveys information from one object to another one. ■ a operation call is labeled with the message being sent and a solid arrow, whereas a return is labeled with the value being returned and shown as a dashed arrow.	aMessage() ReturnValue
A guard condition: ■ represents a test that must be met for the message to be sent.	[aGuardCondition]:aMessage()
For object destruction: ■ an X is placed at the end of an object's lifeline to show that it is going out of existence.	X
A frame: ■ indicates the context of the sequence diagram.	Context

FIGURE 5-2 Sequence Diagram Syntax

The information being returned is used to label the arrow. However, because adding return messages tends to clutter the diagram, unless the return messages add non-obvious information to the diagram, they can be omitted. In Figure 5-1, RequestAppointment is a message sent from the actor aPatient to the actor aReceptionist.

At times a message is sent only if a *condition* is met. The condition is placed in front of the message name. In those cases, the condition is placed between a set of brackets, [ ], e.g., [aPatient Exists] LookupBills() shows that the LookupBills operation is to only be executed if the [aPatient Exists] condition is satisfied. However, when using a sequence diagram to model a specific scenario, conditions are not shown on any single sequence diagram. Instead, conditions are implied only through the existence of different sequence diagrams.

An object can send a message to itself. This is known as *self-delegation*. However, at this point in the evolution of the system requirements, self-delegation is typically ignored. Sometimes, an object is created. For example, in Figure 5-1 the aReceptionist actor sends a Create message to the Appointment class. This is shown by the message being sent directly to the object instead of its lifeline. Also, given that the message is "creating" a new object, there is no object name.

Figure 5-3 portrays two additional examples of instance-specific sequence diagrams. Both represent two different scenarios for the Manage Appointments use case portrayed on the activity diagram in Figure 4-6. In both examples, the diagrams simply represent a single scenario. From a learning point of view, you should be able to see how the sequence diagrams and the activity diagrams relate to one another.

Some use cases call other use cases using the extend and include relationship types. In those cases, we need to show the call to the other use case in the related sequence diagram. For example, the Manage Appointments use case (Figure 3-11) calls or executes the Make Payment Arrangements and the Create New Patient use cases via the extend relationship that points from the parent use case to the two child use cases. To portray this correctly in a sequence diagram requires us to use the frame symbol for each of the two child use cases and to send a call or execute message to the frame. In Figure 5-1, aReceptionist actor sends the Call message to each of the two child use cases.

Some use cases contain iterative processes in which a loop should be modeled (see Figures A1-11 in the Chapter 1 Appendix). For example, Figure 5-4 portrays a sequence diagram that portrays the process that a course registration system might need to model. In this case, the student makes a set of course requests to a registration manager that iterates over a set of classes that are available to enable the student to add courses to their course request. Again, like the previous sequence diagram this is an instant-specific diagram that only portrays the situation in which the courses are available. Notice that the frame not only includes the loop label, but it also includes the condition that terminates the loop: while more courses to request. Other versions of this diagram would be required to portray the situation when a course is not available. For example, the student request could be put onto a waiting list for the courses that were not currently available.

Guidelines for Creating Sequence Diagrams Scott W. Ambler[4] provides a set of guidelines when drawing sequence diagrams. In this section, we review six of them.

- Try to have the messages not only in a top-to-bottom order but also, when possible, in a left-to-right order. If you work in a culture (e.g., Western) that reads left to right and top to bottom, a sequence diagram is much easier to interpret if the messages are ordered as much as possible in the same way. To accomplish this, order the actors and objects along the top of the diagram in the order that they participate in the scenario of the use case. (Naturally, if your development occurs in the culture that reads right to left, such as in Arabic countries, consider the reverse order).

---

[4] S.W. Ambler, *The Elements of UML 2.0 Style* (Cambridge, England: Cambridge University Press, 2005).

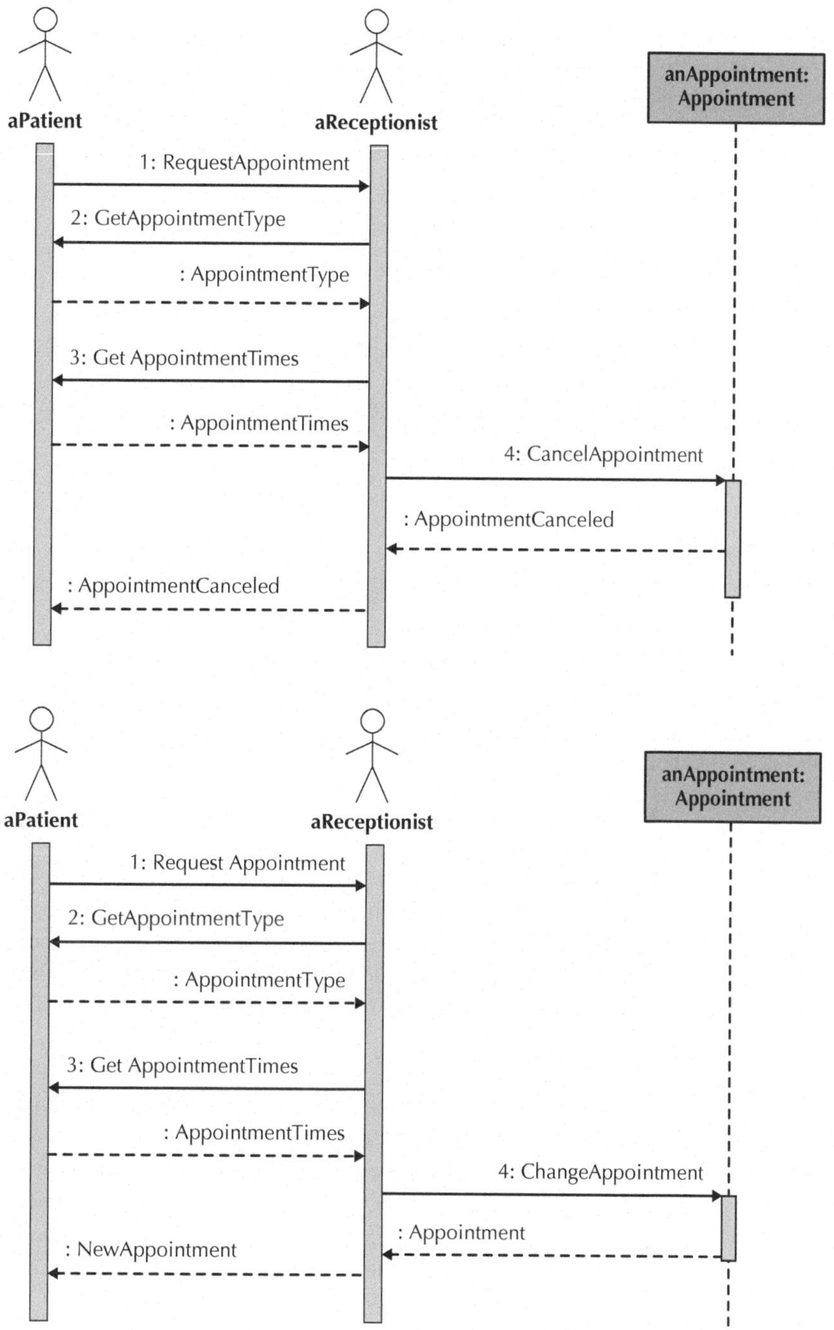

FIGURE 5-3
Additional Sample Instance-Specific Sequence Diagrams

- If an actor and an object conceptually represent the same idea, one inside of the software and the other outside, label them with the same name. In fact, this implies that they exist in both the use-case diagram (as an actor) and in the class diagram (as a class). At first glance, this might seem to lead to confusion. However, if they do indeed represent the same idea, then they should have the same name. For example, a customer actor interacts with the system and the system stores information about the customer. In this case, they do indeed represent the same conceptual idea.

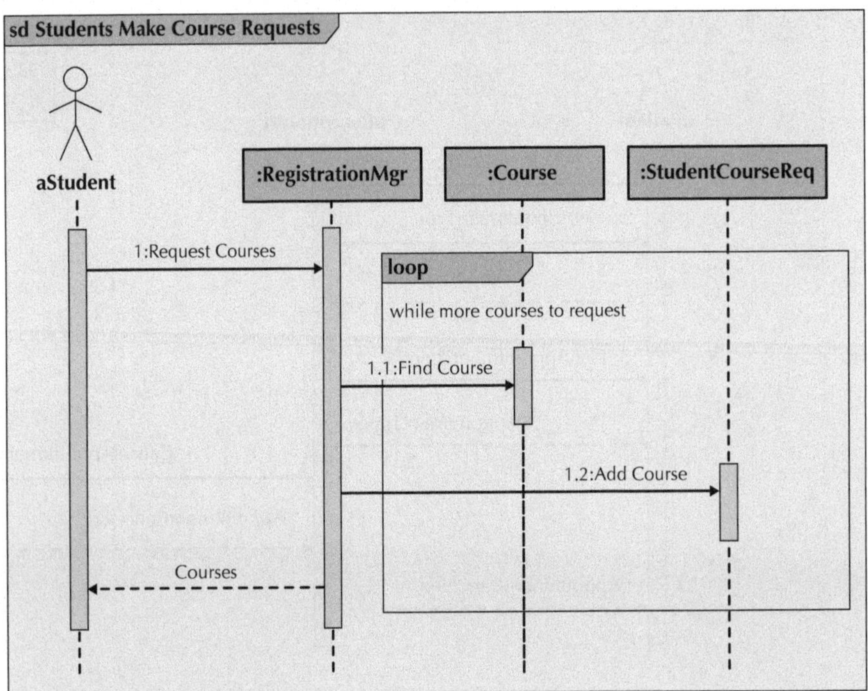

FIGURE 5-4 Example of an Instance-Specific Sequence Diagram that Portrays an Iterative Process

- The initiator of the scenario—actor or object—should be the drawn as the farthest left item in the diagram. This guideline is essentially a specialization of the first guideline. In this case, it relates specifically to the actor or object that triggers the scenario.

- Technically, when sending a message to an object-based lifeline, it is better to include a name for the object in addition to the class of the object. For example, in Figure 5-3, see the anAppointment lifeline. Another option is to simply place a colon in front of the class name instead (see Figure 5-4).

- Show return values only when they are not obvious. Showing all of the returns tends to make a sequence diagram more complex and potentially difficult to comprehend. In many cases, less is more. Only show the returns that actually add information for the reader of the diagram. In our examples in Figures 5-1 and 5-3, we chose to show the returns. This was done to make sure that you see how returns are portrayed. But, since the returns are quite obvious in these examples, there is no need to include them.

- Justify message names and return values near the arrowhead of the message and return arrows, respectively (see Figures 5-1, 5-3, and 5-4). This makes it much easier to interpret the messages and their return values.

Creating a Sequence Diagram

In this section, we describe a six-step process used to create a sequence diagram.[5]

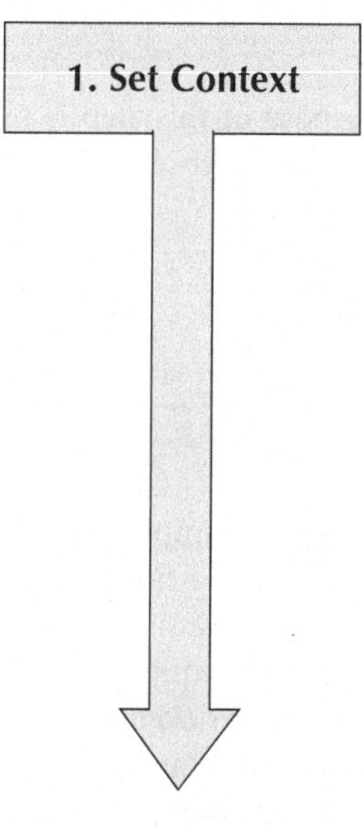

The first step in the process is to determine the context of the sequence diagram. The context of the diagram can be a system, a use case, or a scenario of a use case. The context of the *diagram* is depicted as a labeled *frame* around the diagram (see Figure 5-4). In most cases, it is one use-case scenario. Figure 5-1 portrays an instance-specific sequence diagram for the scenario from the Manage Appointments use case (Figures 3-13 and 4-6) for making an appointment for a new patient. For each possible scenario for the Manage Appointments use case, a separate instance-specific sequence diagram would be created (see Figure 5-3). On the surface, this seems to be a lot of potentially redundant and useless work. However, at this point in the representation of a system, we are still trying to completely understand the problem. This process of creating instance-specific sequence diagrams for each scenario instead of creating a single generic sequence diagram for the entire use case will enable the developers to attain a more complete understanding of the problem being addressed. For example, the instance sequence diagram in Figure 5-1 is much simpler than the activity diagram in Figure 4-6. Each instance-specific sequence diagram is fairly simple to interpret, whereas a generic sequence diagram can be very complex. The testing of a specific use case is accomplished in a much easier manner by validating and verifying the completeness of the set of instance-specific sequence diagrams instead of trying to work through a single complex generic sequence diagram.

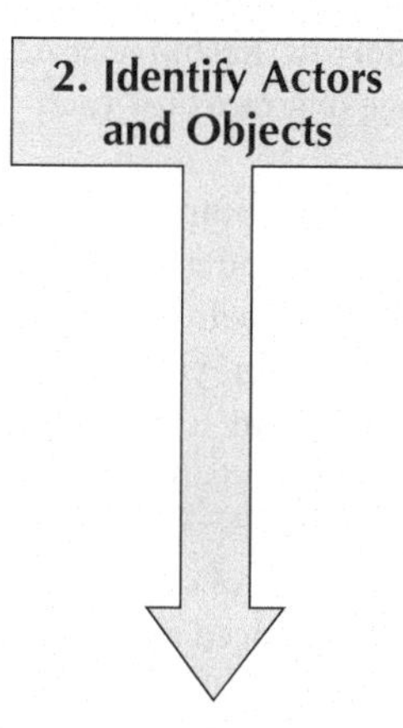

The second step is to identify the actors and objects that participate in the sequence being modeled, i.e., the actors and objects that interact with each other during the use-case scenario. Given that swimlanes were added to the original activity diagram (see Figures 3-7 and 4-16), the actors and objects have already been identified. However, if you *have* not already done so, a very useful approach to identifying all of the scenarios associated with a use case is to role-play the *CRC cards* (see Chapter 4). This can help you identify potentially missing operations that are necessary to support the business process, which the use case is representing, in a complete manner. Also, during role-playing, it is likely that modifications to both the structural model (CRC cards and class diagram) and the functional model (use-case diagram, activity diagrams, and use-case descriptions) will be required. Usually, the sequence diagrams are revised multiple times during the behavioral modeling processes. Don't worry too much about identifying all the actors and objects perfectly; remember that like the functional and structural modeling process, the behavioral modeling process is iterative.

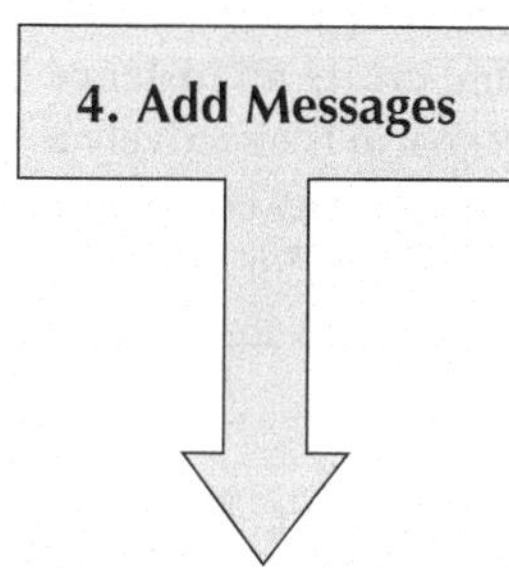

Now that the actors and objects for a scenario has been identified, the third step is to create a lifeline for each. In many of the case tools, actor and object identification and setting a lifeline for each occur at the same time. If the object is a temporary object, such as a web-based shopping cart, an X should be placed below the object at the point on the lifeline where the object goes out of existence.

The fourth step is to add the messages to the diagram. This is done by drawing arrows to represent the messages being passed from actor to actor, actor to object, object to object, and object to actor with the arrow pointing in the message's transmission direction. The arrows should be placed in order from the first message (at the top) to the last (at the bottom) to show time sequence. Any parameters passed along with the messages should be placed in parentheses next to the message's name. As with actor and object identification, in many cases this causes modifications to both the functional and structural models. In this case, activities on activity diagrams, events with use-case descriptions, responsibilities and collaborations on CRC cards, and operations on class diagrams could be effected.

---

[5] The approach described in this section is adapted from Grady Booch, James Rumbaugh, and Ivar Jacobson, *The Unified Modeling Language User Guide* (Reading, MA: Addison-Wesley, 1999).

5. Place Execution Occurrence

The fifth step is to place the execution occurrence on each object's lifeline by drawing a narrow rectangle box over the lifelines to represent when the classes are sending and receiving messages. In most case tools this is automatically done when a *lifeline* sends and receives messages.

6. Validate

The sixth and final step is to validate the sequence diagram. The purpose of this step is to guarantee that the sequence diagram completely represents the underlying process. This is done by *guaranteeing* that the diagram depicts all the steps in the scenario.[6]

APPLYING THE CHAPTER CONCEPTS

Library Management System Example In the last installment of the LMS example, Susan was setting up a meeting with Joe to discuss the current state of the evolving functional and structural models. After the meeting, they decided not to make any substantive modifications to the current models. Instead, they chose to create the instance sequence diagrams and to use them as a basis to continue the iterative and incremental development process. Therefore, Susan went back to the office and had her team create sequence diagrams for each of the scenarios of the Borrow Resource use case as depicted in Figure 4-20. Figures 5-5 through 5-11 portray seven of the 21 scenarios of the Borrow Resource use case. Susan and her team created seven more scenario based sequence diagrams for each patron type: student and guest.

Once the scenario-based sequence diagrams for every use case were completed by Susan's team, she and her team iterated back and modified the functional and structural models. If you look closely at the sequence diagrams, you will see messages being sent to the Patron lifeline that do not have associated activities in the Patron swimlane. Consequently, Susan and her team will need to update the activity diagram to include activities for these messages. Also, the team will need to add appropriate responsibilities to the Patron CRC card and operations to the Patron class in the class diagram. Based on the current state of the evolving models, Susan and her team has identified a set of questions for Joe. For example, in the class diagram (Figure 4-19) does the LMS really need all of the classes? Are the Resource, Physical, and Downloadable classes concrete or abstract? What about the Patron class? However, she decided before setting up another meeting with Joe to go through everything, she would perform CRUDE analysis (next section). This way, she will have a better idea of the interactivity among the actors and the classes.

Campus Housing Service "Your Turn" Exercise In the previous installations of the Campus Housing Service (CHS) "Your Turn" exercise, you identified the functional and structural requirements. In this installment of the Campus Housing Service (CHS) example, using the functional and structural models developed, you should create an instance sequence diagram for each scenario of each use case. Remember, a scenario is effectively a single execution path through the activity diagram that represents the use case. For example, in Figure 4-6 there are thirteen unique paths through the diagram. So, in this case there would be thirteen separate sequence diagrams. We will return to CHS in the next section of the chapter.

---

[6] We describe validation in more detail later in this chapter.

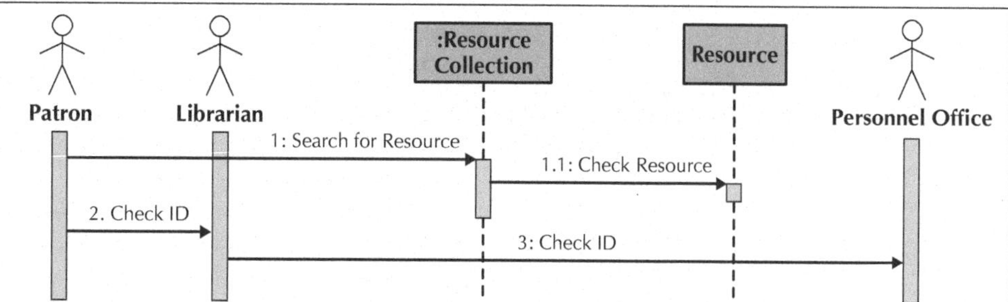

FIGURE 5-5 Borrow Resources Invalid Faculty ID Scenario Sequence Diagram

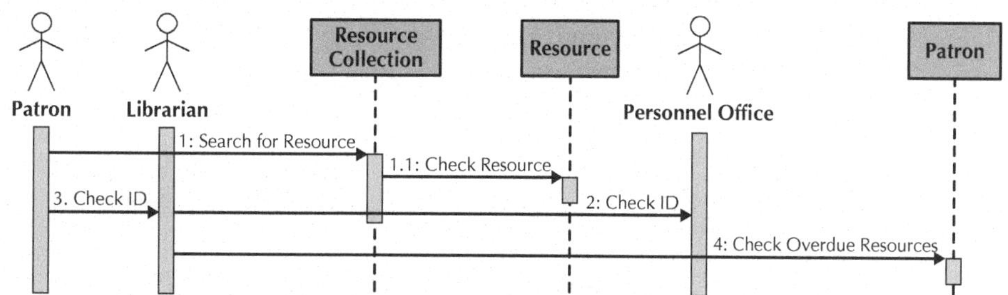

FIGURE 5-6 Borrow Resources Valid Faculty ID, Overdue Resources Scenario Sequence Diagram

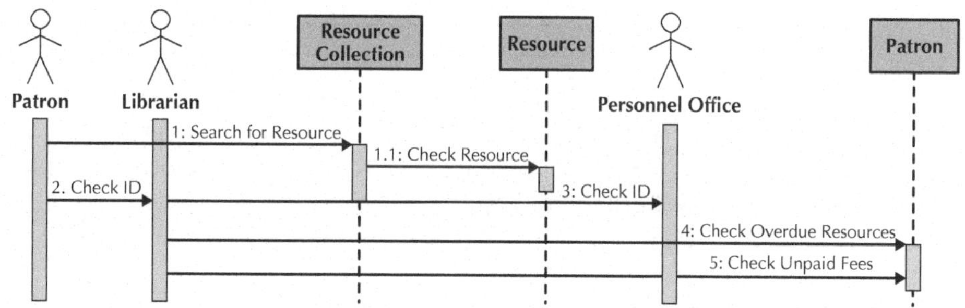

FIGURE 5-7 Borrow Resources Valid Faculty ID, No Overdue Resources, Unpaid Fees Scenario Sequence Diagram

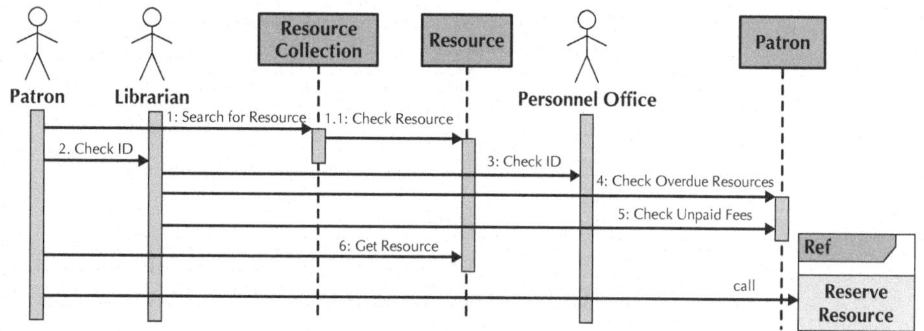

FIGURE 5-8 Borrow Resources Valid Faculty ID, No Overdue Resources, No Unpaid Fees, Resource Not Available, Resource Owned by Library Scenario Sequence Diagram

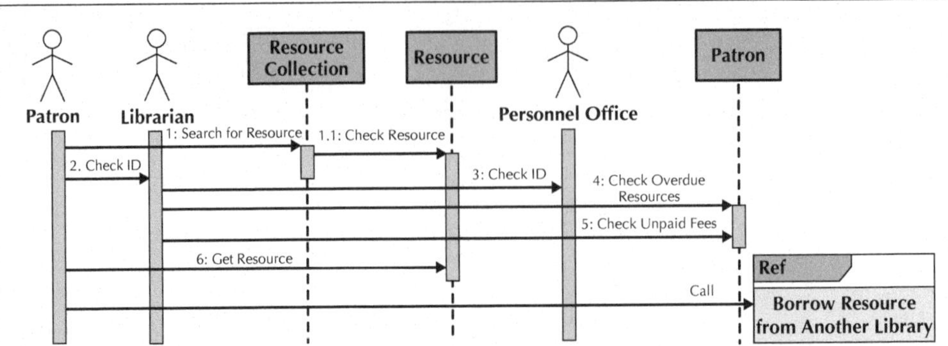

FIGURE 5-9 Borrow Resources Valid Faculty ID, No Overdue Resources, No Unpaid Fees, Resource Not Available, Resource Not Owned by Library Scenario Sequence Diagram

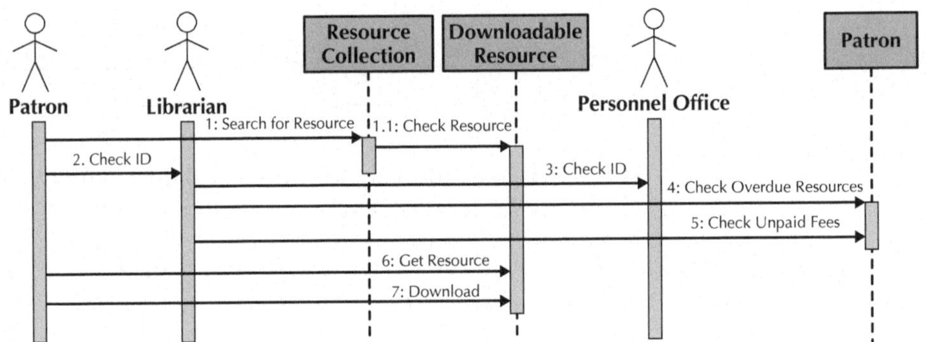

FIGURE 5-10 Borrow Resources Valid Faculty I, No Overdue Resources, No Unpaid Fees, Resource Available, Downloadable Resource Scenario Sequence Diagram

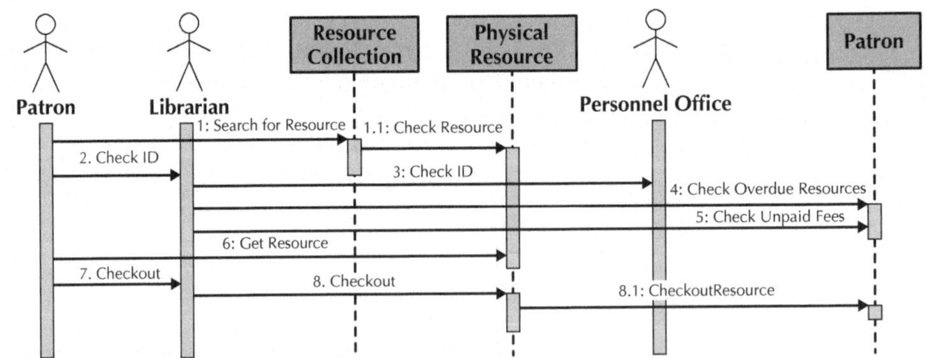

FIGURE 5-11 Borrow Resources Valid Faculty ID, No Overdue Resources, No Unpaid Fees, Resource Available, Physical Resource Scenario Sequence Diagram

CRUDE ANALYSIS

One useful technique to identify how the underlying objects in the problem domain work together to collaborate in support of the use cases is *CRUDE analysis*.[7] CRUDE analysis uses a *CRUDE matrix*, in which each interaction among objects is labeled with a letter for the type of interaction: C for create, R for read or reference, U for update, D for delete, and E for execute. In an object-oriented approach, a class/actor-by-class/actor matrix is used.[8] Each cell in the matrix represents the interaction between instances of the classes. For example, in Figure 5-1, an instance of the Receptionist actor creates an instance of the Appointment class. Assuming a Row:Column ordering, a C is placed in the cell Receptionist:Appointment. In other words, a receptionist actor sends a Create message to the Appointment class to create an instance of the Appointment class. In Figure 5-3, an instance of the Receptionist actor cancels an instance of the Appointments class. This implies a D should be placed in the Receptionist:Appointments cell. Also, in Figure 5-3, an instance of the Receptionist actor changes an instance of the Appointments class. This implies that a U should be placed in the Receptionist:Appointments cell. Figure 5-12 shows the CRUDE matrix based on the Manage Appointments sequence diagrams in Figures 5-1 and 5-3. Obviously, this matrix is not complete. It only represents three of the thirteen scenarios of the Manage Appointments use case. Furthermore, it does not include any of the scenarios of the other six use cases in the Appointment System (see Figure 3-11) nor does it include all of the concrete classes (see Figure 4-8). Obviously, including everything, the matrix would be populated with many more rows, columns, and entries.

Unlike the interaction diagrams, a CRUDE matrix is most useful as a system-wide representation. Once a single CRUDE matrix is completed for the entire system, the matrix can be scanned quickly to ensure that every class can be instantiated. Each type of interaction can be validated for each class. For example, if a class represents only temporary objects, then the column for that class in the matrix should have a D in it somewhere. Otherwise, the instances of the class will never be deleted. Because a data warehouse contains historical data, objects that are to be stored in one should not have any U or D entries in their associated columns. In this way, CRUDE analysis can be used as a way to partially validate the interactions among the objects in an object-oriented system. Finally, the more interactions among a set of classes, the more likely they should be clustered together into a collaboration. However, the number and type of interactions are only an estimate at this point in the development of the system.

	Patient Actor	**Receptionist Actor**	**Appointment Class**
Patient Actor		E	
Receptionist Actor	E		C, U, D
Appointment Class			

FIGURE 5-12   CRUDE Matrix based on Figures 5-1 and 5-3

[7] CRUD analysis has typically been associated with structured analysis and design [see Alan Dennis, Barbara Haley Wixom and Roberta M. Roth, *Systems Analysis Design*, 8th ed. (New York: Wiley, 2022)] and information engineering [see James Martin, *Information Engineering, Book II Planning and Analysis* (Englewood Cliffs, NJ: Prentice Hall, 1990)]. In our case, we have simply adapted it to object-oriented systems development. In the case of object orientation, we have added an E to allow us to document the execution of operations that do not create, read, update, or delete but that instead simply are executed for possible side-effect purposes.

[8] Another useful but more-detailed form of the CRUDE matrix is a Class/Actor: Operation-by-Class/Actor: Operation matrix. For validation and verification purposes, this more-detailed matrix is more useful. Furthermore, this more detailed matrix is useful to begin identifying role-based access control issues related to the security nonfunctional requirements discussed in the design and construction chapters later in the book. However, for our purposes at this point in our discussion, the Class/Actor-by-Class/Actor matrix is sufficient.

Care should be taken when using this technique to cluster classes to identify collaborations. We return to this subject in the next chapter when we deal with partitions and collaborations.

CRUDE analysis also can be used to identify complex objects. The more (C)reate, (U)pdate, or (D)elete entries in the column associated with a class, the more likely the instances of the class have a complex life cycle. As such, these objects are candidates for state modeling with a behavioral state machine (see the next section of this chapter).

APPLYING THE CHAPTER CONCEPTS

Library Management System Example Susan started the creation of a CRUDE matrix that summarized all of the messages being sent in the LMS. Since she and her team weren't exactly sure which classes (see Figure 4-19) should be abstract, she included a row and column for the classes. She also included rows and columns for the faculty/staff, student, and guest actors. Her team believes that this was unnecessary. But everyone believed that it was a lot easier to delete the excess rows and columns that weren't required. So, she created the matrix for the system and filled it out based on the seven faculty/staff scenarios (see Figures 5-5 through 5-11) that described the Borrow Resources use case. Figure 5-13 only shows the rows, columns, and cell values based on 5-5 through 5-11. Next, she handed the matrix to the other team members and had them finish it off by categorizing each of the messages contained on all of the remaining sequence diagrams and recording them in the appropriate cells. Once the matrix is

	Patron Actor	Librarian Actor	Personnel Office Actor	Resource Collection Class	Resource Class	Downloadable Resource Class	Physical Resource Class	Patron Class
Patron Actor		E		R	R	R	R, U	
Librarian Actor			E					R
Personnel Office Actor								
Resource Collection Class					R			
Resource Class								
Downloadable Resource Class								
Physical Resource Class								U
Patron Class								

FIGURE 5-13 LMS CRUDE Matrix based on Figures 5-5 through 5-11

completed, she is going to set up a meeting to discuss everything with Joe. This includes questions regarding the sparseness of the matrix and whether the current functional, structural, and behavioral models are acceptable. Even though the team has not completed any behavioral state machines (these are covered in the next section), the team feels that the current set of models will be in a good enough state for Joe and Susan to meet and clarify anything that is wrong or missing.

Campus Housing Service "Your Turn" Exercise In the previous installation of the Campus Housing Service (CHS) "Your Turn" exercise, you created a sequence diagram for each scenario in each use case. In this installment of the Campus Housing Service (CHS) exercise, you should create a single CRUDE matrix that summarizes all message passing that occurs throughout the evolving system. Remember, you must categorize each message as either a C, R, U, D, or E. We will return to CHS in the next section of the chapter.

BEHAVIORAL STATE MACHINES

Some classes in *class diagrams* represent objects that are quite dynamic in that they pass through a variety of states over the course of their existence. For example, a patient can change over time from being new to current to former based on his or her status with the doctor's office. A behavioral state machine is a dynamic model that shows the different states through which a single object passes during its life in response to events, along with its responses and actions. Typically, *behavioral state machines* are not used for all objects; rather, behavioral state machines are used with complex objects to further define them and to help simplify the design of algorithms for their methods. The behavioral state machine shows the different states of the object and what events cause the object to change from one state to another. Behavioral state machines should be used to help understand the dynamic aspects of a single class and how its instances evolve over time[9] unlike interaction diagrams that show how a particular use case or use-case scenario is executed over a set of classes.

In this section, we describe states, events, transitions, actions, and activities. We also explain how behavioral state machines model the state changes through which complex objects pass. As with interaction diagrams, when we create a behavioral state machine for an object, it is possible that we will uncover additional events that need to be included in the functional model (see Chapter 3) and additional operations that need to be included in the structural model (see Chapter 4), so our interaction diagrams might have to be modified again. Because object-oriented development is iterative and incremental, this continuous modification of the evolving models (functional, structural, and behavioral) of the system is to be expected.

States, Events, Transitions, Actions, and Activities

The *state* of an object is defined by the value of its attributes and its relationships with other objects at a particular point in time. For example, a patient might have a state of new, current, or former. The attributes or properties of an object affect the state that it is in, however, not all attributes or attribute changes will make a difference. For example, think about a patient's address. Those attributes make very little difference to changes in a patient's state. However, if states were based on a patient's geographic location (e.g., in-town patients were treated differently than out-of-town patients), changes to the patient's address would influence state changes.

---

[9] Some authors refer to this as modeling an object's life cycle.

An *event* is something that takes place at a certain point in time and changes a value or values that describe an object, which, in turn, changes the object's state. It can be a designated condition becoming true, the receipt of the call for a method by an object, or the passage of a designated period of time. The state of the object determines exactly what the response will be.

A *transition* is a relationship that represents the movement of an object from one state to another state. Some transitions have a guard condition. A *guard condition* is a Boolean expression that includes attribute values, which allows a transition to occur only if the condition is true. An object typically moves from one state to another based on the outcome of an action triggered by an event. All transitions are associated with an event that must be implemented as an operation with the object's class. Consequently, if there is a transition in a behavioral state machine that is not associated with an operation, then either the transition is in error or an operation is missing.

Elements of a Behavioral State Machine

Figure 5-14 presents an example of a behavioral state machine representing the patient class in the context of a hospital environment. From this diagram, we can tell that a patient enters a hospital and is admitted after checking in. If a doctor finds the patient to be healthy, he or she is released and is no longer considered a patient after two weeks elapse. If a patient is found to be unhealthy, he or she remains under observation until the diagnosis changes.

A *state* is a set of values that describes an object at a specific point in time and represents a point in an object's life in which it satisfies some condition, performs some action, or waits for something to happen (see Figure 5-15). In Figure 5-14 states include entering, admitted, released, and under observation. A state is depicted by a *state symbol*, which is a rectangle with rounded corners with a descriptive label that communicates a particular state. There are two exceptions. An *initial state* is shown using a small, filled-in circle, and an object's *final state* is shown as a circle surrounding a small, filled-in circle. These exceptions depict when an object is created and when an object is deleted, respectively.

Arrows are used to connect the state symbols, representing the transitions between states. Each arrow is labeled with the appropriate event name and any parameters or conditions that may apply. For example, the two transitions from admitted to released and under observation contain guard conditions. As in the other behavioral diagrams, in many cases it is useful to explicitly show the context of the behavioral state machine using a frame.

Figure 5-16 depicts two additional behavioral state machines. The first one depicts a set of states through which a bank account object might experience during its lifetime. In this case,

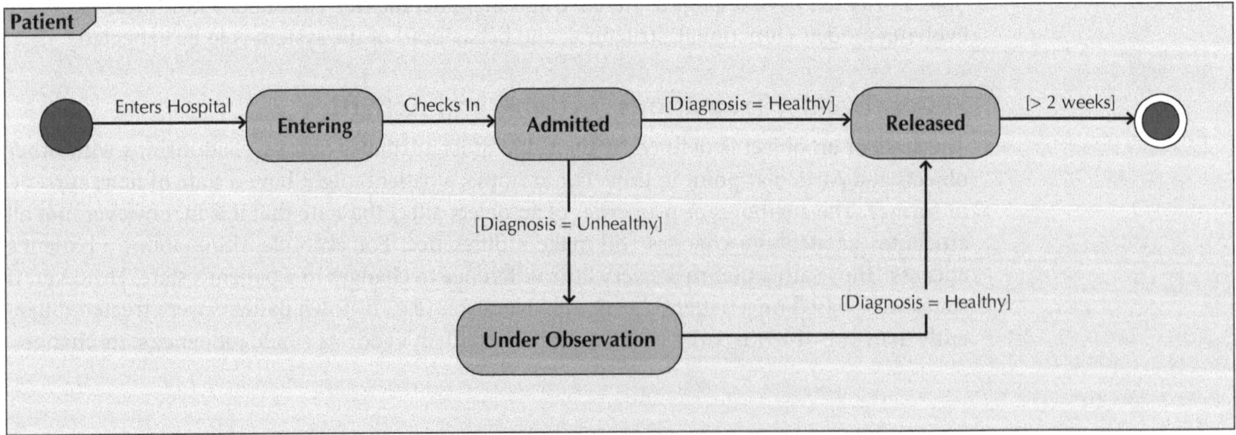

FIGURE 5-14 Sample Behavioral State Machine Diagram

Term and Definition	Symbol
A state: ■ is shown as a rectangle with rounded corners. ■ has a name that represents the state of an object.	aState
An initial state: ■ is shown as a small, filled-in circle. ■ represents the point at which an object begins to exist.	●
A final state: ■ is shown as a circle surrounding a small, filled-in circle (bull's-eye). ■ represents the completion of activity.	◉
An event: ■ is a noteworthy occurrence that triggers a change in state. ■ can be a designated condition becoming true, the receipt of an explicit signal from one object to another, or the passage of a designated period of time. ■ is used to label a transition.	anEvent
A transition: ■ indicates that an object in the first state will enter the second state. ■ is triggered by the occurrence of the event labeling the transition. ■ is shown as a solid arrow from one state to another, labeled by the event name.	⟶
A frame: ■ indicates the context of the behavioral state machine.	Context

FIGURE 5-15 Behavioral State Machine Diagram Syntax

once the account object is created, it is in the Good Standing state until some event occurs and the relevant guard condition is met. For example, if the Balance > Withdrawal Request AND Suspicious Activity guard condition is met, the account object moves into the Frozen state until either the Suspicious Activity Cleared Up or the Account Closed guard conditions are met. If the Suspicious Activity is Cleared Up condition is met, then the Account moves back to the Good Standing state. On the other hand, if the Account Closed condition is met, the account object moves to the final state. The second behavioral state machine deals with the life cycle of an order. The order object is associated with the order processing use portrayed in Figure 3-8. For an order-processing system, additional sequence diagrams would be necessary to completely represent all the processing associated with an order object. Obviously, because behavioral state machines can uncover additional processing requirements, they can be very useful in filling out the complete description of an evolving system.

Sometimes, states and subclasses can be confused. For example, in Figure 5-17, are the classes Freshman, Sophomore, Junior, and Senior subclasses of the class Undergraduate or are they states that an instance of the Undergraduate class goes through during its lifetime? In this case, the latter is the better answer. When trying to identify all potential classes during

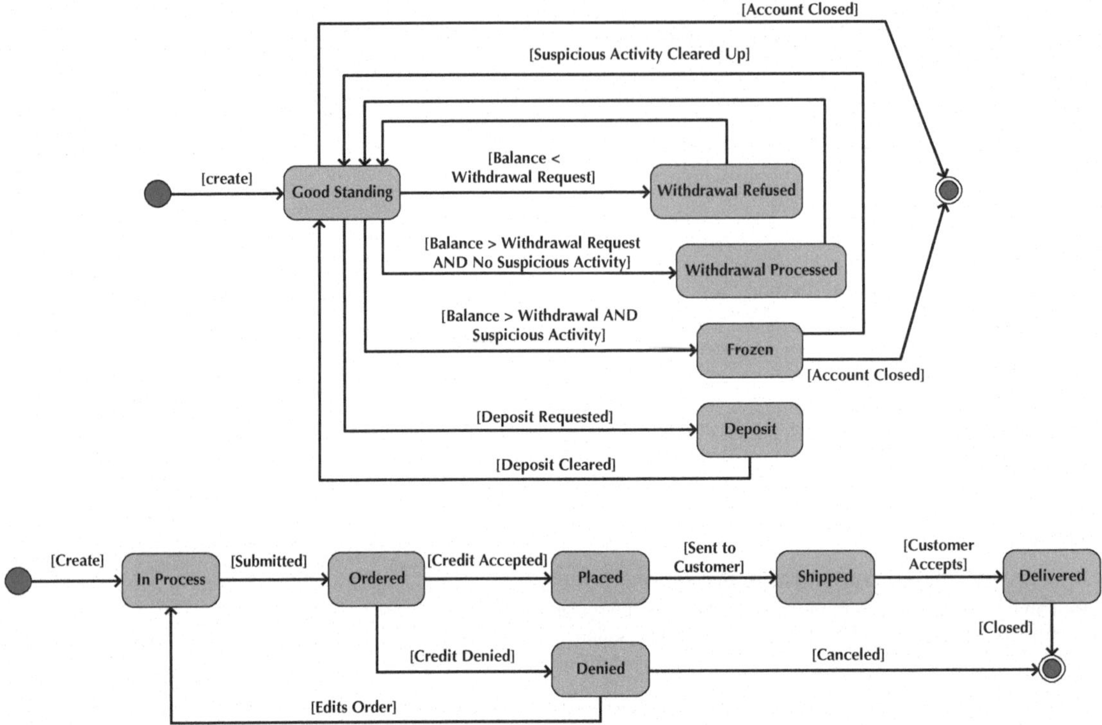

FIGURE 5-16 Additional Behavioral State Machine Diagrams

structural modeling (see Chapter 4), you might actually identify states of the relevant super-class instead of subclasses. This is another example of how tightly intertwined the functional, structural, and behavioral models can be. From a modeling perspective, although we eventually removed the Freshman, Sophomore, Junior, and Senior subclasses from the structural model, capturing that information during structural modeling and removing it based on discoveries made during behavioral modeling were preferable to omitting it and taking a chance of missing a crucial piece of information about the problem domain. Remember, object-oriented development is iterative and incremental. As we progress to a correct model of the problem domain, we will make many mistakes.

Guidelines for Creating Behavioral State Machines

As with the sequence diagrams, Scott W. Ambler suggests a set of guidelines when drawing behavior state machines. In this case, we consider six of his recommendations.[10]

- Create a behavioral state machine for objects whose behavior changes based on the state of the object. In other words, do not create a behavioral state machine for an object whose behavior is always the same regardless of its state. These objects are too simple.

- To adhere to the left-to-right and top-to-bottom reading conventions of Western cultures, the initial state should be drawn in the top left corner of the diagram and the final state should be drawn in the bottom right of the diagram.

---

[10] S.W. Ambler, *The Elements of UML 2.0 Style* (Cambridge, England: Cambridge University Press, 2005).

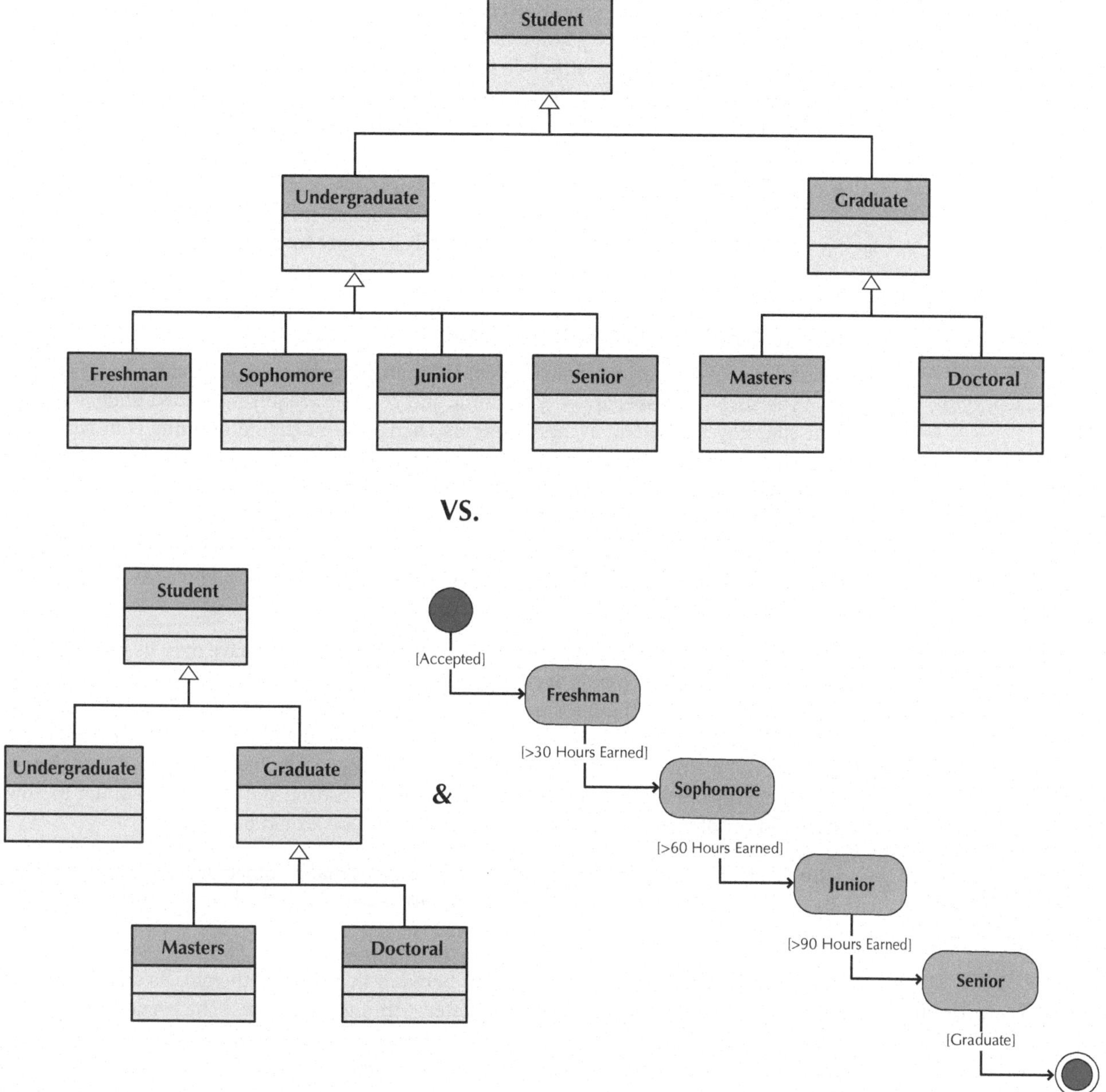

FIGURE 5-17 States versus Subclasses

- Make sure that the names of the states are simple, intuitively obvious, and descriptive. For example, in Figure 5-14, the state names of the patient object are Entering, Admitted, Under Observation, and Released.

- Question black hole and miracle states. These types of states are problematic for the same reason black hole and miracle activities are a problem for activity diagrams (see Chapter 3). *Black hole states*, states that an object goes into and never comes out of, most likely are actually final states. *Miracle states*, states that an object comes out of but never went into, most likely are initial states.

- Be sure that all guard conditions are mutually exclusive (not overlapping). For example, in Figure 5-14, the guard condition [Diagnosis = Healthy] and the guard condition [Diagnosis = Unhealthy] do not overlap. However, if you created a guard condition of [x >= 0] and a second guard condition [x <= 0], the guard conditions overlap when x = 0, and it is not clear to which state the object would transition. This would obviously cause confusion.

- All transitions should be associated with a message and operation. Otherwise, the state of the object could never change. Even though this may be stating the obvious, there have been numerous times that analysts forgot to go back and ensure that this was indeed true.

Creating a Behavioral State Machine

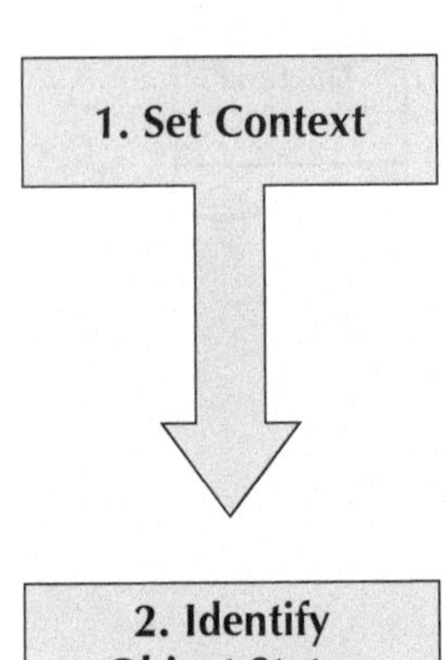

Behavioral state machines are drawn to depict an instance of a single class from a class diagram. Typically, the classes are very dynamic and complex, requiring a good understanding of their states over time and events triggering changes. You should examine your class diagram to identify which classes undergo a complex series of state changes and draw a diagram for each of them. In this section, we describe a five-step process used to build a behavioral state machine.[11] Like the other behavioral models, the first step in the process is determining the context of the behavioral state machine, which is shown in the label of the frame of the diagram. The context of a behavioral state machine is usually a class. However, it also could be a set of classes, a subsystem, or an entire system.

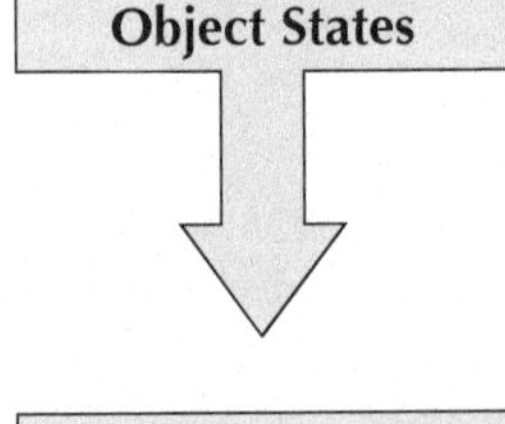

The second step is to identify the various states that an object will have over its lifetime. This includes establishing the boundaries of the existence of an object by identifying the initial and final states of an object. The information necessary to perform this is gleaned from reading the use-case descriptions, talking with users, and relying on the requirements-gathering techniques that you learned about in Chapter 2. An easy way to identify the states of an object is to write the steps of what happens to an object over time, from start to finish, similar to how the normal flow of events section of a use-case description would be created.

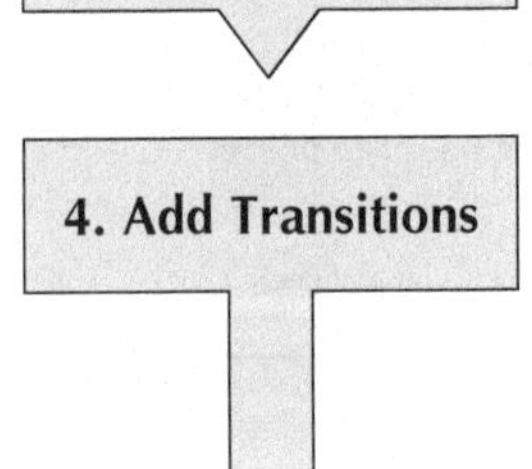

The third step is to determine the sequence of the states that an object will pass through during its lifetime. Using this sequence, the states are placed onto the behavioral state machine in a left-to-right order.

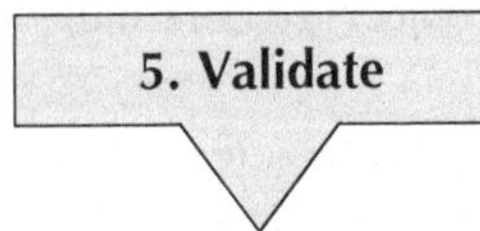

The fourth step is to identify the transitions between the states of the objects and to add the events, actions, and guard conditions associated with the transitions. The events are the *triggers* that cause an object to move from one state to the next state. In other words, an event causes an action to execute that changes the value(s) of an object's attribute(s) in a significant manner. The actions are typically operations contained within the object. Also, guard conditions can model a set of test conditions that must be met for the transition to occur. At this point in the process, the transitions are drawn between the relevant states and labeled with the event, action, or guard condition.

The fifth step is to validate the behavioral state machine by making sure that each state is reachable and that it is possible to leave all states except for final states. Obviously, if an identified state is not reachable, either a transition is missing or the state was identified in error. Only final states can be a dead end from the perspective of an object's life cycle.

---

[11] The approach described in this section is adapted from Booch, Rumbaugh, and Jacobson, *The Unified Modeling Language User Guide*.

APPLYING THE CHAPTER CONCEPTS

Library Management System Example In the last installment we left Susan with setting up a meeting to go through everything that the team had developed. This included the use case, activity, class, and sequence diagrams, the functional requirements, use-case descriptions, CRC cards, and CRUDE matrix. A subset of these is shown in Figures 3-5, 3-9, 3-10, 3-14, 4-19, 4-20, 5-5 through 5-11, and 5-13. After reviewing everything with Joe, Susan told Joe about behavioral state machines and how they could be used to fill out some of the missing requirements and to validate others. Using Figures 5-14 and 5-16, Susan demonstrated how a behavioral state machine actually modeled the lifecycle of a Patient object, a Bank Account Object, and an Order object. Based on Susan's demonstration, Joe understood how useful behavioral state machines could be in further developing the LMS. Next, Susan and Joe carefully reviewed the LMS class diagram (Figure 4-19) and the Borrow Resource use-case sequence diagrams (see Figures 5-5 through 5-11) to pick a set of concrete objects on which to focus the effort on creating a set of behavioral state machine. Based on their careful review, they decided to focus this on books and to deal with the other types of resources later. Based on this decision, Susan headed back to her team to create two behavioral state machines; one for a physical book (Book) and one for a downloadable book (D_Book). Once the team completes these, Susan will go back to Joe to review everything again.

Like Susan and Joe, the team carefully reviewed all of the current representations of the LMS system to determine what states and transitions were relevant to Book and D_Book objects. Based on the use-case diagram (Figure 3-5), the team noticed in addition to checking out, reserving, and returning books, Book and D_Book objects need to be procured and retired. Figures 5-18 and 5-19 show the behavioral state machines that were developed by the team for Book and D_Book objects.

With the completed behavioral state machines for the Book and D_Book objects, Susan and Joe met to discuss the implications for the evolving models. Below is a small excerpt from the discussion.

SUSAN: Joe, I'm glad to be able to sit down with you and review the models again in light of the Book and D_Book behavioral state machines.

JOE: After our last meeting, I hoped that these new diagrams help us along our development. So, let's get started. Why don't you take the lead and explain the diagrams to me.

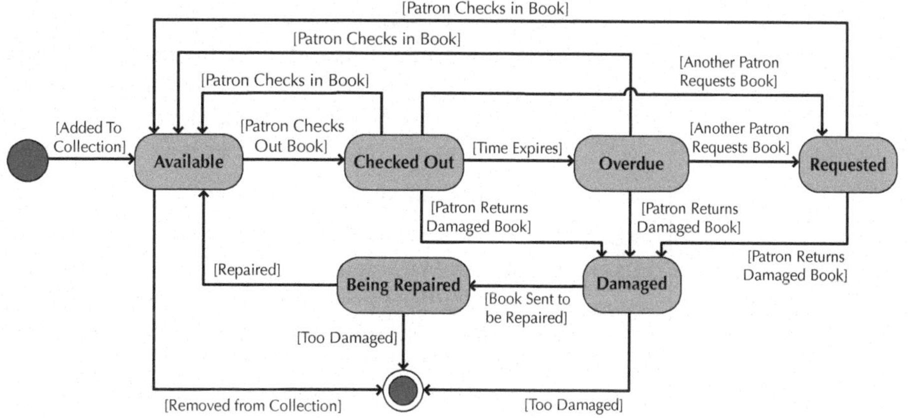

FIGURE 5-18 LMS Book Object Behavioral State Machine

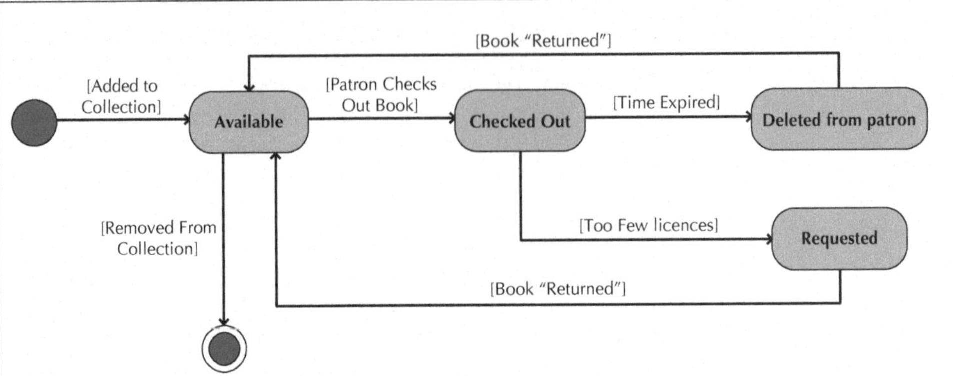

FIGURE 5-19   LMS D_Book Object Behavioral State Machine

SUSAN: Sounds great. To begin with, let's work through the Book object behavioral state machine. As you notice we begin with a book being added to the collection. This implies that somewhere in the use cases, there must be a process to procure new books. When we review the use-case diagram (Figure 3-5), we see that we indeed have a use case that deals with resource procurement. Also, there are three different paths to delete a book object two due to damage and one due to simply removing it from the book collection. Again, when we review the use-case diagram, there is a use case that addresses the need to retire resources. In one case the use case is an extension to the return resource use case and in the other situation, the Librarian simply deletes the resource. These different uses of the Retire use case address the situation of removing both damaged and undamaged books from the collection. So, before we get into the details of checking out and returning books, do you see any problems with the way that a book object is to be created or deleted? Have we left anything out?

JOE: I don't think so. The procurement process is a little more involved, but the actual details of the process don't matter from the perspective of a Book object.

SUSAN: Great, so let's review the states that relate to the checking out and returning books of books. In this case, we identified a set of states and transitions. The first state relates to whether the book is currently in the library or not (Available). If the book is available then a patron can check it out. Once the book has been Checked Out by a patron, the book stays in the Checked Out state until the patron returns the book, the book becomes Overdue, or it is Requested by another patron. If the patron returns a damaged book, the Book goes into the Damaged state. Do you see how all of the transitions and the states are related to the functional, structural, and other behavioral models? Why don't you take a few minutes to work through this diagram and see if we have any omissions or any other errors.

After a few minutes, Joe looked up.

JOE: I think in this case you and your team has nailed it.

SUSAN: Great, now that you have approved this diagram, let's take a step back and look at the use-case diagram (Figure 3-5) and the class diagram (Figure 4-19). As you see, we identified the use cases as dealing with resources; not books. However, if you remember, we originally started with borrowing and returning books (Figure 2-19). We then decided to abstract the idea of books up to resources. In fact, we identified a Book as AKO Physical Resource which was AKO Resource. Now that you have seen the state changes related to a book's life cycle, are these stated related to the other types of resources? Based on this question, I had the team develop a

> behavioral state machine for downloadable books (D_Book). After all, a book is a book isn't? Well, it turned out that the states and transitions of a Book object and a D_Book object do overlap. But they did not seem identical to us. So, could you carefully review the D_Book behavioral state machine for us (see Figure 5-19).
>
> **JOE:** I'm glad you brought this up. At our last meeting, I hadn't thought about the different types of resources and how the use cases might vary depending on the resource type. So, let me work through the D_Book behavioral state machine for a few minutes.
>
> . . .
>
> **JOE:** Now that I have reviewed the D_Object diagram, I noticed that there is an implied invalid assumption in the diagram. You seem to be assuming that once a D_Book object has been checked out, it will be removed from a patron's machine after a certain amount of time has gone by. Not all of the D_Books in our collection expire. So, deleting a D_Book object from a patron's machine may not be relevant. I think we need to rethink this diagram.
>
> **SUSAN** Great, we weren't comfortable with this specific diagram. I think I need to get Jane to come over and work with you on correcting this specific diagram as soon as possible. This misunderstanding on our part has implications throughout our functional, structural, and other behavioral models. For example, should we change the class diagram to have two subclasses of D_Book Expires and Doesn't Expire?
>
> **JOE** I see what you mean. In fact, how should we deal with the idea of expiring downloadable resources? Should they be simply removed from the patron's machine? Could they be renewed? Also, should we or do we treat Podcast, Movie, and Music objects differently (see Figure 4-19).
>
> **SUSAN** And, I'm afraid it's worse than that. Are the states and transitions through which Journal, DVD, and CD objects traverse during their lifetime different than Book objects? Furthermore, are Journal objects physical, downloadable, or both. Once you and Jane have completed all of the behavioral state machines, the team will need to iterate across all of the other models to make sure that everything is consistent. So, as you can see, the creation of the behavioral state machines can raise many questions regarding implicit assumptions in the other models. I'm glad we caught all of these issues now instead of after we have implemented everything based on the current models. Now we will be able to fix everything before we move on to design.
>
> **Campus Housing Service "Your Turn" Exercise** In the previous installation of the Campus Housing Service (CHS) "Your Turn" exercise, you created a CRUDE matrix that summarized all message passing that took place in the CHS system. In this installment of the CHS exercise, you should create a single behavioral state machine for each concrete class identified. We will return to CHS in the next chapter.

VERIFYING AND VALIDATING THE BEHAVIORAL MODEL[12]

In this chapter, we described two different diagrams (sequence diagram and behavioral state machine) and CRUDE matrices that could be used to represent the behavioral model. The sequence diagrams modeled the interaction among the actors and classes that work together to support the business processes included in a system, the CRUDE matrix represented a system-level overview of the interactions among the objects in the system, and the behavioral

---

[12] The material in this section has been adapted from E. Yourdon, *Modern Structured Analysis* (Englewood Cliffs, NJ: Prentice Hall, 1989).

state machine described the state changes through which a concrete object traverses during its lifetime. In this chapter, we combine walkthroughs with CRUDE matrices to more completely verify and validate the behavioral models. Since we covered CRUDE analysis and matrices in an earlier section, we focus only on walkthroughs in this section. We also describe the process in balancing the behavioral models with the functional and structural models. We again use the appointment system and focus on Figures 5-1, 5-3, 5-12, and 5-14 to describe a set of rules that can be used to ensure that the behavioral model is internally consistent.

First, all transitions contained in a behavior state machine must be associated with a message being received on a sequence diagram, and it must be classified as a (C)reate, (U)pdate, or (D)elete message in a CRUDE matrix. For example, in Figure 5-14 the Checks In transition must be associated with a message in the corresponding sequence diagrams that shows a message being received by the Patient object. Furthermore, it should be associated with an (U)pdate entry in the CRUDE matrix associated with the hospital patient system.

Second, all entries in a CRUDE matrix imply a message being sent from an actor or object to another actor or object. If the entry is a (C)reate, (U)pdate, or (D)elete and the execution of the related operation changes the state of the object, then there must be an associated transition in a behavioral state machine that represents the instances of the receiving class. For example, in Figure 5-12 the C, U, and D entries in the Receptionist row and Appointments column imply that instances of the Receptionist actor will create, update, and delete instances of the Appointments class. Thus, there should be create, update, and delete related messages on the sequence diagram corresponding with the appointments processes. Reviewing Figure 5-1, we see that there is a create message sent by the aReceptionist actor to the Appointment class. We also see that in Figure 5-3, there are CancelAppointment and ChangeAppointment messages sent by the aReceptionist actor to the Appointment class. Therefore, the CRUDE matrix and the sequence diagrams are consistent.[13]

Finally, many representation-specific rules have been proposed. However, as in the other models, these rules are beyond the scope of this section on verification and validation.[14]

Balancing Functional and Behavioral Models

As in balancing the functional and structural models, we must ensure the consistency of the two sets of models. In this case, the activity diagrams, use-case descriptions, and use-case diagrams must agree with the sequence diagrams, behavioral state machines, and CRUDE matrix.

First, sequence diagrams must be associated with a use case on the use-case diagram and a use-case description. For example, the sequence diagrams in Figures 5-1 and 5-3 are related to the scenarios of the Manage Appointments use case that appears in the use-case description in Figure 4-7 and the use-case diagram in Figure 3-11.

Second, actors on sequence diagrams and/or CRUDE matrices must be associated with actors on the use-case diagram or referenced in the use-case description, and vice versa. For example, the aPatient actor in the sequence diagram in Figure 5-1, and the Patient Actor row and column in the CRUDE matrix in Figure 5-12 appears in the use-case diagram in Figure 3-11 and the use-case description in Figure 4-7. However, the aReceptionist Actor does not appear in the use-case diagram but is referenced in the events associated with the Manage Appointments use-case description. In this case, the aReceptionist actor is obviously an internal actor, which should not be portrayed on UML's use-case diagram.

---

[13] We have delayed the description of designing operations and methods until Chapter 7. Therefore, the detailed information required to understand a specific message has not been created yet. However, in many cases, enough information will already have been created to validate many of the transitions in behavioral state machines and CRUDE matrices.

[14] A good reference for these types of restrictions is S.W. Ambler, *The Elements of UML 2.0 Style* (Cambridge, England: Cambridge University Press, 2005).

Third, messages on sequence diagrams, transitions on behavioral state machines, and entries in a CRUDE matrix must be related to activities and actions on an activity diagram and events listed in a use-case description, and vice versa. For example, the create message on the sequence diagram (see Figure 5-1) is related to the Create Appointment activity (see Figure 4-6) and the S-1, 3: Create Appointment event and the S-2, 3: Create Appointment event on the use-case description (see Figure 3-11). The C entry in the Receptionist:Appointment cell of the CRUDE matrix is also associated with these messages, activities, and events.

Fourth, all complex objects represented by an object node in an activity diagram must have a behavioral state machine that represents the object's lifecycle, and vice versa. Complex objects tend to be very dynamic and pass through a variety of states during their lifetimes. However, in this case because we no longer have any object nodes in the activity diagram (see Figure 4-6), there is no necessity for a behavioral state machine to be created based on the activity diagram.

Balancing Structural and Behavioral Models

When considering the structural and behavioral models, there are five areas in which we must ensure the consistency between the models.[15] First, objects that appear in a CRUDE matrix must be associated with classes that are represented by CRC cards and appear on the class diagram, and vice versa. For example, the Patient class in the CRUDE matrix in Figure 5-12 is associated with the CRC card in Figure 4-20 and the Patient class in the class diagram in Figure 4-8.

Second, because behavioral state machines represent the life cycle of complex objects, they must be associated with instances (objects) of classes on a class diagram and with a CRC card that represents the class of the instance. For example, the behavioral state machine that describes an instance of a Patient class in Figure 5-15 implies that a Patient class exists on a related class diagram (see Figure 4-8) and that a CRC card exists for the related class (see Figure 4-21).

Third, the objects on a sequence diagram must be an instantiation of a class that is represented by a CRC card and is located on a class diagram. For example, Figure 5-3 has an anAppointment object that is an instantiation of the Appointment class. Therefore, the Appointment class must exist in the class diagram (see Figure 4-8), and a CRC card should exist that describes it. However, when an object on a sequence diagram that is not associated with a class that exists on the class diagram, the analyst must decide to either modify the class diagram by adding these classes or rethink the sequence diagram.

Fourth, messages contained on the sequence diagrams, transitions on behavioral state machines, and cell entries on a CRUDE matrix must be associated with responsibilities and associations on CRC cards and operations in classes and associations connected to the classes on class diagrams. Furthermore, any message sent by a class-based lifeline to another class-based lifeline must be associated with a collaborator on the CRC card of the sending class-based lifeline. For example, in Figure 5-4, the Request Courses message that is received by the RegistrationMgr lifeline must be a responsibility on the RegistrationMgr CRC card and it must be an operation with the RegistrationMgr class on the class diagram. Furthermore, since the RegistrationMgr cascades the FindCourse message to the :Course lifeline and the Add Course message to the :StudentCourseReq lifeline, both the Course and StudentCourseReq classes must be listed as collaborators of the Request Courses responsibility on the RegistrationMgr CRC card (see Figure 5-20).

Fifth, the states in a behavioral state machine must be associated with different values of an attribute or set of attributes that describe an object. For example, the behavioral state machine for the hospital patient object implies that there should be an attribute, possibly current status, which needs to be included in the definition of the class.

---

[15] Role-playing (see Chapter 4) and CRUDE analysis also can be very useful in this undertaking.

Front:

Class Name: RegistrationMgr	ID: 8	Type: Concrete, Domain
Description: Aid student in obtaining courses requested.		Associated Use Cases: 8, 11

Responsibilities	Collaborators
Request Courses	Course, StudentCourseReq

Back:

Attributes:

Student Number

Courses Requested

Relationships:

Generalization (a-kind-of): ______________

Aggregation (has-parts): ______________

Other Associations: Course, StudentCourseReq

FIGURE 5-20
RegistrationMgr CRC
Card

CHAPTER REVIEW

After reading and studying this chapter, you should be able to:

- ☐ Describe the purpose of the behavioral models.
- ☐ Describe the purpose of the interaction diagrams.
- ☐ Describe the different elements of the sequence diagrams.
- ☐ Create a behavioral model using a sequence diagram.

□ Describe the purpose of CRUDE analysis.

□ Create a behavioral model using a CRUDE matrix.

□ Verify and validate the evolving behavioral model using CRUDE analysis and walkthroughs.

□ Explain the purpose of a behavioral state machine.

□ Describe the different elements of the behavioral state machines.

□ Create a behavioral model using a behavioral state machine.

□ Verify and validate the functional model by ensuring the consistency of the behavioral model representations: activity diagrams, sequence diagrams, a CRUDE matrix, and behavioral state machines.

□ Verify and validate both the behavioral models with the functional and structural models by balancing them.

KEY TERMS

Actor	CRUDE analysis	Instance sequence diagram	Sequence diagram
Attributes	CRUDE matrix	Lifeline	State
Behavior	Dynamic model	Message	State symbol
Behavioral models	Event	Method	Swimlanes
Behavioral state machines	Execution occurrence	Miracle states	Temporary object
Black hole states	Final state	Object	Transition
Class	Frame	Operation	Trigger
Class diagram	Generic sequence diagram	Operation call message	Use case
Collaboration	Guard condition	Return message	
Condition	Initial state	Scenario	
CRC cards	Instance	Self-delegation	

QUESTIONS

1. How is behavioral modeling related to functional and structural modeling?

2. What is the difference between an external and internal actor?

3. How does a use-case scenario relate to an activity diagram?

4. How does a use-case relate to a generic sequence diagram?

5. How does a use-case scenario relate to an instance sequence diagram?

6. Contrast the following sets of terms: state, behavior, class, object, message, and transition.

7. Why is iteration important when creating a behavioral model?

8. What are the main building blocks for the sequence diagram? How are they represented on the model?

9. How do you show that a temporary object is to go out of existence on a sequence diagram?

10. Do lifelines always continue down the entire page of a sequence diagram? Explain.

11. Describe the steps used to create a sequence diagram.

12. When drawing a sequence diagram, what guidelines should you follow?

13. What is CRUDE analysis, and what is it used for?

14. Are states always depicted using rounded rectangles on a behavioral state machine? Explain.

15. What kinds of events can lead to state transitions on a behavioral state machine?

16. What are the steps in building a behavioral state machine?

17. When drawing a behavioral state machine, what guidelines should you follow?

18. How are guard conditions shown on a behavioral state machine?

19. Describe the type of class that is best represented by a behavioral state machine. Give two examples of classes that would be good candidates for a behavioral state machine.

20. Identify the models that contain each of the following components: actor, class, final state, guard condition, initial state, message, object, state, transition, and update operation.

EXERCISES

A. Think about sending a first-class letter to an international pen pal. Describe the process that the letter goes through to get from your initial creation of the letter to being read by your friend, from the letter's perspective. Draw a behavioral state machine that depicts the states that the letter moves through.

B. Draw a behavioral state machine that describes the various states that a travel authorization can have through its approval process. A travel authorization form is used in most companies to approve travel expenses for employees. Typically, an employee fills out a blank form and sends it to his or her boss for a signature. If the amount is fairly small (<$300), then the boss signs the form and routes it to accounts payable to be input into the accounting system. The system cuts a check that is sent to the employee for the right amount, and after the check is cashed, the form is filed away with the canceled check. If the check is not cashed within 90 days, the travel form expires. When the amount of the travel voucher is a large amount (>$300), then the boss signs the form and sends it to the CFO, along with a paragraph explaining the purpose of the travel; the CFO signs the form and passes it along to accounts payable. Of course, the boss and the CFO can reject the travel authorization form if they do not feel that the expenses are reasonable. In this case, the employee can change the form to include more explanation or decide to pay the expenses.

C. Think about the system that handles student admissions at your university. The primary function of the system should be able to track a student from the request for information through the admissions process until the student is either admitted to the school or rejected.

1. Write a use-case description that can describe an Admit Student use case.

    Assume that applicants who are children of alumni are handled differently from other applicants. Also, assume that a generic Update Student Information use case is available for your system to use.

2. Create a use-case diagram that includes all of the above use cases.

    Assume that an admissions form includes the contents of the form, SAT information, and references. Additional information is captured about children of alumni, such as their parent's graduation year, contact information, and college major.

3. Create a class diagram for the use cases identified with questions 1 and 2. Also, be sure to include the above information.

    Assume that a temporary student object is used by the system to hold information about people before they send in an admission form. After the form is sent in, these people are considered students.

4. Create an activity diagram with swimlanes for the above use cases.

5. Using the activity diagram, create a sequence diagram for each scenario.

6. Perform a CRUDE analysis to show the interactivity of the objects in the system.

7. Create a behavioral state machine to depict a person as he or she moves through the admissions process.

8. Perform a verification and validation walkthrough of the problem.

D. For the A Real Estate Inc. problem in Chapters 3 (exercises I, J, and K) and 4 (exercises N and O):

1. Create an activity diagram with swimlanes for one of the use cases.

2. Using the activity diagram, create a sequence diagram for each scenario.

3. Perform a CRUDE analysis to show the interactivity of the objects in the system.

4. Create a behavioral state machine to depict one of the classes on the class diagram you created for Chapter 4, exercise N.

5. Perform a verification and validation walkthrough of the problem.

E. For the A Video Store problem in Chapters 3 (exercises L, M, and N) and 4 (exercises P and Q):

1. Create an activity diagram with swimlanes for one of the use cases.

2. Using the activity diagram, create a sequence diagram for each scenario.

3. Perform a CRUDE analysis to show the interactivity of the objects in the system.

4. Create a behavioral state machine to depict one of the classes on the class diagram you created for Chapter 4, exercise P.

5. Perform a verification and validation walkthrough of the problem.

F. For the gym membership problem in Chapters 3 (exercises O, P, and Q) and 4 (exercises R and S):

1. Create an activity diagram with swimlanes for one of the use cases.
2. Using the activity diagram, create a sequence diagram for each scenario.
3. Perform a CRUDE analysis to show the interactivity of the objects in the system.
4. Create a behavioral state machine to depict one of the classes on the class diagram you created for Chapter 4, exercise S.
5. Perform a verification and validation walkthrough of the problem.

G. For the Picnics R Us problem in Chapters 3 (exercises R, S, and T) and 4 (exercises T and U):
   1. Create an activity diagram with swimlanes for one of the use cases.
   2. Using the activity diagram, create a sequence diagram for each scenario.
   3. Perform a CRUDE analysis to show the interactivity of the objects in the system.

4. Create a behavioral state machine to depict one of the classes on the class diagram you created for Chapter 4, exercise T.
5. Perform a verification and validation walkthrough of the problem.

H. For the Of-the-Month-Club problem in Chapters 3 (exercises U, V, and W) and 3 (exercises V and W):
   1. Create an activity diagram with swimlanes for one of the use cases.
   2. Using the activity diagram, create a sequence diagram for each scenario.
   3. Perform a CRUDE analysis to show the interactivity of the objects in the system.
   4. Create a behavioral state machine to depict one of the classes on the class diagram you created for Chapter 4, exercise V.
   5. Perform a verification and validation walkthrough of the problem.

MINICASES

1. Refer to the functional model (use-case diagram, activity diagrams, and use-case descriptions) you prepared for the Professional and Scientific Staff Management (PSSM) Minicase in Chapter 3. Based on your performance, PSSM was so satisfied that it wanted you to develop both the structural and behavioral models so that it could more fully understand both the interaction that would take place between the users and the system and the system itself in greater detail.
   a. Create both CRC cards and a class diagram based on the functional models created in Chapter 3.
   b. Modify the activity diagrams created in Chapter 3 to include swimlanes for each of the use cases.
   c. Create a sequence diagram for each scenario of each use case identified in the functional model.
   d. Perform a CRUDE analysis to show the interactivity of the objects in the system.
   e. Create a behavioral state machine for each of the complex classes in the class diagram.
   f. Perform a verification and validation walkthrough of each model: functional, structural, and behavioral.

2. Refer to the structural model (CRC cards and class diagram) that you created for the Holiday Travel Vehicles Minicase in Chapter 4. Based on your performance, Holiday Travel Vehicles was so satisfied that it wanted you to develop both the functional and behavioral models so that it could more fully understand both the interaction that would take place between the users and the system and the system itself in greater detail.
   a. Based on the structural model you created in Chapter 4 and the problem description in Chapter 4, create a functional model (use-case diagram, activity diagrams, and use-case descriptions) for the business processes associated with the Holiday Travel Vehicles sales system. Be sure to include swimlanes with the activity diagrams.
   b. Create a sequence diagram for each scenario of each use case identified in the functional model.
   c. Perform a CRUDE analysis to show the interactivity of the objects in the system.
   d. Create a behavioral state machine for each of the complex classes in the class diagram.
   e. Perform a verification and validation walkthrough of each model: functional, structural, and behavioral.

PART TWO

DESIGN MODELING

Whereas analysis modeling concentrated on the functional requirements of the evolving system, design modeling incorporates the nonfunctional requirements. That is, design modeling focuses on *how* the system will operate. First, the project team verifies and validates the analysis models (functional, structural, and behavioral). Next, a set of factored and partitioned analysis models are created. The class and method designs are illustrated using the class specifications (using CRC cards and class diagrams), contracts, and method specifications. Next, the data management layer is addressed by designing the actual database or file structure to be used for object persistence, and a set of classes that will map the class specifications into the object persistence format chosen. Concurrently, the team produces the human–computer interaction layer design using use scenarios, windows navigation diagrams, real-use cases, interface templates, storyboards, wireframe diagrams, and user-interface prototypes. The application architecture layer design is created using deployment diagrams and hardware and system software specifications. This collection of deliverables represents the system specification that is handed to the programming team for implementation.

CHAPTER 6 Moving on to Design

Verifying and Validating the Analysis Models

Evolving the Analysis Models into Design Models

Packages and Package Diagrams

Design Criteria

Object Design Activities

Design Strategies

Selecting an Acquisition Strategy

CHAPTER 7 Class and Method Design

Additional Object Design Activities

Constraints and CRC Cards

Constraints and Contracts

Method Specification

Verifying and Validating Class and Method Design

CHAPTER 8 Data Management Layer Design

APPENDICES

CHAPTER 9 Human–Computer Interaction Layer Design

CHAPTER 10 Application Architecture Layer Design

MOVING ON TO DESIGN

Object-oriented system development uses the requirements that were gathered during analysis to create a blueprint for the future system. A successful object-oriented design builds upon what was learned in earlier phases and leads to a smooth implementation by creating a clear, accurate plan of what needs to be done. This chapter describes the initial transition from analysis to design and presents three ways to approach the design for the new system.

OBJECTIVES

- Understand the verification and validation of the analysis models.
- Understand the transition from analysis to design.
- Understand the use of factoring, partitions, and layers.
- Be able to create package diagrams.
- Become familiar with the design criteria of coupling, cohesion, and connascence.
- Be able to extend and restructure the problem domain object designs.
- Be able to identify the reuse of predefined classes, libraries, frameworks, and components.
- Be familiar with the custom, packaged, and outsource design alternatives.

INTRODUCTION

The purpose of analysis is to determine what the business needs are. The purpose of design is to decide how to build the system. The major activity that takes place during *design* is evolving the set of analysis representations into design representations.

Throughout design, the project team carefully considers the new system with respect to the current environment and systems that exist within the organization as a whole. Major considerations in determining how the system will work include environmental factors, such as integrating with existing systems, converting data from legacy systems, and leveraging skills that exist in-house or could be procured elsewhere. Although the planning and analysis are undertaken to develop a possible system, the goal of design is to create a blueprint for a system that can be implemented.

An important initial part of design is to examine several design strategies and decide which will be used to build the system. Systems can be built from scratch, purchased and customized, or outsourced to others, and the project team needs to investigate the viability of each alternative. This decision influences the tasks that are to be accomplished during design.

At the same time, detailed design of the individual classes and methods that are used to map out the nuts and bolts of the system and how they are to be stored must still be completed. Techniques such as CRC cards, class diagrams, contract specification, method specification, and database design provide the final design details in preparation for the construction phase, and they ensure that programmers have sufficient information to build the right system in compliance with the business needs and also efficiently. These topics are covered in Chapters 7 and 8.

Design also includes activities such as designing the user interface, system inputs, and system outputs, which involve the ways that the user interacts with the system. Chapter 9 describes these in detail, along with techniques such as storyboarding and prototyping, which help the project team design a system that meets the needs of its users and is satisfying to use.

Finally, application architecture decisions are made regarding the hardware and software that will be purchased to support the new system and the way that the processing of the system will be organized. For example, the system can be organized so that its processing is centralized at one location, distributed, or both centralized and distributed, and each solution offers unique benefits and challenges to the project team. Because global issues and security influence the implementation plans that are made, they need to be considered along with the system's technical architecture. Application architecture, security, and global issues are described in Chapter 10.

The many steps of design are highly interrelated and, as with the steps in analysis, the analysts often go back and forth among them. For example, prototyping in the interface design step often uncovers additional information that is needed in the system. Alternatively, a system that is being designed for an organization that has centralized systems might require substantial hardware and software investments if the project team decides to change to a system in which all the processing is distributed.

VERIFYING AND VALIDATING THE ANALYSIS MODELS

Before we evolve our analysis representations into design representations, we need to verify and validate the current set of analysis models to ensure that they faithfully represent the problem domain under consideration. This includes testing the fidelity of each model; for example, we must be sure that the activity diagram(s), use-case descriptions, and use-case diagrams all describe the same functional requirements. It also involves testing the fidelity between the models; for instance, transitions on a behavioral state machine are associated with operations contained in a class diagram. Figure 6-1 portrays the fact that the object-oriented analysis models are highly interrelated. This figure reinforces the fact that all modern systems should be built in a use case driven, architecture centric, and incremental and iterative manner. However, if we have completed all of the verifying and validating of the models as described in Chapters 3, 4, and 5, we will have successfully balanced them. However, given the importance of testing, we thought we would bring it up again.[1]

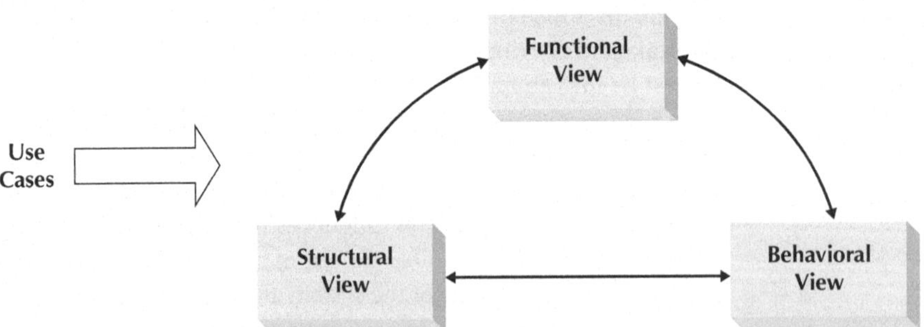

FIGURE 6-1
Object-Oriented
Analysis Models

---

[1] In fact, we return to testing in the follow-on design chapters (Chapters 7 through 10).

EVOLVING THE ANALYSIS MODELS INTO DESIGN MODELS

Now that we have successfully verified and validated our analysis models, we need to begin evolving them into appropriate design models. The purpose of the analysis models was to represent the underlying business problem domain as a set of collaborating objects. In other words, the analysis activities defined the functional requirements. To achieve this, the analysis activities ignored nonfunctional requirements such as performance and the system environment issues (e.g., distributed or centralized processing, user-interface issues, and database issues). In contrast, the primary purpose of the design models is to increase the likelihood of successfully delivering a system that implements the functional requirements in a manner that is affordable and easily maintainable. Therefore, in systems design, we address both the functional and nonfunctional requirements.

From an object-oriented perspective, system design models simply refine the system analysis models by adding system environment (or solution domain) details to them and refining the problem-domain information already contained in the analysis models. When evolving the analysis model into the design model, you should first carefully review the use cases and the current set of classes (their operations and attributes and the relationships between them). Are all the classes necessary? Are there any missing classes? Are the classes fully defined? Are any attributes or methods missing? Do the classes have any unnecessary attributes and methods? Is the current representation of the evolving system optimal? Obviously, if we have already verified and validated the analysis models, quite a bit of this has already taken place. Yet, given that object-oriented systems development is both incremental and iterative, we must review the analysis models again. However, this time we begin looking at the models of the problem domain through a design lens. In this step, we make modifications to the problem-domain models that will enhance the efficiency and effectiveness of the evolving system.

In the following sections, we introduce factoring, partitions and collaborations, and layers as a way to evolve problem domain-oriented analysis models into optimal solution domain-oriented design models. From an enhanced Unified Process perspective (see Figure 1-4), we are moving from the analysis workflow to the design workflow, and we are moving further into the Elaboration phase and partially into the Construction phase.

Factoring

Factoring is the process of separating out a *module* into a stand-alone module. The new module can be a new class or a new method. For example, when reviewing a set of classes, it may be discovered that they have a similar set of attributes and methods. Thus, it might make sense to factor out the similarities into a separate class. Depending on whether the new class should be in a superclass relationship to the existing classes or not, the new class can be related to the existing classes through a *generalization (a-kind-of)* or possibly through an *aggregation (has-parts)* relationship. Using the appointment system example, if the Employee class had not been identified, we could possibly identify it at this stage by factoring out the similar methods and attributes from the Nurse, Receptionist, and Doctor classes. In this case, we would relate the new class (Employee) to the existing classes using the generalization (a-kind-of) relationship. Obviously, by extension we also could have created the Participant class if it had not been previously identified.

Abstraction and *refinement* are two processes closely related to factoring. Abstraction deals with the creation of a higher-level idea from a set of more specific ideas. Identifying the Employee class is an example of abstracting from a set of lower classes to a higher one. In some cases, the abstraction process identifies *abstract classes,* whereas in other situations, it identifies additional *concrete classes*.[2] The refinement process is the opposite of the abstraction process. In the appointment system example, we could identify additional subclasses of the Employee class, such as Secretary and Bookkeeper. Of course, we would add the new classes only if there were sufficient differences among them. Otherwise, the more general class, Employee, would suffice.

Partitions and Collaborations

Based on all the factoring, refining, and abstracting that can take place to the evolving system, the sheer size of the system representation can overload the user and the developer. At this point in the evolution of the system, it might make sense to split the representation into a set of *partitions*. A partition is the object-oriented equivalent of a subsystem,[3] where a subsystem is a decomposition of a larger system into its component systems (e.g., an accounting information system could be functionally decomposed into an accounts-payable system, an accounts-receivable system, a payroll system, etc.). From an object-oriented perspective, partitions are based on the pattern of activity (messages sent) among the objects in an object-oriented system. We describe an easy approach to model partitions and collaborations later in this chapter: packages and package diagrams.

If you recall, an individual class can support multiple use cases. Therefore, an individual class can participate in multiple use-case-based *collaborations*. In cases where classes are supporting multiple use cases, the collaborations should be merged. The class diagram should be reviewed to see how the different classes are related to one another. For example, if attributes of a class have complex object types, such as Person, Address, or Department, and these object types were not modeled as associations in the class diagram, we need to recognize these implied associations. Creating a diagram that combines the class diagram with the message passing on the sequence diagrams can be very useful to show to what degree the classes are coupled.[4] The greater the coupling between classes, the more likely the classes should be grouped together in a collaboration or partition. By looking at a CRUDE matrix, we can use *CRUDE analysis* (see Chapter 5) to identify potential classes on which to merge collaborations.

One of the easiest techniques to identify the classes that could be grouped to form a collaboration is through the use of cluster analysis or multiple dimensional scaling. These statistical techniques enable the team to objectively group classes together based on their affinity for each other. The affinity can be based on semantic relationships, different types of messages being sent between them (e.g., create, read, update, delete, or execute), or some weighted combination of both. There are many different similarity measures and many different algorithms on which the clusters can be based, so one must be careful when using these techniques. Always make sure that the collaborations identified using these techniques make sense from the problem-domain perspective. Just because a mathematical algorithm suggests that the classes belong together does not make it so. However, this is a good approach to create a first-cut set of collaborations.

---

[2] See Chapter 4 for the differences between abstract and concrete classes.

[3] Some authors refer to partitions as subsystems [e.g., see R. Wirfs-Brock, B. Wilkerson, and L. Weiner, *Designing Object-Oriented Software* (Englewood Cliffs, NJ: Prentice Hall, 1990)], whereas others refer to them as layers [e.g., see I. Graham, *Migrating to Object Technology* (Reading, MA: Addison-Wesley, 1994)]. However, we have chosen to use the term *partition* [C. Larman, *Applying UML and Patterns: An Introduction to Object-Oriented Analysis and Design* (Englewood Cliffs, NJ: Prentice Hall, 1998)] to minimize confusion between subsystems in a traditional systems development approach and layers associated with Rational's Unified Approach.

[4] We describe the concept of coupling later in this chapter.

Depending on the complexity of the merged collaboration, it may be useful in decomposing the collaboration into multiple partitions. In this case, in addition to having collaborations between objects, it is possible to have collaborations among partitions. The general rule is the more messages sent between objects, the more likely the objects belong in the same partition. The fewer messages sent, the less likely the two objects belong together.

Another useful approach to identifying potential partitions is to model each collaboration between objects in terms of clients, servers, and contracts. A *client* is an instance of a *class* that sends a *message* to an instance of another class for a *method* to be executed; a *server* is the instance of a class that receives the message; and a *contract* is the specification that formalizes the interactions between the client and server objects (see Chapters 4 and 7). This approach allows the developer to build up potential partitions by looking at the contracts that have been specified between objects. In this case, the more contracts there are between objects, the more likely the objects belong in the same partition, and the reverse is true.

Remember, the primary purpose of identifying collaborations and partitions is to determine which classes should be grouped together in design.

Layers

Until this point in the development of our system, we have focused only on the problem domain; we have totally ignored the system environment (data management, user interface, and application architecture). To successfully evolve the analysis model of the system into a design model of the system, we must add the system environment information. One useful way to do this, without overloading the developer, is to use *layers*. A layer represents an element of the software architecture of the evolving system. We have focused only on one layer in the evolving software architecture: the problem-domain layer. There should be a layer for each of the different elements of the system environment (e.g., data management, user interface, and application architecture). Like partitions and collaborations, layers also can be portrayed using packages and package diagrams (see the next section of this chapter).

The idea of separating the different elements of the architecture into separate layers can be traced back to the *Model–View–Controller (MVC)* architecture of *Smalltalk*.[5] When Smalltalk was first created,[6] the authors decided to separate the application logic from the logic of the user interface. In this manner, it was possible to easily develop different user interfaces that worked with the same application. To accomplish this, they created the *MVC* architecture, where *Models* implemented the application logic (problem domain) and *Views* and *Controllers* implemented the logic for the user interface. Views handled the output, and Controllers handled the input. Because graphical user interfaces were first developed in the Smalltalk language, the MVC architecture served as the foundation for virtually all graphical user interfaces that have been developed today (including the Mac interfaces, the Windows family, and the various Unix-based GUI environments).

---

[5] See S. Lewis, *The Art and Science of Smalltalk: An Introduction to Object-Oriented Programming Using Visual-Works* (Englewood Cliffs, NJ: Prentice Hall, 1995).

[6] Smalltalk was invented in the early 1970s by a software-development research team at Xerox PARC. It introduced many new ideas into the area of programming languages (e.g., object orientation, windows-based user interfaces, reusable class library, and the development environment). In many ways, Smalltalk is the parent of all object-based and object-oriented languages, such as Visual Basic, C++, and Java.

Layers	Examples	Relevant Chapters
Foundation	Date, Enumeration	6, 7
Problem Domain	Employee, Customer	2, 3, 4, 5, 6, 7
Data Accessand Management	DataInputStream, FileInputStream	7, 8
Human Computer Interaction	Button, Panel	7, 9
Application Architecture	ServerSocket, URLConnection	7, 10

FIGURE 6-2
Layers and Sample Classes

Based on Smalltalk's innovative MVC architecture, many different software layers have been proposed.[7] We suggest the following layers for software architecture: foundation, problem domain, data management, human–computer interaction, and application architecture (see Figure 6-2). Each layer limits the types of classes that can exist on it (e.g., only user interface classes may exist on the human–computer interaction layer).

Foundation The *foundation layer* is, in many ways, a very uninteresting layer. It contains classes that are necessary for any object-oriented application to exist. They include classes that represent fundamental data types (e.g., integers, real numbers, characters, and strings), classes that represent fundamental data structures, sometimes referred to as *container classes* (e.g., lists, trees, graphs, sets, stacks, and queues), and classes that represent useful abstractions, sometimes referred to as *utility classes* (e.g., date, time, and money). These classes are rarely, if ever, modified by a developer. They are simply used. Today, the classes found on this layer are typically included with the object-oriented development environments.

Problem Domain The *problem-domain layer* is what we have focused our attention on up until now. The focus of the problem-domain layer was the functional requirements. At this stage in the development of our system, we need to further detail the classes so that we can implement them in an effective and efficient manner. In other words, we need to begin switching our focus from optimizing the user's perspective and start optimizing for the machine's perspective. Many issues need to be addressed when designing classes such that they will be implemented in an efficient manner. For example, there are criteria that are useful in evaluating the "goodness" of the design described in this chapter and there are various design activities that are useful in optimizing the design for the machine described in Chapter 7.

Data Management The *data management layer* addresses the issues involving the persistence of the objects contained in the system. The types of classes that appear in this layer deal with how objects can be stored and retrieved. The classes contained in this layer are called the *Data Access and Manipulation (DAM) classes*. The DAM classes allow the problem-domain classes to be independent of the storage used and, hence, increase the portability of the evolving system. Some of the issues related to this layer include choice of the storage format and optimization.

---

[7] For example, Problem Domain, Human Interaction, Task Management, and Data Management [P. Coad and E. Yourdon, *Object-Oriented Design* (Englewood Cliffs, NJ: Yourdon Press, 1991)]; Domain, Application, and Interface (I. Graham, *Migrating to Object Technology* [Reading, MA: Addison-Wesley, 1994)]; Domain, Service, and Presentation [C. Larman, *Applying UML and Patterns: An Introduction to Object-Oriented Analysis and Design* (Englewood Cliffs, NJ: Prentice Hall, 1998)]; Business, View, and Access [A. Bahrami, *Object-Oriented Systems Development using the Unified Modeling Language* (New York: McGraw-Hill, 1999)]; ApplicationSpecific, Application-General, Middleware, System-Software [I. Jacobson, G. Booch, and J. Rumbaugh, *The Unified Software Development Process* (Reading, MA: Addison-Wesley, 1999)]; Foundation, Architecture, Business, and Application [M. Page-Jones, *Fundamentals of Object-Oriented Design in UML* (Reading, MA: AddisonWesley, 2000)].

There is a plethora of different options in which to choose to store objects. These include sequential files, random access files, relational databases, object/relational databases, object-oriented databases, NoSQL and NewSQL data stores along with data lakes and structured files (e.g., XLM and JSON). Each of these options has been optimized to provide solutions for different access and storage problems. Today, from a practical perspective, there is no single solution that optimally serves all applications. The correct solution is most likely some combination of the different storage options. A complete description of all the issues related to the data management layer is well beyond the scope of this book.[8] However, we do present the fundamentals in Chapter 8.

Human–Computer Interaction

The *human–computer interaction layer* contains classes associated with the View and Controller idea from Smalltalk. The primary purpose of this layer is to keep the specific user-interface implementation separate from the problem-domain classes. This increases the portability of the evolving system. Typical classes found on this layer include classes that can be used to represent buttons, windows, text fields, scroll bars, check boxes, drop-down lists, and many other classes that represent user-interface elements.

When designing the user interface for an application, many issues must be addressed: How important is consistency across different user interfaces? What about differing levels of user experience? How is the user expected to be able to navigate through the system? What about help systems and online manuals? What types of input elements should be included? What types of output elements should be included? Other questions that must be addressed are related to the platform on which the software will be deployed. For example, is the application going to run on a stand-alone computer, is it going to be distributed, or is the application going mobile? If it is expected to run on mobile devices, what type of platform: notebooks, tablets, phones or even wearables? Will it be deployed using Web technology, which runs on multiple devices, or will it be created using apps? Depending on the answer to these questions, different types of user interfaces are possible.

With the advent of social networking platforms, such as Facebook, X, blogs, YouTube, and LinkedIn, the implications for the user interface can be mind boggling. Depending on the application, different social networking platforms may be appropriate for different aspects of the application. Furthermore, each of the different social networking platforms enables (or prevents) consideration of different types of user interfaces. Finally, with the potential audience of your application being global, many different cultural issues will arise in the design and development of culturally aware user interfaces (such as multilingual requirements). Obviously, a complete description of all the issues related to human–computer interaction is beyond the scope of this book.[9] However, from the user's perspective, the user interface is the system. We present the basic issues in user interface design in Chapter 9.

---

[8] There are many good database design books that are relevant to this layer; see, for example, M. Gillenson, *Fundamentals of Database Management Systems* (Hoboken, NJ: John Wiley & Sons, 2005); F. R. McFadden, J. A. Hoffer, and Mary B. Prescott, *Modern Database Management,* 4th Ed. (Reading, MA: Addison-Wesley, 1998); M. Blaha and W. Premerlani, *Object-Oriented Modeling and Design for Database Applications* (Englewood Cliffs, NJ: Prentice Hall, 1998); R. J. Muller, *Database Design for Smarties: Using UML for Data Modeling* (San Francisco: Morgan Kaufmann, 1999).

[9] Books on user interface design that address these issues include B. Schneiderman, *Designing the User Interface: Strategies for Effective Human Computer Interaction*, 3rd Ed. (Reading, MA: Addison-Wesley, 1998); J. Tidwell, *Designing Interfaces: Patterns for Effective Interaction Design*, 2nd Ed. (Sebastopol, CA: O'Reilly Media, 2010); S. Krug, *Don't Make Me Think: A Common Sense Approach to Web Usability* (Berkeley, CA: New Riders Publishing, 2006); N. Singh and A. Pereira, *The Culturally Customized Web Site: Customizing Web Sites for the Global Marketplace* (Oxford, UK: Elsevier, 2005).

Application Architecture The *application architecture layer* addresses how the software will execute on specific computers and networks. This layer includes classes that deal with communication between the software and the computer's operating system and the network. For example, classes that address how to interact with the various ports on a specific computer are included in this layer.

Unlike in the foundation layer, many design issues must be addressed before choosing the appropriate set of classes for this layer. These design issues include the choice of a computing or network architecture, the actual design of a network, hardware and server software specification, and security issues. Other issues that must be addressed with the design of this layer include computer hardware and software configuration (choice of operating systems, such as Linux, Mac OSX, Android and Windows; processor types and speeds; amount of memory; data storage; and input/output technology), standardization, virtualization, grid computing, distributed computing, and Web services. The cloud is essentially a form of distributed computing. In this case, the cloud allows you to treat the platform, infrastructure, software, and even business processes as remote services that can be managed by another firm. In many ways, the cloud allows much of IT to be outsourced (see the discussion of outsourcing later in this chapter). Also as brought up with the human–computer interaction layer, the whole issue of mobile computing is very relevant to this layer. In particular, the different devices, such as phones and tablets, are relevant and the way they will communicate with each other, such as through cellular networks or Wi-Fi, is also important.

Finally, given the amount of power that IT requires today, the whole topic of Green IT must be addressed. Topics that need to be addressed related to Green IT are the location of the data center, data center cooling, alternative power sources, reduction of consumables, the idea of a paperless office, Energy Star compliance, and the potential impact of virtualization, the cloud, and mobile computing. Like the data management and human–computer interaction layers, a complete description of all the issues related to the application architecture is beyond the scope of this book.[10] However, we do present the basic issues in Chapter 10.

PACKAGES AND PACKAGE DIAGRAMS

In UML, collaborations, partitions, and layers can be represented by a higher-level construct: a package.[11] In fact, a package serves the same purpose as a folder on your computer. When packages are used in programming languages such as Java, packages are actually implemented as folders. A *package* is a general construct that can be applied to any of the elements in UML models. In Chapter 3, we introduced the idea of packages as a way to group use cases together to make the use-case diagrams easier to read and to keep the models at a reasonable level of complexity. In Chapter 5 we did the same thing for class diagrams, respectively. In this section, we describe a *package diagram*: a diagram composed only of packages.

The symbol for a package is similar to a tabbed folder (see Figure 6-3). Depending on where a package is used, packages can participate in different types of relationships. For example, in a class diagram, packages represent groupings of classes. Therefore, aggregation and association relationships are possible.

---

[10] Some books that cover these topics include S. D. Burd, *Systems Architecture*, 6th Ed. (Boston: Course Technology, 2011); I. Englander, *The Architecture of Computer Hardware, Systems Software, & Networking: An Information Technology Approach* (Hoboken, NJ: Wiley, 2009); K.K. Hausman and S. Cook, *IT Architecture for Dummies* (Hoboken, NJ: Wiley Publishing, 2011).

[11] This discussion is based on material in Chapter 7 of M. Fowler with K. Scott, *UML Distilled: A Brief Guide to the Standard Object Modeling Language*, 3rd Ed. (Reading, MA: Addison-Wesley, 2004).

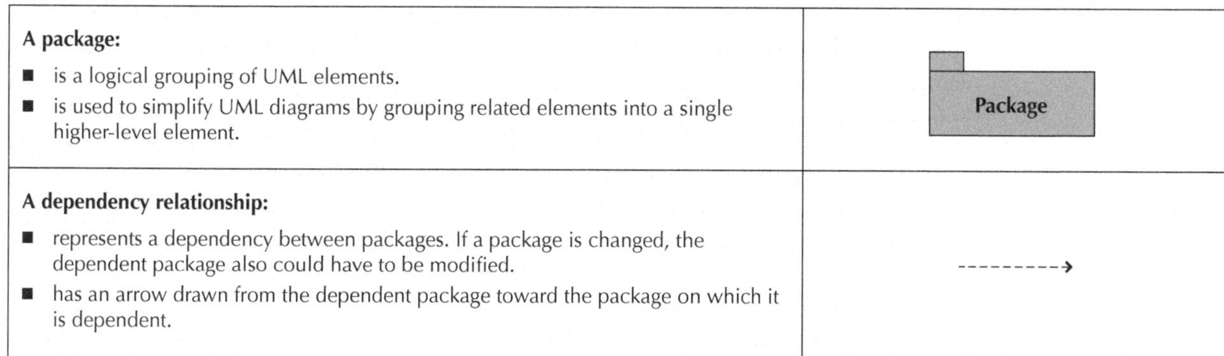

A package:	
■ is a logical grouping of UML elements. ■ is used to simplify UML diagrams by grouping related elements into a single higher-level element.	Package
A dependency relationship: ■ represents a dependency between packages. If a package is changed, the dependent package also could have to be modified. ■ has an arrow drawn from the dependent package toward the package on which it is dependent.	- - - - - - - ->

FIGURE 6-3   Syntax for Package Diagram

In a package diagram, it is useful to depict a new relationship, the *dependency relationship*. A dependency relationship is portrayed by a dashed arrow (see Figure 6-3). A dependency relationship represents the fact that a modification dependency exists between two packages. That is, it is possible that a change in one package could cause a change to be required in another package. Figure 6-4 portrays the dependencies among the different layers (foundation, problem domain, data management, human–computer interaction, and application architecture). For example, if a change occurs in the problem-domain layer, it most likely will cause changes to occur in the human–computer interaction, application architecture, and data management layers. Notice that these layers point to the problem-domain layer and therefore

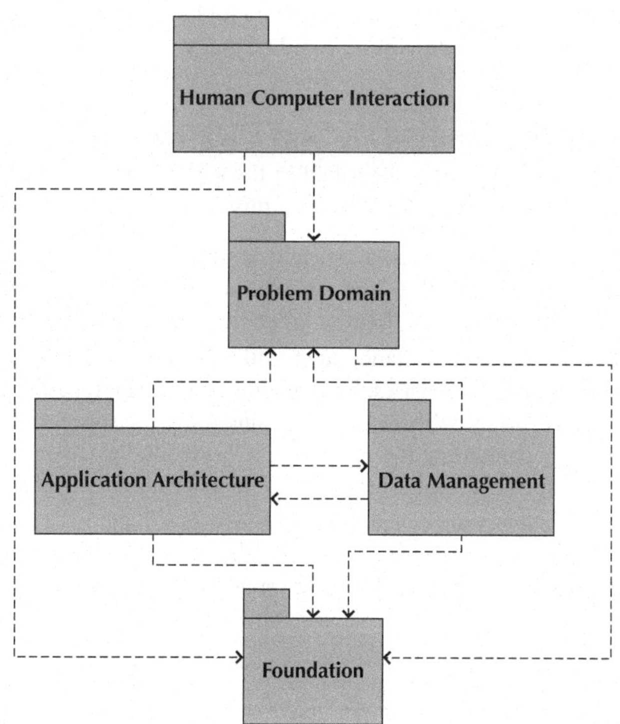

FIGURE 6-4
Package Diagram
of Dependency
Relationships among
Layers

are dependent on it. However, the reverse is not true.[12] Also note that all layers are dependent upon the foundation layer. This is due to the contents of the foundation layer being the fundamental classes from which all other classes will be built. Consequently, any changes made to this layer could have ramifications to all other layers.

At the class level, there could be many causes for dependencies among classes. For example, if the signature for a method is changed, then this causes the interface for all objects of this class to change. In other words, the contract has been modified. Therefore, all classes that have objects that send messages to the instances of the modified class might have to be modified. Capturing dependency relationships among the classes and packages helps the organization in maintaining object-oriented information systems.

Collaborations, partitions, and layers are modeled as packages in UML. Collaborations are normally factored into a set of partitions, which are typically placed on a layer. Partitions can be composed of other partitions. Also, it is possible to have classes in partitions, which are contained in another partition, which is placed on a layer. All these groupings are represented using packages in UML. Remember that a package is simply a generic grouping construct used to simplify UML models through the use of composition.

A simple package diagram, based on the appointment system example from the previous chapters, is shown in Figure 6-5. This diagram portrays only a very small portion of the entire system. In this case, we see that the Patient UI, Patient-DAM, and Patient Table classes depend on the Patient class. Furthermore, the Patient-DAM class depends on the Patient Table class. The same can be seen with the classes dealing with the actual appointments. By isolating the Problem-domain classes (such as the Patient and Appt classes) from the actual object persistence classes (such as the Patient Table and Appt Table classes) through the use of the intermediate Data Management classes (Patient-DAM and Appt-DAM classes), we isolate the Problem-domain classes from the actual storage medium.[13] This greatly simplifies the maintenance and increases the reusability of the Problem-domain classes. Of course, in a complete description of a real system, there would be many more dependencies.

Guidelines for Creating Package Diagrams

As with the UML diagrams described in the earlier chapters, we provide a set of guidelines that we have adapted from Scott W.[14] In this case, we offer six guidelines.

- Use package diagrams to logically organize designs. Specifically, use packages to group classes together when there is an inheritance, aggregation, or composition relationship between them or when the classes form a collaboration.

- In some cases, inheritance, aggregation, or association relationships exist between packages. In those cases, for readability purposes, try to support inheritance relationships vertically, with the package containing the superclass being placed above the package containing the subclass. Use horizontal placement to support aggregation and association relationships, with the packages being placed side by side.

- When a dependency relationship exists on a diagram, it implies that there is at least one semantic relationship between elements of the two packages. The direction of the dependency is typically from the subclass to the superclass, from the whole to the

---

[12] A useful side effect of the dependencies among the layers is that the project manager can divide the project team up into separate teams: one for each design layer. This is possible because each of the design layers is dependent on the problem-domain layer, which has been the focus of analysis. In design, the team can gain some productivity-based efficiency by working on the different layer designs in parallel.

[13] These issues are described in more detail in Chapter 8.

[14] S. W. Ambler, *The Elements of UML 2.0 Style* (Cambridge, UK: Cambridge University Press, 2005).

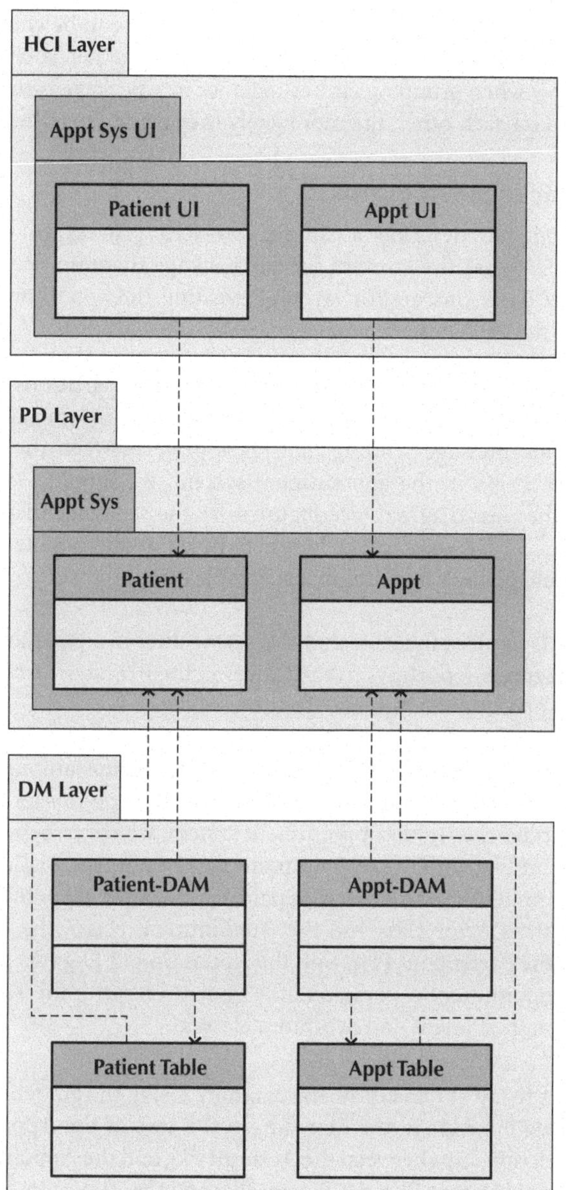

FIGURE 6-5
Partial Package Diagram of the Appointment System

part, and with contracts, from the client to the server. In other words, a subclass is dependent on the existence of a superclass, a whole is dependent upon its parts existing, and a client can't send a message to a nonexistent server.

- When using packages to group use cases together, be sure to include the actors and the associations that they have with the use cases grouped in the package. This will allow the diagram's user to better understand the context of the diagram.

- Give each package a simple, but descriptive name to provide the package diagram user with enough information to understand what the package encapsulates. Otherwise, the user will have to drill-down or open up the package to understand the package's purpose.

■ Be sure that packages are cohesive. For a package to be cohesive, the classes contained in the package, in some sense, belong together. A simple, but not perfect, rule to follow when grouping classes together in a package is that the more the classes depend on each other, the more likely they belong together in a package.

Creating Package Diagrams

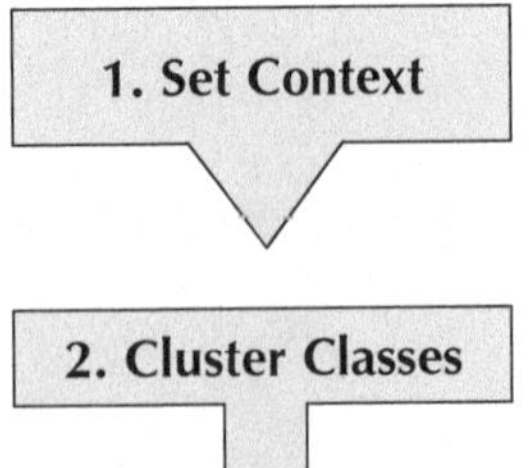

In this section, we describe a simple five-step process to create package diagrams. The first step is to set the context for the package diagram. Remember, packages can be used to model partitions and/or layers. Revisiting the appointment system again, let's set the context as the problem-domain layer.

The second nstep is to cluster the classes together into partitions based on the relationships that the classes share. The relationships include generalization, aggregation, the various associations, and the message sending that takes place between the objects in the system. To identify the packages in the appointment system, we should look at the different analysis models [e.g., the class diagram (see Figure 4-8), the sequence diagrams (see Figures 5-1 and 5-3)], and the CRUDE matrix (see Figure 5-12). If at all possible, classes in a generalization hierarchy should be kept together in a single partition.

The third step is to place the clustered classes together in a partition and model the partitions as packages. Figure 6-6 portrays five packages in the PD Layer: Account Pkg, Participant Pkg, Patient Pkg, Appointment Pkg, and Treatment Pkg.

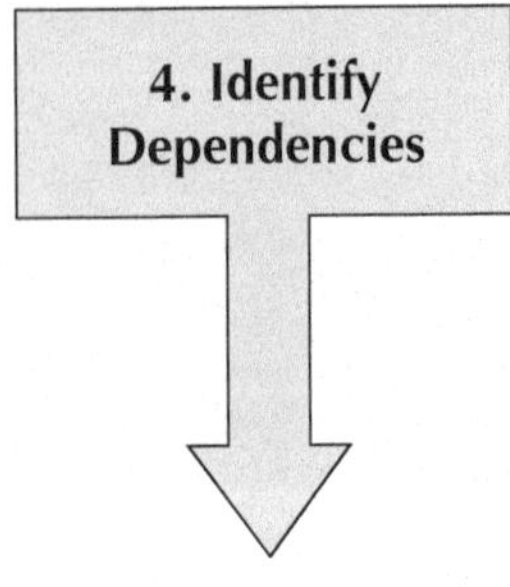

The fourth step is to identify the dependency relationships among the packages. We accomplish this by reviewing the relationships that cross the boundaries of the packages to uncover potential dependencies. In the appointment system, we see association relationships that connect the Account Pkg with the Appointment Pkg (via the associations between the Entry class and the Appointment class), the Participant Pkg with the Appointment Pkg (via the association between the Doctor class and the Appointment class), the Patient Pkg, which is contained within the Participant Pkg, with the Appointment Pkg (via the association between the Patient and Appointment classes), and the Patient Pkg with the Treatment Pkg (via the association between the Patient and Symptom classes).

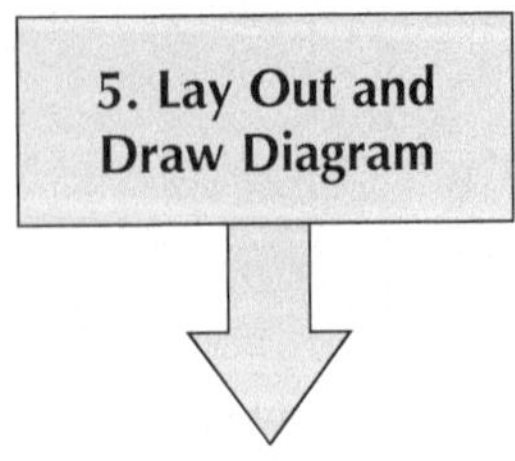

The fifth step is to lay out and draw the diagram. Using the guidelines, place the packages and dependency relationships in the diagram. In the case of the Appointment system, there are dependency relationships between the Account Pkg and the Appointment Pkg, the Participant Pkg and the Appointment Pkg, the Patient Pkg and the Appointment Pkg, and the Patient Pkg and the Treatment Pkg. To increase the understandability of the dependency relationships among the different packages, a pure package diagram that shows only the dependency relationships among the packages can be created (see Figure 6-7).

Verifying and Validating Package Diagrams

Like all the previous models, package diagrams need to be verified and validated. In this case, the package diagrams were derived primarily from the class diagram, the sequence diagrams, and the CRUDE matrix. Only two areas need to be reviewed.

First, the identified packages must make sense from a problem domain or functional requirements point of view. For example, in the context of an appointment system, the packages in Figure 6-7 (Participant, Patient, Appointment, Account, and Treatment) seem to be reasonable.

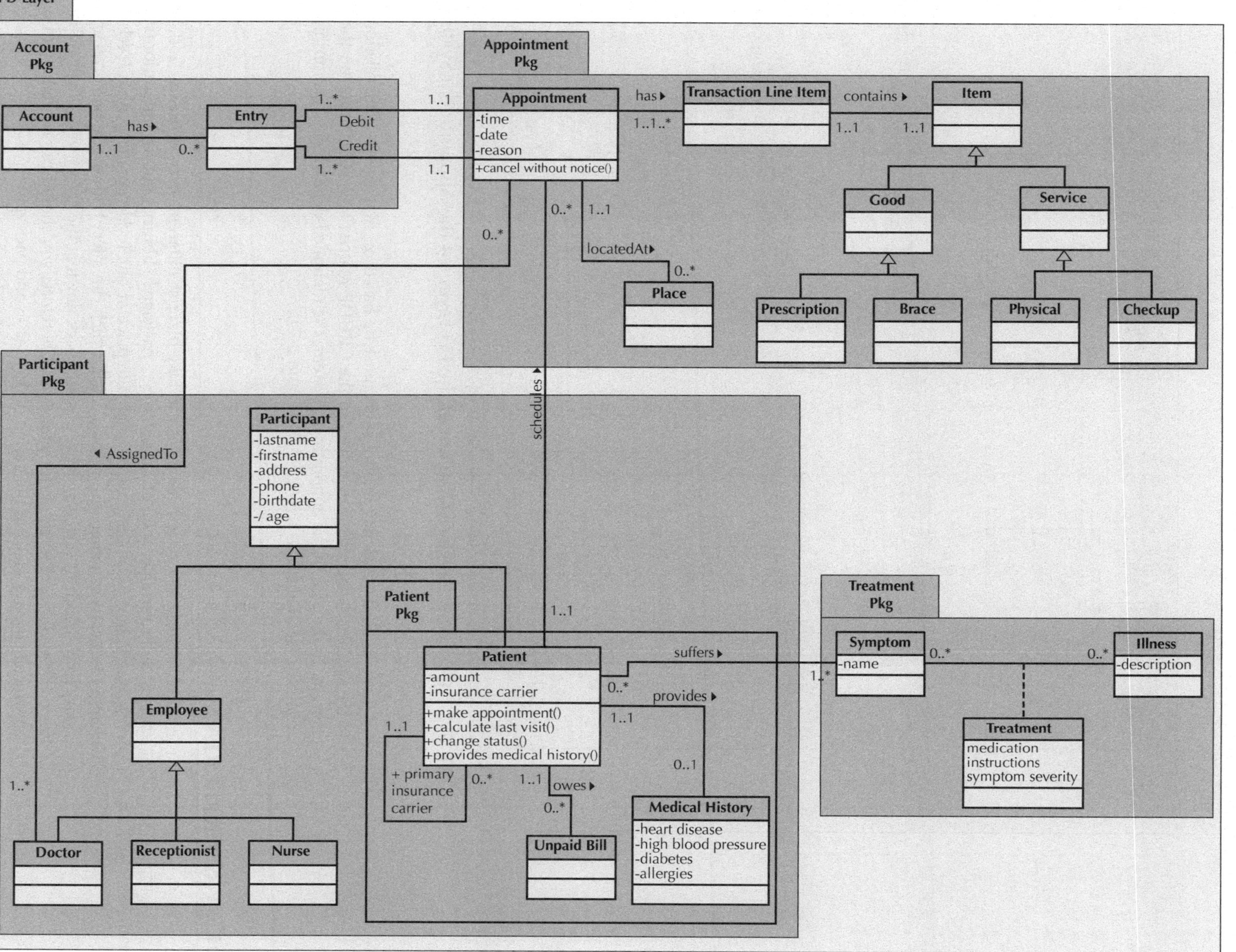

FIGURE 6-6 Package Diagram of the PD Layer of the Appointment Problem

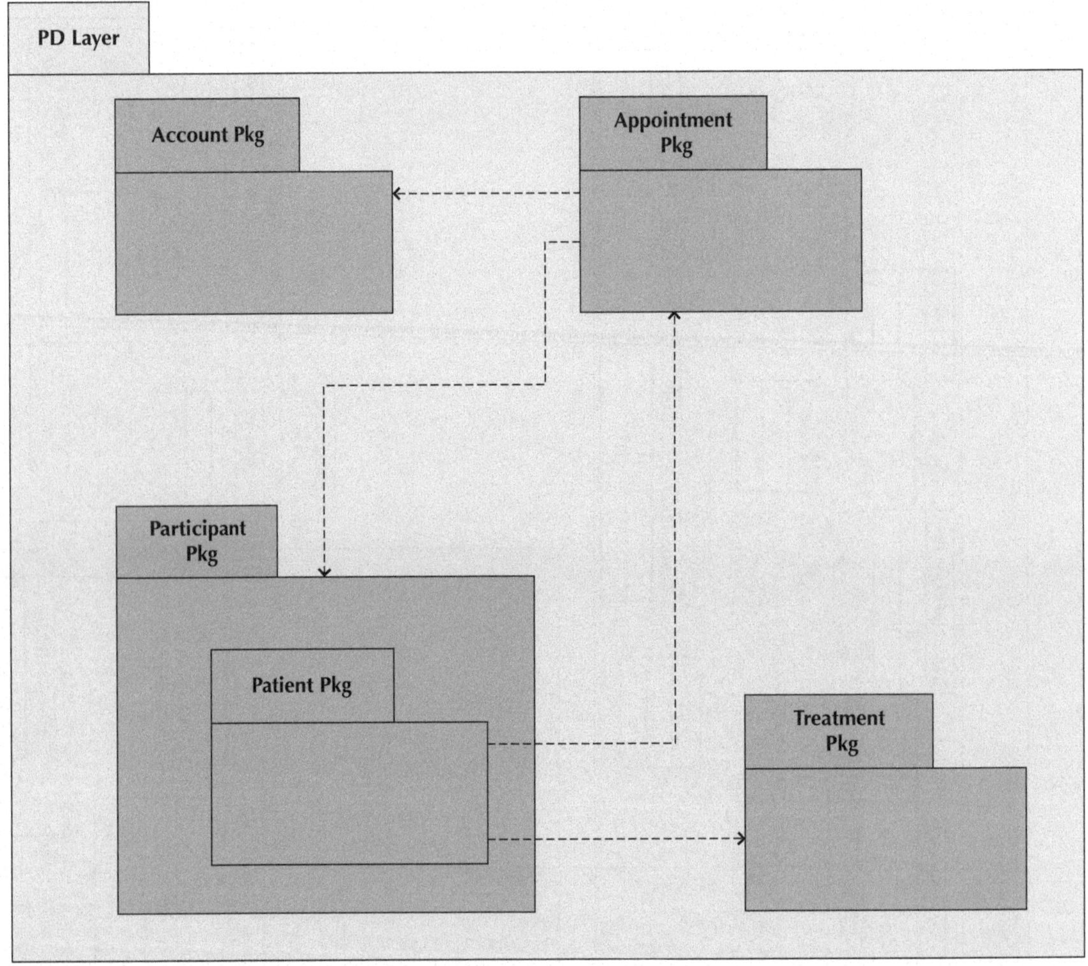

FIGURE 6-7 Overview Package Diagram of the PD Layer for the Appointment System

Second, all dependency relationships must be based on message-sending relationships on the sequence diagrams, cell entries in the CRUDE matrix, and associations on the class diagram. In the case of the appointment system, the identified dependency relationships are reasonable (see Figures 4-8, 5-1, 5-3, 5-12, and 6-7).

DESIGN CRITERIA

In an object-oriented system, changes can take place at different levels of abstraction. These levels include variable, method, class/object, package,[15] library, and/or application/system levels (see Figure 6-8). The changes that take place at one level can affect other levels (e.g., changes to a class can affect the package level, which can affect both the system level and the library level, which in turn can cause changes back down at the class level). Finally, changes can occur at different levels at the same time. Therefore, you should pay careful attention to any and all changes made to the design of the classes and packages.

[15] Other names for a package include cluster, partition, pattern, subject, and subsystem.

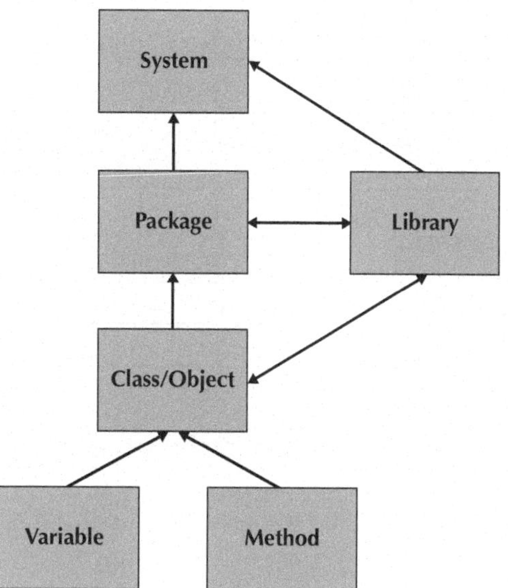

FIGURE 6-8
Levels of Abstraction
in Object-Oriented
Systems

Source: (Based on material from David P. Tegarden, Steven D. Sheetz, and David E. Monarchi, "A Software Complexity Model of Object-Oriented Systems," *Decision Support Systems* 13 (March 1995): 241–262.)

When considering the design of an object-oriented system, a set of criteria exists that can be used to determine whether the design is a good one or a bad one. According to Coad and Yourdon,[16] "A good design is one that balances trade-offs to minimize the total cost of the system over its entire lifetime." These criteria include coupling, cohesion, and connascence.

Coupling

Coupling refers to how interdependent or interrelated the modules (classes, objects, and methods) are in a system. The higher the interdependency, the more likely changes in part of a design can cause changes to be required in other parts of the design. For object-oriented systems, Coad and Yourdon[17] identified two types of coupling to consider: interaction and inheritance.

Interaction coupling deals with the coupling among methods and objects through message passing. Lieberherr and Holland put forth the *Law of Demeter* as a guideline to minimize this type of coupling.[18] Essentially, the law minimizes the number of objects that can receive messages from a given object. The law states that an object should send messages only to one of the following:

- Itself (For example, in Figure 6-9a, Object1 can send Message1 to itself. In other words, a method associated with Object1 can use other methods associated with Object1.[19])
- An object that is contained in an attribute of the object or one of its superclasses (For example, in Figure 6-9b, the PO1 instance of the Purchase Order class should be able to send messages using its Customer, State, and Date attributes.)

[16] Peter Coad and Edward Yourdon, *Object-Oriented Design* (Englewood Cliffs, NJ: Yourdon Press, 1991), p. 128.

[17] Ibid.

[18] Karl J. Lieberherr and Ian M. Holland, "Assuring Good Style for Object-Oriented Programs," *IEEE Software* 6, no. 5 (September, 1989): 38–48; Karl J. Lieberherr, *Adaptive Object-Oriented Software: The Demeter Method with Propagation Patterns* (Boston, MA: PWS Publishing, 1996).

[19] Obviously, this is stating what is expected.

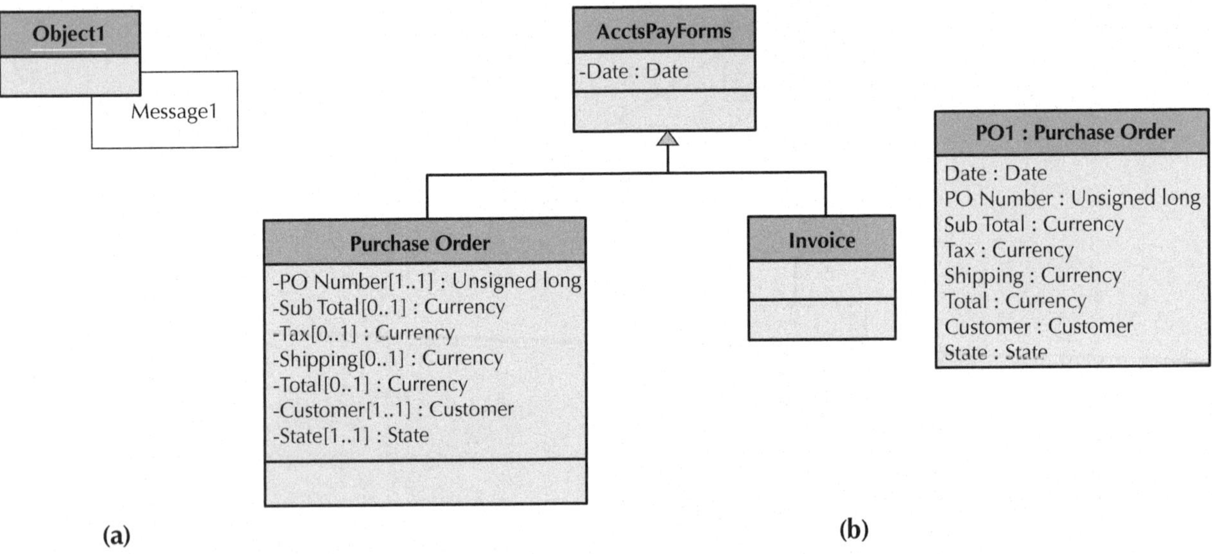

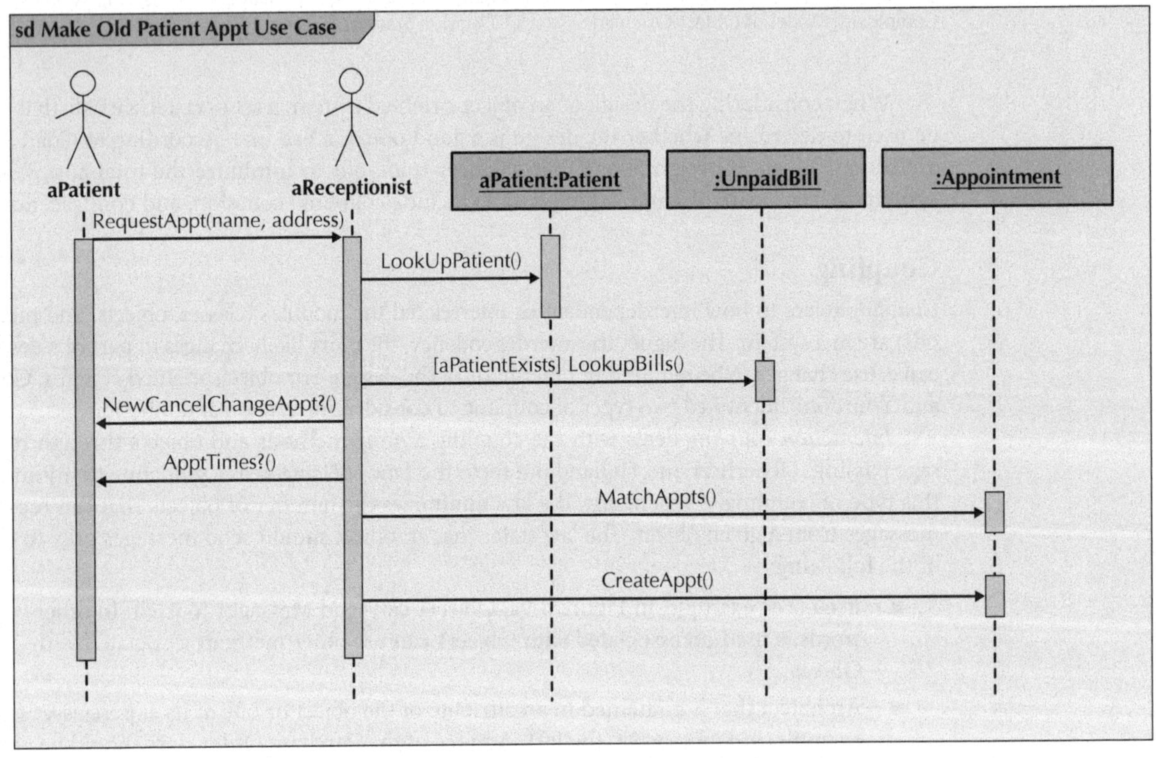

FIGURE 6-9 Examples of Interaction Coupling

- An object that is passed as a parameter to the method (For example, in Figure 6-9c, the aPatient instance sends the message Request Appt(name, address) to the aReceptionist instance, which is allowed to send messages to the instances contained in the name and address parameters.)

- An object that is created by the method (For example, in Figure 6-9c, the method Request Appt associated with the aReceptionist instance creates an instance of the Appointment class. The Request Appt method is allowed to send messages to that instance.)

- An object that is stored in a global variable.[20]

Even though the law of Demeter attempts to minimize interaction coupling among methods and objects, each of the above allowed forms of message sending in fact increases coupling. For example, the coupling increases between the objects if the calling method passes attributes to the called method or if the calling method depends on the value being returned by the called method.

Inheritance coupling, as its name implies, deals with how tightly coupled the classes are in an inheritance hierarchy. Most authors tend to say simply that this type of coupling is desirable. However, depending on the issues raised previously in the appendix of Chapter 1 with inheritance—inheritance conflicts, redefinition capabilities, and dynamic binding—a high level of inheritance coupling might not be a good thing. For example, in Figure 6-10, should Method2() defined in Subclass be allowed to call Method1() defined in Superclass? Or, should Method2() defined in Subclass refer to Attribute1 defined in Superclass? Or, even more confusing, assuming that Superclass is an abstract class, can a Method1() call Method2() or use Attribute2 defined in Subclass? Obviously, the first two examples have some intuitive sense. Using the properties of a superclass is the primary purpose of inheriting from it in the first place. On the other hand, the third example is somewhat counterintuitive. However, owing to the way that different object-oriented programming languages support dynamic binding, polymorphism, and inheritance, all these examples could be possible.

As Snyder has pointed out, most problems with inheritance involve the ability within the object-oriented programming languages to violate the encapsulation and information-hiding principles.[21] From a design perspective, the developer needs to optimize the trade-offs of violating the encapsulation and information-hiding principles and increasing the desirable coupling between subclasses and its superclasses. The best way to solve this conundrum is to ensure that inheritance is used only to support generalization/specialization (a-kind-of) semantics and the principle of substitutability (see Chapter 4). All other uses should be avoided.

Cohesion

Cohesion refers to how self-contained, atomistic and single-minded a module (class, object, or method) is within a system. A class or object should represent only one thing, and a method should solve only a single task. Three general types of cohesion have been identified by Coad and Yourdon for object-oriented systems: method, class, and generalization/specialization.[22]

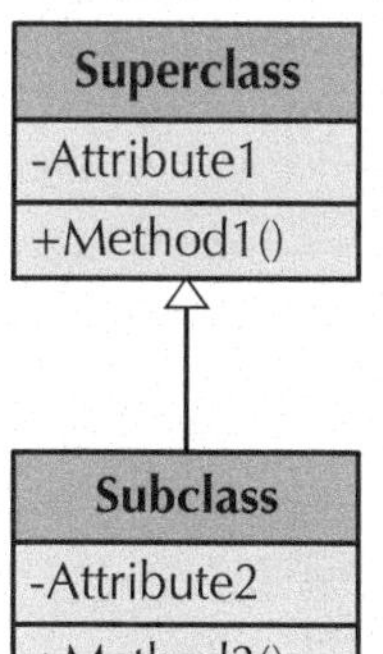

FIGURE 6-10
Example of Inheritance Coupling

---

[20] From a design perspective, global variables should be avoided. Most pure object-oriented programming languages do not explicitly support global variables, and we do not address them any further.

[21] Alan Snyder, "Encapsulation and Inheritance in Object-Oriented Programming Languages," in N. Meyrowitz (Ed.), *OOPSLA '86 Conference Proceedings, ACM SigPlan Notices* 21, no. 11 (November 1986); Alan Snyder, "Inheritance and the Development of Encapsulated Software Components," in B. Shriver and P. Wegner (Eds.), *Research Directions in Object-Oriented Programming* (Cambridge, MA: MIT Press, 1987).

[22] Coad and Yourdon, *Object-Oriented Design*.

Method cohesion addresses the cohesion within an individual method (i.e., how single-minded a method is). Methods should do one and only one thing. A method that actually performs multiple functions is more difficult to understand—and, therefore, to implement and maintain—than one that performs only a single function. In general, method cohesion should be maximized.

Class cohesion is the level of cohesion among the attributes and methods of a class (i.e., how single-minded a class is). A class should represent only one thing, such as an employee, a department, or an order. All attributes and methods contained in a class should be required for the class to represent the thing. For example, an employee class should have attributes that deal with a social security number, last name, first name, middle initial, addresses, and benefits, but it should not have attributes such as door, engine, or hood. Furthermore, there should be no attributes or methods that are never used. In other words, a class should have only the attributes and methods necessary to fully define instances for the problem at hand. In this case, we have *ideal class cohesion*. Glenford Meyers suggested that a cohesive class[23] should have these attributes:

- It should contain multiple methods that are visible outside the class (i.e., a single-method class rarely makes sense).

- Each visible method performs only a single function.

- All methods reference only attributes or other methods defined within the class or one of its superclasses (i.e., if a method is going to send a message to another object, the remote object must be the value of one of the local object's attributes).[24]

Generalization/specialization cohesion addresses the sensibility of the inheritance hierarchy. How are the classes in the inheritance hierarchy related? Are the classes related through a generalization/specialization (a-kind-of) semantics? Or, are they related via some association, aggregation, or membership type of relationship that was created for simple reuse purposes? Recall all the issues raised previously on the use of inheritance. For example, in Figure 6-11, the subclasses Class Rooms and Staff inherit from the superclass Department. Obviously, instances of the Class Rooms and Staff classes are not a-kind-of Department. However, in the early days of object-oriented programming, this use of inheritance was quite common. When a programmer saw that there were some common properties that a set of classes shared, the

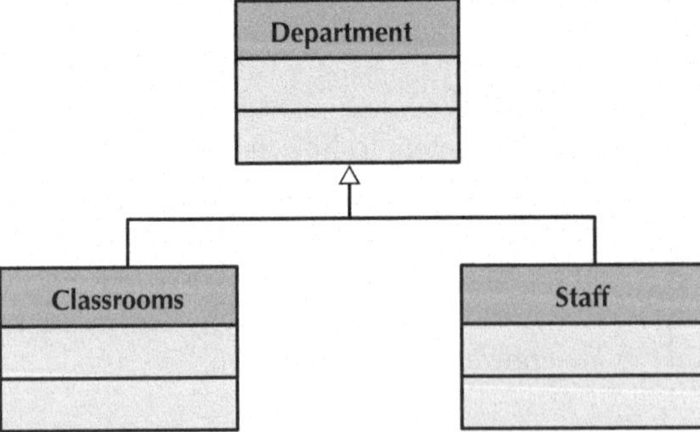

FIGURE 6-11
Generalization/
Specialization vs.
Inheritance Abuse

[23] We have adapted his informational-strength module criteria from structured design to object-oriented design. [See Glenford J. Myers, *Composite/Structured Design* (New York, NY: Van Nostrand Reinhold, 1978).]

[24] This restricts messages passing to only the first, second, and fourth conditions supported by the law of Demeter. For example, in Figure 6-10c, aReceptionist must have attributes associated with it that contains objects for Patients, Unpaid Bills, and Appointments. Furthermore, once an instance of Appointment is created, aReceptionist must have an attribute with the instance as its value to send any additional messages.

programmer would create an artificial abstraction that defined the commonalities. This was potentially useful in a reuse sense, but it turned out to cause many maintenance nightmares. In this case, instances of the Class Rooms and Staff classes are associated with or a-part-of an instance of Department. Today we know that highly cohesive inheritance hierarchies should support only the semantics of generalization and specialization (a-kind-of) and the principle of substitutability.

Connascence

Connascence[25] generalizes the ideas of cohesion and coupling, and it combines them with the arguments for encapsulation. To accomplish this, three levels of encapsulation have been identified. Level-0 encapsulation refers to the amount of encapsulation realized in an individual line of code, level-1 encapsulation is the level of encapsulation attained by combining lines of code into a method, and level-2 encapsulation is achieved by creating classes that contain both methods and attributes. Method cohesion and interaction coupling address primarily level-1 encapsulation. Class cohesion, generalization/specialization cohesion, and inheritance coupling address only level-2 encapsulation. Connascence, as a generalization of cohesion and coupling, addresses both level-1 and level-2 encapsulation.

But what exactly is connascence? Connascence literally means to be born together. From an object-oriented design perspective, it really means that two modules (classes or methods) are so intertwined that if you make a change in one, it is likely that a change in the other will be required. On the surface, this is very similar to coupling and, as such, should be minimized. However, when you combine it with the encapsulation levels, it is not quite that simple. In this case, we want to minimize overall connascence by eliminating any unnecessary connascence throughout the system; minimize connascence across any encapsulation boundaries, such as method boundaries and class boundaries; and maximize connascence within any encapsulation boundary. For example, within a class boundary, it is normally considered a good thing for the methods to use the attributes of the class and to use other methods in the class. However, within a method boundary, use of the attributes and the other methods within the class actually increases the dependency among them. Depending on the size and complexity of the method, this could cause problems with maintaining the method over time. So, as you can see, there are tradeoffs of dependencies across and within the different encapsulation boundaries.

Based on these guidelines, a subclass should never directly access any hidden attribute or method of a superclass [i.e., a subclass should not have special rights to the properties of its superclass(es)]. If direct access to the nonvisible attributes and methods of a superclass by its subclass is allowed—and this is permitted in most object-oriented programming languages— and a modification to the superclass is made, then owing to the connascence between the subclass and its superclass, it is likely that a modification to the subclass also is required.[26] In other words, the subclass has access to something across an encapsulation boundary (the class boundary between the subclass and the superclass). Practically speaking, you should maximize the cohesion (connascence) within an encapsulation boundary and minimize the coupling (connascence) between the encapsulation boundaries.

[25] See Meilir Page-Jones, "Comparing Techniques by Means of Encapsulation and Connascence," *Communications of the ACM* 35, no. 9 (September 1992): 147–151.

[26] Based on these guidelines, the use of the protected visibility, as supported in Java and C++, should be minimized, if not avoided. "Friends" as defined in C++ also should be minimized or avoided. Owing to the level of dependencies these language features create, any convenience afforded to a programmer is more than offset in potential design, understandability, and maintenance problems. These features must be used with great caution and must be fully documented.

OBJECT DESIGN ACTIVITIES

The design activities for classes and methods are really an extension of the analysis and evolution activities presented previously (see Chapters 3, 4, 5, and this chapter). In this case, we expand the descriptions of the partitions, layers, and classes. Practically speaking, the expanded descriptions are created through the activities that take place during the detailed design of the classes and methods. The activities used to design classes and methods include additional specification of the current model, identifying opportunities for reuse, and restructuring the design. Of course, any changes made to a class on one layer can cause the classes on the other layers that are coupled to it to be modified as well.

Adding Specifications

At this point in the development of the system, it is crucial to review the current set of functional, structural, and behavioral models. First, we should ensure that the classes on the problem-domain layer are both necessary and sufficient to solve the underlying problem. To do this, we need to be sure that there are no missing attributes or methods and no extra or unused attributes or methods in each class. Furthermore, are there any missing or extra classes? If we have done our job well during analysis, there will be few, if any, attributes, methods, or classes to add to the models. And it is unlikely that we have any extra attributes, methods, or classes to delete from the models. However, we still need to ensure that we have factored, abstracted, and refined the evolving models and created the relevant partitions and collaborations.

Second, we need to finalize the *visibility* (hidden or visible) of the attributes and methods in each class. Depending on the object-oriented programming language used, this could be predetermined.[27] By default, most object-oriented analysis and design approaches assume Smalltalk's approach.

Third, we need to decide on the signature of every operation (method) in every class. The *signature* of an operation comprises three parts: the name of the operation, the parameters or arguments that must be passed to the operation, including their object type, and the type of value that the operation will return to the calling method. The signature of an operation is also known as the operation's *protocol*.

Fourth, we need to define any constraints that must be preserved by the objects (e.g., an attribute of an object that can have values only in a certain range). There are three different types of constraints: preconditions, postconditions, and invariants.[28] We also must decide how to handle a violation of a constraint. Should the system simply abort? Should the system automatically undo the change that caused the violation? Should the system let the end user determine the approach to correct the violation? In other words, the designer must design the errors that the system is expected to handle. It is best not to leave these types of design decisions for the programmer to solve. Violations of a constraint are known as *exceptions* in languages such as in C++, Java, or Python.

Even though we have described these activities in the context of the problem-domain layer, they are also applicable to the other layers: data management (Chapter 8), human–computer interaction (Chapter 9), and application architecture (Chapter 10).

---

[27] For example, in Smalltalk, attributes are hidden and methods are visible. Other languages allow the programmer to set the visibility of each attribute or method. For example, in C++ and Java, you can set the visibility to private (hidden), public (visible), or protected (visible to subclasses, but not to other classes). It is also possible to control visibility through packages and friends. Finally, in Python, the visibility is always public.

[28] Constraints are described in more detail in Chapter 7.

Identifying Opportunities for Reuse

Previously, we looked at possibly employing reuse in our models in analysis through the use of *patterns* (see Chapter 4). In design, in addition to using analysis patterns, there are opportunities for using design patterns, frameworks, libraries, and components. The opportunities vary depending on which layer is being reviewed. For example, it is doubtful that a class library will be of much help on the problem-domain layer, but a class library could be of great help on the foundation layer.

Like analysis patterns, *design patterns* are simply useful groupings of collaborating classes that provide a solution to a commonly occurring problem. The primary difference between analysis and design patterns is that design patterns are useful in solving "a general design problem in a particular context,"[29] whereas analysis patterns tended to aid in filling out a problem-domain representation. For example, a useful design pattern is the Whole–Part pattern (see Figure 6-12a). The Whole–Part pattern explicitly supports the Aggregation and Composition relationships within the UML. Another useful design pattern is the Iterator pattern (see Figure 6-12b). The primary purpose of the Iterator pattern is to provide the designer with a standard approach to support looping over different types of collections.[30] By using this pattern, regardless of the collection type (Concrete Aggregate), the designer knows that the collection will need to create an iterator (Concrete Iterator) that customizes the standard operations used to traverse the collection: first(), next(), isDone(), and currentItem(). Given the number of collections typically found in business applications, this pattern is one of the more useful ones. For example, in Figure 6-13a, we replicate a portion of the Appointment problem discussed in previous chapters, and in Figure 6-13b we show how the Iterator pattern can be applied to its evolving design. Finally, some of the design patterns support different application architectures (see Chapter 10). For example, the Forwarder–Receiver pattern (see Figure 8-2c) supports a peer-to-peer architecture. Many design patterns are available in C++, Java, C#, or Python.

A *framework* is composed of a set of implemented classes that can be used as a basis for implementing an application. Most frameworks allow us to create subclasses to inherit from classes in the framework. There are object-persistence frameworks that can be purchased and used to add persistence to the problem-domain classes, which would be helpful on the data management layer. Of course, when inheriting from classes in a framework, we are creating a dependency (i.e., increasing the coupling between the problem-domain class and the framework class). Therefore, if we use a framework and the vendor makes changes to the framework, we will have to at least recompile the system when we upgrade to the new version of the framework.

A *class library* is similar to a framework in that it typically has a set of implemented classes that were designed for reuse. However, frameworks tend to be more domain specific. In fact, frameworks may be built using a class library. A typical class library could be purchased to support numerical or statistical processing, natural language processing, file management (data management layer), or user interface development (human–computer interaction layer). In some cases, instances of classes contained in the class library can be created, and in other cases, classes in the class library can be extended by creating subclasses based on them. As with frameworks, if we use classes in a class library, we will run into all the issues dealing with coupling and connascence. If we directly instantiate classes in the class library, we will create a dependency between our object and the class library object based on the signatures of the

---

[29] Erich Gamma, Richard Helm, Ralph Johnson, and John Vlissides, *Design* Patterns: *Elements of Reusable Object-Oriented Software* (Reading, MA: Addison-Wesley, 1995).

[30] The Iterator pattern is related to the DoWhile and DoUntil programming constructs described in the appendix to Chapter 1.

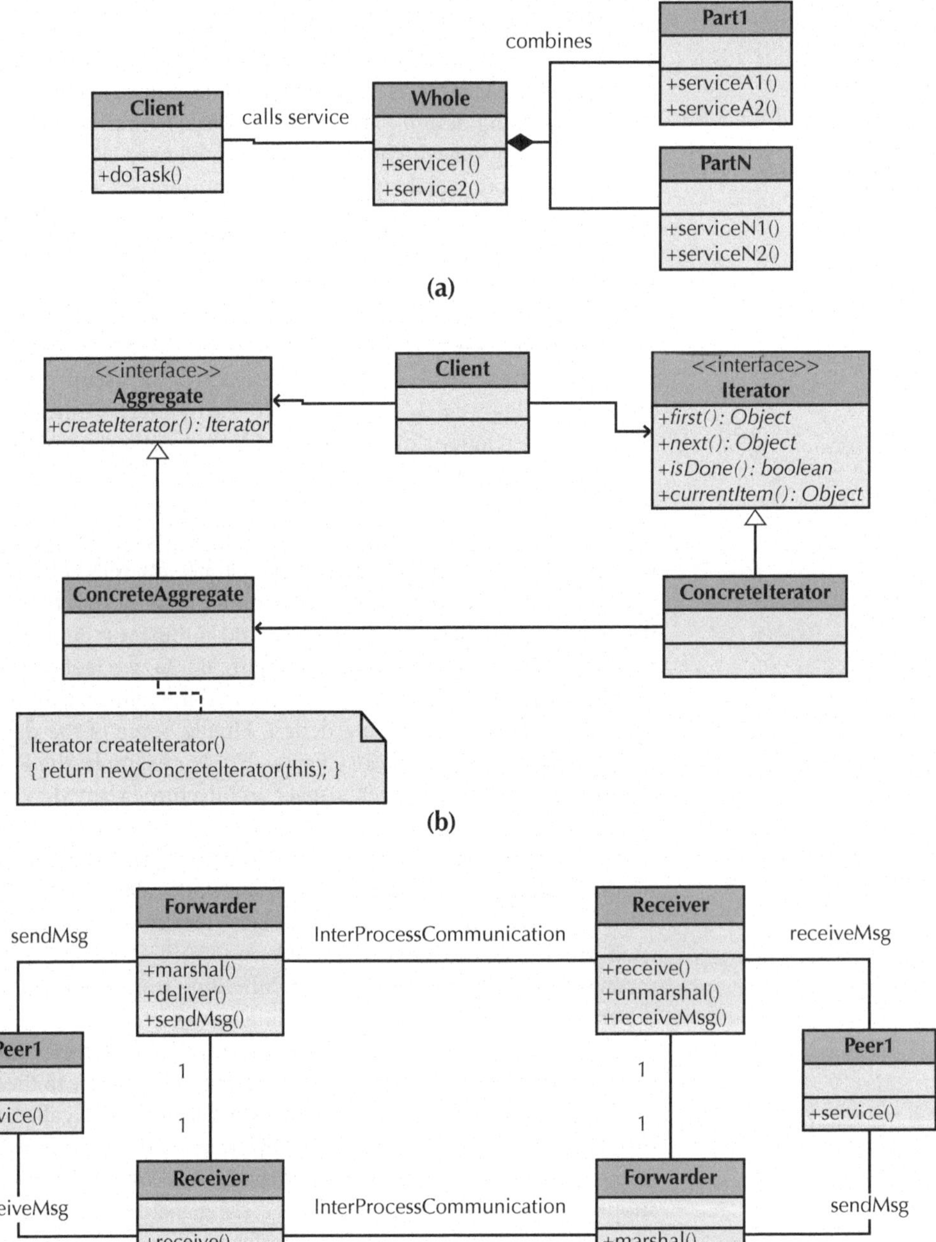

FIGURE 6-12 Sample Design Patterns

Source: Based upon material from F. Buschmann, R. Meunier, H. Rohnert, P. Sommerlad, and M. Stal, *Pattern-Oriented Software Architecture: A System of Patterns* (Chichester, UK: Wiley, 1996); E. Gamma, R. Helm, R. Johnson, and J. Vlissides, *Design Patterns: Elements of Reusable Object-Oriented Software* (Reading, MA: Addison-Wesley, 1995).

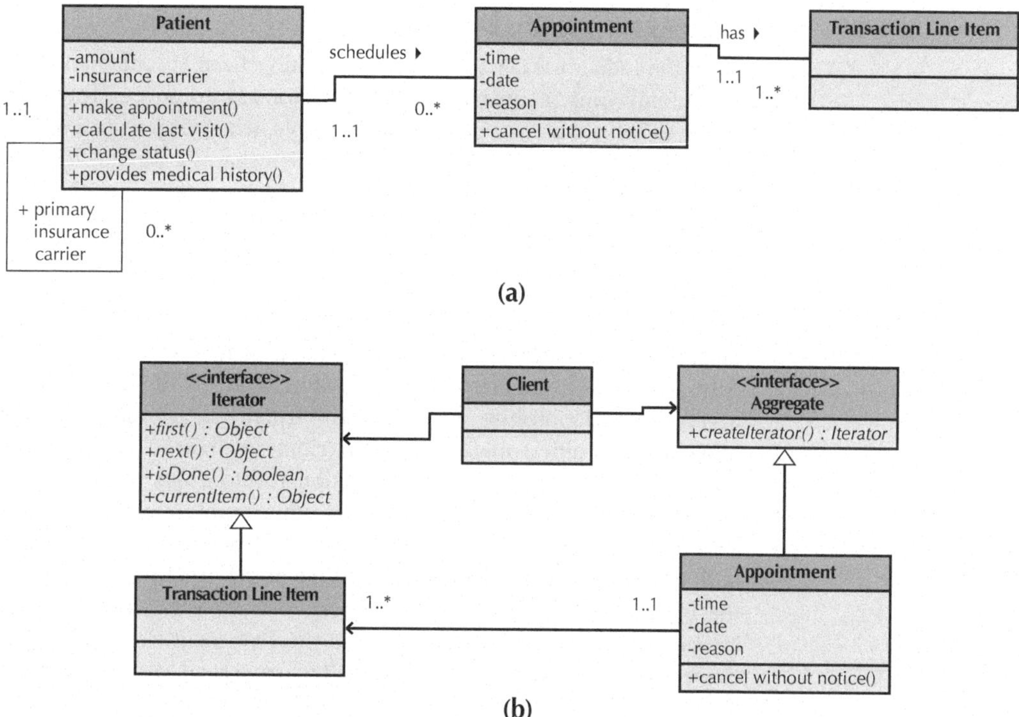

FIGURE 6-13 Iterator Design Pattern Applied to the Appointment Problem

operations in the class library object. This increases the coupling and connascence between the class library object and our object.

A *component* is a self-contained, encapsulated piece of software that can be plugged into a system to provide a specific set of required functionalities. Today, there are many components available for purchase. A component has a well-defined *API (application programming interface)*. An API is essentially a set of method interfaces to the objects contained in the component. The internal workings of the component are hidden behind the API. Components can be implemented using class libraries and frameworks. However, components also can be used to implement frameworks. Unless the API changes between versions of the component, upgrading to a new version normally requires only linking the component back into the application. As such, depending on the programming language, recompilation may not be required.

Which of these approaches should we use? It depends on what we are trying to build. In general, frameworks are used mostly to aid in developing objects on the application architecture, human–computer interaction, or data management layers; components are used primarily to simplify the development of objects on the problem-domain and human–computer interaction layers; and class libraries are used to develop frameworks and components and to support the foundation layer. Whichever of these reuse approaches you use, you must remember that reuse brings many potential benefits and possible problems. For example, the software has previously been verified and validated, which should reduce the amount of testing required for our system. However, as stated before, if the software on which we are basing our system changes, then most likely, we will also have to change our system. Furthermore, if the software is from a third-party firm, we are creating a dependency from our firm (or our client's firm) to the third-party vendor. Consequently, we need to have some confidence that the vendor will be in business for a while.

Restructuring the Design

Once the individual classes and methods have been specified and the class libraries, frameworks, and components have been incorporated into the evolving design, we should use factoring to restructure the design. For example, when reviewing a set of classes on a particular layer, we might discover that a subset of them shares a similar definition. In that case, it may be useful to factor out the similarities and create a new class. Based on the issues related to cohesion, coupling, and connascence, the new class may be related to the old classes via inheritance (generalization) or through an aggregation or association relationship.

Another process that is useful for restructuring the evolving design is *normalization*. Normalization is described in Chapter 8 in relation to relational databases. However, normalization can be useful at times to identify potential classes that are missing from the design. Also related to normalization is the requirement to implement the actual association and aggregation relationships as attributes. Virtually no commercial object-oriented programming language differentiates between attributes and association and aggregation relationships. Therefore, all association and aggregation relationships must be converted to attributes in the classes. For example, in Figure 6-14a, the Appointment and Symptom classes are associated with the Patient class. Furthermore, the Treatment association class is associated with both the Symptom and Illness classes. One of the first things that must be done is to convert the Treatment Association class to a normal class. Notice the multiplicity values for the new associations between the Symptom and the Treatment classes and the Treatment and Illness classes (see Figure 6-14b). Next, we need to convert all associations to attributes that represent the relationships between the affected classes. In this case, the Appointment class must have a

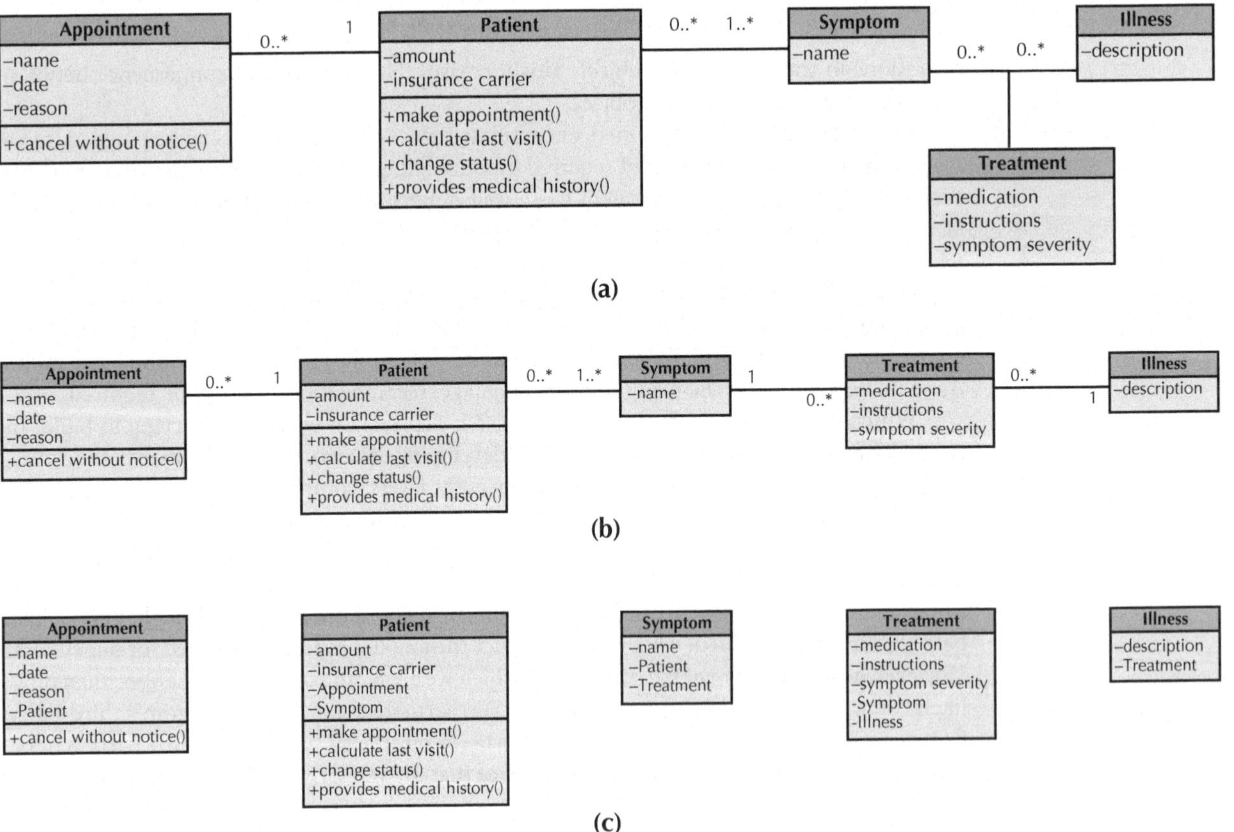

FIGURE 6-14 Converting Associations to Attributes

Patient attribute added to represent an instance of the Patient class; the Patient class must add attributes to reference instances of the Appointment and Symptom classes; the Symptom class must have attributes added to it to reference the instances of the Patient and Treatment classes; the new Treatment class must have attributes that allow an instance of the Symptom class to reference an instance of the Symptom class and one references an instance of the Illness class; and finally, the Illness class must add an attribute that references the relevant instances of the Treatment class (see Figure 6-14c). As you can see, even in this very small example, many changes need to be made to ready the design for implementation.

Finally, all inheritance relationships should be challenged to ensure that they support only a generalization/specialization (a-kind-of) semantics. Otherwise, all the problems mentioned previously with inheritance coupling, class cohesion, and generalization/specialization cohesion will come to pass.

DESIGN STRATEGIES

Until now, we have assumed that the system will be built and implemented by the project team; however, there are actually three ways to approach the creation of a new system: developing a custom application in-house, buying and customizing a packaged system, and relying on an external vendor, developer, or service provider to build the system. Each of these choices has strengths and weaknesses, and each is more appropriate in different scenarios. The following sections describe each design choice in turn, and then we present criteria that you can use to select one of the three approaches for your project.

Custom Development

Many project teams assume that *custom development,* or building a new system from scratch, is the best way to create a system (resources permitting). For one thing, teams have complete control over the way the system looks and functions. Custom development also allows developers to be flexible and creative in the way they solve business problems. Additionally, a custom application is easier to change to include components that take advantage of current technologies that can support such strategic efforts.

Building a system in-house also builds technical skills and functional knowledge within the company. As developers work with business users, their understanding of the business grows and they become better able to align IS with strategies and needs. These same developers climb the technology learning curve so that future projects applying similar technology require much less effort.

Custom application development, however, requires dedicated effort that involves long hours and hard work. Many companies have a development staff that is already overcommitted to filling huge backlogs of systems requests and just does not have time for another project. Also, a variety of skills—technical, interpersonal, functional, project management, and modeling—must be in place for the project to move ahead smoothly. IS professionals, especially highly skilled individuals, are quite difficult to hire and retain.

The risks associated with building a system from the ground up can be quite high, and there is no guarantee that the project will succeed. Developers could be pulled away to work on other projects, technical obstacles could cause unexpected delays, and the business users could become impatient with a growing timeline.

Packaged Software

Many business needs are not unique, and because it makes little sense to reinvent the wheel, many organizations buy *packaged software* that has already been written rather than developing their own custom solution. In fact, there are thousands of commercially available software programs that have already been written to serve a multitude of purposes. Think about your own need for a word processor—did you ever consider writing your own word processing software? That would be very silly considering the number of good software packages available that are relatively inexpensive.

Similarly, most companies have needs that can be met quite well by packaged software, such as payroll or accounts receivable. It can be much more efficient to buy programs that have already been created, tested, and proven. Moreover, a packaged system can be bought and installed in a relatively short time when compared with a custom system. Plus, packaged systems incorporate the expertise and experience of the vendor who created the software.

Packaged software can range from reusable components to small, single-function tools to huge, all-encompassing systems such as *enterprise resource planning (ERP)* applications that are installed to automate an entire business. Implementing ERP systems is a process in which large organizations spend millions of dollars installing packages by companies such as SAP or Oracle and then change their businesses accordingly. Installing ERP software is much more difficult than installing small application packages because benefits can be harder to realize and problems are much more serious.

However, there are problems related to packaged software. For example, companies buying packaged systems must accept the functionality that is provided by the system, and rarely is there a perfect fit. If the packaged system is large in scope, its implementation could mean a substantial change in the way the company does business. Letting technology drive the business can be dangerous.

Most packaged applications allow *customization,* or the manipulation of system parameters to change the way certain features work. For example, the package might have a way to display your company's information or branding that would then appear on input screens. Or an accounting software package could offer a choice of various ways to handle cash flow or inventory control so that it can support the accounting practices in different organizations. If the amount of customization is not enough and the software package has a few features that don't quite work the way the company needs it to work, the project team can create workarounds.

A *workaround* is a custom-built add-on program that interfaces with the packaged application to handle special needs. It can be a nice way to create needed functionality that does not exist in the software package. But workarounds should be a last resort for several reasons. First, workarounds are not supported by the vendor who supplied the packaged software, so upgrades to the main system might make the workaround ineffective. Also, if problems arise, vendors have a tendency to blame the workaround as the culprit and refuse to provide support.

Although choosing a packaged software system is simpler than custom development, it too can benefit from following a formal methodology, just as if a custom application were being built.

Systems integration refers to the process of building new systems by combining packaged software, existing legacy systems, and new software written to integrate these. Many consulting firms specialize in systems integration, so it is not uncommon for companies to select the packaged software option and then outsource the integration of a variety of packages to a consulting firm. (Outsourcing is discussed in the next section.)

The key challenge *in* systems integration is finding ways to integrate the data produced by the different packages and legacy systems. Integration often hinges on taking data produced by one package or system and reformatting it for use in another package or system. The project team starts by examining the data produced by and needed by the different packages or systems and identifying the transformations that must occur to move the data from one to the other. In many cases, this involves fooling the different packages or systems into thinking that the data were produced by an existing program module that the package or system expects to produce the data rather than the new package or system that is being integrated. A third approach is through the use of an *object wrapper*.[31] An object wrapper is essentially an object that "wraps around" a legacy system, enabling an object-oriented system to send messages to the legacy system. Effectively, object wrappers create an application program interface (API) to the legacy system. The creation of an object wrapper protects the corporation's investment in the legacy system.

Outsourcing

The design choice that requires the least amount of in-house resources is *outsourcing*—hiring an external vendor, developer, or service provider to create the system. Outsourcing has become quite popular in recent years. Some estimate that as many as 50 percent of companies with IT budgets of more than $5 million are currently outsourcing or evaluating the approach.

With outsourcing, the decision making and/or management control of a business function is transferred to an outside supplier. This transfer requires two-way coordination, exchange of information, and trust between the supplier and the business. From an IT perspective, IT outsourcing can include hiring consultants to solve a specific problem, hiring contract programmers to implement a solution, hiring a firm to manage the IT function and assets of a company, or actually outsourcing the entire IT function to a separate firm. Today, through the use of application service providers (ASPs), Web services technology, and cloud services, it is possible to use a pay-as-you-go approach for a software package.[32] Essentially, IT outsourcing involves hiring a third party to perform some IT function that traditionally would be performed in-house.

There can be great benefit to having someone else develop a company's system. The outside company may be more experienced in the technology or have more resources, such as experienced programmers. Many companies embark upon outsourcing deals to reduce costs, whereas others see it as an opportunity to add value to the business.

For whatever reason, outsourcing can be a good alternative for a new system. However, it does not come without costs. If you decide to leave the creation of a new system in the hands of someone else, you could compromise confidential information or lose control over future development. In-house professionals are not benefiting from the skills that could be learned from the project; instead, the expertise is transferred to the outside organization. Ultimately, important skills can walk right out the door at the end of the contract. Furthermore, when offshore outsourcing is being considered, we must also be cognizant of language issues, time-zone differences, and cultural differences (e.g., acceptable business practices as understood in one country that may be unacceptable in another). All these concerns, if not dealt with properly, can prevail over any advantage that outsourcing or offshore outsourcing could realize.

Most risks can be addressed if a company decides to outsource, but two are particularly important. First, the company must thoroughly assess the requirements for the project—a company should never outsource what is not understood. If rigorous planning and analysis have occurred, then the company should be well aware of its needs. Second, the company should carefully choose a vendor, developer, or service with a proven track record with the type of system and technology that its system needs.

Three primary types of contracts can be drawn to control the outsourcing deal. A *time-and-arrangements contract* is very flexible because a company agrees to pay for whatever time and expenses are needed to get the job done. Of course, this agreement could result in a large

[31] Ian Graham, *Object-Oriented* Methods: *Principles & Practice*, 3rd Ed. (Reading, MA: Addison-Wesley, 2001).

[32] For an economic explanation of how this could work, see H. Baetjer, *Software as Capital: An Economic Perspective on Software Engineering* (Los Alamitos, CA: IEEE Computer Society Press, 1997).

bill that exceeds initial estimates. This works best when the company and the outsourcer are unclear about what it is going to take to finish the job.

A company will pay no more than expected with a *fixed-price contract* because if the outsourcer exceeds the agreed-upon price, it will have to absorb the costs. Outsourcers are much more careful about defining requirements clearly up front, and there is little flexibility for change.

The type of contract gaining in popularity is the *value-added contract,* whereby the outsourcer reaps some percentage of the completed system's benefits. The company has very little risk in this case, but it must expect to share the wealth once the system is in place.

Creating fair contracts is an art because flexibility must be carefully balanced with clearly defined terms. Often, needs change over time. Therefore, the contract should not be so specific and rigid that alterations cannot be made. Think about how quickly mobile technology has changed. It is difficult to foresee how a project might evolve over a long period of time. Short-term contracts help leave room for reassessment if needs change or if relationships are not working out the way both parties expected. In all cases, the relationship with the outsourcer should be viewed as a partnership where both parties benefit and communicate openly.

Managing the outsourcing relationship is a full-time job. Thus, someone needs to be assigned full time to manage the outsourcer, and the level of that person should be appropriate for the size of the job (a multimillion dollar outsourcing engagement should be handled by a high-level executive). Throughout the relationship, progress should be tracked and measured against predetermined goals. If a company does embark upon an outsourcing design strategy, it should be sure to get adequate information. Many books have been written that provide much more detailed information on the topic.[33] Figure 6-15 summarizes some guidelines for outsourcing.

Selecting a Design Strategy

Each of the design strategies just discussed has its strengths and weaknesses, and no one strategy is inherently better than the others. Thus, it is important to understand the strengths and weaknesses of each strategy and when to use each. Figure 6-16 summarizes the characteristics of each strategy.

Business Need If the business need for the system is common and technical solutions already exist that can meet the business need of the system, it makes little sense to build a custom application. Packaged systems are good alternatives for common business needs.

<table>
<tr><td colspan="1">Outsourcing</td></tr>
<tr><td>

• Keep the lines of communication open between you and your outsourcer.
• Define and stabilize requirements before signing a contact.
• View the outsourcing relationship as a partnership.
• Select the vendor, developer or service provider carefully.
• Assign a person to managing the relationship.
• Don't outsource what you don't understand.
• Emphasize flexible requirements, long-term relationships and short-term contracts.

</td></tr>
</table>

FIGURE 6-15
Outsourcing
Guidelines

---

[33] For more information on outsourcing, we recommend M. Lacity and R. Hirschheim, *Information Systems Outsourcing: Myths, Metaphors, and Realities* (New York, NY: Wiley, 1993); L. Willcocks and G. Fitzgerald, *A Business Guide to Outsourcing Information Technology* (London:Business Intelligence, 1994); E. Carmel, *Offshoring Information Technology: Sourcing and Outsourcing to a Global Workforce* (Cambridge, England: Cambridge University Press, 2005); J. K. Halvey and B. M. Melby, *Information Technology Outsourcing Transactions: Process, Strategies, and Contracts,* 2nd Ed. (Hoboken, NJ: Wiley, 2005); T. L. Friedman, *The World Is Flat: A Brief History of the Twenty-First Century, Updated and Expanded Edition* (New York: Farrar, Straus, and Giroux, 2006).

	Use Custom Development When. . .	Use a Packaged System When. . .	Use Outsourcing When. . .
Business Need	The business need is unique.	The business need is common.	The business need is not core to the business.
In-house Experience	In-house functional and technical experience exists.	In-house functional experience exists.	In-house functional or technical experience does not exist.
Project Skills	There is a desire to build in-house skills.	The skills are not strategic.	The decision to outsource is a strategic decision.
Project Management	The project has a highly skilled project manager and a proven methodology.	The project has a project manager who can coordinate the vendor's efforts.	The project has a highly skilled project manager at the level of the organization that matches the scope of the outsourcing deal.
Time Frame	The time frame is flexible.	The time frame is short.	The time frame is short or flexible.

FIGURE 6-16   Design Strategy Characteristics

A custom alternative should be explored when the business need is unique or has special requirements. Usually, if the business need is not critical to the company, then outsourcing is the best choice—someone outside of the organization can be responsible for the application development.

In-house Experience   If in-house experience exists for all the functional and technical needs of the system, it will be easier to build a custom application than if these skills do not exist. A packaged system may be a better alternative for companies that do not have the technical skills to build the desired system. For example, a project team that does not have mobile technology skills might want to consider outsourcing those aspects of the system.

Project Skills   The skills that are applied during projects are either technical (e.g., Java and SQL) or functional (e.g., security), and different design alternatives are more viable, depending on how important the skills are to the company's strategy. For example, if certain functional and technical expertise that relates to mobile application development is important to an organization because it expects mobile to play an important role in its sales over time, then it makes sense for the company to develop mobile applications in-house, using company employees so that the skills can be developed and improved. On the other hand, some skills, such as network security, may be beyond the technical expertise of employees or not of interest to the company's strategists—it is just an operational issue that needs to be addressed. In this case, packaged systems or outsourcing should be considered so that internal employees can focus on other business-critical applications and skills.

Project Management   Custom applications require excellent project management and a proven methodology. So many things, such as funding obstacles, staffing holdups, and overly demanding business users, can push a project off-track. Therefore, the project team should choose to develop a custom application only if it is certain that the underlying coordination and control mechanisms will be in place. Packaged and outsourcing alternatives also need to be managed; however, they are more shielded from internal obstacles because the external parties have their own objectives and priorities (e.g., it may be easier for an outside contractor to say no to a user than it is for a person within the company). Typically, packaged and outsourcing alternatives have their own methodologies, which can benefit companies that do not have an appropriate methodology to use.

Time Frame When time is a factor, the project team should probably start looking for a system that is already built and tested. In this way, the company will have a good idea of how long the package will take to put in place and what the final result will contain. The time frame for custom applications is hard to pin down, especially when you consider how many projects end up missing important deadlines. If a company must choose the custom development alternative and the time frame is very short, it should consider using techniques such as time-boxing to manage this problem. The time to produce a system using outsourcing really depends on the system and the outsourcer's resources. If a service provider has services in place that can be used to support the company's needs, then a business need could be implemented quickly. Otherwise, an outsourcing solution could take as long as a custom development initiative.

SELECTING AN ACQUISITION STRATEGY

Once the project team has a good understanding of how well each design strategy fits with the project's needs, it must begin to understand exactly *how* to implement these strategies. For example, what tools and technology would be used if a custom alternative were selected? What vendors make packaged systems that address the project's needs? What service providers would be able to build this system if the application were outsourced? This information can be obtained from people working in the IS department and from recommendations by business users. Alternatively, the project team can contact other companies with similar needs and investigate the types of systems that they have put in place. Vendors and consultants usually are willing to provide information about various tools and solutions in the form of brochures, product demonstrations, and information seminars. However, a company should be sure to validate the information it receives from vendors and consultants. After all, they are trying to make a sale. Therefore, they may stretch the capabilities of their tool by focusing on only the positive aspects of the tool while omitting the tool's drawbacks.

It is likely that the project team will identify several ways that a system could be constructed after weighing the specific design options. For example, the project team might have found three vendors that make packaged systems that potentially could meet the project's needs. Or the team may be debating over whether to develop a system using Java as a development tool and the database management system from Oracle or to outsource the development effort to a consulting firm such as Accenture or CGI. Each alternative has pros and cons associated with it that need to be considered, and only one solution can be selected in the end.

To aid in this decision, additional information should be collected. Project teams employ several approaches to gather additional information that is needed. One helpful tool is the *request for proposal (RFP)*, a document that solicits a formal proposal from a potential vendor, developer, or service provider. RFPs describe in detail the system or service that is needed, and vendors respond by describing in detail how they could supply those needs.

Although there is no standard way of writing an RFP, it should include certain key facts that the vendor requires, such as a detailed description of needs, any special technical needs or circumstances, evaluation criteria, procedures to follow, and a timetable. In a large project, the RFP can be hundreds of pages long, since it is essential that all required project details are included.

The RFP is not just a way to gather information. Rather, it results in a vendor proposal that is a binding offer to accomplish the tasks described in the RFP. The vendor proposal includes a schedule and a price for which the work is to be performed. Once the winning vendor proposal is chosen, a contract for the work is developed and signed by both parties.

For smaller projects with smaller budgets, the *request for information (RFI)* may be sufficient. An RFI is a shorter, less detailed request that is sent to potential vendors to obtain general information about their products and services. Sometimes, the RFI is used to determine which vendors have the capability to perform a service. It is often then followed up with an RFP to the qualified vendors.

When a list of equipment is so complete that the vendor need only provide a price, without any analysis or description of what is needed, the *request for quote (RFQ)* may be used. For example, if twenty long-range RFID tag readers are needed from the manufacturer on a certain date at a certain location, the RFQ can be used. If an item is described, but a specific manufacturer's product is not named, then extensive testing will be required to verify fulfillment of the specifications.

Alternative Matrix

An *alternative matrix* can be used to organize the pros and cons of the design alternatives so that the best solution will be chosen in the end (see Figure 6-17). This matrix is created using the same steps as the feasibility analysis, which was presented in Chapter 2. The only difference is that the alternative matrix combines several feasibility analyses into one matrix so that the alternatives can easily be compared. An alternative matrix is a grid that contains the technical, budget, and organizational feasibilities for each system candidate, pros and cons associated with adopting each solution, and other information that is helpful when making comparisons. Sometimes weights are provided for different parts of the matrix to show when some criteria are more important to the final decision.

To create the alternative matrix, draw a grid with the alternatives across the top and different criteria (e.g., feasibilities, pros, cons, and other miscellaneous criteria) along the side. Next, fill in the grid with detailed descriptions about each alternative. This becomes a useful

Evaluation Criteria	Relative Importance (Weight)	Alternative 1: Custom Application Using VB.NET	Score (1–5)*	Weighted Score	Alternative 2: Custom Application Using Java	Score (1–5)*	Weighted Score	Alternative 3: Packaged Software Product ABC	Score (1–5)*	Weighted Score
Technical Issues:										
Criterion 1	20		5	100		3	60		3	60
Criterion 2	10		3	30		3	30		5	50
Criterion 3	10		2	20		1	10		3	30
Economic Issues:										
Criterion 4	25	Supporting	3	75	Supporting	3	75	Supporting	5	125
Criterion 5	10	Information	3	30	Information	1	10	Information	5	50
Organizational Issues:										
Criterion 6	10		5	50		5	50		3	30
Criterion 7	10		3	30		3	30		1	10
Criterion 8	5		3	15		1	5		1	5
TOTAL	100			350			270			360

* This denotes how well the alternative meets the criteria. 1 = poor fit; 5 = perfect fit.

FIGURE 6-17   Sample Alternative Matrix Using Weights

document for discussion because it clearly presents the alternatives being reviewed and comparable characteristics for each one.

Sometimes, weights and scores are added to the alternative matrix to create a weighted alternative matrix that communicates the project's most important criteria and the alternatives that best address them. A scorecard is built by adding a column labeled "weight" that includes a number depicting how much each criterion matters to the final decision. Typically, analysts take 100 points and spread them out across the criteria appropriately. If five criteria were used and all mattered equally, then each criterion would receive a weight of 20. However, if costs were the most important criterion for choosing an alternative, it might receive 60 points, and the other four criteria might get only 10 points each.

Then, the analysts add to the matrix a column called "Score" that communicates how well each alternative meets the criteria. Usually, number ranges like 1 to 5 or 1 to 10 are used to rate the appropriateness of the alternatives by the criteria. So, for the cost criterion, the least expensive alternative may receive a 5 on a 1-to-5 scale, whereas a costly alternative would receive a 1. Weighted scores are computed with each criterion's weight multiplied by the score it was given for each alternative. Then, the weighted scores are totaled for each alternative. The highest weighted score achieves the best match for our criteria. When numbers are used in the alternative matrix, project teams can make decisions quantitatively and on the basis of hard numbers.

It should be pointed out, however, that the score assigned to the criteria for each alternative is nothing more than a subjective assignment. Consequently, it is entirely possible for an analyst to skew the analysis according to his or her own biases. In other words, the weighted alternative matrix can be made to support whichever alternative you prefer and yet retains the appearance of an objective, rational analysis. To avoid the problem of a biased analysis, each analyst on the team could develop ratings independently; then, the ratings could be compared and discrepancies resolved in an open team discussion.

The final step, of course, is to decide which solution to design and implement. The decision should be made by a combination of business users and technical professionals after the issues involved with the different alternatives are well understood. Once the decision is finalized, design can continue as needed, based on the selected alternative.

APPLYING THE CHAPTER CONCEPTS

Library Management System Example　In the last chapter, Susan left Joe with a promise to send Jane over to carefully create behavioral state machines for each concrete class. Once Jane and Joe had all of the behavioral state machines created, Jane brought the results back to the team. Jane pointed out that, based on the behavioral state machines, there were many transitions not associated with any of the operations currently in the representations, i.e., there were many missing operations. This obviously also meant that there were missing responsibilities on the CRC cards, activities in the activity diagram, events with the use case descriptions, and messages in the sequence diagrams. At first, Jane was so appalled at the number of errors in their current representations, she was somewhat hesitant in pointing all of them out to the team. John, one of the programmers on the team, had a fairly volatile reputation. But, before John could explode, Susan spoke up and congratulated Jane on what a good job that Jane and Joe had done uncovering these omissions so early in the development process. Given these identified omissions, Susan had the team divvy up the work of cleaning up all of the representations. Once the team had fixed everything, Susan carefully reviewed the use case diagram (Figure 3-5) and the class diagram (Figure 4-19) to see if there were any opportunities to create packages that could either group use cases together or to group classes together. While she was reviewing the diagrams, she made sure that she considered the coupling, cohesion, and connascence design criteria.

Based on her careful consideration, she decided that the use case diagram and the use cases were simple enough that there was no need to use packages. However, when she reviewed the class diagram, even though there weren't that many classes in the diagram, she saw that creating a Patron package and a Resource package could make sense. So based on this decision, she created the package diagram shown in Figure 6-18.

After creating the package diagram, Susan and her team carefully reviewed the diagram to determine whether any design patterns could be applied. After careful review, Susan and the team decided that the Iterator patter could be applied to the Check Out Transaction, Patron, and Transaction Line Item classes where the Patron class is equivalent to the Client class and the Check Out Transaction class should inherit the interface from the Iterator class and the Transaction Line Item class should inherit the interface from the Aggregate class (see Figure 6-19).

Next, to move into the detailed design of the classes and methods, Susan and her team converted all association and aggregation relationships to attributes (see Figure 6-20). This entailed adding:

- a CheckOutTransaction attribute to the CheckOutDesk class,
- a CheckOutDesk attribute, a TransactionLineItem attribute, and a Patron attribute to the CheckOutTransaction class,
- a CheckOutTransaction attribute, a Resource attribute, and a Patron attribute to the TransactionLineItem class,
- a TransactionLineItem attribute, a Location attribute, and a Collection attribute to the Resource class,
- a Resource attribute to the Location class, and
- a Resource attribute to the Collection class.

Based on the level of expertise that her team possesses, Susan decided that they would follow a custom development approach. Finally, Susan set up another meeting with Joe to work through the above results. We return to this example in the next chapter.

Campus Housing Service "Your Turn" Exercise In the previous installation of the Campus Housing Service (CHS) "Your Turn" exercise, you created a set of behavioral state machines. One for each concrete class. In this installment of the CHS exercise, you should create a package diagram that groups the classes together in appropriate packages for the problem domain. We will return to CHS in the next chapter.

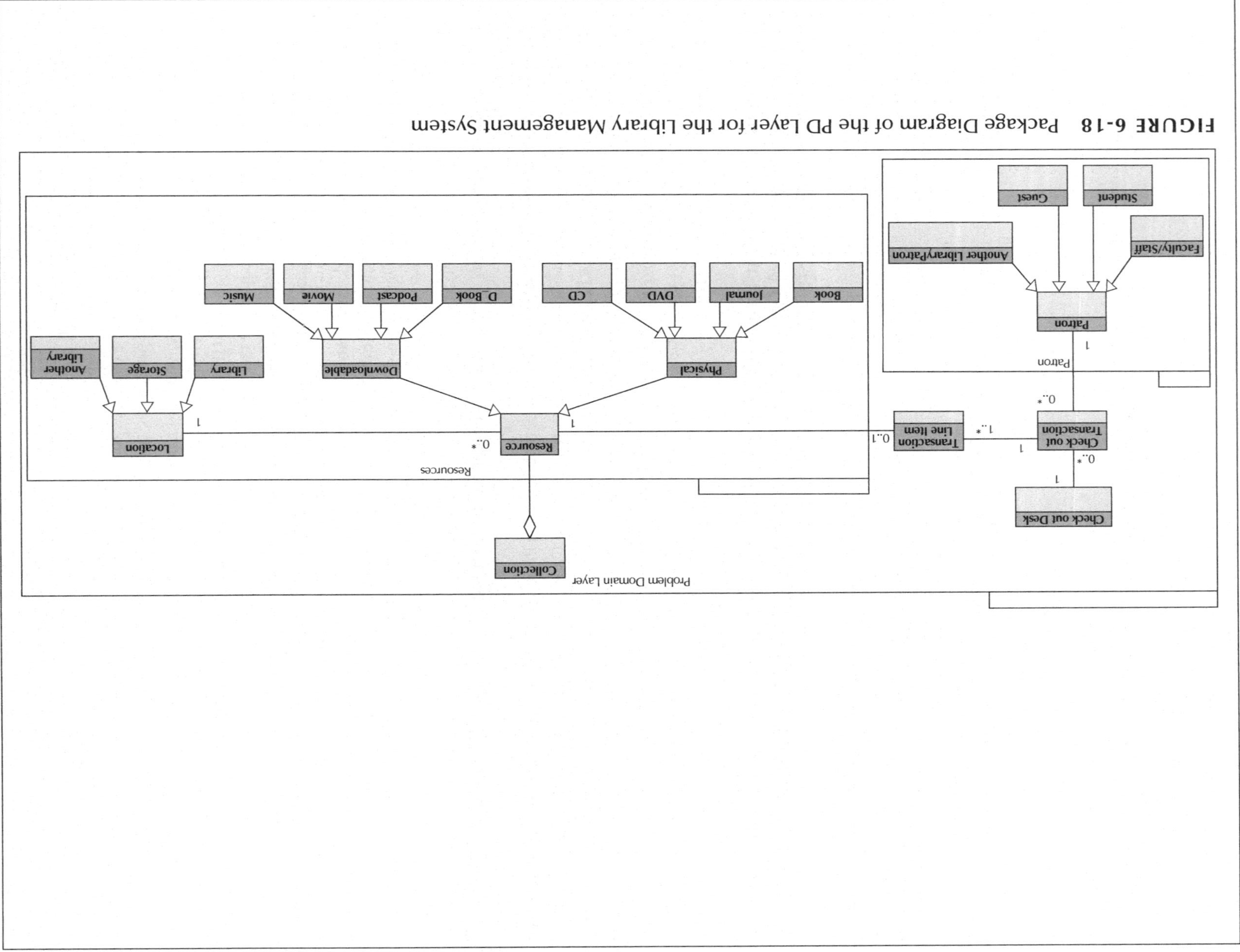

FIGURE 6-18 Package Diagram of the PD Layer for the Library Management System

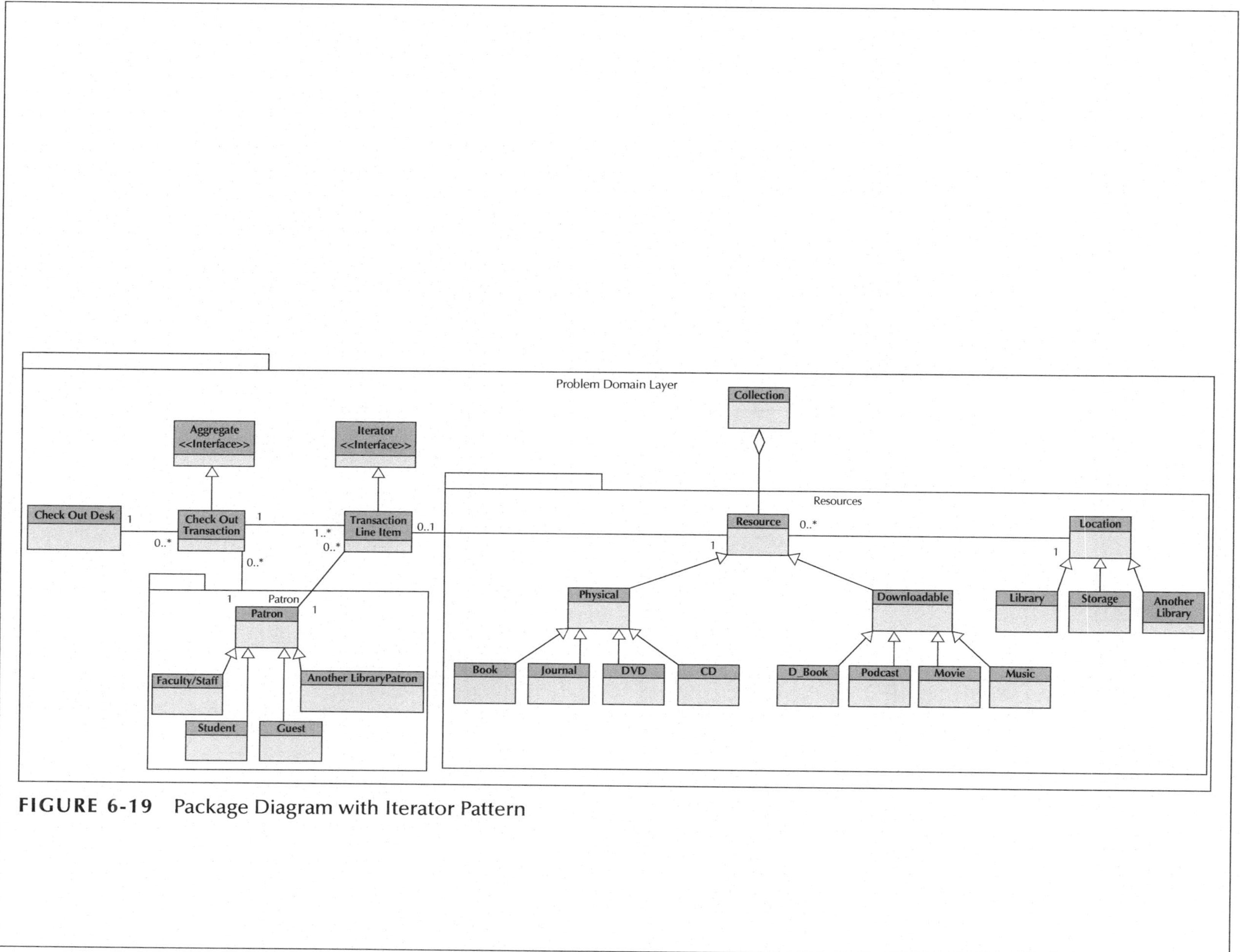

FIGURE 6-19   Package Diagram with Iterator Pattern

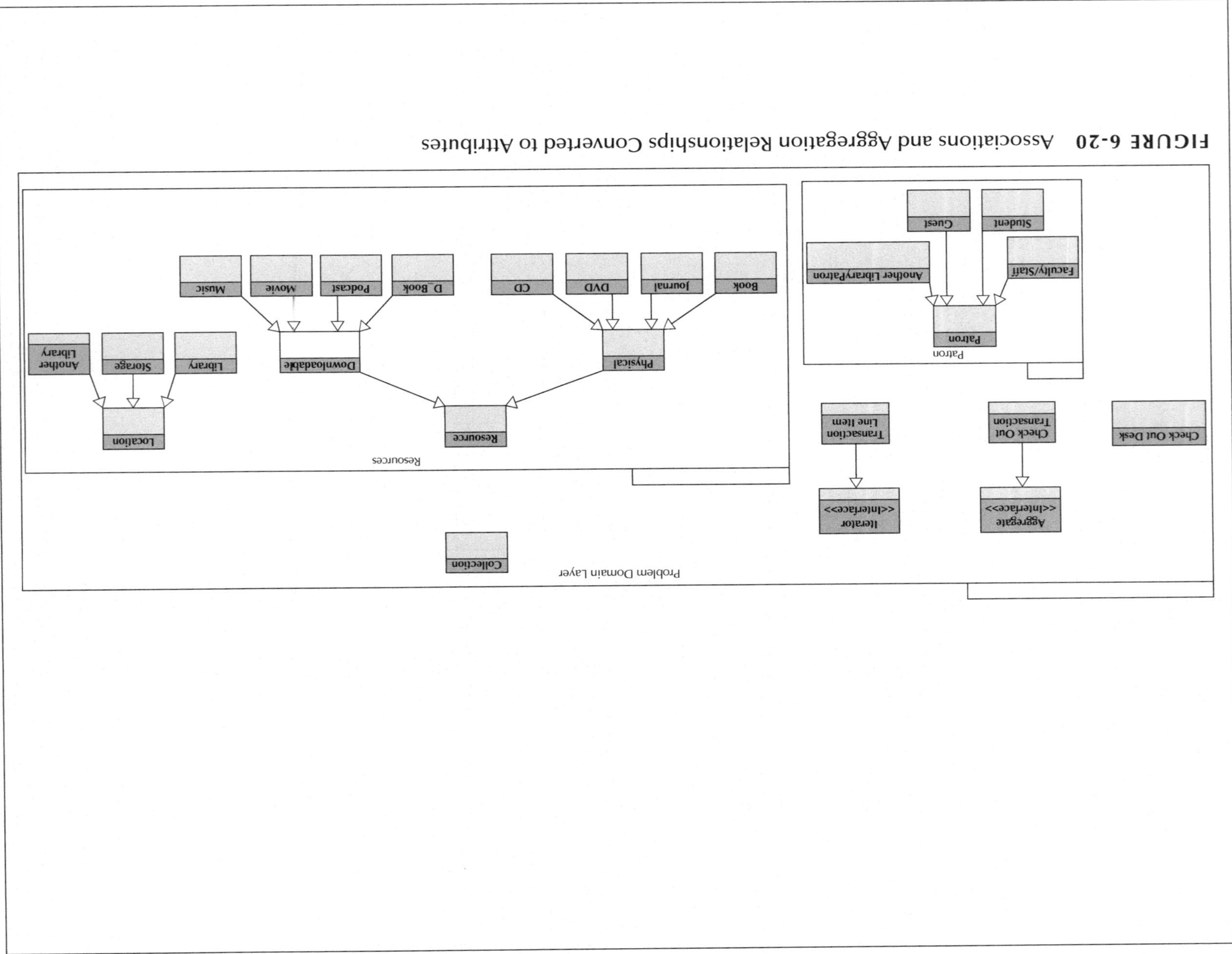

FIGURE 6-20 Associations and Aggregation Relationships Converted to Attributes

CHAPTER REVIEW

After reading and studying this chapter, you should be able to:

- ☐ Describe the purpose of balancing the analysis models.
- ☐ Describe the purpose of the factoring, refinement, and abstraction processes.
- ☐ Describe the purpose of partitions and collaborations.
- ☐ Name and describe the layers.
- ☐ Explain the purpose of a package diagram.
- ☐ Describe the different elements of the package diagram.
- ☐ Create a package diagram to model partitions and layers.
- ☐ Verify and validate package diagrams using walkthroughs.
- ☐ Describe the law of Demeter.
- ☐ Describe the different types of cohesion and why cohesion should be maximized.
- ☐ Describe connascence and how it is related to cohesion and coupling.
- ☐ Describe the need to set the visibility of the attributes and operations, the signature of the operations, and to identify any constraints that the design must enforce.
- ☐ Identify opportunities for reuse through the use of patterns, frameworks, class libraries, and components.
- ☐ Describe the need to restructure the design through the use of factoring and normalization.
- ☐ Describe the pros and cons of the three basic design strategies.

KEY TERMS

A-kind-of
Abstract classes
Abstraction
Aggregation
API (application programming interface)
Application architecture layer
Class
Class cohesion
Class library
Client
Cohesion
Collaboration
Concrete classes
Connascence
Container classes
Contract

Component
Controller
Coupling
CRUDE analysis
Custom development
Customization
Data access and manipulation (DAM) classes
Data management layer
Dependency relationship
Design
Design pattern
Enterprise resource planning (ERP)
Exceptions
Factoring
Foundation layer
Framework

Generalization
Generalization/ specialization cohesion
Has-parts
Human–computer interaction layer
Ideal class cohesion
Inheritance coupling
Interaction coupling
Law of Demeter
Layer
Message
Method
Method cohesion
Model
Model-View-Controller (MVC)
Module

Normalization
Outsourcing
Package
Package diagram
Packaged software
Partition
Patterns
Problem-domain layer
Protocol
Refinement
Server
Signature
Smalltalk
Utility classes
View
Visibility

QUESTIONS

1. Explain the primary difference between an analysis model and a design model.
2. What is meant by balancing the models?
3. What are the interrelationships among the functional, structural, and behavioral models that need to be tested?
4. What does factoring mean? How is it related to abstraction and refinement?
5. What is a partition? How does a partition relate to a collaboration?
6. What is a layer? Name the different layers.
7. What is the purpose of the different layers?

8. Describe the different types of classes that can appear on each of the layers.
9. What issues or questions arise on each of the different layers?
10. What is a package? How are packages related to partitions and layers?
11. What is a dependency relationship? How do you identify them?
12. What are the five steps for identifying packages and creating package diagrams?
13. What needs to be verified and validated in package diagrams?
14. When drawing package diagrams, what guidelines should you follow?
15. What is the law of Demeter?
16. Describe the difference between inheritance and interaction coupling.
17. Describe method cohesion.
18. What is meant by class cohesion? What are the characteristics of ideal class cohesion?
20. Define connascence. How is it related to the ideas of encapsulation, coupling, and cohesion?
21. When designing a specific class, what types of additional specification for a class could be necessary?
22. What situations are most appropriate for a custom development design strategy?
23. What are some problems with using a packaged software approach to building a new system? How can these problems be addressed?
24. When is outsourcing considered a good design strategy? When is it not appropriate?

EXERCISES

A. Describe the difference in meaning between the following two class diagrams. Which is a better model? Why?

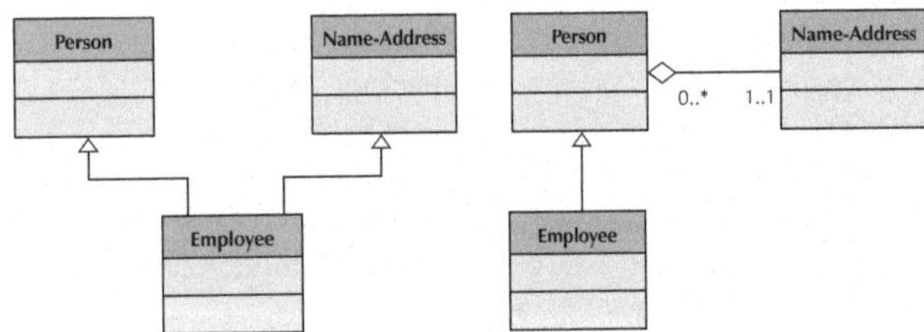

B. From a cohesion, coupling, and connascence perspective, is the following class diagram a good model? Why or why not?

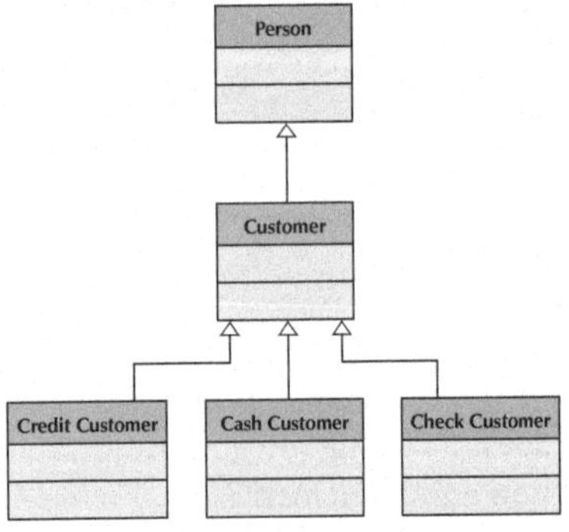

C. From a cohesion, coupling, and connascence perspective, are the following class diagrams good models? Why or why not?

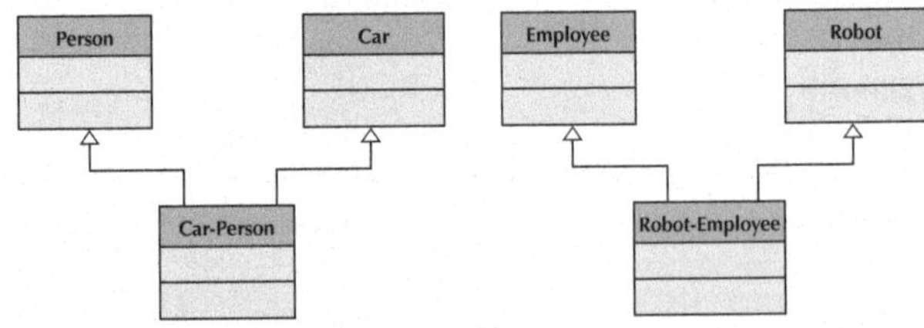

D. For the A Real Estate Inc. problem in Chapters 3 (exercises I, J, and K), 4 (exercises N and O), and 6 (exercise D):
   1. Using the sequence diagrams and the CRUDE matrix, create a package diagram of the problem-domain layer.
   2. Perform a verification and validation walkthrough of the package diagram.
   3. Based on the analysis models that have been created and your current understanding of the firm's position, what design strategy would you recommend? Why?

E. For the A Video Store problem in Chapters 3 (exercises L, M, and N), 4 (exercises P and Q), and 6 (exercise E):

1. Using the sequence diagrams and the CRUDE matrix, create a package diagram of the problem domain layer.

2. Perform a verification and validation walkthrough of the package diagram.

3. Based on the analysis models that have been created and your current understanding of the firm's position, what design strategy would you recommend? Why?

F. For the gym membership problem in Chapters 3 (exercises O, P, and Q), 4 (exercises R and S), and 6 (exercise F):

1. Using the sequence diagrams and the CRUDE matrix, create a package diagram of the problem domain layer.

2. Perform a verification and validation walkthrough of the package diagram.

3. Based on the analysis models that have been created and your current understanding of the firm's position, what design strategy would you recommend? Why?

G. For the Picnics R Us problem in Chapters 3 (exercises R, S, and T), 4 (exercises T and U), and 6 (exercise G):

1. Using the sequence diagrams and the CRUDE matrix, create a package diagram of the problem domain layer.

2. Perform a verification and validation walkthrough of the package diagram.

3. Based on the analysis models that have been created and your current understanding of the firm's position, what design strategy would you recommend? Why?

H. For the Of-the-Month-Club problem in Chapters 3 (exercises U, V, and W), 4 (exercises V and W), and 6 (exercise H):

1. Using the sequence diagrams and the CRUDE matrix, create a package diagram of the problem domain layer.

2. Perform a verification and validation walkthrough of the package diagram.

3. Based on the analysis models that have been created and your current understanding of the firm's position, what design strategy would you recommend? Why?

MINICASES

1. Susan, president of MOTO, Inc., a human resources management firm, is reflecting on the client management software system her organization purchased four years ago. At that time, the firm had just gone through a major growth spurt, and the mixture of automated and manual procedures that had been used to manage client accounts became unwieldy. Susan and Nancy, her IS department head, researched and selected the package that is currently used. Susan had heard about the software at a professional conference she attended, and, at least initially, it worked fairly well for the firm. Some of their procedures had to change to fit the package, but they expected that and were prepared for it.

Since that time, MOTO, Inc., has continued to grow, not only through an expansion of the client base but also through the acquisition of several smaller employment-related businesses. MOTO, Inc., is a much different business than it was four years ago. Along with expanding to offer more diversified human resources management services, the firm's support staff has also expanded. Susan and Nancy are particularly proud of the IS department they have built up over the years. Using strong ties with a local university, an attractive compensation package, and a good working environment, the IS department is well staffed with competent, innovative people, plus a steady stream of college interns that keeps the department fresh and lively. One of the IS teams pioneered the use of the Internet to offer MOTO's services to a whole new market segment, an experiment that has proved very successful.

It seems clear that a major change is needed in the client-management software, and Susan has already begun to plan financially to undertake such a project. This software is a central part of MOTO's operations, and Susan wants to be sure that a high-quality system is obtained this time. She knows that the vendor of their current system has made some revisions and additions to its product line. A number of other software vendors also offer products that may be suitable. Some of these vendors did not exist when the purchase was made four years ago. Susan is also considering Nancy's suggestion that the IS department develop a custom software application.

a. Outline the issues that Susan should consider that would support the development of a custom software application in-house.

   b. Outline the issues that Susan should consider that would support the purchase of a software package.

   c. Within the context of a systems-development project, when should the decision of make-versus-buy be made? How should Susan proceed? Explain your answer.

2. Refer to minicase 1 (West Star Marinas) in Chapter 4. After all the analysis models (both the as-is and to-be models) for West Star Marinas were completed, the director of operations finally understood why it was important to understand the as-is system before delving into the development of the to-be system. However, you now tell him that the to-be models are only the problem-domain portion of the design. He is now very confused. After explaining to him the advantages of using a layered approach to developing the system, he says, "I don't care about reusability or maintenance. I only want the system to be implemented as soon as possible. You IS types are always trying to pull a fast one on the users. Just get the system completed."

     What is your response to the Director of Operations? Do you jump into implementation as he seems to want? What do you do next?

3. Refer to the analysis models that you created for professional and scientific staff management (PSSM) for minicase 2 in Chapter 3 and for minicase 1 in Chapter 5.

   a. Using the sequence diagrams and the CRUDE matrix, create a package diagram of the problem domain layer.

   b. Perform a verification and validation walkthrough of the package diagram.

   c. Based on the analysis models that have been created and your current understanding of the firm's position, what design strategy would you recommend? Why?

4. Refer to the analysis models that you created for Holiday Travel Vehicles for minicase 2 in Chapter 4 and for minicase 2 in Chapter 5.

   a. Using the sequence diagrams and the CRUDE matrix, create a package diagram of the problem domain layer.

   b. Perform a verification and validation walkthrough of the package diagram.

   c. Based on the analysis models that have been created and your current understanding of the firm's position, what design strategy would you recommend? Why?

CHAPTER 7

CLASS AND METHOD DESIGN

The most important step of the design phase is designing the individual classes and methods. Object-oriented systems can be quite complex, so analysts need to create instructions and guidelines for programmers that clearly describe what the system must do. This chapter presents a set of activities and techniques used to design classes and methods. The chapter also covers the designing tests that are necessary to make sure that the design of the classes and methods are implemented correctly. Together they are used to ensure that the object-oriented design communicates how the system needs to be coded.

OBJECTIVES

- Be able to optimize object designs.
- Be able to map an object design to an implementation language.
- Be able to specify constraints and contracts.
- Be able to create a method specification.
- Understand how object-orientation affects software testing.
- Understand the different types of and purpose of unit tests.
- Understand the different types of and purpose of integration tests.
- Understand the different types of and purpose of system tests.
- Understand the different types of and purpose of acceptance tests.

INTRODUCTION

WARNING: *This material may be hazardous to your mental stability.* Not really, but now that we have your attention, you must realize that this material is fairly technical in nature and that it is extremely important in today's "flat" world. Today, much of the actual implementation will be done in a different geographic location than where the analysis and design are performed. We must ensure that the design is specified in a "correct" manner and that there is no, or at least minimal, ambiguity in the design specification.

In today's flat world, the common language spoken among developers is very likely to be UML and some object-oriented language, such as Java, and not English. English has always been and always will be ambiguous. Furthermore, to what variety of English do we refer? As both Oscar Wilde and George Bernard Shaw independently pointed out, the United States and England are divided by a common language.

Practically speaking, Class and Method design is where all the work actually gets done during design. No matter on which layer you are focusing, the classes, which will be used to create the system objects, must be designed. Some people believe that with reusable class libraries and off-the-shelf components, this type of low-level, or detailed, design is a waste of time and that we should jump immediately into the "real" work: coding the system. However, experience shows that low-level, or detailed, design is critical despite the use of libraries and components. Detailed design is still very important for three reasons. First, with today's modern CASE tools, quite a bit of the actual code can be generated by the tool from the detailed design. Second, even preexisting classes and components need to be understood, organized, and pieced together. Third, it is still common for the project team to have to write some code and produce original classes that support the application logic of the system.

Jumping right into coding will guarantee disastrous results. For example, even though the use of layers can simplify the individual classes, they can increase the complexity of the interactions between them. If the classes are not designed carefully, the resulting system can be very inefficient. Or worse, the instances of the classes (i.e., the objects) will not be capable of communicating with each other, which will result in the system's not working properly.

The good news is that the detailed design of the individual classes and methods is fairly straightforward. The interactions among the objects on the problem-domain layer have been designed, in some detail, during analysis (see Chapters 3 through 6). The other layers (data management, human–computer interaction, and application architecture) are highly dependent on the problem-domain layer. Therefore, if the problem-domain classes are designed correctly, the design of the classes on the other layers will fall into place, relatively speaking.

That being said, it has been our experience that many project teams are much too quick at jumping into writing code for the classes without first designing them. Some of this has been caused by the fact that object-oriented systems analysis and design has evolved from object-oriented programming. Furthermore, with the growing popularity of agile approaches (see Chapter 13) and their focus on the idea that the code is the design, this problem could become overwhelming. Until recently there has been a general lack of accepted guidelines on how to design and develop effective object-oriented systems. However, with the acceptance of UML as a standard object notation, standardized approaches based on work of many object methodologists have emerged.[1]

ADDITIONAL OBJECT DESIGN ACTIVITIES

In earlier chapters (Chapters 3–6), we focused on creating a problem-domain model that represents the problem space. To accomplish this, we expanded the descriptions of the partitions, layers, and classes by including additional specification of the current model, identifying opportunities for reuse, and restructuring the design. In this section, we delve deeper into some of the more technical aspects of object-oriented design. Specifically, we describe optimizing the design and how to map our problem-domain model to an actual implementation language such as Java.

Optimizing the Design[2]

Up until now, we have focused our energy on developing an understandable design. With all the classes, patterns, collaborations, partitions, and layers designed and with all the class libraries, frameworks, and components included in the design, understandability has been our primary focus. However, increasing the understandability of a design typically creates an

---

[1] For example, OPEN [I. Graham, B. Henderson-Seller, and H. Yanoussi, *The Open Process Specification* (Reading, MA: Addison-Wesley, 1997)], RUP [P. Kruchten, *The Rational Unified Process: An Introduction*, 2nd ed. (Reading, MA: Addison-Wesley, 2000)], and the Enhanced Unified Process (see Chapter 1).

[2] The material contained in this section is based on James Rumbaugh, Michael Blaha, William Premerlani, Frederick Eddy, and William Lorensen, *Object-Oriented Modeling and Design* (Englewood Cliffs, NJ: Prentice Hall, 1991); Bernd Brugge and Allen H. Dutoit, *Object-Oriented Software Engineering: Conquering Complex and Changing Systems* (Englewood Cliffs, NJ: Prentice Hall, 2000).

inefficient design. Conversely, focusing on efficiency issues will deliver a design that is more difficult to understand. A good practical design manages the inevitable trade-offs that must occur.[3]

The first optimization to consider is to review the access paths between objects. In some cases, a message from one object to another has a long path to traverse (i.e., it goes through many objects). If the path is long and the message is sent frequently, a redundant path should be considered. Adding an attribute to the calling object that will store a direct connection to the object at the end of the path can accomplish this.

A second optimization is to review each attribute of each class. It should be determined which methods use the attributes and which objects use the methods. If the only methods that use an attribute are read and update methods and only instances of a single class send messages to read and update the attribute, then the attribute may belong with the calling class (client) instead of the called class (server). Moving the attribute to the calling class will substantially speed up the system.

A third optimization is to review the direct and indirect fan-out of each method. *Fan-out* refers to the number of messages sent by a method. The direct fan-out is the number of messages sent by the method itself, whereas the indirect fan-out also includes the number of messages sent by the methods called by the other methods in a message tree. If the fan-out of a method is high relative to the other methods in the system, the method should be optimized.

A fourth optimization is to look at the execution order of the statements in often-used methods. In some cases, it is possible to rearrange some of the statements to be more efficient. For example, if based on the objects in the system, it is known that a search routine can be narrowed by searching on one attribute before another one, then the search algorithm should be optimized by forcing it to always search in a predefined order.

A fifth optimization is to avoid recomputation by creating a *derived attribute* (or *active value*) (e.g., a total that stores the value of the computation). This is also known as *caching computational results,* and it can be accomplished by adding a *trigger* to the attributes contained in the computation (i.e., attributes on which the derived attribute is dependent). This would require a recomputation to take place only when one of the attributes that go into the computation is changed. Another approach is to simply mark the derived attribute for recomputation and delay the recomputation until the next time the derived attribute is accessed. This last approach delays the recomputation as long as possible. In this manner, a computation does not occur unless it must occur. Otherwise, every time a derived attribute needs to be accessed, a computation will be required.

A sixth optimization that should be considered deals with objects that participate in a one-to-one association; that is, they both must exist for either to exist. In this case, it might make sense, for efficiency purposes, to collapse the two defining classes into a single class. However, this optimization might need to be reconsidered when storing the "fatter" object in a database. Depending on the type of object persistence used (see Chapter 8), it can be more efficient to keep the two classes separate. Alternatively, it could make more sense for the two classes to be combined on the problem-domain layer but kept separate on the data management layer.

Mapping Problem-Domain Classes to Implementation Languages[4]

Up until this point, it has been assumed that the classes and methods in the models would be implemented directly in an object-oriented programming language. However, now it is

---

[3] The optimizations described here are only suggestions. In all cases, the decision to implement one or more of these optimizations really depends on the problem domain of the system and the environment on which the system will reside, i.e., the data management layer (see Chapter 8), the human–computer interaction layer (see Chapter 9), and the application architecture layer (see Chapter 10).

[4] The mapping rules presented in this section are based on material in Coad and Yourdon, *Object-Oriented Design.*

important to map the current design to the capabilities of the programming language used. For example, if we have used multiple inheritance in our design but we are implementing in a language that supports only single inheritance, then the multiple inheritance must be factored out of the design. If the implementation is to be done in an object-based language, one that does not support inheritance,[5] or a non–object-based language, such as C, we must map the problem-domain objects to programming constructs that can be implemented using the chosen implementation environment.

Implementing Problem-Domain Classes in a Single-Inheritance Language The only issue associated with implementing problem-domain objects is the factoring out of any multiple inheritance—i.e., the use of more than one superclass—used in the evolving design. For example, if you were to implement the solution in Java, C#, or Visual Basic.net, you must factor out any multiple inheritance. The easiest way to do this is to use the following rule:

> **RULE 1a:** Convert the additional inheritance relationships to association relationships. The multiplicity of the new association from the subclass to the superclass should be 1..1. If the additional superclasses are concrete, that is, they can be instantiated themselves, then the multiplicity from the superclass to the subclass is 0..1. Otherwise, it is 1..1. Furthermore, an exclusive-or (XOR) constraint must be added between the associations. Finally, you must add appropriate methods to ensure that all information is still available to the original class.

or

> **RULE 1b:** Flatten the inheritance hierarchy by copying the attributes and methods of the additional superclass(es) down to all of the subclasses and remove the additional superclass from the design.[6]

Figure 7-1 demonstrates the application of these rules. Figure 7-1a portrays a simple example of multiple inheritance where Flying Car inherits from both Airplane and Car, and Amphibious Car inherits from both Car and Boat. Assuming that Car is concrete, we apply Rule 1a to Figure 7-1a, and we end up with the diagram in Figure 7-1b, where we have added the association between Flying Car and Car and the association between Amphibious Car and Boat. The multiplicities have been added correctly, and the XOR constraint has been applied. If we apply Rule 1b to Figure 7-1a, we end up with the diagram in Figure 7-1c, where all the attributes of Car have been copied down into Flying Car and Amphibious Car. In this latter case, you might have to deal with the effects of inheritance conflicts.

The advantage of Rule 1a is that all problem-domain classes identified during analysis are preserved. This allows maximum flexibility of maintenance of the design of the problem-domain layer. However, Rule 1a increases the amount of message passing required in the system, and it has added processing requirements involving the XOR constraint, thus reducing the overall efficiency of the design. Accordingly, our recommendation is to limit Rule 1a to be applied only when dealing with "extra" superclasses that are concrete because they have an independent existence in the problem domain. Use Rule 1b when they are abstract because they do not have an independent existence from the subclass.

---

[5] In this case, we are talking about implementation inheritance, not the interface inheritance. Interface inheritance supported by Visual Basic and Java supports only inheriting the requirements to implement certain methods, not any implementation. Java and Visual Basic.net also support single inheritance as described in this text.

[6] It is also a good idea to document this modification in the design so that in the future, modifications to the design can be maintained easily.

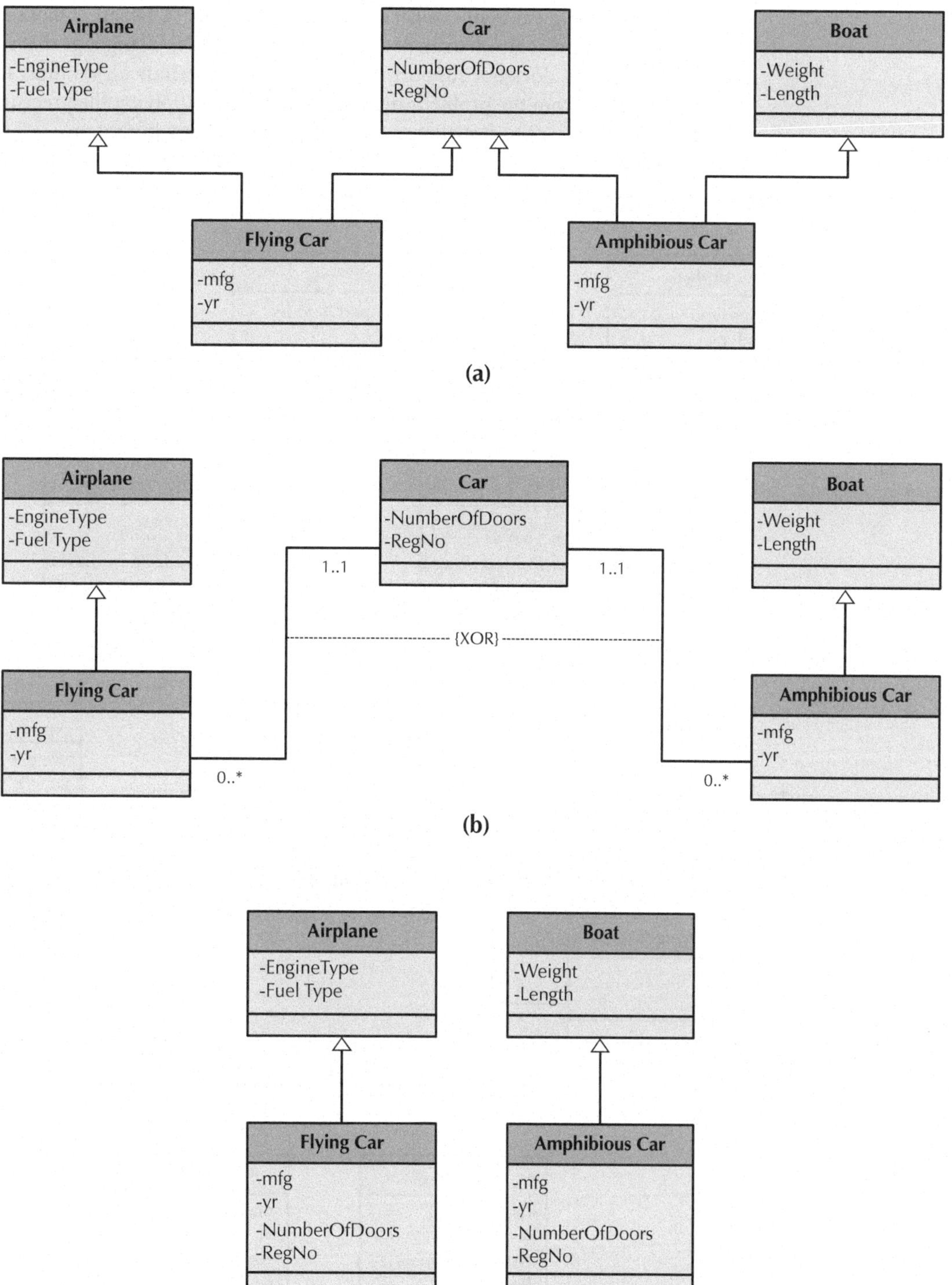

FIGURE 7-1 Factoring Out Multiple-Inheritance Effect for a Single-Inheritance Language

Implementing Problem-Domain Objects in an Object-Based Language If we are going to implement our solution in an *object-based language* (i.e., a language that supports the creation of objects but does not support implementation inheritance), we must factor out all uses of inheritance from the problem-domain class design. Applying the preceding rule to all superclasses enables us to restructure our design without any inheritance.

Figure 7-2 demonstrates the application of the preceding rules. Figure 7-2a shows the same simple example of multiple inheritance portrayed in Figure 7-1, where Flying Car

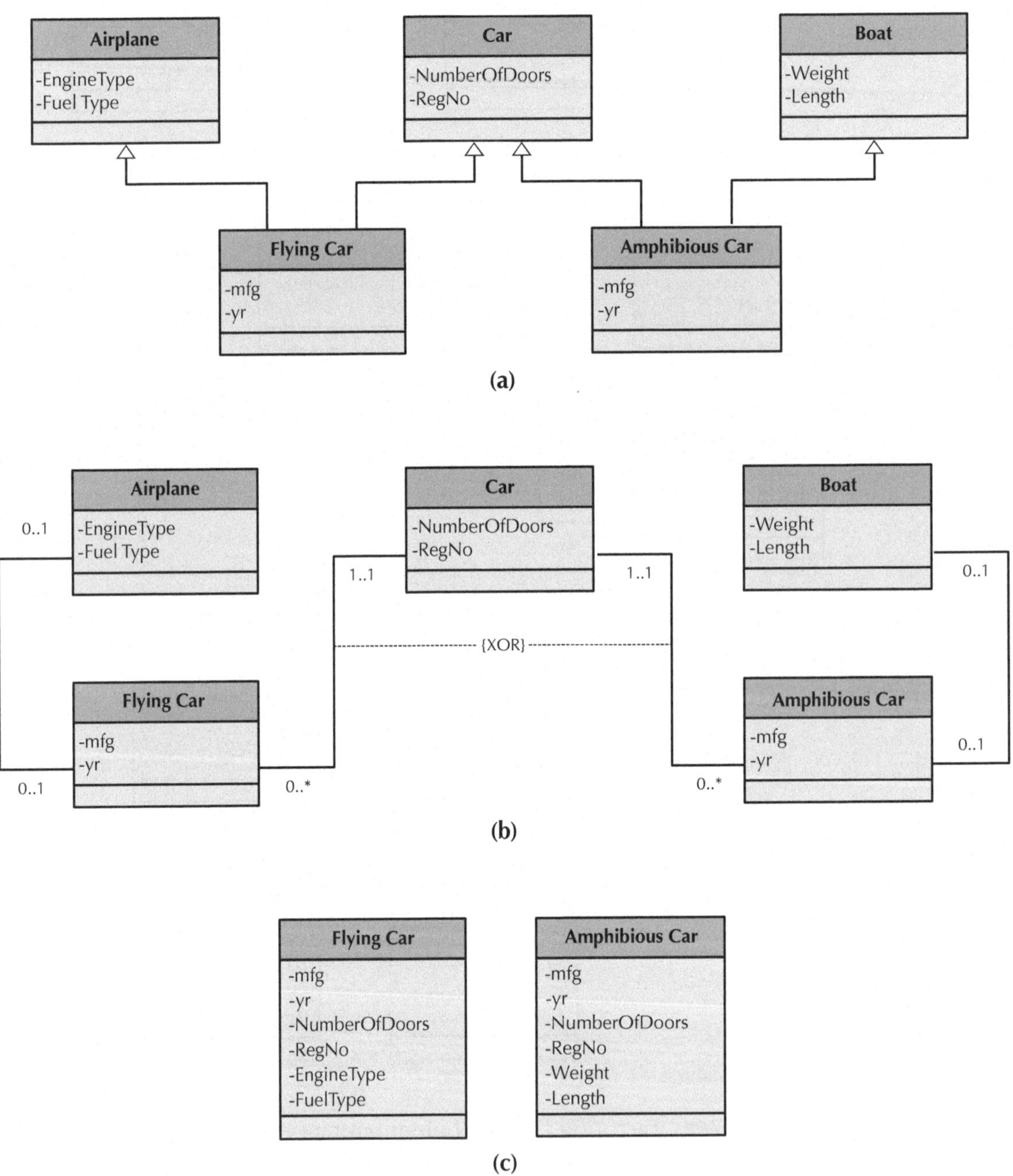

FIGURE 7-2 Factoring Out Multiple Inheritance Effect for an Object-Based Language

inherits from both Airplane and Car, and Amphibious Car inherits from both Car and Boat. Assuming that Airplane, Car, and Boat are concrete, we apply Rule 1a to Figure 7-2a and we end up with the diagram in Figure 7-2b, where we have added the associations, the multiplicities, and the XOR constraint. If we apply Rule 1b to Figure 7-2a, we end up with the diagram in Figure 7-2c, where all the attributes of the superclasses have been copied down into Flying Car and Amphibious Car. In this latter case, you might have to deal with the effects of inheritance conflicts. In this case, we again recommend to limit Rule 1a to be applied only when dealing with superclasses that are concrete because they have an independent existence in the problem domain. Use Rule 1b when they are abstract because they do not have an independent existence from the subclass.

Implementing Problem-Domain Objects in a Traditional Language From a practical perspective, we are much better off implementing an object-oriented design in an object-oriented programming language, such as C++, Java, Objective-C, C#, or Visual Basic.net. Practically speaking, the gulf between an object-oriented design and a traditional programming language is simply too great for mere mortals to be able to cross. The best advice that we can give about implementing an object-oriented design in a traditional programming language is to run away as fast and as far as possible from the project. However, if we are brave (foolish?) enough to attempt this, we must realize that in addition to factoring out inheritance from the design, we must factor out all uses of polymorphism, dynamic binding, encapsulation, and information hiding. This is quite a bit of additional work to be accomplished. The way we factor these object-oriented features out of the detailed design of the system tends to be language dependent. Therefore, this is beyond the scope of this text.

CONSTRAINTS AND CRC CARDS

Contracts were introduced in Chapter 4 in association with collaborations. A *contract* formalizes the interactions between the client and server objects, where a *client (consumer)* object is an instance of a class that sends a message to a *server (supplier)* object that executes one of its methods in response to the request. Contracts are modeled on the legal notion of a contract, where both parties, client and server objects, have obligations and rights. Practically speaking, a contract is a set of constraints and guarantees. If the constraints are met, then the server object guarantees certain behavior.[7] Constraints can be written in a natural language (e.g., English), a semiformal language (e.g., *Structured English*[8]), or a formal language (e.g., UML's Object Constraint Language). Given the need for precise, unambiguous specification of constraints, we recommend using UML's Object Constraint Language.

The *Object Constraint Language (OCL)*[9] is a complete language designed to specify constraints. In this section, we provide a short overview of some of the more useful constructs contained in the language (see Figure 7-3). Essentially, all OCL expressions are simply a declarative statement that evaluates to either being true or false. If the expression evaluates to true, then the constraint has been satisfied. For example, if a customer had to have a less than a one hundred dollar balance owed to be allowed to place another credit order, the OCL expression would be:

balance owed <= 100.00

[7] The idea of using contracts in design evolved from the "Design by Contract" technique developed by Bertrand Meyer. See Bertrand Meyer, *Object-Oriented Software Construction* (Englewood Cliffs, NJ: Prentice Hall, 1988).

[8] We describe Structured English with Method Specification later in this chapter.

[9] For a complete description of the object constraint language, see Jos Warmer and Anneke Kleppe, *The Object Constraint Language: Precise Modeling with UML* (Reading, MA: Addison-Wesley, 1999).

Operator Type	Operator	Example
Comparison	=	a = 5
	<	a < 100
	<=	a <= 100
	>	a > 100
	>=	a >= 100
	<>	a <> 100
Logical	and	a and b
	or	a or b
	xor	a xor b
	not	not a
Math	+	a + b
	-	a - b
	*	a * b
	/	a / b
String	concat	a = b.concat(c)
Relationship Traversal	.	relationshipAttributeName.b
	::	superclassName::propertyName
Collection	size	a.size
	count(object)	a.count(b)
	includes(object)	a.includes(b)
	isEmpty	a.isEmpty
	sum()	a.sum(b,c,d)
	select(expression)	a.select(b > d)

FIGURE 7-3
Sample OCL
Constructs

otherwise, an error has occurred. OCL also has the ability to traverse relationships between objects, e.g., if the amount on a purchase order is required to be the sum of the values of the individual purchase order lines, this can be modeled as:

$$amount = OrderLine.sum(get Price())$$

This is a constraint test, not an assignment statement. So, if the purchase order amount attribute's value does not equal to the summation of the results of sending the getPrice() message to all of the relevant OrderLine objects, an error has occurred. OCL also provides the ability to model more-complex constraints with a set of logical operators: and, or, xor, and not. For example, if customers were to be given a discount only if they were a senior citizen or a "prime" customer, OCL could be used to model the constraint as:

$$age > 65 \text{ or customer Type} = \text{"prime"}$$

OCL provides many other constructs that can be used to build unique constraints. These include math-oriented operators, string operators, and relationship traversal operators. For example, if the printed name on a customer order should be the concatenation of the customer's first name and last name, then OCL could represent this constraint as:

$$printedName = firstName.concat(lastName)$$

As with the OrderLine example above, this is a constraint, not an assignment statement. So, again if this "test" is not true, an error has occurred. We already have seen an example of the '.' operator being used to traverse a relationship from Order to OrderLine above. The '::' operator allows the modeling of traversing inheritance relationships.

OCL also provides a set of operations that are used to support constraints over a collection of objects. For example, we demonstrated the use of the sum() operator above where we wanted to guarantee that the amount was equal to the summation of all of the prices of the items in the collection. The size operation returns the number of items in the collection. The count operation returns the number of occurrences in the collection of the specific object passed as its argument. The includes operation tests whether the object passed to it is already included in the collection. The isEmpty operation determines whether the collection is empty or not. The select operation provides support to model the identification of a subset of the collection based on the expression that is passed as its argument. Obviously, OCL provides a rich set of operators and operations in which to model constraints.

Types of Constraints

Three different types of *constraints* are typically captured in object-oriented design: preconditions, postconditions, and invariants.

Contracts are used primarily to establish the preconditions and postconditions for a method to be able to execute properly. A *precondition* is a constraint that must be met for a method to execute. For example, the parameters passed to a method must be valid for the method to execute. Otherwise, an exception should be raised. A *postcondition* is a constraint that must be met after the method executes, or the effect of the method execution must be undone. For example, the method cannot make any of the attributes of the object take on an invalid value. In this case, an exception should be raised, and the effect of the method's execution should be undone.

Whereas preconditions and postconditions model the constraints on an individual method, *invariants* model constraints that must always be true for all instances of a class. Examples of invariants include domains or types of attributes, multiplicity of attributes, and the valid values of attributes. This includes the attributes that model association and aggregation relationships. For example, if an association relationship is required, an invariant should be created that will enforce it to have a valid value for the instance to exist. Invariants are normally attached to the class. We can attach invariants to the CRC cards or class diagram by adding a set of assertions to them.

In Figure 7-4, the back of the CRC cards constrains the values of the attributes of a Patient object and an Appointment object to specific types. For example, a Patient's amount must be a float and an appt must be an instance of the Appointment class. Furthermore, a Patient's amount is optional, but it can't have more than one value [i.e., a multiplicity of (0..1)], and it must have the same value as the result of the Appointment.getTotalCost() message sent to the instance of Appointment stored in the appt attribute. Also shown is the constraint for an Appointment object to exist, instances of the Entry, Transaction Line Item, Place, Patient, and Doctor classes class must exist (see the Relationships section of the CRC card where the minimum value of the multiplicities are always one). In some cases the upper limit constrains the number of value to one (..1) and in other cases the number of values are many (..*). With regards to instances of an Appointment class, there are many additional OCL constraints. For example, the value of the totalCost attribute must be equal to the sum of the values of the LineItem.getAmt() messages that are actually sent to instances of the TransactionLineItem class (see LineItem attribute of the Appointment class in Figure 7-4b). Alternatively, it is possible to have all the invariants contained in the class diagram (see Figure 7-5). However, if all

Front:

Class Name: Patient	ID: 3	Type: Concrete, Domain
Description: An individual who needs to receive or has received medical attention		Associated Use Cases: 2

Responsibilities	Collaborators
Make appointment	Appointment
Calculate last visit	
Change status	
Provide medical history	Medical history

Back:

Attributes:

amount (0..1) (float) {amount = Appointment.getTotalCost()}

insurance carrier (0..*) (string)

appt (0..*) (Appointment)

medical history (0..1) (Medical History)

Relationships:

Generalization (a-kind-of): Participant

Aggregation (has-parts):

Other Associations: Appointment (0..*), Medical History (0..1)

(a)

FIGURE 7-4
Invariants on a
CRC Card

invariants are placed on a class diagram for all classes, the diagram becomes very difficult to understand. Consequently, we recommend either extending the CRC card to document the OCL invariants instead of attaching them all to the class diagram, as we did in Figure 7-4, or creating a separate text document that contains them (see Figure 7-6).

Front:

Class Name: Appointment	**ID:** 5	**Type:** Concrete, Domain
Description: A scheduled appointment between a patient and a doctor		**Associated Use Cases:** 5

Responsibilities	**Collaborators**
Cancel without notice	
Create	
Get total cost	TransactionLineItem
Get office	Place
Get insurance carrier	Patient
Get last visit	Patient
Get medical history	Patient
Get doctor	Doctor
Get debit amount	Entry
Get credit amount	Entry

Back:

Attributes:

appointmentNumber (1..1) (unsigned long)	
time (1..1) (Time)	
date (1..1) (Date)	
reason (1..1) (String)	
totalCost (1..1) (float)	{totalCost = sum(LineItem.getAmt())}
Debit (1..*) (Entry)	{Debit = sum(Entry.getAmt())}
Credit (1..*) (Entry)	{Credit = sum(Entry.getAmt())}
LineItem (1..*) (TransactionLineItem)	
Office (1..1) (Place)	{Office = Place.getAddress()}
PatientID (1..1) (String)	{PatientID = Patient.concat(getLastname(),getFirstname())}
DoctorID (1..*) (String)	{DoctorID = Doctor.concat(getLastname(),getFirstname())}

Relationships:

Generalization (a-kind-of):

Aggregation (has-parts):

Other Associations: Entry (1..*), Entry (1..*), Transaction Line Item(1..*), Place (1..1), Patient (1..1), Doctor (1..*)

FIGURE 7-4
Continued

(b)

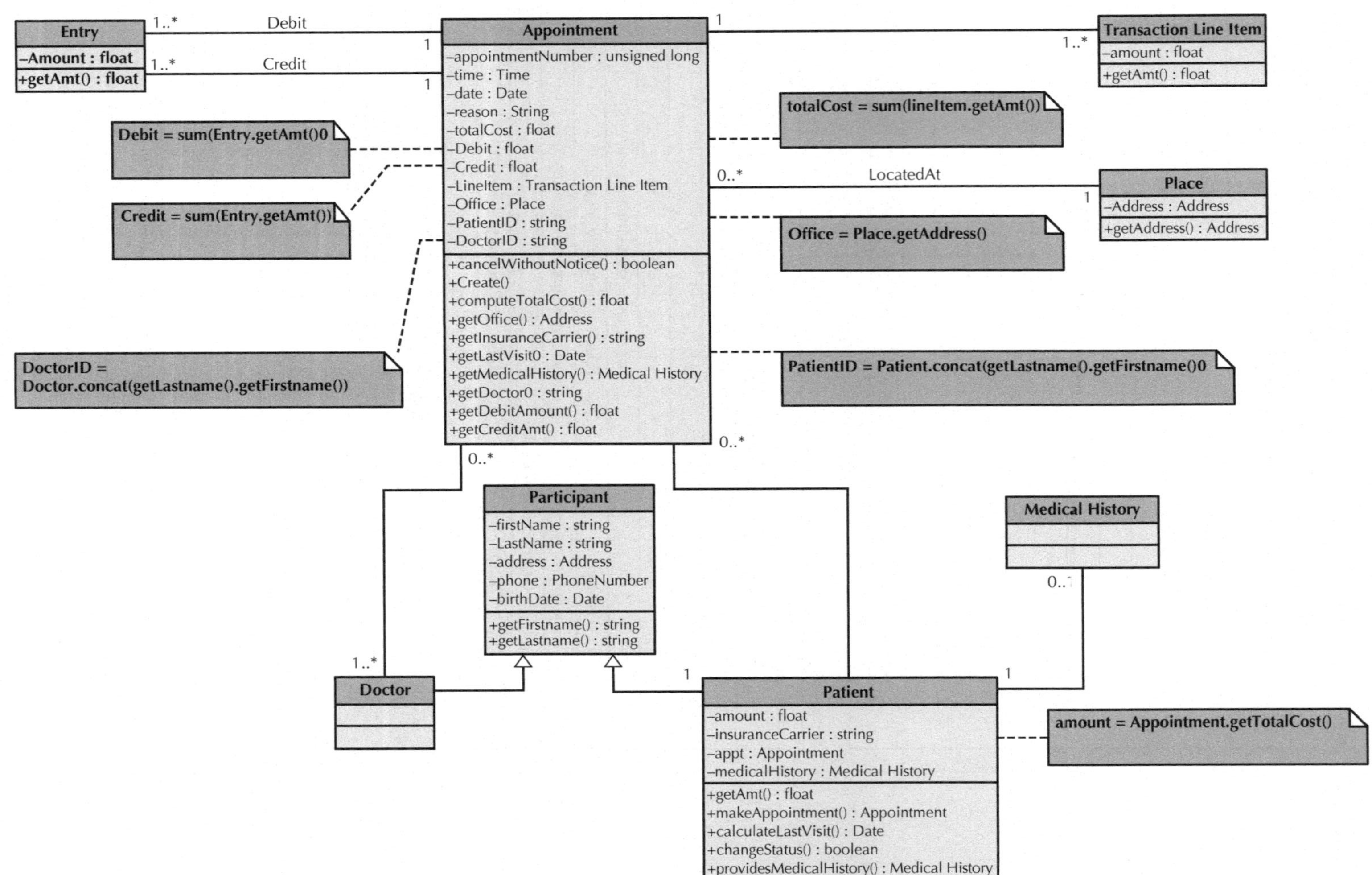

FIGURE 7-5   Invariants on a Class Diagram

Appointment Invariants:

totalCost = sum(LineItem.getAmt())

Debit = sum(Entry.getAmt())

Credit = sum(Entry.getAmt())

Office = Place.getAddress()

PatientID = Patient.concat(getLastname(),getFirstname())

DoctorID = Doctor.concat(getLastname(),getFirstname())

Patient Invariants:

Amount = Appointment.getTotalCost()

FIGURE 7-6
Invariants in a
Text File

APPLYING THE CHAPTER CONCEPTS

Library Management System (LMS) Example In the previous installment of the Library Management System (LMS) example, Susan and her team had created a package diagram, applied the Iterator design pattern to the transaction classes, and had converted the association and aggregation relationships to attributes. Upon completing this, Susan decided to go back once again and meet with Joe to make sure that everything completed to date was correct. In particular, she wanted to validate the current package diagram. Below is a small excerpt from her meeting with Joe.

SUSAN: Joe, I'm glad to be able to sit down with you and review our latest version of our structural model. In this case, I would like to go through the model to make sure that we have not included anything unnecessarily.

JOE: To be honest, I hoped that our meetings would start to slow down somewhat. I guess when you stated that the process would be very iterative and incremental, you weren't kidding. So, let's get started.

SUSAN: In the past, we had raised questions as to whether all of the subclasses in the model were really necessary. We had decided to delay that decision until later. Well, now is later.

JOE: That's right, we procrastinated certain decisions. So, I guess we really did need to meet again.

SUSAN: Okay, let's review the classes in the Patron package (see Figure 6-20). I realize that when considering the subclasses of the Patron class, there are differences between the subclasses. However, from the library's perspective, are the differences relevant? Or are the differences primarily a difference in an attribute's value? Remember, we are now moving into design of the solution where we attempt to optimize the classes.

JOE: I guess from the library's point of view, the additional attributes in the subclasses are not relevant to the process of checking out and returning resources. So, I guess we could consider removing the subclasses. That would simplify the model. However, the process of validating the IDs is different for the different subclasses. What should we do about that?

SUSAN: Now that we know that we do not need the subclasses for the additional attributes, there are two different ways in which we can handle the different process requirements. From your perspective, it really will not make a difference as to which way

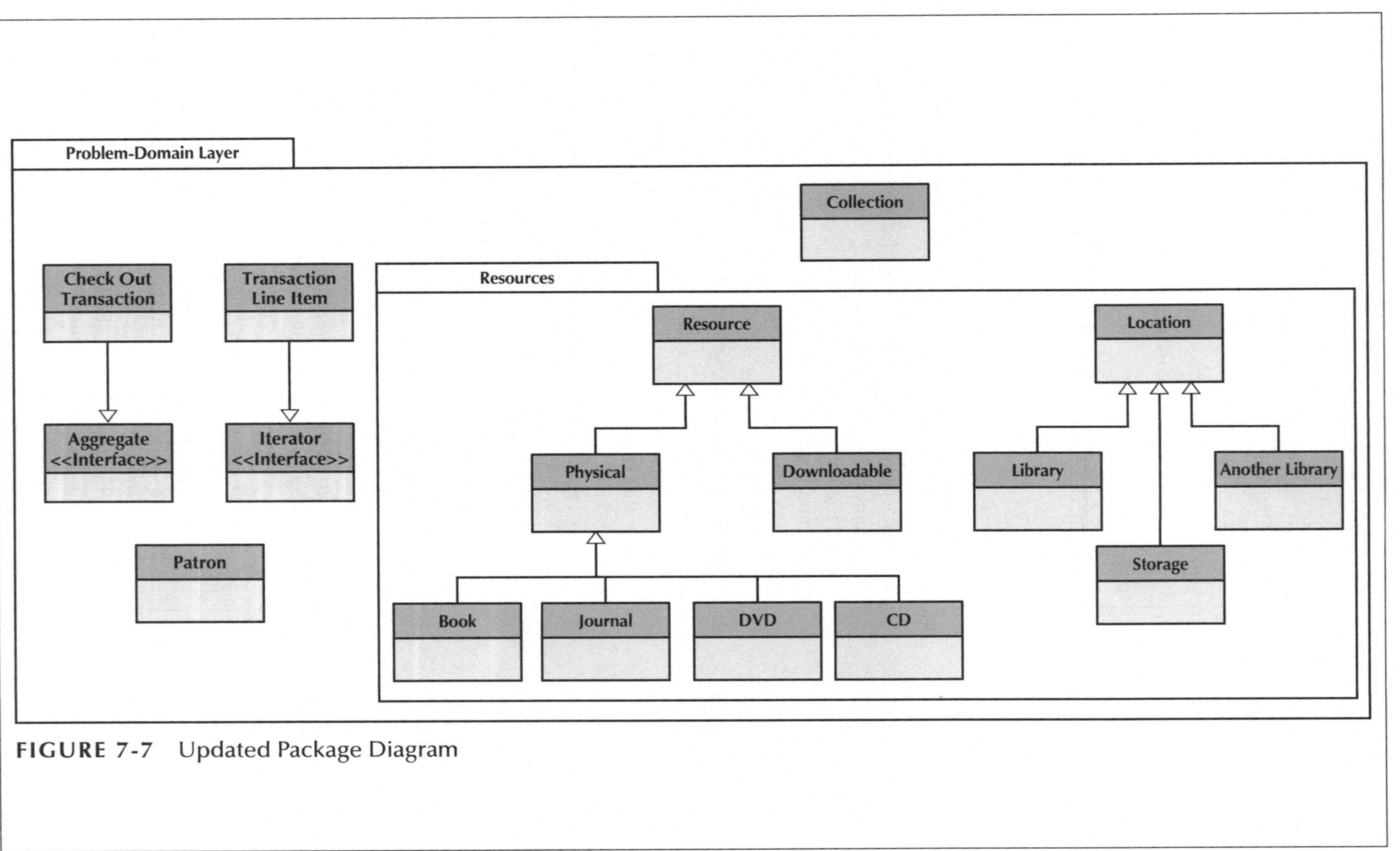

FIGURE 7-7   Updated Package Diagram

is chosen. Therefore, I will defer that decision to our programmers so that they can choose the most efficient way to implement the processes. So, let's move on to my next concern. Given that there is only one physical library, do we really need to have a Check Out Desk class?

JOE: That's a good question. We do have multiple check out desks. But we really don't need to keep track of any information regarding which desk is used to check out a resource.

SUSAN: Next, let's review the Resource package. Do we need to keep the subclasses of the Location class?

JOE: Yes. Not only the value of the attributes can be different, the additional attributes in the subclasses are also different. For example, in the library, we need to know on which floor the resource is located. While, with the warehouse, we need to know which aisle and bin the resource is stored in the warehouse. And with another library, we just need to know the contact information for the other library.

SUSAN: Okay, let's move on to the subclasses of Resource.

Joe and Susan discussed the need for those subclasses and created a new package diagram (see Figure 7-7) Using this diagram, Susan modified the CRC cards accordingly and added the invariants to them. A sample of the CRC cards are shown in Figure 7-8. Once Susan

---

Front:

Class Name: Patron	**ID:** 25	**Type:** Concrete, Domain

Description: Describes the common properties of the Faculty/Staff, Student, and Guest subclasses	**Associated Use Cases:** 1

Responsibilities	**Collaborators**
Checkout	
CheckUnpaidFees	
CheckOverdueResources	
GetPatron	

Back:

Attributes:
Name (1..1) (String)
IDnumber (1..1) (String)
Address (1..1) (Address)
CheckOutTransaction (0..*) (CheckOutTransaction)

Relationships:
Generalization (a-kind-of):

(a)

FIGURE 7-8   Sample CRC cards

Front:

Class Name: Resource	**ID:** 26	**Type:** Abstract, Domain
Description: Describes the common properties of the Physical and Downloadable classes		**Associated Use Cases:** 1,2

Responsibilities	**Collaborators**
Checkout	
GetResource	

Back:

Attributes:

Title

IDnumber

Publisher

TransactionLineItem (0..1) (TransactionLineItem)

Location (1..1) (Location)

Relationships:
Generalization (a-kind-of):

(b)

FIGURE 7-8 *Continued*

had the CRC cards updated, she ran them over to Joe to validate them again. When comparing the Patron and Resource CRC cards back to the original cards (see Figure 4-6) you will notice many changes. First, the attributes have all added invariant constraints to their definitions. Second, the association and aggregation relationships have been converted to attributes. Third, the Patron and Resource classes are no longer directly related to each other. Instead, since the Iterator pattern was added, they are now indirectly related to each other via the Iterator-based classes.

Front:

Class Name: TransactionLineItem	ID: 29	Type: Concrete, Domain
Description: Describes a line item with a resource checkout transaction		**Associated Use Cases:** 1,2

Responsibilities	Collaborators
create	

Back:

Attributes:

resource (1..1) (Resource)

Relationships:
Generalization (a-kind-of):

(c)

FIGURE 7-8 *Continued*

Campus Housing Service "Your Turn" Exercise In the previous installation of the Campus Housing Service (CHS) "Your Turn" exercise, you created a package diagram. In this installment of the CHS exercise, you should choose one of the classes and create a set of invariants for attributes and relationships and add them to the CRC card for the class.

CONSTRAINTS AND CONTRACTS

Contracts document the message passing that takes place between objects. Consequently, from a constraint perspective, they are used to document the pre- and post- conditions of a method. Technically speaking, a contract should be created for each message sent and received by each object, one for each interaction. However, there would be quite a bit of duplication if this were done. In practice, a contract is created for each method that can receive messages from other objects (i.e., one for each visible method).

A contract should contain the information necessary for a programmer to understand what a method is to do (i.e., they are declarative in nature). This information includes the method name, class name, ID number, client objects, associated use cases, description, arguments received, type of data returned, and the pre- and post-conditions.[10] Contracts do not have a detailed algorithmic description of how the method is to work. Detailed algorithmic descriptions typically are documented in a method specification (as described later in this chapter). In other words, a contract is composed of the information required for the developer of a client object to know what messages can be sent to the server objects and what the client can expect in return. Figure 7-9 shows a sample format for a contract.

Because each contract is associated with a specific method and a specific class, the contract must document them. The ID number of the contract is used to provide a unique identifier for every contract. The Clients (Consumers) element of a contract is a list of classes and methods that send a message to this specific method. This list is determined by reviewing the sequence diagrams associated with the server class.[11] The Associated Use Cases element is a list of use cases in which this method is used to realize the implementation of the use case. The use cases listed here can be found by reviewing the server class's CRC card and the associated sequence diagrams. Also, as described in Chapter 4, by associating the use cases with the individual classes allows the analyst to be able to track back to determine who the primary actor and stakeholders are. This provides the information required to limit the access to the instances of the class to the individuals who play the roles identified by the primary actors and stakeholders. Between the Clients (Consumers) and the Associated Use Cases list, the information to support role-based access control to address the security nonfunctional requirements can be identified. We cover security issues in more detail in Chapters 8, 9, and 10.

The Description of Responsibilities provides an informal description of what the method is to perform, not how it is to do it. The arguments received are the data types of the parameters passed to the method, and the value returned is the data type of the value that the method returns to its clients. Together with the method name, they form the signature of the method.

The pre-condition and post-condition elements are where the pre- and post-conditions for the method are recorded. Recall that pre- and post-conditions can be written in a natural language, a semiformal language, or a formal language. As with invariants, we recommend that you use UML's Object Constraint Language.[12]

Example

In this example, we return to the order example shown in Figures 7-4, 7-5, and 7-6. In this case, we limit the discussion to the design of the MakeAppointment method of the Patient class. The first decision we must make is how to specify the design of the relationship from Patient to Appointment. By reviewing Figures 7-4 and 7-5, we see that the relationship has a multiplicity of 0..* which means that an instance of Patient may exist without having any appointment or an instance of Patient could have many appointments. As shown in Figure 7-4a, the relationship has been converted to an attribute that can contain many instances of the Appointment class.

However, an important question that would not typically come up during analysis is whether the Appointment objects should be kept in sorted order or not. Another question that is necessary to have answered for design purposes is how many appointments could be expected

---

[10] Currently, there is no standard format for a contract. The contract in Figure 7-9 is based on material contained in Ian Graham, *Migrating to Object Technology* (Reading, MA: Addison-Wesley, 1995); Craig Larman, *Applying UML and Patterns: An Introduction to Object-Oriented Analysis and Design* (Englewood Cliffs, NJ: Prentice Hall, 1998); Meyer, *Object-Oriented Software Construction*; R. Wirfs-Brock, B. Wilkerson, and L. Wiener, *Designing Object-Oriented Software* (Englewood Cliffs, NJ: Prentice Hall, 1990).

[11] The Clients (Consumers) list can also be derived from the more detailed form of the CRUDE matrix (Class/Actor: Operation-by-Class/Actor: Operation). Furthermore, this more detailed matrix is useful to begin identifying role-based access control issues related to the security nonfunctional requirements discussed later in the book.

[12] See Warmer and Kleppe, *The Object Constraint Language: Precise Modeling with UML.*

Method Name:	Class Name:		ID:
Clients (Consumers):			
Associated Use Cases:			
Description of Responsibilities:			
Arguments Received:			
Type of Value Returned:			
Pre-Conditions:			
Post-Conditions:			

FIGURE 7-9
Sample Contract
Form

by a patient. The answers to these two questions will determine how we should organize the appointments from the patient object's perspective. If the number of appointments is going to be relatively small and the appointments don't have to be kept in sorted order, then using a built-in programming language construct such as a vector is sufficient. However, if the number of orders is going to be large or the orders must be kept in sorted order, then some form of a sorted data structure, such as a linked list, is necessary. For example, we assume that the number of appointments for a specific patient will be relatively small. We also assume that it would be better if the appointments should be kept in sorted order. Therefore, we will retrieve the appointments in sorted order from the database (see Chapter 8) and store them in a vector.[13]

Using Figure 7-9, a contract for the Make Appointment method of the Patient class is specified (see Figure 7-10a). We see that only instances of the Appointment class use the method (see Clients section), that the method implements part of the logic that supports the Manage Appointments use case (see Associated Use-Cases section), and that the contract includes a short description of the methods responsibilities. We also see that the method receives a single argument of type Appointment and that it does returns a Boolean value. Finally, we see that both a precondition and a postcondition were specified. The precondition simply states that the new Appointment object cannot be in the vector of appts; that is, the appointment cannot have previously been associated with this patient. The postcondition, on the other hand, specifies that the new value of appts must be equal to the old value (@pre) plus the new appointment object (including). In Figure 7-10b, we see the contract for the Create method of the Appointment class. In this case, the Create method is not used by any object. Instead, it is called by a Receptionist actor (see Figure 5-1). Like the MakeAppointment contract, the Create method is associated with the Manage Appointments use case. In this case, the Create method creates a new instance of the Appointment class. To create an appointment, the arguments passed (time, date, reason, PatientID) must have values in them (see the Pre-Conditions section).

---

[13] Notice, this is a very detailed design and implementation concern. This is an example of where detailed programming knowledge is required by the development team.

Method Name: MakeAppointment	**Class Name:**	Patient	**ID:**	16

Clients (consumers): Appointment

Associated Use Cases: Manage Appointments

Description of Responsibilities: To associate a new appointment with a Patient object

Arguments Received: anAppointment:Appointment

Type of Value Returned: Boolean

Pre-Conditions: not appt.includes(anAppointment)

Post-Conditions: appt = appt@pre.including(anAppointment)

(a)

Method Name: Create	**Class Name:**	Appointment	**ID:**	18

Clients (consumers):

Associated Use Cases: Manage Appointments

Description of Responsibilities: Create a new instance of the Appointment class

Arguments Received: time:Time, date:Date, reason:String, PatientID:String

Type of Value Returned: anAppointment:Appointment

Pre-Conditions: not time = null not date = null nor reason = null not PatientID = null

Post-Conditions: None

FIGURE 7-10
Sample Contracts for the Make Appointment method of the Patient Class and the Create method of the Appointment Class

(b)

This is a good example of moving from the problem domain to the solution domain. While we were focusing on the problem domain during analysis, the actual implementation of patients and their appointments was never considered. However, because we now are designing the implementation of the relationship between the Patient objects and the Appointment objects, we have had to move away from the language of the end user and toward the language of the programmer. During design, the focus moves toward optimizing the code to run faster on the computer and not worrying about the end user's ability to understand the inner workings of the system; from an end user's perspective, the system should become more of a black box with which they interact. As we move farther into the detailed design of the implementation of the problem-domain classes, some solution domain classes, such as the approach to implement relationships, will creep into the specification of the problem-domain layer.

APPLYING THE CHAPTER CONCEPTS

Library Management System (LMS) Example Upon completing the validation of the invariants recorded on the CRC cards, Susan had her team develop a set of contracts that documented the pre- and post-conditions for every method contained in the system. A sample of the contracts developed are shown in Figure 7-11. Even though the contracts are mostly for the programmers, Susan decided to take them over to Joe and work through them to make sure that all invariants were documented correctly. The pre-conditions and the post-conditions of the contracts took a little explaining (see Figure 7-11). For example, the pre- and post-conditions in Figure 11c essentially ensures that the resource has not been previously checked out and that once the checkout method finishes, the resource is checked out. Once Joe understood the reason (not necessarily the OCL) for the pre- and

Method Name: Checkout Resource	**Class Name:** Patron	**ID:** 15
Clients (consumers):		
Associated Use Cases: 1		
Description of Responsibilities: To start the process of checking out a resource, e.g, a book		
Arguments Received: resourceList:List		
Type of Value Returned: Boolean		
Pre-Conditions: not resourceList = null		
Post-Conditions: none		

(a)

FIGURE 7-11 Sample Contracts for the Library Management System

Method Name:	create	**Class Name:**	CheckoutTransaction	**ID:**	16

Clients (consumers):   Resource

Associated Use Cases:
1

Description of Responsibilities:

To create a CheckoutTransaction object that contains a Patron object

Arguments Received:
patron:Patron

Type of Value Returned: Boolean

Pre-Conditions:
not patron = null

Post-Conditions:
none

(b)

Method Name:	Add	**Class Name:**	CheckoutTransaction	**ID:**	17

Clients (consumers):   Resource

Associated Use Cases:
1

Description of Responsibilities:

Insert a TransactionLineItem object into a CheckoutTransaction object

Arguments Received:
aTransactionLineItem: TransactionLineItem

Type of Value Returned: Boolean

Pre-Conditions:
not aTransactionLineItem = Null
not transactionsLineItems.includes(aTransactionLineItem
.includes(getResource))

Post-Conditions:
transactionsLineItems = transactionsLineItems@pre.including
(aTransactionLineItem.includes(getResource))

(c)

FIGURE 7-11   *Continued*

post-conditions, with a little help from Susan, Joe was able to validate the remaining contracts. Once this was done, Susan had the team iterate back and modify the earlier documentation including the activity diagrams and sequence diagrams.

Campus Housing Service "Your Turn" Exercise In the previous installation of the Campus Housing Service (CHS) "Your Turn" exercise, you chose one of the classes and created a set of invariants for attributes and relationships and added them to the CRC card for the class. In this installation, you should choose one of the methods in the class that you chose and create a contract for it. Use OCL to specify any pre- or postcondition.

METHOD SPECIFICATION

Once the analyst has communicated the big picture of how the system needs to be put together, he or she needs to describe the individual classes and methods in enough detail so that programmers can take over and begin writing code. Methods on the CRC cards, class diagram, and contracts are described using *method specifications*. Method specifications are written documents that include explicit instructions on how to write the code to implement the method. Typically, project team members write a specification for each method and then pass them all along to programmers who write the code during implementation of the project. However, with agile development approaches, the creation of method specifications is never done. Instead, given that the developers are programmers, the developers simply write the code and skip the specifications. Specifications need to be very clear and easy to understand, or programmers will be slowed down trying to decipher vague or incomplete instructions.

There is no formal syntax for a method specification, so every organization uses its own format, often using a form like the one in Figure 7-12. Typical method specification forms contain four components that convey the information that programmers will need for writing the appropriate code: general information, events, message passing, and algorithm specification.

General Information

The top of the form in Figure 7-12 contains general information, such as the name of the method, name of the class in which this implementation of the method will reside, ID number, Contract ID (which identifies the contract associated with this method implementation), programmer assigned, the date due, and the target programming language. This information is used to help manage the programming effort.

Events

The second section of the form is used to list the events that trigger the method. An *event* is a thing that happens or takes place. Clicking the mouse generates a mouse event, pressing a key generates a keystroke event—in fact, almost everything the user does generates an event.

In the past, programmers used procedural programming languages that contained instructions that were implemented in a predefined order, as determined by the computer system, and users were not allowed to deviate from the order. Many programs today are *event driven* (e.g., programs written in languages such as Visual Basic, Objective C, C++, C#, Python, or Java), and event-driven programs include methods that are executed in response to an event initiated by the user, system, or another method. After initialization, the system waits for an event to occur. When it does, a method is fired that carries out the appropriate task, and then the system waits once again.

We have found that many programmers still use method specifications when programming in event-driven languages, and they include the event section on the form to capture when the method will be invoked. Other programmers have switched to other design tools that capture event-driven programming instructions, such as the behavioral state machine described in Chapter 5.

Method Name:	Class Name:	ID:
Contract ID:	Programmer:	Date Due:

Programming Language:

    ❑ Visual Basic   ❑ Python   ❑ C++   ❑ Java

Triggers/Events:

Arguments Received: Data Type:	Notes:

Messages Sent & Arguments Passed: ClassName.MethodName:	Argument Data Type:	Notes:

Arguments Returned: Data Type:	Notes:

Algorithm Specification:

Misc. Notes:

FIGURE 7-12
Method
Specification Form

Message Passing

The next section of the method specification describes the message passing to and from the method, which are identified on the sequence diagrams. Programmers need to understand what arguments are being passed into, passed from, and returned by the method because the arguments ultimately translate into attributes and data structures within the actual method.

Algorithm Specifications

Algorithm specifications can be written in Structured English or some type of formal language.[14] Structured English is simply a formal way of writing instructions that describe the steps of a process. Because it is the first step toward the implementation of the method, it looks much like a simple programming language. Structured English uses short sentences that clearly describe exactly what work is performed on what data. There are many versions of Structured English because there are no formal standards; each organization has its own type of Structured English. Figure 7-13 shows some examples of commonly used Structured English statements.[15]

Action statements are simple statements that perform some action. An If statement controls actions that are performed under different conditions, and a For statement (or a While statement) performs some actions until some condition is reached, i.e., these support the iteration or looping constructs of programming languages. A Case statement is an advanced form of an If statement that has several mutually exclusive branches.

If the algorithm of a method is complex, a tool that can be useful for algorithm specification is UML's *activity diagram* (Chapters 3 and 4). Recall that activity diagrams can be used to specify any type of process. Obviously, an algorithm specification represents a process. However, owing to the nature of object orientation, processes tend to be highly distributed over many little methods over many objects. Needing to use an activity diagram to specify the algorithm of a method can, in fact, hint at a problem in the design. For example, the method should be further decomposed or there could be missing classes.

The last section of the method specification provides space for other information that needs to be communicated to the programmer, such as calculations, special business rules,

Common Statements	Example
Action Statement	Profits = Revenues − Expenses Generate Inventory-Report
If Statement	IF Customer Not in the Customer Object Store THEN Add Customer record to Customer Object Store ELSE Add Current-Sale to Customer's Total-Sales Update Customer record in Customer Object Store

For Statement	FOR all Customers in Customer Object Store DO
	
	    Generate a new line in the Customer-Report
	
	    Add Customer's Total-Sales to Report-Total

Case Statement	CASE
	
	    IF Income < 10,000: Marginal-tax-rate = 10 percent
	
	    IF Income < 20,000: Marginal-tax-rate = 20 percent
	
	    IF Income < 30,000: Marginal-tax-rate = 31 percent
	
	    IF Income < 40,000: Marginal-tax-rate = 35 percent
	
	    ELSE Marginal-tax-rate = 38 percent
	
	ENDCASE

FIGURE 7-13
Structured
English

---

[14] For our purposes, Structured English will suffice. However, there has been some work with the Catalysis, Fusion, and Syntropy methodologies to include formal languages, such as VDM and Z, into specifying object-oriented systems.

[15] The Structured English statements are associated with the programming constructs described in the appendix to Chapter 1.

calls to subroutines or libraries, and other relevant issues. This also can point out changes or improvements that will be made to any of the other design documentation based on problems that the analyst detected during the specification process.[16]

Example

This example continues the addition of an appointment for a patient described in the previous section (see Figure 7-14). The general information section of the specification documents the method's name (Create), its class (Appointment), its unique ID number (18), the

Method Name: Create	Class Name: Appointment	ID: 18
Contract ID: 18	**Programmer:** J. Doe	**Date Due:** Aug. 3

Programming Language:

❑ **Visual Basic** ❑ **Python** ❑ **C++** ❑ **Java**

Triggers/Events:

The Receptionist attempts to create an appointment for a patient

Arguments Received: Data Type:	Notes:
time:Time	
date:Date	
reason:String	
PatientID:String	

Messages Sent & Arguments Passed: ClassName.MethodName:	Argument Data Type:	Notes:
Patient.MakeAppointment()	Appointment	

Arguments Returned: Data Type:	Notes:
anAppointment:Appointment	

Algorithm Specification:

```
IF type(time) == Time AND time Not Equal to Null
        AND IF type(date) == Date AND date Not Equal to Null
        AND IF type(reason) == String AND Not Equal to Null
        AND IF type(PatientID) == String) AND IF PatientID Not Equal to Null
            Create new Appointment object
            Send MakeAppointment() message to Patient object
            Return an Appointment object

ELSE
        Return an error
```

Misc. Notes:

FIGURE 7-14 Method Specification for the Create method of the Appointment class

[16] Remember that the development process is very incremental and iterative. Therefore, changes could be cascaded back to any point in the development process (e.g., to use-case descriptions, use-case diagrams, CRC cards, class diagrams, object diagrams, sequence diagrams, behavioral state machines, and package diagrams).

ID number of its associated contract (18), the programmer assigned (J. Doe), the date that its implementation is due (Aug. 3), and the programming language to be used (Python). Second, the trigger/event that caused this method to be executed is identified (The Receptionist attempts to create an appointment for a patient.). Third, the data type of the arguments passed to this method is documented (Time, Date, String, and String). Fourth, the method sends a message to another object. In this case, it sends a MakeAppointment() message to an instance of the Patient class. Fifth, we specify the type of return value that the method produces (Appointment). Finally, we specify the actual algorithm. In this example, we provide a Structured English-based specification). If the algorithm is complex, you can use an activity diagram to specify it.

APPLYING THE CHAPTER CONCEPTS

Library Management System (LMS) Example Once the team had iterated back and "fixed" the earlier documentation (use-case diagram, use-case descriptions, activity diagrams, CRC cards, class diagram, sequence diagrams, CRUDE matrix, and behavioral state machines), the team tackled the method specifications using the contracts, the activity diagrams, and sequence diagrams. In most cases, the algorithms were simple enough that they were specified using Structured English. Figure 7-15 shows the method specification for the Checkout method of the Patron class.

Based on the details contained in the method specifications, Susan and the team iterated back over the earlier representations. For example, using the method specification for the Checkout Resource method of the Patron class, Susan created Figure 7-16a that portrays the updated version of the CRC card for the Patron class and the updated sequence diagram that showed the logic of the scenario the Borrow Resource use case is shown in Figure 7-16b. You should compare the previous versions of the CRC card (see Figure 7-8a) and the sequence diagram (see Figure 5-11) with the updated versions. Even this late in the process, Susan and her team had to add quite a bit of detail.

Campus Housing Service "Your Turn" Exercise In the previous installation of the Campus Housing Service (CHS) "Your Turn" exercise, you created a contract using OCL for one of the methods in the class that you chose. In this installation, you should create a method specification for the same method. You should use both Structured English and an activity diagram to specify the algorithm.

Method Name:	Checkout Resource	Class Name:	Patron	ID:	15

Contract ID:	15	Programmer:	J. Doe	Date Due:	Aug. 10

Programming Language:

❏ **Visual Basic**   ❏ **Python**   ❏ **C++**   ❏ **Java**

Triggers/Events:

The Patron requests to checkout a resource such as a book

Arguments Received:
Data Type: **Notes:**

resourceList:List

Messages Sent & Arguments Passed: ClassName.MethodName:	Argument Data Type:	Notes:
CheckoutTransaction.create	Patron	
Resource.GetResource	String	
TransactionLineItem.create	Resource	
CheckoutTransaction.Add	TransactionLineItem	

Arguments Returned:
Data Type: **Notes:**

Boolean

Algorithm Specification:

```
IF resourceList not == null
    Create new CheckoutTransaction object passing the Patron object
    FOR each item in resourceList
        Get the associated Resource object
        Create a new TransactionLineItem object passing the Resource object
        Add the TransactionLineItem object to the CheckoutTransaction object
    Close out transaction
```

Misc. Notes:

FIGURE 7-15   Method Specification for the Checkout Method of the Patron Class

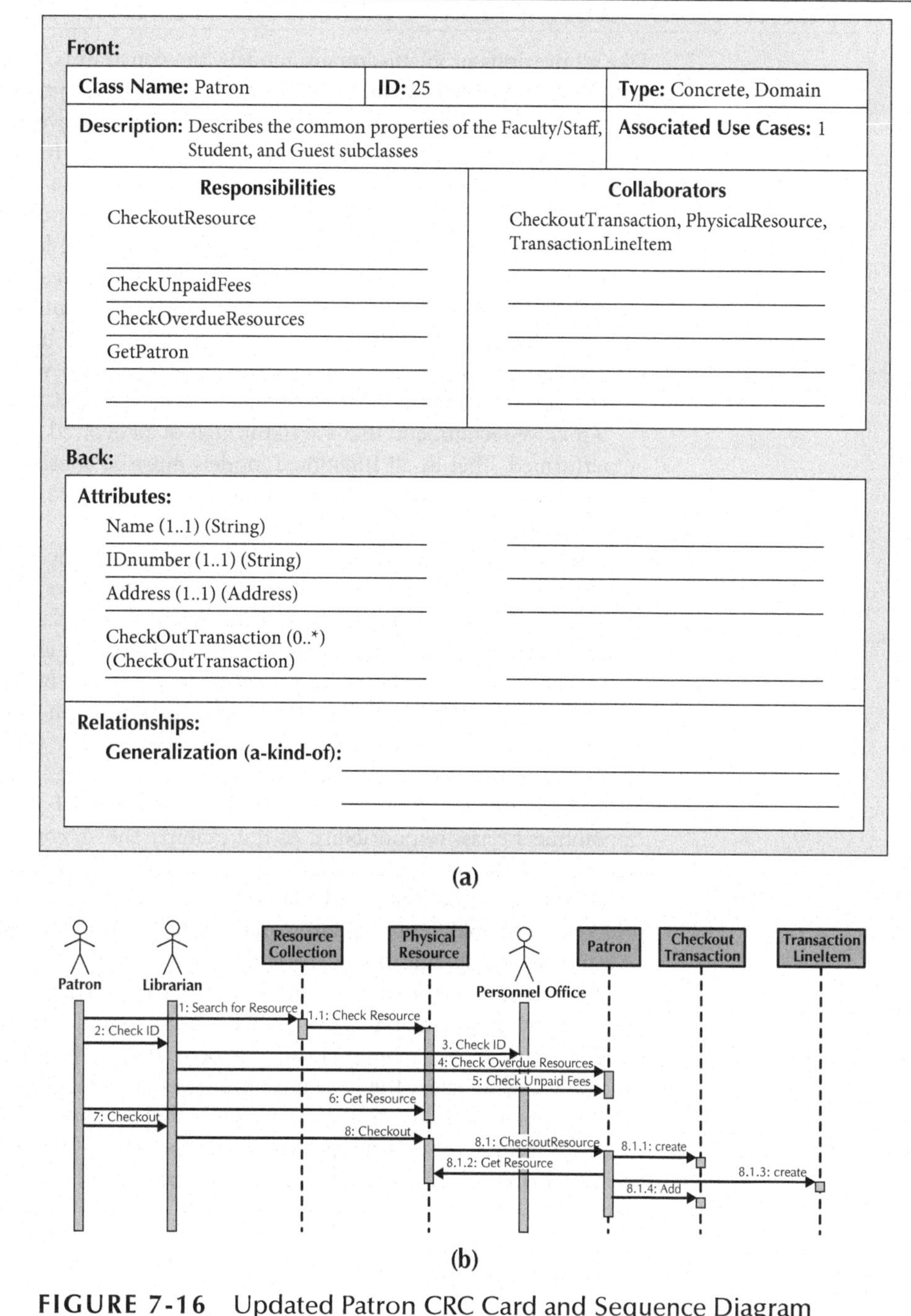

FIGURE 7-16 Updated Patron CRC Card and Sequence Diagram

VERIFYING AND VALIDATING CLASS AND METHOD DESIGN

Like all previous problem-domain models, the constraints, contracts, and method specifications need to be verified and validated. Given that we are primarily dealing with the problem domain in this chapter, the constraints and contracts were derived from the functional requirements and the problem-domain representations. However, they are applicable to the other layers. In that case, they would be derived from the solution domain representations associated with the data management (see Chapter 8), human–computer interaction (see Chapter 9), and application architecture (see Chapter 10) layers. Given the issues described earlier with the design criteria, additional specifications, reuse opportunities, design restructuring, design optimization, and mapping to implementation languages (see Chapter 6 and this chapter), it is likely that many modifications have taken place to the analysis representations of the problem domain. Consequently, virtually everything must be re-verified and re-validated.

First, we recommend that a walkthrough of all evolved problem-domain representations be performed. That is, all functional models must be consistent; all structural models must be consistent; all behavioral models must be consistent; and the functional, structural, and behavioral models must be balanced.

Second, all constraints, contracts, and method specifications must be tested. For example, the CRC cards for the Patient and Appointment classes (see Figure 7-4) and the method specification for the Create method of the Appointment class (see Figure 7-11) have a small disagreement. The CRC cards assert that the Appointment class is a Collaborator of the Make appointment responsibility of the Patient class. However, the method specification states just the opposite, i.e., the client of the MakeAppointment method is an Appointment object, i.e., an Appointment object sends a MakeAppointment message to an instance of the Patient class. Therefore, we need to go back and remove the Appointment collaborator from the Patient class's Make appointment responsibility and to add a Patient collaborator to the Create method of the Appointment class's responsibility. As this example shows, continuous testing is invaluable. The best way to do this is to role-play the system using the different scenarios of the use cases. In this case, we must enforce the invariants on the evolved CRC cards (see Figure 7-4), the pre- and postconditions on the contract forms (see Figure 7-10), and the design of each method specified with the method specification forms (see Figure 7-14).

Given the amount of verifying and validating of the models that we have performed on the evolving system, it might seem like overkill to perform the above again. However, given the pure volume of changes that can take place during design, it is crucial to thoroughly test the models again before the system is implemented. In fact, testing is so important to the agile development approaches, testing forms the virtual backbone of those methodologies. Without thorough testing, there is no guarantee that the system being implemented will address the problem being solved. Given that testing is applicable to the development of all layers (see Figure 6-4), we overview software testing next.

Software Testing

In object-oriented systems, the temptation is to minimize testing. After all, using patterns, frameworks, class libraries, and components, much of the system has been tested previously. Therefore, we should not have to test as much. Right? Wrong! Testing is more critical to object-oriented systems than to systems developed in the past. Based on encapsulation (and information hiding), polymorphism (and dynamic binding), inheritance, reuse, and the actual object-oriented products, thorough testing is much more difficult and critical. Given the complexity of the development processes used and the global nature of information systems development, testing becomes even more crucial. Thus, object-oriented testing must be done systematically, and the results must be documented so that the project team knows what has and has not been tested. Testing object-oriented systems is therefore very complex. Consequently, a complete coverage of the topic is beyond the scope of this book.[17]

The purpose of testing is not to demonstrate that the system is free of errors. It is not possible to prove that a system is error free. The purpose of testing is to uncover differences between what the system is doing and what the system should do. In other words, the purpose of testing is to try and break the system. This is like theory testing. You cannot prove a theory. If a test fails to find problems with a theory, your confidence in the theory is increased. However, if a test succeeds in finding a problem, then the theory has been falsified. Software testing is similar in that it can only show the existence of errors. So, the point of testing is to uncover as many errors as feasible. It is simply not cost-effective to try to get every error out of the software. Except in simple examples, it is, in fact, impossible. There are simply too many combinations to check.

With our functional requirements, we focused our testing approach to ensure the fidelity of our problem-domain representations using role-playing and walkthroughs (see Chapters 3, 4, 5, 6, and this chapter). These included the balancing of the analysis models and ensuring that all constraints (invariant, pre-conditions, and post-conditions) and method specifications were completed in such a way that they removed any ambiguity from the developer's intention of the detailed design of the classes that addressed the functional requirements.

With the design of the data management layer (Chapter 8), the focus of the verification and validation activities deal with confirming that the problem-domain classes are mapped properly to the type of object persistence chosen and that a set of data access and manipulation classes were designed. Testing the design of the human–computer interaction layer (Chapter 9) includes the validation of all data input by using the constraints to guarantee that only valid data is allowed to enter the system. When considering testing the application architecture layer (Chapter 10), the fidelity of the design of the network, hardware, and the deployment of the software must be guaranteed. As with the other layers, performing walkthroughs to balance the high-level and low-level designs of the network and to confirm that the hardware specifications and the specifications of the software over the network and workstations were consistent is necessary.

In addition to testing the functional requirements across all layers, testing must also address all nonfunctional requirements: operational, performance, security, and ethical, legal, cultural and political requirements (see Chapter 2). For example, performance testing of all interactions with the implementation of the system becomes important. For example, if queries run too slow, the optimization approaches described in this chapter may be required on the problem domain, data management, human-computer interaction, and application architecture layers. And, of course, once these optimizations have been designed and implemented, the optimizations will need to be further tested. As you can see, regardless of the system development methodology used, testing is paramount to delivering successful information systems.

In general, there are four general types or levels of tests: unit tests, integration tests, system tests, and acceptance tests (see Figure 7-17). Although each application system is different, most errors are found during integration and system testing. Before describing the specific types of tests, we describe the effect that the object-oriented characteristics have on testing and the necessary planning and management activities that must take place to have a successful testing program. Next, we describe the four general types of tests. Finally, given the importance of the security nonfunctional requirements, we describe how security requirements affect testing.

Testing and Object Orientation

Most testing techniques have been developed to support non–object-oriented development. Therefore, most of the testing approaches have had to be adapted to object-oriented systems.

---

[17] For a good introduction to testing object-oriented software, see John D. McGregor and David A. Sykes, *A Practical Guide to Testing Object-Oriented Software* (Boston: Addison-Wesley, 2001). For a thorough coverage of testing object-oriented software, see Robert V. Binder, *Testing Object-Oriented Systems: Models, Patterns, and Tools* (Reading, MA: Addison-Wesley, 1999), this book provides more than 1,000 pages of information with regard to how to test the different artifacts and processes included in object-oriented systems development.

Stage	Type of Tests	Test Plan Source	When to Use	Notes
Unit Testing	**Black-Box Testing** Treats class as "black-box"	CRC Cards Class Diagram Contracts	For normal unit testing	• Tester focuses on whether the class meets the requirements stated in the specifications.
	White-Box Testing Looks inside the class to test its major elements.	Method Specifications Behavioral State Machine	When complexity is high	• By looking inside the class to review the code itself the tester may discover additional errors or assumptions.
Integration Testing	**User Interface Testing** The tester tests each interface function.	HCI Design	For normal integration testing	• Testing is done by moving through each and every menu item in the interface either in a top-down or bottom-up manner.
	Use-Case Testing The tester tests each use case.	Use-Case Diagram Activity Diagrams Sequence Diagrams	When the user interface is important	• Testing is done by moving through each use case to ensure they work correctly. This is usually combined with user interface testing because it does not test all interfaces.
	Interaction Testing Tests each process in a step-by-step fashion.	Use-Case Diagram Activity Diagrams Sequence Diagrams CRC Cards Class Diagrams Contracts	When the system performs data processing	• The entire system begins as a set of stubs. Each class is added in turn and the results of the class compared to the correct result from the test data; when a class passes, the next class is added and the test re-run. This is done for each package. Once each package has passed all tests, then the process repeats integrating the packages.
	System Interface Testing Tests the exchange of with other systems	Use-Case Diagram Activity Diagrams Sequence Diagrams	When the system exchanges data	• Because data transfers between systems are often automated and not monitored directly by the users it is critical to design tests to ensure they are being done correctly.
System Testing	**Requirements Testing** Tests to whether original business requirements are met.	Use-Case Diagram Activity Diagrams Sequence Diagrams	For normal system testing	• Ensures that changes made as a result of integration testing did not create new errors.
	Usability Testing Tests how convenient the system is to use	HCI Design Use-Case Diagram Activity Diagrams Sequence Diagrams	When user interface is important	• Often done by analyst with experience in how users think and in good interface design. Can use formal usability testing procedures discussed in Chapter 9.
	Security Testing Tests disaster recovery & unauthorized access	Data Management Design HCI Design Physical Architecture Design	When the system is important	• Security testing is a complex task, usually done by an infrastructure analyst assigned to the project. In extreme cases, a professional firm may be hired.
	Performance Testing Examines the ability to perform under high loads	Data Management Design HCI Design Physical Architecture Design	When the system is important	• High volumes of transactions are generated and given to the system. This is often done by using special purpose testing software.
	Documentation Testing Tests the accuracy of the documentation	Help System Procedures Tutorials	For normal system testing	• Analysts spot check or check every item on every page to ensure that the documentation items and examples work properly.

FIGURE 7-17 Types of Tests

Stage	Type of Tests	Test Plan Source	When to Use	Notes
Acceptance Testing	**Alpha Testing** Conducted by users to ensure they accept the system.	System Tests	For normal accept-ance testing	• Often repeats previous tests but are conducted by users themselves to ensure they accept the system.
	Beta Testing Uses real data, not test data	No plan	When the system is important	• Users closely monitor system for errors or useful improvements.

FIGURE 7-17   *Continued*

The characteristics of object-oriented systems that affect testing the most are encapsulation (and information hiding); polymorphism (and dynamic binding); inheritance; and the use of patterns, class libraries, frameworks, and components. Also, the sheer volume of products that come out of a typical object-oriented development process has increased the importance of testing in object-oriented systems development.

Encapsulation and Information Hiding Encapsulation and information hiding allow processes and data to be combined to create holistic entities (i.e., objects). They support hiding everything behind a visible interface. Although this allows the system to be modified and maintained in an effective and efficient manner, it makes testing the system problematic. What do you need to test to build confidence in the system's ability to meet the user's need? You need to test the business process that is represented in the use cases. However, the business process is distributed over a set of collaborating classes and contained in the methods of those classes. The only way to know the effect that a business process has on a system is to look at the state changes that take place in the system. But in object-oriented systems, the instances of the classes hide the data behind a class boundary. How is it possible then to see the impact of a business process?

A second issue raised by encapsulation and information hiding is the definition of a "unit" for unit testing. What is the unit to be tested? Is it the package, class, or method? In traditional approaches, the answer would be the process that is contained in a function. However, the process in object-oriented systems is distributed over a set of classes. Therefore, testing individual methods makes no sense. The answer is the class. This dramatically changes the way unit testing is done.

A third issue raised is the impact on integration testing. In this case, objects can be aggregated to form aggregate objects; for instance, a car has many parts, or they can be grouped together to form collaborations. Furthermore, they can be used in class libraries, frameworks, and components. Based on all of these different ways classes can be grouped together, how does one effectively do integration testing?

Polymorphism and Dynamic Binding Polymorphism and dynamic binding dramatically affect both unit and integration testing. Because an individual business process is implemented through a set of methods distributed over a set of objects, as shown before, the unit test makes no sense at the method level. However, with polymorphism and dynamic binding, the same method (a small part of the overall business process) can be implemented in many different objects. Therefore, testing individual implementations of methods makes no sense. Again, the unit that makes sense to test is the class. Except for trivial cases, dynamic binding makes it impossible to know which implementation is going to be executed until the system does it. Therefore, integration testing becomes very challenging.

Inheritance When taking into consideration the issues raised about inheritance, it should not be a surprise that inheritance affects the testing of object-oriented systems. Through the use of inheritance, bugs can be propagated instantaneously from a superclass to all its direct and indirect subclasses. However, the tests that are applicable to a superclass are also applicable to all its subclasses. As usual, inheritance is a double-edged sword. Finally, even though we have stated this many times before, inheritance should support only a generalization and specialization type of semantics. Remember, when using inheritance, the principle of substitutability is critical (see Chapter 4). All these issues affect unit and integration testing.

Reuse On the surface, reuse should decrease the amount of testing required. However, each time a class is used in a different context, the class must be tested again. Therefore, any time a class library, framework, or component is used, unit testing and integration testing are important. In the case of a component, the unit to test is the component itself. Remember that a component has a well-defined API (application program interface) that hides the details of its implementation.

Object-Oriented Development Process and Products In most textbooks, testing is covered near the end of system development. This seems to imply that testing is something that takes place only after the programming has ended. However, every product[18] that comes out of the object-oriented development process must be tested. For example, it is a lot easier to ensure that the requirements are captured and modeled correctly through testing the use cases, and it is a lot cheaper to catch this type of error back in the inception or elaboration phases than it is in construction. Obviously, this is also true for testing collaborations. By the time we have implemented a collaboration as a set of layers and partitions, we could have expended a great deal of time—and time is money—on implementing the wrong thing. So, testing collaborations by role-playing the CRC cards in analysis actually saves the team lots of time and money.

Testing is something that must take place throughout system development, not simply at the end. However, the type of testing that can take place on nonexecutable representations, such as use cases and CRC cards, is different from those on code written in an object-oriented programming language. The primary approach to testing nonexecutable representations is some form of an inspection or walkthrough of the representation.[19] In the earlier chapters, we focused on verifying and validating the different analysis and design representations. We also made sure that the different representations were consistent and balanced. As such, we have dealt with testing the nonexecutable representations throughout the development process.

Test Planning

Testing starts with the development of a *test plan,* which defines a series of tests that will be conducted. One of the concerns that must be addressed through a comprehensive set of tests is to not limit the testing to the so-called *happy path* where testing only focusses on the *normal flow of events* of the use cases. Furthermore, happy path testing is limited to only ensuring that the code works when the tester provides the expected values. Not only should testing include the alternative paths through the use cases, but testing must also include all possible combinations of input data that could be in error. In other words, testing should include the *sad paths* through the use cases also. Because testing takes place throughout the development of an object-oriented system, a test plan should be developed at the very beginning of system development and continuously updated as the system evolves. For example, the representation of a class evolves from a simplistic CRC card to a set of classes that are implemented in a programming language. In Figure 7-4 we see CRC cards for the Patient and Appointment classes that contain invariants. Each of these invariants must be tested

---

[18] For example, activity diagrams, use-case descriptions, use-case diagrams, CRC cards, class diagrams, object diagrams, sequence diagrams, behavioral state machines, package diagrams, contracts, method specifications, use scenarios, window navigation diagrams, storyboards, wireframe diagrams, real use cases, and source code.

[19] See Michael Fagan, "Design and Code Inspections to Reduce Errors in Program Development," *IBM Systems Journal* 15, no. 3 (1976); Daniel P. Freedman and Gerald M. Weinberg, *Handbook of Walkthrough, Inspections, and Technical Reviews: Evaluating Programs, Projects, and Products,* 3rd Ed. (New York: Dorset House Publishing, 1990). Also, Chapters 3, 4, 5, and 6 describe the walkthrough process in detail in relation to the verification and validation of the analysis models.

and enforced for the classes to be considered to be of sufficient quality. One simple invariant test would be to attempt to assign a value to the appointmentNumber that contains a String value. Another invariant test would be to try and assign more than one date to the date attribute of the Appointment class. Finally, a trickier invariant test would be to try to assign an integer value to the totalCost attribute. This one is more difficult because most programming languages allow an integer to be automatically "cast" to a float. If the value contained in the totalCost attribute really is supposed to be a float, then casting the integer value to a float would be an error. These tests could be done using a walkthrough approach when the class is specified, as we did in Chapters 3, 4, 5, and 6. Furthermore, once the class has been fully implemented, a more rigorous approach is necessary. In fact, with agile and DevOps approaches, it is recommended that testing be fully automated.[20]

The test plan should address all products that are created during the development of the system. For example, tests should be created that can be used to test completeness of a CRC card. Each individual test has a specific objective and describes a set of very specific *test cases* to examine. In the case of invariant-based tests, a description of the invariant is given, and the original values of the attribute, the event that will cause the attribute value to change, the actual results observed, the expected results, and whether it passed or failed are shown. *Test specifications* are created for each type of constraint that must be met by the class.

Testing should not be limited to the functional requirements. Instead, testing must also consider all the nonfunctional requirements. In this text, this includes operations testing, performance testing, security testing, and the testing of all cultural and political considerations. Given the incremental and iterative development nature of object-oriented systems development, the nonfunctional requirements should be verified and validated during the design and construction phases of the Unified Process. However, the nonfunctional requirements need to be thoroughly tested once they have been implemented during the construction and transition phases. Consequently, testing should be performed throughout the development process. Obviously, it is a lot easier to design tests when you are creating the different analysis and design representations than to wait and design them during the construction of the system. In fact, many of the agile approaches suggest creating the test either before or concurrently with the identification of the requirements that drive the creation of the system (see Chapter 2).

When testing an object-oriented system, given that the systems are built incrementally, being able to toggle on/off the different features that the system is supporting is useful. In this way, the testing can be somewhat localized and controlled. For example, for testing purposes, only certain user interface features could be toggled on. The other features could be toggled off by "graying" them out. Once the set of features have been tested, they can be toggled off and others toggled on. Obviously, this type of testing is not available until some code has been created. Also, in most cases, all classes that are supporting an application will not likely be finished at the same time. In those cases, depending on the language, toggles could be useful to test the parts of the system that has been implemented. With other languages, the programmer will have to write *stubs* for the unfinished classes to enable the completed classes around them to be tested. A stub is a placeholder for a class that usually displays a simple test message on the screen or returns some *hardcoded* value[21] when it is selected. For example, consider an application system that provides creating, changing, deleting, finding, and printing functions for some object such as patients or appointments. Depending on the final design, these different functions could end up in different objects on different layers. Therefore, to test the functionality associated with the classes on the problem-domain layer, a stub would be written for each of the classes on the other layers that interact with the problem-domain classes. These stubs

---

[20] Gene Kim, Jez Humble, Patrick Debois, John Willis, *The DevOps Handbook: How to Create World-Class Agility, Reliability, & Security in Technology Organizations* (Portland, OR: IT Revolution Press, 2016); Steve Freeman, Nat Pryce, *Growing Object-Oriented Software, Guided By Tests* (Boston, NA: Pearson Education, 2010); Kent Beck, *Test-Driven Development by Example* (Boston, NA: Pearson Education, 2003).

[21] *Hardcoded* means written into the program. For example, suppose you were writing a unit to calculate the net present value of a loan. The stub might be written to always display (or return to the calling module) a value of 100 regardless of the input values.

would be the minimal interface necessary to be able to test the problem-domain classes. For example, they would have methods that could receive the messages being sent by the problem-domain layer objects and methods that could send messages to the problem-domain layer objects. Typically, the methods would display a message on the screen notifying the tester that the method was successfully reached (e.g., Delete item from Database method reached). In this way, the problem-domain classes could pass class testing before the classes on the other layers were completed.

In fact, testing could need to continue even after deployment. For example, Netflix uses a tool that they call *Chaos Monkey* that simulates major failures by constantly and randomly killing servers to ensure that their systems are fully recoverable.[22] Finally, realize that the results from testing could be the uncovering of additional functional and nonfunctional requirements. Again, given the nature of object-oriented systems development, this is somewhat expected.

Unit Tests

Unit tests focus on a single unit—the class. There are two approaches to unit testing: black-box testing and white-box testing (see Figure 7-17). *Black-box testing* is the most used because each class represents an encapsulated object. Black-box testing is driven by the CRC cards, class diagrams, and contracts associated with a class, not by the programmers' interpretation. In this case, the test plan is developed directly from the specification of the class: each item in the specification becomes a test, and several test cases are developed for it. *White-box testing* is based on the method specifications and the behavioral state machine associated with each class. However, white-box testing has had limited impact in object-oriented development. This is due to the rather small size of the individual methods in a class. Most approaches to testing classes use black-box testing to ensure their correctness.

Black-box tests should be based on the invariants on the CRC cards and the pre- and post-conditions captured with the contracts for each method. Assuming all the constraints have been captured on the CRC cards and contracts, individual test cases can be developed easily. Figure 7-18 shows a typical template for a test plan for a class. In this case, a description for the requirements for invariant testing, contract-based testing, and state-based testing is

<table>
<tr><td colspan="3">Class Test Plan</td><td>Page ___ of ___</td></tr>
<tr><td>Class Name: ______________</td><td>Date Designed : _______</td><td colspan="2">Date Conducted : _______</td></tr>
<tr><td colspan="4">Class Objective:

</td></tr>
<tr><td colspan="4">Associated Contract IDs: ___________________________________</td></tr>
<tr><td colspan="4">Associated Use-Case IDs: ___________________________________</td></tr>
<tr><td colspan="4">Associated Superclass(es): ___________________________________</td></tr>
<tr><td colspan="4">Invariant-Based Test Requirements:</td></tr>
<tr><td colspan="4">Contract-Based Test Requirements:</td></tr>
<tr><td colspan="4">State-Based Test Requirements:</td></tr>
</table>

FIGURE 7-18
Sample Class
Test Plan

---

[22] Gene Kim, Jez Humble, Patrick Debois, John Willis, *The DevOps Handbook: How to Create World-Class Agility, Reliability, & Security in Technology Organizations* (Portland, OR: IT Revolution Press, 2016).

included. For example, suppose the CRC card for a patient class gave an invariant that the value of the amount attribute must be between $20 and $200. The tester would develop a series of test cases to ensure that the value is validated before the system accepts it. It is impossible to test every possible combination of input and situation; there are simply too many possible combinations. In this example, the test requires a minimum of three test cases: one with a valid value (e.g., $25), one with a low invalid value (e.g., $7), and one with a high invalid value (e.g., $250). Most tests would also include a test case with a nonnumeric value to ensure the data types were checked (e.g., ABCD). A good test would include a test case with nonsensical but potentially valid data (e.g., $21.4). In most cases, simple class test plan is insufficient to describe all the invariant tests that would need to be included. For example, in addition to creating a set of tests based on a valid range of values, the tester should also test for valid data types and multiplicity. In these cases, testers should also include an invariant test specification for all attributes of a class. Figure 7-19 shows a form that can be used to specify the tests for the invariants describe earlier with the CRC cards.

In the case of a contract, a set of tests for each pre- and post-condition is required. For example, the contract of the Create method of the Appointment class shown in Figure 7-4b has a pre-condition that essentially requires that valid values must be passed to the method

---

Class Invariant Test Specification　　　　　　　　　　　　Page ___ of ___

Class Name: ______________　　**Version Number:** _______　　**CRC Card ID:** _______

Tester: ______________　　**Date Designed:** _______　　**Date Conducted:** _______

Testing Objectives:

Test Cases

Invariant Description	Original Attribute Value	Event	New Attribute Value	Expected Result	Result P/F
Attribute Name:					
1) ___________	___________	___________	___________	___________	____
2) ___________	___________	___________	___________	___________	____
3) ___________	___________	___________	___________	___________	____
Attribute Name:					
1) ___________	___________	___________	___________	___________	____
2) ___________	___________	___________	___________	___________	____
3) ___________	___________	___________	___________	___________	____
Attribute Name:					
1) ___________	___________	___________	___________	___________	____
2) ___________	___________	___________	___________	___________	____
3) ___________	___________	___________	___________	___________	____

FIGURE 7-19　Class Invariant Test Specification

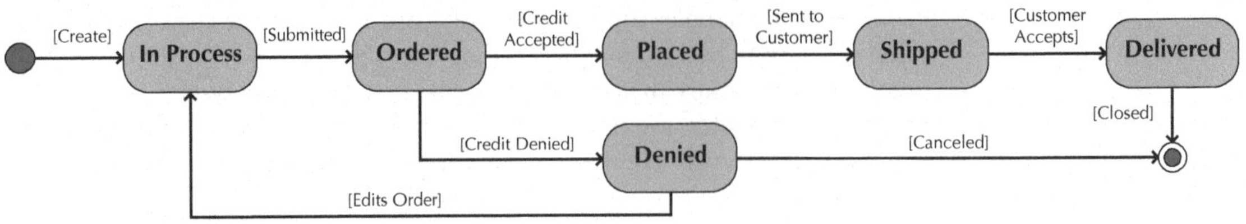

FIGURE 7-20 Order Behavioral State Machine (see Figure 5-16)

for it to successfully create a new Appointment. Also, notice that each argument that is being passed into the method is typed. As you can see in the method specification (see Figure 7-14), we have shown the algorithm that specifies the implementation of both sets of constraints. Tests must be created to enforce these constraints. This would be a form of white-box testing. If the class is a subclass of another class, then all the tests associated with the superclass must be executed again. The interactions among the constraints, invariants, and the pre- and post-conditions in the subclass and the superclass(es) must be addressed also.

Using a behavioral state machine is another useful way to identify white-box tests for a class. Any class that has a behavioral state machine associated with it has a potentially complex life cycle. It is possible to create a series of tests to guarantee that each state can be reached. For example, Figure 7-20 portrays the behavioral state machine for the Order class associated with the order processing example (see Figure 3-8). In this case, there are many transitions between the different states of an instance of the Order class. Tests should be created to guarantee that the only transitions allowed from an instance of the Order class are the ones specifically defined. In this case, it should be impossible for an Order object to go from the In process state to the Shipped state without traversing the Ordered and Placed states. In other words, the Submitted, Credit Accepted, and Sent to Customer guard conditions must have been traversed successfully. This state-based testing can be done throughout the development of the class via walkthroughs and role-playing early in the evolution of the class and more rigorous testing once it has been implemented in a programming language.

Finally, owing to good object-oriented design, to fully test a class, special testing methods might have to be added to the class being tested. For example, how can invariants be tested? The only way to really test them is to have methods that are visible to the outside of the class that can be used to manipulate the values of the class's attributes. However, adding these types of methods to a class does two things. First, they add to the testing requirements because they themselves must be tested. Second, if they are not removed from the deployed version of the system, the system will be less efficient, and the advantage of information hiding effectively is lost. As is readily apparent, testing classes is complex. Therefore, great care must be taken when designing tests for classes.

Integration Tests

Integration tests assess whether a set of classes that must work together do so without error. They ensure that the interfaces and linkages between different parts of the system work properly. At this point, the classes have passed their individual unit tests, so the focus now is on the flow of control among the classes and on the data exchanged among them. Integration testing follows the same general procedures as unit testing: The tester develops a test plan that has a series of tests, which, in turn, have a test. Integration testing is often done by a set of programmers and/or systems analysts.

From an object-oriented systems perspective, integration testing can be difficult. A single class can be in many different aggregations, because of the way objects can be combined to form new objects, class libraries, frameworks, components, and packages. Where is the best

<table>
<tr><td colspan="3">Use-Case Test Plan</td><td>Page ___ of ___</td></tr>
<tr><td>Use-Case Name: _______________</td><td>Version Number _______</td><td colspan="2">Use-Case ID: _______</td></tr>
<tr><td>Tester: _____________</td><td>Date Designed _______</td><td colspan="2">Date Conducted: _______</td></tr>
<tr><td colspan="4">Use-Case Objective:

</td></tr>
<tr><td colspan="4">Associated Class IDs: ______________________________________</td></tr>
<tr><td colspan="4">Associated Use-Case IDs: ______________________________________</td></tr>
<tr><td colspan="4">Testing Objectives:</td></tr>
<tr><td colspan="4">Scenario-Based Test Requirements:</td></tr>
</table>

FIGURE 7-21
Sample Use-Case
Test Plan

place to start the integration? Typically, the answer is to begin with the set of classes, a collaboration, that are used to support the highest-priority use case (see Chapter 3). Also, dynamic binding makes it crucial to design the integration tests carefully to ensure that the combinations of methods are tested.

There are four approaches to integration testing: *user interface testing,*[23] *use-case testing, interaction testing,* and *system interface testing* (see Figure 7-17). Most projects use all four approaches. However, like unit testing, integration testing must be carefully planned. In the case of use-case testing, only the aspects of the class, class invariants, and contract-based constraints related to the specific use case are included in these use-case context-dependent class tests (see Figures 7-18 and 7-19). In fact, typically use-case testing is performed one scenario at a time. Obviously, reviewing the scenario-based sequence diagrams would be helpful here. Figure 7-21 shows a typical form that can be used to plan a use-case test. In many ways, use-case testing can be viewed as a more rigorous role-playing exercise (see Chapter 4).

Like unit testing, integration testing should be performed throughout the evolution of the system. In the early stages of the system's development, you should be working with the CRC cards and role-playing them. Later, you will have the contracts and method specifications completed. Gradually, you will have implemented the problem-domain classes, the user interface classes, and the data management layer classes in a programming language. As in unit testing, each time a new representation (diagram, text, and program) is created, a new integration test needs to be performed. Therefore, as the system evolves to support the use case more completely, we can more rigorously test whether the use case is fully supported or not.

One of the major problems with integration testing and object-oriented systems is the difficulty caused by the interaction of inheritance and dynamic binding. This specific problem has become known as the *yo-yo problem.* The yo-yo problem occurs when the analyst or designer must bounce up and down through the inheritance graph to understand the control flow through the methods being executed. In most cases, this is caused by a rather deep inheritance graph; that is, the subclass has many superclasses above it in the inheritance graph. The yo-yo problem becomes even more of a nightmare in testing object-oriented systems when inheritance conflicts exist and when multiple inheritance is used. About the only realistic approach to testing through the yo-yo problem is through an interactive debugger that is typically part of a systems development environment, such as Eclipse or Visual Studio.

---

[23] We describe some of the different types of user interface testing in Chapter 9.

System Tests

To ensure that all classes work together without error, systems analysts usually conduct the *system tests*. System testing is like integration testing but is much broader in scope. Whereas integration testing focuses on whether the classes work together without error, system tests examine how well the system meets both the functional and nonfunctional requirements, e.g., usability, documentation, performance, and security (see Figure 7-17).

The purpose of functional *requirements testing* is to ensure that the functional requirements uncovered are indeed met. Like integration testing, this is primarily driven by the system's use cases and their scenarios. However, in many cases, integration testing requires modifications to the system. So, the focus of requirements testing is to ensure that the modifications made did not cause new errors.

Usability testing is essentially a combination of the user interface and use-case testing that takes place during integration testing. Where user interface and use-case testing focused on whether the user interface works and whether the use case was supported, respectively, usability testing focuses on how *well* the user interface supports the use cases. That is, how efficient and effective the user interface is. In many cases, this could include formal usability testing (see Chapter 9).

Obviously, in today's networked world, *security testing* is crucial. *Security testing* involves three primary areas: authentication, authorization, and virus control.[24] *Authentication testing* deals with ensuring that the logged in user is who he or she claims to be. Typically, this has been addressed with user IDs and passwords and with encryption techniques. *Authorization testing* deals with ensuring that the logged in user has the authority to use the system(s) being accessed. Authorization has been controlled using roles, access control lists, and capability lists. Security *roles* are the same as actor roles in a use-case model. Depending on the role being played by a user, different capabilities are made available to the user in the form of a *capability list*. Also, an *access control list* can be associated with each use case and with each class. In this case, an access control list specifies which roles have access to the resource (use case or class). Given that many system break-ins are a function of viruses, *virus controls* also need to be enforced. Obviously, security requirements will impact the performance of the system. Therefore, trade-offs between these two sets of requirements may be necessary.

Given that documentation is basically a system, *documentation testing* should involve both unit and integration testing. In this case, the unit is a documentation entry, and the user interface is either the paper or help screen. From an integration testing perspective, the focus is on whether the documentation works or not. And, like system testing of the software, the focus of system testing of the documentation is how well the documentation works. The reason that documentation is not typically tested in parallel with the system, i.e., when the classes, use cases, and user interface are tested, is to minimize the amount of documentation testing required.[25]

Performance testing focuses on trying to break the system with regard to the amount of work the system can handle. These types of tests typically fall into two categories: stress tests and volume tests. The purpose of *stress tests*, also known as *load tests*, is to ensure that the system can handle a certain number of simultaneous requests. For example, if the system is supposed to be able to handle 10,000 simultaneous requests, a stress test would attempt to push the system into handling more than that. If the performance of the test is insufficient, various software and database optimizations can be investigated. In other cases, additional hardware could be required. The purpose of *volume tests* is to push the implementation so that

---

[24] We discuss security issues in more detail in Chapter 10.

[25] We discuss the developing documentation in Chapter 12 with the Infrastructure Management workflow.

it may break when there is a large amount of data required to answer a user request. Again, if it is discovered that the system fails this type of test, then database and software optimizations and additional hardware could be required. You typically do not want the user to make a request for a report and wait "too long" for the report to be processed. In some cases, giving up some functionality to improve performance can be crucial to the success of the system. So, the results of performance testing can make or break a system.

Acceptance Tests

Acceptance testing is done primarily by the users with support from the project team. The goal is to confirm that the system is complete, meets the business needs that prompted the system to be developed, and is acceptable to the users. Acceptance testing is done in two stages: *alpha testing*, in which users test the system using made-up data, and *beta testing*, in which users begin to use the system with real data but are carefully monitored for errors (see Figure 7-17).

APPLYING THE CHAPTER CONCEPTS

Library Management System (LMS) Example Now that Susan and her team had virtually completed the design of the functional or problem domain-based classes, the team had one thing left to do before moving on to design the data management (Chapter 8), human–computer interaction (Chapter 9), and application architecture (Chapter 10) layers; the team needed to develop a set of tests that can be used to verify and validate the problem domain-based software as it was being developed. So, she sat down with Alan (her head of the testing group) and discussed the different types of software test that should be considered (see Figure 7-17). With regard to unit testing, she and Alan decided that they should perform both Black-Box and White-Box testing. To begin with, using Figure 7-18 as a template, they created a Class Test Plan for each class in the problem-domain models. For example, the team carefully reviewed the CRC card, contracts, method specifications, and behavioral state machine for the Patron class. Based on the review, they created the test plan for the Patron class (see Figure 7-22). The test plan included documenting which contracts, use cases, and superclasses that are associated with the class. It also includes a specific invariant test that would guarantee that the value of the IDnumber attribute is unique and a specific contract-based test that would ensure that the values being passed to the CheckoutResource method are valid. Given the simplistic nature of the state changes in which a Patron object goes through during its lifetime, Alan suggested that there was no reason to specify any tests based on the Patron behavioral state machine.

Using the class test plans, CRC cards, contracts, method specifications, and behavioral state machines the team created a set of unit tests for each class. Susan decided that Alan needed to specify the invariant tests in more detail than was included with the class test plans. For example, using Figure 7-19 as a template, the team created a class invariant test specification for the Patron class. Figure 7-23 shows part of the created class invariant test specification. Specifically, the included tests checks for valid multiplicities and data type.

Next, Susan and Alan moved on to develop a set of integration tests. However, given the current state of the development effort, the only relevant tests that could be designed was use-case testing. She and Alan would need to design the other type of integration tests as the data management, human-computer interaction, and application architecture layers were designed. For example, until the user interface has been designed, it really isn't possible to develop a set of user interface tests. Therefore, Susan and Alan focused on developing a set of tests for the use cases. In this case, Susan and Alan focused on the use case, activity, and sequence diagrams. For example, to check out a physical resource, such as a

<table>
<tr><td colspan="3">Class Test Plan</td><td>Page 5 of 25</td></tr>
<tr><td>Class Name: Patron</td><td>Version Number: 1</td><td colspan="2">CRC Card ID: 25</td></tr>
<tr><td>Tester: Susan</td><td>Date Designed: 6/30</td><td colspan="2">Date Conducted: _______</td></tr>
<tr><td colspan="4">Class Objective:
To keep track of all relevant information associated with patrons of the library</td></tr>
<tr><td colspan="4">Associated Contract IDs: 13, 14, 15</td></tr>
<tr><td colspan="4">Associated Use-Case IDs: 1</td></tr>
<tr><td colspan="4">Associated Superclass(es): None</td></tr>
<tr><td colspan="4">Invariant-Based Test Requirements:
IDnumber is unique</td></tr>
<tr><td colspan="4">Contract-Based Test Requirements:
CheckoutResource received value (resourceList) is not null and is a ResourceList object</td></tr>
<tr><td colspan="4">State-Based Test Requirements:
None</td></tr>
</table>

FIGURE 7-22   Class Test Plan for the Patron Class

book, requires an interaction with at least five classes: Checkout Transaction, Patron, Physical Resource, Resource Collection, and Transaction Line Item (see Figure 7-16b). Using Figure 7-21 as a template, Alan created a test plan for the Borrow Resources use case (see Figure 7-24). Essentially, using the sequence diagrams (see Figures 5-5 through 5-11 and Figure 7-16b), Alan used the scenarios of the Borrow Resource use case to identify the scenario-based test requirements. Basically, for the Borrow Resource use case to succeed, each of the scenarios must be able to complete. Therefore, the relevant class-based unit tests (see Figures 7-19 and 7-20) had to be executed again. To accomplish this now, Alan initiated a set of role-playing exercises that was completed by a few librarians. Next, Alan set up a meeting with John to go over the tests that have been designed. In this way, John would be able to test the software as it is being developed instead of waiting to the end. However, once the software is completed, Alan will use these same tests to make sure that the implementation works as designed. While Alan was going over the tests, John pointed out that downloadable resources were "checked out" using a different process (see Figure 4-9). Thus, tests will need to be developed for downloadable resources also. Alan went back to work on identifying the additional scenarios. Once he completed all of these, he went back John again.

Now that the problem-domain layer, along with all of its relevant tests, have been designed, the team could start implementing the classes on the problem-domain layer. She tasked John with implementing and working with Alan the testing of the problem-domain layer as the other layers were being designed. She also split off some members of the team to design the classes for the other three layers. She had Jane head up the design of the data management layer, Beth head up the design of the human-computer interaction layer, and Phil head up the design of the physical architecture layer. She reminded everyone that they

<table>
<tr><td colspan="6">Class Invariant Test Specification</td><td>Page ___ of ___</td></tr>
<tr><td colspan="3">Class Name: Patron</td><td colspan="2">Version Number: 1</td><td colspan="2">CRC Card ID: 25</td></tr>
<tr><td colspan="3">Tester: Susan</td><td colspan="2">Date Designed: 6/30</td><td colspan="2">Date Conducted: _______</td></tr>
<tr><td colspan="7">Testing Objectives:
To guarantee the attributes can only have valid values</td></tr>
<tr><td colspan="7">Test Cases</td></tr>
</table>

Invariant Description	Original Attribute Value	Event	New Attribute Value	Expected Result	Result P/F
Attribute Name: Name					
1) (1..1)	Null	create	Null	F	____
2) (String)	Null	create	1234	F	____
3) (String)	Null	create	John	P	____
Attribute Name: IDnumber					
1) (1..1)	Null	create	Null	F	____
2) (String)	Null	create	1234	F	____
3) (String)	Null	create	John	P	____
Attribute Name: Address					
1) (1..1)	Null	create	Null	F	____
2) (Address)	Null	create	123 X Ln City, ST, Zip	F	____
3) (Address)	Null	create	address Obj	P	____

FIGURE 7-23 Partial Class Invariant Test Specification for the Patron Class

must stay in contact with John and Alan to make sure that what was designed could be implemented and tested in an optimal manner. In the next chapter, we visit Jane as she is designing the data management layer.

Campus Housing Service "Your Turn" Exercise In the previous installation of the Campus Housing Service (CHS) "Your Turn" exercise, using both Structured English and an activity diagram to specify the algorithm you created a method specification. In this installation, you should:

1. Create a class test plan for each class in the problem domain.
2. Using one of the class test plans, create a class invariant test specification.
3. Choose a use case and create a use case test plan for it. (Hint: Look through the activity and sequence diagrams for the chosen use case.)

We will return to CHS in the next chapter.

<table>
<tr><td colspan="3">Use-Case Test Plan</td><td>Page 1 of 15</td></tr>
<tr><td colspan="2">Use-Case Name: Borrow Resource</td><td>Version Number: 1</td><td>Use-Case ID: 1</td></tr>
<tr><td>Tester: Susan</td><td>Date Designed: 6/30</td><td colspan="2">Date Conducted: _______</td></tr>
</table>

Use-Case Objective:
To support the loaning of library resources to the library's patrons

Associated Class IDs: 25, 26, 28, 29, 30
Associated Use-Case IDs: None

Testing Objectives:
To make sure that all possible scenarios of a use case are supported

Scenario-Based Test Requirements:
- Invalid Faculty/Staff ID
- Valid Faculty/Staff ID, Overdue Resources
- Valid Faculty/Staff ID, No Overdue Resources, Unpaid Fees
- Valid Faculty/Staff ID, No Overdue Resources, No Unpaid Fees, Resource Not Available, Resource Owned by Library
- Valid Faculty/Staff ID, No Overdue Resources, No Unpaid Fees, Resource Not Available, Resource Not Owned by Library
- Valid Faculty/Staff ID, No Overdue Resources, No Unpaid Fees, Resource Available, Downloadable Resource
- Valid Faculty/Staff ID, No Overdue Resources, No Unpaid Fees, Resource Available, Physical Resource
- Invalid Student ID
- Valid Student ID, Overdue Resources
- Valid Student ID, No Overdue Resources, Unpaid Fees
- Valid Student ID, No Overdue Resources, No Unpaid Fees, Resource Not Available, Resource Owned by Library
- Valid Student ID, No Overdue Resources, No Unpaid Fees, Resource Not Available, Resource Not Owned by Library
- Valid Student ID, No Overdue Resources, No Unpaid Fees, Resource Available, Downloadable Resource
- Valid Student ID, No Overdue Resources, No Unpaid Fees, Resource Available, Physical Resource
- Invalid Student ID
- Valid Guest ID, Overdue Resources
- Valid Guest ID, No Overdue Resources, Unpaid Fees
- Valid Guest ID, No Overdue Resources, No Unpaid Fees, Resource Not Available, Resource Owned by Library
- Valid Guest ID, No Overdue Resources, No Unpaid Fees, Resource Not Available, Resource Not Owned by Library
- Valid Guest ID, No Overdue Resources, No Unpaid Fees, Resource Available, Downloadable Resource
- Valid Guest ID, No Overdue Resources, No Unpaid Fees, Resource Available, Physical Resource

FIGURE 7-24
Use Case Test Plan for the Borrow Resource Use Case

CHAPTER REVIEW

After reading and studying this chapter, you should be able to:

- ☐ Optimize a design.
- ☐ Map the problem-domain classes to a single-inheritance language.
- ☐ Map the problem-domain classes to an object-based language.
- ☐ Understand the difficulties in implementing an object-oriented design in a traditional programming language.
- ☐ Use the OCL to define precondition, postcondition, and invariant constraints.
- ☐ Create contracts to specify the interaction between client and server objects.
- ☐ Specify methods using the method specification form.
- ☐ Specify the logic of a method using Structured English and activity diagrams.
- ☐ Understand how to verify and validate both the design of the classes and the design of their methods.
- ☐ Describe how object-orientation affects software testing.
- ☐ Describe and discuss unit testing.
- ☐ Describe and discuss integration testing.
- ☐ Describe and discuss system testing.
- ☐ Describe and discuss acceptance testing.

KEY TERMS

Acceptance testing	Contract	Object constraint	System test
Access control list	Derived attribute	language (OCL)	Test case
Active value	Documentation testing	Performance testing	Test plan
Activity diagram	Event	Postcondition	Test specification
Alpha test	Event driven	Precondition	Trigger
Authentication testing	Fan-out	Requirements testing	Unit test
Authorization testing	Happy path	Role	Usability testing
Beta test	Hardcoded	Sad path	Use-case testing
Black-box testing	Integration test	Security testing	User interface testing
Caching computational results	Interaction testing	Server	Virus controls
Capability list	Invariant	Stress test	Volume test
Chaos Monkey	Load test	Structured English	White-box testing
Client	Method specification	Stub	Yo-yo problem
Constraint	Normal flow of events	Supplier	
Consumer	Object-based language	System interface testing	

QUESTIONS

1. What are exceptions?
2. What are constraints? What are the three different types of constraints?
3. What is the purpose of a contract? How are contracts used?
4. What is the Object Constraint Language? What is its purpose?
5. What is the Structured English? What is its purpose?
6. What is an invariant? How are invariants modeled in a design of a class? Give an example of an invariant for an hourly employee class using the Object Constraint Language.
7. Create a contract for a compute pay method associated with an hourly employee class. Specify the preconditions and postconditions using the Object Constraint Language.
8. How do you specify a method's algorithm?
9. Give an example of an algorithm specification for a compute pay method associated with an hourly employee class using Structured English.

10. Give an example of an algorithm specification for a compute pay method associated with an hourly employee class using an activity diagram.
11. How are methods specified? Give an example of a method specification for a compute pay method associated with an hourly employee class.
12. Why is testing important?
13. What is the purpose of testing?
14. Describe how object orientation affects testing.
15. Compare and contrast the terms test, test plan, and test case.
16. What is a stub and why is it used in testing?
17. What is the primary goal of unit testing?
18. How are the test cases developed for unit tests?
19. Compare and contrast black-box testing and white-box testing.
20. What are the different types of class tests?
21. What is the primary goal of integration testing?
22. How are the test cases developed for integration tests?
23. Describe the yo-yo problem. Why does it make integration testing difficult?
24. What is the primary goal of system testing?
25. How are the test cases developed for system tests?
26. What is the primary goal of acceptance testing?
27. How are the test cases developed for acceptance tests?
28. Compare and contrast alpha testing and beta testing.

EXERCISES

A. For the A Real Estate Inc. problem in Chapters 4 (exercises I, J, and K), 5 (exercises N and O), 6 (exercise D), and 7 (exercise D):

1. Choose one of the classes and create a set of invariants for attributes and relationships and add them to the CRC card for the class.
2. Choose one of the methods in the class that you chose and create a contract and a method specification for it. Use OCL to specify any pre- or postcondition and use both Structured English and an activity diagram to specify the algorithm.
3. Create an invariant test specification for the class you chose.
4. Create a use-case test plan, including the specific class plans and invariant tests, for a use case from the A Real Estate Inc. exercises in the previous chapters.

B. For the A Video Store problem in Chapters 4 (exercises L, M, and N), 5 (exercises P and Q), 6 (exercise E), and 7 (exercise E):

1. Choose one of the classes and create a set of invariants for attributes and relationships and add them to the CRC card for the class.
2. Choose one of the methods in the class that you chose and create a contract and a method specification for it. Use OCL to specify any pre- or postcondition and use both Structured English and an activity diagram to specify the algorithm.
3. Create an invariant test specification for the class you chose.
4. Create a use-case test plan, including the specific class plans and invariant tests, for a use case from the A Video Store exercises in the previous chapters.

C. For the gym membership problem in Chapters 4 (exercises O, P, and Q), 5 (exercises R and S), 6 (exercise F), and 7 (exercise F):

1. Choose one of the classes and create a set of invariants for attributes and relationships and add them to the CRC card for the class.
2. Choose one of the methods in the class that you chose and create a contract and a method specification for it. Use OCL to specify any pre- or postcondition and use both Structured English and an activity diagram to specify the algorithm.
3. Create an invariant test specification for the class you chose.
4. Create a use-case test plan, including the specific class plans and invariant tests, for a use case from the gym membership exercises in the previous chapters.

D. For the Picnics R Us problem in Chapters 4 (exercises R, S, and T), 5 (exercises T and U), 6 (exercise G), and 7 (exercise G):

1. Choose one of the classes and create a set of invariants for attributes and relationships and add them to the CRC card for the class.
2. Choose one of the methods in the class that you chose and create a contract and a method specification for it. Use OCL to specify any pre- or postcondition and use both Structured English and an activity diagram to specify the algorithm.
3. Create an invariant test specification for the class you chose.
4. Create a use-case test plan, including the specific class plans and invariant tests, for a use case from the Picnics R Us exercises in the previous chapters.

E. For the Of-the-Month-Club problem in Chapters 4 (exercises U, V, and W), 5 (exercises V and W), 6 (exercise H), and 7 (exercise H):

1. Choose one of the classes and create a set of invariants for attributes and relationships and add them to the CRC card for the class.

2. Choose one of the methods in the class that you chose and create a contract and a method specification for it. Use OCL to specify any pre- or postcondition and use both Structured English and an activity diagram to specify the algorithm.

3. Create an invariant test specification for the class you chose.

4. Create a use-case test plan, including the specific class plans and invariant tests, for a use case from the Of-the-Month-Club exercises in the previous chapters.

MINICASES

1. Your boss has been in the software development field for thirty years. He has always prided himself on his ability to adapt his skills from one approach to developing software to the next approach. For example, he had no problem learning structured analysis and design in the early 1980s and information engineering in the early 1990s. He even understands the advantage of rapid application development. But the other day, when you and he were talking about the advantages of object-oriented approaches, he became totally confused. He thought that characteristics such as polymorphism and inheritance were an advantage for object-oriented systems. However, when you explained the problems with inheritance conflicts, redefinition capabilities, and the need for semantic consistency across different implementations of methods, he was ready to simply give up. To make matters worse, you then went on to explain the importance of contracts in controlling the development of the system. At this point in the conservation, he basically threw in the towel. As he walked off, you heard him say something like "I guess it's true, it's too hard to teach an old dog new tricks."

   Being a loyal employee and friend, you decided to write a short tutorial to give your boss on object-oriented systems development. As a first step, create a detailed outline for the tutorial. As a subtle example, use good design criteria, such as coupling and cohesion, in the design of your tutorial outline.

2. You have been working with the professional and scientific management (PSSM) problem for quite a while. You should go back and refresh your memory about the problem before attempting to solve this situation. Refer back to your solutions to Minicase 3 in Chapter 6.

   a. For each class in the structural model, using OCL, create a set of invariants for attributes and relationships and add them to the CRC cards for the classes.

   b. Choose one of the classes in the structural model. Create a contract for each method in that class. Be sure to use OCL to specify the preconditions and the postconditions. Be as complete as possible.

   c. Create an invariant test specification for the class you chose for question b.

   d. Create a method specification for each method in the class you chose for question b. Use both Structured English and activity diagrams for the algorithm specification.

   e. Create a use-case test plan, including the specific class plans and invariant tests, for a use case from the exercises in the previous chapters.

3. You have been working with the Holiday Travel Vehicle problem for quite a while. You should go back and refresh your memory about the problem before attempting to solve this situation. Refer back to your solutions Minicase 4 in Chapter 6.

   In the new system for Holiday Travel Vehicles, the system users follow a two-stage process to record complete information on all of the vehicles sold. When an RV or trailer first arrives at the company from the manufacturer, a clerk from the inventory department creates a new vehicle record for it in the computer system. The data entered at this time include basic descriptive information on the vehicle such as manufacturer, name, model, year, base cost, and freight charges. When the vehicle is sold, the new vehicle record is updated to reflect the final sales terms and the dealer-installed options added to the vehicle. This information is entered into the system at the time of sale when the salesperson completes the sales invoice.

   When it is time for the clerk to finalize the new vehicle record, the clerk selects a menu option from the system, which is called Finalize New Vehicle Record. The tasks involved in this process are described below.

When the user selects Finalize New Vehicle Record from the system menu, the user is immediately prompted for the serial number of the new vehicle. This serial number is used to retrieve the new vehicle record for the vehicle from system storage. If a record cannot be found, the serial number is probably invalid. The vehicle serial number is then used to retrieve the option records that describe the dealer-installed options that were added to the vehicle at the customer's request. There may be zero or more options. The cost of the option specified on the option record(s) is totaled. Then, the dealer cost is calculated using the vehicle's base cost, freight charge, and total option cost. The completed new vehicle record is passed back to the calling module.

a. Update the structural model (CRC cards and class diagram) with this additional information.

b. For each class in the structural model, using OCL, create a set of invariants for attributes and relationships and add them to the CRC cards for the classes.

c. Choose one of the classes in the structural model. Create a contract for each method in that class. Be sure to use OCL to specify the preconditions and the postconditions. Be as complete as possible.

d. Create a method specification for each method in the class you chose for question c. Use both Structured English and activity diagrams for the algorithm specification.

e. Create an invariant test specification for the class you chose for question c.

f. Create a use-case test plan, including the specific class plans and invariant tests, for a use case from the exercises in the previous chapters.

CHAPTER 8

DATA MANAGEMENT LAYER DESIGN

A project team designs the data management layer of a system using a three-step process: selecting the format of the storage, mapping the problem domain classes to the selected format, and then designing the necessary data access and manipulation classes. This chapter describes the different ways objects can be stored and several important characteristics that should be considered when choosing among object persistence formats. It describes a problem domain class to object persistence format mapping process for the most important object persistence formats. Next, the chapter describes how to design data access and manipulation classes and describes how to ensure the fidelity of the data management layer. We describe the effect that nonfunctional requirements have on the data-management layer. Finally, since the most popular storage format today is the relational database and that most database administrators use the entity-relationship diagram to represent the relational database design, the chapter provides an appendix on the optimization of relational databases from both storage and access perspectives, and a description of how to map the class diagram based design of the relational database to an entity relationship diagram.

OBJECTIVES

- Become familiar with several object persistence formats.
- Be familiar with the different approaches to data distribution.
- Be able to map problem domain objects to different object persistence formats.
- Be able to design the data access and manipulation classes.
- Understand the effect of nonfunctional requirements on the data management layer.
- Understand how to verify and validate the data management layer.
- Be able to optimize storage efficiency and speed of a relational database used for object storage and access.
- Be able to estimate the size of a relational database.

INTRODUCTION

Applications are of little use without the data that they support. How useful is a multimedia application that can't support images or sound? Why would someone log into a system to find information if it would take less time to locate the information manually? One of the leading complaints by end users is that the final system is too slow, so to avoid such complaints project team members must allow time during design to carefully make sure that the file or database performs as fast as possible. At the same time, the team must keep hardware and environmental costs down by minimizing the storage space that the application will require. The goals of maximizing access to the objects and minimizing the amount of space taken to store objects can conflict, and designing object persistence efficiency usually requires trade-offs.

The design of the *data management layer* addresses these concerns. It includes both the design of data access and manipulation classes and the actual data storage. The design of the data access and manipulation classes should ensure the independence of the problem domain classes from the data storage format. As such, the data access and manipulation classes handle all communication with the database. In this manner, the problem domain is decoupled from the object storage, allowing the object storage to be changed without affecting the problem domain classes.

The data storage component manages how data are stored and handled by the programs that run the system. The data storage component is composed of a set of object persistence classes. Effective object persistence design decreases the chances of ending up with inefficient systems, long system response times, and users and other systems that cannot get to the information that they need in the way that they need it—all of which can affect the success of the project. From a practical perspective, there are five basic types of formats that can be used to store objects for application systems: files (sequential and random), object-oriented databases, object-relational databases, relational databases, and NoSQL datastores.[1] Each type has certain characteristics that make it more appropriate for some types of systems over others. Once the object persistence format is selected to support the system, the problem-domain objects need to drive the design of the actual object storage. Then the object storage needs to be designed to optimize its processing efficiency.

OBJECT PERSISTENCE FORMATS

Each of the *object persistence* types is described in this section. *Files* are electronic lists of data that have been optimized to perform a particular transaction. For example, Figure 8-1 shows a customer order file with information about customers' orders, in the form in which it is used, so that the information can be accessed and processed quickly by the system.

A *database* is a collection of groupings of information, each of which is related to each other in some way (e.g., through common fields). Logical groupings of information could include such categories as customer data, information about an order, product information, and so on. A *database management system (DBMS)* is software that creates and manipulates these databases (see Figure 8-2 for a relational database example). Such *end-user DBMSs* as Microsoft Access support small-scale databases that are used to enhance personal productivity, whereas *enterprise DBMSs,* such as SQL Server, MongoDB, and Oracle, can manage huge volumes of data and support applications that run an entire company. An end-user DBMS is significantly less expensive and easier for novice users to use than its enterprise counterpart, but it does not have the features or capabilities that are necessary to support mission-critical or large-scale systems.

Sequential and Random-Access Files

From a practical perspective, most object-oriented programming languages support sequential and random-access files as part of the language.[2] In this section, we describe what sequential access and random access files are.[3] We also describe how sequential access and random

---

[1] There are other types of files, such as relative, indexed sequential, and multi-indexed sequential, and databases, such as hierarchical, network, and multidimensional. However, these formats typically are not used for object persistence.

[2] For example, see the FileInputStream, FileOutputStream, and RandomAccessFile classes in the java.io package.

[3] For a more complete coverage of issues related to the design of files, see Owen Hanson, *Design of Computer Data Files* (Rockville, MD: Computer Science Press, 1982).

Order Number	Date	Cust ID	Last Name	First Name	Amount	Tax	Total	Prior Customer	Payment Type
234	11/23/00	2242	DeBerry	Ann	$ 90.00	$5.85	$ 95.85	Y	MC
235	11/23/00	9500	Chin	April	$ 12.00	$0.60	$ 12.60	Y	VISA
236	11/23/00	1556	Fracken	Chris	$ 50.00	$2.50	$ 52.50	N	VISA
237	11/23/00	2242	DeBerry	Ann	$ 75.00	$4.88	$ 79.88	Y	AMEX
238	11/23/00	2242	DeBerry	Ann	$ 60.00	$3.90	$ 63.90	Y	MC
239	11/23/00	1035	Black	John	$ 90.00	$4.50	$ 94.50	Y	AMEX
240	11/23/00	9501	Kaplan	Bruce	$ 50.00	$2.50	$ 52.50	N	VISA
241	11/23/00	1123	Williams	Mary	$120.00	$9.60	$129.60	N	MC
242	11/24/00	9500	Chin	April	$ 60.00	$3.00	$ 63.00	Y	VISA
243	11/24/00	4254	Bailey	Ryan	$ 90.00	$4.50	$ 94.50	Y	VISA
244	11/24/00	9500	Chin	April	$ 24.00	$1.20	$ 25.20	Y	VISA
245	11/24/00	2242	DeBerry	Ann	$ 12.00	$0.78	$ 12.78	Y	AMEX
246	11/24/00	4254	Bailey	Ryan	$ 20.00	$1.00	$ 21.00	Y	MC
247	11/24/00	2241	Jones	Chris	$ 50.00	$2.50	$ 52.50	N	VISA
248	11/24/00	4254	Bailey	Ryan	$ 12.00	$0.60	$ 12.60	Y	AMEX
249	11/24/00	5927	Lee	Diane	$ 50.00	$2.50	$ 52.50	N	AMEX
250	11/24/00	2242	DeBerry	Ann	$ 12.00	$0.78	$ 12.78	Y	MC
251	11/24/00	9500	Chin	April	$ 15.00	$0.75	$ 15.75	Y	MC
252	11/24/00	2242	DeBerry	Ann	$132.00	$8.58	$140.58	Y	MC
253	11/24/00	2242	DeBerry	Ann	$ 72.00	$4.68	$ 76.68	Y	AMEX

FIGURE 8-1   Customer Order File

access files are used to support an application. For example, they can be used to support master files, look-up files, transaction files, audit files, and history files.

Sequential access files allow only sequential file operations to be performed (e.g., read, write, and search). Sequential access files are very efficient for sequential operations that process all the objects consecutively, such as report writing. However, for random operations, such as finding or updating a specific object, they are very inefficient. On the average, 50 percent of the contents of a sequential access file will have to be searched before finding the specific object of interest in the file. They come in two flavors: ordered and unordered.

An *unordered sequential access file* is basically an electronic list of information stored on disk. Unordered files are organized serially (i.e., the order of the file is the order in which the objects are written to the file). Typically, new objects simply are added to the file's end.

Ordered sequential access files are placed into a specific sorted order (e.g., in ascending order by customer number). There is overhead associated with keeping files in a particular sorted order. The file designer can keep the file in sorted order by always creating a new file each time a delete or addition occurs, or by keeping track of the sorted order via the use of a *pointer,* which is information about the location of the related record. A pointer is placed at the end of each record, and it "points" to the next record in a series or set. The underlying data/file structure in this case is the *linked list*[4] data structure.

[4] For more information on various data structures, see Ellis Horowitz and Sartaj Sahni, *Fundamentals of Data Structures* (Rockville, MD: Computer Science Press, 1982); Michael T. Goodrich and Roberto Tamassia, *Data Structures and Algorithms in Java* (New York: Wiley, 1998).

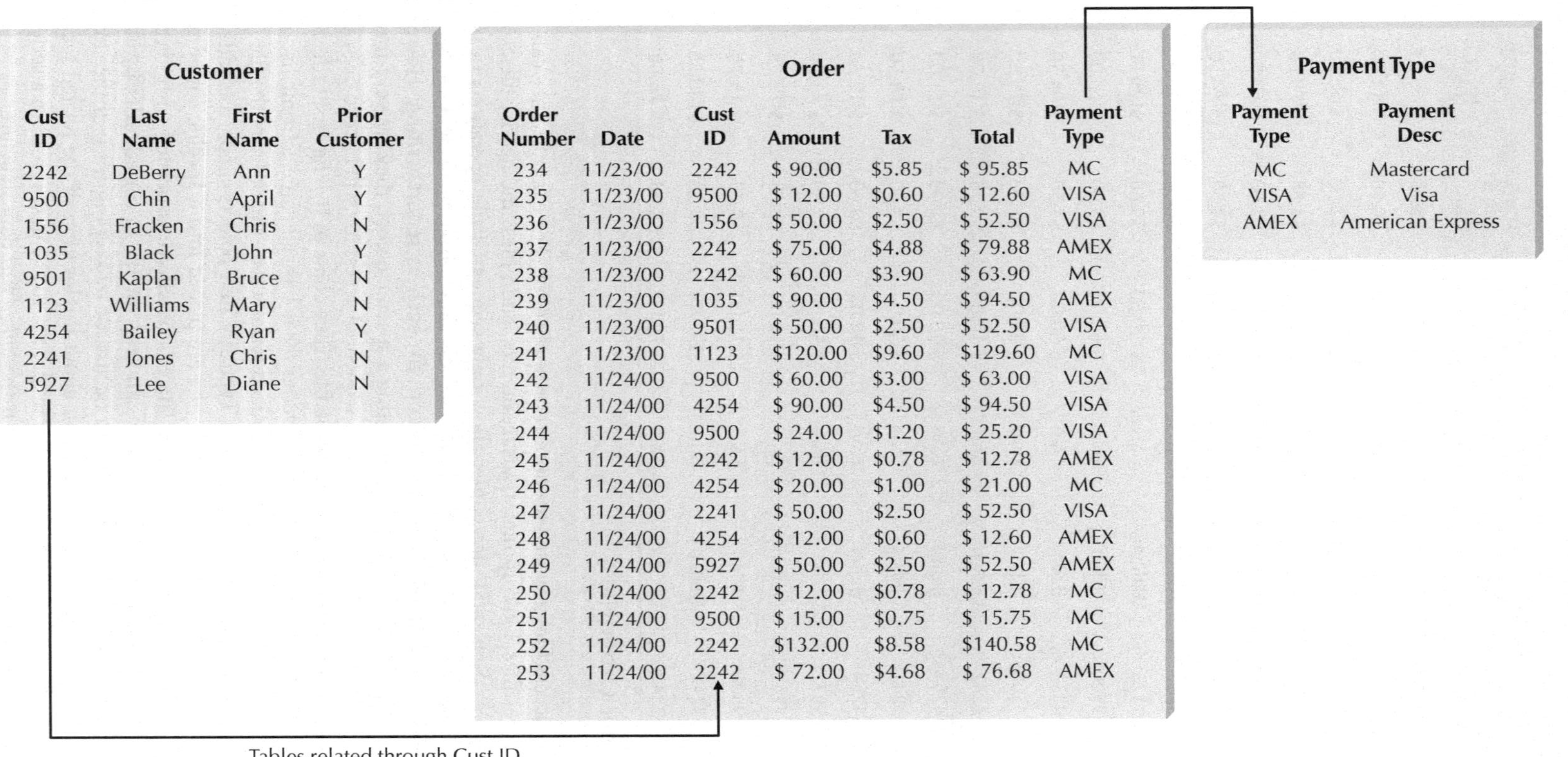

Customer

Cust ID	Last Name	First Name	Prior Customer
2242	DeBerry	Ann	Y
9500	Chin	April	Y
1556	Fracken	Chris	N
1035	Black	John	Y
9501	Kaplan	Bruce	N
1123	Williams	Mary	N
4254	Bailey	Ryan	Y
2241	Jones	Chris	N
5927	Lee	Diane	N

Order

Order Number	Date	Cust ID	Amount	Tax	Total	Payment Type
234	11/23/00	2242	$ 90.00	$5.85	$ 95.85	MC
235	11/23/00	9500	$ 12.00	$0.60	$ 12.60	VISA
236	11/23/00	1556	$ 50.00	$2.50	$ 52.50	VISA
237	11/23/00	2242	$ 75.00	$4.88	$ 79.88	AMEX
238	11/23/00	2242	$ 60.00	$3.90	$ 63.90	MC
239	11/23/00	1035	$ 90.00	$4.50	$ 94.50	AMEX
240	11/23/00	9501	$ 50.00	$2.50	$ 52.50	VISA
241	11/23/00	1123	$120.00	$9.60	$129.60	MC
242	11/24/00	9500	$ 60.00	$3.00	$ 63.00	VISA
243	11/24/00	4254	$ 90.00	$4.50	$ 94.50	VISA
244	11/24/00	9500	$ 24.00	$1.20	$ 25.20	VISA
245	11/24/00	2242	$ 12.00	$0.78	$ 12.78	AMEX
246	11/24/00	4254	$ 20.00	$1.00	$ 21.00	MC
247	11/24/00	2241	$ 50.00	$2.50	$ 52.50	VISA
248	11/24/00	4254	$ 12.00	$0.60	$ 12.60	AMEX
249	11/24/00	5927	$ 50.00	$2.50	$ 52.50	AMEX
250	11/24/00	2242	$ 12.00	$0.78	$ 12.78	MC
251	11/24/00	9500	$ 15.00	$0.75	$ 15.75	MC
252	11/24/00	2242	$132.00	$8.58	$140.58	MC
253	11/24/00	2242	$ 72.00	$4.68	$ 76.68	AMEX

Payment Type

Payment Type	Payment Desc
MC	Mastercard
VISA	Visa
AMEX	American Express

FIGURE 8-2 Customer Order Database

Random access files allow only random or direct file operations to be performed. This type of file is optimized for random operations, such as finding and updating a specific object. Random access files typically have a faster response time to find and update operations than any other type of file. However, because they do not support sequential processing, applications such as report writing are very inefficient. The various methods to implement random access files are beyond the scope of this book.[5]

There are times when it is necessary to be able to process files in both a sequential and random manner. One simple way to do this is to use a sequential file that contains a list of the keys (the field in which the file is to be kept in sorted order) and a random-access file for the actual objects. This minimizes the cost of additions and deletions to a sequential file while allowing the random file to be processed sequentially by simply passing the key to the random file to retrieve each object in sequential order. It also allows fast random processing to occur by using only the random-access file, thus optimizing the overall cost of file processing. However, if a file of objects needs to be processed in both a random and sequential manner, the developer should consider using a database instead.

There are many different application types of files—e.g., master files, lookup files, transaction files, audit files, and history files. *Master files* store core information that is important to the business and, more specifically, to the application, such as order information or customer mailing information. They usually are kept for long periods of time, and new records are appended to the end of the file as new orders or new customers are captured by the system. If changes need to be made to existing records, programs must be written to update the old information.

Lookup files contain static values, such as a list of valid ZIP/postal codes or the names of the states/provinces. Typically, the list is used for validation. For example, if a customer's mailing address is entered into a master file, the state name is validated against a lookup file that contains U.S. states to make sure that the operator entered the value correctly.

A *transaction file* holds information that can be used to update a master file. The transaction file can be destroyed after changes are added, or the file may be saved in case the transactions need to be accessed again in the future. Customer address changes, for one, would be stored in a transaction file until a program is run that updates the customer address master file with the new information.

For control purposes, a company might need to store information about how data change over time. For example, as human resources clerks change employee salaries in a human resources system, the system should record the person who made the changes to the salary amount, the date, and the actual change that was made. An *audit file* records before and after images of data as they are altered so that an audit can be performed if the integrity of the data is questioned.

Sometimes files become so large that they are unwieldy, and much of the information in the file is no longer used. The *history file* (or archive file) stores past transactions (e.g., old customers and past orders) that are no longer needed by system users. Typically, the file is stored off-line, yet it can be accessed on an as-needed basis. Other files, such as master files, can then be streamlined to include only active or very recent information.

Relational Databases

A relational database is the most popular kind of database for application development. A relational database is based on collections of tables with each table having a *primary key*—a field or fields whose values are unique for every row of the table. The tables are related to one another by placing the primary key from one table into the related table as a *foreign key* (see Figure 8-3). Most *relational database management systems (RDBMS)* support *referential integrity*,

---

[5] For a more-detailed look at the underlying data and file structures of the different types of files, see Mary E. S. Loomis, *Data Management and File Structures*, 2nd Ed. (Englewood Cliffs, NJ: Prentice Hall, 1989); Michael J. Folk and Bill Zoeellick, *File Structures: A Conceptual Toolkit* (Reading, MA: Addison-Wesley, 1987).

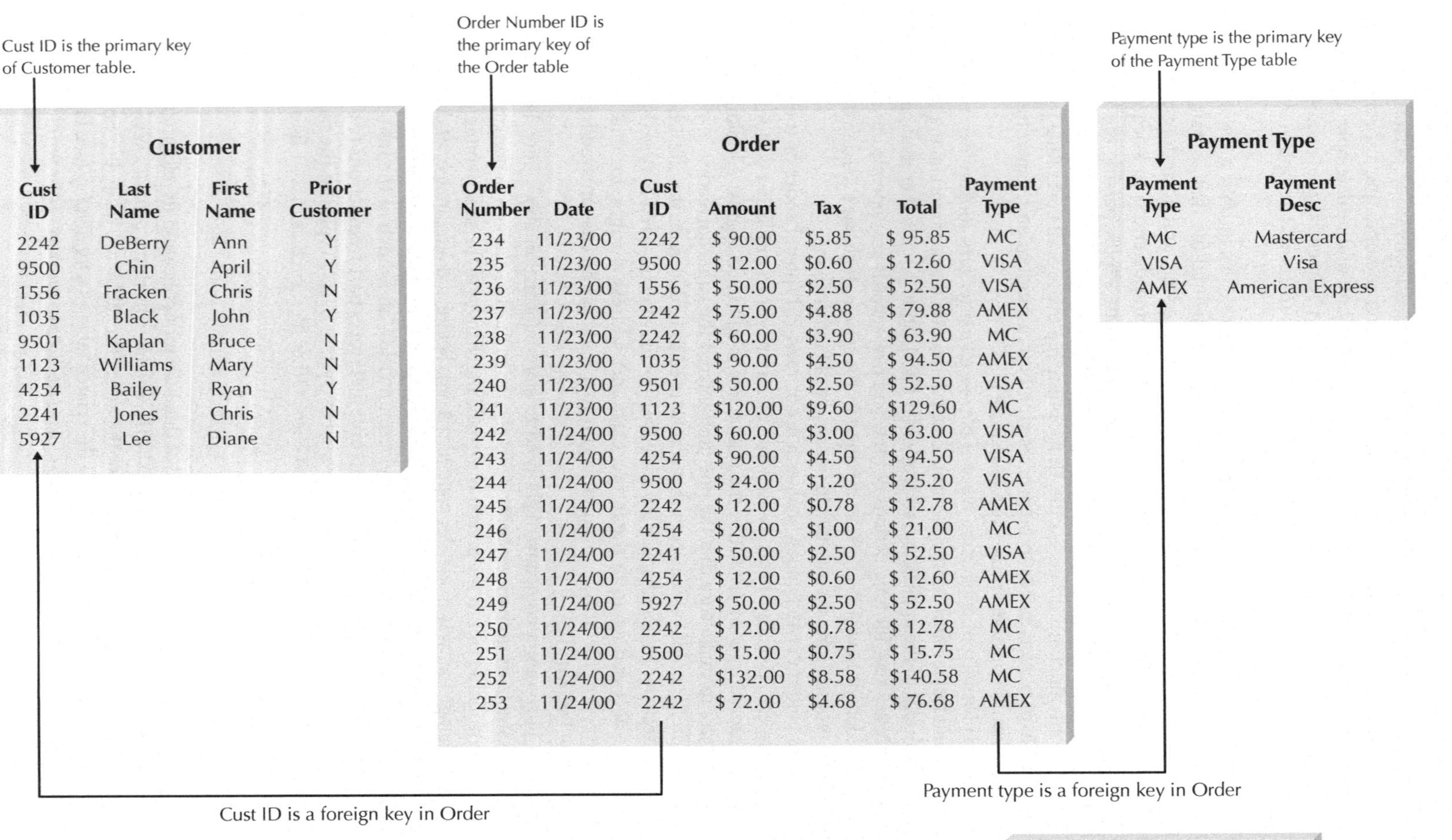

Customer

Cust ID	Last Name	First Name	Prior Customer
2242	DeBerry	Ann	Y
9500	Chin	April	Y
1556	Fracken	Chris	N
1035	Black	John	Y
9501	Kaplan	Bruce	N
1123	Williams	Mary	N
4254	Bailey	Ryan	Y
2241	Jones	Chris	N
5927	Lee	Diane	N

Order

Order Number	Date	Cust ID	Amount	Tax	Total	Payment Type
234	11/23/00	2242	$ 90.00	$5.85	$ 95.85	MC
235	11/23/00	9500	$ 12.00	$0.60	$ 12.60	VISA
236	11/23/00	1556	$ 50.00	$2.50	$ 52.50	VISA
237	11/23/00	2242	$ 75.00	$4.88	$ 79.88	AMEX
238	11/23/00	2242	$ 60.00	$3.90	$ 63.90	MC
239	11/23/00	1035	$ 90.00	$4.50	$ 94.50	AMEX
240	11/23/00	9501	$ 50.00	$2.50	$ 52.50	VISA
241	11/23/00	1123	$120.00	$9.60	$129.60	MC
242	11/24/00	9500	$ 60.00	$3.00	$ 63.00	VISA
243	11/24/00	4254	$ 90.00	$4.50	$ 94.50	VISA
244	11/24/00	9500	$ 24.00	$1.20	$ 25.20	VISA
245	11/24/00	2242	$ 12.00	$0.78	$ 12.78	AMEX
246	11/24/00	4254	$ 20.00	$1.00	$ 21.00	MC
247	11/24/00	2241	$ 50.00	$2.50	$ 52.50	VISA
248	11/24/00	4254	$ 12.00	$0.60	$ 12.60	AMEX
249	11/24/00	5927	$ 50.00	$2.50	$ 52.50	AMEX
250	11/24/00	2242	$ 12.00	$0.78	$ 12.78	MC
251	11/24/00	9500	$ 15.00	$0.75	$ 15.75	MC
252	11/24/00	2242	$132.00	$8.58	$140.58	MC
253	11/24/00	2242	$ 72.00	$4.68	$ 76.68	AMEX

Payment Type

Payment Type	Payment Desc
MC	Mastercard
VISA	Visa
AMEX	American Express

FIGURE 8-3 Relational Database

or the idea of ensuring that values linking the tables together through the primary and foreign keys are valid and correctly synchronized. For example, if an order-entry clerk using the tables in Figure 8-3 attempted to add order 254 for customer number 1111, this would be a mistake because no customer exists in the Customer table with that number. If the RDBMS supported referential integrity, it would check the customer numbers in the Customer table, discover that the number 1111 is invalid, and return an error to the entry clerk. The clerk would then go back to the original order form and recheck the customer information.

Tables have a set number of columns and a variable number of rows that contain occurrences of data. *Structured query language (SQL)* is the standard language for accessing the data in the tables. SQL operates on complete tables, as opposed to the individual rows in the tables. Thus, a query written in SQL is applied to all the rows in a table all at once, which is different from a lot of programming languages, which manipulate data row by row. When queries must include information from more than one table, the tables first are *joined* based on their primary key and foreign key relationships and treated as if they were one large table. Examples of RDBMS software are Microsoft SQL Server, Oracle, DB2, and MySQL.

To use a RDBMS to store objects, objects must be converted so that they can be stored in a table. From a design perspective, this entails mapping a UML class diagram to a relational database schema.

Object-Relational Databases

Object-relational database management systems (ORDBMSs) are relational database management systems with extensions to handle the storage of objects in the relational table structure. This is typically done through the use of user-defined types. For example, an attribute in a table could have a data type of map, which would support storing a map. This is an example of a complex data type. In pure RDBMSs, attributes are limited to simple or atomic data types, such as integers, floats, or chars.

ORDBMSs, because they are simply extensions to their RDBMS counterparts, also have very good support for the typical data management operations that business has come to expect from RDBMSs, including an easy-to-use query language (SQL), authorization, concurrency-control, and recovery facilities. However, because SQL was designed to handle only simple data types, it too has been extended to handle complex object data. Currently, vendors deal with this issue in different manners. For example, DB2, Informix, and Oracle all have extensions that provide some level of support for objects.

Many of the ORDBMSs on the market still do not support all object-oriented features that can appear in an object-oriented design (e.g., inheritance). As described in Chapter 1 Appendix, one of the problems in supporting inheritance is that inheritance support is language dependent. For example, the way Smalltalk supports inheritance is different from C++s' approach, which is different from Java's approach. Thus, vendors currently must support many different versions of inheritance, one for each object-oriented language, or decide on a specific version and force developers to map their object-oriented design (and implementation) to their approach. Like RDBMSs, a mapping from a UML class diagram to an object-relational database schema is required.

Object-Oriented Databases

The next type of database management system that we describe is the *object-oriented database management systems (OODBMS)*. There have been two primary approaches to supporting object persistence within the OODBMS community: adding persistence extensions to an object-oriented programming language and creating an entirely separate database management system.

With an OODBMS, collections of objects are associated with an extent. An *extent* is simply the set of instances associated with a particular class (i.e., it is the equivalent of a table in a RDBMS). Technically speaking, each instance of a class has a unique identifier assigned to it by the OODBMS: the *Object ID*. However, from a practical point of view, it is still a good idea to have a semantically meaningful primary key (even though from an OODBMS perspective this is unnecessary). Referential integrity is still very important. In an OODBMS, from the user's perspective, it looks as if the object is contained within the other object. However, the OODBMS keeps track of these relationships through the use of the Object ID, and therefore foreign keys are not technically necessary.[6]

OODBMSs provide support for some form of inheritance. However, as already discussed, inheritance tends to be language dependent. Currently, most OODBMSs are tied closely to either a particular *object-oriented programming language (OOPL)* or a set of OOPLs. Originally, most OODBMSs supported either Smalltalk or C++. Today, many of the commercially available OODBMSs provide support for C++, Java, and Smalltalk.

OODBMSs also support the idea of *repeating groups* (fields) or *multivalued attributes*. These are supported through the use of *attribute sets* and *relationship sets*. RDBMSs do not explicitly allow multivalued attributes or repeating groups. This is considered a violation of the first normal form (discussed in the appendix to this chapter) for relational databases. Some ORDBMSs do support repeating groups and multivalued attributes.

Until recently, OODBMSs have mainly been used to support multimedia applications or systems that involve complex data (e.g., graphics, video, and sound). Application areas, such as computer-aided design and manufacturing (CAD/CAM), financial services, geographic information systems, health care, telecommunications, and transportation, have been the most receptive to OODBMSs. They are also becoming popular technologies for supporting electronic commerce, online catalogs, and large Web multimedia applications. Examples of pure OODBMSs include Gemstone, Objectivity, and Versant.

Although pure OODBMS exist, most organizations currently invest in *ORDBMS* technology. The market for OODBMS is expected to grow, but its ORDBMS and RDBMS counterparts dwarf it. One reason for this situation is that there are many more experienced developers and tools in the RDBMS arena. Furthermore, relational users find that using an OODBMS comes with a fairly steep learning curve.

NoSQL Data Stores[7]

NoSQL data stores are the more recent type of object persistence available. Depending on whom you talk to, NoSQL either stands for No SQL or Not Only SQL. Regardless, the data stores that are described as NoSQL typically do not natively support SQL. Currently, there is no standard for NoSQL data stores. Most NoSQL data stores were created to address problems associated with storing large amounts of distributed data in RDBMSs. NoSQL data stores tend to support very fast queries. However, when it comes to updating, NoSQL data stores normally do not support a locking mechanism, and consequently, all copies of a piece of data are not required to be consistent at all times. Instead, they tend to support an eventually consistent based model. Therefore, it is technically possible to have different values for different copies of the same object stored in different locations in a distributed system.

---

[6] Depending on the storage and updating requirements, it usually is a good idea to use a foreign key in addition to the Object ID. The Object ID has no semantic meaning. Therefore, in the case of needing to rebuild relationships between objects, Object IDs are difficult to validate. Foreign keys, by contrast, should have some meaning outside of the DBMS.

[7] For a more complete description of NoSQL data stores see Pramod J. Sadalage and Martin Fowler, *NoSQL Distilled: A Brief Guide to the Emerging World of Polyglot Persistence* (Upper Saddle River, NJ: Addison Wesley, 2013).

Depending on the application, this could cause problems for decision makers. Therefore, their applicability is limited and are not applicable to many traditional business transaction processing systems. Some of the better-known NoSQL data stores include Bigtable, DynamoDB, HBase, CouchDB, Neo4J, and Cassandra. There are many different types of NoSQL data stores, including key-value stores, document stores, column-oriented stores, and graph databases.

Key-value data stores essentially provide a distributed index (primary key) to where a BLOB (binary large object) is stored. A BLOB treats a set of attributes as one large object. A good example of this type of NoSQL data store is DynamoDB. DynamoDB provides support for many of the core services for Amazon. Obviously, as one of the largest e-commerce sites in the world, Amazon needed a solution for object persistence that was scalable, distributable, and reliable. Typical RDBMS-based solutions would not work for some of these applications. Applications that typically use key-value data stores are Web-based shopping carts, product catalogs, and bestseller lists. These types of applications do not require updating the underlying data. For example, you do not update the title of a book in your shopping cart when you are making a purchase at Amazon. Given the scale and distributed nature of this type of system, there are bound to be many failures across the system. Being fault tolerant and temporarily sacrificing some consistency across all copies of an object is a reasonable trade-off.

Document data stores, as the name suggests, are built around the idea of documents. The idea of document databases has been around for a long time. These types of stores are considered to be schema free. By that we mean there is no detailed design of the database. A good example of an application that would benefit from this type of approach is a business card database. In a relational database, multiple tables would need to be designed. In a document data store, the design is done more in a "just in time" manner. As new business cards are input into the system, attributes not previously included are simply added to the evolving design. Previously entered business cards would simply not have those attributes associated with them. One major difference between key-value data stores and document data stores is that the "document" has structure and can be easily searched based on the non-key attributes contained in the document, whereas the key-value data store simply treats the "value" as one big monolithic object. MongoDB and CouchDB are examples of this type of data store.

Columnar data stores organize the data into columns instead of rows. However, there seems to be some confusion as to what this actually implies. In the first approach to columnar data stores, the rows represent the attributes and the columns represent the objects. In contrast, relational databases represent attributes in columns and represent objects in rows. This type of columnar data store is very effective in business intelligence, data mining, and data warehousing applications where the data are fairly static and many computations are performed over a single or a small subset of the available attributes. In comparison to a relational database where you would have to select a set of attributes from all rows, with this type of data store, you would simply have to select a set of rows. This should be a lot faster than with a relational database. A few good examples of this type of columnar data store include Oracle's Retail Predictive Application Server, Vertica, and SAP IQ. The second approach to columnar data stores, which includes HBase and Cassandra, is designed to handle very large data sets (petabytes of data) that can be accessed as if the data are stored in columns. However, in this case, the data are actually stored in a three-dimensional map composed of object ID, attribute name, timestamp, and value instead of using columns and rows. This approach is highly scalable and distributable. These types of data stores support social applications such as Twitter and Facebook and support search applications such as Google Maps, Earth, and Analytics.

Given the popularity of social computing, business intelligence, data mining, data warehousing, e-commerce, and their need for highly scalable, distributable, and reliable data storage, NoSQL data stores are an area that should be considered as part of an object persistence solution. However, given the overall diversity and complexity of NoSQL data stores, we do not consider them any further in this text.

Graph databases organize data as connected nodes and edges, along with their properties. Graph databases have their roots in network databases of 1970s, but offer greater sophistication of querying, improved data retrieval performance, higher scalability, and more advanced data structures. They are also more user-friendly and easier to deploy (as integration with other systems and support for SQL is becoming common). While most databases (including relational) have the ability to connect objects (tables and rows), graph databases are especially good at storing and querying relationship-related data. For example, if in a relational database, relationships are not explicitly stored and are enacted each time related tables are joined together, graph databases store relationships (node edges) explicitly and typically index them to optimize their access. This greatly improves the query performance and permits complex queries that traverse multiple graph nodes. For example, graph database can support questions such as: how many friends do my friends have in common? Such a query would be quite tricky for a relational database. An example of graph database is Neo4J, optimized for fast management, storage, and traversal of nodes and edges. Other vendors (e.g., MongoDB) also offer graphing capabilities. Graph databases are especially prominent in social networks (e.g., for strong personal or professional connections), but are also used in such diverse areas as supply chain management, bioinformatics, knowledge management, and artificial intelligence (where knowledge graphs are used to supply machine learning with relational facts that are hard to retrieve from text or tabular data).

Selecting an Object Persistence Format

Each of the file and database storage formats that have been presented has its strengths and weaknesses, and no one format is inherently better than the others. In fact, sometimes a project team chooses multiple formats to support a specific application. For example, a team could choose a relational database for structured data, a file for video data, and a NoSQL datastore for social media data. Thus, it is important to understand the strengths and weaknesses of each format and when to use each one. Figure 8-4 presents a summary of the characteristics of each and the scenarios that can help identify when each type of format is more appropriate.

Major Strengths and Weaknesses The major strengths of files include the following: Some support for sequential and random-access files is normally part of an OOPL, files can be designed to be very efficient, and they are a good alternative for temporary or short-term storage. However, all file manipulation must be done through the OOPL. Files do not have any form of access control beyond that of the underlying operating system. Finally, in most cases, if files are used for permanent storage, redundant data most likely will result. This can cause many update anomalies.

RDBMSs bring with them proven commercial technology. They are the leaders in the DBMS market. Furthermore, they can handle very diverse data needs. However, they cannot handle complex data types, such as images. Therefore, all objects must be converted to a form that can be stored in tables composed of atomic or simple data. They provide no support for object orientation. This lack of support causes an *impedance mismatch* between the objects contained in the OOPL and the data stored in the tables. An impedance mismatch refers to the amount of work done by both the developer and DBMS and the potential information loss that can occur when converting objects to a form that can be stored in tables.

Because ORDBMSs are typically object-oriented extensions to RDBMSs, they inherit the strengths of RDBMSs. They are based on established technologies, such as SQL, and unlike their predecessors, they can handle complex data types. However, they provide only limited

	Sequential and Random Access Files	Relational DBMS	Object Relational DBMS	Object-Oriented DBMS	NoSQL data store
Major Strengths	Usually part of an object-oriented programming language Files can be designed for fast performance Good for short-term data storage	Leader in the database market Can handle diverse data needs	Based on established, proven technology, e.g., SQL Able to handle complex data	Able to handle complex data Direct support for object orientation	Able to handle complex data
Major Weaknesses	Redundant data Data must be updated using programs, i.e., no manipulation or query language No access control	Cannot handle complex data No support for object orientation Impedance mismatch between tables and objects	Limited support for object orientation Impedance mismatch between tables and objects	Technology is still maturing Skills are hard to find	Technology is still maturing Skills are hard to find
Data Types Supported	Simple and Complex	Simple	Simple and Complex	Simple and Complex	Simple and Complex
Types of Application Systems Supported	Transaction processing	Transaction processing and decision making	Transaction processing and decision making	Transaction processing and decision making	Primarily decision making
Existing Storage Formats	Organization dependent	Organization dependent	Organization dependent	Organization dependent	Organization dependent
Future Needs	Poor future prospects	Good future prospects	Good future prospects	Good future prospects	Good future prospects

FIGURE 8-4   Comparison of Object Persistence Formats

support for object orientation. The level of support varies among the vendors; therefore, ORDBMSs may also suffer from the impedance mismatch problem.

OODBMSs support complex data types and have the advantage of directly supporting object orientation. Therefore, they do not suffer from the impedance mismatch that the previous DBMSs do. However, the OODBMS community is still maturing. Therefore, this technology might still be too risky for some firms. The other major problems with OODBMS are the lack of skilled labor and the perceived steep learning curve of the RDBMS community. NoSQL data stores support complex data types. However, they can suffer from some forms of impedance mismatch. The primary problems with NoSQL data stores are their lack of maturity and the lack of skilled labor who knows how to effectively use them.

Data Types Supported   The first issue is the type of data that will need to be stored in the system. Most applications need to store simple data types, such as text, dates, and numbers. All files and DBMSs are equipped to handle this kind of data. The best choice for simple data storage, however, is usually the RDBMS because the technology has matured over time and has continuously improved to handle simple data very effectively. Increasingly, applications are incorporating complex data, such as video, images, or audio. ORDBMSs, OODBMSs, or NoSQL data stores are best able to handle data of this type. Complex data stored as objects can be manipulated much faster than with other storage formats. However, one possibility to handle data that includes both simple and complex data is to use a combination of object persistence formats.

Type of Application System There are many kinds of application systems that can be developed. *Transaction-processing systems* are designed to accept and process many simultaneous requests (e.g., order entry, distribution, and payroll). In transaction-processing systems, the data are continuously updated by a large number of users, and the queries that these systems require typically are predefined or targeted at a small subset of records (e.g., List the orders that were backordered today or What products did customer #1234 order on May 12, 2019?).

Another set of application systems is the set designed to support decision making, such as *decision support systems (DSS), management information systems (MIS), executive information systems (EIS),* and *expert systems (ES).* These decision-making support systems are built to support users who need to examine large amounts of read-only historical data. The questions that they ask are often ad hoc, and include hundreds or thousands of records at a time (e.g., List all customers in the West region who purchased a product costing more than $500 at least three times, or What products had increased sales in the summer months that have not been classified as summer merchandise?).

Transaction-processing systems and DSSs thus have very different data storage needs. Transaction-processing systems need data storage formats that are tuned for a lot of data updates and fast retrieval of predefined, specific questions. Files, relational databases, object-relational databases, and object-oriented databases can all support these kinds of requirements. By contrast, systems to support decision making are usually only reading data (not updating it), often in ad hoc ways. The best choices for these systems usually are RDBMSs because these formats can be configured specially for needs that may be unclear and less apt to change the data. However, depending on the type of data needed to support the decision-making application, RDBMSs may not be appropriate. In that case, ORDBMS, OODBMS, a NoSQL data store, or some combination of object persistence formats may be the better solution.

Existing Storage Formats The storage format should be selected primarily on the basis of the kind of data and application system being developed. However, project teams should consider the existing storage formats in the organization when making design decisions. In this way, they can better understand the technical skills that already exist and how steep the learning curve will be when the storage format is adopted. For example, a company that is familiar with RDBMS will have little problem adopting a relational database for the project, whereas an OODBMS or a NoSQL data store might require substantial developer training.

Future Needs Not only should a project team consider the storage technology within the company, but it should also be aware of current trends and technologies that are being used by other organizations. A large number of installations of a specific type of storage format suggest that skills and products are available to support the format. Therefore, the selection of that format is safe. For example, it would probably be easier and less expensive to find RDBMS expertise when implementing a system than to find help with an OODBMS or a NoSQL data store.

Other Miscellaneous Criteria Other criteria that should be considered include cost, licensing issues, concurrency control, ease of use, security and access controls, version management, storage management, lock management, query management, language bindings, and APIs. We also should consider performance issues, such as cache management, insertion, deletion, retrieval, and updating of complex objects. Finally, the level of support for object orientation (such as objects, single inheritance, multiple inheritance, polymorphism, encapsulation and information hiding, methods, multivalued attributes, and repeating groups) is critical.

APPROACHES TO DATA DISTRIBUTION

Given the complexity of the business environment today, distributing data over a set of machines located in different geographical locations is a practical necessity. There are many different approaches to distributing data. Virtually all object persistence formats described above can be distributed. In this section, we overview some of issues that a data distribution approach must address.

First, *replicate* data over every data node in the network. This approach increases the fault tolerance of the data, and it decreases the data retrieval speed. However, given that there are multiple copies of the data, creating, updating, and deleting data is much slower. Furthermore, while the data is being updated, the different copies will have different values. Consequently, policies that address the required level of consistency must be created and enforced to address these potential anomalies.

Second, *partition data* in such a way that only a single copy of the data exists. In this case, the primary decision is to determine where each partition should be stored. Typically, the location of the data is determined based on the volume of activities that will be using the data. That is, you place the data closest to the activities in the network. Overall, as with the replicated approach, this approach can decrease the retrieval speed while not raising the issues with updating the data. However, given that there is only a single copy of the data, fault tolerance is only increased between the different partitions.

Third, data can be partially replicated and partitioned. This approach is a compromise between the replicated and partitioned approaches. In this case, some of the data is replicated across different partitions. This allows the fault tolerance of the replicated data to be increased and the retrieval speed of the data to be decreased. However, the issues with consistency of data values with the replicated data still must be addressed.

Fourth, with data distribution, *concurrency controls* become even more important. Depending on the distribution approach, these controls may have to be enforced across multiple data nodes in the network.

Fifth, depending on the data distribution approached used, *query optimization* can be more challenging than typical query optimization. For example, with the replicated approach, a typical query optimization method would work. With the partitioned approach, the query optimization method needs to consider the location of the data being queried. Finally, with the partially replicated and partitioned approach, the query optimization approach needs to take into consideration what is the "closest" location of the data being queried.

Sixth, there are many tools that can be used to support data distribution. For example, a distributed file system such as Hadoop or distributed NoSQL databases such as Cassandra, MongoDB, and Azure Cosmos DB. Each of these tools have their own advantages and disadvantages in supporting data distribution. However, coverage of these tools is beyond the scope of this book.

Finally, the distribution of the data is fully dependent on the architecture of the underlying network. For example, peer-to-peer networks, client-server networks, and server-based networks. We describe the different network architectures in Chapter 10.

MAPPING PROBLEM DOMAIN OBJECTS TO OBJECT PERSISTENCE FORMATS

There are many different formats from which to choose to support object persistence. Each of the formats can have some conversion requirements. Regardless of the object persistence format chosen, we suggest supporting primary keys and foreign keys by adding them to the problem domain classes at this point. However, this does imply that some additional processing will be required. The developer must set the value for the foreign key when adding the relationship to an object.

From a practical perspective, mapping to different file formats is essentially the same approach as used in mapping to a RDBMS format. Consequently, we do not present a set of separate rules. Also, given that there are multiple types of NoSQL data stores, when it comes to mapping an object-oriented design to a NoSQL data store, the approach depends on the type of datastore. For example:

- in a key-value data store (e.g., Redis or DynamoDB), you can map each instance of a class to a key and have the attributes serialized as a value,
- in a document store (e.g., MongoDB or CouchDB), each instance of a class can be represented as a document and the attributes map to fields in the document, and
- in a columnar data store (e.g., Cassandra), the mapping is very similar to mapping to a RDBMS format.
- in a graph database (e.g., Neo4J), each node is typically an instance of a class and its properties are class attributes.

Furthermore, given that there are language specific (C++, Java, Python, etc.) data mappers for the different NoSQL vendors, we do not go into any further detail here in this textbook.

We also recommend that data management functionality specifics, such as retrieval and updating of data from the object storage, be included only in classes contained in the data management layer. This will ensure that the data management classes are dependent on the problem domain classes and not vice versa. This allows the design of problem domain classes to be independent of any specific object persistence environment, thus increasing their portability and their potential for reuse. Like our previous recommendation, this also implies additional processing.

Mapping Problem Domain Objects to an OODBMS Format

If we support object persistence with an OODBMS, the mappings between the problem domain objects and the OODBMS tend to be fairly straightforward. As a starting point, we suggest that each concrete problem domain class should have a corresponding object persistence class in the OODBMS. There will also be a data access and manipulation (DAM) class (described later in this chapter) that contains the functionality required to manage the interaction between the object persistence class and the problem domain layer. For example, using the appointment system example from the previous chapters, the Patient class is associated with an OODBMS class (see Figure 8-5). The Patient class essentially will be unchanged from analysis. The Patient-OODBMS class will be a new class that is dependent on the Patient class, whereas the Patient-DAM class will be a new class that depends on both the Patient class and the Patient-OODBMS class. The Patient-DAM class must be able to read from and write to the OODBMS. Otherwise, it will not be able to store and retrieve instances of the Patient class. Even though this does add overhead to the installation of the system, it allows the problem domain class to be independent of the OODBMS being used. If at a later time another OODBMS or object persistence format is adopted, only the DAM classes will have to be modified. This approach increases both the portability and the potential for reuse of the problem domain classes.

Even though we are implementing the DAM layer using an OODBMS, a mapping from the problem domain layer to the OODBMS classes in the data access and management layer may be required. If multiple inheritance is used in the problem domain but not supported by the OODBMS, then the multiple inheritance must be factored out of the OODBMS classes. For each case of multiple inheritance (i.e., more than one superclass),

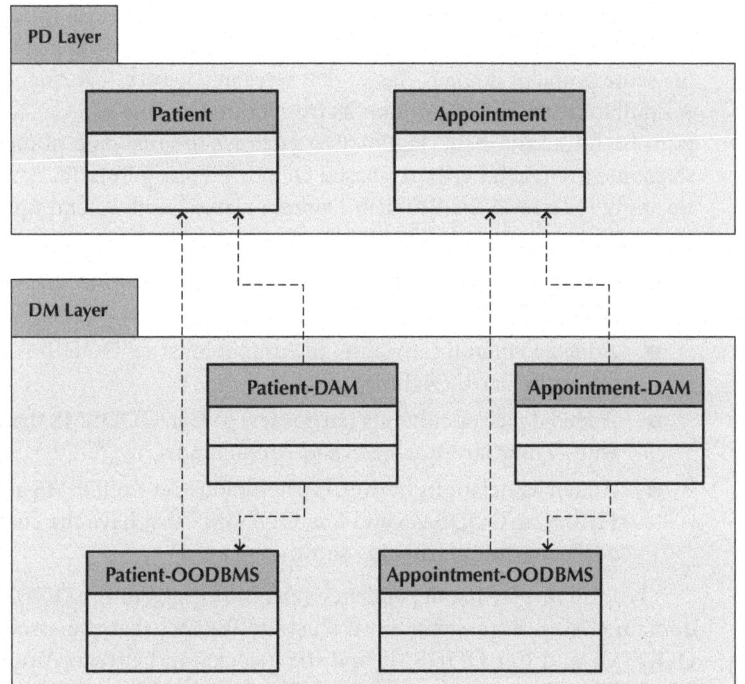

FIGURE 8-5
Appointment System
Problem-Domain and
DM Layers

the following rules can be used to factor out the multiple inheritance effects in the design of the OODBMS classes.[8]

> **Rule 1a:** Add a column(s) to the OODBMS class(es) that represents the subclass(es) that will contain an Object ID of the instance stored in the OODBMS class that represents the "additional" superclass(es). This is similar in concept to a foreign key in an RDBMS. The multiplicity of this new association from the subclass to the "superclass" should be 1..1. Add a column(s) to the OODBMS class(es) that represents the superclass(es) that will contain an Object ID of the instance stored in the OODBMS class that represents the subclass(es). If the superclasses are concrete, that is, they can be instantiated themselves, then the multiplicity from the superclass to the subclass is 0..1, otherwise, it is 1..1. An exclusive-or (XOR) constraint must be added between the associations. Do this for each "additional" superclass.

or

> **Rule 1b:** Flatten the inheritance hierarchy of the OODBMS classes by copying the attributes and methods of the additional OODBMS superclass(es) down to all of the OODBMS subclasses and remove the additional superclass from the design.[9]

---

[8] The rules presented in this section are based on material in Ali Bahrami, *Object-Oriented Systems Development Using the Unified Modeling Language* (New York: McGraw-Hill, 1999); Michael Blaha and William Premerlani, *Object-Oriented Modeling and Design for Database Applications* (Upper Saddle River, NJ: Prentice Hall, 1998); Akmal B. Chaudri and Roberto Zicari, *Succeeding with Object Databases: A Practical Look at Today's Implementations with Java and XML* (New York:Wiley, 2001); Peter Coad and Edward Yourdon, *Object-Oriented Design* (Upper Saddle River, NJ: Yourdon Press, 1991); Paul R. Read, Jr., *Developing Applications with Java and UML* (Boston: Addison-Wesley, 2002).

[9] It is also a good idea to document this modification in the design so that in the future, modifications to the design can be easily maintained.

These multiple inheritance rules are very similar to those described in Chapter 7. Figure 8-6 demonstrates the application of these rules. The right side of the figure portrays the same problem domain classes that were in Chapter 7: Airplane, Car, Boat, FlyingCar, and AmphibiousCar. FlyingCar inherits from both Airplane and Car, and AmphibiousCar inherits from both Car and Boat. Figure 8-6a portrays the mapping of multiple inheritance relationships into a single inheritance-based OODBMS using Rule 1a. Assuming that Car is concrete, we apply Rule 1a to the Problem Domain classes, and we end up with the OODBMS classes on the left side of Part a, where we have:

- Added a column (attribute) to FlyingCar-OODBMS that represents an association with Car-OODBMS;
- Added a column (attribute) to AmphibiousCar-OODBMS that represents an association with Car-OODBMS;
- Added a pair of columns (attributes) to Car-OODBMS that represents an association with FlyingCar-OODBMS and AmphibiousCar-OODBMS and for completeness sake;
- Added associations between AmphibiousCar-OODBMS and Car-OODBMS and FlyingCar-OODBMS and Car-OODBMS that have the correct multiplicities and the XOR constraint explicitly shown.

We also display the dependency relationships from the OODBMS classes to the problem domain classes. Furthermore, we illustrate the fact that the association between FlyingCar-OODBMS and Car-OODBMS and the association between AmphibiousCar-OODBMS and Car-OODBMS are based on the original factored-out inheritance relationships in the problem domain classes by showing dependency relationships from the associations to the inheritance relationships.

On the other hand, if we apply Rule 1b to map the Problem Domain classes to a single inheritance-based OODBMS, we end up with the mapping in Figure 8-6b, where all the attributes of Car have been copied into the FlyingCar-OODBMS and AmphibiousCar-OODBMS classes. In this latter case, you may have to deal with the effects of inheritance conflicts (see Chapter 1 Appendix).

The advantage of Rule 1a is that all problem domain classes identified during analysis are preserved in the database. This allows maximum flexibility of maintenance of the design of the data management layer. However, Rule 1a increases the amount of message passing required in the system, and it has added processing requirements involving the XOR constraint, thus reducing the overall efficiency of the design. Our recommendation is to limit Rule 1a to be applied only when dealing with "extra" superclasses that are concrete because they have an independent existence in the problem domain. Use Rule 1b when they are abstract because they do not have an independent existence from the subclass.

In either case, additional processing will be required. In the first case, cascading of deletes will work, not only from the individual object to all its elements but also from the superclass instances to all the subclass instances. In the second case, there will be a lot of copying and pasting of the structure of the superclass to the subclasses. In the case that a modification of the structure of the superclass is required, the modification must be cascaded to all the subclasses. However, multiple inheritance is rare in most business problems. In most situations, the preceding rules will never be necessary.

When instantiating problem domain objects from OODBMS objects, additional processing will be required also. The additional processing will be in the retrieval of the OODBMS objects and taking their elements to create a problem domain object. Also, when storing the problem domain object, the conversion to a set of OODBMS objects is required. Basically speaking, any time that an interaction takes place between the OODBMS and the system, if

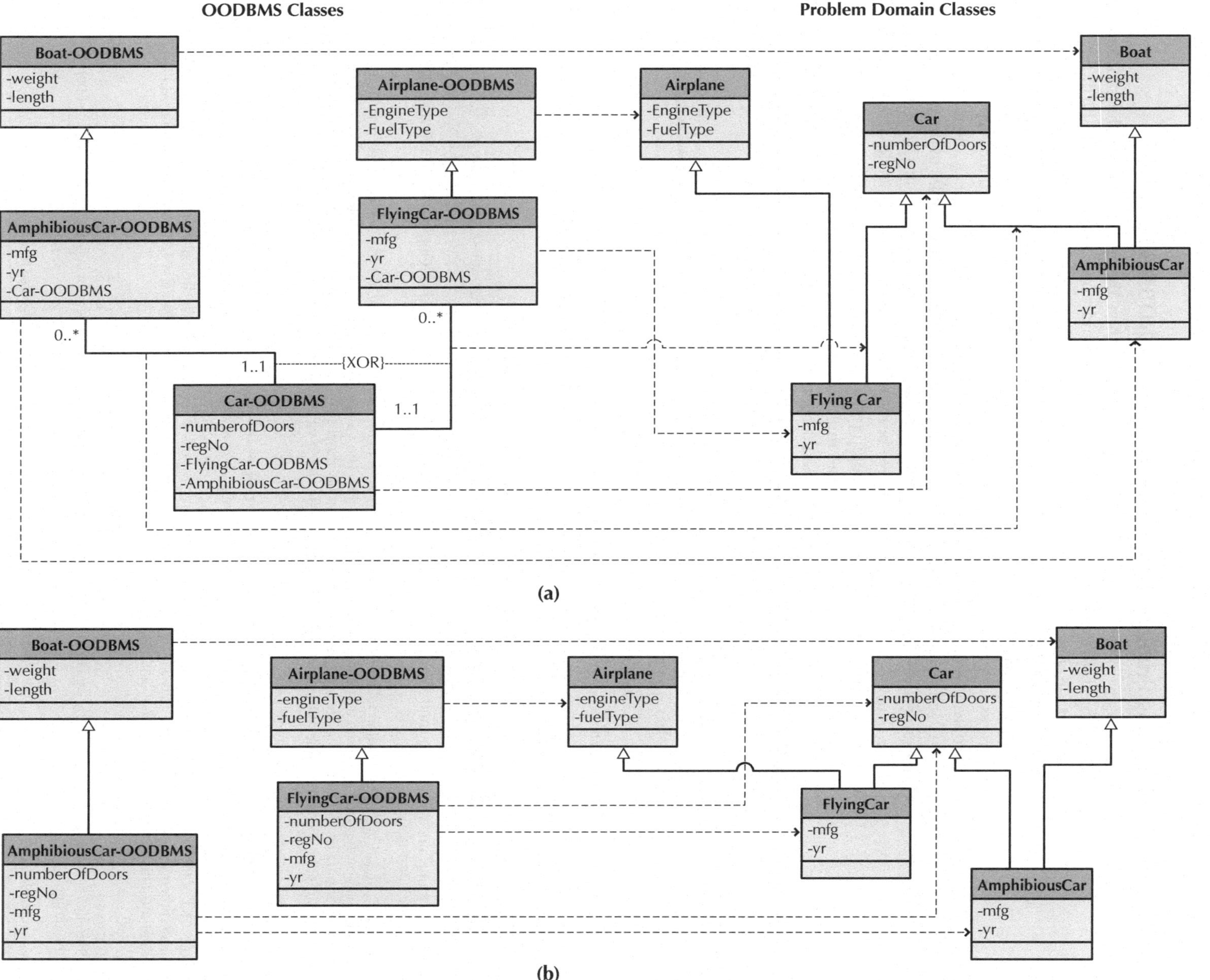

FIGURE 8-6 Mapping Problem Domain Objects to a Single Inheritance-Based OODBMS

multiple inheritance is involved and the OODBMS supports only single inheritance, a conversion between the two formats will be required.

Mapping Problem Domain Objects to an ORDBMS Format

If we support object persistence with an ORDBMS, then the mapping from the problem domain objects to the data management objects is much more involved. Depending on the level of support for object orientation, different mapping rules are necessary. For our purposes, we assume that the ORDBMS supports Object IDs, multivalued attributes, and stored procedures. However, we assume that the ORDBMS does not provide any support for inheritance. Based on these assumptions, Figure 8-7 lists a set of rules that can be used to design the mapping from the Problem Domain objects to the tables of the ORDBMS-based data management layer.

First, all concrete Problem Domain classes must be mapped to the tables in the ORDBMS. For example, in Figure 8-8 the Patient class has been mapped to Patient-ORDBMS table. Notice that the Participant class has also been mapped to an ORDBMS table. Even though the Participant class is abstract, this mapping was done because in the complete class diagram (see Figure 6-6), the Participant class had multiple direct subclasses (Employee and Patient).

Second, single-valued attributes should be mapped to columns in the ORDBMS tables. Again, referring to Figure 8-8, we see that the amount attribute of the Patient class has been included in the Patient Table class.

Rule 1: Map all concrete Problem Domain classes to the ORDBMS tables. Also, if an abstract problem domain class has multiple direct subclasses, map the abstract class to an ORDBMS table.

Rule 2: Map single-valued attributes to columns of the ORDBMS tables.

Rule 3: Map methods and derived attributes to stored procedures or to program modules.

Rule 4: Map single-valued aggregation and association relationships to a column that can store an Object ID. Do this for both sides of the relationship.

Rule 5: Map multivalued attributes to a column that can contain a set of values.

Rule 6: Map repeating groups of attributes to a new table and create a one-to-many association from the original table to the new one.

Rule 7: Map multivalued aggregation and association relationships to a column that can store a set of Object IDs. Do this for both sides of the relationship.

Rule 8: For aggregation and association relationships of mixed type (one-to-many or many-to-one), on the single-valued side (1..1 or 0..1) of the relationship, add a column that can store a set of Object IDs. The values contained in this new column will be the Object IDs from the instances of the class on the multivalued side. On the multivalued side (1..,* or 0..*), add a column that can store a single Object ID that will contain the value of the instance of the class on the single-valued side.

For generalization/inheritance relationships:

Rule 9a: Add a column(s) to the table(s) that represents the subclass(es) that will contain an Object ID of the instance stored in the table that represents the superclass. This is similar in concept to a foreign key in an RDBMS. The multiplicity of this new association from the subclass to the "superclass" should be 1..1. Add a column(s) to the table(s) that represents the superclass(es) that will contain an Object ID of the instance stored in the table that represents the subclass(es). If the superclasses are concrete, that is, they can be instantiated themselves, then the multiplicity from the superclass to the subclass is 0..1, otherwise, it is 1..1. An exclusive-or (XOR) constraint must be added between the associations. Do this for each superclass.

or

Rule 9b: Flatten the inheritance hierarchy by copying the superclass attributes down to all of the subclasses and remove the superclass from the design.*

* It is also a good idea to document this modification in the design so that in the future, modifications to the design can be maintained easily.

FIGURE 8-7 Schema for Mapping Problem Domain Objects to ORDBMS

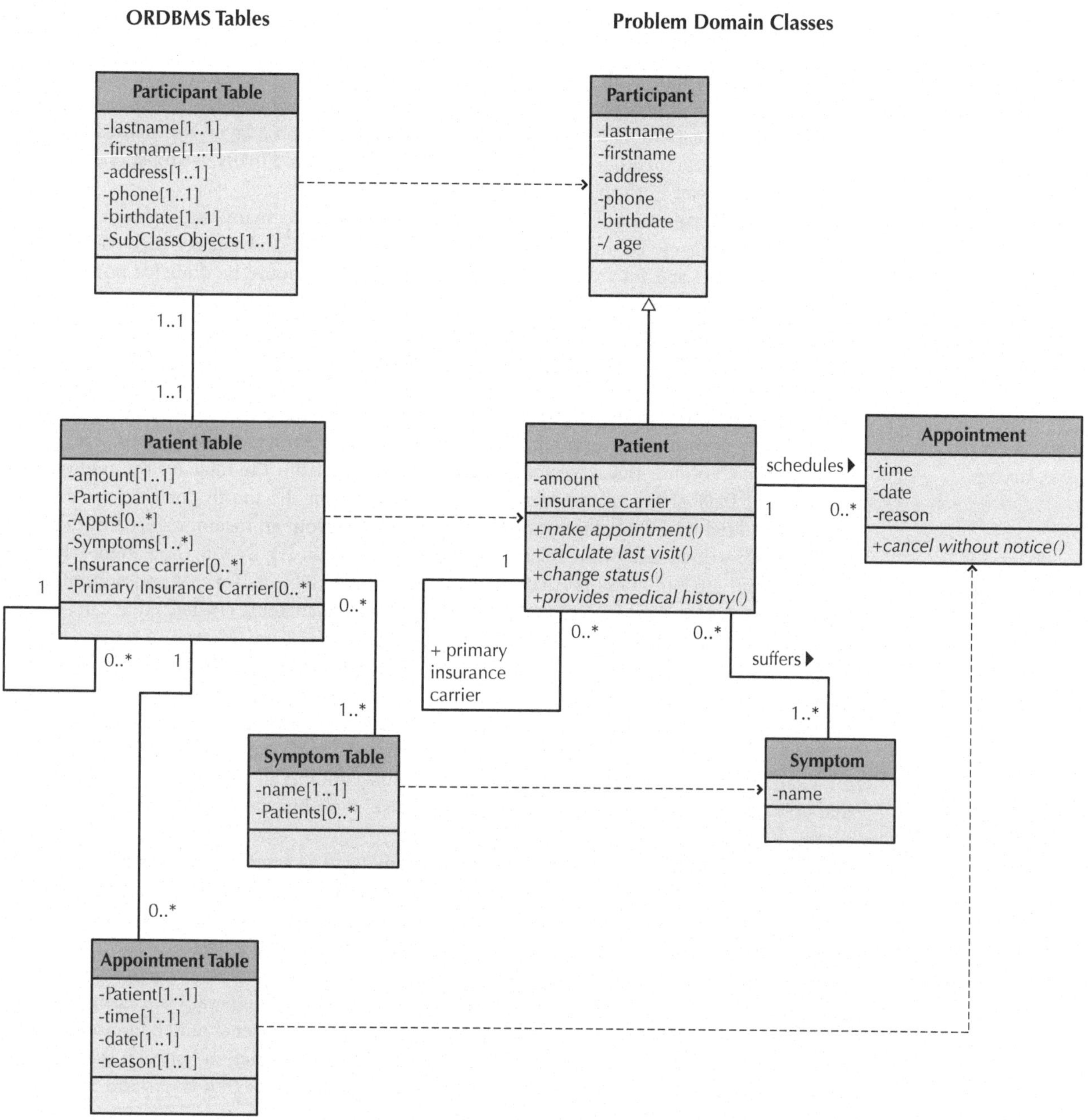

FIGURE 8-8 Example of Mapping Problem Domain Objects to ORDBMS Schema

Third, depending on the level of support of stored procedures, the methods and derived attributes should be mapped either to stored procedures or program modules.

Fourth, single-valued (one-to-one) aggregation and association relationships should be mapped to a column that can store an Object ID. This should be done for both sides of the relationship.

Fifth, multivalued attributes should be mapped to columns that can contain a set of values. For example, in Figure 8-8, the insurance carrier attribute in the Patient class may contain multiple values because a patient may have more than one insurance carrier. Thus, in the Patient table, a multiplicity has been added to the insurance carrier attribute to portray this fact.

The sixth mapping rule addresses repeating groups of attributes in a problem domain object. In this case, the repeating group of attributes should be used to create a new table in the ORDBMS. It can imply a missing class in the problem domain layer. Normally, when a set of attributes repeats together as a group, it implies a new class. Finally, we must create a one-to-many association from the original table to the new one.

The seventh rule supports mapping multivalued (many-to-many) aggregation and association relationships to columns that can store a set of Object IDs. Basically, this is a combination of the fourth and fifth rules. Like the fourth rule, this should be done for both sides of the relationships. For example, in Figure 8-8, the Symptom table has a multivalued attribute (Patients) that can contain multiple Object IDs to Patient Table objects, and Patient table has a multivalued attribute (Symptoms) that can contain multiple Object IDs to Symptom Table objects.

The eighth rule combines the intentions of Rules 4 and 7. In this case, the rule maps one-to-many and many-to-one relationships. On the single-valued side (1..1 or 0..1) of the relationship, a column that can store a set of Object IDs from the table on the multivalued side (1..* or 0..*) of the relationship should be added. On the multivalued side, a column should be added to the table that can store an Object ID from an instance stored in the table on the single-valued side of the relationship. For example, in Figure 8-8, the Patient table has a multivalued attribute (Appts) that can contain multiple Object IDs to Appointment Table objects, whereas the Appointment table has a single-valued attribute (Patient) that can contain an Object ID to a Patient Table object.

The ninth, and final, rule deals with the lack of support for generalization and inheritance. In this case, there are two different approaches. These approaches are virtually identical to the rules described with the preceding OODBMS object persistence formats. For example, in Figure 8-8, the Patient table contains an attribute (Participant) that can contain an Object ID for a Participant Table object, and the Participant table contains an attribute (SubClassObjects) that contains an Object ID for an object, in this case, stored in the Patient table. In the other case, the inheritance hierarchy is flattened.

Of course, additional processing is required any time an interaction takes place between the database and the system. Every time an object must be created or retrieved from the database, updated, or deleted, the ORDBMS object(s) must be converted to the problem domain object, or vice versa. The only other choice is to modify the problem domain objects. However, such a modification can cause problems between the problem domain layer and the application architecture and human–computer interface layers. Generally speaking, the cost of conversion between the ORDBMS and the problem domain layer should be more than offset by the savings in development time associated with the interaction between the problem domain and application architecture and human–computer interaction layers and the ease of maintenance of a semantically clean problem domain layer.

Mapping Problem Domain Objects to a RDBMS Format

If we support object persistence with an RDBMS, then the mapping from the problem domain objects to the RDBMS tables is similar to the mapping to an ORDBMS. However, the assumptions made for an ORDBMS are no longer valid. Figure 8-9 lists a set of rules that can be used to design the mapping from the problem domain objects to the RDBMS-based data management layer tables.

The first four rules are basically the same set of rules used to map problem domain objects to ORDBMS-based data management objects. First, all concrete problem domain classes must be mapped to tables in the RDBMS. Second, single-valued attributes should be mapped to

Rule 1: Map all concrete-problem domain classes to the RDBMS tables. Also, if an abstract Problem Domain class has multiple direct subclasses, map the abstract class to a RDBMS table.

Rule 2: Map single-valued attributes to columns of the tables.

Rule 3: Map methods to stored procedures or to program modules.

Rule 4: Map single-valued aggregation and association relationships to a column that can store the key of the related table, i.e., add a foreign key to the table. Do this for both sides of the relationship.

Rule 5: Map multivalued attributes and repeating groups to new tables and create a one-to-many association from the original table to the new ones.

Rule 6: Map multivalued aggregation and association relationships to a new associative table that relates the two original tables together. Copy the primary key from both original tables to the new associative table, i.e., add foreign keys to the table.

Rule 7: For aggregation and association relationships of mixed type, copy the primary key from the single-valued side (1..1 or 0..1) of the relationship to a new column in the table on the multivalued side (1..* or 0..*) of the relationship that can store the key of the related table, i.e., add a foreign key to the table on the multivalued side of the relationship.

For generalization/inheritance relationships:

Rule 8a: Ensure that the primary key of the subclass instance is the same as the primary key of the superclass. The multiplicity of this new association from the subclass to the "superclass" should be 1..1. If the superclasses are concrete, that is, they can be instantiated themselves, then the multiplicity from the superclass to the subclass is 0..1, otherwise, it is 1..1. Furthermore, an exclusive-or (XOR) constraint must be added between the associations. Do this for each superclass.

or

Rule 8b: Flatten the inheritance hierarchy by copying the superclass attributes down to all of the subclasses and remove the superclass from the design.*

* It is also a good idea to document this modification in the design so that in the future, modifications to the design can be maintained easily.

FIGURE 8-9   Schema for Mapping Problem Domain Objects to RDBMS

columns in the RDBMS table. Third, methods should be mapped to either stored procedures or program modules, depending on the complexity of the method. Fourth, single-valued (one-to-one) aggregation and association relationships are mapped to columns that can store the foreign keys of the related tables. This should be done for both sides of the relationship. For example, in Figure 8-10, we needed to include tables in the RDBMS for the Participant, Patient, Symptom, and Appointment classes.

The fifth rule addresses multivalued attributes and repeating groups of attributes in a problem domain object. In these cases, the attributes should be used to create new tables in the RDBMS. As in the ORDBMS mappings, repeating groups of attributes can imply missing classes in the Problem Domain layer. In that case, a new problem domain class may be required. Finally, we should create a one-to-many or zero-to-many association from the original table to the new one. For example, in Figure 8-10, we needed to create a new table for insurance carrier because it was possible for a patient to have more than one insurance carrier.

The sixth rule supports mapping multivalued (many-to-many) aggregation and association relationships to a new table that relates the two original tables. In this case, the new table should contain foreign keys back to the original tables. For example, in Figure 8-10, we needed to create a new table that represents the suffer association between the Patient and Symptom problem domain classes.

The seventh rule addresses one-to-many and many-to-one relationships. With these types of relationships, the multivalued side (0..* or 1..*) should be mapped to a column in its table that can store a foreign key back to the single-valued side (0..1 or 1..1). It is possible that we have already taken care of this situation because we earlier recommended inclusion of both primary and foreign key attributes in the problem domain classes. In the case of Figure 8-10,

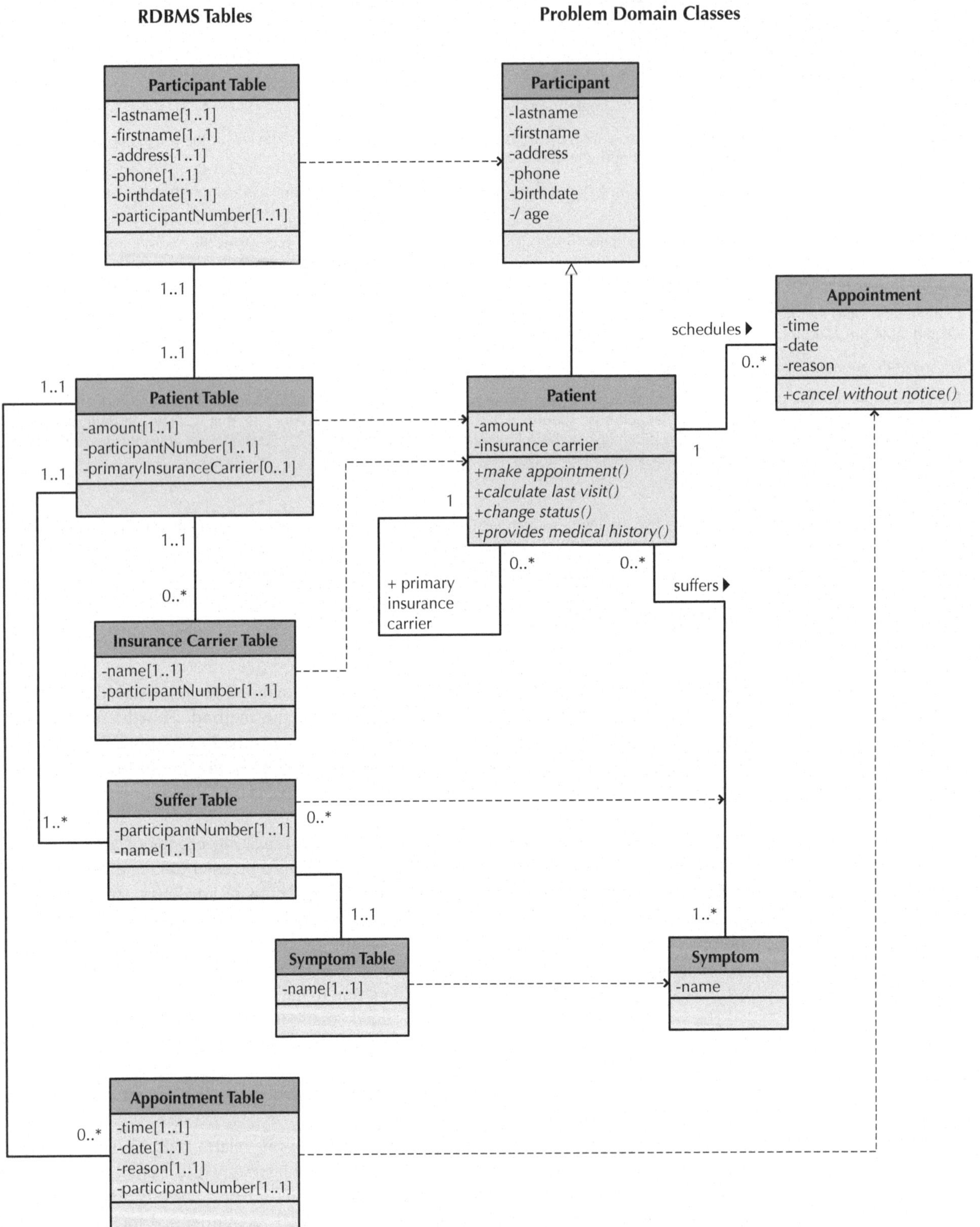

FIGURE 8-10 Example of Mapping Problem Domain Objects to RDBMS Schema

we had already added the primary key from the Patient class to the Appointment class as a foreign key (see participantNumber). However, in the case of the reflexive relationship, primary insurance carrier, associated with the Patient class, we need to add a new attribute (primaryInsuranceCarrier) to be able to store the relationship.

The eighth, and final, rule deals with the lack of support for generalization and inheritance. As in the case of an ORDBMS, there are two different approaches. These approaches are virtually identical to the rules described with OODBMS and ORDBMS object persistence formats given earlier. The first approach is to add a column to each table that represents a subclass for each of the concrete superclasses of the subclass. Essentially, this ensures that the primary key of the subclass is the same as the primary key for the superclass. If we had previously added the primary and foreign keys to the problem domain objects, as we recommended, then we do not have to do anything else. The primary keys of the tables will be used to rejoin the instances stored in the tables that represent each of the pieces of the problem domain object. Conversely, the inheritance hierarchy can be flattened and the rules (Rules 1 through 7) can be reapplied.

As in the case of the ORDBMS approach, additional processing will be required any time that an interaction takes place between the database and the system. Every time an object must be created, retrieved from the database, updated, or deleted, the mapping between the problem domain and the RDBMS must be used to convert between the two different formats. In this case, a great deal of additional processing will be required.

DESIGNING DATA ACCESS AND MANIPULATION CLASSES

The final step in developing the data management layer is to design the *data access and manipulation classes* that act as a translator between the object persistence and the problem domain objects. Thus, they should always be capable of at least reading and writing both the object persistence and problem domain objects. As described earlier, the object persistence classes are derived from the concrete problem domain classes, whereas the data access and manipulation classes depend on both the object persistence and problem domain classes.

Depending on the application, a simple rule to follow is that there should be one data access and manipulation class for each concrete problem domain class. In some cases, it might make sense to create data access and manipulation classes associated with the human–computer interaction classes (see Chapter 9). However, this creates a dependency from the data management layer to the human–computer interaction layer. Adding this additional complexity to the design of the system normally is not recommended.

Returning to the ORDBMS solution for the Appointment system example (see Figure 8-8), we see that we have four problem domain classes and four ORDBMS tables. Following the previous rule, the DAM classes are rather simple. They have to support only a one-to-one translation between the concrete problem domain classes and the ORDBMS tables (see Figure 8-11). Because the Participant problem domain class is an abstract class, only three data access and manipulation classes are required: Patient-DAM, SymptomDAM, and Appointment-DAM. However, the process to create an instance of the Patient problem domain class can be fairly complicated. The Patient-DAM class might have to be able to retrieve information from all four ORDBMS tables. To accomplish this, the Patient-DAM class retrieves the information from the Patient table. Using the Object-IDs stored in the attribute values associated with the Participant, Appts, and Symptoms attributes, the remaining information required to create an instance of Patient is easily retrieved by the Patient-DAM class.

In the case of using an RDBMS to provide persistence, the data access and manipulation classes tend to become more complex. For example, in the Appointment system, there are still four problem domain classes, but, owing to the limitations of RDBMSs, we have to support six RDBMS tables (see Figure 8-10). The data access and manipulation class for the Appointment

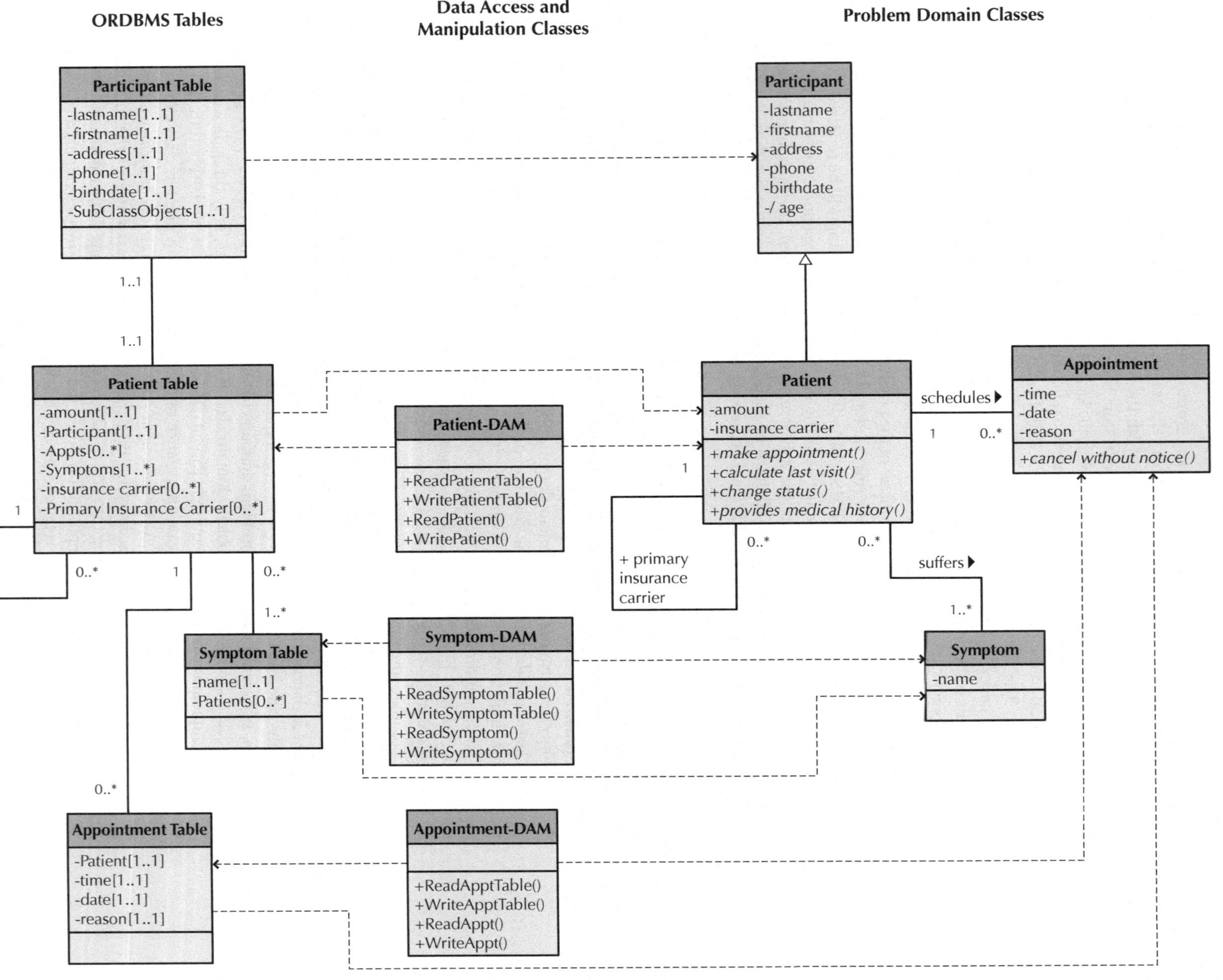

FIGURE 8-11   Managing Problem Domain Objects to ORDBMS Using DAM Classes

problem domain class and the Appointment RDBMS table is no different from those supported for the ORDBMS solution (see Figures 8-11 and 8-12). However, owing to the multivalued attributes and relationships associated with the Patient and Symptom problem domain classes, the mappings to the RDBMS tables were more complicated. Consequently, the number of dependencies from the data access and manipulation classes (Patient-DAM and Symptom-DAM) to the RDBMS tables (Patient table, Insurance Carrier table, Suffer table, and the Symptom table) has increased. Furthermore, because the Patient problem domain class is associated with the other three problem domain classes, the actual retrieval of all information necessary to create an instance of the Patient class could involve joining information from all six

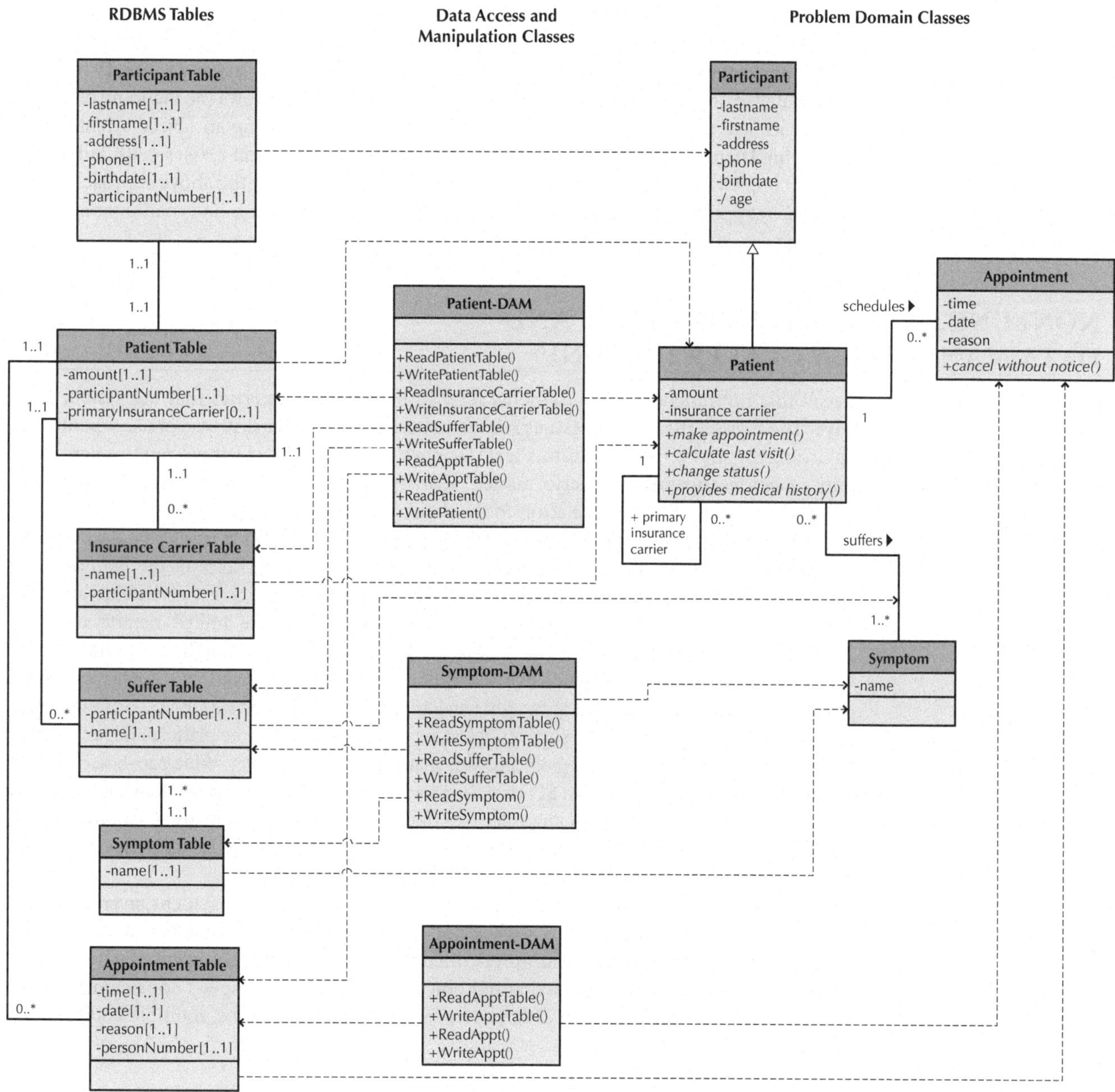

FIGURE 8-12   Mapping Problem Domain Objects to RDBMS Using DAM Classes

RDBMS tables. To accomplish this, the Patient-DAM class must first retrieve information from the Patient table, Insurance Carrier table, Suffer table, and the Appointment table. Because the primary keys of the Patient table and the Participant table are identical, the Patient-DAM class can either directly retrieve the information from the Participant table, or the information can be joined using the participantNumber attributes of the two tables, which act as both primary and foreign keys. Finally, using the information contained in the Suffer table, the information in the Symptom table can also be retrieved. Obviously, the farther we get from the object-oriented problem domain class representation, the more work must be performed. However, as in the case of the ORDBMS example, notice that absolutely no modifications were made to the problem domain classes. Therefore, the data access and manipulation classes again have prevented data management functionality from creeping into the problem domain classes.

One specific approach that has been suggested to support the implementation of data access and manipulation classes is to use an object-relational mapping library such as Hibernate.[10] Hibernate, developed within the JBoss community, allows the mapping of objects written in Java that are to be stored in an RDBMS. Instead of using an object-oriented programming language to implement the data access and manipulation classes, with Hibernate, they are implemented in XML files that contain the mapping. As in the above approach, modeling the mapping in an XML file prevents the details on data access and manipulation from sneaking into the problem domain representation.

NONFUNCTIONAL REQUIREMENTS AND DATA MANAGEMENT LAYER DESIGN[11]

Recall that nonfunctional requirements refer to behavioral properties that the system must have. These properties include issues related to performance, security, ease of use, operational environment, and reliability. In this text, we have grouped nonfunctional requirements into four categories: operational, performance, security, and cultural and political requirements. We describe each of these in relation to the data management layer.

The *operational requirements* for the data management layer include issues that deal with the technology being used to support object persistence. However, the choice of the *hardware and operating system* limits the choice of the technology and format of the object persistence available. This is especially true when you consider mobile computing. Given the limited memory and storage available on these devices, the choices to support object persistence are limited. One possible choice to support object persistence that works both on Google's Android and Apple's iOS-based platforms is SQLite. SQLite is a lightweight version of SQL that supports RDBMS. However, there are many different approaches to support object persistence that are more platform dependent; for example, Android supports storing objects with shared preferences (a key-value pair-based NoSQL approach), internal storage, on an SD card, in a local cache, or on a remote system. This, in turn, determines which set of the mapping rules described earlier will have to be used. Another operational requirement could be the ability to import and export data using XML. Again, this could limit the object stores under consideration.

The primary *performance requirements* that affect the data management layer are speed and capacity. As described before, depending on the anticipated—and, afterwards, actual—usage patterns of the objects being stored, different indexing and caching approaches may be necessary. When considering distributing objects over a network, speed considerations can cause objects to be replicated on different nodes in the network. Thus, multiple copies of the

---

[10] For more information on Hibernate, see www.hibernate.org.

[11] Because the vast majority of nonfunctional requirements affect the application architecture layer, we provide additional details in Chapter 10.

same object may be stored in different locations on the network. This raises the issue of update anomalies. Depending on the application being built, NoSQL data stores that support an eventually consistent update model may be appropriate. Also, depending on the estimated size and growth of the system, different DBMSs may need to be considered. An additional requirement that can affect the design of the data management layer deals with the availability of the objects being stored. It might make sense to limit the availability to different objects based on the time of day. For example, one class of users may be allowed to access a set of objects only from 8 to 12 in the morning and a second set of users may be able to access them only from 1 to 5 in the afternoon. Through the DBMS, these types of restrictions could be set.

The *security requirements* deal primarily with access controls, encryption, and backup. Through a modern DBMS, different types of access can be set (e.g., Create, Read, Update, or Delete) granting access only to users (or class of users) who have been authorized. Furthermore, *access control* can be set to guarantee that only users with "administrator" privileges are allowed to modify the object storage schema or access controls.[12] Much of the required information to support access controls for this layer is contained in the CRUDE matrices and CRC cards used during analysis. For example, the CRC cards refer to the associated use cases which contain the list of roles (primary actors and stakeholders) that should have access to the data stored in the DBMS. Furthermore, the more detailed version of the CRUDE matrix (see footnote 8 in Chapter 5), allows the specific type of access that should be granted to each role. Encryption requirements on this layer deal with whether the object should be stored in an encrypted format or not. Even though encrypted objects are more secure than unencrypted objects, the process of encrypting and decrypting the objects will slow down the system. Depending on the application architecture being used, the cost of encryption may be negligible. For example, if we plan on encrypting the objects before transmitting them over a network, there may be no additional cost of storing them in the encrypted format. Backup requirements deal with ensuring that the objects are routinely copied and stored in case the object store becomes corrupted or unusable. Having a backup copy made on a periodic basis and storing the updates that have occurred since the last backup copy was made ensure that the updates are not lost, and the object store can be reconstituted by running the copies of the updates against the backup copy to create a new current copy.

There are a few *political and cultural requirements* that can affect the data management layer. These include issues related to the expected number of characters that should be allocated for a data field, the format of a data field, and the considerations of any applicable laws. For example, how many characters should be allocated for a last name field that is part of an Employee object, what format should a date be stored, or where will the data be physically located—different parts of the world have different laws regarding the protection of data. Finally, there could be a corporate IT bias toward different hardware and software platforms. If so, this could limit the type of object store available.

VERIFYING AND VALIDATING THE DATA MANAGEMENT LAYER

Like the models on the problem domain layer, the specifications for the data management layer need to be verified and validated. By now, it might seem a little heavy handed to insist on more verifying and validating. However, depending on the object persistence chosen, the changes that have been applied to the design of the evolving system may be very substantial. Consequently, it is crucial to thoroughly test the fidelity of the design again before the system

---

[12] We cover access controls in more detail in Chapter 10.

is implemented. Without thoroughly testing the data management layer, there is no guarantee that an efficient and effective system will be implemented. Verifying and validating the design of the data management layer fall into three basic groups.

First, we recommend verifying and validating any changes made to the problem domain by performing walkthroughs of the modified functional, structural, and behavioral models. Furthermore, all of the models must be consistent and balanced. And, if any problem domain class was modified that was associated with a use-case scenario, that scenario should be tested again through role-playing.

Second, the dependency of the object persistence instances on the problem domain must be enforced. For example, all invariants associated with a problem domain class need to be verified and validated. For example, if a name data field is specified in a problem domain class as being thirty-five characters long and as being a required field, then similar constraints must be enforced when the field is stored.

Third, the design of the data access and manipulation classes need to be tested to ensure that they are dependent on the problem domain classes and the object persistence format, not the other way around. For example, in Figure 8-11, we see that the Patient-DAM class is dependent on both the Patient problem domain class and the Patient table.

Once the system has been implemented, testing of the data management layer becomes even more important. One issue that should be addressed is the testing of the nonfunctional requirements. In this case, tests must be designed and performed for each of the nonfunctional requirements. For example, for the performance requirements, load testing must be performed to identify possible performance bottlenecks in the database (see Chapter 7).

APPLYING THE CHAPTER CONCEPTS

Library Management System (LMS) Example In the previous installation of the LMS example, the John and Alan was tasked to move on to implement and create the relevant tests for the problem domain layer. At this point, the team also started working on the detailed design of the data management, human–computer interaction, and the application architecture layers. Even though the team still coordinated everything, they developed the design for these three layers somewhat independently of each other. In this installation of the LMS example, we only deal with the data management layer. Consequently, we drop in to see what Jane is up to.

The first thing that Jane did was to schedule another meeting with Joe to discuss the various options to enable the storage of the library's data. During the discussion, Joe informed Jane that the library has been using MySQL with other applications and wondered if it would be a good candidate to use in this case. In this way, their own IT staff could be an asset in developing and maintaining the actual database. Given the design of the classes (see package diagram in Figure 7-7), Jane assured Joe that MySQL, being a RDBMS, would work for the structured data in the design. However, Jane wasn't quite sure about the downloadable resources that the library supported. After Jane and Joe talked about them, it turned out that all downloadable resources were "stored" outside of the library. For example, the downloadable journals were based on subscriptions to a database. The same was true for the books, music, and movies. Consequently, to allow the patrons to have access to the downloadable resources, the only additional information that the library needed to keep track of was the location of the resource. Armed with this information and the package diagram, Jane was able to go back to the team and design the RDBMS tables and the DAM classes. Part of

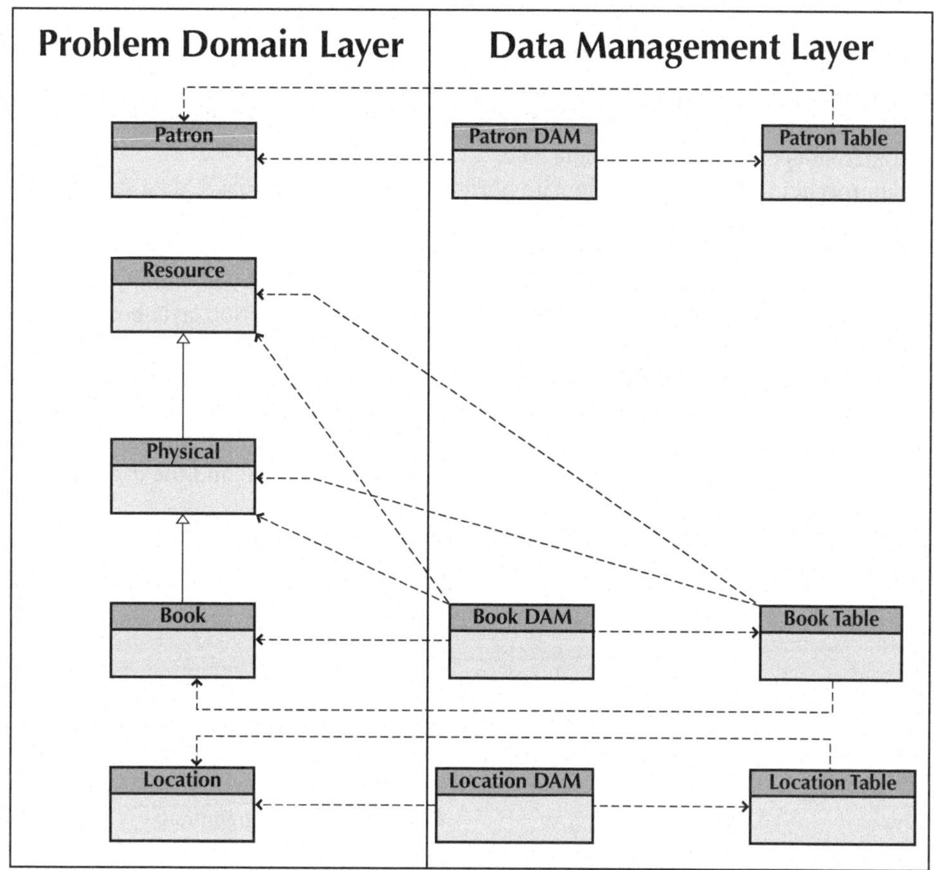

Figure 8-13 LMS Partial Data Management Layer Design

this design is shown in Figure 8-13. We chose to flatten the inheritance hierarchy using Rule 8b (see Figure 8-9) Notice the dependency relationships. All DAM classes are dependent on both the actual object persistence format chosen (RDBMS) and the Problem Domain classes. Also, the object persistence format is based on the Problem Domain classes. All SQL statements are contained in the DAM classes and all attributes are contained in the tables of the RDBMS of the Data Management layer. In the next installation of this example we see how Beth is doing on the design of the Human-Computer Interaction Layer.

Campus Housing Service "Your Turn" Exercise In the previous installation of the Campus Housing Service (CHS) "Your Turn" exercise, you created a class test plan for each class in the problem-domain, you specified a set of invariant tests for one of the classes, and you created a use-case test plan for one of the use cases. In this installation, you should use the mapping rules for a RDBMS to design the data management layer. This should also include the design of the DAM classes. We will return to CHS in the next chapter.

CHAPTER REVIEW

After reading and studying this chapter, you should be able to:

- [ ] Describe the different types of object persistence formats.
- [ ] Select the appropriate object persistence format based on its strengths and weaknesses.
- [ ] Describe the different approaches to distribute data.
- [ ] Describe the approaches to map problem domain objects to the different NoSQL data store formats.
- [ ] Map a set of problem domain objects to an OODBMS format.
- [ ] Map a set of problem domain objects to an ORDBMS format.
- [ ] Map a set of problem domain objects to an RDBMS format.
- [ ] Create a set of data access and manipulation classes that act as a communication layer between the problem domain layer and the actual object persistence used.
- [ ] Describe why the operational and performance nonfunctional requirements of the object persistence format are constrained by decisions made regarding the application architecture layer.
- [ ] Describe how the nonfunctional requirements of the object persistence format may influence the actual design of the data management layer; these include both the object persistence format and the data access and manipulation classes.
- [ ] Understand how to verify and validate both the design of both the object persistence format and the data access and manipulation classes.

KEY TERMS

Access control
Attribute sets
Audit file
Columnar data stores
Concurrency controls
Data access and
    manipulation classes
Data management layer
Database
Database management
    system (DBMS)
Decision support
    systems (DSS)
Document data stores
End-user DBMS
Enterprise DBMS
Executive information
    systems (EIS)
Expert system (ES)

Extent
File
Foreign key
Graph databases
Hardware and operating
    system
History file
Impedance mismatch
Join
Key-value data stores
Linked list
Lookup file
Management information
    system (MIS)
Master file
Multivalued attributes (fields)
NoSQL data stores
Object ID

Object-oriented database
    management system
    (OODBMS)
Object-oriented programming
    language (OOPL)
Object persistence
Object-relational database
    management system
    (ORDBMS)
Operational requirements
Ordered sequential access file
Partition data
Performance requirements
Pointer
Political and cultural
    requirements
Primary key
Query optimization
Random access files

Referential integrity
Relational database
    management sys-
    tem (RDBMS)
Relationship sets
Repeating groups
Replicated data
Security requirements
Sequential access files
Structured query
    language (SQL)
Transaction file
Transaction-
    processing system
Unordered sequential
    access file
Update anomaly

QUESTIONS

1. Describe the steps in object persistence design.
2. How are a file and a database different from each other?
3. What is the difference between an end-user database and an enterprise database? Provide an example of each one.
4. What are the differences between sequential and random access files?
5. Name five types of files and describe the primary purpose of each type.

6. What is the most popular kind of database today? Provide three examples of products that are based on this database technology.

7. What is referential integrity and how is it implemented in an RDBMS?

8. List some of the differences between an ORDBMS and an RDBMS.

9. What are the advantages of using an ORDBMS over an RDBMS?

10. List some of the differences between an ORDBMS and an OODBMS.

11. What are the advantages of using an ORDBMS over an OODBMS?

12. What are the advantages of using an OODBMS over an RDBMS?

13. What are the advantages of using an OODBMS over an ORDBMS?

14. What are the factors in determining the type of object persistence format that should be adopted for a system? Why are these factors so important?

15. Why should you consider the storage formats that already exist in an organization when deciding upon a storage format for a new system?

16. What are the different approaches to distribute data?

17. When implementing the object persistence in an ORDBMS, what types of issues must you address?

18. When implementing the object persistence in an RDBMS, what types of issues must you address?

19. What are some of the nonfunctional requirements that can influence the design of the data management layer?

20. What is the primary purpose of the data access and manipulation classes?

21. Why should the data access and manipulation classes be dependent on the problem domain classes instead of the other way around?

22. Why should the object persistence classes be dependent on the problem domain classes instead of the other way around?

EXERCISES

A. Using the Web or other resources, identify a product that can be classified as an end-user database and a product that can be classified as an enterprise database. How are the products described and marketed? What kinds of applications and users do they support? In what kinds of situations would an organization choose to implement an end-user database over an enterprise database?

B. Visit a commercial website (e.g., Amazon.com). If files were being used to store the data supporting the application, what types of files would be needed? What access type would be required? What data would they contain?

C. Using the Web, review one of the following products. What are the main features and functions of the software? In what companies has the DBMS been implemented, and for what purposes? According to the information that you found, what are three strengths and weaknesses of the product?

1. Relational DBMS

2. Object-relational DBMS

3. Object-oriented DBMS

D. What is the most popular kind of database today? Provide three examples of products that are based on this database technology.

E. What is referential integrity and how is it implemented in an RDBMS?

F. When implementing the object persistence in an RDBMS, what types of issues must you address?

G. Jim Smith's dealership sells Fords, Hondas, and Toyotas. The dealership keeps information about each car manufacturer with whom it deals so that the dealership can get in touch with them easily. The dealership also keeps information about the models of cars that it carries from each manufacturer. It keeps information like list price, the price the dealership paid to obtain the model, and the model name and series (e.g., Honda Civic LX). It also keeps information about all sales that it has made (e.g., it records a buyer's name, the car bought, and the amount paid for the car). To contact the buyers in the future, contact information is also kept (e.g., address and phone number).

1. Create a problem-domain class diagram for this situation.

2. Create a class diagram that shows the mapping of the problem domain classes to a RDBMS for format.

3. Add the DAM classes between the problem-domain classes and the RDBMS classes.

H. For the A Real Estate Inc. problem in Chapter 3 (exercises I, J, and K), Chapter 4 (exercises N and O),

Chapter 5 (exercise D), Chapter 6 (exercise D), and Chapter 7 (exercise A):

1. Create a class diagram that shows the mapping of the problem domain classes to a RDBMS for format.
2. Add the DAM classes between the problem-domain classes and the RDBMS classes.

I. For the A Video Store problem in Chapter 3 (exercises L, M, and N), Chapter 4 (exercises P and Q), Chapter 5 (exercise E), Chapter 6 (exercise E), and Chapter 7 (exercise B):

J. Create a class diagram that shows the mapping of the problem domain classes to a RDBMS for format.

K. Add the DAM classes between the problem-domain classes and the RDBMS classes.

L. For the gym membership problem in Chapter 3 (exercises O, P, and Q), Chapter 4 (exercises R and S), Chapter 5 (exercise F), Chapter 6 (exercise F), and Chapter 7 (exercise C):

1. Create a class diagram that shows the mapping of the problem domain classes to a RDBMS for format.

2. Add the DAM classes between the problem-domain classes and the RDBMS classes.

M. For the Picnics R Us problem in Chapter 3 (exercises R, S, and T), Chapter 4 (exercises T and U), Chapter 5 (exercise G), Chapter 6 (exercise G), and Chapter 7 (exercise D):

1. Create a class diagram that shows the mapping of the problem domain classes to a RDBMS for format.

2. Add the DAM classes between the problem-domain classes and the RDBMS classes.

N. For the Of-the-Month-Club problem in Chapter 3 (exercises U, V, and W), Chapter 4 (exercises V and W), Chapter 5 (exercise H), Chapter 6 (exercise H), and Chapter 7 (exercise E):

1. Create a class diagram that shows the mapping of the problem domain classes to a RDBMS for format.

2. Add the DAM classes between the problem-domain classes and the RDBMS classes.

MINICASES

1. Refer to the Professional and Scientific Staff Management (PSSM) minicase in Chapters 3, 5, 6, and 7.

   a. Create a class diagram that shows the mapping of the problem domain classes to a RDBMS for format.

   b. Add the DAM classes between the problem-domain classes and the RDBMS classes.

2. Refer to the Holiday Travel minicase in Chapters 4, 5, 6, and 7.

   a. Create a class diagram that shows the mapping of the problem domain classes to a RDBMS for format.

   b. Add the DAM classes between the problem-domain classes and the RDBMS classes.

APPENDIX 8-1: OPTIMIZING RDBMS-BASED OBJECT STORAGE

Once the object persistence format (that is, storage type and medium) is selected, the object persistence should be optimized for processing efficiency. The methods of optimization vary based on the format that you select; however, the basic concepts remain the same. Once you understand how to optimize a particular type of object persistence, you will have some idea as to how to approach the optimization of other formats. This section focuses on the optimization of the most popular storage format: relational databases.

There are two primary dimensions in which to optimize a relational database: for storage efficiency and for speed of access. Unfortunately, these two goals often conflict because the best design for access speed may take up a great deal of storage space as compared to other, less-speedy designs. Ultimately, the project team will go through a series of trade-offs until the ideal balance is reached.

Optimizing Storage Efficiency

The most efficient tables in a relational database in terms of storage space have no redundant data and very few null values. The presence of null values suggests that space is being wasted (and more data to store means higher data storage hardware costs). For example, the table in Figure A8-1 repeats customer information, such as name and state, each time a customer places an order, it also contains many null values in the product-related columns. These nulls occur whenever a customer places an order for fewer than three items (the maximum number on an order).

In addition to wasting space, redundancy and null values also allow more room for error and increase the likelihood that problems will arise with the integrity of the data. What if customer 1035 moved from Maryland to Georgia? In the case of Figure A8-1, a program must be written to ensure that all instances of that customer are updated to show Georgia as the new state of residence. If some of the instances are overlooked, then the table will contain an *update anomaly*, whereby some of the records contain the correctly updated value for state and other records contain the old information. Similar anomalies can occur when adding or deleting records from this table.

Nulls threaten data integrity because they are difficult to interpret. A blank value in the Order table's product fields could mean the customer did not want more than one or two products, the operator forgot to enter in all three products on the order, or the customer canceled part of the order and the products were deleted by the operator. It is impossible to be sure of the actual meaning of the nulls. This ambiguity is especially problematic when the records are later processed automatically, such as when training machine learning models. Lacking context and ability to make clarifying inquiries, machines generally struggle to handle

Order

- -Order Number : unsigned long
- -Date : Date
- -Cust ID : unsigned long
- -Last Name : String
- -First Name : String
- -State : String
- -Tax Rate : float
- -Product 1 Number : unsigned long
- -Product 1 Desc. : String
- -Product 1 Price : double
- -Product 1 Qty. : unsigned long
- -Product 2 Number : unsigned long
- -Product 2 Desc. : String
- -Product 2 Price : double
- -Product 2 Qty. : unsigned long
- -Product 3 Number : unsigned long
- -Product 3 Desc. : String
- -Product 3 Price : double
- -Product 3 Qty. : unsigned long

Redundant Data

Null Cells

Sample Records:

Order Number	Date	Cust ID	Last Name	First Name	State	Tax Rate	Prod. 1 Number	Prod. 1 Desc.	Prod. 1 Price	Prod. 1 Qty.	Prod. 2 Number	Prod. 2 Desc.	Prod. 2 Price	Prod. 2 Qty.	Prod. 3 Number	Prod. 3 Desc.	Prod. 3 Price	Prod. 3 Qty.
239	11/23/00	1035	Black	John	MD	0.05	555	Cheese Tray	$45.00	2								
260	11/24/00	1035	Black	John	MD	0.05	444	Wine Gift Pack	$60.00	1								
273	11/27/00	1035	Black	John	MD	0.05	222	Bottle Opener	$12.00	1								
241	11/23/00	1123	Williams	Mary	CA	0.08	444	Wine Gift Pack	$60.00	2								
262	11/24/00	1123	Williams	Mary	CA	0.08	222	Bottle Opener	$12.00	2								
287	11/27/00	1123	Williams	Mary	CA	0.08	222	Bottle Opener	$12.00	2								
290	11/30/00	1123	Williams	Mary	CA	0.08	555	Cheese Tray	$45.00	3								
234	11/23/00	2242	DeBerry	Ann	DC	0.065	555	Cheese Tray	$45.00	2								
237	11/23/00	2242	DeBerry	Ann	DC	0.065	111	Wine Guide	$15.00	1	444	Wine Gift Pack	$60.00	1				
238	11/23/00	2242	DeBerry	Ann	DC	0.065	444	Wine Gift Pack	$60.00	1								
245	11/24/00	2242	DeBerry	Ann	DC	0.065	222	Bottle Opener	$12.00	1								
250	11/24/00	2242	DeBerry	Ann	DC	0.065	222	Bottle Opener	$12.00	1								
252	11/24/00	2242	DeBerry	Ann	DC	0.065	222	Bottle Opener	$12.00	1	444	Wine Gift Pack	$60.00	2				
253	11/24/00	2242	DeBerry	Ann	DC	0.065	222	Bottle Opener	$12.00	1	444	Wine Gift Pack	$60.00	1				
297	11/30/00	2242	DeBerry	Ann	DC	0.065	333	Jams & Jellies	$20.00	2								
243	11/24/00	4254	Bailey	Ryan	MD	0.05	555	Cheese Tray	$45.00	2								
246	11/24/00	4254	Bailey	Ryan	MD	0.05	333	Jams & Jellies	$20.00	3								
248	11/24/00	4254	Bailey	Ryan	MD	0.05	222	Bottle Opener	$12.00	1	333	Jams & Jellies	$20.00	2	111	Wine Guide	$15.00	1
235	11/23/00	9500	Chin	April	KS	0.05	222	Bottle Opener	$12.00	1								
242	11/23/00	9500	Chin	April	KS	0.05	333	Jams & Jellies	$20.00	3								
244	11/24/00	9500	Chin	April	KS	0.05	222	Bottle Opener	$12.00	2								
251	11/24/00	9500	Chin	April	KS	0.05	111	Wine Guide	$15.00	2								

FIGURE A8-1 Optimizing Storage

different types of null values appropriately, resulting in potentially erroneous decisions, such as to impute nulls with some value (e.g., column average) in cases where no value is applicable (such as amount of tax paid by a tax-exempt non-resident).[1]

For both these reasons—wasted storage space and data integrity threats—project teams should remove redundancy and nulls from the table. During design, the class diagram is used to examine the design of the RDBMS tables (e.g., see Figure 8-12) and to optimize it for storage efficiency. If you follow the modeling instructions and guidelines that were presented in Chapter 4, you will have little trouble creating a design that is highly optimized in this way because a well-formed logical data model does not contain redundancy or many null values.

Sometimes, however, a project team needs to start with a model that was poorly constructed or with one that was created for files or a nonrelational type of format. In these cases, the project team should follow a series of steps that serve to check the model for storage efficiency. These steps make up a process called normalization.[2] *Normalization* is a process whereby a series of rules are applied to the RDBMS tables to assess and ensure the efficiency of the tables (see Figure A8-2). These rules help analysts identify tables that are not represented correctly. Here, we describe three normalization rules that are applied regularly in practice.

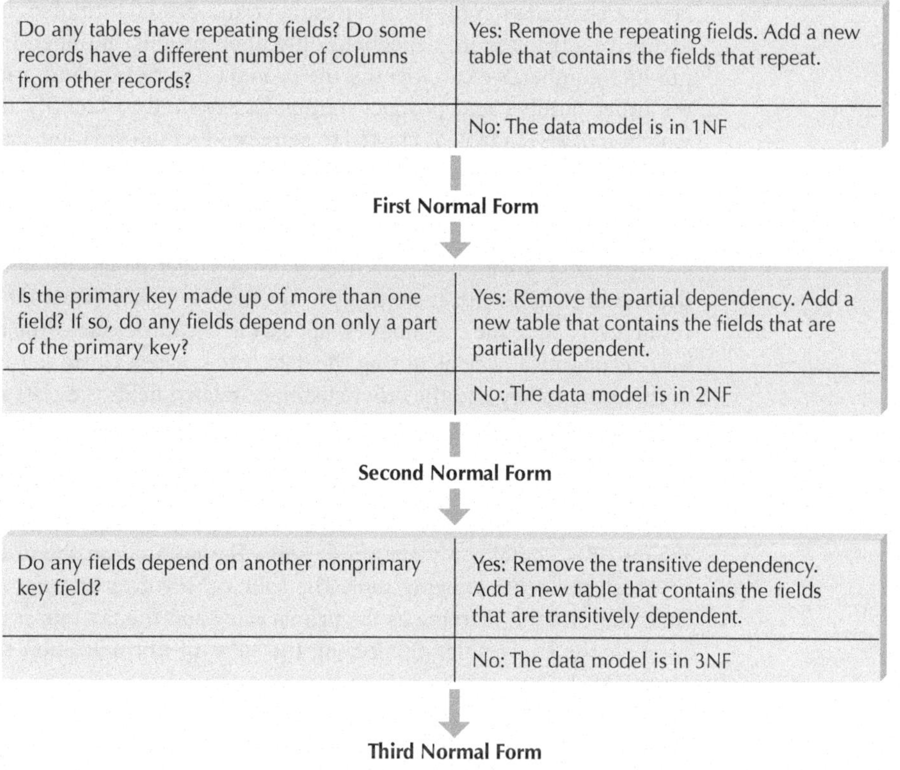

FIGURE A8-2
The Steps of
Normalization

[1] For more information, see: Lukyanenko, R., Castellanos, A. Parsons, J., Tremblay M.C., and Storey, V. C. (2019). "Using Conceptual Modeling to Support Machine Learning" in CAiSE Forum 2019 Proceedings, LNBIP 350, Rome, Italy, June 3–7, 2019, pp. 170–181.

[2] Normalization also can be performed on the problem domain layer (see Chapter 6). However, the normalization process should be used on the problem domain layer only to uncover missing classes. Otherwise, optimizations that have nothing to do with the semantics of the problem domain can creep into the problem domain layer.

Figure A8-1 shows a model in 0 Normal Form, which is an unnormalized model before the normalization rules have been applied.

A model is in *first normal form (1NF)* if it does not lead to multivalued fields, fields that allow a set of values to be stored, or repeating fields, which are fields that repeat within a table to capture multiple values. The rule for 1NF says that all tables must contain the same number of columns (i.e., fields) and that all the columns must contain a single value. Notice that the model in Figure A8-1 violates 1NF because it causes product number, description, price, and quantity to repeat three times for each order in the table. The resulting table has many records that contain nulls in the product-related columns, and orders are limited to three products because there is no room to store information for more.

A much more efficient design (and one that conforms to 1NF) leads to a separate table to hold the repeating information; to do this, we create a separate table on the model to capture product order information. A zero-to-many relationship would then exist between the two tables. As shown in Figure A8-3, the new design eliminates nulls from the Order table and supports an unlimited number of products that can be associated with an order.

Second normal form (2NF) requires first that the data model is in 1NF and second that the data model leads to tables containing fields that depend on a whole *primary key*. This means that the primary key value for each record can determine the value for all the other fields in the record. Sometimes fields depend on only part of the primary key (i.e., *partial dependency*), and these fields belong in another table.

For example, in the new Product Order table that was created in Figure A8-3, the primary key is a combination of the order number and product number, but the product description and price attributes are dependent only upon product number. In other words, by knowing product number, we can identify the product description and price. However, knowledge of the order number and product number is required to identify the quantity. To rectify this violation of 2NF, a table is created to store product information, and the description and price attributes are moved into the new table. Now, product description is stored only once for each instance of a product number as opposed to many times (every time a product is placed on an order).

A second violation of 2NF occurs in the Order table: customer first name and last name depend only upon the customer ID, not the whole key (Cust ID and Order Number). As a result, every time the customer ID appears in the Order table, the names also appear. A much more economical way of storing the data is to create a Customer table with the Customer ID as the primary key and the other customer-related fields (i.e., last name and first name) listed only once within the appropriate record. Figure A8-4 illustrates how the model would look when placed in 2NF.

Third normal form (3NF) occurs when a model is in both 1NF and 2NF and, in the resulting tables, none of the fields depend on nonprimary key fields (i.e., *transitive dependency*). Figure A8-4 contains a violation of 3NF: The tax rate on the order depends upon the state to which the order is being sent. The solution involves creating another table that contains state abbreviations serving as the primary key and the tax rate as a regular field. Figure A8-5 presents the end results of applying the steps of normalization to the original model from Figure A8-1.

Optimizing Data Access Speed

After you have optimized the design of the object storage for efficiency, the end result is that data are spread out across a number of tables. When data from multiple tables need to be accessed or queried, the tables must be first joined. For example, before a user can print out a list of the customer names associated with orders, first the Customer and Order tables need

Revised Model:

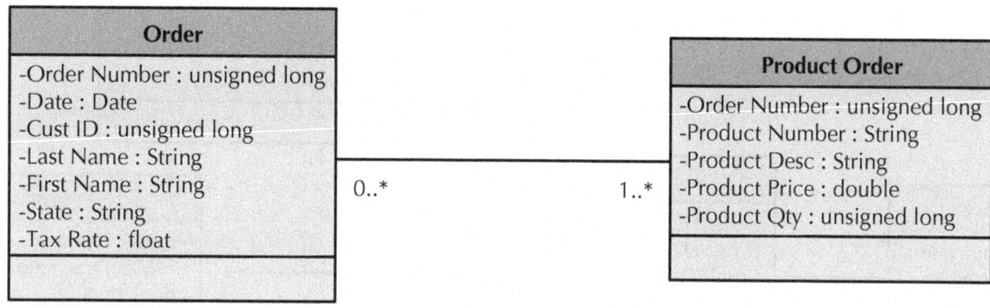

Note: Order Number will serve as part of the primary key of Order

Note: Cust ID also will serve as part of the primary key of Order

Note: Order Number will serve as part of the primary key of Product Order

Note: Product Number will serve as part of the primary key of Product Order

Note: Order Number also will serve as a foreign key in Product Order

(a)

Order 237 has 2 products

Sample Records:

Order Table

Order Number	Date	Cust ID	Last Name	First Name	State	Tax Rate
239	11/23/00	1035	Black	John	MD	0.05
260	11/24/00	1035	Black	John	MD	0.05
273	11/27/00	1035	Black	John	MD	0.05
241	11/23/00	1123	Williams	Mary	CA	0.08
262	11/24/00	1123	Williams	Mary	CA	0.08
287	11/27/00	1123	Williams	Mary	CA	0.08
290	11/30/00	1123	Williams	Mary	CA	0.08
234	11/23/00	2242	DeBerry	Ann	DC	0.065
237	11/23/00	2242	DeBerry	Ann	DC	0.065
238	11/23/00	2242	DeBerry	Ann	DC	0.065
245	11/24/00	2242	DeBerry	Ann	DC	0.065
250	11/24/00	2242	DeBerry	Ann	DC	0.065
252	11/24/00	2242	DeBerry	Ann	DC	0.065
253	11/24/00	2242	DeBerry	Ann	DC	0.065
297	11/30/00	2242	DeBerry	Ann	DC	0.065
243	11/24/00	4254	Bailey	Ryan	MD	0.05
246	11/24/00	4254	Bailey	Ryan	MD	0.05
248	11/24/00	4254	Bailey	Ryan	MD	0.05
235	11/23/00	9500	Chin	April	KS	0.05
242	11/23/00	9500	Chin	April	KS	0.05
244	11/24/00	9500	Chin	April	KS	0.05
251	11/24/00	9500	Chin	April	KS	0.05

Product Order Table

Order Number	Product Number	Product Desc	Product Price	Product Qty
239	555	Cheese Tray	$45.00	2
260	444	Wine Gift Pack	$60.00	1
273	222	Bottle Opener	$12.00	1
241	444	Wine Gift Pack	$60.00	2
262	222	Bottle Opener	$12.00	2
287	222	Bottle Opener	$12.00	2
290	555	Cheese Tray	$45.00	3
234	555	Cheese Tray	$45.00	2
237	111	Wine Guide	$15.00	1
237	444	Wine Gift Pack	$60.00	1
238	444	Wine Gift Pack	$60.00	1
245	222	Bottle Opener	$12.00	1
250	222	Bottle Opener	$12.00	1
252	222	Bottle Opener	$12.00	1
252	444	Wine Gift Pack	$60.00	2
253	222	Bottle Opener	$12.00	1
253	444	Wine Gift Pack	$60.00	1
297	333	Jams & Jellies	$20.00	2
243	555	Cheese Tray	$45.00	2
246	333	Jams & Jellies	$20.00	3
248	222	Bottle Opener	$12.00	1
248	333	Jams & Jellies	$20.00	2
248	111	Wine Guide	$15.00	1
235	222	Bottle Opener	$12.00	1
242	333	Jams & Jellies	$20.00	3
244	222	Bottle Opener	$12.00	2
251	111	Wine Guide	$15.00	2

Order 248 has 3 products

(b)

FIGURE A8-3 1NF: Remove Repeating Fields

Product Order

-Order Number : unsigned long
-Product Number : unsigned long
-Qty : unsigned long

Customer

-Cust ID : unsigned long
-Last Name : String
-First Name : String

Order

-Order Number : unsigned long
-Date : Date
-Cust ID : unsigned long
-State : String
-Tax Rate : float

Product

-Product Number : unsigned long
-Product Desc : String
-Price : double

1..1   0..*

0..*   1..*

Note: Cust ID will serve as the primary key of Customer.

Note: Order Number will serve as the primary key of Order.

Note: Cust ID will serve as a foreign key in Order.

Note: Order Number will serve as part of the primary key of Product Order.

Note: Order Number also will serve as a foreign key in Product Order.

Note: Product Number will serve as part of the primary key in Product Order.

Note: Product Number also will serve as a foreign key in Product Order.

Note: Product Number will serve as part of the primary key of Product Order.

Sample Records:

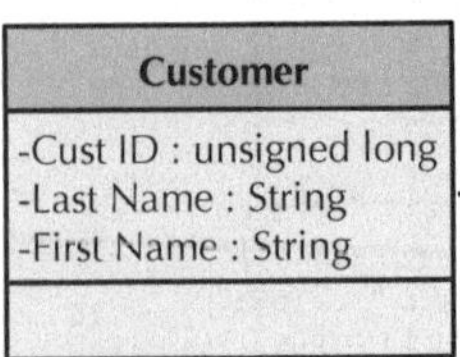

Customer Table

Cust ID	Last Name	First Name
1035	Black	John
1123	Williams	Mary
2242	DeBerry	Ann
4254	Bailey	Ryan
9500	Chin	April

Last Name and First Name were moved to the Customer table to eliminate redundancy

Order Table

Order Number	Date	Cust ID	State	Tax Rate
239	11/23/00	1035	MD	0.05
260	11/24/00	1035	MD	0.05
273	11/27/00	1035	MD	0.05
241	11/23/00	1123	CA	0.08
262	11/24/00	1123	CA	0.08
287	11/27/00	1123	CA	0.08
290	11/30/00	1123	CA	0.08
234	11/23/00	2242	DC	0.065
237	11/23/00	2242	DC	0.065
238	11/23/00	2242	DC	0.065
245	11/24/00	2242	DC	0.065
250	11/24/00	2242	DC	0.065
252	11/24/00	2242	DC	0.065
253	11/24/00	2242	DC	0.065
297	11/30/00	2242	DC	0.065
243	11/24/00	4254	MD	0.05
246	11/24/00	4254	MD	0.05
248	11/24/00	4254	MD	0.05
235	11/23/00	9500	KS	0.05
242	11/23/00	9500	KS	0.05
244	11/24/00	9500	KS	0.05
251	11/24/00	9500	KS	0.05

Product Order Table

Order Number	Product Number	Product Qty
239	555	2
260	444	1
273	222	1
241	444	2
262	222	2
287	222	2
290	555	3
234	555	2
237	111	1
237	444	1
238	444	1
245	222	1
250	222	1
252	222	1
252	444	2
253	222	1
253	444	1
297	333	2
243	555	2
246	333	3
248	222	1
248	333	2
248	111	1
235	222	1
242	333	3
244	222	2
251	111	2

Product Table

Product Number	Product Desc	Product Price
111	Wine Guide	$15.00
222	Bottle Opener	$12.00
333	Jams & Jellies	$20.00
444	Wine Gift Pack	$60.00
555	Cheese Tray	$45.00

Product Desc and Price were moved to the Product table to eliminate redundancy

FIGURE A8-4   2NF Partial Dependencies Removed

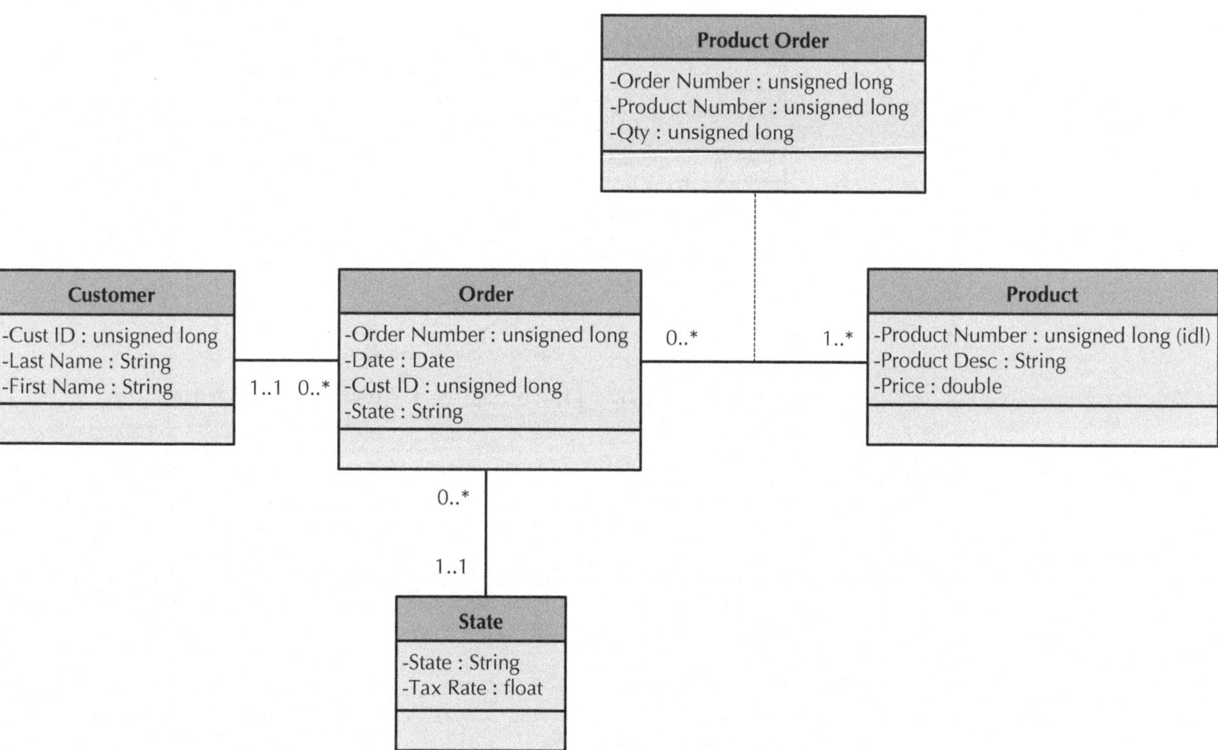

FIGURE A8-5 3NF Normalized Field

to be joined, based on the customer number field (see Figure A8-5). Only then can both the order and customer information be included in the query's output. *Joins* can take a lot of time, especially if the tables are large or if many tables are involved.

Consider a system that stores information about 10,000 different products, 25,000 customers, and 100,000 orders, each averaging three products per order. If an analyst wanted to investigate whether there were regional differences in music preferences, the analyst would need to combine all the tables to be able to look at products that have been ordered while knowing the state of the customers placing the orders. A query of this information would result in a huge table with 300,000 rows (i.e., the number of products that have been ordered) and 11 columns (the total number of columns from all of the tables combined).

The project team can use several techniques to try to speed up access to the data, including denormalization, clustering, and indexing.

Denormalization After the object storage is optimized, the project team may decide that increased data retrieval speed is more important than storage efficiency or data update speed and elect to denormalize or add redundancy back into the design. *Denormalization* reduces the number of joins that need to be performed in a query, thus speeding up access. Figure A8-6 shows a denormalized model for customer orders. The customer last name was added back into the Order table because the project team learned during analysis that queries about orders usually require the customer last name field. Instead of joining the Order table repeatedly to the Customer table, the system now needs to access only the Order table because it contains all of the relevant information needed to solve the music preference question posed above.

Denormalization is ideal in situations in which information is queried frequently but updated rarely. However, due to the additional storage required and the potential update anomalies, denormalization should be applied sparingly. There are three cases in which you

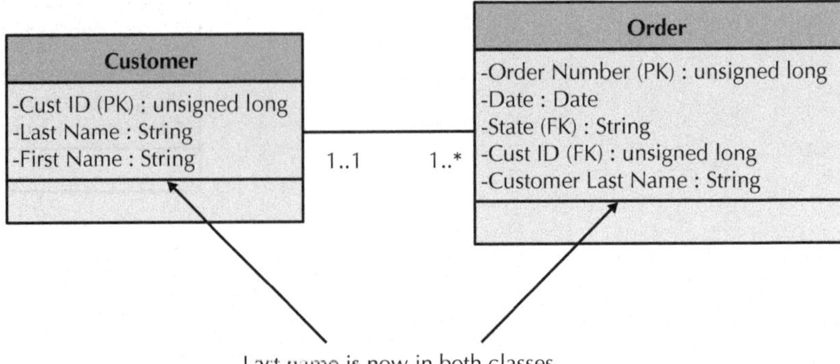

FIGURE A8-6   Denormalized Physical Data Model

may rely upon denormalization to reduce joins and improve performance. First, denormalization can be applied in the case of look-up tables, which are tables that contain descriptions of values (e.g., a table of product descriptions or a table of payment types). Because descriptions of codes rarely change, it may be more efficient to include the description along with its respective code in the main table to eliminate the need to join the look-up table each time a query is performed (see Figure A8-7a).

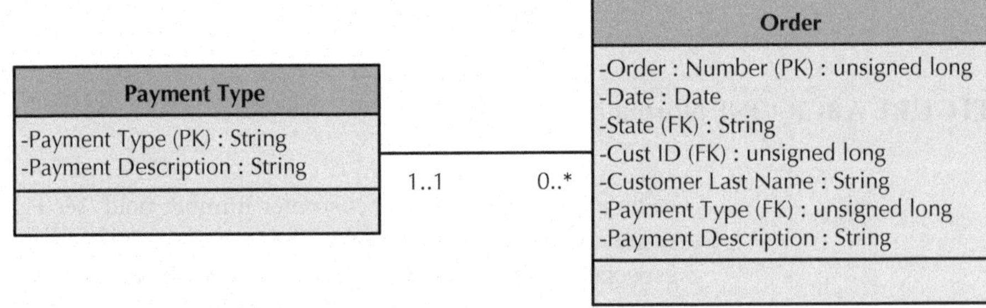

(a)

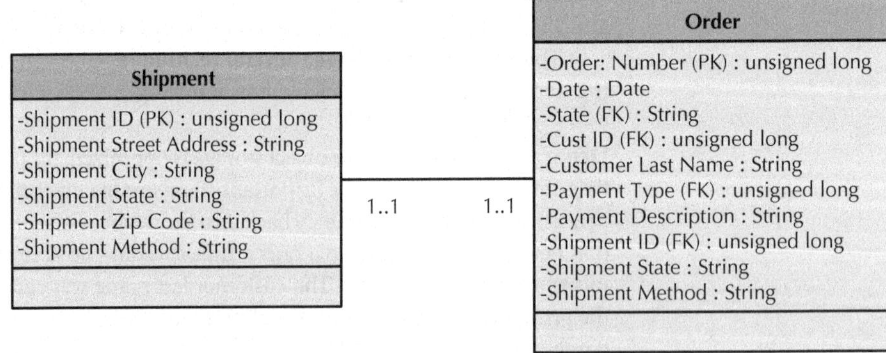

(b)

FIGURE A8-7   Denormalization Situations (FK, foreign key; PK, primary key)

Second, one-to-one relationships are good candidates for denormalization. Although logically two tables should be separated, from a practical standpoint the information from both tables may regularly be accessed together. Think about an order and its shipping information. Logically, it might make sense to separate the attributes related to shipping into a separate table, but as a result the queries regarding shipping will probably always need a join to the Order table. If the project team finds that certain shipping information, such as state and shipping method, is needed when orders are accessed, they may decide to combine the tables or include some shipping attributes in the Order table (see Figure A8-7b).

Third, at times it is more efficient to include a parent entity's attributes in its child entity on the physical data model. For example, consider the Customer and Order tables in Figure A8-6, which share a one-to-many relationship, with Customer as the parent and Order as the child. If queries regarding orders continuously require customer information, the most popular customer fields can be placed in Order to reduce the required joins to the Customer table, as was done with Customer Last Name.

Clustering Speed of access also is influenced by the way that the data are retrieved. Think about shopping in a grocery store. If you have a list of items to buy but you are unfamiliar with the store's layout, you need to walk down every aisle to make sure that you don't miss anything from your list. Likewise, if records are arranged in no particular order (or in an order that is irrelevant to your data needs), then any query of the records results in a *table scan* in which the DBMS has to access every row in the table before retrieving the result set. Table scans are the most inefficient of data retrieval methods.

One way to improve access speed is to reduce the number of times that the storage medium needs to be accessed during a transaction. One method is to *cluster* records together physically so that similar records are stored close together. With *intrafile clustering*, like records in the table are stored together in some way, such as in order by primary key or, in the case of a grocery store, by item type. Thus, whenever a query looks for records, it can go directly to the right spot on the disk (or other storage medium) because it knows in what order the records are stored, just as we can walk directly to the bread aisle to pick up a loaf of bread. *Interfile clustering* combines records from more than one table that typically are retrieved together. For example, if customer information is usually accessed with the related order information, then the records from the two tables may be physically stored in a way that preserves the customer-order relationship. Returning to the grocery store scenario, an interfile cluster would be similar to storing peanut butter, jelly, and bread next to each other in the same aisle because they are usually purchased together, not because they are similar types of items. Of course, each table can have only one clustering strategy because the records can be arranged physically in only one way.

Indexing A familiar time saver is an index located in the back of a textbook, which points directly to the page or pages that contain a topic of interest. Think of how long it would take to find all the times that relational database appears in this textbook without the index to rely on! An *index* in data storage is like an index in the back of a textbook; it is a minitable that contains values from one or more columns in a table and the location of the values within the table. Instead of paging through the entire textbook, we can move directly to the right pages and get the information we need. Indexes are one of the most important ways to improve database performance. Whenever there are performance problems, the first place to look is an index.

A query can use an index to find the locations of only those records that are included in the query answer, and a table can have an unlimited number of indexes. Figure A8-8 shows an index that orders records by payment type. A query that searches for all the customers who

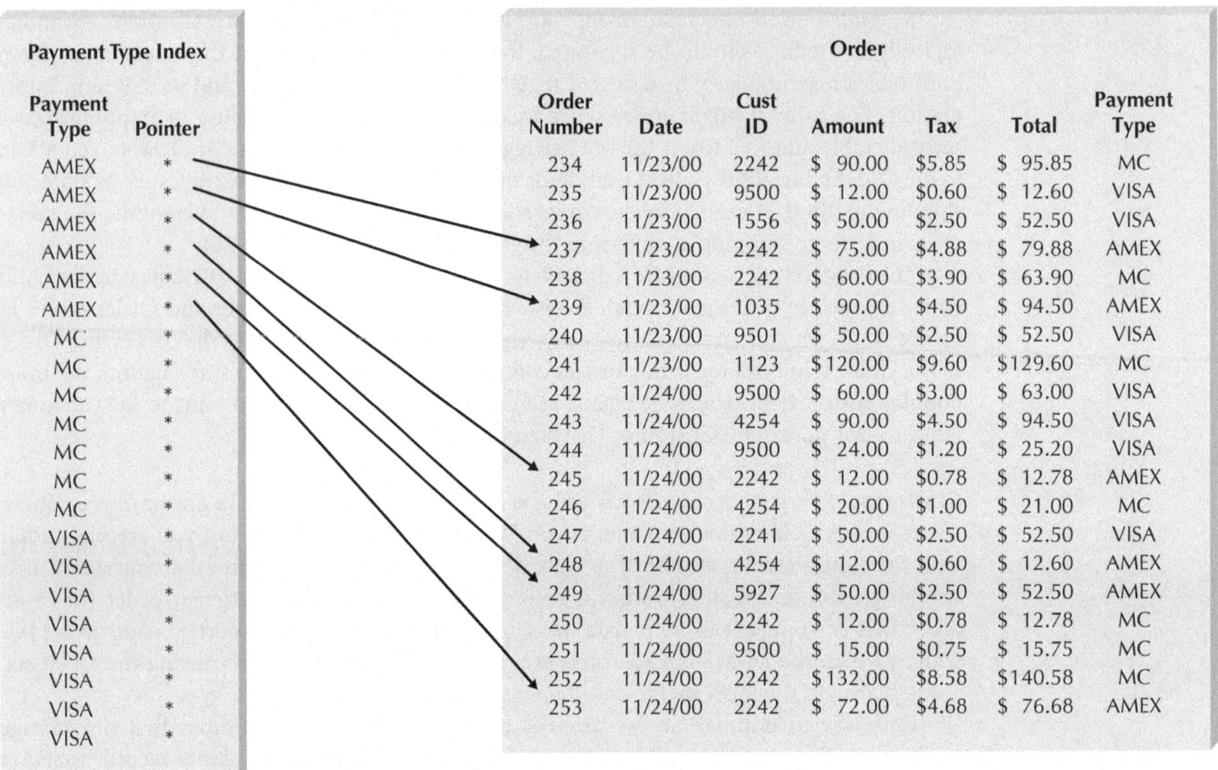

FIGURE A8-8 Payment Type Index

used American Express can use this index to find the locations of the records that contain American Express as the payment type without having to scan the entire Order table.

Project teams can make indexes perform even faster by placing them into the main memory of the data storage hardware. Retrieving information directly from memory is much faster than retrieving it from a hard disk—Think about how much faster it is to retrieve a memorized phone number versus one that must be looked up in a phone book. Similarly, when a database has an index in memory, it can locate records very, very quickly.

Of course, indexes require overhead in that they take up space on the storage medium. Also, they need to be updated as records in tables are inserted, deleted, or changed. Thus, although indexes lead to faster access to the data, they slow down the update process. In general, we should create indexes sparingly for transaction systems or systems that require a lot of updates, but we should apply indexes generously when designing systems for decision support (see Figure A8-9).

Estimating Data Storage Size Even if we have denormalized our physical data model, clustered records, and created indexes appropriately, the system will perform poorly if the database server cannot handle its volume of data. Therefore, one last way to plan for good performance is to apply *volumetrics*, which means estimating the amount of data that the hardware will need to support. You can incorporate your estimates into the database server hardware specification to make sure that the database hardware is sufficient for the project's

FIGURE A8-9
Guidelines for
Creating Indexes

> Use indexes sparingly for transaction systems.
>
> Use many indexes to increase response times in decision support systems.
>
> For each table, create a unique index that is based on the primary key.
>
> For each table, create an index that is based on the foreign key to improve the performance of joins.
>
> Create an index for fields that are used frequently for grouping, sorting, or criteria.

FIGURE A8-10
Calculating
Volumetrics

Field	Average Size
Order Number	8
Date	7
Cust ID	4
Last Name	13
First Name	9
State	2
Amount	4
Tax Rate	2
Record Size	49
Overhead	30%
Total Record Size	63.7
Initial Table Size	50,000
Initial Table Volume	3,185,000
Growth Rate/Month	1,000
Table Volume @ 3 years	5,478,200

needs. The size of the database is based on the amount of raw data in the tables and the overhead requirements of the DBMS. To estimate size, you will need to have a good understanding of the initial size of your database as well as its expected growth rate over time.

Raw data refers to all the data that are stored within the tables of the database, and it is calculated based on a bottom-up approach. First, write down the estimated average width for each column (field) in the table and sum the values for a total record size (see Figure A8-10). For example, if a variable-width Last Name column is assigned a width of 20 characters, you can enter 13 as the average character width of the column. In Figure A8-10, the estimated record size is 49.

Next, calculate the *overhead* for the table as a percentage of each record. Overhead includes the room needed by the DBMS to support such functions as administrative actions and indexes, and it should be assigned based on past experience, recommendations from technology vendors, or parameters that are built into software that was written to calculate volumetrics. For example, your DBMS vendor might recommend that you allocate 30 percent of the records' raw data size for overhead storage space, creating a total record size of 63.7 in the Figure A8-10 example.

Finally, record the number of initial records that will be loaded into the table, as well as the expected growth per month. This information should have been collected during analysis. According to Figure A8-10, the initial space required by the first table is 3,185,000, and future sizes can be project based on the growth figure. These steps are repeated for each table to get a total size for the entire database.

Many CASE tools provide you with database-size information based on how you set up the object persistence, and they calculate volumetrics estimates automatically. Ultimately, the size of the database needs to be shared with the design team so that the proper technology can be put in place to support the system's data and potential performance problems can be addressed long before they affect the success of the system.

APPENDIX 8-2: CONVERTING CLASS DIAGRAMS TO ENTITY-RELATIONSHIP DIAGRAMS

The *entity-relationship diagram (ERD)* is the primary diagram used to design databases. The ERD was originally created to provide a semantically sound way to perform *data modeling*. Specifically, it was created as a means to semantically model and design relational databases. In this book, we used the class diagram both as our structural modeling and our database design tool. Like the class diagram, the ERD is a static model. However, unlike the class diagram, the ERD can only model data. Consequently, anything that can be done with an ERD can be done with a class diagram; but not vice versa. In this appendix, we introduce the syntax of the ERD and we describe how to map a class diagram to an ERD.

The ERD was created by Peter Chen to provide an easy, but yet comprehensive, way to model/design a relational database that represented the data and their relationships in a problem domain.[3] AN ERD is made up of entities and relationships. An *entity* is the data equivalent of a *class*, while *relationships* are the equivalent of *associations*. Where an association has *multiplicities*, relationships have *cardinalities*. However, unlike the multiplicities associated with the class diagram, cardinalities cannot show specified range of connections, e.g., 2..4, nor can show multiple disjoint relationships, e.g., 1..3,5. Figure A8-11 compares the class diagram and ERD syntax. With the class diagram, the multiple ends were shown with an*, the optional association was shown as a 0, and a mandatory or required association is shown by a 1. Notice, with the ERD, the multiple end is shown as a "crows foot," the optional relationship is shown with a circle on the line, and a required relationship is shown by a vertical line crossing the relationship line. Finally, to convert a class diagram to an ERD, you simply follow the rules for mapping a problem domain class diagram to the RDBMS tables described in Figure 8-9. Once this is done, then simply convert all classes to entities, all associations to

Class Diagram Syntax		Entity-Relationship Diagram Syntax	
Class	**ClassName** -attributeName -methodName	Entity	**Entity Name** attribute name attribute name
Associations and Multiplicities		**Relationships and Cardinalities**	
0..*	1	>O——————‖	
1..*	1	>┤——————‖	
0..*	0..1	>O——————O┤	
1..*	0..1	>┤——————O┤	

FIGURE A8-11 Class Diagram and ERD Syntax Comparison

[3] P. Chen, "The Entity-Relationship Model – Toward a Unified View of Data" *ACM Transactions on Database Systems*, 1, 1976, 9–36.

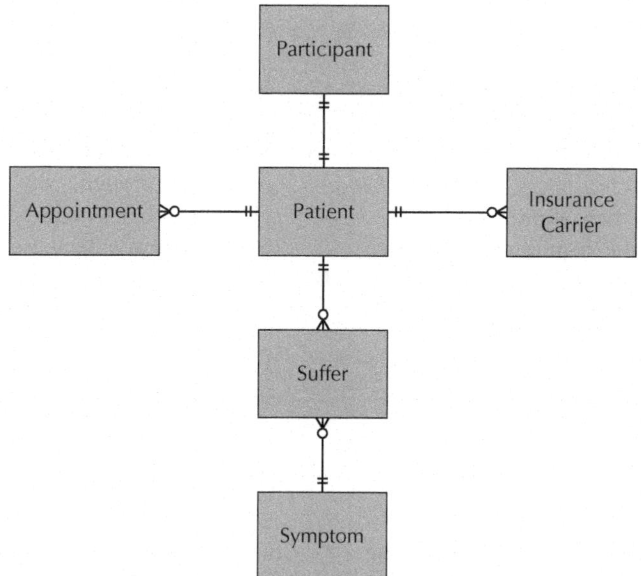

FIGURE A8-12
ERD equivalent of
RDBMS Tables in
Figures 8-10 and 8-12

relationships, and all multiplicities to cardinalities by using Figure A8-11. Figure A8-12 portrays the results of this process of converting the RDBMS Tables portion of the class diagram in Figures 8-10 and 8-12 to an ERD. In this case, we are showing the entities with their names only. Optionally, we could have also shown the attributes.

APPENDIX REVIEW

After reading and studying this appendix, you should be able to:

- [ ] Use normalization to minimize update anomalies and to increase storage efficiency.
- [ ] Describe the first three normal forms.
- [ ] Describe when to use denormalization, clustering, and indexing to increase the speed of data access.
- [ ] Explain why denormalization, clustering, and indexing can slow down updating.
- [ ] Apply volumetrics to estimate the amount of data storage required.
- [ ] Map a class diagram to an entity-relationship diagram.

KEY TERMS

Association	Entity-relationship	Multiplicity	Second normal form (2NF)
Cardinality	diagram (ERD)	Normalization	Table scan
Class	First normal form (1NF)	Overhead	Third normal form (3NF)
Cluster	Index	Partial dependency	Transitive dependency
Data modeling	Interfile clustering	Primary key	Update anomaly
Denormalization	Intrafile clustering	Raw data	Volumetrics
Entity	Join	Relationship	

QUESTIONS

1. Name three ways null values can be interpreted in a relational database. Why is this problematic?
2. What are the two dimensions in which to optimize a relational database?
3. What is the purpose of normalization?
4. How does a model meet the requirements of third normal form?
5. Describe three situations that can be good candidates for denormalization.
6. Describe several techniques that can improve performance of a database.
7. What is the difference between interfile and intrafile clustering? Why are they used?
8. What is an index and how can it improve the performance of a system?
9. Describe what should be considered when estimating the size of a database.
10. Why is it important to understand the initial and projected size of a database during design?

EXERCISES

A. You have been given a file that contains the following fields relating to CD information. Using the steps of normalization, create a model that represents this file in third normal form. The fields include:

Musical group name	CD title 2
Musicians in group	CD title 3
Date group was formed	CD 1 length
Group's agent	CD 2 length
CD title 1	CD 3 length

Assumptions:

- Musicians in group contain a list of the members of the people in the musical group.
- Musical groups can have more than one CD, so both group name and CD title are needed to uniquely identify a particular CD.

B. For Jim Smith dealership problem in exercise G of Chapter 8:

1. Describe how you would denormalize the model that you created. Draw the new class diagram based on your suggested changes. How would performance be affected by your suggestions?
2. Examine the model that you created. Develop a clustering and indexing strategy for this model. Describe how your strategy will improve the performance of the database.
3. Calculate the size of the database. Provide size estimates for the initial size of the database as well as for the database in one year's time. Assume that the dealership sells ten models of cars from each manufacturer to approximately 20,000 customers a year. The system will be set up initially with one year's worth of data.
4. Create an ERD based on the class diagram you created in 1.

C. For the A Real Estate Inc. problem in exercise H:

1. Apply the rules of normalization to the class diagram to check the diagram for processing efficiency.
2. Develop a clustering and indexing strategy for this model. Describe how your strategy will improve the performance of the database.
3. Create an ERD based on the class diagram you created in 1.

D. For the A Video Store problem in exercise I:

1. Apply the rules of normalization to the class diagram to check the diagram for processing efficiency.
2. Develop a clustering and indexing strategy for this model. Describe how your strategy will improve the performance of the database.
3. Create an ERD based on the class diagram you created in 1.

E. For the gym membership problem in exercise J:

1. Apply the rules of normalization to the class diagram to check the diagram for processing efficiency.
2. Develop a clustering and indexing strategy for this model. Describe how your strategy will improve the performance of the database.
3. Create an ERD based on the class diagram you created in 1.

F. For the Picnics R Us problem in exercise K:

1. Apply the rules of normalization to the class diagram to check the diagram for processing efficiency.

2. Develop a clustering and indexing strategy for this model. Describe how your strategy will improve the performance of the database.

3. Create an ERD based on the class diagram you created in 1.

G. For the Of-the-Month-Club problem in exercise L:

1. Apply the rules of normalization to the class diagram to check the diagram for processing efficiency.

2. Develop a clustering and indexing strategy for this model. Describe how your strategy will improve the performance of the database.

3. Create an ERD based on the class diagram you created in 1.

MINICASES

1. The system development team at the Wilcon Company is working on developing a new customer order entry system. In the process of designing the new system, the team has identified the following class and its attributes:

Inventory Order
Order Number (PK)
Order Date
Customer Name
Street Address
City
State
Zip
Customer Type
Initials
District Number
Region Number
1 to 22 occurrences of: Item Name
    Quantity Ordered
    Item Unit
    Quantity Shipped
    Item Out
    Quantity Received

a. State the rule that is applied to place a class in first normal form. Based on the above class, create a class diagram that will be in 1NF.

b. State the rule that is applied to place a class into second normal form. Revise the class diagram for the Wilcon Company using the class and attributes described (if necessary) to place it in 2NF.

c. State the rule that is applied to place a class into third normal form. Revise the class diagram to place it in 3NF.

d. When planning for the physical design of this database, can you identify any likely situations where the project team might choose to denormalize the class diagram? After going through the work of normalizing, why would this be considered?

2. In the new system under development for Holiday Travel Vehicles, seven tables will be implemented in the new relational database. These tables are: New Vehicle, Trade-in Vehicle, Sales Invoice, Customer, Salesperson, Installed Option, and Option. The expected average record size for these tables and the initial record count per table are given here.

Table Name	Average Record Size	Initial Table Size (Records)
New Vehicle	65 characters	10,000
Trade-in Vehicle	48 characters	7,500
Sales Invoice	76 characters	16,000
Customer	61 characters	13,000
Salesperson	34 characters	100
Installed Option	16 characters	25,000
Option	28 characters	500

a. Perform a volumetrics analysis for the Holiday Travel Vehicle system. Assume that the DBMS that will be used to implement the system requires 35 percent overhead to be factored into the estimates. Also, assume a growth rate for the company of 10 percent per year. The systems development team wants to ensure that adequate hardware is obtained for the next three years.

b. Map the class diagram that you have created for the Holiday Travel Vehicle system to an ERD.

3. Refer to the Professional and Scientific Staff Management (PSSM) minicase in Chapters 3, 5, 6, and 7.

a. Apply the rules of normalization to the class diagram to check the diagram for processing efficiency.

b. Develop a clustering and indexing strategy for this model. Describe how your strategy will improve the performance of the database.

c. Create an ERD based on the class diagram you created in a.

CHAPTER 9

HUMAN–COMPUTER INTERACTION LAYER DESIGN

A user interface is the part of the system with which the users interact. From the user's point of view, the user interface is the system. It includes the screen displays that provide navigation through the system, the screens and forms that capture data, and the reports that the system produces (whether on paper, on the screen, or via some other medium). This chapter introduces the basic principles and processes of interface design and discusses how to design the interface structure and standards, navigation design, input design, and output design. The chapter introduces the issues related to designing user interfaces for the mobile computing environment, social media, games, multidimensional information visualizations, and immersive environments. It also introduces the issues that need to be considered when designing user interfaces for a global audience. Finally, the chapter describes the effect of the nonfunctional requirements on designing the human–computer interaction layer.

OBJECTIVES

- Understand fundamental user interface design principles.
- Understand the process of user interface design.
- Understand how to design the user interface structure.
- Understand how to design the user interface standards.
- Understand commonly used principles and techniques for navigation design.
- Understand commonly used principles and techniques for input design.
- Understand commonly used principles and techniques for output design.
- Be able to design a user interface.
- Understand the unique design issues for user interface design for mobile computing, social media, games, multidimensional information visualization, and immersive applications.
- Understand the issues that need to be addresses when designing user interfaces for international and multicultural audiences.
- Understand the effect of nonfunctional requirements on the human–computer interaction layer.

INTRODUCTION

Interface design is the process of defining how a system will interact with external entities (e.g., customers, suppliers, and other systems). In this chapter, we focus on the design of *user interfaces*, but it is also important to remember that there are sometimes *system interfaces*, which exchange information with other systems. System interfaces are typically designed as part of a systems integration effort. They are defined in general terms as part of the application architecture and data management layers. The human–computer interaction layer defines the way in which the users interact with the system and the nature of the inputs and outputs that the system accepts and produces.

Up until now, the entire development process has been focused on getting the problem-domain layer and its storage on the data management layer right. However, from the user's point of view, the user interface on the human–computer interaction layer is the system. Users do not really care about how the problem domain objects are stored. But, they do care about how they can use the system to support them in their activities. Based on our layered based design approach, the user interface of the human–computer interaction layer is independent of the data management layer. But it is dependent on both the problem domain and application architecture layers. Depending on the type of device that the human–computer interaction layer is deployed on will set both opportunities and constraints as to what user interface features can be implemented. For example, deploying the human computer interaction layer on both a smartphone and a desktop computer will cause two different user interfaces to be designed.

Even though there are command-line user interfaces (e.g., Terminal on Mac OSX), we are only focusing on *graphical user interfaces (GUI)* that use windows, menus, icons, etc.[1] Today, GUI-based interfaces are the most common type of interfaces that we use.[2] Regardless of the underlying hardware being used, a GUI-based user interface comprises three fundamental parts. The first is the *navigation mechanism*, the way in which the user gives instructions to the system and tells it what to do (e.g., buttons and menus). The second is the *input mechanism*, the way in which the system captures information (e.g., forms for adding new customers). The third is the *output mechanism*, the way in which the system provides information to the user or to other systems (e.g., reports and Web pages). Each of these is conceptually differ-ent, but they are closely intertwined. All GUI-based displays contain navigation mechanisms, and most contain input and output mechanisms. Therefore, navigation design, input design, and output design are tightly coupled and must be performed in an incremental and itera-tive manner.

In this chapter, even though we focus primarily on designing user interfaces that run in a laptop or desktop type of environment, we also provide general guidelines for mobile com-puting, social media applications, advanced technology interfaces, such as 3D augmented and virtual reality applications, and finally, issues related to going global with the user interface.

PRINCIPLES FOR USER INTERFACE DESIGN

In many ways, user interface design is an art. The goal is to make the interface pleasing to the eye and simple to use while minimizing the effort the users need to accomplish their work. The system is never an end in itself; it is merely a means to accomplish the business of an organization or some tasks of an individual.

We have found that the greatest problem facing experienced designers is using space effectively. Simply put, often there is much more information that needs to be presented on a

---

[1] Many people attribute the origin of GUI interfaces to Apple or Microsoft. Some people know that Microsoft copied from Apple, which, in turn, "borrowed" the whole idea from a system developed at the Xerox Palo Alto Research Center (PARC) in the 1970s. Very few know that the Xerox system was based on a system developed by Doug Englebart of Stanford that was first demonstrated at the Western Computer Conference in 1968. Around the same time, he also invented the mouse, desktop video conferencing, groupware, and a host of other things we now take for granted. Doug is a legend in the computer science community and has won too many awards to count but is relatively unknown by the general public.

[2] A set of good books on GUI design include Jennifer Tidwell, *Designing Interfaces*, 2nd Ed. (Sebastopol, CA: O'Reilly Media, 2010); Ben Shneiderman, *Designing the User Interface: Strategies for Effective Human–Computer Interaction*, 3rd Ed. (Reading, MA: Addison-Wesley, 1998); Alan Cooper, *About Face 3: The Essentials of Interaction Design* (Indianapolis, IN: Wiley, 2007).

Principle	Description
Layout	The interface should be a series of areas on the screen that are used consistently for different purposes—for example, a top area for commands and navigation, a middle area for information to be input or output, and a bottom area for status information.
Content Awareness	Users should always be aware of where they are in the system and what information is being displayed.
Aesthetics	Interfaces should be functional and inviting to users through careful use of white space, colors, and fonts. There is often a trade-off between including enough white space to make the interface look pleasing without losing so much space that important information does not fit on the screen.
User Experience	Although ease of use and ease of learning often lead to similar design decisions, sometimes there is a trade-off between the two. Novice or infrequent users of software prefer ease of learning, whereas frequent users prefer ease of use.
Consistency	Consistency in interface design enables users to predict what will happen before they perform a function. It is one of the most important elements in ease of learning, ease of use, and aesthetics.
Minimal User Effort	The interface should be simple to use. Most designers plan on having no more than three mouse clicks from the starting menu until users perform work.

FIGURE 9-1
Principles of User
Interface Design

screen or report or form than will fit comfortably. Analysts must balance the need for simplicity and pleasant appearance against the need to present the information across multiple pages or screens, which decreases simplicity. In this section, we discuss some fundamental interface design principles, which are common for navigation design, input design, and output design[3] (see Figure 9-1).

Layout

The first element of design is the basic *layout* of the *screen, form,* or *report*. Most software designed for personal computers follows the standard Microsoft Windows or Apple Macintosh approach for screen design. The screen is divided into three boxes. The top box is the navigation area, through which the user issues commands to navigate through the system. The bottom box is the status area, which displays information about what the user is doing. The middle—and largest—box for accomplishing the task; it commonly displays reports and presents forms for data entry.

This use of multiple layout areas also applies to inputs and outputs. Data areas on reports and forms are often subdivided into subareas, each of which is used for a different type of information. These areas are almost always rectangular, although sometimes space constraints or aesthetics require odd shapes. Nonetheless, the margins on the edges of the screen should be consistent. Each of the areas within the report or form is designed to hold different information. For example, on an order form (or order report), one part may be used for customer information (e.g., name and address), one part for information about the order in general (e.g., date and payment information), and one part for the order details (e.g., how many units of which items at what price each). Each area is self-contained so that information in one area does not run into another.

The areas and information within areas should have a natural intuitive flow to minimize the users' movement from one area to the next. People in Europe, parts of Asia, Africa, and the

---

[3] A good book on the design of interfaces is Susan Weinschenk, Pamela Jamar, and Sarah Yeo, *GUI Design Essentials* (New York: Wiley, 1997).

Americas (e.g., United States, Canada, Mexico, Brazil, France, Russia, India, and Nigeria) tend to read left-to-right, top-to-bottom, so related information should be placed so that it is used in this order (e.g., address lines, followed by city, state or province, and then ZIP code or postal code). In contrast, when communicating in Arabic, Hebrew, or Persian, people tend to read right-to-left. Many East Asian cultures, such as Korean, Japanese, and Chinese, traditionally use a bi-orientational system, which means content can be laid out vertically (top-to-bottom) or horizontally (right-to-left, but also left-to-right). These and other (discussed later) cultural differences should be considered when designing forms and reports.

Sometimes the content sequence is in chronological order, or from the general to the specific, or from most frequently to least frequently used. In any event, before the areas are placed on a form or report, the analyst should have a clear understanding of what arrangement makes the most sense for how the form or report will be used. The flow between sections should also be consistent, whether horizontal or vertical. Ideally, the areas will remain consistent in size, shape, and placement for the forms used to enter information (whether paper or on screen) and the reports used to present it.

Content Awareness

Content awareness refers to the ability of an interface to make the user aware of the information it contains with the least amount of effort on the user's part. All parts of the interface, whether navigation, input, or output, should provide as much content awareness as possible, but it is particularly important for forms or reports that are used quickly or irregularly. Content awareness applies to the interface in general. All interfaces should have titles (on the screen frame, for example). Menus should show where the user is and, if possible, where the user came from to get there.

Content awareness also applies to the areas within forms and reports. All areas should be clear and well-defined so that it is difficult for the user to become confused about the information in any area. Then users can quickly locate the part of the form or report that is likely to contain the information they need. Sometimes the areas are marked by lines, colors, or headings; in other cases, the areas are only implied.

Content awareness also applies to the *fields* within each area. Fields are the individual elements of data that are input or output. The *field labels* that identify the fields on the interface should be short and specific—objectives that often conflict. There should be no uncertainty about the format of information within fields, whether for entry or display. For example, a date of 10/5/15 is different depending on whether you are in the United States (October 5, 2015) or in Canada (May 10, 2015). Any fields for which there is the possibility of uncertainty or multiple interpretations should provide explicit explanations.

Content awareness also applies to the information that a form or report contains. In general, all forms and reports should contain a preparation date (i.e., the date printed or the date completed) so that the age of information is obvious. Likewise, all printed forms and software should provide version numbers so that users, analysts, and programmers can identify outdated materials.

Aesthetics

Aesthetics refers to designing interfaces that are pleasing to the eye. Interfaces do not have to be works of art, but they do need to be functional and inviting to use. In most cases, less is more, meaning that a simple, minimalist design is the best.

Space is usually at a premium on forms and reports, and often there is the temptation to squeeze as much information as possible onto a page or a screen. Unfortunately, this can make a form or report so unpleasant that users do not want to use it. In general, all forms and reports need a minimum amount of *white space* that is intentionally left blank.

In general, novice or infrequent users of an interface, whether on a screen or on paper, prefer interfaces with low density, often one with a density of less than 50 percent (i.e., less than 50 percent of the interface occupied by information). More-experienced users prefer higher densities, sometimes approaching 90 percent occupied, because they know where information is located and high densities reduce the amount of physical movement through the interface.

The design of text is equally important. As a general rule, all text should be in the same font and about the same size. Fonts should be no smaller than 8 points, but 10 points or higher is preferred, particularly if the interface will be used by older people. Changes in font and size are used to indicate changes in the type of information that is presented (e.g., headings and status indicators). In general, italics and underlining should be avoided because they make text harder to read.

Serif fonts (i.e., those having letters with serifs, or tails, such as Times Roman) are the most readable for printed reports, particularly for small letters. Sans serif fonts (i.e., those without serifs, such as Helvetica or Arial) are the most readable for computer screens and are often used for headings in printed reports. Never use all capital letters, except possibly for titles.

Color and patterns should be used carefully and sparingly and only when they serve a purpose. (About 10 percent of men are color blind, so the improper use of color can impair their ability to read color text.) A quick trip around the Web will demonstrate the problems caused by indiscriminate use of colors and patterns. Remember, in most business settings, the goal is pleasant readability, not art; color and patterns should be used to strengthen the message, not overwhelm it. Color is best used to separate and categorize items, such as showing the difference between headings and regular text, or to highlight important information. Therefore, colors with high contrast should be used (e.g., black and white). In general, black text on a white background is the most readable, and blue on red is the least readable. Also, when it comes to the proper use of color, cultural issues come into play. We discuss this later in the chapter.

User Experience

User experience can essentially be broken down into two levels: those with experience and those without. Interfaces should be designed for both types of users. Novice users usually are most concerned with *ease of learning*—how quickly they can learn new systems. Expert users are usually most concerned with *ease of use*—how quickly they can use the system once they have learned how to use it. Often these two are complementary and lead to similar design decisions, but sometimes there are trade-offs. Novices, for example, often prefer menus that show all available system functions, because these promote ease of learning. Experts, on the other hand, sometimes prefer fewer menus organized around the most commonly used functions.

Research shows that expert and novice users have different requirements and behavior patterns in some cases. For example, novices virtually never look at the bottom area of a screen that presents status information, whereas experts refer to the status bar when they need information. Most systems should be designed to support frequent users, except for systems designed to be used infrequently or when many new users or occasional users are expected. Likewise, systems that contain functionality that is used only occasionally must contain a highly intuitive interface or an interface that contains clear, explicit guidance regarding its use. The balance of quick access to commonly used and well-known functions and guidance through new and less-well-known functions is challenging to the interface designer, and this balance often requires elegant solutions.

Systems that will end up being used by many people on a daily basis are more likely to have a majority of expert users (e.g., order-entry systems). Although interfaces should try to balance ease of use and ease of learning, these types of systems should put more emphasis on ease of use rather than ease of learning. Users should be able to access the commonly used functions quickly, with few keystrokes or a small number of menu selections. In many other systems (e.g., decision-support systems), most people remain occasional users for the lifetime of the system. In this case, greater emphasis may be placed on ease of learning rather than ease of use.

Consistency

Consistency in design is probably the single most important factor in making a system simple to use because it enables users to predict what will happen. When interfaces are consistent, users can interact with one part of the system and then know how to interact with the rest, aside from elements unique to those parts. Consistency usually refers to the interface within one computer system, so that all parts of the same system work in the same way. Ideally, the system should also be consistent with other computer systems in the organization and with commercial software that is used. Many software development tools support consistent system interfaces by providing standard interface objects (e.g., list boxes, pull-down menus, and radio buttons).

Consistency occurs at many different levels. Consistency in the *navigation controls* conveys how actions in the system should be performed. For example, using the same icon or command to change an item clearly communicates how changes are made throughout the system. Consistency in terminology is also important. This refers to using the same words for elements on forms and reports (e.g., not customer in one place and client in another). We also believe that consistency in report and form design is important, although a study suggests that being *too* consistent can cause problems.[4] When reports and forms are very similar except for very minor changes in titles, users sometimes mistakenly use the wrong form and either enter incorrect data or misinterpret its information. The implication for design is to make the reports and forms similar but give them some distinctive elements (e.g., color, size of titles icons, and graphics) that enable users to immediately detect differences.

Minimizing User Effort

Interfaces should be designed to minimize the amount of effort needed to accomplish tasks. This means using the fewest possible mouse clicks or keystrokes to move from one part of the system to another. Most interface designers follow the *three-clicks rule:* Users should be able to go from the start or main menu of a system to the information or action they want in no more than three mouse clicks or three keystrokes. However, with regard to this point, you need to be aware of Krug's principles (discussed later).

USER INTERFACE DESIGN PROCESS

User interface design is a use-case driven, incremental, and iterative process. Analysts often move back and forth between the different parts (navigation, input, and output) of the user interface, rather than proceeding sequentially from one part to another part. Given that the design process is use case driven, the analysts begin the user interface design process by

---

[4] John Satzinger and Lorne Olfman, "User Interface Consistency Across End-User Application: The Effects of Mental Models," *Journal of Management Information Systems* (Spring 1998): 167–193.

examining the *use cases* (see Chapter 3) and their associated *activity* and *sequence diagrams* (see Chapters 4 and 5) developed in analysis. Analysts then typically sit down with users to develop *use scenarios* that describe commonly employed patterns of actions the users will perform so that the interface enables users to quickly and smoothly perform these scenarios. In some cases, additional requirements are uncovered. Depending on the importance of the newly uncovered requirements, this can cause the problem domain layer to be modified, which in turn can cause the data management layer to be modified. However, many times, these new requirements can be delayed until the next iteration of the system. With agile approaches, user interface design and requirements modeling is intertwined and new requirements are uncovered on a regular basis. Consequently, depending on the stability of the modeling of the problem domain, user interface design could occur concurrently with functional modeling. Even though functional and behavioral modeling is associated with the analysis workflow and user interface design is associated with the design workflow, the level of activity associated with the two workflows overlaps (see Figures 1-3 and 1-4). As such, performing user interface design along side of functional and behavioral modeling is compatible with both the Unified Process and the Enhanced Unified Process.

Once a basic set of use scenarios have been developed, the actual user interface is designed. As we stated earlier, all GUI-based user interfaces comprise three parts: navigation, input, and output. To some degree, all three parts tend to be designed together. Consequently, the user interface design process tends to follow a prototyping style of development wherein the analyst and user will incrementally build a design by iterating across all three parts of the user interface using different design tools. For example, when designing the structure of the navigation, a *windows navigation diagram (WND)* is very useful; when designing the layout of the user interface, a *wireframe diagram* is very useful; and when attempting to try and tie the navigation, input, and output designs together, *storyboards*, and *user interface prototypes* are very useful. Another useful idea when developing a user interface is to have a set of accepted *interface standards* that can be used across multiple applications. For example, a standard set of menus, icons, and user interface templates simplify the entire design of the human–computer interaction layer. Once the basic design has been completed for a specific use case, then the *essential use case* developed in functional modeling should be converted to a *real use case* that, along with the other tools used to design the interface, can be used as a basis for documentation, training, and testing.

Use Scenario Development

A *use scenario* is an outline of the steps that the users perform to accomplish some part of their work. A use scenario is one path through an essential use case. For example, Figure 9-2 shows the use-case diagram for the Appointment System. This figure shows that the Create New Patient use case is distinct from the Make Payment Arrangements use case. We model these two use cases separately because they represent separate processes that are used by the Manage Appointments use case.

The use-case diagram was designed to model all possible uses of the system at a fairly high level of abstraction. In one use scenario, an existing patient makes a request with the receptionist regarding an appointment with the doctor. The receptionist looks up the patient, asks the patient if they need to update any information, and checks to see if the patient has any bills to be paid. The receptionist then asks the patient whether he or she wants to set up a new appointment, cancel an existing appointment, or change an existing appointment. If the patient wants to make a new appointment, the receptionist asks the patient for some suggested appointment times, which the receptionist matches against potential times available. The receptionist finally creates a new appointment (see Figures 3-12, 4-7, 5-1, and 5-3).

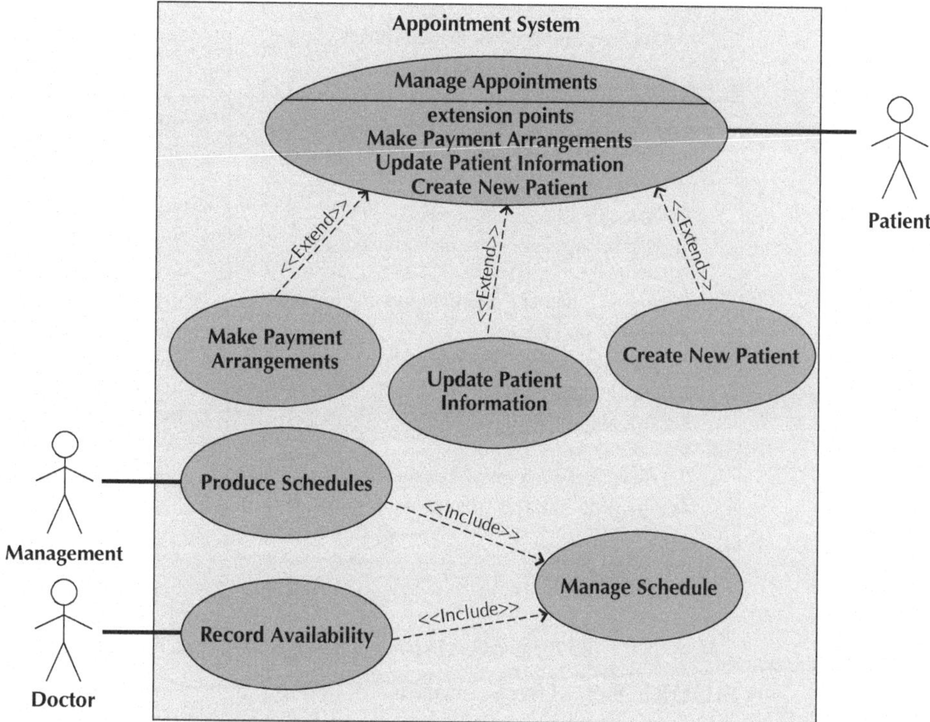

FIGURE 9-2 Appointment System Use-Case Diagram (see Figure 3-11)

In another use scenario, a patient simply wants to cancel an appointment. In this case, the receptionist looks up the patient, asks the patient if they need to update any information, and checks to see if the patient has any bills to be paid. The receptionist then asks the patient for the time of the appointment to be canceled. Finally, the receptionist deletes the appointment.

Use scenarios are presented in a simple narrative description that is tied to the essential use cases developed during analysis (see Chapter 3). Figure 9-3 shows the two use scenarios just described. The key point with using use cases for interface design is *not* to document all possible use scenarios within a use case. The goal is to document two or three of the most common use scenarios so that the interface can be designed to enable the most common uses to be performed simply and easily.

Navigation Structure Design

The navigation structure defines the basic components of the interface and how they work together to provide functionality to users. A *windows navigation diagram (WND)*[5] is used to show how all the screens, forms, and reports used by the system are related and how the user moves from one to another. Most systems have several WNDs, one for each major part of the system.

A WND is very similar to a behavioral state machine (see Chapter 5), in that they both model state changes. A behavioral state machine typically models the *state* changes of an object, whereas a WND models the state changes of the user interface. In a WND, each state of the user interface is represented as a box. A box typically corresponds to a user interface

---

[5] A WND is based on the behavioral state machine and object diagrams [see Meilir Page-Jones, *Fundamentals of Object-Oriented Design in UML* (New York: Dorset House, 2000)].

<table>
<tr><th>Use scenario: Existing Patient Makes New Appointment</th><th>Use scenario: Existing Patient Cancels Appointment</th></tr>
<tr><td>

1. Patient contacts the office regarding an appointment (1) and gives the receptionist their name and address (2).
2. The receptionist looks up the patient (3a).
3. The receptionist asks if the patient needs to update their information (S-2, 1 or S-2, 1a) and determines whether the patient has any unpaid bills (S-2, 2 or S-2, 2a).
4. The receptionist then asks the patient for a set of possible times to set up a new appointment and matches them with the times available (S-2, 3).
5. The receptionist informs the patient that their appointment time was created (4).

</td><td>

1. Patient contacts the office regarding an appointment (1) and gives the receptionist their name and address (2).
2. The receptionist looks up the patient (3a).
3. The receptionist asks if the patient needs to update their information (S-2, 1 or S-2, 1a) and determines whether the patient has any unpaid bills (S-2, 2 or S-2, 2a).
4. The receptionist asks the patient for the appointment time to be canceled and deletes the appointment (S-2, 3a).
5. The receptionist informs the patient that their appointment time was canceled (4).

</td></tr>
</table>

The numbers in parentheses refer to specific events in the essential use case (see Figure 3-13).

FIGURE 9-3 Use Scenarios

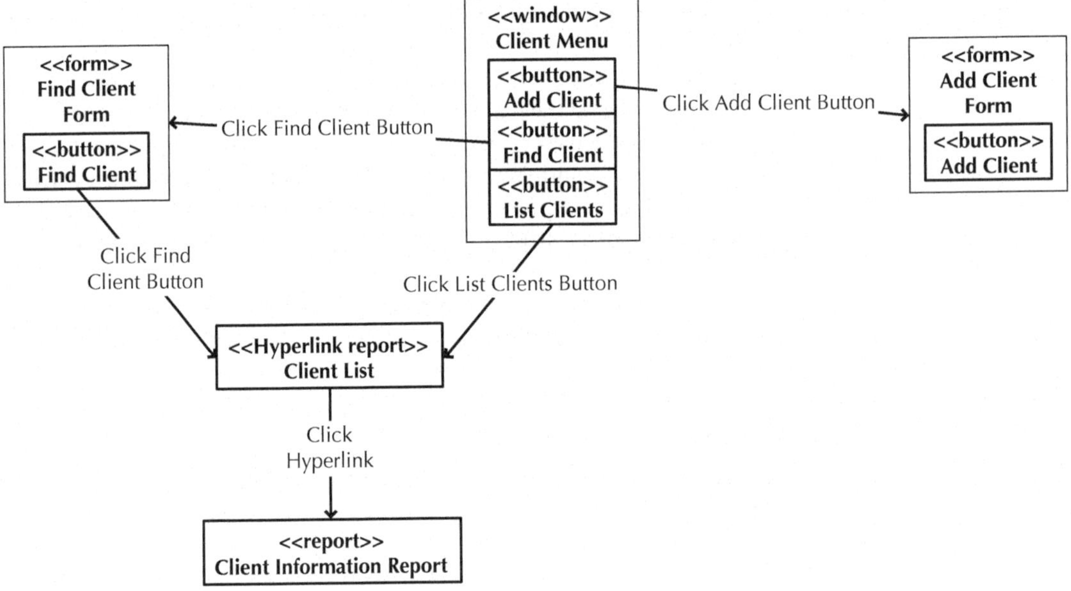

FIGURE 9-4 Sample WND

component, such as a *window, form, button,* or *report.* For example, in Figure 9-4, there are five separate states: Client Menu, Find Client Form, Add Client Form, Client List, and Client Information Report.

Transitions are modeled as either a single-headed or double-headed arrow. A single-headed arrow indicates that a return to the calling state is not required, whereas a double-headed arrow represents a required return. For example in Figure 9-4, the transition from the Client Menu state to the Find Client Form state does not require a return. The arrows are labeled with the action that causes the user interface to move from one state to another. For example, in Figure 9-4, to move from the Client Menu state to the Find Client Form state, the user must click the Find Client Button on the Client Menu.

The last item to be described in a WND is the *stereotype*. A stereotype is modeled as a text item enclosed within guillemets or angle brackets (<< >>). The stereotype represents the type of user interface component of a box on the diagram. For example, the Client Menu is a window, whereas Find Client Form is a form.

The basic navigation structure of an interface follows the basic structure of the business process itself as defined in the use cases and behavioral models. The analyst starts with the essential use cases and develops the fundamental flow of control of the system as it moves from object to object. The analyst then examines the use scenarios to see how well the WND supports them. Quite often, the use scenarios identify paths through the WND that are more complicated than they should be. The analyst then reworks the WND to simplify the ability of the interface to support the use scenarios, sometimes by making major changes to the menu structure, sometimes by adding shortcuts.

Interface Standards Design

Interface standards are the basic design elements that are common across the individual screens, forms, and reports within the system. Depending on the application, there may be several sets of interface standards for different parts of the system (e.g., one for Web screens, one for mobile screens, one for paper reports, and one for input forms). For example, the part of the system used by data entry operators might mirror other data entry applications in the company, whereas a Web interface for displaying information from the same system might adhere to some standardized Web format. Likewise, each individual interface might not contain all of the elements in the standards (e.g., a report screen might not have an edit capability), and they might contain additional characteristics beyond the standard ones, but the standards serve as the touchstone that ensures the interfaces are consistent across the system. The following sections discuss some of the main areas in which interface standards should be considered: metaphors, objects, actions, icons, and templates.

Interface Metaphor First of all, the analysts must develop the fundamental interface metaphor(s) that defines how the interface will work. An *interface metaphor* is a concept from the real world that is used as a model for the computer system. The metaphor helps the user understand the system and enables the user to predict what features the interface might provide, even without actually using the system. Sometimes systems have one metaphor, whereas in other cases there are several metaphors in different parts of the system.

Often, the metaphor is explicit. Quicken, for example, uses a checkbook metaphor for its interface, even to the point of having the users type information into an on-screen form that looks like a real check. In other cases, the metaphor is implicit or unstated, but it is there, nonetheless. Many Windows systems use the paper form or table as a metaphor.

In some cases, the metaphor is so obvious that it requires no thought. For example, most online stores use a shopping cart metaphor to temporarily store the items that the customer is considering purchasing. In other cases, a metaphor is hard to identify. In general, it is better not to force a metaphor that really doesn't fit a system, because an ill-fitting metaphor will confuse users by promoting incorrect assumptions.

Interface Templates An *interface template* defines the general appearance of all screens in the information system and the paper-based forms and reports that are used. The template design, for example, specifies the basic layout of the screens (e.g., where the navigation area(s), status area, and form/report area(s) will be placed) and the color scheme(s) that will be applied. It defines whether windows will replace one another on the screen or will cascade over the top of each other. The template defines a standard placement and order for common interface actions (e.g., File Edit View rather than File View Edit). In short, the template draws together the other major interface design elements: metaphors, objects, actions, and icons.

Interface Objects The template specifies the names that the interface will use for the major *interface objects,* the fundamental building blocks of the system, such as the classes. In many cases, the object names are straightforward, such as calling the shopping cart the "shopping cart." In other cases, it is not so simple. For example, Amazon.com sells much more than books. In some cases, the user might not know whether he or she is looking for a physical book, digital music, or Kindle download. In those cases, the user can use a catchall search item: All Departments. In the case that the user knows the type of item that he or she wants to buy, the user can limit the search by specifying more-specific types of search items, such as Apps for Android, Books, Kindle Store, or Music. Obviously, the object names should be easily understood and help promote the interface metaphor.

In general, in cases of disagreements between the users and the analysts over names, whether for objects or actions (discussed later), the users should win. A more understandable name always beats a more precise or more accurate one.

Interface Actions The template also specifies the navigation and command language style (e.g., menus) and grammar (e.g., object-action order; see the navigation design section later in this chapter). It gives names to the most commonly used *interface actions* in the navigation design (e.g., buy versus purchase or modify versus change).

Interface Icons The interface objects and actions and their status (e.g., deleted or overdrawn) may be represented by *interface icons*. Icons are pictures that appear on command buttons as well as in reports and forms to highlight important information. Icon design is very challenging because it means developing a simple picture less than half the size of a postage stamp that needs to convey an often-complex meaning. The simplest and best approach is to simply adopt icons developed by others (e.g., a blank page to indicate create a new file, a diskette to indicate save).[6] This has the advantage of quick icon development, and the icons might already be well understood by users because they have seen them in other software.

Commands are actions that are especially difficult to represent with icons because they are in motion, not static. Many icons have become well known from widespread use, but icons are not as well understood as first believed. Use of icons can sometimes cause more confusion than insight. Icon meanings become clearer with use, but sometimes a picture is not worth even one word; when in doubt, use a word, not a picture.

Interface Design Prototyping

An *interface design prototype* is a mock-up or a simulation of a computer screen, form, or report. A prototype is prepared for each interface in the system to show the users and the programmers how the system will perform. In the "old days," an interface design prototype was usually specified on a paper form that showed what would be displayed on each part of the screen. Paper forms are still used today, but more and more interface design prototypes

---

[6] However, given that diskettes are rarely used anymore, the value of using the diskette icon may be fading away.

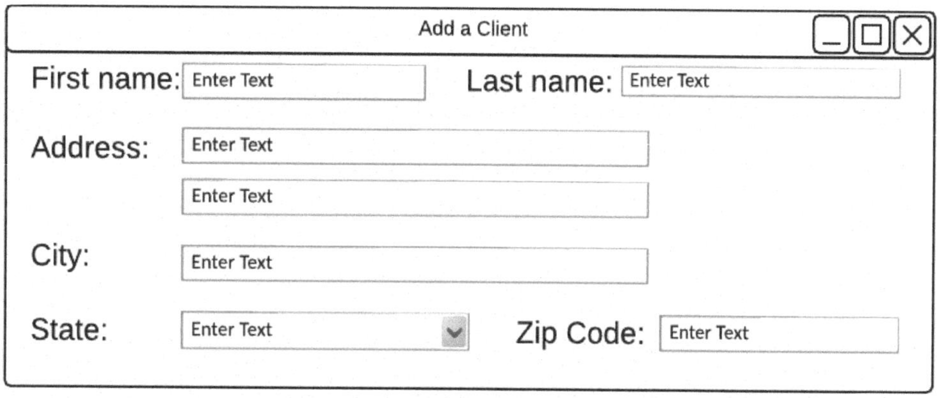

FIGURE 9-5   Sample Wireframe Diagram

are being built using computer tools instead of paper. The most common approaches to interface design prototyping are wireframe diagrams, storyboards, and language prototypes.

Wireframe Diagram A *wireframe diagram* is simply a picture that resembles the actual user interface that the user will gradually receive. Typically, it is created using a tool such as Microsoft's Visio or Google's Lucidchart. Using this type of tool, the designer can quickly drag and drop the user interface components onto the canvas to lay out the design of the user interface. For example, Figure 9-5 portrays a simple wireframe diagram. Even though there is no executable capability associated with a wireframe diagram, it does allow the user to quickly get a feel for the look of the user interface that will be delivered.

Storyboard At its simplest, an interface design prototype is a paper-based *storyboard*. The storyboard shows hand-drawn pictures of what the screens will look like and how they flow from one screen to another, in the same way a storyboard for a cartoon shows how the action will flow from one scene to the next (see Figure 9-6). Storyboards are the simplest technique because all they require is paper (often a flip chart) and a pen—and someone with some artistic ability. Storyboards also combine both the navigation information of the windows navigation diagram and to some degree the layout information of the wireframe diagram. However, with today's graphics tools, the designer can work effectively with a set of users to design both the look and feel of the evolving system without having to actually implement anything, by combining the wireframe diagrams with the windows navigation diagram into a single better storyboard type of diagram (see Figure 9-7).

User Interface Prototypes With today's programming environments, such as Visual Studio and NetBeans, it is fairly easy to develop executable prototypes (see Figure 9-8) of the user interface that would allow the user to be able to interact with the user interface by clicking on buttons and entering pretend data into forms (but because there is no **code and database** behind the pages, the data are never processed). The different parts of the user interface are linked together so that as the user clicks on buttons, the requested part of the system appears. These executable prototypes take longer to develop than windows navigation diagrams, wireframe diagrams, and storyboards but have the distinct advantage of showing *exactly* what the screens will look like. The user does not have to guess about the shape or position of the elements on the screen. However, one of the potential issues that can arise when developing user

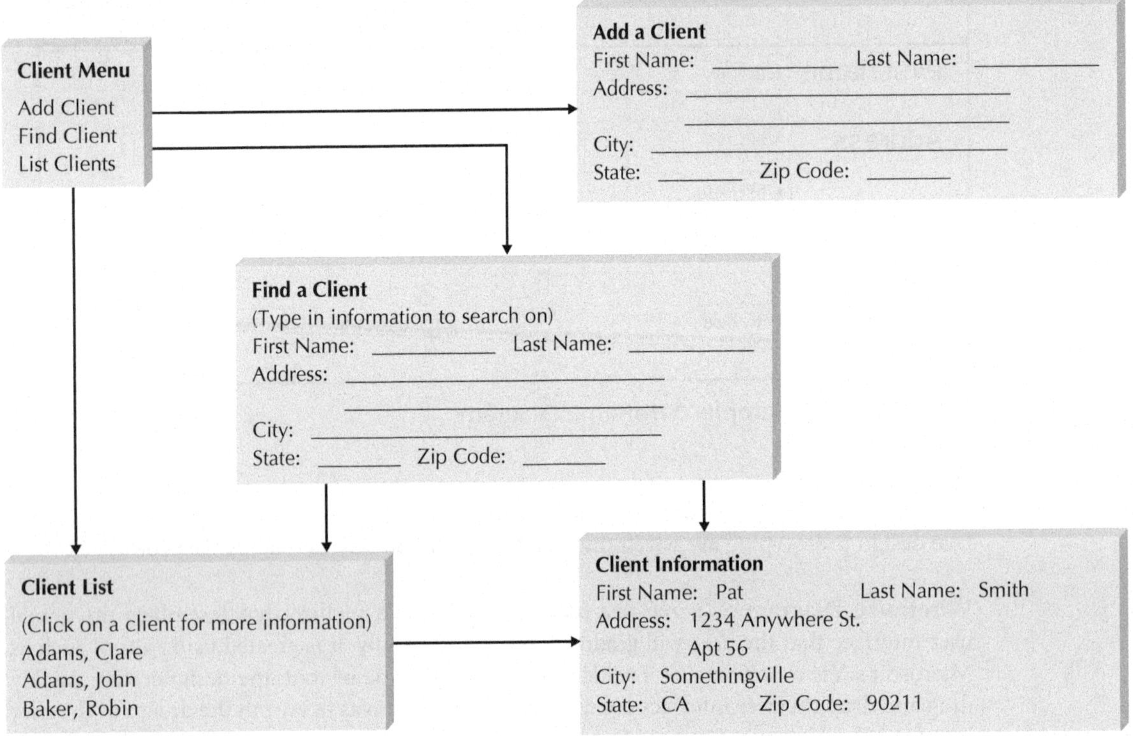

FIGURE 9-6 Sample Storyboard

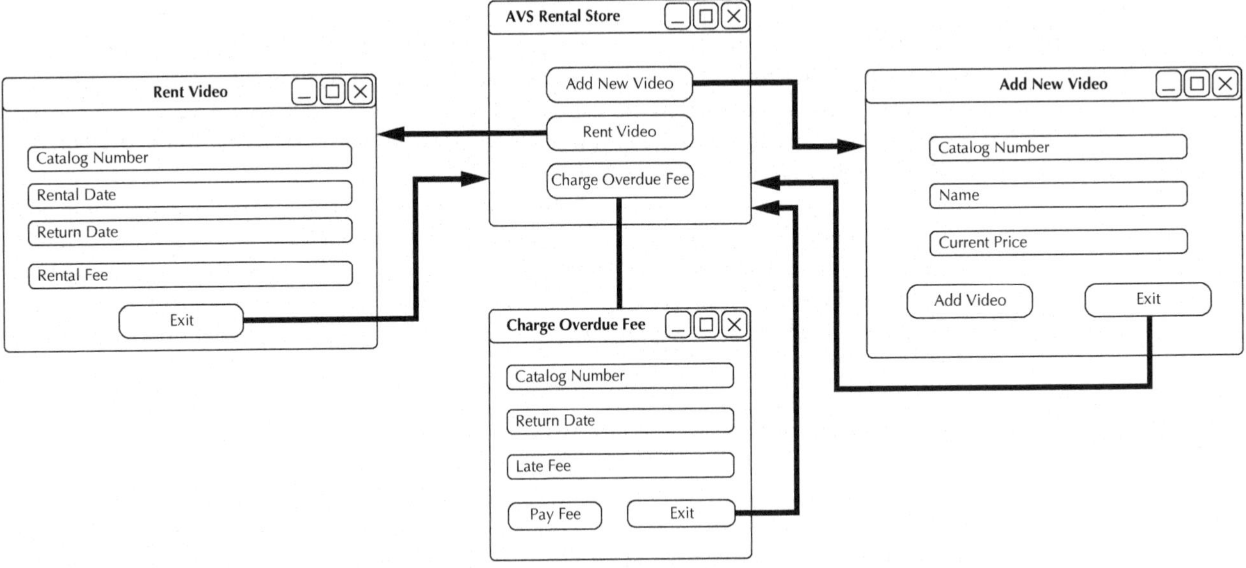

FIGURE 9-7 Sample Combined Windows Navigation and Wireframe Diagrams

interface prototypes is that the user's expectations of when the systems will be completed can become unrealistic. To actually connect the prototype to the problem domain such that the system actually works is not a trivial problem. So, user expectations need to be carefully managed. Otherwise, a system that meets all of its specifications could end up being considered a failure.

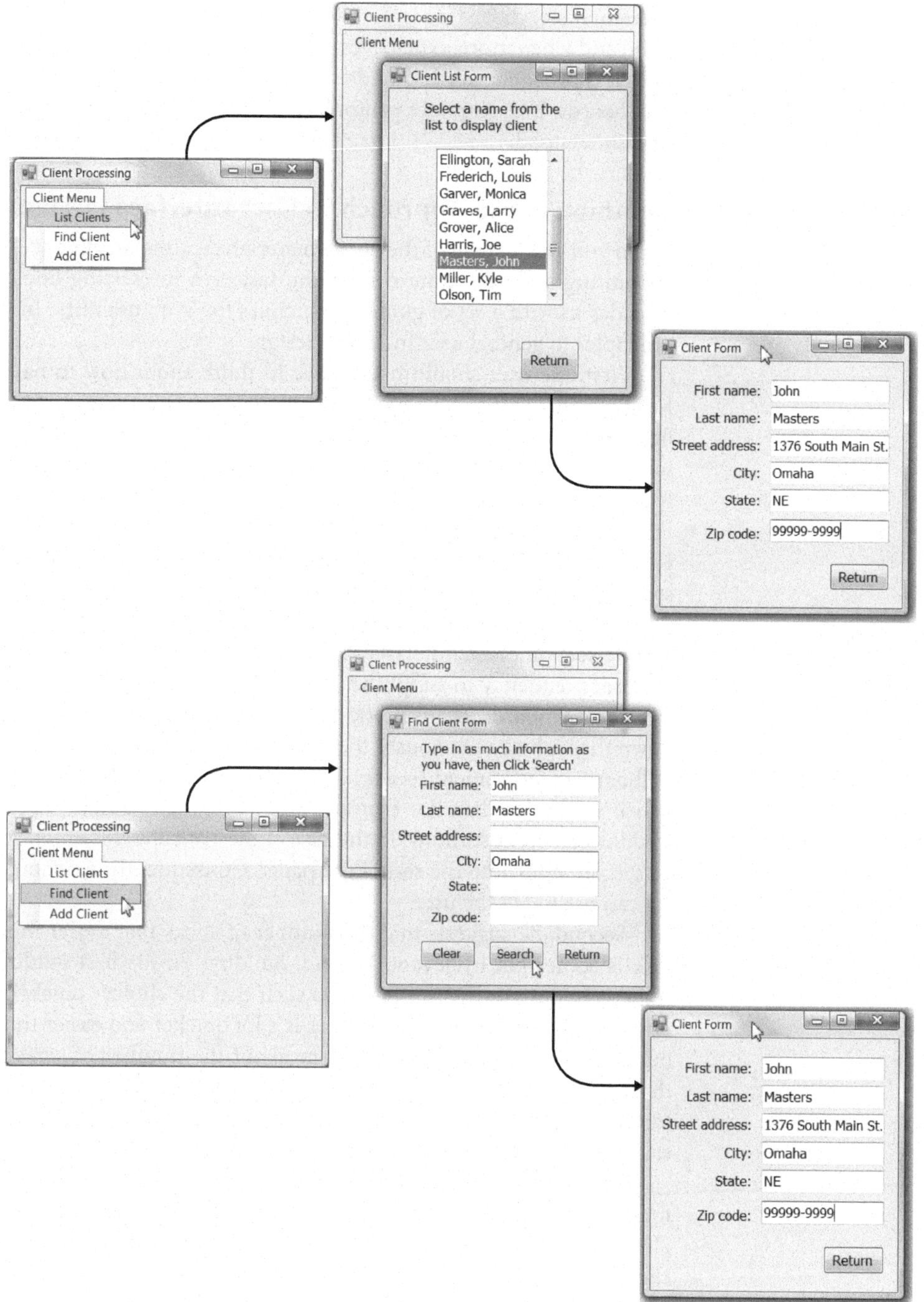

FIGURE 9-8 Sample User Interface Prototype

Selecting the Appropriate Techniques Projects often use a combination of different interface design prototyping techniques for different parts of the system. Storyboarding is the fastest and least expensive but provides the least amount of detail. Wireframe diagrams provide more of a feel that the user will experience, while remaining fairly inexpensive to develop. User interface prototypes are the slowest, most expensive, and most detailed approach.

Therefore, storyboarding is used for parts of the system in which the interface is well understood and when more-expensive prototypes are thought to be unnecessary. However, in most cases it is probably worth the additional cost of developing wireframe diagrams in addition to storyboards. User interface prototypes are used for parts of the system that are critical, yet not well understood.

Common Sense Approach to User Interface Design

When you consider all of the above material, creating an effective user interface design can be a daunting and very time-consuming task. An interesting book by Steve Krug,[7] however, provides us with a set of guiding principles for Web usability. In this section, we adapt these principles to general user interface design.

First, the user should never have to think about how to navigate the user interface. As Krug puts it, "Don't make me think." Cognitively speaking, any time the user has to stop and figure out how to use the user interface, the creator of the user interface has failed. That might seem a little harsh, but it is true. From the user's perspective, the user interface is the system. If the developers have done their homework, the user interface should be intuitive to use. From a practical perspective, we should study how the user really uses the system. Based on Krug's observations of users, he found that users do not read Web pages; instead, they tend to scan them. As a general user interface design guideline, we suggest that you make it easy for users to identify the different parts of the user interface so that they simply scan the screen to see the section of the interface that is applicable to the problem that they are solving. Given the user's tendency to simply scan the user interface, Krug suggests that we should consider studying billboards for inspiration. Billboards are designed to be "read" at 70 mph as you drive down the highway. Obviously, the most relevant information must catch your attention for the billboard advertisement to work. He suggests that we should use the set of conventions with which we are familiar. For example, when looking at a newspaper you know that it is organized into different sections. In the case of the *Wall Street Journal*, you know that the front page acts as an index into the rest of the paper. Consequently, we should look for conventions that we can use to aid the user.

Second, he suggests that the number of clicks that a user must perform to complete the task is somewhat irrelevant. Instead, building on his first guiding principle, the important thing is to design the user interface such that the choices (clicks) to be made are unambiguous. Making a lot of obvious choices is a lot quicker and easier than a few vague and ambiguous ones. Consequently, don't worry about the number of screens that the user must work through. However, like any other rule, this can be taken to an extreme. Too many clicks is still too many clicks. The overall goal is to minimize the user's effort. Simply focus on making it easier for the user to complete the task.

Third, minimize the number of words on the screen. Given that users scan the screen to find for what they are searching, make it easier by not cluttering the screen with lots of noise. He suggests that in the case of Web interfaces, 50 percent to 75 percent of the words can be eliminated without losing any information contained on the screen. Obviously, this may be somewhat extreme, but it does suggest that following the KISS[8] principle is critical when designing effective user interfaces.

---

7 Steve Krug, *Don't Make Me Think: A Common Sense Approach to Web Usability*, 2nd Ed. (Berkeley, CA: 2nd Ed. New Riders, 2006).

8 Keep it simple, stupid!

NAVIGATION DESIGN

The navigation component of the interface enables the user to enter commands to navigate through the system and perform actions to enter and review information it contains. The navigation component also presents messages to the user about the success or failure of his or her actions. The goal of the navigation system is to make the system as simple as possible to use. A good navigation component is one the user never really notices. It simply functions the way the user expects, and thus the user gives it little thought. In other words, keep Krug's three guiding principles in mind as you work through the next three sections of the text.

Basic Principles

One of the hardest things about using a computer system is learning how to manipulate the navigation controls to make the system do what you want. Analysts should assume that users have not read the manual, attended training, nor have external help readily at hand. All controls should be clear and understandable and placed in an intuitive location on the screen. Ideally, the controls should anticipate what the user will do. For example, many setup programs are designed so that for a typical installation, the user can simply keep pressing the Next button.

Prevent Mistakes The first principle of designing navigation controls is to prevent the user from making mistakes. A mistake costs time and causes frustration. Worse still, a series of mistakes can cause the user to discard the system. Mistakes can be reduced by labeling commands and actions appropriately and by limiting choices. Too many choices can confuse the user, particularly when the choices are similar and hard to describe in the short space available on the screen. When there are many similar choices on a menu, consider creating a second menu level or a series of options for basic commands.

Never display a command that cannot be used. Many Windows applications gray out commands that cannot be used; they are displayed on pull-down menus in a very light-colored font, but they cannot be selected. This shows that they are available but cannot be used in the current context. It also keeps all menu items in the same place.

When the user is about to perform a critical function that is difficult or impossible to undo (e.g., deleting a file), it is important to confirm the action with the user (and make sure the selection was not made by mistake). Having the user respond to a confirmation message, which explains what the user has requested and asks the user to confirm that this action is correct, usually does this.

Simplify Recovery from Mistakes No matter what the system designer does, users will make mistakes. The system should make it as easy as possible to correct these errors. Ideally, the system has an Undo button that makes mistakes easy to override; however, writing the software for such buttons can be very complicated.

Use Consistent Grammar Order One of the most fundamental decisions is the *grammar order*. Most commands require the user to specify an object (e.g., file, record, and word), and the action to be performed on that object (e.g., copy and delete). The interface can require the user to first choose the object and then the action (an *object–action order*) or first choose the action and then the object (an *action–object order*). Most Windows applications use an object–action grammar order (e.g., think about copying a block of text in your word processor).

The grammar order should be consistent throughout the system, both at the data element level and at the overall menu level. Experts debate about the advantages of one approach over the other, but because most users are familiar with the object–action order, most systems today are designed using that approach.

Types of Navigation Controls

There are two traditional hardware devices that can be used to control the user interface: the keyboard and a pointing device such as a mouse, trackball, or touch screen. Today, depending on the hardware being used, voice recognition systems can also be used to control the user interface. There are three basic software approaches for defining user commands: languages, menus, and direct manipulation.

Languages

With a *command language,* the user enters commands using a special language developed for the computer system (e.g., UNIX and SQL editor both use command languages). Command languages sometimes provide greater flexibility than other approaches because the user can combine language elements in ways not predetermined by developers. However, they put a greater burden on users because users must learn syntax and type commands rather than select from a well-defined, limited number of choices. Systems today use command languages sparingly, except in cases where there is an extremely large number of command combinations that make it impractical to try to build all combinations into a menu (e.g., SQL queries for databases).

Natural language interfaces are designed to understand the user's own language (e.g., English, Spanish, and Arabic). These interfaces attempt to interpret what the user means, and often they present back to the user a list of interpretations from which to choose. An example of the use of natural language is Google's search engine. Google's search engine enables users to use free-form text to search the Web for topics of interest. Another example is OpenAI's ChatGPT that uses artificial intelligence to respond to natural language prompts.

Menus

The most common type of navigation system today is the *menu.* A menu presents a user with a list of choices, each of which can be selected. Menus are easier to learn than languages because a limited number of available commands are presented to the user in an organized fashion. Clicking on an item with a pointing device or pressing a key that matches the menu choice (e.g., a function key) takes very little effort. Therefore, menus are usually preferred to languages.

Menus need to be designed with care because the submenus behind a main menu are hidden from users until they click on the menu item. It is better to make menus broad and shallow (i.e., each menu containing many items with only one or two layers of menus) rather than narrow and deep (i.e., each menu containing only a few items, but each leading to three or more layers of menus). A broad and shallow menu presents the user with the most information initially so that he or she can see many options and requires only a few mouse clicks or keystrokes to perform an action. A narrow and deep menu makes users hunt for items hidden behind menu items and requires many more clicks or keystrokes to perform an action.

Research suggests that in an ideal world, any one menu should contain no more than eight items, and it should take no more than two mouse clicks or keystrokes from any menu to perform an action (or three from the main menu that starts a system).[9] However, analysts sometimes must break this guideline in the design of complex systems by grouping menu

---

[9] Kent L. Norman, *The Psychology of Menu Selection* (Norwood NJ: Ablex Publishing Corp., 1991).

items separated by a horizontal line. Often menu items have *hot keys* that enable experienced users to quickly invoke a command with keystrokes in lieu of a menu choice (e.g., on a Windows machine, Ctrl-F tends to invoke the Find command across many applications; on a Mac Command-F is commonly used instead).

Menus should put together like items so that the user can intuitively guess what each menu contains. Most designers recommend grouping menu items by interface objects (e.g., customers, purchase orders, and inventory) rather than by interface actions (e.g., new, update, and format), so that all actions pertaining to one object are in one menu, all actions for another object are in a different menu, and so on. However, this is highly dependent on the specific interface. Some of the more common types of menus include *menu bars, drop-down menus, pop-up menus, tab menus,* and *toolbars.*

Direct Manipulation

With *direct manipulation,* the user enters commands by working directly with interface objects. For example, users can change the size of objects in Microsoft PowerPoint by clicking on them and moving their sides, or they can move files in Windows Explorer by dragging the filenames from one folder to another. Direct manipulation can be simple, but it suffers from two problems. First, users familiar with language- or menu-based interfaces don't always expect it. Second, not all commands are intuitive. [How do you copy (not move) files in Windows Explorer? On the Macintosh, why does moving a folder to the trash delete the file if it is on the hard disk, but eject the DVD if the file is on a DVD?]

Messages

Messages are the way the system responds to a user and informs the user of the status of the interaction. There are many different types of messages, such as *error messages, confirmation messages, acknowledgment messages, delay messages,* and *help messages.* In general, messages should be clear, concise, and complete, which are sometimes conflicting objectives. All messages should be grammatically correct and free of jargon and abbreviations (unless they are the users' jargon and abbreviations). Avoid negatives because they can be confusing (e.g., replace Are you sure you do not want to continue? with Do you want to quit?). Likewise, avoid humor, because it wears off quickly after the same message appears dozens of times.

Messages should require the user to acknowledge them (by clicking, for example), rather than being displayed for a few seconds and then disappearing. The exceptions are messages that inform the user of delays in processing, which should disappear once the delay has passed. In general, messages are text, but sometimes, standard icons are used. For example, Windows displays an hourglass when the system is busy. All messages should be carefully crafted, but error and help messages require particular care. Messages (and especially error messages) should always explain the problem in polite, succinct terms (e.g., what the user did incorrectly) and explain corrective action as clearly and as explicitly as possible so that the user knows exactly what needs to be done. In the case of complicated errors, the error message should display what the user entered, suggest probable causes for the error, and propose possible user responses. When in doubt, provide either more information than the user needs or the ability to get additional information. Error messages should provide a message number. Message numbers are not intended for users, but their presence makes it simpler for help desks and customer support lines to identify problems and help users because many messages use similar wording.

Navigation Design Documentation

The design of the navigation for a system is done through the use of WNDs and real use cases. Real use cases are derived from the essential use cases (see Chapter 3), use scenarios, and WNDs. Recall that an essential use case is one that describes only the minimum essential issues necessary to understand the required functionality. A real use case describes a specific set of steps that a user performs to use a specific part of a system. Hence, real use cases are very useful when developing role-based access controls to support the security nonfunctional requirements (see Chapter 10), the documentation of the system (see Chapter 12), and when designing the tests (Chapter 7) and user training (see Chapter 12). However, since real use cases are implementation dependent, there may need to be customized versions for each platform on which the system is to be deployed.

To evolve an essential use case into a real use case, two changes must be made. First, the use-case type must be changed from essential to real. Second, all events must be specified in terms of the actual user interface. And, given the peculiarities of different platforms, e.g., desktops, tablets, and smartphones, real use cases will need to be developed for each platform on which the use case is being deployed. Therefore, the normal flow of events, subflows, and alternative/exceptional flows must be modified. The normal flow of events, subflows, and alternative/exceptional flows for the real use case associated with the storyboard user interface prototype given in Figure 9-6 is shown in Figure 9-9. For example, step 2 of the normal flow

<table>
<tr><td colspan="2">Use-Case Name: Maintain Client List</td><td>ID: 12</td><td>Importance Level: High</td></tr>
<tr><td colspan="2">Primary Actor: Sales Rep</td><td colspan="2">Use-Case Type: Detail, Real</td></tr>
<tr><td colspan="4">Stakeholders and Interests: Sales Rep – wants to add, find, or list clients</td></tr>
<tr><td colspan="4">Brief Description: Describes how sales representatives can search and maintain the client lists</td></tr>
<tr><td colspan="4">Trigger: Sales rep requests to find a client, add a new client, list the existing clients</td></tr>
<tr><td colspan="4">Type: External</td></tr>
<tr><td colspan="4">Relationships:
        Association: Sales Rep
        Include:
        Extend:
        Generalization:</td></tr>
<tr><td colspan="4">Normal Flow of Events:
   1. The Sales Rep starts up the system.
   2. The system provides the Sales Rep with the Main Menu for the system.
   3. Call S-1: List Clients
   4. The system returns the Sales Rep to the Main Menu of the system.</td></tr>
<tr><td colspan="4">Subflows:
  S-1: List Clients
     1. System creates a list of all clients.
     2. Sales Rep selects a specific client from the list.
     3. System produces a Client Information Report.
  S-2: Find Client
     1. System asks Sales Rep for search criteria.
     2. Sales Rep types search criteria into form.
     3. Sales Rep submits search criteria to system.
     4. System creates a list of the clients that meet the search criteria.
     5. Sales Rep selects a specific client from the list.
     6. System produces a Client Information Report.
  S-3: New Clients
     1. The System asks the Sales Rep for the information describing the new client.
     2. Sales Rep types information into form.
     3. Sales Rep submits the information to the system.</td></tr>
<tr><td colspan="4">Alternate/Exceptional Flows:
   3a. Call S-2, Find Client
   3b. Call S-3, New Client</td></tr>
</table>

FIGURE 9-9
Real Use-Case
Example

of events states that "The System provides the Sales Rep with the Main Menu for the System," which allows the Sales Rep to interact with the Maintain Client List aspect of the system.

INPUT DESIGN

Inputs facilitate the entry of data into the computer system, whether highly structured data, such as order information (e.g., item numbers, quantities, and costs) or unstructured information (e.g., comments). Input design means designing the screens used to enter the information as well as any forms on which users write or type information (e.g., timecards and expense claims).

Basic Principles

The goal of the input mechanism is to simply and easily capture accurate information for the system. The fundamental principles for input design reflect the nature of the inputs (whether batch or online) and ways to simplify their collection.

Online versus Batch Processing There are two general formats for entering inputs into a computer system: online processing and batch processing. With *online processing* (sometimes called *transaction processing*), each input item (e.g., a customer order and a purchase order) is entered into the system individually, usually at the same time as the event or transaction prompting the input. For example, when you check a book out from the library, buy an item at the store, or make an airline reservation, the computer system that supports that process uses online processing to immediately record the transaction in the appropriate database(s). Online processing is most commonly used when it is important to have *real-time information* about the business process. For example, when you reserve an airline seat, the seat is no longer available for someone else to use.

With *batch processing*, all the inputs collected over some time period are gathered together and entered into the system at one time in a batch. Some business processes naturally generate information in batches. For example, most hourly payrolls are done using batch processing because time cards are gathered together in batches and processed at once. Batch processing is also used for transaction processing systems that do not require real-time information. For example, most stores send sales information to district offices so that new replacement inventory can be ordered. This information can be sent in real time as it is captured in the store so that the district offices are aware within a second or two that a product is sold. If stores do not need this up-to-the-second real-time data, they will collect sales data throughout the day and transmit it every evening in a batch to the district office. This batching simplifies the data communications process and often saves in communications costs, but it does mean that inventories are accurate only at the end of the day, not in real time, after the batch has been processed.

Capture Data at the Source Perhaps the most important principle of input design is to capture the data in an electronic format at its original source or as close to the original source as possible. In the early days of computing, computer systems replaced traditional manual systems that operated on paper forms. As these business processes were automated, many of the original paper forms remained, either because no one thought to replace them or because it was too expensive to do so. Instead, the business process continued to contain manual forms that were taken to the computer center in batches to be typed into the computer system by a *data entry operator*.

Many business processes still operate this way today. For example, most organizations have expense claim forms that are completed by hand and submitted to an accounting department, which approves them and enters them into the system in batches. There are three problems with this approach. First, it is expensive because it duplicates work (the form is filled out twice, once by hand, once by keyboard). Second, it increases processing time because the paper forms must be physically moved through the process. Third, it increases the cost and probability of error, because it separates the entry from the processing of information; someone might misread the handwriting on the input form, data may be entered incorrectly, or the original input could contain an error that invalidates the information.

Most transaction-processing systems today are designed to capture data at its source. *Source data automation* refers to using special hardware devices to automatically capture data without requiring anyone to type it. Stores commonly use *bar-code readers* that automatically scan products and enter data directly into the computer system. No intermediate formats such as paper forms are used. Similar technologies include *optical character recognition,* which can read printed numbers and text (e.g., on checks), *magnetic stripe readers,* which can read information encoded on magnetic strip (e.g., credit cards), and *smart cards,* which contain microprocessors, memory chips, and batteries (much like credit card–sized calculators). As well as reducing the time and cost of data entry, these systems reduce errors because they are far less likely to capture data incorrectly. Today, portable computers and scanners allow data to be captured at the source even in mobile settings (e.g., air courier deliveries and use of rental cars).

These automatic systems are not capable of collecting a lot of information, so the next-best option is to capture data immediately from the source using a trained entry operator. Many airline and hotel reservations, loan applications, and catalog orders are recorded directly into a computer system, while the customer provides the operator with answers to questions. Some systems eliminate the operator altogether and allow users to enter their own data. For example, most universities no longer accept paper-based applications for admissions; all applications are typed by students into electronic forms.

The forms for capturing information (on a screen, on paper, etc.) should support the data source. That is, the order of the information on the form should match the natural flow of information from the data source, and data-entry forms should match paper forms used to initially capture the data.

Minimize Keystrokes Another important principle is to minimize keystrokes. Keystrokes cost time and money, whether they are performed by a customer, user, or trained data-entry operator. The system should never ask for information that can be obtained in another way (e.g., by retrieving it from a database or by performing a calculation). Likewise, a system should not require a user to type information that can be selected from a list; selecting reduces errors and speeds entry.

In many cases, some fields have values that recur often. These frequent values should be used as the *default value* for the field so that the user can simply accept the value and not have to retype it time and time again. Examples of default values are the current date, the area code held by the majority of a company's customers, and a billing address, which is based on the customer's residence. Most systems permit changes to default values to handle data-entry exceptions as they occur.

Types of Inputs

Each data item that has to be input is linked to a field on the form into which its value is typed. Each field also has a field label, which is the text beside, above, or below the field that tells the user what type of information belongs in the field. Often the field label is similar to the name of the data element, but they do not have to have identical words. In some cases, a field displays a template over the entry box to show the user exactly how data should be typed. There are many different types of inputs, in the same way that there are many different types of fields.

Text As the name suggests, a *text box* is used to enter text. Text boxes can be defined to have a fixed length or can be scrollable and can accept a virtually unlimited amount of text. In either case, boxes can contain single or multiple lines of textual information. We never use a text box if we can use a selection box.

Text boxes should have field labels placed to the *left* of the entry area, their size clearly delimited by a box (or a set of underlines in a non-GUI interface). If there are multiple text boxes, their field labels and the left edges of their entry boxes should be aligned. Text boxes should permit standard GUI functions, such as cut, copy, and paste.

Numbers A *number box* is used to enter numbers. Some software can automatically format numbers as they are entered, so that 3452478 becomes $34,524.78. Dates are a special form of numbers that sometimes have their own type of number box. Never use a number box if you can use a selection box.

Selection Box A *selection box* enables the user to select a value from a predefined list. The items in the list should be arranged in some meaningful order, such as alphabetical for long lists or in order of most frequently used. The default selection value should be chosen with care. A selection box can be initialized as unselected. However, it is better to start with the most commonly used item already selected.

Input Validation

All data entered into the system need to be validated to ensure their accuracy. Input *validation* (also called *edit checks*) can take many forms. Ideally, computer systems should not accept data that fail any important validation check to prevent invalid information from entering the system. However, even though this can be very difficult and invalid data can sometimes slip past data-entry operators and the users providing the information, enforcing the constraints discussed in Chapter 7 is a good place to start. Remember, there are three types of constraints that must be captured: *invariants*, *preconditions*, and *postconditions*. By reviewing the *contracts* and *assertions* that captured the constraints, most, if not all, data validation issues can be identified.

There are six different types of validation checks: *completeness check, format check, range check, check digit check, consistency check,* and *database check* (see Figure 9-10). Every system should use at least one validation check on all entered data and, ideally, perform all appropriate checks where possible. One thing that we should remember, in many cases the data that comes into a program via a user interface is typically formatted as a string. Consequently, the system must perform a format check on the string contents before any of the other validation checks can be performed. If the value is not the right data type, then none of the other tests will matter. For example, if an invariant states that the value of an attribute must be an integer, then a format check of the string value must test whether the value passed into the system can be cast to an integer or not. Only after it is shown that the value can be cast to an integer can the other checks be performed.

Type of Validation	When to Use	Notes
Completeness check Ensures all required data have been entered	When several fields must be entered before the form can be processed	If required information is missing, the form is returned to the user unprocessed.
Format check Ensures data are of the right type (e.g., numeric) and in the right format (e.g., month, day, year)	When fields are numeric or contain coded data	Ideally, numeric fields should not permit users to type text data, but if this is not possible, the entered data must be checked to ensure it is numeric. Some fields use special codes or formats (e.g., license plates with three letters and three numbers) that must be checked.
Range check Ensures numeric data are within correct minimum and maximum values	With all numeric data, if possible	A range check permits only numbers between correct values. Such a system can also be used to screen data for "reasonableness"—e.g., rejecting birthdates prior to 1880 because people do not live to be a great deal over 100 years old (most likely, 1980 was intended).
Check digit check Check digits are added to numeric codes	When numeric codes are used	Check digits are numbers added to a code as a way of enabling the system to quickly validate correctness. For example, U.S. Social Security numbers and Canadian Social Insurance numbers assign only eight of the nine digits in the number. The ninth number—the check digit—is calculated using a mathematical formula from the first eight numbers. When the identification number is typed into a computer system, the system uses the formula and compares the result with the check digit. If the numbers don't match, then an error has occurred.
Consistency checks Ensure combinations of data are valid	When data are related	Data fields are often related. For example, someone's birth year should precede the year in which he or she was married. Although it is impossible for the system to know which data are incorrect, it can report the error to the user for correction.
Database checks Compare data against a database (or file) to ensure they are correct	When data are available to be checked	Data are compared against information in a database (or file) to ensure they are correct. For example, before an identification number is accepted, the database is queried to ensure that the number is valid. Because database checks are more expensive than the other types of checks (they require the system to do more work), most systems perform the other checks first and perform database checks only after the data have passed the previous checks.

FIGURE 9-10 Types of Input Validation

OUTPUT DESIGN

Outputs are what the system produces, whether on the screen, on paper, or in other media, such as the Web. Outputs are perhaps the most visible part of any system because a primary reason for using an information system is to access the information that it produces.

Basic Principles

The goal of the output mechanism is to present information to users so that they can accurately understand it with the least effort. The fundamental principles for output design reflect how the outputs are used and ways to make it simpler for users to understand them.

Understand Report Usage The first principle in designing reports is to understand how they are used. Reports can be used for many different purposes. In some cases—but not very often—reports are read cover to cover because all information is needed. In most cases, reports are used to identify specific items or used as references to find information, so the order in which items are sorted on the report or grouped within categories is critical. This is particularly important for the design of electronic or Web-based reports. Web reports that are intended to be read from start to finish should be presented in one long scrollable page, whereas reports that are used primarily to find specific information should be broken into multiple pages, each with a separate link. Page numbers and the date on which the report was prepared are also important for reference reports.

The frequency of the report can also play an important role in its design and distribution. *Real-time reports* provide data that are accurate to the second or minute at which they were produced (e.g., stock market quotes). *Batch reports* are those that report historical information that may be months, days, or hours old, and they often provide additional information beyond the reported information (e.g., totals, summaries, and historical averages).

There are no inherent advantages to real-time reports over batch reports. The only advantages lie in the time value of the information. If the information in a report is time critical (e.g., stock prices and air-traffic control information), then real-time reports have value. This is particularly important because real-time reports are often expensive to produce; unless they offer some clear business value, they might not be worth the extra cost.

Manage Information Load Most managers get too much information, not too little (i.e., the *information load* that the manager must deal with is too great). The goal of a well-designed report is to provide all the information needed to support the task for which it was designed. This does not mean that the report needs to provide all the information available on the subject—just what the users decide they need in order to perform their jobs. In some cases, this can result in the production of several different reports on the same topics for the same users because they are used in different ways. This is not a bad design.

For users in Westernized countries, the most important information should always be presented first in the top-left corner of the screen or paper report. Information should be provided in a format that is usable without modification. The user should not need to re-sort the report's information; instead critical information should be highlighted so that users can find it more easily amid a mass of data, or perform additional mathematical calculations.

Minimize Bias No analyst sets out to design a biased report. The problem with bias is that it can be very subtle; analysts can introduce it unintentionally. *Bias* can be introduced by the way lists of data are sorted because entries that appear first in a list can receive more attention than those later in the list. Data are often sorted in alphabetical order, making those entries starting with the letter *A* more prominent. Data can be sorted in chronological order (or reverse chronological order), placing more emphasis on older (or most recent) entries. Data may be sorted by numeric value, placing more emphasis on higher or lower values. For example, consider a monthly sales report by state. Should the report be listed in alphabetical order by state name, in descending order by the amount sold, or in some other order (e.g., geographic region)? There are no easy answers to this, except to say that the order of presentation should match the way the information is used.

Graphical displays and reports can present particularly challenging design issues.[10] The scale on the axes in graphs is particularly subject to bias. For most types of graphs, the scale should always begin at zero; otherwise, comparisons among values can be misleading. For

---

[10] Two of the best books on the design of charts and graphical displays are by Edward R. Tufte, *The Visual Display of Quantitative Information, Envisioning Information* (Cheshire, CT: Graphics Press, 2001) and *Visual Explanations: Images and Quantities, Evidence and Narrative* (Cheshire, CT: Graphics Press, 1997). Another good book is by William Cleveland, *Visualizing Data* (Summit, NJ: Hobart Press, 1993).

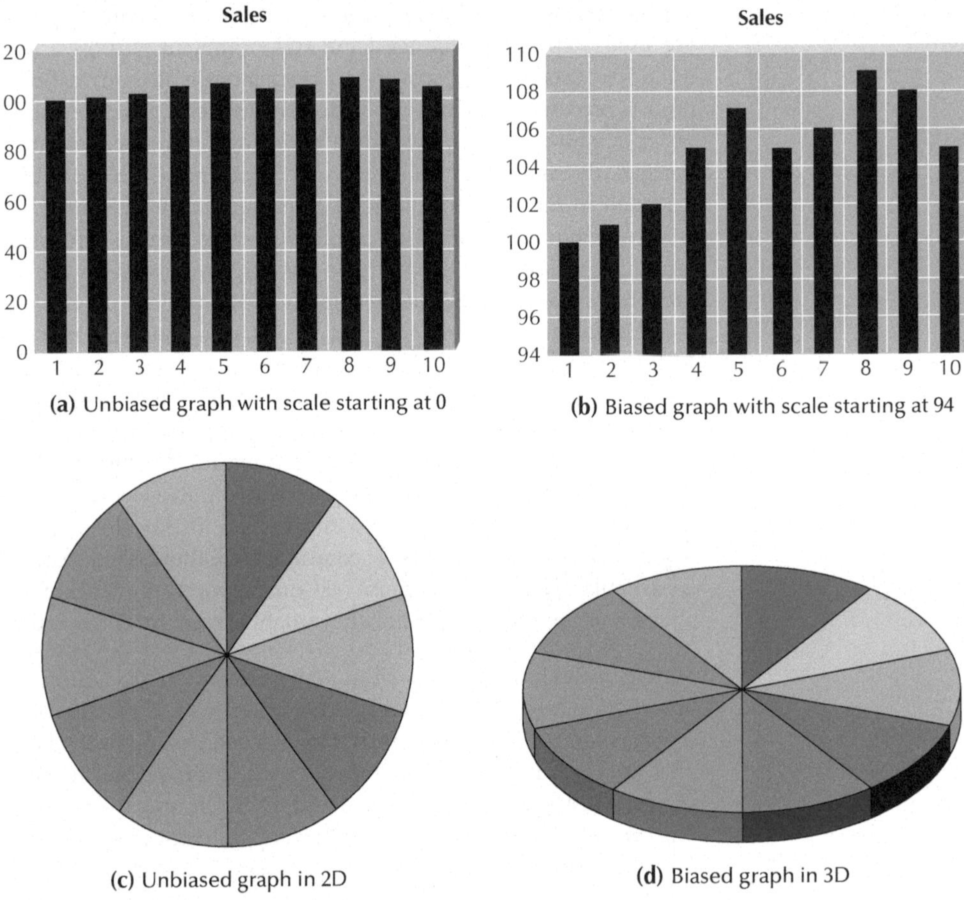

(a) Unbiased graph with scale starting at 0

(b) Biased graph with scale starting at 94

(c) Unbiased graph in 2D

(d) Biased graph in 3D

FIGURE 9-11   Bias in Graphs

example, have sales increased by very much since year 1 (see Figure 9-11a and b)? The numbers in both charts are the same, but the visual images the two present are quite different. A glance at Figure 9-11a would suggest only minor changes, whereas a glance at Figure 9-11b might suggest that there have been some significant increases. In fact, sales have increased by a total of 15 percent over five years, or 3 percent per year. Figure 9-11a presents the most accurate picture; Figure 9-11b is biased because the scale starts very close to the lowest value in the graph and misleads the eye into inferring that there have been major changes. You should also be beware of the so-called 3D effects. For example, the pie charts in Figures 9-11c and d represent the same data; in fact the data itself are constant. However, owing to the "3D" pie chart, the slices nearer the front look bigger.

Types of Outputs

There are many different types of reports, such as *detail reports, summary reports, exception reports, turnaround documents,* and *graphs* (see Figure 9-12). Classifying reports is challenging because many reports have characteristics of several different types. For example, some detail reports also produce summary totals, making them summary reports.

Type of Report	When to Use	Notes
Detail report Lists detailed information about all the items requested	When user needs full information about the items	This report is usually produced only in response to a query about items matching some criteria. This report is usually read cover to cover to aid understanding of one or more items in depth.
Summary report Lists summary information about all items	When user needs brief information on many items	This report is usually produced only in response to a query about items matching some criteria, but it can be a complete database. This report is usually read for the purpose of comparing several items to each other. The order in which items are sorted is important.
Turnaround document Outputs that "turn around" and become inputs	When a user (often a customer) needs to return an output to be processed	Turnaround documents are a special type of report that are both outputs and inputs. For example, most bills sent to consumers (e.g., credit-card bills) provide information about the total amount owed and also contain a form that consumers fill in and return with payment.
Graphs Charts used in addition to and instead of tables of numbers	When users need to compare data among several items	Well-done graphs help users compare two or more items or understand how one has changed over time. Graphs are poor at helping users recognize precise numeric values and should be replaced by or combined with tables when precision is important. Bar charts tend to be better than tables of numbers or other types of charts when it comes to comparing values between items (but avoid three-dimensional charts that make comparisons difficult). Line charts make it easier to compare values over time, whereas scatter charts make it easier to find clusters or unusual data. Pie charts show proportions or the relative shares of a whole.

FIGURE 9-12 Types of Reports

Media

Many different types of media are used to produce reports. Today, most organizations have moved toward "printing" reports electronically. One popular format is Adobe's PDF. These "reports" are stored in electronic format on file servers or Web servers so that users can easily access them. Often the reports are available in more predesigned formats than their paper-based counterparts because the cost of producing and storing different formats is minimal. Electronic reports also can be produced on demand as needed, and they enable the user to search for certain words more easily. Furthermore, electronic reports can provide a means of supporting ad hoc reports, where users customize the contents of the report at the time the report is generated. Some users still print the electronic report on their own printers, but the reduced cost of electronic delivery over distance and the ease of enabling more users to access the reports than when they were only in paper form usually offset the cost of local printing.

MOBILE COMPUTING AND USER INTERFACE DESIGN[11]

From a user interface design perspective, going mobile is both exciting and challenging. Obviously, with today's smartphones, such as the iPhone[TM], there are many possibilities. However, just because these phones have the ability to surf the Web doesn't mean that a simple Web interface is the answer. These devices have limited screen space and have capabilities, such as *touch screens* and *haptic feedback* (such as vibration or pulses), which regular computers do not. Consequently, you really need to focus on designing the interface for the device and not simply porting the Web interface over to it. Furthermore, you need to realize that a *tablet*, such as the iPad, is not a big *smartphone*; it is in its own category with its own challenges and capabilities. Consequently, you really need to design the interface for *mobile devices* from the ground up. In this section, we discuss some challenges and provide some guidelines to develop effective mobile interfaces. However, before we begin, you should realize that all of the material described previously is still applicable. It's just that when you are dealing with these devices, additional issues must be considered.

Jenifer Tidwell[12] identifies six challenges that a mobile user interface designer must face. The screen of a phone is small. There simply is not a lot of "real estate" available to use. Not only are the screens small, but they come in different sizes. What works on one screen might not work on another screen. Some screens have haptic abilities: They respond to touch and orientation, and in some case, they vibrate. Obviously, these abilities are not available on all mobile devices. However, they do provide interesting possibilities for user interface design. Virtual and actual physical keypads are tiny. Consequently, too much typing can be challenging for the user to input the right information. People use their mobile devices, especially their phones, in all kinds of environments. They use them in dark places (like a poorly lit classroom). They use them in bright sunlight. They use them in quiet places (like the library or movie theater) and they use them in noisy places (such as at a football game). These devices are simply used everywhere today. Because these devices are used everywhere, the users can be easily distracted from the device. For example, have you ever texted someone when you aren't supposed to be using your phone, like during class? Or, what about out on a date? In other words, users are typically multitasking while using their phone. They do not want to spend a lot of energy on trying to navigate a mobile site or app. Consequently, Krug's three design principles described earlier are very important, especially the first one: Don't make me think!

Based on these challenges, Tidwell provides a set of suggestions that you should follow in designing a user interface for these devices. First, given the mobile context, you really need to focus on what the user needs and not what the user might want. In other words, you really should go back to business process and functional modeling (Chapter 3). In this case, only focus on the tasks that users need to perform when they are in the mobile context. This is a good example of a nonfunctional requirement (mobile computing) affecting the possible functional requirements.

Second, if you are porting an application or website to a mobile device, remove all "fluff" from the site: Strip the site down to its bare essentials. If the user needs access to the full site, be sure to provide a link to it in an obvious location. Alternatively, you could provide a complete mobile version of the application or website to the user. Obviously, the design of the user interface will be different, but the functionality should be the same.

---

[11] Obviously, in a short section we cannot cover all of the issues related to developing mobile applications. For anyone who is seriously considering developing mobile applications, we recommend that you begin by looking at books that deal with the specific devices on which you will be deploying your application. For example, Donn Felker, *Android[TM] Application Development for Dummies[TM]* (Hoboken, NJ: Wiley, 2011); Neal Goldstein and Tony Bove, *iPhone[TM] Application Development All-In-One for Dummies[TM]* (Hoboken, NJ: Wiley, 2010); Neal Goldstein and Tony Bove, *iPad[TM] Application Development for Dummies[TM]* (Hoboken, NJ: Wiley, 2010); Chris Stevens, *Designing for the iPad[TM]: Building Applications that Sell* (Chichester, UK: Wiley, 2011).

[12] Jenifer Tidwell, *Designing Interfaces: Patterns for Effective Design,* 2nd Ed. (Sebastopol, CA: O'Reilly, 2010).

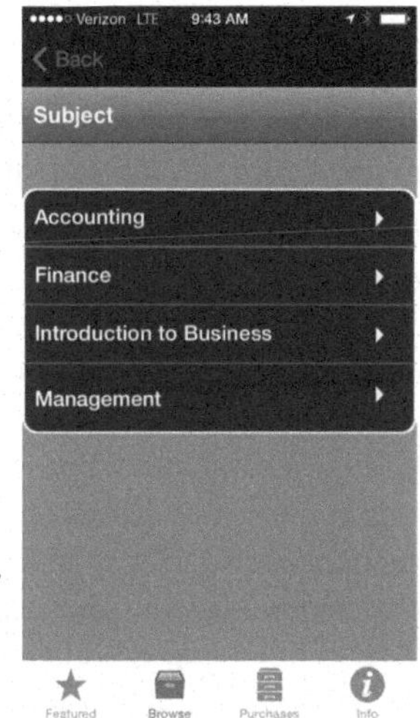

FIGURE 9-13
Linearization Example,
Wiley Business Study
Center, used with
permission.

Third, whenever possible, take advantage of the unique capabilities built into these devices. Some of the devices have *GPS* built in, and many can approximate a geographic location of the device based on Wi-Fi or cellular network connections points. Depending on your application, knowing where the user is could change the results. In other cases, the device has an accelerometer that allows the app to "know" the orientation of the device. Most of these devices have speech recognition capabilities, cameras that can be used for scanning, touch screens that allow sophisticated gestures to be used, and haptic feedback, such as bumps and vibrations. All of these capabilities could prove useful in developing different mobile applications.

Fourth, when considering a phone, you tend to have a limited width from which to work. Consequently, you should try to linearize the content of the application (see Figure 9-13). By that we mean, take advantage of vertical scrolling and try to minimize, if not eliminate, horizontal scrolling. It is simply more natural for users to scroll up and down instead of left to right on these devices.

Fifth, optimize your mobile application for the user. This includes minimizing the number of times the device must interact with a server to download or upload information with a server. Not everyone has access to 4G, alone 5G, networks. In many cases, uploading and downloading are still very slow. Optimization also includes the user's interaction with the device. Instead of using a lot of typing, scrolling, and taps on a touch screen, consider using the speech recognition capability. It's a lot easier to speak slowly to a smartphone than it is to have to type a lot into a virtual or physical keyboard.

Tidwell also provides a set of reusable patterns that have been customized for mobile devices. These include things such as a vertical stack, filmstrip, and bottom navigation.[13]

In addition to the general suggestions that Tidwell provides, the whole area of interaction must be designed. With traditional GUI-based interfaces, the interactions tended to be limited to typing on a keyboard; using a mouse to click, scroll, or zoom in an interface; or using a combination of keyboard and the mouse to rotate part of the content in the interface. Overall, it is a fairly limited set of interactions. However, with the new mobile devices that have speech recognition, voice generation, touch screens, haptic feedback (via vibration), accelerometers that allow the device to know its orientation, and cameras that can be used for scanning input, the number of options for designing the navigation and input and output parts of the user interface have increased substantially. From our perspective, we are just now detecting the tip of the proverbial iceberg of possibilities with these devices. However, the general prototyping approach suggested earlier in the chapter works. Just the number of options to consider has increased substantially.

When it comes to the navigation part of the user interface, the primary additional option is the use of the touchscreen.[14] In fact, there is an entire vocabulary when it comes to the way users interact with touchscreens. Today, the designer needs to consider tapping, pinching, spreading, flicking, scrolling (one-finger vs. two-finger), and dragging to name a few. For example:

- Tapping can be used to open or activate an app, to select an object in the interface, or to stop an action, such as scrolling.
- Pinching is used to shrink or zoom out.
- Spreading is used to enlarge or zoom in.
- Flicking can be used to move an object or for interacting with a slider to scroll.

---

[13] Tidwell also suggests that the Design for Mobile (patterns.design4mobile.com) pattern library provides many good patterns to use when developing mobile applications.

[14] A good reference to gestural design is Dan Saffer, *Designing Gestural Interfaces* (Sebastopol, CA: O'Reilly, 2008).

- Scrolling can be accomplished by using a single finger on a scroll bar or by using two fingers on anywhere on the interface.
- Move an object on the screen by placing a finger on the object and dragging it to another location. This is similar to using a mouse to drag an object to another location.

Different mobile devices may implement each of these slightly differently. Obviously, the number of choices to support navigation has greatly expanded.

For the input part of the user interface, the primary additional options to consider are the use of the camera as a device to scan items; microphone as a speech input device; and accelerometer to detect acceleration, orientation, and vibrations. For example, Google Maps™ supports a voice recognition interface to find a location. Also, there are numerous apps that use the accelerometer to detect acceleration and vibration (e.g., Wavefront Labs' Accelerometer Data Pro™). Furthermore, many games available on mobile devices use the accelerometer as an input device.

The primary additional options to consider for the output part of the user interface include voice generation and haptic feedback. For example, Google Maps and Waze support a voice generation capability that provides driving directions. Additionally, virtually all smartphones support a vibrate option when the phone rings and when alerts or text messages arrive.

SOCIAL MEDIA AND USER INTERFACE DESIGN[15]

Given the impact that such social media platforms as Facebook and X (formerly Twitter), have had in today's world, developing applications for *social media* has obviously come to the forefront. In many ways, mobile computing and social media have grown up together. Like mobile computing, each social media platform has its own capabilities and challenges. Social media platforms range from sites that allow you to simply upload material to them, such as Flickr and YouTube, to sites that support a virtual existence in the metaverse, such as Second Life. During your career, you might need to develop applications for a specific social media platform, such as Facebook or X, or possibly develop your own social media site.

When developing your own social media presence, you must understand who is your target audience. Is the audience employees of your firm, or is the audience outside of the firm? In this section, we only focus on an external audience. Once you know who the audience is, you need to know what they are saying about the firm. In many ways, social media is simply another channel for marketing the firm's products and capabilities. Before you can deploy a social media presence, you really need to understand what the users' needs (desires) are. In other words, back to requirements determination. In this case, the problem is that the users are "out there" somewhere, so typical approaches to gathering requirements, such as interviews and observation, don't work. Instead, you need to hunt through the Web to root out your requirements. Some of the more useful places to look are blogs or other social media outlets that address issues that would be of interest to your firm. When all else fails, you can always use a search engine such as Google. Regardless, you obviously have to understand the functional requirements before you can design your social media presence.

Once you understand your functional requirements, you need to determine what type of social media presence is necessary to address the requirements effectively. Each social media platform has its own niche. Consequently, you might need to deploy many different applications across different platforms to effectively meet the firm's social media presence requirements. Also, you must look at your social media site as a means for your firm to build and maintain a positive image or brand. Therefore, the social media site must contain material that your potential customers want to consume. You must remember that the underlying purpose of marketing is to "manufacture" wants

---

[15] Much of the material in this section has been based upon material from Jenifer Tidwell, *Designing Interfaces: Patterns for Effective Design*, 2nd Ed. (Sebastopol, CA: O'Reilly, 2010).

and then "convert" the wants into needs. Given that your social media site is effectively another marketing channel, your site must be able to draw in new customers and to get current customers to regularly return. In this section, we provide some general guidelines for developing your own social media site so that both new customers visit and current customers return.[16]

First, you really need to post to your site regularly. If the content of the site becomes stagnant, no one will want to visit. The content of the site should contain a mixture of media: videos, podcasts, sound clips, and so on. The site's material should include a mixture of firm-driven material, material from customers, and links to relevant content that is located on other sites. Also, be sure to include ways for visitors to join in a "conversation" with the firm, such as Facebook[TM] comments or X[TM] tweets.

Second, make sure that you understand the difference between *push* and *pull* approaches. If the user must come to you to find out something, then you are using a pull-based approach. On the other hand, if you put the information out to the user, then you are using a push-based approach. When it comes to social media, you really need to use a combination of the approaches. For example, in Facebook[TM] if someone posts on your wall or sends you a request, Facebook[TM] will send you an e-mail message to try and entice you back to the Facebook[TM] site. The act of posting to your site was a pull-based action, and the e-mail message sent to you is a push-based action. In a nutshell, you want to focus on more of a push-based approach. You want your content to get to your customers in as an effective manner as possible. You don't want them to have to come looking for you. Encourage them to opt in for update notifications to come to them in a form that they prefer. Some might prefer e-mail notifications, and others might prefer you post to their Facebook[TM] or X[TM] accounts. Also, be sure to include links to your social media sites on your home page. But be sure not to overwhelm the customer. Not every customer wants to know every tidbit regarding the firm. Only give the customer what the customer wants. Remember, Krug's first principle: Don't make me think! A corollary to this principle for social media would be: Don't make me work! Make it easy for the customer to find only what they want (or maybe what we want them to want).

Third, be sure that your home page and your social media sites are all synced together so that when one is updated, the other sites "know" about the update. This makes your job of maintaining the different sites much easier, and it allows your customers to have a consistent experience across all sites. However, don't overdo this. It is obvious that different sites have different media and, potentially, different audiences. You aren't going to use Facebook[TM] in the same way you would use X[TM], YouTube[TM], or a blog. Be sure to include crosslinks among the different sites. This enables your customer to easily navigate through your different sites.

Fourth, enable the customers to share the great content that you have created. You can include buttons that allow them to email the content to their closest "friends" or other followers in their own social network. You also should provide a means to gather feedback from your customers regarding your content. One way is to include the ability for customers to make and share comments regarding your content. Another way is to provide a voting or "like" mechanism to encourage the customer to become engaged with your site.

Fifth, be sure to design your sites so that not only your customers can easily find the material for which they are searching, but also search engines can find the material. Search engines are at least as likely to bring new customers to your sites as other customers. Design the site so that once the customer lands on your site, he or she stays there for a while. One way that you can accomplish this is by providing the customer with links to "related" material. If you decided to include a voting or "like" mechanism, be sure to enable the customer to see the "best" or, at least, the most popular material first. Another possibility is to create a leaderboard that displays the most shared material. You need to leverage the information gained by implementing the fourth guideline.

---

[16] Two good books devoted to developing applications for social media in general are Erin Malone, *Designing Social Interfaces* (Sebastopol, CA: O'Reilly, 2009) and Gavin Bell, *Building Social Web Applications: Establishing Community at the Heart of Your Site* (Sebastopol, CA: O'Reilly, 2009). There are a couple of books devoted to two specific social media platforms. Two good books are Jesse Stay, *Facebook[TM] Application Development for Dummies[TM]* (Hoboken, NJ: Wiley, 2011) and Dusty Reagan, *Twitter[TM] Application Development for Dummies[TM]* (Hoboken, NJ: Wiley, 2010).

Sixth, one of the more difficult things to accomplish is to have your sites become a place that your customers feel that they belong. You want your customers to feel that they are members of something; you want to try to build a feeling of community. The more they feel that they belong, the more likely they will recommend your site to their friends. One way to accomplish this is to encourage employees, at least the "right" employees, to author their own "independent" sites that discuss topics of interest to your customers. This will give a more personal feel to the firm and possibly entice customers to stick around on the site longer.

Finally, in most cases, your customers visit your sites using a variety of hardware platforms. The platforms range from the desktop to the notebook to the tablet to the smartphone. Consequently, all of the material related to general user interface design and to mobile computing is applicable. Because you have a global audience, you need to be sure to take into account international and cultural issues in your design.

GAMES, MULTIDIMENSIONAL INFORMATION VISUALIZATIONS, AND IMMERSIVE ENVIRONMENTS[17]

With the advent of games and multidimensional information visualizations being used in business and the potential of applying immersive technologies, such as the Oculus Rift™, to solve business problems using augmented and virtual reality, the design of the human–computer interaction layer is becoming even more important in information systems development. In many ways, user interface design for games, multidimensional information visualizations, and immersive environments is very similar to designing a user interface for more traditional application areas. However, in other ways, it is very different.

Games, Gamification, and User Interface Design

Games have been around for a very, very long time. They have been very successful in many different areas because they are fun and engaging.[18] When applying games to business situations, there are two general approaches to consider: development of games that support business processes and gamification of business processes. The development of games to solve business problems is relatively new. Traditionally, they have been used primarily with academic simulations. However, given the popularity of games in our culture, business games are being developed and deployed to increase customer and employee engagement.[19] *Gamification* deals with applying gaming mechanics to non-gaming situations. Gamification has been used to redesign classrooms and to support learning, and, like games, it too has been used to increase customer and employee engagement.[20]

In both using games and gamification, the secret to success deals with motivating the customer and/or employee to remain engaged with the business process. Even though traditional

---

[17] Obviously, in a short section we cannot cover all of the issues related to developing games, multidimensional information visualizations, or using immersive environments to solve business applications. However, in this section we provide with an overview of the types of issues that you may run into when using these technologies. We also provide pointers to many references that have been useful in our development efforts.

[18] Jane McGonigal, *Reality Is Broken: Why Games Make Us Better and How They Can Change the World* (New York: Penguin Books, 2011); James Paul Gee, *Why Video Games Are Good for Your Soul* (Champaign, IL: Common Ground Publishing, 2005); Bernard Suits, *The Grasshopper: Games, Life, and Utopia* (Ontario, CA: Broadview Press, 2005).

[19] Jesse Schell, *The Art of Game Design: A Book of Lenses* (Boca Raton, FL: CRC Press, 2008); Jon Radoff, *Game On: Energize Your Business with Social Media Games* (Indianapolis, IN: Wiley, 2011); Bryon Reeves and J. Leighton Read, *Total Engagement: Using Games and Virtual Worlds to Change the Way People Work and Businesses Compete* (Boston, MA: Harvard Business Press, 2009).

[20] Lee Sheldon, *The Multiplayer Classroom: Designing Coursework as a Game* (Boston, MA: Course Technology, 2012); Rajat Paharia, *Loyalty 3.0: How Big Data and Gamification Are Revolutionizing Customer and Employee Engagement* (New York: McGraw-Hill, 2013); Gabe Zichermann and Joselin Linder, *The Gamification Revolution: How Leaders Leverage Game Mechanics to Crush the Competition* (New York: McGraw-Hill, 2013); Kris Duggin and Kate Shoup, *Business Gamification for Dummies* (Hoboken, NJ: Wiley, 2013).

motivation approaches have worked to motivate employees in the past, due to the nature of the changing types of work performed, they no longer function in an efficient or effective manner (see Chapter 11). Traditional approaches typically used a "stick and carrot" approach to motivation. If an individual (child, student, or employee) did something undesired, he or she was punished. On the other hand, if they did something desired, they were rewarded. In other words, motivation was based entirely on extrinsic benefits. Games and gamification focus primarily on intrinsic benefits; not extrinsic benefits.[21] Typically, you play games because you enjoy the game. When was the last time that you played a game because you had to and not wanted to? Did you play it for money? Was it so that you could please someone else? Or, was it so that you could be part of something larger than yourself? How enjoyable was it? Are you motivated to play it again? Why? Chances are that money was not a sufficient motivator to play it again. But, playing a game for the fun of it will probably motivate you to play it over and over again. In fact, depending on your gaming personality type, playing a game to please someone else or to be part of something larger than yourself may motivate you to play it again.[22]

Given the success of business game development and the gamification of business processes, there are a few things that we can learn to improve user interfaces. One of the first things is that games are designed explicitly to be fun.[23] Typically, when we design business information systems, one of the last things we think about is whether the system is fun to use or not. When was the last time you considered using an accounting information system as being fun? However, in this case, the fun component of a business information system deals specifically with how engaging the user interface is.[24] Therefore, there are a few things that we can apply from games to develop more engaging user interfaces.[25]

First, games are about creating a *user experience*. Obviously, when creating an experience, the user interface designer must pay close attention to all of the issues that we have described earlier. Otherwise, not only will the experience be light on the engagement factor, but it could also create a negative experience instead of the positive one hoped for.

Second, game experiences are all about the ideas and themes woven throughout the game. The ideas of story telling (see Chapter 2) and use cases (see Chapter 3) provide a basis to design and develop the user(s)' engagement experience.

Third, game developers worry a lot about the player (user). This brings a better focus to the roles (actors) that the users play in our system (see Chapter 3). When it comes to game design, not only do we have to worry about the tasks in which the user will be engaged, but we also have to start thinking about the individual psychological and cognitive differences among the different users.[26] This applies both to different types of customers and employees.

Fourth, game developers also tend to try and build a community around the game. In this way, users have a built-in support mechanism. Schell[27] suggests a set of tips to develop a strong community that can be applied to general business information systems development. He suggests that we should foster friendships by encouraging the users to talk with each other about the system and we should try to create community property by having the users (and developers)

---

[21] Kevin Werbach and Dan Hunter, *For the Win: How Game Thinking Can Revolutionize Your Business* (Philadelphia, AA: Wharton Digital Press, 2012).

[22] Ralph Koster, *A Theory of Fun for Game Design*, 2nd Ed. (Sebastopol, CA: O'Reilly Media, 2014); Jesse Schell, *The Art of Game Design: A Book of Lenses* (Boca Raton, FL: CRC Press, 2008); Kevin Werbach and Dan Hunter, *For the Win: How Game Thinking Can Revolutionize Your Business* (Philadelphia, AA: Wharton Digital Press, 2012).

[23] Ralph Koster, *A Theory of Fun for Game Design*, 2nd Ed. (Sebastopol, CA: O'Reilly Media, 2014).

[24] Jon Radoff, Game On: *Energize Your Business with Social Media Games* (Indianapolis, IN: Wiley, 2011) and Bryon Reeves and J. Leighton Read, *Total Engagement: Using Games and Virtual Worlds to Change the Way People Work and Businesses Compete* (Boston, MA: Harvard Business Press, 2009).

[25] Jesse Schell, *The Art of Game Design: A Book of Lenses* (Boca Raton, FL: CRC Press, 2008).

[26] Chaomei Chen, *Information Visualization and Virtual Environments* (London: Springer-Verlag, 1999); Howard Gardner, *Frames of Mind: The Theory of Multiple Intelligences* (New York: Basic Books, 1983).

[27] Jesse Schell, *The Art of Game Design: A Book of Lenses* (Boca Raton, FL: CRC Press, 2008).

take joint responsibility for the system. However, one of his more relevant suggestions is to support multiple levels of users based on their level of experience. By having the system detect the level of expertise of the user in using the system, the system can introduce features, such as short cuts, once a specific "level" has been reached. This is associated with "leveling up" in games. This would help in addressing the trade-offs between ease of learning and ease of use when developing a user interface. This could also encourage users to "buy in" to the system.

Fifth, when it comes to successful game design, you must consider the aesthetics. As such, without a focus on aesthetics, the experience that you want the customer or employee to incur may be less than desirable. In fact, it could discourage them from returning to your site.

Multidimensional Information Visualization Design

There have been many different types of *multidimensional information visualizations* that have been used in business.[28] However, the different types fall into two basic categories: multidimensional information visualizations in *2D space* and multidimensional information visualizations in *nonimmersive 3D space*. Those visualizations that are displayed in 2D space include the basic business charts and graphs you would find in a spreadsheet or statistics package, e.g., heat maps, maps, node-link diagrams, parallel coordinates, radar charts, scatterplots, and treemaps.[29] The primary issue related to the use of these types of charts and diagrams deals with the potential of bias creeping into the display (see earlier in the chapter). However, when considering visualizations that are displayed in nonimmersive 3D space, additional issues are raised.[30]

The first issue that comes up is the issue of being able to determine a specific value that is being represented. For example, in Figure 9-14, which portrays a multidimensional surface chart, it is virtually impossible to determine specific values represented in the 3D space. In this case, there are four separate values being plotted: one for the X-axis, one for the Y-axis, one for the Z-axis, and one that uses the color of the surface. Only the last value, due to the legend, can be easily determined. Another example of this problem is portrayed in Figure 9-15 that shows a multidimensional bar chart. Again, four separate values are depicted. There are two basic approaches used to address this problem: being able

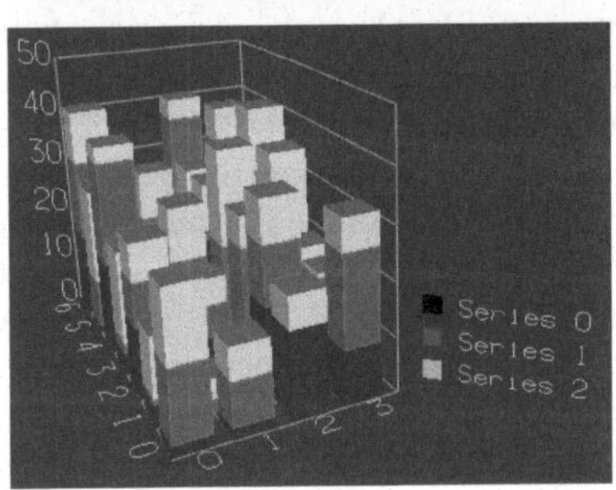

FIGURE 9-14
Multidimensional Surface Chart in 3D Space

FIGURE 9-15
Multidimensional Bar Chart in 3D Space

[28] David Tegarden, "Business Information Visualization," *Communications of the Association for Information Systems*, Vol. 1, Article 4 (1999) (http://aisel.aisnet.org/cais/vol1/iss1/4).

[29] A set of good books that address these types of information visualizations are: Ben Fry, *Visualizing Data* (Sebastopol, CA: O'Reilly Media, 2008); Derek L. Hansen, Ben Shneiderman, and Marc A. Smith, *Analyzing Social Media Networks with NodeXL: Insights from a Connected World* (Burlington, MA: Morgan Kaufmann, 2011); Nathan Yau, *Visualize This: The FlowingData Guide to Design, Visualization, and Statistics* (Indianapolis, IN: Wiley, 2011); Nathan Yau, *Data Points: Visualization That Means Something* (Indianapolis, IN: Wiley, 2013).

[30] A set of good books that address these types of information visualizations are: Judith R. Brown, Rae Earnshaw, Mikael Jern, and John Vince, *Visualization: Using Computer Graphics to Explore Data and Present Information* (New York: Wiley, 1995); Robert Spence, *Information Visualization* (Harlow England: ACM Press, 2001); Chaomei Chen, *Information Visualization: Beyond the Horizon*, 2nd Ed. (London: Springer-Verlag, 2004); Usama Fayyad, Georges Grinstein, and Andreas Wierse (eds.), *Information Visualization in Data Mining and Knowledge Discovery* (San Francisco: Morgan Kaufmann, 2002).

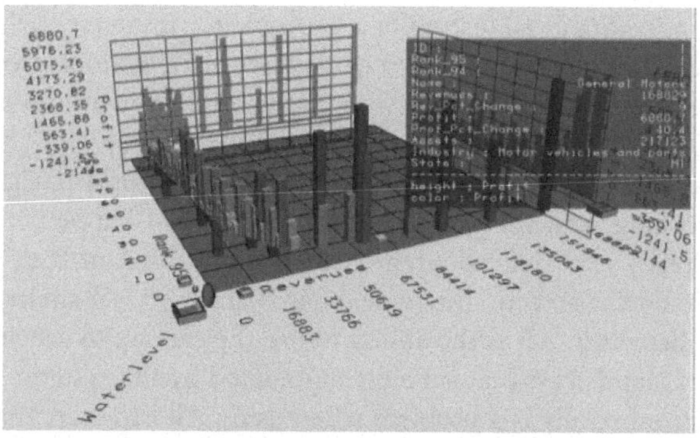

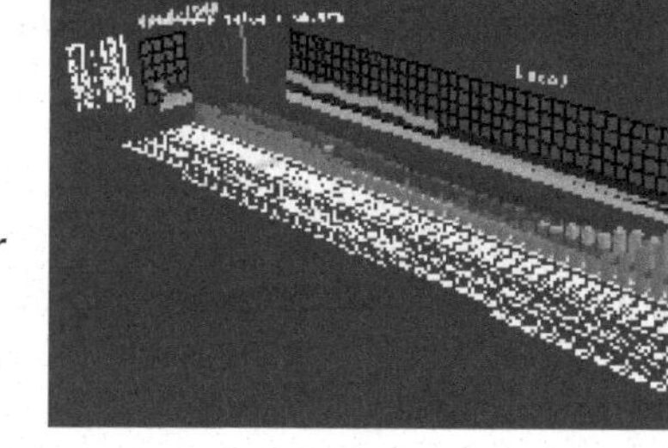

FIGURE 9-16
Multidimensional Bar Chart on Floors and Walls in 3D Space

FIGURE 9-17
Multidimensional Bar Chart on Floor with Line Graphs on Walls in 3D Space

to rotate and zoom the visualization and providing a *drill-down capability* that allows the specific values to be displayed (see Figure 9-16).

Another issue that comes up when displaying data in 3D space is *occlusion*; that is, when viewing data in 3D, some of the visualization may be covered up, hidden, by other parts of the visualization. For example, in Figure 9-15, the values drawn at the "back" of the visualization cannot be easily determined. In Figure 9-16, the negative values are drawn below the surface of the floor of the visualization. As such, the negative values cannot be seen. However, by rotating the visualization "up" and being able to click on a specific value, the values associated with that observation can be drilled down into and displayed in a semi-transparent window. In Figure 9-17, the visualization displays the basic values on the floor. With this visualization, in addition to supporting displays on the walls, the user can also use a slicing plane that "cuts through" the visualization to help better understand the data being visualized. These types of visualizations have been used quite extensively in supporting business decision making.

There are many more types of multidimensional information visualizations that have been used in business, e.g., volumes, floors and walls, maps, and surfaces. Each has its own strengths, weaknesses, and challenges. Furthermore, today there are many specialized tools that can be used to aid in designing and developing these types of visualizations. However, the basic design process is essentially the same user interface design process described earlier. You still have to design the navigation controls, the input mechanisms, and the output. To begin with, you will have to understand the underlying problem domain and the tasks that the user needs to perform. Next, you will need to choose the type of visualization to be designed based on the task that the user needs supported. This is still an art form. Our recommendation is to sit down with the user and go through different types of information visualizations to try and determine which of the information visualizations are reasonable. This decision should be based on whether the mapping of the data to the visualization is "intuitive" from the user's perspective or not. Also, remember that just because you can implement a complex, multidimensional information visualization does not mean that you should do it. In many cases, simple business charts and graphics are more than sufficient. Like game design, be sure to focus on aesthetics. If the visualization is not pleasing to the eye of the user, then it is probably the wrong visualization. Finally, given that visualization design is more of an art than a science, testing the visualization's effectiveness with many users is critical.

User Interface Design and Immersive Environments

Augmented and virtual reality using immersive technologies, such the Oculus Rift™, is among the latest and exciting application areas being utilized to solve business problems.

Where *virtual reality (VR)* technologies completely immerse the user into an artificial simulated digital environment, *augmented reality (AR)* technologies are used to augment or enhance the view of the real world. There are both opportunities and challenges with deploying both of these technologies.

AR has primarily been used in advertising, real-world navigation, room design, games, social networking, and medical applications.[31] If you happen to watch the NFL[TM] on TV, you have already experienced augmented reality: Think of the "first down" line that magically appears on the screen. The typical hardware used is a smartphone or tablet. One of the primary challenges in AR is the ability to use the camera to see and the software to interpret the real-world landscape that is being augmented by the system. This is known as *object recognition*. This especially is a problem when using AR browsers that "connects" the real world with content on the Web. In this case, a browser must recognize where it is physically located and add "links" to allow the user to look up additional information about the locations that it sees. To do this, the browser must use the camera, the GPS, and the accelerometer of the smartphone. Another major issue with regard to AR is of a social nature. For example, using AR devices while talking with someone can raise issues about privacy, such as are you paying attention to the other person or are you looking at the information being displayed and what exactly is the information being displayed. There are also apps available today that support facial recognition, which obviously raises even more issues with privacy. However, there are all kinds of possible benefits from using this technology, e.g., think about the advertising that takes place in the movie *Minority Report*. Using AR could allow you to see information that has been personalized about the locations around you as you walk down the street.

A prototyping approach, similar to the user interface design approach described earlier is used to design AR applications.[32] All of the issues related to traditional user interface design, game design, and multidimensional information visualization design are relevant and must be addressed, e.g., imagine using a heads-up display while driving your car to provide information about your location. Are you focusing on the road or are you simply experiencing another form of distraction? Consequently, testing the AR system in real-world situations is essential.

VR has been both overhyped and under utilized. Even though today VR has primarily been associated with games, it has been used in business for a long time.[33] It has been used in areas such as derivatives trading, financial risk management, industrial process control, marketing analysis, network modeling, operations management, organizational modeling, portfolio management, product design and manufacturing, room layout design, sensitivity analysis, simulated meetings, stock market analysis, and training. However, from a user interface design perspective, VR raises additional issues that need to be addressed.

It is believed that VR attains its power by captivating the user's attention and inducing a sense of *immersion*, the feeling of being present in the space being simulated. The challenge of creating the feeling of immersion has two primary dimensions: sensory and affective. In the sensory dimension, the combination of stimuli employed must be of sufficient vividness that an individual's automatic perceptual processes are triggered, resulting in the simulation being perceived as life-like. In the affective dimension, the user should be cast in an interactive, exploratory role. When considering these dimensions, one should remember that virtual reality resides in an individual's consciousness and, therefore, the relative contribution of

---

[31] A good book to get a basic overview of augmented reality is Gregory Kipper and Joseph Rampolla, *Augmented Reality: An Emerging Technologies Guide to AR* (Waltham, MA: Syngress, 2013).

[32] Tony Mullen, *Prototyping Augmented Reality* (Indianapolis, IN: Syngress, 2011).

[33] David Tegarden, "Business Information Visualization," *Communications of the Association for Information Systems*, Vol. 1, Article 4 (1999) (http://aisel.aisnet.org/cais/vol1/iss1/4); Alan Wexelblat (ed.), *Virtual Reality: Applications and Explorations* (Boston, MA: Academic Press, 1993); Dimitris Chorafas and Heinrich Steinmann, *Virtual Reality: Practical Applications in Business and Industry* (Englewood Cliffs, NJ: Prentice Hall, 1995); Robert Thierauf, *Virtual Reality Systems for Business* (Westport, CN: Quorum Books, 1995).

each of these dimensions in creating a sense of immersion will vary across individuals. Thus, immersion is a function of both technology and perceiver. This raises the issue of individual psychological and cognitive differences.[34]

Interaction with a virtual world may take the form of *wayfinding* through the virtual space, rearranging existing, or creating new, 3D objects, or communicating with another agent (person or automaton) sharing the same virtual space. Visitors to large virtual worlds are often unable to comprehend the overall topological structure of the space. They may wander aimlessly when attempting to find a particular location for the first time and may subsequently have difficulty finding their way back to locations already visited. Wayfinding tasks require the user to be able to conceptualize the virtual space as a whole and to develop a *cognitive map* of it.[35] A cognitive map consists of not only spatial relationships, but also of auditory, sensory, and emotional impressions. In games, a map is typically provided to help with understanding where one is in the virtual space and from where one has come. Like the immersion issue, wayfinding also raises issues related to individual psychological and cognitive differences.

The last challenge with regard to using VR as a user interface platform deals with collaboration. When considering multiuser, distributed VR systems, such as many of today's video games, occlusion can become a very large problem. Not only can objects in the VR space hide other VR objects, but they can also hide other users. Also, it is possible for one user to see something of interest that the other users may not. In this case, the issue of wayfinding comes back up. For example, if user A finds an interesting piece of information, then user A must communicate how to navigate to a location in which the other users will be able to observe the finding. There are multiple possibilities here, including providing wayfinding directions from a specified "viewpoint," "teleporting" the other users from their individual current locations to the current location of user A, having user A go find the other users and bring them to the appropriate location, or having user A simply "drive" all other users to the appropriate location by taking over their ability to navigate through the visualization. Furthermore, once the other users are at the appropriate location, how do they return to their previous location?

Obviously, designing effective and efficient VR applications is very difficult.[36] Again, the overall design process is similar to the general user interface design process described earlier. However, given the potential for VR to support business decision making by combining gaming and information visualization technologies into a single seamless distributed environment and that the investment in specialized hardware and software is dropping, VR could provide large payoffs.

INTERNATIONAL AND CULTURAL ISSUES AND USER INTERFACE DESIGN[37]

With the World Wide Web, virtually any firm can have a global presence. With this capability, a firm must be cognizant of a set of international and cultural issues. These issues include multilingual requirements, color, and *cultural differences.*

---

[34] Chaomei Chen, *Information Visualization and Virtual Environments* (London: Springer-Verlag, 1999); Howard Gardner, *Frames of Mind: The Theory of Multiple Intelligences* (New York: Basic Books, 1983).

[35] Reginald Golledge (ed.), *Wayfinding Behavior: Cognitive Mapping and Other Spatial Processes* (Baltimore, MD: The John Hopkins University Press, 1999); Rob Kitchin and Scott Freundschuh, *Cognitive Mapping: Past, Present and Future* (London: Routledge, 2000).

[36] A recent book that tackles how to design a VR system is Ann Lantham Cudworth, *Virtual World Design* (Boca Raton, FL: CRC Press, 2014).

[37] A set of books that provide a good introduction to building information systems for a multicultural audience include Elisa M. del Galdo and Jakob Nielsen, *International User Interfaces* (New York, NY: Wiley, 1996); Nitish Singh and Arun Pereira, *The Culturally Customized Web Site: Customizing Web Sites for the Global Marketplace* (Oxford, UK: Elsevier Butterworth Heinemann, 2005); John Yunker, *Beyond Borders: Web Globalization Strategies* (Berkley, CA: New Riders, 2003).

Multilingual Requirements

The first and most obvious difference between applications used in one region and those designed for global use is language. Global applications often have *multilingual requirements,* which means that they have to support users who speak different languages and write using non-English letters (e.g., those with accents, Cyrillic, and Japanese). One of the most challenging aspects in designing global systems is getting a good translation of the original language messages into a new language. Words often have similar meanings but can convey subtly different meanings when they are translated, so it is important to use translators skilled in translating technical words. A few rules that you should follow are to:

- Keep the writing short and simple. It is much easier to avoid mistranslations.
- Avoid humor, jargon, slang, clichés, puns, analogies, and metaphors. These tend to be too culturally specific. Consequently, the underlying point being made will most likely be lost in translation.
- Use good grammar. Be sure to punctuate everything correctly. Even though you might be tempted to ignore grammar and punctuation rules to try to make a point, it makes translating more difficult, especially for automated translation systems. Don't depend on automated spelling and grammar checkers to enforce this.

Another challenge is often screen space. In general, English-language messages usually take 20 percent to 30 percent fewer letters than their French or Spanish counterparts. Designing global systems requires allocating more screen space to messages than might be used in the English-language version.

Some systems are designed to handle multiple languages on the fly so that users in different countries can use different languages concurrently; that is, the same system supports several different languages simultaneously (a concurrent multilingual system). Other systems contain separate parts that are written in each language and must be reinstalled before a specific language can be used; that is, each language is provided by a different version of the system so that any one installation will use only one language (i.e., a discrete multilingual system). Either approach can be effective, but this functionality must be designed into the system well in advance of implementation.

Finally, one other consideration that must be considered is reading direction. In most Western societies, readers read from left to right and top to bottom. This is not true for many cultures. For example, in Arabic countries, readers typically read right to left and top to bottom.

Color

To begin with, color is not black and white. The meaning associated with a *color* can be culturally dependent. In fact, black and white isn't necessarily black and white; they could be white and black. In most Western cultures, black is associated with death, mourning, and grief or with respect and formality. For example, in the United States, we typically wear black to a funeral, or you would expect to see religious leaders in black (think about the robes typically worn by a Catholic priest). In many Eastern cultures, on the other hand, white is associated with death or the color of robes worn by religious leaders. In an example reported by Singh and Pereira, when senior citizens in the United States and India were asked to "visualize the following statement: A lady dressed in white, in a place of worship," the results that came back were as near to the opposite as one could get. In India, the lady would be a widow, but in the United States she would be expected to be a bride.[38]

---

[38] Nitish Singh and Arun Pereira, *The Culturally Customized Web Site: Customizing Web Sites for the Global Marketplace* (Oxford, UK: Elsevier Butterworth Heinemann, 2005).

Other colors that have meanings that are culturally driven include green, blue, red, yellow, and purple. In the United States, red implies excitement, spice, passion, sex, and even anger; in Mexico, it indicates religion; in the United Kingdom, it indicates authority, power, and government; in Scandinavian countries, it indicates strength; and in China, it means communism, joy, and good luck. Blue is associated with holiness in Israel; cleanliness in Scandinavia; love and truth in India; loyalty in Germany; and trust, justice, and "official" business in the United States. In Ireland, green signifies nationalism and Catholicism, and in the United States it denotes health, environmentalism, safety, greed, and envy. Green is a very confusing color for Americans. In the Arab Middle East green is a sign of holiness, in France it represents criminality, and in Malaysia it signifies danger and disease. Yellow also has many culturally dependent meanings. In the United States, it is associated with caution and cowardice; in Scandinavia, warmth; in Germany, envy; and in India, commerce. Purple signifies death, nobility, or the Church in Latin America, the United States, and Italy, respectively. Obviously, when building an information system for a global audience, colors must be chosen carefully; otherwise, unintentional messages will be sent.

Cultural Differences

The *New York Times* columnist Tom Friedman talks about the need for a firm to use its own local capabilities as a basis for competitive advantage in a global market. He refers to this process as *glocalization*. In some ways, when developing a website for an international audience, you need to consider the opposite of glocalization. You need to think about what message needs to be sent to a local culture from your global organization to achieve the business goals of the firm. Consequently, you need to be able to understand the different local cultures. Cultural issues have been studied at both organizational and national levels. Different researchers have emphasized different dimensions on which to focus our attention. In this section, we limit our discussion to cultural issues that effect designing effective user interfaces. In particular, we only address the research of Edward Hall and Geert Hofstede.[39]

Hall identified three dimensions that are directly relevant to user interface design: speed of messages, context, and time. The *speed of messages* dimension deals with how fast a member of a culture is expected to understand a message and how "deep" the content of a typical message will be in a culture. The deeper the message content, the longer it will take for a member of a culture to understand the message. For example, two different approaches to describe a historical event would be a news headline (fast and shallow) and a documentary (slow and deep). According to Hall, different cultures have different expectations of the content of and response to a message. This particular dimension has implications for the content of the message contained in the user interface. Krug's third design principle turns out to be culturally driven. For a Western audience, minimizing the number of words contained in a user interface makes sense. Westerners prefer to get to the point as fast as possible. However, this is not true for Eastern cultures.[40] Consequently, for a firm like Amazon.com, providing detailed reviews and short excerpts from a book provides support for a slow and deep culture, while providing bullet point types of comments supports the fast and shallow culture. By providing both, Amazon.com addresses both needs.

The second dimension, *context*, deals with the level of implicit information that is used in the culture versus the information needing to be made explicit. In *high-context* cultures,

---

[39] See Geert Hofstede, *Culture's Consequences: Comparing Values, Behaviors, Institutions and Organizations Across Nations*, 2nd Ed. (Thousand Oaks, CA: Sage, 2001); Geert Hofstede, Gert Jan Hofstede, and Michael Minkov, *Cultures and Organizations: Software of the Mind*, 3rd Ed. (New York: McGraw-Hill, 2010); Edward T. Hall, *Beyond Culture* (New York: Anchor Books, 1981).

[40] See Richarde E. Nisbett, *The Geography of Thought: How Asians and Westerners Think Differently . . . And Why* (New York: Free Press, 2003).

most information is known intrinsically and does not have to be made explicit. Therefore, the actual content of the message is fairly limited. However, in *low-context* cultures, everything must be spelled out explicitly to avoid any ambiguity, and therefore the message needs to be very detailed. You will find this dimension causing problems when attempting to close a business deal. In most Western societies, the lawyers want everything spelled out. In contrast, in most Eastern societies, it may, in fact, be considered insulting to have to spell everything out. From a system design perspective, a high-context culture would want the design to focus on aesthetics, politeness, and humility, but in a low-context culture, things such as the terms and conditions of a purchase, the "rank" of the product and firm, and the use of superlatives in describing the product and firm are critical attributes of a successful system.

Hall's third dimension, *time*, addresses how a culture deals with many different things going on simultaneously. In a *polychronic time* culture, members of the culture tend to do many things at the same time but are easily distracted and view time commitments as very flexible. With *monochronic time* cultures, members of the culture solve many things by focusing on one thing at a time, are single-minded, and consider time commitments as something that is set in stone. When designing for a polychronic culture, the liberal use of "pop-up" messages might be fun and engaging, while in a monochronic culture, pop-up messages simply annoy the user. In the past, Northern Hemisphere cultures have been monochronic and Southern Hemisphere cultures have been polychronic. However, with the use of e-mail interruptions and text messaging, this could change over time. Regardless, allowing interruptions to occur does in fact distract the users from their current task. Depending on the culture, this could be a good or bad thing to support.

Hofstede also has identified cultural dimensions that are relevant to the user interface. These include power distance, uncertainty avoidance, individualism versus collectivism, and masculinity versus femininity. The first dimension, *power distance*, addresses how the distribution of social power is dealt with in the culture. In cultures with a high power distance, members of the culture believe in the authority of the social hierarchy. In cultures with low power distance, members of the culture believe that power should be more equally distributed. Consequently, in cultures with a high power distance, emphasis on the "greatness" of the leaders of the firm, the use of "proper titles" for members of the firm, and the posting of testimonials on behalf of the firm by "prominent" members of society is important. International awards won by the firm, its members, or its products should also be posted prominently on the website.

The second dimension, *uncertainty avoidance*, addresses to what degree a culture is comfortable with uncertainty. In a culture with a high uncertainty avoidance, members avoid taking risks, value tradition, and are much more comfortable in a rule-driven society. In cultures that score high on uncertainty avoidance, more customer service needs to be provided, more important "local" contacts need to be available, the firm's and product's history and tradition need to be provided on the website, and, in the case of software, the use of free trials and downloads is critical. In other words, you need to build trust and reduce perceived risk between the customer and the firm. This can be supported through product seals of approval or the use of WebTrust^{TM} certifications for the website.[41] Merely translating a website from a low uncertainty avoidance culture to a high uncertainty avoidance culture is not sufficient. You also need to point out relationships between the local culture and the firm's products.

The third dimension, *individualism* versus *collectivism*, is based on the level of emphasis the culture places on the individual or the collective, or group. In North America and Europe,

---

[41] See https://www.cpacanada.ca/en/business-and-accounting-resources/audit-and-assurance/overview-of-webtrust-services

individualism is rewarded. However, in East Asia, it is believed that by focusing on optimizing the group, the individual will be most successful. In other words, it is the group that is the most important. In a collective society, presenting information on how the firm "gives back" to the community; supports "member" clubs, "loyalty" programs, and "chat" facilities; and provides links to "local" sites of interest are very important characteristics for a website. In contrast, in an individualistic society, providing support for personalization of the user's experience with the website, emphasizing the uniqueness of the products that the user is viewing, and emphasizing the privacy policy of the site are critical.

Hofstede's fourth dimension, *masculinity* versus *femininity*, does not mean how men and women are treated by the culture. Instead, this dimension addresses how well masculine and feminine characteristics are valued by the culture. For example, in a masculine culture, characteristics such as being assertive, ambitious, aggressive, and competitive are valued, whereas in a feminine culture, characteristics such as being encouraging, compassionate, thoughtful, gentle, and cooperative are valued. In masculine cultures, a focus on the effectiveness of the firm's products is essential. Also, clearly separating male- and female-oriented topics and placing them on different sections of a website can be critical. Relative to male-cultures, feminine cultures value a focus on aesthetics and using more of a soft-sell approach, where the focus on more affective, intangible aspects of the firm, its members, and its products is more appropriate.

Obviously, operationalizing Hall's and Hofstede's dimensions for effective user interface design is not easy. Furthermore, given all of the different platforms on which a user interface can be deployed, the level of complexity and difficulty in designing effective and efficient user interfaces that take into consideration the global and multicultural world in which we live is increasing. However, in a global market, ignoring cultural issues in user interface design, whether it is for an internal system used only by employees of the firm or an external system that is used by customers, will most certainly cause a system to fail.

NONFUNCTIONAL REQUIREMENTS AND HUMAN–COMPUTER INTERACTION LAYER DESIGN

The human–computer interaction layer is heavily influenced by nonfunctional requirements. In this chapter, we dealt with issues such as layout of the user interface, awareness of content, aesthetics, user experience, and consistency. We also have provided information on how to design the navigation, inputs, and outputs of the user interface. Finally, we have considered mobile computing, social media, immersive and multidimensional environments, and international and cultural issues in user-interface design. None of these have anything to do with the functional requirements of the system. However, if they are ignored, the system can be unusable. As with the data management layer, there are four primary types of nonfunctional requirements that can be important in designing the human–computer interaction layer: operational, performance, security, and cultural and political requirements.

Operational requirements, such as choice of hardware and software platforms, influence the design of the human–computer interaction layer. For example, something as simple as the number of buttons on a mouse (one, two, three, or more) changes the interaction that the user will experience. Other operational nonfunctional requirements that can influence the design of the human–computer interaction layer include system integration and portability. In these cases, a Web-based solution may be required, which can affect the design; not all features of a user interface can be implemented efficiently and effectively on the Web. This can require additional user interface design. Obviously, the entire area of mobile computing can affect the success or failure of the system.

Performance requirements, over time, have become less of an issue for this layer. However, speed requirements are still paramount, especially with mobile computing. Most users do not care for hitting return or clicking the mouse and having to take a coffee break while they are waiting for the system to respond, so efficiency issues must be still addressed. Depending on the user interface toolkit used, different user interface components may be required. Furthermore, the interaction of the human–computer interaction layer with the other layers must be considered. For example, if the system response is slow, incorporating more-efficient data structures with the problem domain layer, including indexes in the tables with the data management layer, and/or replicating objects across the application architecture layer could be required.

Security requirements affecting the human–computer interaction layer deal primarily with the access controls implemented to protect the objects from unauthorized access, the authorization controls that support limiting log-ins, and the possibility of encrypting any and all data that is transmitted between the user interface and the system. Most of the information necessary to support these controls can be derived from the real use case descriptions and the CRC cards and CRUDE matrices referenced in previous chapters. However, most of these controls are enforced through the DBMS on the data management layer (Chapter 8) and the operating system on the application architecture layer (Chapter 10). However, through the expansion of the validation of inputs to the system to include the security requirements, the design of this layer can be critical. [42]

In addition to the international and cultural issues described previously, unstated norms effect the cultural and political requirements that can affect the design of the human–computer interaction layer. Unstated norm requirements include having the date displayed in the appropriate format (MM/DD/YYYY versus DD/MM/YYYY). For a system to be truly useful in a global environment, the user interface must be customizable to address local cultural requirements.

VERIFYING AND VALIDATING THE HUMAN–COMPUTER INTERACTION LAYER[43]

In addition to performing input validation, verifying and validating the human–computer interaction layer design is necessary to understand how to improve the user interface before the system is complete. Most interface designers intentionally or unintentionally design an interface that meets their personal preferences, which might or might not match the preferences of the users. The key message, therefore, is to have as many people as possible evaluate the interface, and the more users the better. Most experts recommend involving at least ten potential users in the evaluation process.

Interface evaluations almost always identify improvements, so the interface design process is repeated in a cyclical process until no new improvements are identified. In practice, most analysts interact closely with the users during the interface design process so that users have many chances to see the interface as it evolves, rather than waiting for one overall interface evaluation at the end of the interface design process. It is better for all concerned (both analysts and users) if changes are identified sooner rather than later. For example, if the interface structure or standards need improvements, it is better to identify changes before most of the screens that use the standards have been designed.[44] Ideally, interface evaluation should be performed while the system is being designed—before it is built—so that any major design problems can be identified and corrected before the time and cost of programming have been spent on a weak design. It is not uncommon for the system to undergo one or two major

---

[42] We describe security requirements in more detail in Chapter 11.

[43] Verifying and validation approaches, in general, were described in Chapters 4 through 7. Also, further approaches to testing the evolving system are described in Chapter 12. In this section, we describe approaches that have been customized to the human–computer interaction layer.

[44] A good source for more information on user interface evaluation is Deborah Hix and H. Rex Hartson, *Developing User Interfaces, Ensuring Usability Through Product & Process* (New York: Wiley, 1993).

changes after the users see the first interface design prototype because they identify problems that are overlooked by the project team. However, many organizations save interface evaluation for the very last step in the systems development before the system is installed.

As with interface design prototyping, interface evaluation can take many different forms, each with different costs and different amounts of detail. In addition to all of the types of input validation described earlier, there are five common approaches to interface evaluation: heuristic evaluation, walkthrough evaluation, interactive evaluation, A/B testing, and formal usability testing. As with interface design prototyping, the different parts of a system can be evaluated using different techniques.

A *heuristic evaluation* examines the interface by comparing it to a set of heuristics or principles for interface design. The project team develops a checklist of interface design principles—from the list at the start of this chapter, for example, as well as the list of principles in the navigation, input, and output design sections later in this chapter. At least three members of the project team then individually work through the interface design prototype, examining every interface to ensure that it satisfies each design principle on a formal checklist. After each has gone through the prototype separately, they meet as a team to discuss their evaluations and identify specific improvements that are required.

An interface design *walkthrough evaluation* is a meeting conducted with the users who ultimately have to operate the system. The project team presents the prototype to the users and walks them through the various parts of the interface. The project team shows the storyboard and wireframe diagrams or actually demonstrates the user interface prototype and explains how the interface will be used. The users identify improvements to each of the interfaces that are presented.

With an *interactive evaluation,* the users themselves actually work with the user interface prototype in a one-person session with member(s) of the project team (an interactive evaluation cannot be used with a storyboard or wireframe diagrams). As the user works with the prototype (often by going through the use scenarios, using the real use cases described later in this chapter, or just navigating at will through the system), he or she tells the project team member(s) what he or she likes and doesn't like and what additional information or functionality is needed. As the user interacts with the prototype, team member(s) records the cases when he or she appears to be unsure of what to do, makes mistakes, or misinterprets the meaning of an interface component. If the pattern of uncertainty, mistakes, or misinterpretations reoccurs across several of the users participating in the evaluation, it is a clear indication that those parts of the interface need improvement.

A/B testing is a form of interactive evaluation. These techniques were originally developed in marketing to ascertain which marketing campaign would be the best. In our case, multiple user interface prototypes are created instead of different marketing campaigns. Potential users are assigned to the different versions of the user interface. The effectiveness of the user interfaces are tested and statistically analyzed to determine which of the user interfaces should be further developed and deployed.

Formal *usability testing* is commonly done with commercial software products and products developed by large organizations that will be widely used through the organization. As the name suggests, it is a very formal—almost scientific—process that can be used only with language prototypes (and systems that have been completely built awaiting installation or shipping).[45] As with interactive evaluation, usability testing is done in one-person sessions in which a user works directly with the software. However, it is typically done in a special lab equipped with video cameras and special software that records every keystroke and mouse operation so that they can be replayed to understand exactly what the user did.

The user is given a specific set of tasks to accomplish (usually the use scenarios), and after some initial instructions, the project team's members are not permitted to interact with the

---

[45] A good source for usability testing is Jakob Nielsen and Robert Mack (eds.), *Usability Inspection Methods* (New York: Wiley, 1994). See also www.useit.com/papers.

user to provide assistance. The user must work with the software without help, which can be hard on the users if they become confused with the system. It is critical that users understand that the goal is to test the interface, not their abilities, and if they are unable to complete the task, the interface—not the user—has failed the test.

Formal usability testing is very expensive, because each one-user session can take one to two days to analyze depending on the volume of detail collected in the computer logs and videos. Sessions typically last one to two hours. Most usability testing involves five to ten users, because if there are fewer than five users, the results depend too much on the specific individual users who participated, and more than ten users are often too expensive to justify (unless a large commercial software developer is involved).

APPLYING THE CHAPTER CONCEPTS

Library Management System (LMS) Example In the previous installation of the LMS example, Jane had visited with Joe to determine how the Data Management Layer should be implemented. In that case, Jane decided to simply use the RDBMS (MySQL) that the library was already using with other applications. In this installation, we catch up with Beth and her design of the Human–Computer Interaction Layer.

To begin with, Beth decided that she should go back and review the latest use case diagram with Joe. After her meeting with Joe, she realized that there should be an external actor that represented the external "databases" from which downloadable resources could be acquired. Based on this, she modified the use case diagram (see Figure 9-18). After fixing the use case diagram, Beth and Joe decided that the user interface for the Borrow Resource use case should be done first. To accomplish this, Beth sat down with Joe and reviewed the latest activity diagram of the Borrow Resource use case (see Figure 9-19).

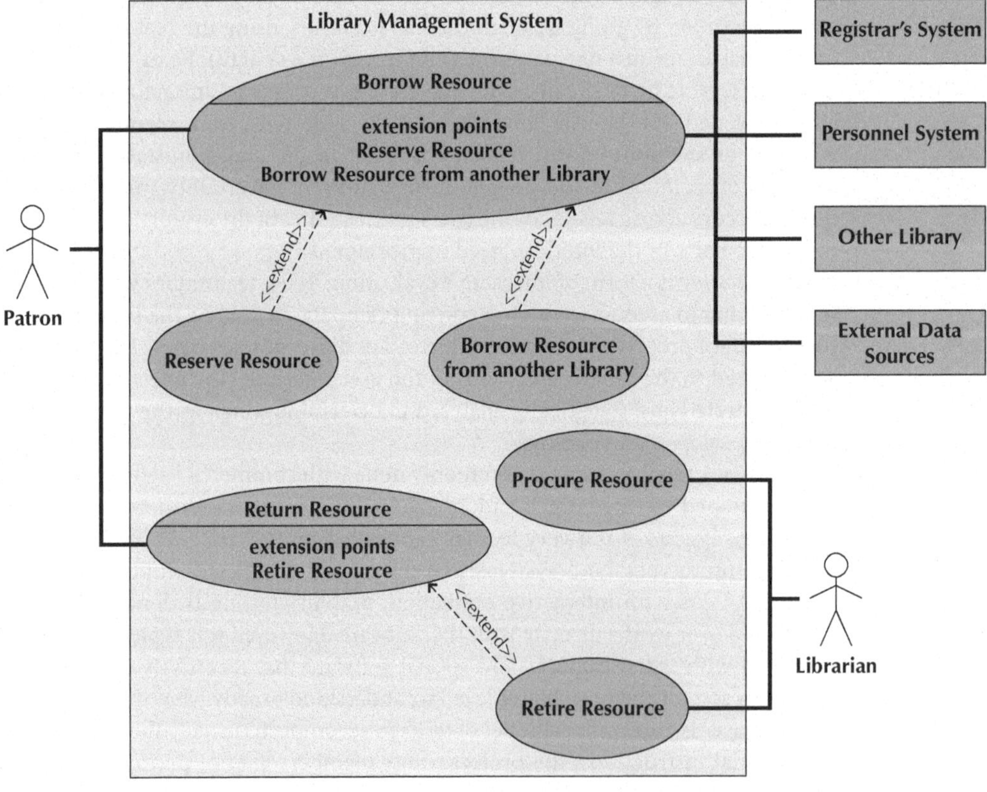

FIGURE 9-18 Updated LMS Use Case Diagram

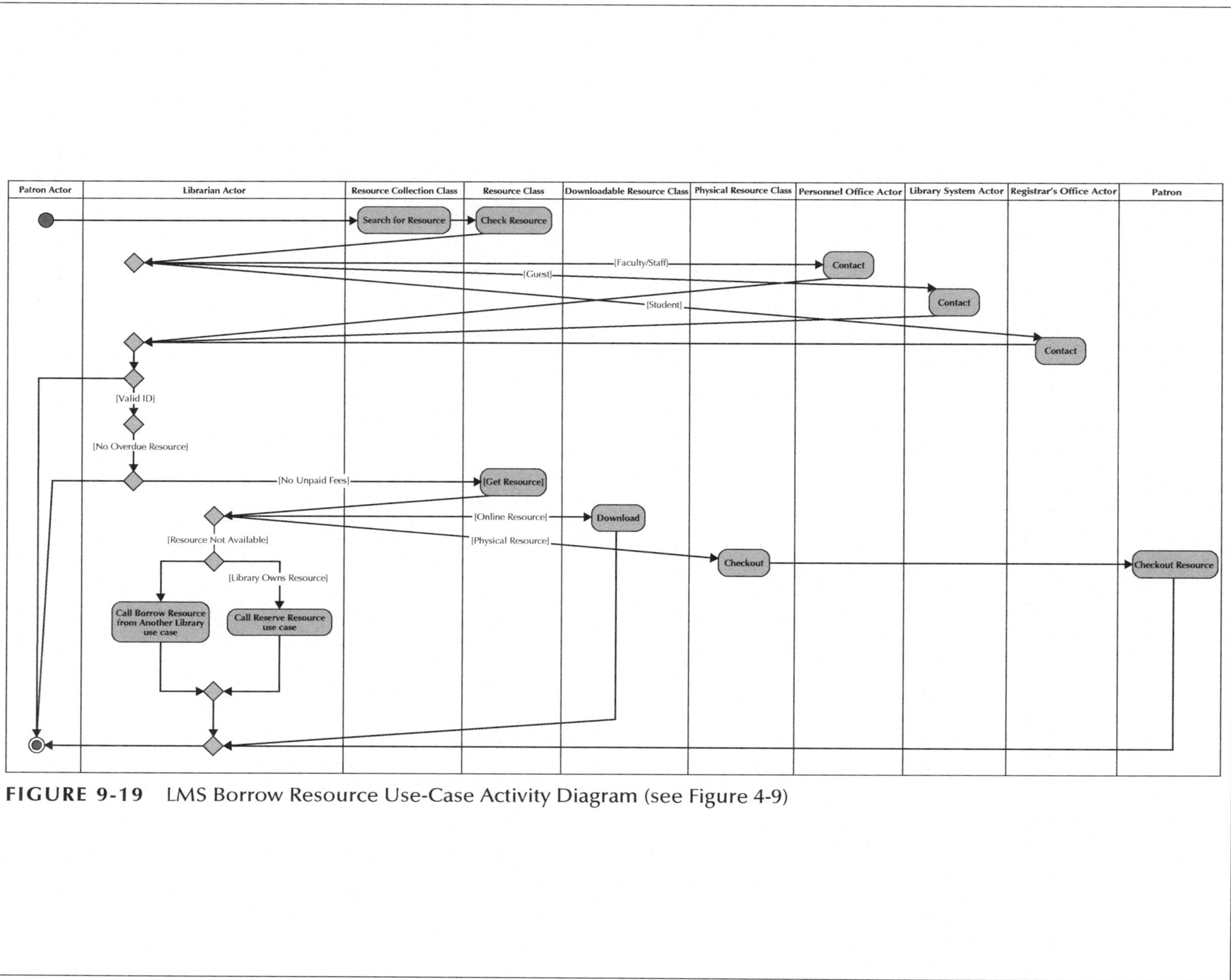

FIGURE 9-19 LMS Borrow Resource Use-Case Activity Diagram (see Figure 4-9)

Based on the review, Beth and Joe realized that there were different tasks that needed to be supported. First, the Patron needed to be able to search for resources. Second, if the resource was a physical resource, the Patron would need to get the actual resource and bring it to the checkout desk where the librarian would interact with the system to determine whether the Patron would be allowed to check out the resource or not. And if the Patron was allowed to check out the resource, the librarian would perform the checkout activity. Third. if the resource was downloadable and available, then for the Patron to "check out" the resource, the system (not the librarian) would need to verify the Patron's identity, make sure that the Patron did not have any overdue resources, and make sure that the Patron did not owe any fees. Finally, how should the system behave if the Patron did not have a valid ID, they had overdue resources, or they had unpaid fees. The activity diagram nor the sequence diagrams (see Figures 5-5 through 5-11, and 7-16) addressed these contingencies. Consequently, Beth and Joe needed to sit down and modify the activity and sequence diagrams before designing the human–computer interaction layer. Based on the modifications, Beth designed the HCI layer using combined wireframe and window navigation diagrams.

Figures 9-20 and 9-21 show her first cut at the design for the user interface that supports the Borrow Resource use case for the patrons and the librarians, respectively. Once she completed these, she set a meeting with Joe to explain how the user interface would work. Below is a transcript of the meeting.

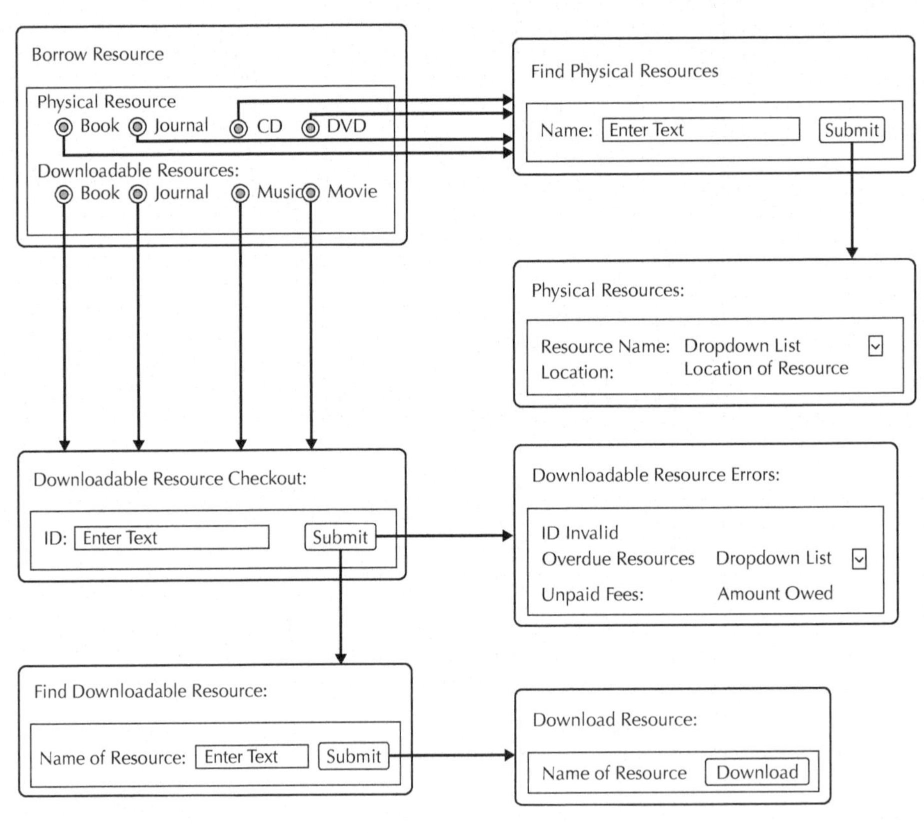

FIGURE 9-20
Patron HCI Design
for the Borrow
Resource use case

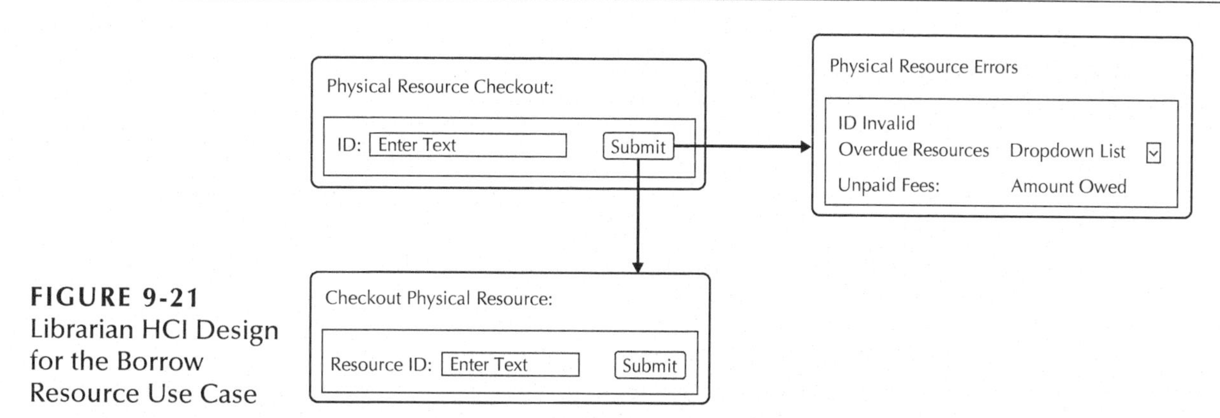

FIGURE 9-21
Librarian HCI Design
for the Borrow
Resource Use Case

BETH: Joe, I'm glad to be able to sit down with you and review our first cut at the design for the user interface that supports the Borrow Resource use case for the patrons and the librarians. In this case, I would like to go through the design to make sure that both the layout and navigation makes sense from your point of view.

JOE: This is great. It seems to me that we are finally getting somewhere.

BETH: Joe, you do need to realize, these are just designs, once we know we are in the ballpark, we can start implementing them. But you should realize that user interface code is the majority of the code for any system to be implemented.

JOE: Okay, I get it. So, let's get started.

BETH: When a patron wants to borrow a resource, they will use this first screen to choose the type of resource that they want to checkout. If the patron wants to checkout a physical resource, they will pick either a Book, Journal, CD, or DVD. Once they pick one of those, the system will automatically bring up the Find Physical Resources window to the right. As you can see, the arrows show this. Next, in the Find Physical Resources window, the patron will type in the name of the resource in which they are interested and submit it to the system. Once the system finds the resource, it will display the Physical Resources window that will contain a dropdown list that contains a list of possible matches. As the poatron scrolls through the dropdown list, the location of the current dropdown list value will display its location. At this time, the patron can go and get the actual resource. Do you see how the window's layout and navigation is designed?

JOE: Yes.

BETH: Based on your understanding of this scenario, can you try to explain what happens with regards to a downloadable resource?

JOE: I think so. Should I try?

BETH: Yes.

JOE: Okay, here goes nothing. If the patron wants to checkout a downloadable resource, they will pick either a Book, Journal, Music, or Movie. Once they pick one of those, the system will automatically bring up the Downloadable Resource Checkout window. Here, the patron will type in their ID and submit it to the system. If an error occurs, the system will display the Downloadable Resource Errors window. Otherwise, the system will display the Find Downloadable Resource window where the patron will type in the name of the resource in which they are interested and submit it to the system. Next the system will display the Download Resource window that contains a dropdown list of possible matches. The patron can then scroll through the matches to find the specific one in which they are interested. Once they see it, they can press the Download button to download the resource. So, how did I do?

> **BETH:** Perfect. Based on your performance, I suspect that the design for the librarian (see Figure 9-21) is also very straightforward.
>
> **JOE:** I agree. I see how the user interface should work. Even though this design is only a first cut and therefore incomplete, what happens once the patron is done. For example, what happens once the patron downloads the resource or once they get an error? In other words, how does a patron close out the system?
>
> **BETH:** That's a really good observation. But as you said, this was only our first cut design. We intentionally left out those details. We wanted to make sure that the basic design and navigation worked for you before we added all of those details. So, does the design work?
>
> **JOE:** It does provide the necessary functionality. But it also seems a little clunky. Instead of having multiple windows popping up all over the place, is it possible to simply keep extending the relevant content?
>
> **BETH:** Yes. Now that I understand your preference, the next time I come over, I'll bring a working prototype that does exactly that. I'll also have the missing functionality included.
>
> **JOE:** That would be great. See you next time.
>
> In the next installation of this example, we see how Phil is doing on the design of the Application Architecture Layer.
>
> **Campus Housing Service "Your Turn" Exercise** In the previous installation of the Campus Housing Service (CHS) "Your Turn" exercise, you used the mapping rules for a RDBMS to design the data management layer including the design of the DAM classes. In this installation, you should design the HCI layer using a set of wireframe diagrams that portrays the layout of the user interface and a WND that shows the navigation between the objects in the wireframe diagrams. We will return to CHS in the next chapter.

CHAPTER REVIEW

After reading and studying this chapter, you should be able to:

- [ ] Describe the six basic principles of user interface design.
- [ ] Apply the use-case driven process described to design a user interface.
- [ ] Describe the purpose of use scenarios in user interface design.
- [ ] Describe how to use windows navigation diagrams, wireframe diagrams, storyboards, and user interface prototypes during the design of a user interface.
- [ ] Describe the difference between essential and real use cases.
- [ ] Describe the importance and use of interface standards in user interface design.
- [ ] Discuss the relationship between user interface design and requirements determination.
- [ ] Design efficient and effective navigation controls that are easy to use, prevent users from making mistakes, support obvious approaches for users to recover from mistakes, and use a consistent grammar order.
- [ ] Design efficient and effective input mechanisms that capture the necessary information for the system.
- [ ] Design efficient and effective output that supports the users in their tasks.
- [ ] Describe the unique issues related to designing user interfaces for mobile computing platforms.
- [ ] Describe the unique navigation controls, input mechanisms, and outputs that mobile computing platforms possess.
- [ ] Describe the unique issues related to designing user interfaces for social applications.
- [ ] Describe the unique issues related to designing user interfaces for immersive and multidimensional applications.
- [ ] Discuss the international and cultural issues that can affect the design of the human–computer interaction layer.
- [ ] Describe how nonfunctional requirements may influence the actual design of the human–computer interaction layer.
- [ ] Describe the five common approaches used to evaluate user interfaces.

KEY TERMS

A/B testing
Acknowledgment message
Action–object order
Aesthetics
Assertions
Augmented reality (AR)
Bar-code reader
Batch processing
Batch report
Bias
Button
Check digit check
Cognitive map
Collectivism
Color
Command language
Completeness check
Confirmation message
Consistency
Consistency check
Content awareness
Context
Cultural differences
2D space
Database check
Default value
Delay message
Detail report
Direct manipulation
Drill-down capability
Drop-down menu
Ease of learning
Ease of use
Edit check
Error message

Essential use case
Exception report
Femininity
Field
Field label
Form
Format check
Gamification
GPS
Grammar order
Graph
Graphical user interface (GUI)
Haptic feedback
Help message
Heuristic evaluation
High-context
Hot key
Immersion
Individualism
Information load
Input mechanism
Interactive evaluation
Interface action
Interface design prototype
Interface evaluation
Interface icon
Interface metaphor
Interface object
Interface standards
Interface template
Invariants
Layout
Low-context
Magnetic stripe readers
Masculinity

Menu
Menu bar
Mobile device
Monochronic time
Multilingual requirements
Multidimensional information
  visualization
Natural language
Navigation controls
Navigation mechanism
Nonimmersive 3D
Number box
Object–action order
Object recognition
Occlusion
Online processing
Optical character recognition
Output mechanism
Polychronic time
Pop-up menu
Postcondition
Power distance
Precondition
Pull
Push
Range check
Real-time information
Real-time report
Real use case
Report
Screen
Selection box
Sequence diagrams
Smart card
Smartphone

Social media
Source data automation
Speed of messages
State
Stereotype
Storyboard
Summary report
System interface
Tab menu
Tablet
Text box
Three-clicks rule
Time
Toolbar
Touch screens
Transaction processing
Transition
Turnaround document
Uncertainty avoidance
Usability testing
Use case
Use scenario
User experience
User interface
User interface prototype
Validation
Virtual reality (VR)
Wayfinding
Walkthrough evaluation
White space
Window
Wireframe diagram
Windows navigation
  diagram (WND)

QUESTIONS

1. Explain three important user interface design principles.
2. What are three fundamental parts of most user interfaces?
3. Why is content awareness important?
4. What is white space, and why is it important?
5. Under what circumstances should densities be low? High?
6. How can a system be designed to be used by both experienced and first-time users?
7. Why is consistency in design important? Why can too much consistency cause problems?
8. How can different parts of the interface be consistent?
9. Describe the basic process of user interface design.
10. What are use cases, and why are they important?
11. What is a WND, and why is it used?

12. Why are interface standards important?
13. Explain the purpose and contents of interface metaphors, interface objects, interface actions, interface icons, and interface templates.
14. Why do we prototype the user interface design?
15. What are Krug's three design principles?
16. Describe three basic principles of navigation design.
17. How can you prevent mistakes?
18. Explain the differences between object-action order and action-object order.
19. Describe four types of navigation controls
20. Why are menus the most commonly used navigation control?
21. Compare and contrast four types of menus.
22. Under what circumstances would you use a drop-down menu versus a tab menu?
23. Under what circumstances would you use an image map versus a simple list menu?
24. Describe five types of messages.
25. What are the key factors in designing an error message?
26. What is context-sensitive help? Does your word processor have context-sensitive help?
27. How do an essential use case and a real use case differ?
28. What is the relationship between essential use cases and use scenarios?
29. What is the relationship between real use cases and use scenarios?
30. Explain three principles in the design of inputs.
31. Compare and contrast batch processing and online processing. Describe one application that would use batch processing and one that would use online processing.
32. Why is capturing data at the source important?
33. Describe four devices that can be used for source data automation.
34. Describe five types of inputs.
35. Why is input validation important?
36. Describe five types of input validation methods.
37. Describe how invariants, preconditions, and postconditions are useful in input validation.
38. Explain three principles in the design of outputs.
39. Describe five types of outputs.
40. What do you think are three common mistakes that novice analysts make in navigation design?
41. What do you think are three common mistakes that novice analysts make in input design?
42. What do you think are three common mistakes that novice analysts make in output design?
43. What are the six challenges you face when developing mobile applications?
44. What are the six suggestions to address the mobile computing challenges?
45. What are the unique navigation controls, input mechanisms, and outputs that mobile computing supports?
46. With regard to social media, what is the difference between "push" and "pull" approaches to interacting with customers?
47. Why is it important to keep your social media sites synced?
48. How can you keep your customers engaged with your social media sites?
49. Why do people play games?
50. What is gamification?
51. What is occlusion? Why is it an issue when developing multidimensional information visualizations? Augmented reality systems? Virtual reality systems?
52. What is augmented reality?
53. Name some of potential business applications of augmented reality.
54. What is virtual reality?
55. Name some of potential business applications of virtual reality.
56. When developing a virtual reality system, what are some of the issues that need to be addresses?
57. What is a cognitive map?
58. What are some of the multilingual issues that you may face when developing for a global audience?
59. How important is the proper use of color when developing websites for a global audience? Give some examples of potential pitfalls that you could run into.
60. Name the three cultural dimensions that are relevant to user interface design identified by Hall. Why are they relevant?
61. Name the four cultural dimensions that are relevant to user interface design identified by Hofstede. Why are they relevant?
62. What are some of the nonfunctional requirements that can influence the design of the human–computer interaction layer?
63. Why is it important to perform an interface evaluation before the system is built?
64. Compare and contrast the five types of interface evaluation.
65. Under what conditions is heuristic evaluation justified?

EXERCISES

A. Develop two use scenarios for a website that sells some retail products (e.g., books, music, and clothes).

B. Create a storyboard for a website that sells some retail products (e.g., books, music, and clothes).

C. Draw a WND for a website that sells some retail products (e.g., books, music, and clothes).

D. Create a wireframe diagram for the home page of a website that sells some retail products (e.g., books, music, and clothes).

E. Describe the primary components of the interface standards for a website that sells some retail products (metaphors, objects, actions, icons, and template).

F. Using the Web, identify a set of games that are useful in some aspect of business, for example, advertising or training.

G. Using the Web, identify a set of multidimensional information visualizations that are used to support business decision-making.

H. Using the Web, find businesses that are currently using augmented and virtual reality systems.

I. For the A Real Estate Inc. problem in Chapter 3 (exercises I, J, and K), Chapter 4 (exercises N and O), Chapter 5 (exercise D), Chapter 6 (exercise D), Chapter 7 (exercise A), and Chapter 8 (exercise H):
1. Develop two use scenarios.
2. Draw a WND.
3. Design a storyboard.

J. Based on your solution to exercise I:
1. Create wireframe diagrams for the interface design.
2. Develop a real use case.

K. For the A Video Store problem in Chapter 4 (exercises L, M, and N), Chapter 5 (exercises P and Q), Chapter 6 (exercise E), Chapter 7 (exercise E), Chapter 8 (exercise B), and Chapter 9 (exercise I):
1. Develop two use scenarios.
2. Draw a WND.
3. Design a storyboard.

L. Based on your solution to exercise K:
1. Create wireframe diagrams for the interface design.
2. Develop a real use case.

M. For the gym membership problem in Chapter 4 (exercises O, P, and Q), Chapter 5 (exercises R and S),

Chapter 6 (exercise F), Chapter 7 (exercise F), Chapter 8 (exercise C), and Chapter 9 (exercise J):
1. Develop two use scenarios.
2. Draw a WND.
3. Design a storyboard.

N. Based on your solution to exercise M:
1. Create wireframe diagrams for the interface design.
2. Develop a real use case.

O. For the Picnics R Us problem in Chapter 4 (exercises R, S, and T), Chapter 5 (exercises T and U), Chapter 6 (exercise G), Chapter 7 (exercise G), Chapter 8 (exercise D), and Chapter 9 (exercise K):
1. Develop two use scenarios.
2. Draw a WND.
3. Design a storyboard.

P. Based on your solution to exercise O:
1. Create wireframe diagrams for the interface design.
2. Develop a real use case.

Q. For the Of-the-Month-Club problem in Chapter 4 (exercises U, V, and W), Chapter 5 (exercises V and W), Chapter 6 (exercise H), Chapter 7 (exercise H), Chapter 8 (exercise E), and Chapter 9 (exercise L):
1. Develop two use scenarios.
2. Draw a WND.
3. Design a storyboard.

R. Based on your solution to exercise Q:
1. Create wireframe diagrams for the interface design.
2. Develop a real use case.

S. Create a user interface design for a mobile solution for the:
1. A Real Estate Inc. problem.
2. A Video Store problem.
3. Gym membership problem.
4. Picnics R Us problem.
5. Of-the-Month-Club problem.

T. How would your answers change to exercises I through S if you were developing for a global marketplace?

MINICASES

1. Tots to Teens is a catalog retailer specializing in children's clothing. A project has been under way to develop a new order entry system for the company's catalog clerks. The old system had a character-based user interface that corresponded to the system's COBOL underpinnings. The new system will feature a graphical user interface more in keeping with up-to-date PC products in use today. The company hopes that this new user interface will help reduce the turnover it has experienced with its order entry clerks. Many newly hired order entry staff found the old system very difficult to learn and were overwhelmed by the numerous mysterious codes that had to be used to communicate with the system.

   A user interface walkthrough evaluation was scheduled for today to give the user a first look at the new system's interface. The project team was careful to invite several key users from the order entry department. In particular, Norma was included because of her years of experience with the order entry system. Norma was known to be an informal leader in the department; her opinion influenced many of her associates. Norma had let it be known that she was less than thrilled with the ideas she had heard for the new system. Owing to her experience and good memory, Norma worked very effectively with the character-based system and was able to breeze through even the most convoluted transactions with ease. Norma had trouble suppressing a sneer when she heard talk of such things as "icons" and "buttons" in the new user interface.

   Cindy was also invited to the walkthrough because of her influence in the order entry department. Cindy has been with the department for just one year, but she quickly became known because of her successful organization of a sick child daycare service for the children of the department workers. Sick children are the number-one cause of absenteeism in the department, and many of the workers could not afford to miss workdays. Never one to keep quiet when a situation needed improvement, Cindy has been a vocal supporter of the new system.

   a. Drawing upon the design principles presented in the text, describe the features of the user interface that will be most important to experienced users like Norma.

   b. Drawing upon the design principles presented in the text, describe the features of the user interface that will be most important to novice users like Cindy.

2. The members of a systems development project team have gone out for lunch together, and as often happens, the conversation turns to work. The team has been working on the development of the user interface design, and so far, work has been progressing smoothly. The team should be completing work on the interface prototypes early next week. A combination of storyboards and language prototypes has been used in this project. The storyboards depict the overall structure and flow of the system, but the team developed language prototypes of the actual screens because they felt that seeing the actual screens would be valuable for the users.

   Chris (the youngest member of the project team): I read an article last night about a really cool way to evaluate a user interface design. It's called usability testing, and it's done by all the major software vendors. I think we should use it to evaluate our interface design.

   Heather (systems analyst): I've heard of that, too, but isn't it really expensive?

   Mark (project manager): I'm afraid it is expensive and I'm not sure we can justify the expense for this project.

   Chris: But we really need to know that the interface works. I thought this usability testing technique would help us prove we have a good design.

   Amy (systems analyst): It would, Chris, but there are other ways too. I assumed we'd do a thorough walkthrough with our users and present the interface to them at a meeting. We can project each interface screen so that the users can see it and give us their reaction. This is probably the most efficient way to get the users' response to our work.

Heather: That's true, but I'd sure like to see the users sit down and work with the system. I've always learned a lot by watching what they do, seeing where they get confused, and hearing their comments and feedback.

Ryan (systems analyst): It seems to me that we've put so much work into this interface design that all we really need to do is review it ourselves. Let's just make a list of the design principles we're most concerned about and check it ourselves to make sure we've followed them consistently. If we have, we should be fine. We want to get moving on the implementation, you know.

Mark: These are all good ideas. It seems like we've all got a different view of how to evaluate the interface design. Let's try to sort out the technique that's best for our project.

Develop a set of guidelines that can help a project team like this one select the most appropriate interface evaluation technique for their project.

3. The menu structure for Holiday Travel Vehicle's existing character-based system is shown here. Develop and prototype a new interface design for the system's functions using a graphical user interface. Also, develop a set of real use cases for your new interface. Assume the new system will need to include the same functions as those shown in the menus provided. Include any messages that will be produced as a user interacts with your interface (error, confirmation, status, etc.). Also, prepare a written summary that describes how your interface implements the principles of good interface design as presented in the textbook.

```
              Holiday Travel Vehicles

                   Main Menu

            1 Sales Invoice
            2 Vehicle Inventory
            3 Reports
            4 Sales Staff

       Type number of menu selection here:____
```

```
              Holiday Travel Vehicles

                Sales Invoice Menu

            1 Create Sales Invoice
            2 Change Sales Invoice
            3 Cancel Sales Invoice

       Type number of menu selection here:____
```

```
              Holiday Travel Vehicles

              Vehicle Inventory Menu

            1 Create Vehicle Inventory Record
            2 Change Vehicle Inventory Record
            3 Delete Vehicle Inventory Record

       Type number of menu selection here:____
```

```
              Holiday Travel Vehicles

                  Reports Menu

            1 Commission Report
            2 RV Sales by Make Report
            3 Trailer Sales by Make Report
            4 Dealer Options Report

       Type number of menu selection here:____
```

```
              Holiday Travel Vehicles

           Sales Staff Maintenance Menu

            1 Add Salesperson Record
            2 Change Salesperson Record
            3 Delete Salesperson Record

       Type number of menu selection here:____
```

4. One aspect of the new system under development at Holiday Travel Vehicles will be the direct entry of the sales invoice into the computer system by the salesperson as the purchase transaction is being completed. In the current system, the salesperson fills out a paper form (shown on the next page).

Design and prototype an input screen that will permit the salesperson to enter all the necessary information for the sales invoice. The following information may be helpful in your design process. Assume that Holiday Travel Vehicles sells recreational vehicles and trailers from four different manufacturers. Each manufacturer has a fixed number of names and models of RVs and trailers.

For the purposes of your prototype, use this format:

Mfg-A	Name-1 Model-X
Mfg-A	Name-1 Model-Y
Mfg-A	Name-1 Model-Z
Mfg-B	Name-1 Model-X
Mfg-B	Name-1 Model-Y
Mfg-B	Name-2 Model-X
Mfg-B	Name-2 Model-Y
Mfg-B	Name-2 Model-Z
Mfg-C	Name-1 Model-X
Mfg-C	Name-1 Model-Y
Mfg-C	Name-1 Model-Z
Mfg-C	Name-2 Model-X
Mfg-C	Name-3 Model-X
Mfg-D	Name-1 Model-X
Mfg-D	Name-2 Model-X
Mfg-D	Name-2 Model-Y

Also, assume there are ten different dealer options that could be installed on a vehicle at the customer's request. The company currently has ten salespeople on staff.

Holiday Travel Vehicles
Sales Invoice

Invoice #: _____________
Invoice Date: _________

Customer Name: _______________________________
Address: _______________________________
City: _______________________________
State: _______________________________
Zip: _______________________________
Phone: _______________________________

New RV/TRAILER
(circle one)

Name: _______________________________
Model: _______________________________
Serial #: ______________________ Year: _________
Manufacturer: _______________________________

Trade-in RV/TRAILER
(circle one)

Name: _______________________________
Model: _______________________________
Year: _______________________________
Manufacturer: _______________________________

Options:

Code	Description	Price
_______	_______________________	_______
_______	_______________________	_______
_______	_______________________	_______
_______	_______________________	_______

Vehicle Base Cost: _______________
Trade-in Allowance: _______________   _______________________
Total Options: _______________   (Salesperson Name)
Tax: _______________
License Fee: _______________
Final Cost: _______________   _______________________
(Customer Signature)

5. Refer to the Professional and Scientific Staff Management (PSSM) Minicase in Chapters 4, 6, 7, 8, and 9.

   a. Develop two use scenarios, draw a WND, and design a storyboard.

   b. Based on your answers to part a, create wireframe diagrams for the user interface and develop a set of real use cases for the user interface.

   c. How would your user interface design have to be modified if you were to deploy it on a tablet? What about a smartphone?

   d. What, if any, social media sites should PSSM consider?

   e. How would your answers change if you were developing the system for a global audience?

CHAPTER 10

APPLICATION ARCHITECTURE LAYER DESIGN

An important component of the design of an information system is the design of the application architecture layer, which describes the distribution of the software over the system's hardware and network environment. The application architecture layer design flows primarily from the nonfunctional requirements, such as operational, performance, security, cultural, and political requirements. This chapter describes the use of the UML deployment diagram as a way to portray the design of the application architecture layer.

OBJECTIVES

- Understand the different application architecture components.
- Understand server-based, client-based, client–server, peer-to-peer, and cloud application architectures.
- Be familiar with ubiquitous computing and the Internet of things (IoT).
- Be able to create a network model using a deployment diagram.
- Be familiar with how to create a hardware and software specification.
- Understand how operational, performance, security, cultural, and political requirements affect the design of the application architecture layer.

INTRODUCTION

In today's environment, most information systems are spread across multiple computers. A Web-based system, for example, runs in the browser on a desktop computer but interacts with the Web server (and possibly other computers) over the Internet. A system that operates completely inside a company's network may have a Visual Basic program installed on one computer but interact with a database server elsewhere on the network. Therefore, an important step of design is the creation of the application architecture layer design, the plan for how the system will be distributed across the computers.

In many cases, systems are built to use the existing hardware and software in the organization. Therefore, the current architecture restricts the design choices. Other factors such as corporate standards, existing site-licensing agreements, and product–vendor relationships also can mandate what architecture the project team must use. However, many organizations now have a variety of infrastructures available or are openly looking for pilot projects to test new architectures that enable a project team to select one on the basis of other important factors.

Designing the application architecture layer can be quite difficult; therefore, many organizations hire expert consultants or assign very experienced analysts to the task. In this chapter, we examine the key factors in application architecture layer design, but it is important to remember that it takes lots of experience to do it well. The nonfunctional requirements developed during analysis (see Chapter 2) play a key role in application architecture layer design.

These requirements are reexamined and refined into more-detailed requirements that influence the system's architecture.

ELEMENTS OF THE APPLICATION ARCHITECTURE LAYER

The objective of designing the application architecture layer is to determine what parts of the application software will be assigned to what hardware. Although there are numerous ways the software components can be placed on the hardware components, we describe five of the application architectures in use today: *server-based architectures*, *client-based architectures*, *client–server architectures*, *peer-to-peer architectures*, and *cloud computing*.

Architectural Components

The major *architectural components* of any system are the software and the hardware. The major software components of the system being developed have to be identified and then allocated to the various hardware components on which the system will operate. Each of these components can be combined in a variety of different ways.

All software systems can be divided into four basic functions. The first is *data storage* (associated with the object persistence located on the data management layer—see Chapter 8). Most application programs require data to be stored and retrieved, whether the information is a small file such as a memo produced by a word processor or a large database that stores an organization's accounting records. These are the data documented in the structural model (CRC cards and class diagrams). The second function is *data access logic* (associated with the data access and manipulation classes located on the data management layer—see Chapter 8), the processing required to access data, which often means database queries in *SQL (structured query language)*. The third function is the *application logic* (located on the problem-domain layer—see Chapters 3 through 7), which can be simple or complex, depending on the application. This is the logic documented in the functional (activity diagrams and use cases) and behavioral models (sequence and behavioral state machines). The fourth function is the *presentation logic* (located on the human–computer interaction layer—see Chapter 9), the presentation of information to the user, and the acceptance of the user's commands (the user interface). These four functions (data storage, data access logic, application logic, and presentation logic) are the basic building blocks of any application.

The three primary hardware components of a system are *client computers*, *servers*, and the *network* that connects them. Client computers are the input/output devices employed by the user and are usually desktop or laptop computers, but they can also be handheld devices, cell phones, special-purpose terminals, and so on. Servers are computers running software to handle system needs and requests (e.g., store data). Servers can be accessed by anyone who has permission. The network that connects the computers can vary in speed from a slow cell phone, to medium-speed always-on frame relay networks, to fast always-on broadband connections such as cable modem, DSL, or T1 circuits, to high-speed always-on ethernet, T3, or ATM circuits.[1]

Server-Based Architectures

The very first computing architectures were server-based architectures, with the server performing all four functions. The clients enabled users to send and receive messages to and from

---

[1] For more information on networks, see Alan Dennis, *Networking in the Internet Age* (New York: Wiley, 2002).

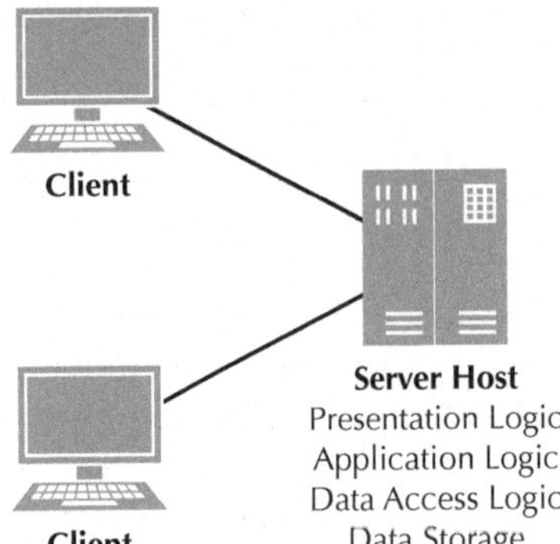

FIGURE 10-1
Server-Based
Architecture

the server. The clients merely captured keystrokes and sent them to the server for processing and accepted instructions from the server on what to display (see Figure 10-1).

This very simple architecture often works very well. Application software is developed and stored on one computer, and all data are on the same computer. There is one point of control, because all messages flow through the one central server. The fundamental problem with server-based networks is that the server must process all messages. As the demands for more and more applications grow, many server computers become overloaded and unable to quickly process all the users' demands. Response time becomes slower, and network managers are required to spend increasingly more money to upgrade the server computer. Unfortunately, upgrades come in large increments and are expensive; it is difficult to upgrade "a little."

Client-Based Architectures

With client-based architectures, the clients are personal computers on a local area network (LAN), and the server computer is a server on the same network. The application software on the client computers is responsible for the presentation logic, the application logic, and the data access logic; the server simply stores the data (see Figure 10-2).

This simple architecture also often works well. However, as the demands for more and more network applications grow, the network circuits can become overloaded. The fundamental problem in client-based networks is that all data on the server must travel to the client for processing. For example, suppose the user wishes to display a list of all employees with company life insurance. All the data in the database must travel from the server where

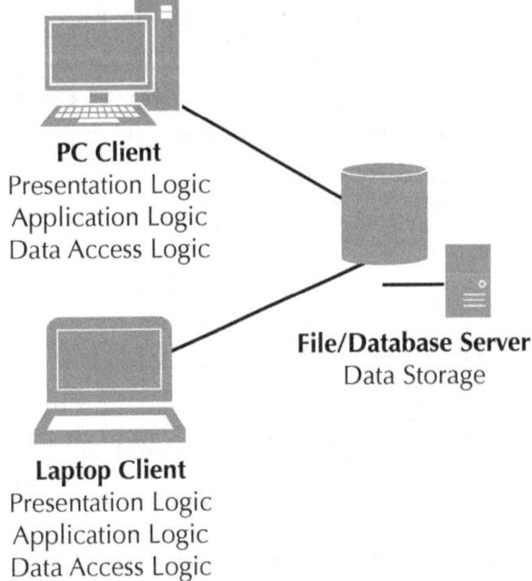

FIGURE 10-2
Client-Based
Architectures

the database is stored over the network to the client, which then examines each record to see whether it matches the data requested by the user. This can overload both the network and the power of the client computers.

Client–Server Architectures

Most organizations today use client–server architectures, which attempt to balance the processing between the client and the server by having both do some of the application functions. In these architectures, the client is responsible for the presentation logic, whereas the server is responsible for the data access logic and data storage. The application logic may reside on either the client or the server or be split between both (see Figure 10-3). The client shown in Figure 10-3 can be referred to as a *thick,* or *fat, client* if it contains the bulk of application logic. A current practice is to create client–server architectures using *thin clients* because there is less overhead and maintenance in supporting thin-client applications. For example, many Web-based systems are designed with the Web browser performing presentation, with only minimal application logic using programming languages like Java and the Web server having the application logic, data access logic, and data storage.

Client–server architectures have four important benefits. First, they are *scalable*. That means it is easy to increase or decrease the storage and processing capabilities of the servers. If one server becomes overloaded, you simply add another server so that many servers are used to perform the application logic, data access logic, or data storage. The cost to upgrade is much more gradual, and you can upgrade in smaller steps rather than spending hundreds of thousands to upgrade a mainframe server.

Client–server architectures can support many different types of clients and servers. It is possible to connect computers that use different operating systems so that users can choose which type of computer they prefer (e.g., combining both Windows and Apple computers on the same network). We are not locked into one vendor, as is often the case with server-based networks. *Middleware* is a type of system software designed to translate between different vendors' software. Middleware is installed on both the client computer and the server computer. The client software communicates with the middleware, which can reformat the message into a standard language that can be understood by the middleware assisting the server software.

For thin-client server architectures that use Internet standards, it is simple to clearly separate the presentation logic, the application logic, and the data access logic and design so that each is somewhat independent. For example, the presentation logic can be designed in HTML or XML to specify how the page will appear on the screen (see Chapter 9). Simple

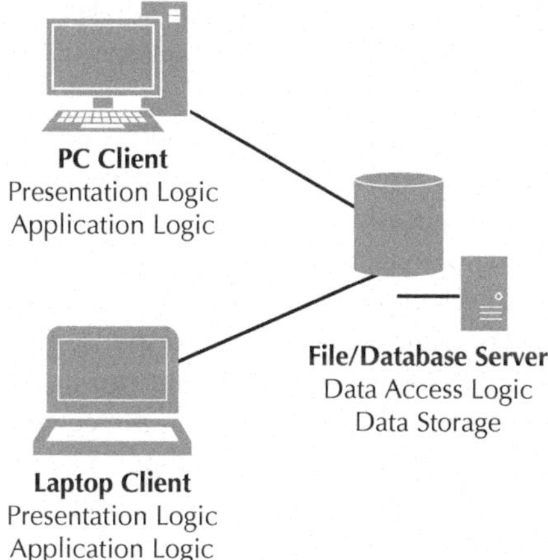

FIGURE 10-3
Client–Server
Architecture

program statements are used to link parts of the interface to specific application logic modules that perform various functions. These HTML or XML files defining the interface can be changed without affecting the application logic. Likewise, it is possible to change the application logic without changing the presentation logic or the data, which are stored in databases and accessed using SQL commands.

Finally, because no single server computer supports all the applications, the network is generally more reliable. There is no central point of failure that will halt the entire network if it fails, as there is in server-based computing. If any one server fails in a client–server environment, the network can continue to function using all the other servers (but, of course, any applications that require the failed server will not work).

Client–server architectures also have some critical limitations, the most important of which is its complexity. All applications in client–server computing have two parts, the software on the client and the software on the server. Writing this software is more complicated than writing the traditional all-in-one software used in server-based architectures. Updating the network with a new version of the software is more complicated, too. In server-based architectures, there is one place where application software is stored; to update the software, we simply replace it there. With client–server architectures, we must update all clients and all servers.

Much of the debate about server-based versus client–server architectures has centered on cost. One of the great claims of server-based networks in the 1980s was that they provided economies of scale. Manufacturers of big mainframes claimed it was cheaper to provide computer services on one big mainframe than on a set of smaller computers. The personal computer revolution changed this. Since the 1980s, the cost of personal computers has continued to drop, whereas their performance has increased significantly. Today, personal computer hardware is more than 1,000 times cheaper than mainframe hardware for the same amount of computing power.

With cost differences like these, it is easy to see why client–server computing is so popular. The problem with these cost comparisons is that they ignore the *total cost of ownership*, which includes factors other than obvious hardware and software costs. For example, many cost comparisons overlook the increased complexity associated with developing application software for client–server networks. Most experts believe that it costs four to five times more to develop and maintain application software for client–server computing than it does for server-based computing.

Client–Server Tiers There are many ways the application logic can be partitioned between the client and the server. The example in Figure 10-3 is one of the most common. In this case, the server is responsible for the data, and the client is responsible for the application and presentation. This is called a *two-tiered architecture* because it uses only two sets of computers, clients, and servers.

A *three-tiered architecture* uses three sets of computers (see Figure 10-4). In this case, the software on the client computer is responsible for presentation logic, an application server (or servers) is responsible for the application logic, and a separate database server (or servers) is responsible for the data access logic and data storage.

An *n-tiered architecture* uses more than three sets of computers. In this case, the client is responsible for presentation, database servers are responsible for the data access logic and data storage, and the application logic is spread across two or more different sets of servers. This type of architecture is common in today's e-commerce systems (see Figure 10-5). The first component is the Web browser on the client computer employed by a user to access the system and enter commands (presentation logic). The second is a Web server that responds to the user's requests, either by providing (HTML) pages and graphics (application logic) or by

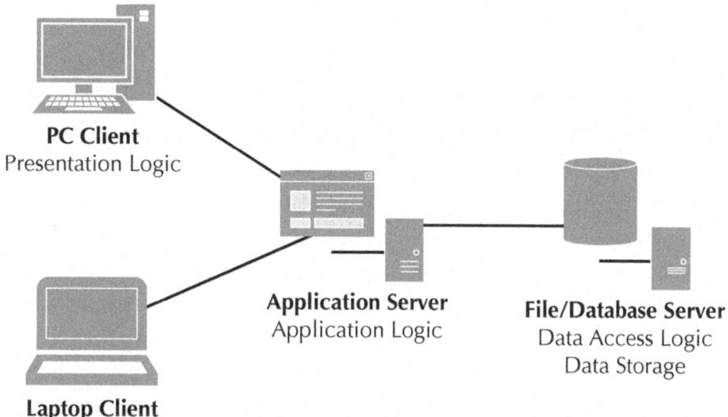

FIGURE 10-4
Three-Tiered Client–
Server Architecture

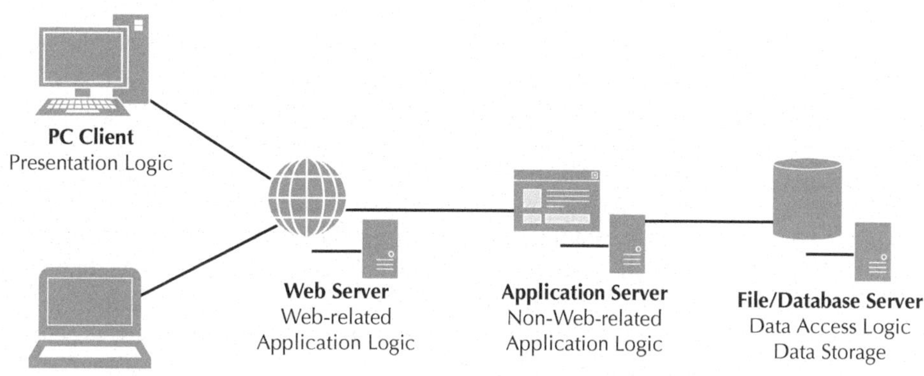

FIGURE 10-5
Four-Tiered Client–
Server Architecture

sending the request to the third component on another application server that performs various functions (application logic). The fourth component is a database server that stores all the data (data access logic and data storage). Each of these four components is separate, making it easy to spread the different components on different servers and to partition the application logic on two different servers.

The primary advantage of an n-tiered client–server architecture compared with a two-tiered architecture (or a three-tiered architecture with a two-tiered architecture) is that it separates the processing that occurs to better balance the load on the different servers; it is more scalable. In Figure 10-5, we have three separate servers, a configuration that provides more power than if we had used a two-tiered architecture with only one server. If we discover that the application server is too heavily loaded, we can simply replace it with a more powerful server or just put in several more application servers. Conversely, if we discover the database server is underused, we could store data from another application on it.

There are two primary disadvantages to an n-tiered architecture compared with a two-tiered architecture (or a three-tiered architecture with a two-tiered architecture). First, the configuration puts a greater load on the network. If you compare Figures 10-3, 10-4, and 10-5, you will see that the n-tiered model requires more communication among the servers; it generates more network traffic, so you need a higher-capacity network. It is also much more difficult to program and test software in n-tiered architectures than in two-tiered architectures because more devices have to communicate to complete a user's transaction.

Peer-to-Peer Architectures

Peer-to-peer architectures have been around for quite a while. Essentially, peer-to-peer architectures support the sharing of a machine's resources with any other machine on the network. These resources can be shared data, software, and even CPUs. One of the earliest successes with peer-to-peer networks was SETI where the shared resource was the actual CPU. In this case, when a machine wasn't using its full processing capacity, the SETI[2] application would use the unused power to analyze the data that it was collecting in its search for life on other planets. Another famous peer-to-peer application was Napster; the music sharing application.[3] With peer-to-peer networks, every machine on the network can be both a server and a client. Consequently, the four architectural components (presentation logic, application logic, data access logic, and data storage) can be located on every machine. It just depends on which applications and/or resources are being shared by each machine. Figure 10-6 shows a typical peer-to-peer architecture.

Cloud Computing[4]

Cloud computing is the idea of treating IT as a utility or commodity. Essentially, cloud computing is the latest approach to support distributed computing in a client–server type of architecture where the server is "on the cloud" and the client is on the desktop (see Figure 10-7). The cloud can be the firm's corporate data center, an external data center, or some combination of the two; however, more and more it generally is seen as an external, rather than an internal, service. Consequently, the idea of *multitenancy*, where the cloud vendor has multiple customers using the same resource at the same time, becomes a real issue for both the cloud vendor and the cloud customer. Cloud computing may become the greatest enabler for IT *outsourcing* (see Chapter 11).

There are three different classifications of clouds: private, public, and hybrid. *Private clouds* are available only to employees of the firm, *public clouds* are available to the general public, and *hybrid clouds* combine the private and public cloud ideas to form a single cloud. In some senses, all e-commerce sites could run in a hybrid cloud environment where the customer sales transaction portion of the system would need to be public while all other aspects would be private.

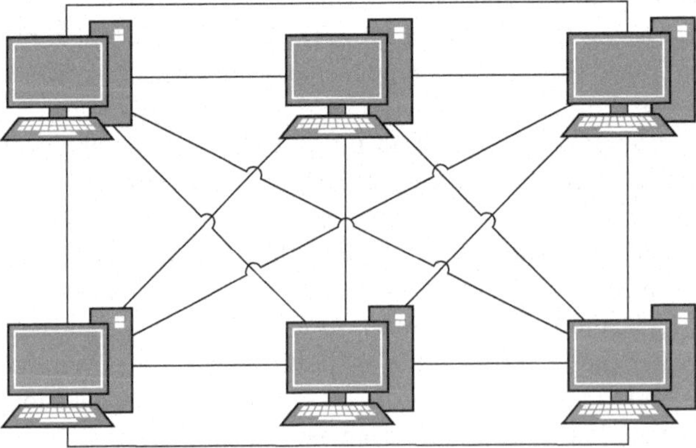

FIGURE 10-6
Peer-To-Peer
Architecture

[2] www.seti.org.

[3] www.napster.com.

[4] Judith Hurwitz, Marcia Kaufman, Fern Halper, and Robin Bloor, *Cloud Computing for Dummies*[TM] (Hoboken, NJ: Wiley 2010).

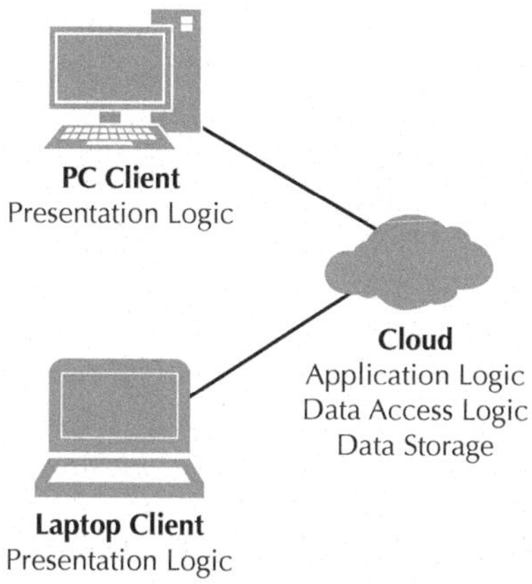

FIGURE 10-7
Cloud Architecture

Fundamentally, cloud computing is an umbrella technology that encompasses the ideas of virtualization, service-oriented architectures, and grid computing. The idea of virtualization is not new. *Virtualization* is the idea of treating any computing resource, regardless of where it is located, as if it is "in" the client machine. This idea evolved from *virtual memory*. Virtual memory was developed originally in the 1960s. Virtual memory allowed the user/ programmer to act as if the amount of main memory in the computer was unlimited. This was done by swapping "pages" of main memory out to disk when the content of the pages was not being used and by swapping a page from disk back to main memory when it was needed. Before virtual memory was created, the programmer had to write code to perform the paging function for each application. Virtualization is simply the scaling up of this idea to all computing resources, not simply main memory. This includes treating a mainframe computer as if it is a set of virtual servers, each of which can be running different operating and/or application systems.

Web services basically support connections between different *services* to form *service-oriented architectures*.[5] Basically, a service is a piece of software that supports some aspect of a business process. A service can be an implementation of part of a business process, it can be an implementation of an entire business process, or it can be object persistence support for the data management layer (see Chapter 8). These services can be either internal or external to the firm. Services can be combined to support *business processes*. A service-oriented architecture allows business processes to be supported by "plugging and playing" services together in a static and/or dynamic manner.[6] Some of the pluggable and playable services can be purchased outright, or they can be billed to the firm based on their use, a sort of pay-as-you-go model.

Grid computing[7] tends to be the underlying hardware technology that supports the cloud. A grid is a very large set of networked computers that tend to be geographically dispersed. For example, the grid that supports SalesForce.com's CRM application contains about 1,000 computers. The computers do not have to be of the same type. For example, they can be a mixture of Linux servers and mainframes. With grid computing, firms have the ability to add and remove computers to support a business process based on the current level of activity taking place in that particular business process. This provides an enormous amount of flexibility in configuring the underlying application architecture that supports business processes.

---

[5] Douglas K. Barry, *Web Services and Service-Oriented Architectures* (San Francisco: Morgan Kaufman, 2003).

[6] P. Ghandforoush, T.K. Sen, and D. Tegarden, R. Ramaswamy, "Designing Systems Using Business Components: A Case Study in Call Center Automation." *International Journal of Electronic Customer Relationship Management* 4, no. 2 (2010): 161–179.

[7] Pawel Plaszczak and Richard Welner Jr., *Grid Computing* (San Francisco: Morgan Kaufman, 2006).

Combining virtualization, service-oriented architectures, and grid computing is what all the hoopla is about with regard to cloud computing. Cloud computing is highly elastic and scalable, it supports a demand-driven approach to provisioning and deprovisioning of resources, and it supports a billing model that only charges for the resources being used. From a business perspective, cloud computing supports the idea of IT being a commodity.

The cloud can contain the firm's IT infrastructure, IT platform, and software. *Infrastructure as a Service (IaaS)* refers to the cloud providing the computing hardware to the firm as a remote service. The hardware typically includes the computing hardware that supports application servers, networking, and data storage. Amazon's EC2 (aws.amazon.com/ec2/) service is a good example of this. With *Platform as a Service (PaaS)*, the cloud vendor not only provides hardware support to a customer but also provides the customer with either package-based solutions, different services that can be combined to create a solution, or the development tools necessary to create custom solutions in the PaaS vendor's cloud. SalesForce.com is a good example of the vendor providing a package-based solution, Amazon's SimpleDB and Simple Query Service are examples of different services being supported, and Google's App Engine is an example of a cloud vendor providing good development tools. Like most things in IT, *Software as a Service (SaaS)* is not a new idea. SaaS has been around for more than thirty years. In the 1970s, there were many "service bureaus" that supported *timesharing* of hardware and software to many different customers; that is, they supported multitenancy. For example, ADP has supported payroll functions for many firms for a very long time. Today, SalesForce.com's CRM system is a good example of a SaaS cloud-based solution.

However, cloud computing must overcome certain obstacles before it becomes the primary approach to provision the application architecture layer.[8] The first obstacle is the mixed level of cloud performance. One issue is whether the vendor has the resources to provide the firm with enough "power" during a peak load. The issue here is that a typical cloud vendor is supporting many different firms. If the vendor does not have enough computing resources to handle all of the firms' peak loads at the same time, then there will have to be some degradation of some or all of the firms' support. This is primarily a result of the unpredictability of the overall performance requirements with disk I/O and network traffic. Given the multitenancy typical of a cloud vendor's hardware, bottlenecks with disks will occur. However, given the dependency on networks, data transfer rates are critical. In an enlightening example, Armbrust and colleagues show that when dealing with large volumes of data, it is faster to transfer data using overnight shipping. In their example, they showed that if you were to transfer 10 terabytes of data with an average transfer rate of 20 Mbits/sec, then it would take more than 45 days to complete the transfer. If you shipped the data overnight instead, you would effectively be using a transfer rate of 1,500 Mbits/sec.[9]

The second obstacle deals with the level of dependency that a customer's firm has on a cloud vendor. Firms are dependent on cloud vendors based on the type of service that they are using the actual level of service availability, and the potential of data lock-in. Currently, most cloud vendor's API to storage is proprietary. Consequently, the customer's data become "locked in" to the specific cloud vendors storage. This is also true for much of the actual service APIs. Consequently, customers find themselves hoping that the cloud vendor will be the equivalent of a benevolent dictator that will act in the interest of the customer; otherwise, actual level of service being provided could suffer. Given the potential for data and/or

---

[8] Michael Armbrust, Armando Fox, Rean Griffith, Anthony D. Joseph, Randy Katz, Andy Konwinski, Gunho Lee, David Patterson, Areil Rabkin, Ion Stoica, and Matei Zahara, "A View of Cloud Computing," *Communications of the ACM* 53, no. 4 (2010): 50–58.

[9] AWS has a service called Snowball that helps with this for large data migrations. See https://aws.amazon.com/snowball/.

service lock-in, a customer must pay close attention to the viability of the cloud vendor. If the vendor goes out of business, the customer could be following suit very quickly. If the cloud vendor also has outsourced to other cloud vendors, such as to a disk farm company, then they could find themselves in the same situation. This could lead to a cascading effect of business failures. Although there is some competition among the major cloud vendors today (mainly Google Cloud, Microsoft Azure, and Amazon AWS), customers should have a back-up plan to not grow overly dependent on any one of them. Consequently, when a firm is considering outsourcing its IT area into the cloud, the firm had better understand the total risk involved.

The third major obstacle to cloud adoption is the perceived level of security available in the cloud. Not only does a firm have to worry about security from the outside, but due to multitenancy, the firm must seriously consider potential attacks from within its cloud from other cloud users. From a service availability perspective, a denial-of-service attack against another tenant within the cloud can cause performance degradation of the firm's systems. Finally, a firm must consider protecting itself from the cloud vendor. The cloud vendor is responsible only for physical security and firewalls. All application-level security tends to be the responsibility of the cloud customer. Obviously, security in the cloud is a very complex endeavor. Given the confidentiality and auditability requirements of Sarbanes–Oxley (SOX) and the Health and Human Services Health Insurance Portability and Accountability Act (HIPAA), security in the cloud becomes a major concern when a firm considers moving any of its confidential data, including e-mail, to the cloud. In many ways, when using a cloud a firm is simply taking a leap of faith that the cloud is secure.

Selecting an Application Architecture

Most systems are built to use the existing infrastructure in the organization, so often the current infrastructure restricts the choice of architecture. For example, if the new system will be built for a mainframe-centric organization, a server-based architecture may be the best option. Other factors such as corporate standards, existing licensing agreements, and product/vendor relationships can also mandate what architecture the project team needs to design. However, many organizations now have a variety of infrastructures available or are openly looking for pilot projects to test new architectures and infrastructures, enabling a project team to select an architecture based on other important factors.

Each of the computing architectures just discussed has its strengths and weaknesses, and no architecture is inherently better than the others. Thus, it is important to understand the strengths and weaknesses of each computing architecture and when to use each. Figure 10-8 presents a summary of a set of important characteristics of each.

Characteristic	Server-Based	Client-Based	Client–Server	Peer-to-Peer	Cloud
Cost of Infrastructure	Very High	Low	Medium-High	Low	Medium
Cost of Development	Medium-High	Low	Medium-High	Medium-High	Medium-High
Ease of Development	Medium	Medium	Medium	Medium-High	Medium
Interface Capabilities	Low	High	High	High	High
Control and Security	High	Low	Medium	Low	Medium
Scalability	Low	Low	High	High	High
Data Distribution	Low	Low	Low-Medium	Low-High	Low-High

FIGURE 10-8 Characteristics of Application Architectures

Cost of Infrastructure One of the strongest driving forces to the cloud is cost of infrastructure (the hardware, software, and networks that will support the application). Simply put, server-based architectures are very expensive. Even though client-based and peer-to-peer architectures are very cheap, they have many limitations (see below). The cost of client–server architectures is low compared to server-based architectures but greater than the client-based or peer-to-peer architectures. Finally, the cost of the cloud varies depending on exactly what services are necessary.

Cost of Development The cost of developing systems is an important factor when considering the actual cost of the different architectures. Depending on the application, developing software for client–server and peer-to-peer architectures can be extremely complex and expensive. This is due to the networking expertise required. Developing application software for client-based architectures is usually fairly cheap. Depending on the machine used for a server, the cost can vary quite a bit. For example, depending on the expertise of the development team, the complexity of mainframe software can cause the cost to be relatively high. On the other hand, with a simple PC-based server, the development cost can be relatively low. As with the cost of infrastructure, the cost of developing cloud based solutions vary based on the type of service that are required to support the application.

Ease of Development In most organizations today, there is a huge backlog of applications that have been approved but that lack the staff to implement them. In many cases, the backlog has been caused by the lack of expertise available with the different architectures. For example, years ago developing software for a mainframe was only of a moderate level of difficulty. However, given the lack of mainframe expertise available, developing mainframe software has become difficult. The tools for mainframe-based systems often are not user friendly and require highly specialized skills—skills that new graduates often don't have and aren't interested in acquiring. In contrast, client-based, client–server, and cloud-based architectures can rely on *graphical user interface (GUI)* development tools that can be intuitive and easy to use. The development of applications for these architectures can be fast and painless. However, given that client–server and peer-to-peer systems must be built for several layers of hardware (e.g., database servers, Web servers, and client workstations) that need to communicate effectively with one another, applications can be very complex. Project teams often underestimate the effort involved in creating secure, efficient applications.

Interface Capabilities Typically, server-based applications contain plain, character-based interfaces. For example, think about airline reservation systems such as SABRE, which can be quite difficult to use unless the operator is well trained on the commands and hundreds of codes that are used to navigate through the system. Today, most users of systems expect a GUI or a Web-based interface that they can operate using a mouse and graphical objects. GUI and Web development tools typically are created to support client-based, client–server, peer-to-peer, or cloud applications; rarely can server-based environments support these types of applications.

Control and Security The server-based architecture was originally developed to control and secure data. Given that all of the data is in a single location, it is much easier to control and secure a server-based architecture. In contrast, with client-based and peer-to-peer architectures, data is stored on the local machines. This raises serious concerns as to whether each machine is secured sufficiently. Depending on which architectural components are located on the server, client–server architectures can be as secure as the server-based architecture or they can require a high degree of coordination among the components which raises the chance for security holes or control problems. With cloud architectures, the level of control and security depends on exactly what is in the cloud and what is on the client machines. Therefore, from a practical perspective, the cloud is similar to client–server. When an organization has a system that absolutely must be secure, then the project team may be more comfortable with the server-based alternative on highly secure and control-oriented mainframe computers or deploying the application to the cloud.

Scalability *Scalability* refers to the ability to increase or decrease the capacity of the computing infrastructure in response to changing capacity needs. Given that "machines" can be added or removed on the fly when the processing requirements change, the most scalable architecture is the cloud. Peer-to-peer networks can be expanded by simply purchasing and adding an additional machine to the network. Of course this will also require additional coordination among the peer machines. Like peer-to-peer networks, client–server-based architectures can be expanded by purchasing and adding additional servers. But again, this can cause issues with coordinating the different servers. For example, is the data being replicated, partitioned, or some combination across the servers (see Chapter 8). In contrast, server-based architectures that rely on mainframe hardware needs to be scaled up in large, expensive increments. While client-based architectures have ceilings above which the application cannot grow because increases in use and data can result in increased network traffic to the extent that performance is unacceptable.

Level of Data Distribution *Level of data distribution* refers to the ease of distributing data over the application architecture. The ability to distribute data with server-based and client-based architectures tend to be low. With client–server applications, the level of data distribution is dependent on how many different servers are involved and whether the data is replicated or partitioned over the architecture (see Chapter 8). If there is only a single server, then the level of data distribution is the same as the server-based architecture; low. Depending on the application the level of data distribution with peer-to-peer and cloud architectures can range from low to high.

UBIQUITOUS COMPUTING AND THE INTERNET OF THINGS[10]

Often, *ubiquitous computing* and the *Internet of Things (IoT)* are the beginning of the realization of the dreams (or nightmares) of science fiction writers. This ranges from the dystopian views portrayed in *Blade Runner* and the *Terminator* movies to the Precrime unit of *Minority Report* and finally to the extremely optimistic future portrayed in *The Jetsons* cartoon of the 1960s and, more recently, in the movie *Wall-E*. Essentially, ubiquitous computing is the idea that computing takes place everywhere and in everything. With ubiquitous computing, computing becomes so ingrained into everyday things that computing effectively disappears into the background. In other words, computing becomes so deeply rooted into everyday things

---

[10] This section is based on material contained in Adam Greenfield, *Everywhere: The Dawning If the Age of Ubiquitous Computing* (Berkeley, CA: New Riders, 2006); Bo Begole, *Ubiquitous Computing for Business* (Upper Saddle River, NJ: FT Press, 2011); Adrian McEwen and Hakim Cassimally, *Designing the Internet of Things* (Chichester, West Sussex, UK: Wiley, 2014); David Rose, *Enchanted Objects: Design, Human Desire, and the Internet of Things* (New York, NY: Scribner, 2014); Gershon Dublon and Joseph A. Paradiso, "Extra Sensory Perception," *Scientific American* 311, no. 1 (July 2014): 36–41.

that the things themselves seem to become magical. The IoT is the idea that, in addition to things having some form of computing capacity built into them, everyday things become connected via the Internet. So, in addition to having some form of computing capacity, everyday things can communicate with each other. This raises the importance of understanding mobile computing, social media, and cloud computing even further. Obviously, the opportunities (or pitfalls) that this provides may be endless.

Currently, there are two major approaches to support ubiquitous computing: general computing devices and specialized computing devices. General computing devices include devices such as smartphones and tablets. These devices can be loaded with many different apps that provide all types of computing and communication support. For example, your smartphone can be used as a GPS, an e-book reader, a music or video player, a game console, a web interface, a camera, an audio recorder, a restaurant advisor, a dating app, etc. In other words, if there is an app for it, you can have it loaded on your smartphone to give you that capability. Today's smartphones are essentially general computers that happen to support voice communications, i.e., it also is a phone. And, like general-purpose computers, the smartphone typically requires you to activate the app before it can do anything for you. Even though it is very impressive to have that amount of computing capability in your hands, it only supports the dream of ubiquitous computing in a very limited manner. Essentially, from an information systems development perspective, this is not new; it is no different than having a computer connected to the Internet. Thus, developing apps for these devices should follow the same basic development approach used throughout this book.

The second approach, having specialized computing devices, goes a long way toward realizing the dream of ubiquitous computing. With this approach, we have so-called *enchanted objects* that can interact with each other. An enchanted object is an everyday object that has a very specialized processor embedded in it that augments the object such that the object seems to be magical. For example, an umbrella that, since there is a good chance of rain, lets you know that you should take it with you today, or a wallet that lets you know that you are reaching your monthly budget limits or that your account just received a deposit. In the case of the umbrella, the umbrella is connected to a weather app. If the forecast is for rain, the umbrella activates a set of LEDs in the handle that informs you that you should take it with you when you leave. In the case of the wallet, as you deplete your monthly budget, the wallet becomes more difficult to open, or if you receive a deposit to your account, the wallet "puffs" up to let you know that your wallet is fatter, i.e., you have more cash available.

The general information systems development approach used in this book is applicable to the development of enchanted objects. However, given that enchanted objects, by definition, are enhanced everyday things, additional issues must also be addressed. These issues include a set of unique design principles, a set of characteristics, and a set of levels of enchantment.

McEwen and Cassimally identify a set of unique design principles that need to be considered when developing enchanted objects.[11] First, enchanted objects should be in the background simply providing its message for you to receive at your leisure, not "in your face." This is in contrast with most apps today. Typically, apps will notify you about some topic at their leisure by interrupting you. Second, magic is a useful metaphor for people to adopt an enchanted object. The umbrella mentioned earlier is a good example of this principle. The umbrella simply sits by the door letting you know whether it wants to be taken with you or not. Third is the whole issue of privacy. With all of these enchanted objects "sharing" data about you, all of the issue related to Orwell's "Big Brother" creeps into focus. How will you keep anything secret and, possibly even more important, who actually owns the data being

---

[11] Adrian McEwen and Hakim Cassimally, *Designing the Internet of Things* (Chichester, West Sussex, UK: Wiley, 2014).

collected? However, this issue is not unique to enchanted objects. It is equally applicable to smartphones and their apps. Fourth, we need to consider how to "mash-up" a set of enchanted objects that are loosely connected to support a larger purpose. In fact, Brynjolfsson and McAfee suggest that innovation that uses recombination may provide the basis for a new type of economy that will increase both progress and prosperity.[12] Fifth, the idea of affordances becomes increasingly important. For an enchanted object to be adopted, it must be very simple to use. The object itself must imply how to use it. The umbrella, for example, simply lets you know that you should take it with you by drawing your attention to it.

Rose provides a set of characteristics that enchanted objects should possess if we are to adopt them.[13] First, they should be glanceable. The umbrella, again, is a great example. You don't have to do anything but glance at the umbrella to know whether you should take it with you or not. Second, enchanted objects should be gestureable. This is related to the idea of affordances. It must be intuitively obvious as to how to use an enchanted object. For example, years ago The A.T. Cross Company sold a notebook and pen combination (CrossPad™) that you could use to take notes. The affordance of this product was the fact that you simply used a special pen to write your notes on the paper contained in the notebook. The enchanted part was the fact that the product also had a radio transmitter built into the pen that enabled it to store your notes in electronic form that could be uploaded to your computer later. Third, the enchanted object must be affordable. In this case, given the falling cost of computing hardware, if the object isn't that affordable at first, it should be fairly quickly. Fourth, the objects should be wearable. The Fitbit™ is a perfect example. You simply wear it like a watch. Fifth, an enchanted object should be indestructible. Obviously, this one would only be true as it is related to the underlying object. For example, the enchanted umbrella is as indestructible as any normal umbrella, but it is not as indestructible as other things in the real world. Sixth, an enchanted object must be capable of doing its thing with minimal interaction with the user. For example, you simply wear the Fitbit™ and plug it up at night to your computer, and it will update itself, recharge itself, update your profile, and be waiting for you to put it on in the morning. Seventh, an enchanted object should be loveable. By that we mean that they should be easy to anthropomorphize. We should enjoy using them, and we should miss them when we don't. Obviously, you should recognize that there are trade-offs among some of the characteristics and, as such, not all objects will possess all of them. However, as a designer, your enchanted objects should have as many as possible.

Rose also suggests a set of levels (or steps) of enchantment of which enchanted objects designers should be aware. For the first level, he suggests that enchanted objects should be augmented everyday objects that are connected to the network. This allows them to send and receive data that can be used by other enchanted objects or other systems. Given the amount of data to be collected about ourselves and everyone else for both current time and in the future, the second level for enchanted objects is to be able to be personalized such that they can interact with us in a customized manner. Currently, to a small degree Amazon and Netflix are already doing this, e.g., with their list of recommendations that they make to you. Their recommendations are based on your past interactions with them and matching those interactions to the interactions of others. The potential for this type of activity in health systems is enormous. The third level is where our enchanted objects interact with our social networks to automatically inform our colleagues, or a special subset of them, of our activities with the enchanted object. This again could be very useful in health systems where the object informs our physician's system or our health support group of certain types of positive (or negative)

---

[12] Erik Brynjolfsson and Andrew McAfee, *The Second Machine Age: Work, Progress, and Prosperity in a Time of Brilliant Technologies* (New York, NY: Norton, 2014).

[13] David Rose, Enchanted Objects: *Design, Human Desire, and the Internet of Things* (New York, NY: Scribner, 2014).

activities. The fourth level adapts gaming ideas to our enchanted objects, i.e., gamification. Fitbit™ is a perfect example of using gamification to keep a user intrinsically motivated to reach his or her individual goals by allowing competition with friends or groups. The last level is that designers of enchanted objects will improve their adoption if the objects can be part of a story; Rose refers to this as storyification. Through the use of stories, users can more easily understand the purpose of and the utility provided by the enchanted objects, thus increasing the likelihood of a user "bonding" with the enchanted object.

Given the potential of ubiquitous computing and the IoT, you should begin considering possible applications that may benefit from them. For example, today, through the use of RFID and GPS, it is possible to know the location of each and every one of a firm's inventory items. Even though it can be argued that an inventory item with an RFID tag and GPS isn't an enchanted object, it is useful one. And even though the cost of these types of augmentations is dropping, it can be further argued that you may not want to tag each and every item. However, before the enchanted object vision can become a reality, two possible technical problems will need to be addressed.[14] First, given the current set of communication networks, can existing networks handle the additional communication volume required? Do the Internet, cell phone, and Wi-Fi networks have sufficient bandwidth to support all of these additional objects? When you start to connect everything to networks, it is doubtful that the capacity is available. Second, is it reasonable to expect the simple special-purpose devices that are embedded in enchanted objects to handle the complexity of the required communication protocols of existing networks? To address these problems could mean that a new physical architecture is necessary. It may even be necessary to rely on hubs that connect devices and their different protocols together in one easy-to-use interface.

INFRASTRUCTURE DESIGN

In most cases, a system is built for an organization that has a hardware, software, and communications infrastructure already in place. Thus, project teams are usually more concerned with how an existing infrastructure needs to be changed or improved to support the requirements that were identified during analysis, as opposed to how to design and build an infrastructure from scratch. Coordination of infrastructure components is very complex, and it requires highly skilled technical professionals. As a project team, it is best to allow the infrastructure analysts to recommend and lead changes to the computing infrastructure.

Deployment Diagram

Deployment diagrams are used to represent the relationships between the hardware components used in the physical infrastructure of an information system. For example, when designing a distributed information system that will use a wide area network, a deployment diagram can be used to show the communication relationships among the different nodes in the network. They also can be used to represent the software components and how they are deployed over the application architecture or infrastructure of an information system. In this case, a deployment diagram represents the environment for the execution of the software.

The elements of a deployment diagram include nodes, artifacts, and communication paths (see Figure 10-9). Other elements can also be included in this diagram. In our case, we include only the three primary elements and the element that portrays an artifact being deployed onto a node.

[14] Francis da Costa, *Rethinking the Internet of Things: A Scalable Approach to Connecting Everything* (New York, NY: Apress Media, 2013).

<table>
<tr>
<td>

A node:

- is a computational resource, e.g., a client computer, server, separate network, or individual network device.
- is labeled by its name.
- may contain a stereotype to specifically label the type of node being represented, e.g., device, client workstation, application server, mobile device, etc.

</td>
<td>

<<stereotype>>
Node Name

</td>
</tr>
<tr>
<td>

An artifact:

- is a specification of a piece of software or database, e.g., a database or a table or view of a database, a software component or layer.
- is labeled by its name.
- may contain a stereotype to specifically label the type of artifact, e.g., source file, database table, executable file, etc.

</td>
<td>

<<stereotype>>
Artifact Name

</td>
</tr>
<tr>
<td>

A node with a deployed artifact:

- portrays an artifact being placed on a physical node.

</td>
<td>

<<stereotype>>
Node Name

<<stereotype>>
Artifact Name

</td>
</tr>
<tr>
<td>

A communication path:

- represents an association between two nodes.
- allows nodes to exchange messages.
- may contain a stereotype to specifically label the type of communication path being represented (e.g., LAN, Internet, serial, parallel).

</td>
<td>

<<stereotype>>

</td>
</tr>
</table>

FIGURE 10-9 Development Diagram Syntax

A *node* represents any piece of hardware that needs to be included in the model of the application architecture layer design. For example, nodes typically include client computers, servers, separate networks, or individual network devices. Typically, a node is labeled with its name and, possibly, with a stereotype. The stereotype is modeled as a text item surrounded by "<< >>" symbols. The stereotype represents the type of node being represented on the diagram. For example, typical stereotypes include device, mobile device, database server, Web server, and application server. There are times that the notation of a node should be extended to better communicate the design of the application architecture layer. Figure 10-10 includes a set of typical network node symbols that can be used instead of the standard notation.

An *artifact* represents a piece of the information system that is to be deployed onto the application architecture (see Figure 10-9). Typically, an artifact represents a software component, a subsystem, a database table, an entire database, or a layer (data management, human–computer interaction, or problem domain). Artifacts, like nodes, can be labeled with both a name and a stereotype. Stereotypes for artifacts include source file, database table, and executable file.

A *communication path* represents a communication link between the nodes of the application architecture (see Figure 10-9). Communication paths are stereotyped based on the

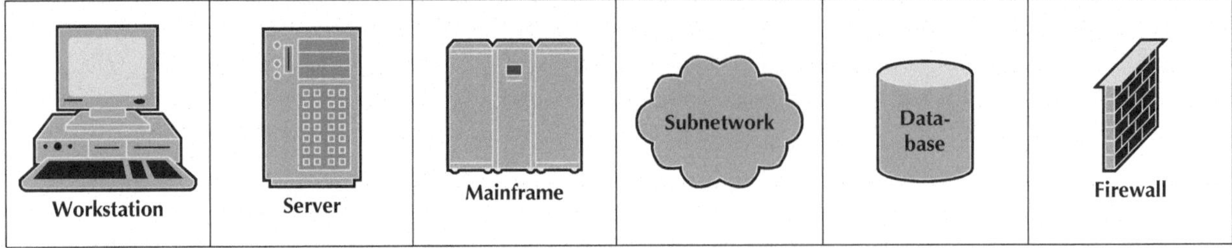

FIGURE 10-10 Extended Node Syntax for Development Diagram

type of communication link they represent (e.g., LAN, Internet, serial, parallel, or USB) or the protocol that is being supported by the link (e.g., TCP/IP).

Figure 10-9 portrays three different versions of a deployment diagram. Figure 10-11a only uses the basic standard notation. Figure 10-11b introduces the idea of deploying an artifact onto a node (see Figure 10-9). In this case, the artifacts represent the different layers of the appointment system described in earlier chapters. Figure 10-11c uses the extended notation to represent the same architecture as portrayed in Figure 10-11b. As you can see, all three versions have their strengths and weaknesses. When comparing Figure 10-11a and Figure 10-11b, the user can glean more information from Figure 10-11b with little additional effort. However, when comparing Figure 10-11a to Figure 10-11c, the extended node notation

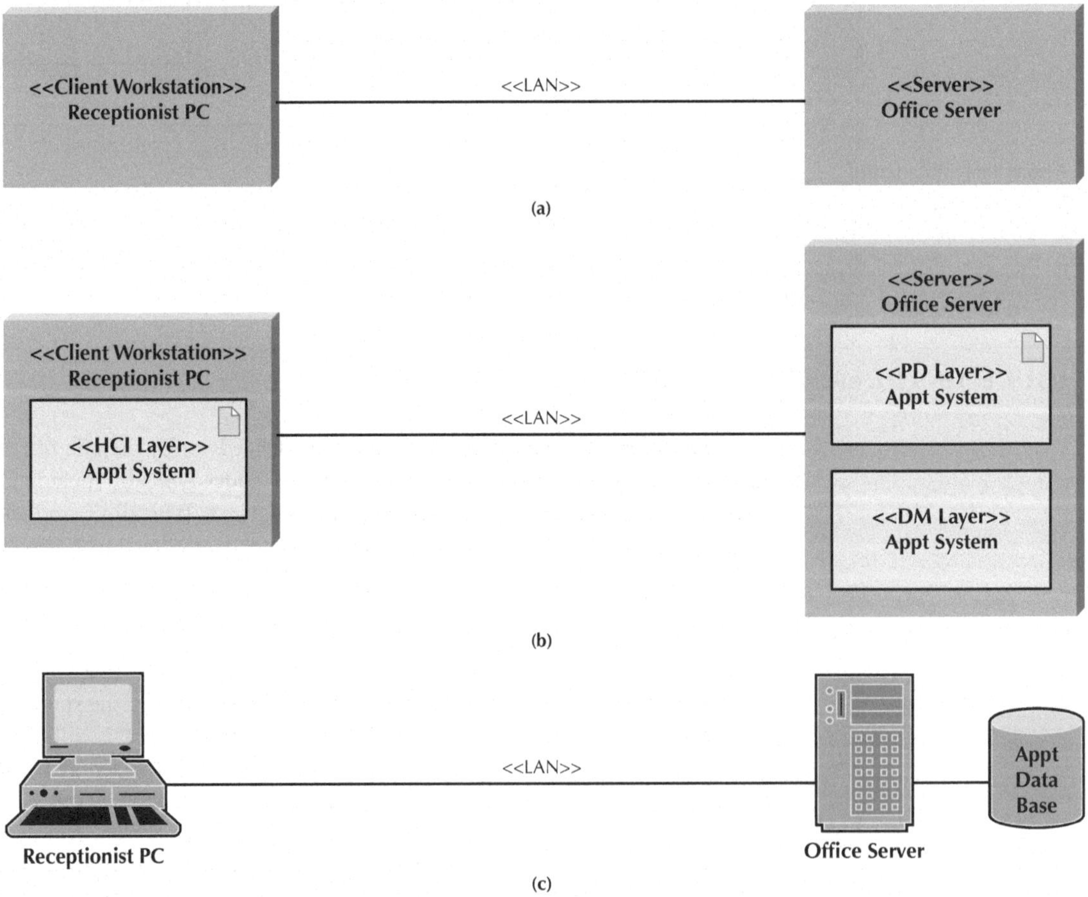

FIGURE 10-11 Three Versions of Appointment System Deployment Diagram

enables the user to quickly understand the hardware requirements of the architecture. When comparing Figure 10-11b to Figure 10-11c, Figure 10-11b supports the software distribution explicitly but forces the user to rely on the stereotypes to understand the required hardware, whereas Figure 10-11c omits the software distribution information entirely. We recommend that you use the combination of symbols to best portray the application architecture to the user community.

Network Model

The *network model* is a diagram that shows the major components of the information system (e.g., servers, communication lines, and networks) and their geographic locations throughout the organization. There is no one way to depict a network model, and in our experience, analysts create their own standards and symbols, using presentation applications (e.g., PowerPoint) or diagramming tools (e.g., Visio). In this text, we use UML's deployment diagram.

The purpose of the network model is twofold: to convey the complexity of the system and to show how the system's software components will fit together. The components of the network model are the various clients (e.g., personal computers and kiosks), servers (e.g., database, network, communications, and printer), network equipment (e.g., Wi-Fi connections, ethernet, cell phone network, and satellite links), and external systems or networks (e.g., Internet service providers) that support the application. *Locations* are the geographic sites related to these components. For example, if a company created an application for users at four of its plants in Canada and eight plants in the United States with one external system to provide Internet service, the network model to depict this would contain twelve locations (4 + 8 = 12).

Creating the network model is a top-down exercise whereby we first graphically depict all the locations where the application will reside. Placing symbols that represent the locations for the components on a diagram and then connecting them with lines that are labeled with the approximate amount of data or types of network circuits between the separated components accomplish this.

Companies seldom build networks to connect distant locations by buying land and laying cable (or sending up their own satellites). Instead, they usually lease services provided by large telecommunications firms such as AT&T, Lumen, and Verizon. Figure 10-12 shows a typical network. The clouds in the diagram represent the networks at different locations (e.g., Toronto, Atlanta). The lines represent network connections between specific points (e.g., Toronto to Brampton). In other cases, a company might lease connections from many points to many others, and rather than trying to show all the connections, a separate cloud may be drawn to represent this many-to-many type of connection (e.g., the cloud in the center of Figure 10-12 represents a network of many-to-many connections provided by a telecom firm like Verizon).

This high-level diagram has several purposes. First, it shows the locations of the components needed to support the application; therefore, the project team can get a good understanding of the geographic scope of the new system and how complex and costly the communications infrastructure will be to support. (For example, an application that supports one site will probably have less communications costs as compared to a more-complex application that will be shared all over the world.) The diagram also indicates the external components of the system (e.g., customer systems and supplier systems), which may impact security or global needs (discussed later in this chapter).

The second step of the network model is to create low-level network diagrams for each of the locations shown on the top-level diagram. First, hardware is drawn on the model in a way that depicts how the hardware for the new system will be placed throughout the location. It usually helps to use symbols that resemble the hardware that will be used. The amount of detail to include on the network model depends on the needs of the project. Some low-level network models contain text descriptions below each of the hardware components that

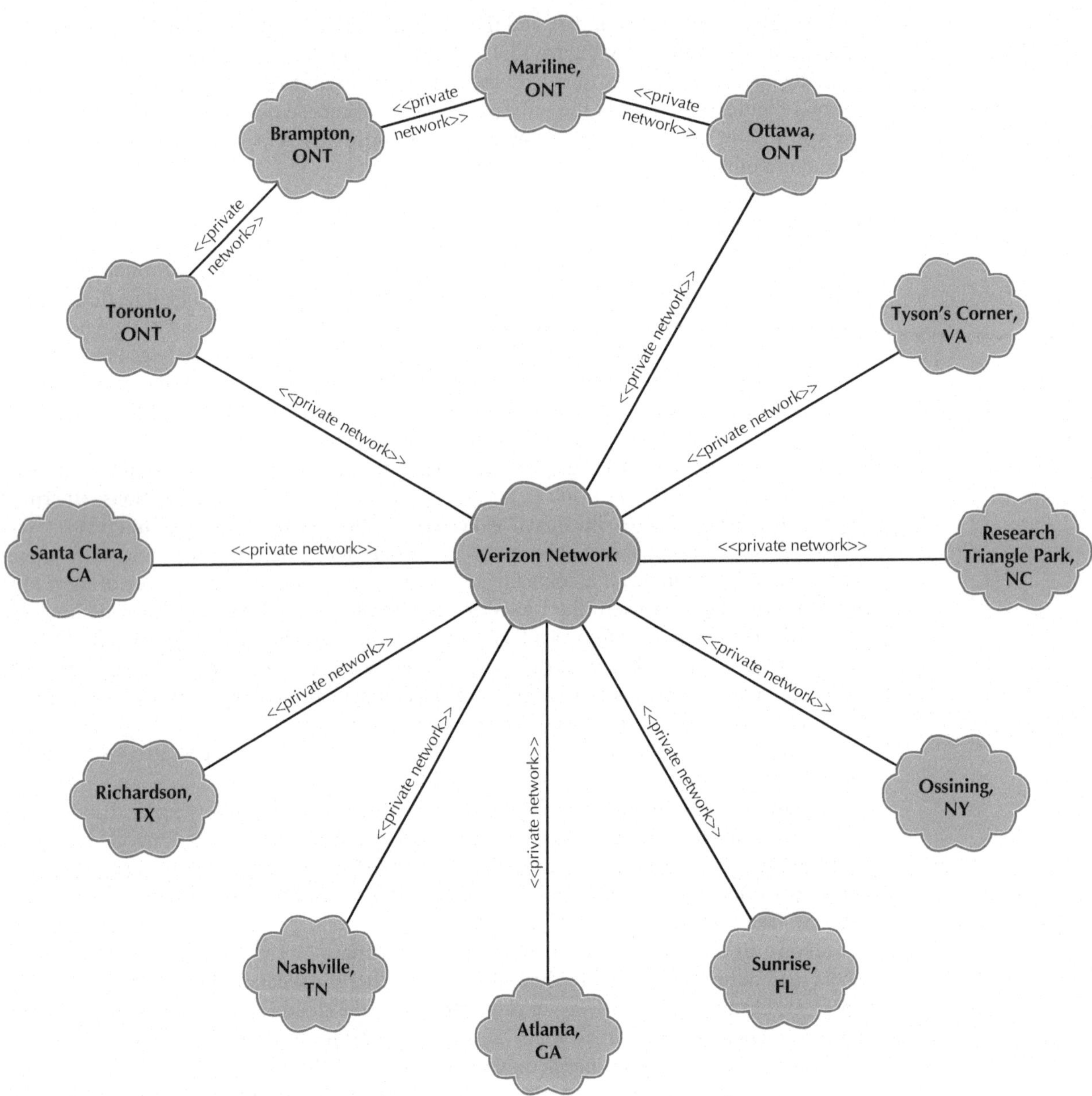

FIGURE 10-12 Deployment Diagram Representation of a Top-Level Network Model

describe in detail the proposed hardware configurations and processing needs; others include only the number of users that are associated with the different parts of the diagram.

Next, lines are drawn connecting the components that will be physically attached to each other. In terms of software, some network models list the required software for each network model component right on the diagram, whereas other times, the software is described in a memo attached to the network model. Figure 10-13 shows a deployment diagram that portrays two levels of detail of a low-level network model. Notice, we use both the standard and extended node notation in this figure. In this case, we have included a package (see Chapter 6) to represent a set of connections to the router in the MFA building. By including a package, we

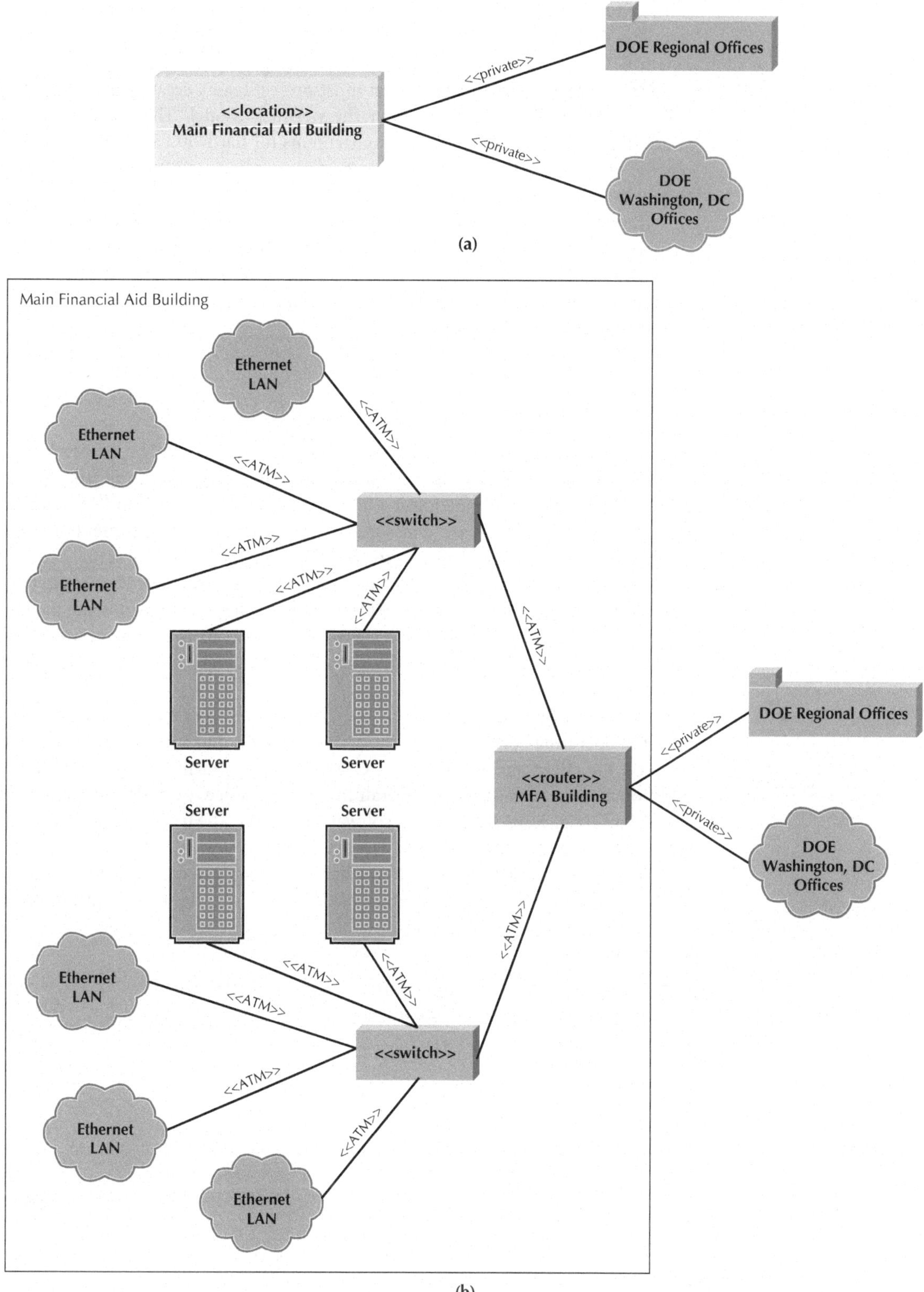

FIGURE 10-13   Deployment Diagram Representation of a Low-Level Network Model

show only the detail necessary. The extended notation in many cases aids the user in understanding the topology of the application architecture layer much better than the standard notation. We recommend using the symbols that get the message across best.

Our experiences have shown that most project teams create a memo for the project files that provides additional detail about the network model. This memo can include special issues that affect communications, requirements for hardware and software that might not be obvious from the network model, or specific hardware or software vendors or products that should be acquired.

The primary purpose of the network model diagram is to present the proposed infrastructure for the new system. The project team can use the diagrams to understand the scope of the system, the complexity of its structure, any important communication issues that might affect development and implementation, and the actual components that need to be acquired or integrated into the environment.

HARDWARE AND SYSTEM SOFTWARE SPECIFICATIONS

The time to begin acquiring the hardware and software that will be needed for a future system is during the design of the system. In many cases, the new system will simply run on the existing equipment in the organization. Other times, however, new hardware and software must be purchased. The *hardware and software specification* is a document that describes what hardware and software are needed to support an application. The actual acquisition of hardware and software should be left to the purchasing department or the area in the organization that handles capital procurement. However, the project team writes the hardware and software specification to communicate the project needs to the appropriate people. There are several steps involved in creating the document. Figure 10-14 shows a sample hardware and software specification.

First, we need to define the software that will run on each component. This usually starts with the operating system (e.g., Windows and Linux) and includes any special-purpose software on the client and servers (e.g., Oracle database). This document should consider any additional costs, such as technical training, maintenance, extended warranties, and licensing agreements (e.g., a site license for a software package). The listed needs are influenced by decisions that are made in the other design activities.

Second, we must create a list of the hardware that is needed to support the future system. With the advent of mobile computing (see Chapter 10), cloud computing (see earlier in this

Specification	Standard Client	Standard Web Server	Standard Application Server	Standard Database Server
Operating System	• Windows	• Linux	• Linux	• Linux
Special Software	• Adobe Reader • VLC	• Apache	• Java	• Oracle
Hardware	• 32 GB Memory • 500 GB SSD • Intel Core i7 • 24″ Touch Screen	• 128 GB Memory • 1 TB disk drive • Intel Core i9	• 128 GB Memory • 2-1 TB disk drives • Intel Core i9	• 128 GB Memory • 25 TB RAID • Intel Core i9
Network	• 500 Mbps Ethernet • Wi-Fi	• 1 GPS Ethernet	• 1 GPS Ethernet	• 1 GPS Ethernet

FIGURE 10-14   Sample Hardware and Software Specification

chapter), the IoT (see earlier in this chapter), and Green IT (see earlier in this chapter), this step is much more involved than it used to be. However, the low-level network model provides a good starting point for recording the project's hardware needs because each component on the diagram corresponds to an item on this list. In general, the list can include things like database servers, network servers, peripheral devices (e.g., printers and scanners), backup devices, storage components, and any other hardware component that is needed to support an application. At this time, you also should note the quantity of each item that will be needed.

Third, we must describe, in as much detail as possible, the minimum requirements for each piece of hardware. Typically, the project team must convey requirements like the amount of processing capacity, the amount of storage space, and any special features that should be included. Many organizations have standard lists of approved hardware and software that must be used; so in many cases, this step simply involves selecting items from the lists. Other times, however, the team is operating in new territory and is not constrained by the need to select from an approved list. This step becomes easier with experience; however, there are some hints that can help you describe hardware needs (see Figure 10-15). For example, consider the hardware standards within the organization or those recommended by vendors. Talk with experienced system developers or other companies with similar systems. Finally, think about the factors that affect hardware performance, such as the response-time expectations of the users, data volumes, software memory requirements, the number of users accessing the system, the number of external connections, and growth projections.

The last step to consider is to evaluate vendor proposals (see Chapter 7). The easiest way to do this is to create an *alternative matrix* (see Chapters 2 and 7). In this case, the evaluation criteria in the alternative matrix should include all architectural requirements, both optional and mandatory, and each criterion should be weighted. Some general criteria include CPU speed, bus speed, disk size, disk access time, cache size, cache speed, RAM size, RAM speed, data transfer rate, video RAM size and speed, monitor size, and printer resolution. Of course, in today's connected world, the networking hardware and software would also need to be specified, including routers, print servers, hubs, and switches. Mobile devices such as smartphones and tablets may be part of the physical architecture solution. Depending on the problem-domain requirements, additional hardware and system software could be required, such as speech recognition and generation software and hardware, digitizing tablets, and possibly head-mounted displays, shutter glasses, force feedback pointing devices, and 3D printers. Each of these types of specialized devices has its own specialized evaluation criteria. In a

<table>
<tr><td>

FIGURE 10-15
Factors in Hardware and Software Selection

</td><td>

Functions and Features   What specific functions and features are needed (e.g., size of monitor, software features)?

Performance   How fast does the hardware and software operate (e.g., processor, number of database writes per second)?

Legacy Databases and Systems   How well does the hardware and software interact with legacy systems (e.g., can it write to this database)?

Hardware and OS Strategy   What are the future migration plans (e.g., the goal is to have all of one vendor's equipment)?

Cost of Ownership   What are the costs beyond purchase (e.g., incremental license costs, annual maintenance, training costs, salary costs)?

Political Preferences   People are creatures of habit and are resistant to change, so changes should be minimized.

Vendor Performance   Some vendors have reputations or future prospects that are different from those of a specific hardware or software system they currently sell.

</td></tr>
</table>

nutshell, when creating a hardware and system software specification, most systems analysts find that they need help from IT and CS personnel.

Depending on the overall cost and size of the project, one thing that should be seriously considered is the use of a benchmark. A *benchmark* is essentially a sample of programs that would be expected to run on the new physical architecture. Even though benchmarks can be expensive to create, they tend to provide a more realistic picture of how the proposed physical architecture layer will perform.

When evaluating hardware, there is a set of issues that you should recognize.[15]

- Not only should you provide sample programs for the benchmarks, but you also need to provide actual data. Otherwise, the benchmark results could be misleading.

- You need to carefully review the mix of system software and hardware. For example, in many cases, Linux performs better on the same hardware when compared against Windows, but some applications might not be available under Linux. Consequently, there may be some trade-offs that should be considered.

- When considering adding additional hardware, be sure to evaluate the additional hardware based on marginal utility, not actual utility.

- Do not specify the physical architecture before you understand the problem-domain requirements. This might seem obvious, but when you consider the time it takes for a mainframe computer, a large number of servers, or a large number of client machines to be specified, ordered, and delivered, it can be tempting to specify the hardware and system software prematurely. This could lead to either under- or over-specification.

- Recognize the reality of *Parkinson's Law*. From an IT perspective, Parkinson's Law implies that regardless of the users' real needs, their imagined needs will always fill up whatever capacity the system has. Consequently, it is imperative that the physical architecture layer design be based on the current and expected future architecture of the problem-domain layer.

- Do not limit choices to a single vendor. This is especially true when you consider commodity hardware, such as displays, desktops, and department-size servers.

- Given the rate of technological change that is taking place in IT, consider leading-edge ideas. For example, even though tablet computers have been around for a while, the iPad™ was not on most people's radar. Today, it is considered to be a game changer when considering client-based hardware. Consequently, you really must stay up to date when it comes to the design of the physical architecture layer.

NONFUNCTIONAL REQUIREMENTS AND APPLICATION ARCHITECTURE LAYER DESIGN

The design of the application architecture layer specifies the overall architecture and the placement of software and hardware that will be used. Each of the architectures discussed before has its strengths and weaknesses. Most organizations use client–server architectures for cost reasons, so in the event that there is no compelling reason to choose one architecture over another, cost usually suggests client–server.

---

[15] Alton R. Kindred, *Data Systems and Management: An Introduction to Systems Analysis and Design*, 2nd Ed. (Englewood Cliffs, NJ: Prentice Hall, 1980).

Creating an application architecture layer design begins with the nonfunctional requirements. The first step is to refine the nonfunctional requirements into more-detailed requirements that are then used to help select the architecture to be used (server-based, client-based, or client–server) and what software components will be placed on each device. In a client–server architecture, one also has to decide whether to use a two-tier, three-tier, or *n*-tier architecture. Then the nonfunctional requirements and the architecture design are used to develop the hardware and software specification.

Four primary types of nonfunctional requirements can be important in designing the architecture: operational requirements, performance requirements, security requirements, and cultural/political requirements. Furthermore, each of these requirements must be fully verified and validated.

Operational Requirements

Operational requirements specify the operating environment(s) in which the system must perform and how those might change over time. This usually refers to operating systems, system software, and information systems with which the system must interact, but on occasion it also includes the physical environment if the environment is important to the application (e.g., it's located on a noisy factory floor, so no audible alerts can be heard). Figure 10-16 summarizes four key operational requirement areas and provides some examples of each.

Technical Environment Requirements *Technical environment requirements* specify the type of hardware and software system on which the system will work. These requirements usually focus

Type of Requirement	Definition	Examples
Technical Environment Requirements	Special hardware, software, and network requirements imposed by business requirements	• The system will work over the Web environment with Internet Explorer. • All office locations will have an always-on network connection to enable real-time database updates. • A version of the system will be provided for customers connecting over the Internet via a tablet or smartphone.
System Integration Requirements	The extent to which the system will operate with other systems	• The system must be able to import and export Excel spreadsheets. • The system will read and write to the main inventory database in the inventory system.
Portability Requirements	The extent to which the system will need to operate in other environments	• The system must be able to work with different operating systems (e.g., Linux, Mac OS, and Windows). • The system might need to operate with handheld devices, such as Android and Apple iOS devices.
Maintainability Requirements	Expected business changes to which the system should be able to adapt	• The system will be able to support more than one manufacturing plant with six months' advance notice. • New versions of the system will be released every six months.

FIGURE 10-16 Operational Requirements

on the operating system software (e.g., Windows, Linux, and Mac OS), database system software (e.g., Oracle), and other system software (e.g., Firefox). In today's distributed world, issues related to mobile computing (see Chapter 9) and cloud computing (see the earlier section in this chapter), are very relevant. Consequently, it also includes all of the different types of hardware from mainframe computers to smartphones to IoT devices. Depending on the applications being deployed over the application architecture, specialized hardware could be required, such as 3D displays, 3D printing, 3D sound systems, and tablets with accelerometers. With today's technology, the possible combinations of hardware that can be used to solve a problem are nearly endless. Consequently, this is one area where additional expertise might be required.

System Integration Requirements *System integration requirements* are those that require the system to operate with other information systems, either inside or outside the company. These typically specify interfaces through which data will be exchanged with other systems.

Portability Requirements Information systems never remain constant. Business needs change and operating technologies change, so the information systems that support them and run on them must change, too. *Portability requirements* define how the technical operating environments might change over time and how the system must respond (e.g., the system currently runs on Windows, whereas in the future the system might have to be deployed on Linux). Portability requirements also refer to potential changes in business requirements that drive technical environment changes. For example, in the future, users might want to access a website from their cell phones.

Maintainability Requirements *Maintainability requirements* specify the business requirement changes that can be anticipated. Not all changes are predictable, but some are. For example, suppose a small company has only one manufacturing plant but is anticipating the construction of a second plant in the next five years. All information systems must be written to make it easy to track each plant separately, whether for personnel, budgeting, or inventory systems. The maintainability requirements attempt to anticipate future requirements so that the systems designed today will be easy to maintain if and when those future requirements appear. Maintainability requirements can also define the update cycle for the system, such as the frequency with which new versions will be released.

Performance Requirements

Performance requirements focus on performance issues, such as response time, capacity, and reliability. Figure 10-17 summarizes three key performance requirement areas and provides some examples.

Speed Requirements *Speed requirements* are exactly what they say: How fast should the system operate? First is the *response time* of the system: How long it takes the system to respond to a user request. Although everyone would prefer low response times, with the system responding immediately to each user request, this is not practical. We could design such a system, but it would be expensive and unrealistic as systems need time for updates (e.g., software patches) and maintenance. Most users understand that certain parts of a system will respond quickly, whereas others are slower. Actions that are performed locally on the user's computer must be almost immediate (e.g., typing, dragging, and dropping), whereas others that require communicating across a network can have longer response times (e.g., a Web request).

The second aspect of speed requirements is how long it takes transactions in one part of the system to be reflected in other parts. For example, how soon after an order is placed will

Type of Requirement	Definition	Examples
Speed Requirements	The time within which the system must perform its functions	• Response time must be less than 7 seconds for any transaction over the network. • The inventory database must be updated in real time. • Orders will be transmitted to the factory floor every 30 minutes.
Capacity Requirements	The total and peak number of users and the volume of data expected	• There will be a maximum of 100–200 simultaneous users at peak use times. • A typical transaction will require the transmission of 10K of data.
Availability and Reliability Requirements	The extent to which the system will be available to the users and the permissible failure rate due to errors	• The system will store data on approximately 5,000 customers for a total of about 2 MB of data. • Scheduled maintenance shall not exceed one 6-hour period each month. • The system shall have 99% uptime performance.

FIGURE 10-17   Performance Requirements

the items it contained be shown as no longer available for sale to someone else? If the inventory is not updated immediately, then someone else could place an order for the same item, only to find out later it is out of stock. This is especially true when one considers NoSQL database that does not update all copies of the data immediately (see Chapter 8). Or how soon after an order is placed is it sent to the warehouse to be picked from inventory and shipped?

Capacity Requirements *Capacity requirements* attempt to predict how many users the system will have to support, both in total and simultaneously. Capacity requirements are important in understanding the size of the databases, the processing power needed, and so on. The most important requirement is usually the peak number of simultaneous users because this has a direct impact on the processing power of the computer(s) needed to support the system.

It is often easier to predict the number of users for internal systems designed to support an organization's own employees than it is to predict the number of users for customer-facing systems, especially those on the Web. How *does* Weather.com estimate the peak number of users who will simultaneously seek weather information? This is as much an art as a science, so often the team provides a range of estimates, with wider ranges used to signal a less-accurate estimate.

Availability and Reliability Requirements *Availability and reliability requirements* focus on the extent to which users can assume that the system will be available for them to use. Although some systems are intended to be used only during the forty-hour work week, some systems are designed to be used by people around the world. For such systems, project team members need to consider how the application can be operated, supported, and maintained *24/7*. This 24/7 requirement means that users might need help or have questions at any time, and a support desk that is available eight hours a day will not be sufficient support. It is also important to consider what reliability is needed in the system. A system that requires high reliability (e.g., a medical device or telephone switch) needs far greater planning and testing than one that does not have such high-reliability needs (e.g., personnel system or Web catalog).

It is more difficult to predict the peaks and valleys in use of the system when the system has a global audience. Typically, applications are backed up on weekends or late evenings when users are no longer accessing the system. Such maintenance activities need to be rethought with global initiatives. For example, what day(s) of the week is considered a "down" day. In different parts of the world, business does not take place every day. In some parts, Friday is sacred; in other parts, it's Saturday or Sunday. Consequently, political and cultural issues (described below and in Chapter 9) can impact the performance requirements. The development of Web interfaces, in particular, has escalated the need for 24/7 support; by default, the Web can be accessed by anyone at any time. For example, the developers of a Web application for U.S. outdoor gear and clothing retailer Orvis were surprised when the first order after going live came from Japan.

Security Requirements[16]

The primary purpose of the security requirements is actually to increase the trust that the users have with the system and its data and to protects the information system from disruption and data loss, whether caused by an intentional act (e.g., a hacker or a terrorist attack) or a random event (e.g., disk failure or tornado). In the past, security has been primarily the responsibility of the operations group—the staff responsible for installing and operating security controls, such as firewalls, intrusion-detection systems, and routine backup and recovery operations. However today, developers of new systems must ensure that the system's *security requirements* produce reasonable precautions to prevent problems; system developers are responsible for ensuring security within the information systems themselves. Furthermore, with DevSecOps (i.e., Development + Security + Operations) "continuous delivery" approaches to developing and deploying IS, security must be at the forefront of any and all decisions.[17]

Security is an ever-increasing problem in today's Internet-enabled world. Historically, the greatest security threat has come from inside the organization itself. Ever since the early 1980s when the FBI first began keeping computer crime statistics and security firms began conducting surveys of computer crime, organizational employees have perpetrated the vast majority of computer crimes. For years, 80 percent of unauthorized break-ins, thefts, and sabotage have been committed by insiders, leaving only 20 percent to hackers external to the organizations.

In 2001, that changed. Depending on what survey you read, the percentage of incidents attributed to external hackers in 2001 increased to 50 to 70 percent of all incidents, meaning that the greatest risk facing organizations is now from the outside. Although some of this shift may be due to better internal security and better communications with employees to prevent security problems, much of it is simply due to an increase in attacks over the Internet, such as denial of service attacks, malware, phishing, ransomware, social engineering, spyware, Trojan horses, and many others, by external hackers. Furthermore, given cloud computing and the IoT, security must be taken very seriously and be addressed as the system is being designed instead of simply an add-on that is considered after the system has been implemented.

An emerging security challenge is due to the rise of quantum computing. *Quantum computing* uses the principles of quantum mechanics (such as superposition and entanglement) to perform calculations and transmit information using quantum particles (electrons,

---

[16] For more information, see Brett C. Tjaden, *Fundamentals of Secure Computer Systems* (Wilsonville, OR: Franklin, Beedle, and Associates, 2004); for security controls associated with the Sarbanes–Oxley act, see Dennis C. Brewer, *Security Controls for Sarbanes–Oxley Section 404 IT Compliance: Authorization, Authentication, and Access* (Indianapolis: Wiley, 2006); William Stallings, *Effective Cybersecurity: A Guide to Using Best Practices and Standards* (Upper Saddle River, NJ: Pearson Education, 2019); O. Sami Saydjari, *Engineering Trustworthy Systems: Get Cybersecurity Design Right the First Time* (New York, NY: McGraw-Hill, 2018).

[17] See for example, https://www.microsoft.com/en-us/security/business/security-101/what-is-devsecops.

photons, and ions). Quantum computers can perform some computations in a matter of hours, whereas regular computers could take billions of years to accomplish the same tasks. While mainstream commercially viable quantum computers may not be available for many years, experts are already worried about the ability of quantum computers to break common encryption standards (discussed later). In fact, it is possible that some malicious actors are already harvesting data (such as credit card transactions, medical files, phone calls) in hopes of using quantum computers in the future to decrypt these data. It is hence prudent to be aware of such possibilities, so as not to be taken off-guard when the ability to break common encryption becomes reality.

Developing security requirements usually starts with some assessment of the value of the system and its data. This helps pinpoint extremely important systems so that the operations staff is aware of the risks. Security within systems usually focuses on specifying who can access what data, identifying the need for encryption and authentication, and ensuring the application prevents the spread of viruses (see Figure 10-18).

System Value The most important computer asset in any organization is not the equipment; it is the organization's data. For example, suppose someone destroyed a mainframe computer worth $10 million. The mainframe could be replaced, simply by buying a new one. It would be expensive, but the problem would be solved in a few weeks. Now suppose someone destroyed all the student records at your university so that no one knew what courses anyone had taken or their grades. The cost would far exceed the cost of replacing a $10 million computer. The lawsuits alone would easily exceed $10 million, and the cost of staff to find paper records and reenter the data from them would be enormous and certainly would take more than a few weeks.

In some cases, the information system itself has value that far exceeds the cost of the equipment as well. For example, for an online bank that has no brick and mortar branches, the website is a *mission-critical system*. If the website crashes, the bank cannot conduct business with its customers. A mission-critical application is an information system that is literally critical to the survival of the organization. It is an application that cannot be permitted to fail, and if it does fail, the network staff drops everything else to fix it. Mission-critical applications are usually clearly identified so that their importance is not overlooked.

Type of Requirement	Definition	Examples
System Value Estimates	Estimated business value of the system and its data	• The system is not mission critical, but a system outage is estimated to cost $50,000 per hour in lost revenue. • A complete loss of all system data is estimated to cost $20 million.
Access Control Requirements	Limitations on who can access what data	• Only department managers will be able to change inventory items within their own department. • Telephone operators will be able to read and create items in the customer file but cannot change or delete items.
Encryption and the Authentication Requirements	Defines what data will be encrypted where and whether authentication will be needed for user access	• Data will be encrypted from the user's computer to website to provide secure ordering. • Users logging in from outside the office will be required to authenticate.
Virus Control Requirements	Requirements to control the spread of viruses	• All uploaded files will be checked for viruses before being saved in the system.

FIGURE 10-18   Security Requirements

Even temporary disruptions in service can have significant costs. The costs of disruptions to a company's primary website or the LANs and backbones that support telephone sales operations are often measured in the millions of dollars. Amazon.com, for example, has revenues of more than $10 million per hour, so if its website were unavailable for an hour or even part of an hour, it would lose millions of dollars in revenue. Companies that do less e-business or do telephone sales have lower costs, but recent surveys suggest losses of $100,000 to $200,000 per hour are not uncommon for major customer-facing information systems.

Access Control Requirements Some of the data stored in the system need to be kept confidential; some data need special controls on who is allowed to change or delete it. Personnel records, for example, should be readable only by the personnel department and the employee's supervisor; changes should be permitted to be made only by the personnel department. *Access control requirements* state who can access what data and what type of access is permitted: whether the individual can create, read, update and/or delete the data. The requirements reduce the chance that an authorized user of the system can perform unauthorized actions. The vast majority of these requirements have already been captured in the form of the actors and stakeholders with the real use-case descriptions (Chapter 9), the associated classes with the CRC cards (Chapters 4 and 7), and the detailed version of the CRUDE matrix (Chapter 5).

There are several approaches to address access control. An *access control list* is associated with the asset for which you want to control access. For example, a file that you wanted to restrict access to a subset of users would have the users, along with the type of access being granted to them, listed in the access control list for the file. If a user was not in the list, the user would not be able to access the file. Furthermore, if a user was only granted read access, then the user could only read the file. We could actually implement this detailed level of control by capturing the access control lists in the pre-conditions of a method contract (see Chapter 7). Another approach would be to create a *capabilities list* with each user profile. In this case, the access controls would be associated with a specific user instead of a file. With the previous example, the capabilities list would show that the user had read access to the file. Finally, we could combine the access control and capabilities list approaches and require that access is only granted to an IT asset if both the access control list and the capabilities list match. This is the basis for the *access control matrix* approach. However, in terms of processing power requirements, the actual cost of these very low-level approaches may be prohibitive.

Role-based access control attempts to address some of the overhead associated with the access control list, the capability list, and the access control matrix approaches. With *role-based access controls*, access is limited by the role that the user is assigned. So instead of keeping track of the level of access being granted by the individual user, the controls are maintained at the role level. This could be captured with documentation associated with the actors that will be using the system. This is obviously a variation of the capabilities list approach. Furthermore, using operating system file level controls or using controls implemented through the DBMS would provide access controls at a less granular level. These approaches obviously require less processing power and less storage. As usual, it always comes back to cost-benefit analysis of the amount of risk a firm is willing to take on with regard to the cost of security.

Encryption and Authentication Requirements One of the best ways to prevent unauthorized access to data is *encryption*, which is a means of disguising information by the use of mathematical algorithms (or formulas). Encryption can be used to protect data stored in databases or data that are in transit over a network from a database to a computer. There are two fundamentally different types of encryption: symmetric and asymmetric. A *symmetric encryption algorithm* [such as Data Encryption Standard (DES) or Advanced Encryption Standard (AES)] is one in which the key used to encrypt a message is the *same* as the one used to decrypt it, which means that it is essential to protect the key and that a separate key must be used for each person or organization with whom the system shares information (or else everyone can read all the data).

An *asymmetric encryption algorithm* (such as *public key encryption*) is one in which the key used to encrypt data (called the *public key*) is different from the one used to decrypt it (called the *private key*). Even if everyone knows the public key, once the data are encrypted, they cannot be decrypted without the private key. Public key encryption greatly reduces the key-management problem. Each user has its public key that is used to encrypt messages sent to it. These public keys are widely publicized (e.g., listed in a telephone book style directory)— that's why they're called public keys. The private key, in contrast, is kept secret.

Public key encryption also permits *authentication* (or digital signatures). When one user sends a message to another, it is difficult to legally prove who actually sent the message. Legal proof is important in many communications, such as bank transfers and buy/sell orders in currency and stock trading, which normally require legal signatures. Public key encryption algorithms are *invertible*, meaning that text encrypted with either key can be decrypted by the other. Normally, we encrypt with the public key and decrypt with the private key. However, it is possible to do the reverse: encrypt with the private key and decrypt with the public key. Because the private key is secret, only the real user can use it to encrypt a message. Thus, a digital signature or authentication sequence is used as a legal signature on many financial transactions. This signature is usually the name of the signing party plus other unique information from the message (e.g., date, time, or dollar amount). This signature and the other information are encrypted by the sender using the private key. The receiver uses the sender's public key to decrypt the signature block and compares the result to the name and other key contents in the rest of the message to ensure a match.

The only problem with this approach lies in ensuring that the person or organization that sent the document with the correct private key is the actual person or organization. Anyone can post a public key on the Internet, so there is no way of knowing for sure who actually used it. For example, it would be possible for someone other than Organization A in this example to claim to be Organization A when, in fact, they are an imposter.

This is where the Internet's public key infrastructure (PKI) becomes important.[18] The PKI is a set of hardware, software, organizations, and polices designed to make public key encryption work on the Internet. PKI begins with a *certificate authority (CA)*, which is a trusted organization that can vouch for the authenticity of the person or organization using authentication (e.g., VeriSign). A person wanting to use a CA registers with the CA and must provide some proof of identity. There are several levels of certification, ranging from a simple confirmation from a valid e-mail address to a complete government-style background check with an in-person interview. The CA issues a digital certificate that is the requestor's public key, encrypted using the CA's private key as proof of identity. This certificate is then attached to the user's e-mail or Web transactions in addition to the authentication information. The receiver then verifies the certificate by decrypting it with the CA's public key and must also contact the CA to ensure that the user's certificate has not been revoked by the CA.

The encryption and authentication requirements state what encryption and authentication requirements are needed for what data. For example, will sensitive data such as customer credit-card numbers be stored in the database in encrypted form, or will encryption be used to take orders over the Internet from the company's website? Will users be required to use a digital certificate in addition to a standard password?

Virus Control Requirements *Virus control requirements* address the single most common security problem: *viruses*. Studies have shown that almost 90 percent of organizations suffer

---

[18] For more on the PKI, see http://datatracker.ietf.org/wg/pkix/charter/.

a virus infection each year. Viruses cause unwanted events—some harmless (such as nuisance messages), some serious (such as the destruction of data). Any time a system permits data to be imported or uploaded from a user's computer, there is the potential for a virus infection. Many systems require that all information systems that permit the import or upload of user files to check those files for viruses before they are stored in the system.

Testing[19] There are many different types of security threats with which testing can help address, e.g., denial of service attacks, malware, phishing, ransomware, social engineering, spyware, Trojan horses, and many others. The first way to address security threats is to incorporate security concerns throughout the development process. This begins with identifying the different types of threats that could occur as early as possible with the development of the system. Once the different types of potential threats have been identified, then the appropriate approaches to security can be designed for both the IT artifacts created during the development process, e.g., CRC cards, and the most effective way to incorporate the security requirements into the actual system can be developed. As described above, there are different ways in which to address the security requirements. For example, there are different approaches to implement access controls. Depending on the approach chosen, different types of testing are appropriate. Next, we extend our coverage of security testing to include the unit and integration levels.

Typical unit testing attempts to uncover missing requirements. However, when unit testing the security requirements, we want to ensure that only authorized users will be able to execute the different methods of each class. As described in Chapter 7, this could be implemented as a set of pre-conditions that would be part of the method specification and implementation. Moreover, when considering the data management layer, we could implement access controls directly in the DBMS. We also could decide to encrypt all data stored in the DBMS. However, depending on the volume of data and the different types of access to the data that needed to be supported, this level of detailed security requirements implementation could be prohibitive in terms of the process power required.

With integration testing, testers should be sure to incorporate both authorization and access control types of tests when testing the user interface and use cases. The basis of these tests should come from the use-case descriptions, contracts, and method specifications. In addition to the typical input validations that must be performed, tests that can detect code insertions should also be performed. This simply implies a more detailed set of user interface tests that guarantee only valid data is allowed to pass from the user interface to the system. Furthermore, if encryption is to be used on the data captured by the user interface, appropriate tests must be performed to make sure that it works as expected. In many ways, this takes us back to the unit testing level. However, instead of testing classes, the unit is the individual field.

Cultural and Political Requirements

Cultural and political requirements are those specific to the countries in which the system will be used. In today's global business environment, organizations are expanding their systems to reach users around the world. Although this can make great business sense, its impact on application development should not be underestimated. Yet another important part of the design of the system's application architecture is understanding the global cultural and political requirements for the system (see Chapter 9 and Figure 10-19).

---

[19] For more information, see William Stallings, *Effective Cybersecurity: A Guide to Using Best Practices and Standards* (Upper Saddle River, NJ: Pearson Education, 2019); O. Sami Saydjari, *Engineering Trustworthy Systems: Get Cybersecurity Design Right the First Time* (New York, NY: McGraw-Hill, 2018); Len Bass, Ingo Weber, Liming Zhu, *DevOps: A Software Architect's Perspective* (Upper Saddle River, NJ: Pearson Education, 2015); Gene Kim, Jez Humble, Patrick Debois, John Willis, *The DevOps Handbook: How to Create World-Class Agility, Reliability, & Security in Technology Organizations* (Portland, OR: IT Revolution Press, 2016).

Type of Requirement	Definition	Examples
Customization Requirements	Specification of what aspects of the system can be changed by local users	• Country managers will be able to define new fields in the product database to capture country-specific information. • Country managers will be able to change the format of the telephone number field in the customer database.
Legal Requirements	The laws and regulations that impose requirements on the system	• Personal information about customers cannot be transferred out of European Union countries into the United States. • It is against U.S. federal law to divulge information on who rented what videotape, so access to a customer's rental history is permitted only to regional managers.

FIGURE 10-19   Cultural and Political Requirements

Customization Requirements For global applications, the project team needs to give some thought to *customization requirements:* How much of the application will be controlled by a central group, and how much of the application will be managed locally? For example, some companies allow subsidiaries in some countries to customize the application by omitting or adding certain features. This decision has trade-offs between flexibility and control because customization often makes it more difficult for the project team to create and maintain the application. It also means that training can differ among different parts of the organization, and customization can create problems when staff moves from one location to another.

Owing to the use of different languages, in some cases, specialized hardware that has been customized to the local culture is required. For example, having specialized keyboards makes sense for any language that does not use the typical Roman alphabet, e.g., Arabic, Hebrew, Greek, Japanese, Korean, Mandarin, or Russian. There are also emulators available for many different languages. Depending on the users being served, assistive devices could be required, such as Braille devices, eye-tracking devices, head pointers, head/mouth stick keyboards, or adaptive ability switches. Depending on the cultural and political requirements, many different hardware platforms might need to be considered.

Legal Requirements *Legal requirements* are requirements imposed by laws and government regulations. System developers sometimes forget to think about legal regulations; unfortunately, forgetting comes at some risk because ignorance of the law is no defense. For example, in 1997 a French court convicted the Georgia Institute of Technology of violating French language law. Georgia Tech operated a small campus in France that offered summer programs for American students. The information on the campus Web server was primarily in English because classes are conducted in English, which violated the law requiring French to be the predominant language on all Internet servers in France. By formally considering legal regulations, you are less likely to overlook them. Another major example is the recent European court ruling regarding the user's right to be forgotten.

Another area that legal requirements can cause problems is with the *end user license agreements*. When is the last time that you carefully have read the end user license agreement when you installed software on your machine? From an organizational perspective, this could cause problems. Some agreements commit an organization to allow access to the data that is processed by the software. Other agreements require that an organization be bound by the laws of a foreign country. Or, with a federal government system such as in the United States, the agreement could require that an organization follow the laws of another nation. So, from an organizational perspective, organizations should restrict the installation of any software until an organization's lawyers give approval. Otherwise, a user could be granting access to an outside organization to organizational data and possibly to intellectual property. In other words, we need to have the "fine print" of the agreement read by an expert to prevent the accidental loss of organizational assets.

Synopsis

In many cases, the technical environment requirements as driven by the business requirements can simply define the application architecture layer. In this case, the choice is simple: Business requirements dominate other considerations. For example, the business requirements might specify that the system needs to work over the Web using the customer's Web browser. In this case, the architecture probably should be a thin client–server. Such business requirements are most likely in systems designed to support external customers. Internal systems can also impose business requirements, but usually they are not as restrictive.

In the event that the technical environment requirements do not stipulate a specific architecture, then the other nonfunctional requirements become important. Even in cases when the business requirements drive the architecture, it is still important to work through and refine the remaining nonfunctional requirements because they are important in later stages of design and implementation.

VERIFYING AND VALIDATING THE APPLICATION ARCHITECTURE LAYER

Like the models on the other layers, the infrastructure design and the hardware and software specifications of the application architecture layer need to be verified and validated. Verifying and validating the design of the application architecture layer fall into three basic groups.

First, we recommend verifying and validating deployment diagrams by ensuring that all of them are in fact consistent and balanced. For example, each of the nodes in a top-level network model deployment diagram should be associated with a separate deployment diagram that represents the low-level network model for the node.

Second, the hardware and software specifications should be consistent with the "lowest-level" network models. For example, if a low-level network model for an office describes a set of workstations, servers, printers, switches, routers, etc., then the hardware and software specification for that location should be the details for each of the IT artifacts for that location.

Third, once the system has been implemented, testing of the nonfunctional requirements becomes crucial. In this case, tests must be designed and performed for each of the nonfunctional requirements. For example, for the performance requirements, load testing must be performed to identify possible performance bottlenecks in the network.

APPLYING THE CHAPTER CONCEPTS

Library Management System (LMS) Example In the previous installation of the LMS example, Beth had taken her first cut design of the HCI layer that would support the Borrow Resource use case to Joe to get his feedback. In this installation we check in with Phil to see how everything is going with the design of the Application Architecture layer.

During a regular team meeting, Jane and Beth described the current status for the design of the Data Management and Human–Computer Interaction layers. Here is a small excerpt from the meeting.

SUSAN: Jane, could you tell us the current status of the data management layer design?

JANE: After meeting with Joe, I found out that the library staff is currently using the MySQL RDBMS for data storage for other applications. So, based on the package diagram for the problem-domain layer, we decided to leverage that expertise for all structured data. Which meant that we only needed to deal with designing something for the Downloadable resources. Furthermore, literally all the downloadable resources are available with some type of subscription. So, we only will need to design the DAM classes for the downloadable resources. And these will have to be customized to each subscription. Our next step is to go ahead and develop both the data access and storage logic for the structured data and to bring John in so that we can get each subscription's API specified in enough detail to be implemented in an efficient manner.

SUSAN: Jane, it sounds that regarding the data management layer, we really lucked out. Beth, how is it going with the human–computer interaction layer design?

BETH: Well, I met with Joe to go over a partial design of the HCI layer. In this case Joe had wanted a slightly different layout. Based on his suggestions, we felt that a web-based design would be the best approach for this specific application. I called Joe and made the suggestion. He was very interested in pursuing this approach. In fact, he would like to treat this application as a possible foundation to upgrade their other systems. So, we are off and running on designing a web-based HCI layer.

SUSAN: Beth, this sounds promising. We just might be able to get additional contracts to work with the library. Phil, I suspect that armed with this information, you now can set out a design for the application architecture layer.

PHIL: Yes, but before I do anything, I'm going to call Joe to find out what the application architectures that they currently have in place for the other applications. Based on the library using MySQL, I think we can design an architecture that could support evolving the other applications to a more modern architecture. So, I'll set up a meeting with Joe and his current staff to see what they are currently doing. Once I know this, I'll design an architecture that will support our current application and that could support their other applications.

After Phil met with Joe and his staff, he realized that the other applications were using a server-based architecture (see Figure 10-1). Also, Phil realized that they really wanted to allow patrons to be able to lookup the location of physical resources and to checkout downloadable resources remotely. So, he sat down with John to design the application architecture. The architecture that they came up with was essentially a four-tiered client server architecture (see Figure 10-5) that also included a fire wall and the cloud for the storage of the downloadable resources. Figure 10-20 portrays this design. Given the current designs of the data management, human–computer interaction, and application architecture layers, Alan was able to design the remaining tests to make sure that the quality of the system was sufficient, and John was able to implement the designs.

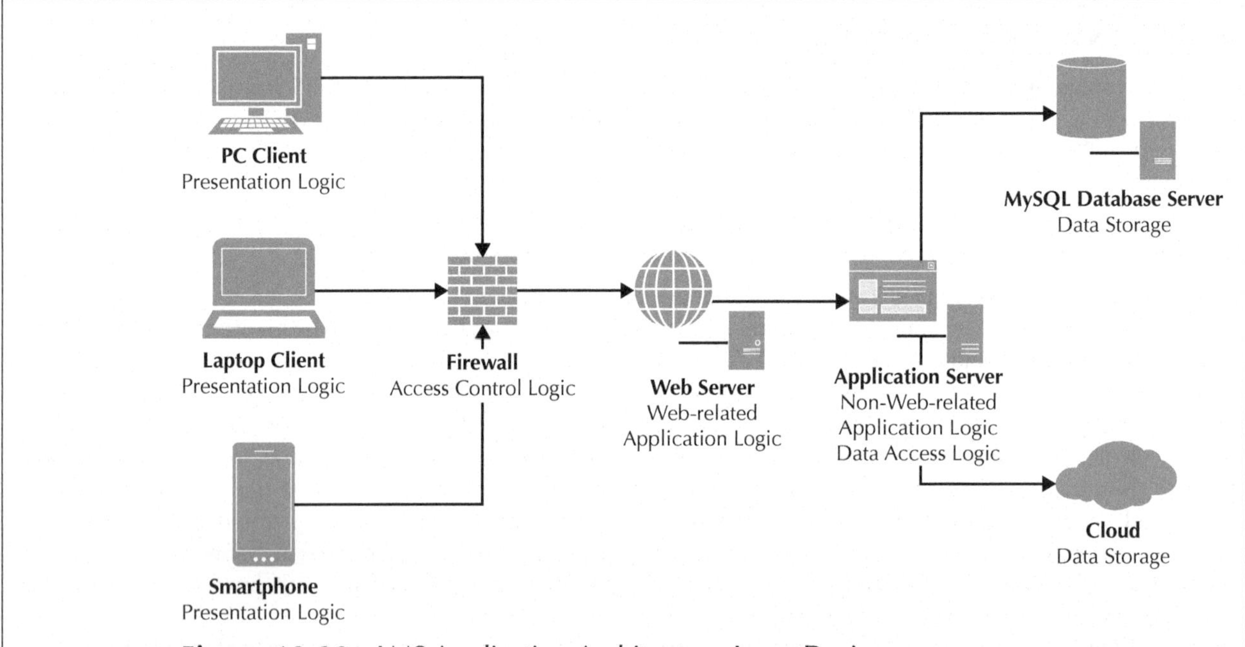

Figure 10-20   LMS Application Architecture Layer Design

Campus Housing Service "Your Turn" Exercise   In the previous installation of the Campus Housing Service (CHS) "Your Turn" exercise, you designed the HCI layer using a set of wireframe diagrams that portrayed the layout of the user interface and a WND that showed the navigation between the objects in the wireframe diagrams. In this installation, you should use a deployment diagram to show the topology of the application architecture of the CHS network. In this case, you should use a client–server architecture. Furthermore, you should write a justification of this decision.

CHAPTER REVIEW

After reading and studying this chapter, you should be able to:

- ☐ Describe the four major architectural components.
- ☐ Describe the five major application architectures.
- ☐ Describe Infrastructure as a Service, Platform as a Service, and Software as a Service.
- ☐ Describe the three primary obstacles to cloud computing.
- ☐ Discuss the trade-offs in selecting an application architecture.
- ☐ Discuss the potential impact of ubiquitous computing and the Internet of Things.
- ☐ Describe enchanted objects.
- ☐ Create an infrastructure design using deployment diagrams.
- ☐ Create a high-level hardware and software specification.
- ☐ Describe how nonfunctional requirements may influence the actual design of the application architecture layer.

KEY TERMS

24/7
Access control list
Access control matrix
Access control requirements
Application logic
Architectural component
Artifact
Asymmetric encryption
  algorithm
Authentication
Availability and reliability
  requirements
Business process
Capabilities list
Capacity requirements
Certificate authority (CA)
Client-based architecture
Client computer
Client–server architecture
Cloud computing
Communication path
Cultural and political
  requirements
Customization requirements

Data access logic
Data storage
Deployment diagrams
Enchanted objects
Encryption
End user license agreement
Fat client
Graphical user interface (GUI)
Grid computing
Hardware and software
  specification
Hybrid cloud
Infrastructure as a
  service (IaaS)
Internet of Things (IoT)
Invertible
Legal requirements
Locations
Maintainability requirements
Middleware
Mission-critical system
Multitenancy
Network
Network model

Node
N-tiered architecture
Operational requirements
Outsourcing
Parkinson's law
Peer-to-peer architecture
Performance requirements
Platform as a service (PaaS)
Portability requirements
Presentation logic
Private cloud
Private key
Public cloud
Public key
Public key encryption
Quantum computing
Response time
Role-based access control
Scalable
Security requirements
Server
Server-based architecture
Service
Service-oriented architecture

Software as a service (SaaS)
Speed requirements
SQL (structured
  query language)
Symmetric encryp-
  tion algorithm
System integration
  requirements
Technical environment
  requirements
Thick client
Thin client
Three-tiered architecture
Timesharing
Total cost of ownership
Two-tiered architecture
Ubiquitous computing
Virtual memory
Virtualization
Virus
Virus control requirements
Web services

QUESTIONS

1. What are the four basic functions of any information system?

2. What are the three primary hardware components of any application architecture?

3. Name two examples of a server.

4. Compare and contrast server-based architectures, client-based architectures, client–server-based architectures, peer-to-peer architectures, and cloud architectures.

5. What is the biggest problem with server-based computing?

6. What is the biggest problem with client-based computing?

7. Describe the major benefits and limitations of thin client–server architectures.

8. Describe the major benefits and limitations of thick client–server architectures.

9. Describe the differences among two-tiered, three-tiered, and *n*-tiered architectures.

10. Describe the major benefits and limitations of peer-to-peer architectures.

11. Name the three different types of clouds. How do they differ from one another?

12. What is meant by a service-oriented architecture?

13. Define virtualization. How does it relate to the cloud?

14. What are the differences among IaaS, PaaS, and SaaS?

15. What are the obstacles for provisioning the application architecture layer with cloud technologies?

16. What, if any, are the issues related to security in the cloud?

17. What are SOX and HIPAA, and how could they affect a firm's decision to adopt cloud technology?

18. Define *scalable*. Why is this term important to system developers?

19. What seven criteria are helpful to use when comparing the appropriateness of computing alternatives?

20. Why should the project team consider the existing application architecture in the organization when designing the application architecture layer of the new system?

21. What is meant by ubiquitous computing? How about the Internet of Things?

22. What additional hardware- and software-associated costs might need to be included on the hardware and software specification?

23. Who is ultimately in charge of acquiring hardware and software for a project?

24. What is a benchmark, and why is it important?

25. Why is Parkinson's Law relevant to the design of the physical architecture layer?

26. What do you think are three common mistakes that novice analysts make in architecture design and hardware and software specification?
27. Describe the major nonfunctional requirements and how they influence application architecture layer design.
28. Why is it useful to define the nonfunctional requirements in more detail even if the technical environment requirements dictate a specific architecture?
29. What does the network model communicate to the project team?
30. What are the differences between the top-level network model and the low-level network model?
31. Are some nonfunctional requirements more important than others in influencing the architecture design?
32. What do you think are the most important security issues for a system?
33. Describe the different approaches to access control.
34. Why is it important to have end user license agreements examined?

EXERCISES

A. Using the Web (or past issues of computer industry magazines such as *Computerworld*), locate a system that runs in a server-based environment. Based on your reading, why do you think the company chose that computing environment?

B. Using the Web (or past issues of computer industry magazines such as *Computerworld*), locate a system that runs in a client–server environment. Based on your reading, why do you think the company chose that computing environment?

C. Using the Web, locate examples of a mainframe component, a minicomputer component, and a microcomputer component. Compare the components in terms of price, speed, available memory, and disk storage. Did you find large differences in prices when the performances of the components are considered?

D. You have been selected to find the best client–server architecture for a Web-based order entry system that is being developed for L.L. Bean. Write a short memo that describes to the project manager your reason for selecting an *n*-tiered architecture over a two-tiered architecture. In the memo, give some idea as to what different components of the architecture you would include.

E. Think about the system that your university currently uses for career services and suppose that you are in charge of replacing the system with a new one. Describe how you would decide on the computing architecture for the new system using the criteria presented in this chapter. What information will you need to find out before you can make an educated comparison of the alternatives?

F. Using the Web, find examples of firms using the cloud as a basis for the application architecture layer. Describe exactly what they are doing.

G. Locate a consumer products company on the Web and read its company description (so that you get a good understanding of the geographic locations of the company). Pretend that the company is about to create a new application to support retail sales over the Web. Create a high-level network model that depicts the locations that would include components that support this application.

H. Create a low-level network diagram for the building that houses the computer labs at your university. Choose an application (e.g., course registration and student admissions) and include only the components that are relevant to that application.

I. An energy company with headquarters in Dallas, Texas, is thinking about developing a system to track the efficiency of its oil refineries in North America. Each week, the ten refineries—as far as Valdez, Alaska, and as close as San Antonio, Texas—will upload performance data via satellite to the corporate mainframe in Dallas. Production managers at each site will use a personal computer to connect to an Internet service provider and access reports via the Web. Create a high-level network model that depicts the locations that have components supporting this system.

J. Suppose that the admissions office in your university has a Web-based application so that students can apply for admission online. Recently, there has been a push to admit more international students into the university. What do you recommend that the application include to ensure that it supports this global requirement?

K. Based on the A Real Estate Inc. problem in Chapter 3 (exercises I, J, and K), Chapter 4 (exercises N and O), Chapter 5 (exercise D), Chapter 6 (exercise D), Chapter 7 (exercise A), Chapter 8 (exercise H), and Chapter 9 (exercises I and J), suggest an application architecture design and portray it with a deployment diagram.

L. Based on the A Video Store problem in Chapter 3 (exercises L, M, and N), Chapter 4 (exercises P and Q), Chapter 5 (exercise E), Chapter 6 (exercise E), Chapter 7 (exercise B), Chapter 8 (exercise I), and Chapter 9 (exercises K and L), suggest an application architecture design and portray it with a deployment diagram.

M. Based on the gym membership problem in Chapter 3 (exercises O, P, and Q), Chapter 4 (exercises R and S), Chapter 5 (exercise F), Chapter 6 (exercise F), Chapter 7 (exercise C), Chapter 8 (exercise J), and Chapter 9 (exercises M and N), suggest an application architecture design and portray it with a deployment diagram.

N. Based on the Picnics R Us exercises in Chapter 3 (exercises R, S, and T), Chapter 4 (exercises T and U), Chapter 5 (exercise G), Chapter 6 (exercise G), Chapter 7 (exercise D), and Chapter 8 (exercise K), and Chapter 9 (exercises O and P), suggest an application architecture design and portray it with a deployment diagram.

O. Based on the Of-the-Month-Club problem in Chapter 3 (exercises U, V, and W), Chapter 4 (exercises V and W), Chapter 5 (exercise H), Chapter 6 (exercise H), Chapter 7 (exercise E), Chapter 8 (exercise L), and Chapter 9 (exercises Q and R), suggest an application architecture design and portray it with a deployment diagram.

MINICASES

1. The system development project team at Birdie Masters golf schools has been working on defining the application architecture design for the system. The major focus of the project is a networked school location operations system, allowing each school location to easily record and retrieve all school location transaction data. Another system element is the use of the Internet to enable current and prospective students to view class offerings at any of the Birdie Masters' locations, schedule lessons and enroll in classes at any Birdie Masters location, and maintain a student progress profile—a confidential analysis of the student's golf skill development.

The project team has been considering the globalization issues that should be factored into the architecture design. The school's plan for expansion into the golf-crazed Japanese market is moving ahead. The first Japanese school location is tentatively planning to open about six months after the target completion data for the system project. Therefore, it is important that issues related to the international location be addressed now during design.

Assume that you have been given the responsibility of preparing a summary memo on the globalization issues that should be factored into the design. Prepare this memo discussing the globalization issues that are relevant to Birdie Masters' new system.

2. Jerry is a relatively new member of a project team that is developing a retail store management system for a chain of sporting goods stores. Company headquarters is in Las Vegas, and the chain has twenty-seven locations throughout Nevada, Utah, and Arizona. Several cities have multiple stores.

The new system will be a networked client–server architecture. Stores will be linked to one of three regional servers, and the regional servers will be linked to corporate headquarters in Las Vegas. The regional servers also link to one another. Each retail store will be outfitted with similar configurations of two PC-based point-of-sale terminals networked to a local file server. Jerry has been given the task of developing a network model that will document the geographic structure of this system. He has not faced a system of this scope before and is a little unsure how to begin.

a. Prepare a set of instructions for Jerry to follow in developing this network model.

b. Using a deployment diagram, draw a network model for this organization.

3. Refer to the Professional and Scientific Staff Management (PSSM) minicase in Chapters 3, 5, 6, 7, 8, and 9. Based on the solutions developed for those problems, suggest an application architecture design and portray it with a deployment diagram.

4. Refer to the Holiday Travel Vehicles minicase in Chapters 4, 5, 6, 7, 8, and 9. Based on the solutions developed for those problems, suggest an application architecture design and portray it with a deployment diagram.

PART THREE

SUPPORTING UNIFIED PROCESS WORKFLOWS

The supporting workflows of the Unified process include Project Management, Configuration and Change Management, Environment, Operations and Support, and Infrastructure Management. These workflows focus on the managerial aspects of information systems development. In addition to these supporting workflows, aspects of the Implementation and Deployment engineering workflows are described. Without successfully executing these workflows, the information system development effort can easily fail.

CHAPTER 11 Project Management

CHAPTER 12 Finishing Touches: Final Unified Process Workflows

CHAPTER 11

PROJECT MANAGEMENT

This chapter primarily describes the project management workflow of the Unified Process. On this workflow, analysts perform a feasibility analysis to determine the technical, economic, and organizational feasibility of the system; if appropriate, the system is selected and the development project begins. They must staff the project team taking into considerations the project requirements and the characteristics of the personnel that will be needed. This workflow also addresses the effective management of meetings, the project development schedule, the scope of the project, and risk management. These issues will be managed using different scheduling, monitoring, and estimation tools.

OBJECTIVES

- Be able to perform a feasibility analysis.
- Understand how to assess technical, economic, and organizational feasibility.
- Understand how projects are selected in some organizations.
- Understand the ethical considerations when selecting a project.
- Understand how Green IT considerations can affect project selection.
- Become familiar with how to staff a project.
- Understand how to effectively manage meetings.
- Understand how to manage the scope, refine the estimates, and manage the risk of a project.
- Be familiar with project assessment activities.
- Become familiar with traditional project management tools including work breakdown structures, Gantt charts, and network diagrams.
- Become familiar with use-case–driven effort estimation.
- Be able to create an iterative project workplan.

INTRODUCTION

Most projects occurring in people's lives, such as weddings or graduation celebrations, require planning and management. Months are spent in advance identifying and performing all the tasks that need to get done, such as sending out invitations and selecting a menu, and time and money are carefully allocated among them. Along the way, decisions are recorded, problems are addressed, and changes are made. The increasing popularity of the party planner, a person whose sole job is to coordinate a party, suggests how tough this job can be. In the end, the success of any party has a lot to do with the effort that went into planning along the way. System development projects can be much more complicated than the projects we encounter in our personal lives—usually, more people are involved (e.g., the organization, software vendors, IT consultants, and potential customers), the costs are higher, and more tasks need to be completed. Owing to the complexity of software and software development, it is virtually impossible to "know" all of the possible things that could happen during system development projects. Therefore, it is not surprising that "party planners" exist for information systems projects: They are called *project managers.*

In the information systems context, *project management* is the process of planning and controlling the development of a system within a specified time frame at a minimum cost with the right functionality.[1] In general, a *project* is a set of activities with a starting point and an ending point meant to create a system that brings value to the business. A project manager has the primary responsibility for managing the hundreds of tasks and roles that need to be carefully coordinated. Today, project management is an actual profession, and analysts spend years working on projects before tackling the management of them. However, in many cases, unreasonable demands set by *project sponsors* and business managers can make project management very difficult. Too often, the approach of the holiday season, the chance at winning a proposal with a low bid, or a funding opportunity pressures project managers to promise systems long before they can deliver them. These overly optimistic timetables are thought to be one of the biggest problems that projects face; instead of pushing a project forward faster, they result in delays. Another source is the changing nature of information technology. An innovation in information technology may look so attractive that organizations embrace projects using this technology without assessing whether the technology adds value to the organization; instead, the technology itself seems important in its own right. Problems can usually be traced back to the very beginning of the development of the system, where too little attention was given to identifying the *business value* and understanding the risks associated with the project.

A *feasibility* analysis plays an important role in deciding whether to proceed with an information systems development project. It examines the technical, economic, and organizational, and ethical pros and cons of developing the system, and it gives the organization a slightly more detailed picture of the advantages of investing in the system as well as any obstacles that could arise. In most cases, the project sponsor works closely with the development team to develop the feasibility analysis. Once the feasibility analysis has been completed, it is submitted to the *approval committee*, along with a revised *system request*. The committee then decides whether to approve the project, decline the project, or table it until additional information is available. Projects are selected by weighing risks and returns and by making trade-offs at the organizational level.

Once the committee has approved a project, the development team must carefully plan for the actual development of the system. Because we are following a Unified Process-based approach, the systems development workplan will evolve throughout the development process. Given this evolutionary approach, one critical success factor for project management is to start with a realistic assessment of the work that needs to be accomplished and then manage the project according to that assessment. This can be achieved by carefully creating and managing the workplan, estimating the effort to develop the system, staffing the project, and coordinating project activities.

In addition to covering the above material, this chapter also covers three traditional project management tools that are very useful to manage object-oriented systems development projects (work breakdown structures, Gantt charts, and network diagrams).

---

[1] For a very good comprehensive description of project management for information systems, see R.K. Wysocki, *Effective Project Management: Traditional, Agile, Extreme,* 5th Ed. (Indianapolis, IN: Wiley Publishing, 2009). Also, the Project Management Institute (www.pmi.org) and the Information Systems Community of Practice of the Project Management Institute (is.vc.pmi.org) have valuable resources on information systems project management. Finally, the following are good books on project management for object-oriented projects: G. Booch, *Object Solutions: Managing the Object-Oriented Project* (Menlo Park, CA: Addison-Wesley, 1996); M. R. Cantor, *Object-Oriented Project Management with UML* (New York: Wiley, 1998); A. Cockburn, *Surviving Object-Oriented Projects: A Manager's Guide* (Reading, MA: Addison-Wesley, 1998); I. Jacobson, G. Booch, and J. Rumbaugh, *The Unified Software Development Process* (Reading, MA: Addison-Wesley, 1999); W. Royce, *Software Project Management: A Unified Framework* (Reading, MA: Addison-Wesley, 1998).

FEASIBILITY ANALYSIS

Once the need for the system and its *business requirements* have been defined, it is time to create a more detailed business case to better understand the opportunities and limitations associated with the proposed project. Feasibility analysis guides the organization in determining whether to proceed with a project. Feasibility analysis also identifies the important *risks* associated with the project that must be addressed if the project is approved. As with the system request, each organization has its own process and format for the feasibility analysis, but most include three types: technical feasibility, economic feasibility, and organizational feasibility. The results of these analyses are combined into a *feasibility study*, which is given to the approval committee (see Figure 11-1).

Although we now discuss feasibility analysis within the context of initiating a project, most project teams will revise their feasibility study throughout the development process and revisit its contents at various checkpoints during the project. If at any point the project's risks and limitations outweigh its benefits, the project team may decide to cancel the project or make necessary improvements.

Technical Feasibility

The first type of feasibility analysis addresses the *technical feasibility* of the project: the extent to which the system can be successfully designed, developed, and installed by the IT group. Technical feasibility analysis is in essence a *technical risk analysis* that strives to answer this question: *Can* we build it?[2]

Many risks can endanger the successful completion of a project. First is the users' and analysts' lack of *familiarity with the functional area*. When analysts are unfamiliar with the business functional area, they have a greater chance of misunderstanding the users or of missing opportunities for improvement. The risk increases dramatically when the users themselves are less familiar with an application, such as with the development of a system to support a business innovation. In general, developing new systems is riskier than producing extensions to an existing system because existing systems tend to be better understood.

Technical Feasibility: Can We Build It?
- Familiarity with Functional area: Less familiarity generates more risk
- Familiarity with Technology: Less familiarity generates more risk
- Project Size: Large projects have more risk
- Compatibility: The harder it is to integrate the system with the company's existing technology, the higher the risk

Economic Feasibility: Should We Build It?
- Development costs
- Annual operating costs
- Annual benefits (cost savings and revenues)
- Intangible costs and benefits

Organizational Feasibility: If We Build It, Will They Come?
- Is the project strategically aligned with the business?
- Project champion(s)
- Senior management
- Users
- Other stakeholders

FIGURE 11-1
Feasibility Analysis Assessment Factors

---

[2] We use *build it* in the broadest sense. Organizations can also choose to buy a commercial software package and install it, in which case, the question might be, Can we select the right package and successfully install it?

Familiarity with the technology is another important source of technical risk. When a system uses technology that has not been used before *within the organization*, there is a greater chance that problems will occur and delays will be incurred because of the need to learn how to use the technology. Risk increases dramatically when the technology itself is new.

Project size is an important consideration, whether measured as the number of people on the development team, the length of time it will take to complete the project, or the number of distinct features in the system. Larger projects present more risk, both because they are more complicated to manage and because there is a greater chance that important system requirements will be overlooked or misunderstood. Furthermore, the extent to which the project is highly integrated with other systems can cause problems because complexity increases when many systems must work together.

Finally, project teams need to consider the *compatibility* of the new system with the technology that already exists in the organization. Systems are rarely built in a vacuum—they are built in organizations that already have numerous systems in place. New technology and applications need to integrate with the existing environment for many reasons. They might rely on data from existing systems, they might produce data that feed other applications, and they might have to use the company's existing communications infrastructure.

The assessment of a project's technical feasibility is not cut and dried because in many cases, some interpretation of the underlying conditions is needed. One approach is to compare the project under consideration with prior projects undertaken by the organization. Another option is to consult with experienced IT professionals in the organization or external IT consultants; often they can judge whether a project is feasible from a technical perspective.

Economic Feasibility

The second element of a feasibility analysis is to perform an *economic feasibility* analysis (also called a *cost–benefit analysis*), which identifies the financial risk associated with the project. It attempts to answer the question, *Should* we build the system? Economic feasibility is determined by identifying costs and benefits associated with the system, assigning values to them, and then calculating the cash flow and return on investment for the project. The more expensive the project, the more rigorous and detailed the analysis should be. Figure 11-2 lists the steps in performing a cost–benefit analysis; each step is described in the following sections.

Identifying Costs and Benefits The first task when developing an economic feasibility analysis is to identify the kinds of costs and benefits the system will have and list them along the left-hand column of a spreadsheet. Figure 11-3 lists examples of costs and benefits that may be included.

Costs and benefits can be broken down into four categories: development costs, operational costs, tangible benefits, and intangibles. *Development costs* are tangible expenses incurred during the construction of the system, such as salaries for the project team, hardware and software expenses, consultant fees, training, and office space and equipment. Development costs are usually thought of as one-time costs. *Operational costs* are tangible costs required to operate the system, such as the salaries for operations staff, software licensing fees, equipment upgrades, and communications charges. Operational costs are usually thought of as ongoing costs.

Revenues and cost savings are the *tangible benefits* the system enables the organization to collect or the tangible expenses the system enables the organization to avoid. Tangible benefits could include increased sales, reductions in staff, and reductions in inventory. Of course, a project also can affect the organization's bottom line by reaping *intangible benefits* or incurring *intangible costs*. Intangible costs and benefits are more difficult to incorporate into the economic feasibility because they are based on intuition and belief rather than "hard numbers." Nonetheless, they should be listed in the spreadsheet along with the tangible items.

<table>
<tr><td>**1. Identifying Costs and Benefits**</td><td>List the tangible costs and benefits for the project. Include both one-time and recurring costs.</td></tr>
<tr><td>**2. Assigning Values to Costs and Benefits**</td><td>Work with business users and IT professionals to create numbers for each of the costs and benefits. Even intangibles should be valued if at all possible.</td></tr>
<tr><td>**3. Determining Cash Flow**</td><td>Project what the costs and benefits will be over a period of time, usually three to five years. Apply a growth rate to the numbers, if necessary.</td></tr>
<tr><td>**4. Determining Net Present Value (NPV)**</td><td>Calculate what the value of future costs and benefits are if measured by today's standards. You will need to select a rate of growth to apply the NPV formula.</td></tr>
<tr><td>**5. Determining Return on Investment (ROI)**</td><td>Calculate how much money the organization will receive in return for the investment it will make using the ROI formula.</td></tr>
<tr><td>**6. Determining the Break-Even Point**</td><td>Find the first year in which the system has greater benefits than costs. Apply the break-even formula using figures from that year. This will help you understand how long it will take before the system creates real value for the organization.</td></tr>
<tr><td>**7. Graphing the Break-Even Point**</td><td>Plot the yearly costs and benefits on a line graph. The point at which the lines cross is the break-even point.</td></tr>
</table>

FIGURE 11-2
Steps for Conducting
Economic Feasibility

Development Costs	Operational Costs
Development Team Salaries	Software Upgrades
Consultant Fees	Software Licensing Fees
Development Training	Hardware Repairs
Hardware and Software	Hardware Upgrades
Vendor Installation	Operational Team Salaries
Office Space and Equipment	Communications Charges
Data Conversion Costs	User Training
Tangible Benefits	**Intangible Benefits**
Increased Sales	Increased Market Share
Reductions in Staff	Increased Brand Recognition
Reductions in Inventory	Higher Quality Products
Reductions in IT Costs	Improved Customer Service
Better Supplier Prices	Better Supplier Relations

FIGURE 11-3
Example Costs and
Benefits for
Economic Feasibility

Assigning Values to Costs and Benefits Once the types of costs and benefits have been identified, analysts assign specific dollar values to them. This might seem impossible; how can someone quantify costs and benefits that haven't happened yet? And how can those predictions be realistic? Although this task is very difficult, analysts have to do the best they can to come up with reasonable numbers for all the costs and benefits. Only then can the approval committee make an educated decision about whether to move ahead with the project.

The best strategy for estimating costs and benefits is to rely on the people who have the clearest understanding of them. For example, costs and benefits related to the technology or the project itself can be provided by the company's IT group or external consultants, and business users can develop the numbers associated with the business (e.g., sales projections and order levels). Analysts can also consider past projects, industry reports, and vendor information, although these approaches probably will be a bit less accurate. All the estimates will probably be revised as the project proceeds.

Sometimes it is acceptable for analysts to list intangible benefits, such as improved customer service, without assigning a dollar value, whereas other times they must make estimates regarding the value of an intangible benefit. If possible, they should quantify intangible costs or benefits. Otherwise, it will not be apparent whether the costs and benefits have been realized. Consider a system that is supposed to improve customer service. This is an intangible benefit, but assume that the greater customer service will decrease the number of customer complaints by 10 percent each year over three years and that $200,000 is spent on phone charges and phone operators who handle complaint calls. Suddenly there are some very tangible numbers with which to set goals and measure the original intangible benefit.

Figure 11-4 shows costs and benefits along with assigned dollar values. Notice that the customer service intangible benefit has been quantified based on fewer customer complaint phone calls. The intangible benefit of being able to offer services that competitors currently offer was not quantified, but it was listed so that the approval committee will consider the benefit when assessing the system's economic feasibility.

Benefits[a]	
Increased sales	500,000
Improved customer service[b]	70,000
Reduced inventory costs	68,000
Total benefits	**638,000**
Development costs	
2 servers @ $125,000	250,000
Printer	100,000
Software licenses	34,825
Server software	10,945
Development labor	1,236,525
Total development costs	**1,632,295**
Operational costs	
Hardware	54,000
Software	20,000
Operational labor	111,788
Total operational costs	**185,788**
Total costs	**1,818,083**

[a]An important yet intangible benefit will be the ability to offer services that our competitors currently offer.

[b]Customer service numbers have been based on reduced costs for customer complaint phone calls.

FIGURE 11-4
Assigning Values to Costs and Benefits

Determining Cash Flow A formal cost–benefit analysis usually contains costs and benefits over a selected number of years (usually three to five years) to show cash flow over time (see Figure 11-5). When using this *cash-flow method,* the years are listed across the top of the spreadsheet to represent the time period for analysis, and numeric values are entered in the appropriate cells within the spreadsheet's body. Sometimes fixed amounts are entered into the columns. For example, Figure 11-5 lists the same amount for customer complaint calls and inventory costs for all five years. Usually, amounts are augmented by some rate of growth to adjust for inflation or business improvements, as shown by the 6 percent increase that is added to the sales numbers in the sample spreadsheet. Finally, totals are added to determine what the overall benefits will be; the higher the overall total, the greater the economic feasibility of the solution.

	1	2	3	4	5	Total
Increased sales	500,000	530,000	561,800	595,508	631,238	
Reduction in customer complaint calls	70,000	70,000	70,000	70,000	70,000	
Reduced inventory costs	68,000	68,000	68,000	68,000	68,000	
TOTAL BENEFITS:	638,000	668,000	699,800	733,508	769,238	
PV OF BENEFITS:	**619,417**	**629,654**	**640,416**	**651,712**	**663,552**	**3,204,752**
PV OF ALL BENEFITS:	**619,417**	**1,249,072**	**1,889,488**	**2,541,200**	**3,204,752**	
2 Servers @ $125,000	250,000	0	0	0	0	
Printer	100,000	0	0	0	0	
Software licenses	34,825	0	0	0	0	
Server software	10,945	0	0	0	0	
Development labor	1,236,525	0	0	0	0	
TOTAL DEVELOPMENT COSTS:	1,632,295	0	0	0	0	
Hardware	54,000	81,261	81,261	81,261	81,261	
Software	20,000	20,000	20,000	20,000	20,000	
Operational labor	111,788	116,260	120,910	125,746	130,776	
TOTAL OPERATIONAL COSTS:	185,788	217,521	222,171	227,007	232,037	
TOTAL COSTS:	1,818,083	217,521	222,171	227,007	232,037	
PV OF COSTS:	**1,765,129**	**205,034**	**203,318**	**201,693**	**200,157**	**2,575,331**
PV OF ALL COSTS:	**1,765,129**	**1,970,163**	**2,173,481**	**2,375,174**	**2,575,331**	
TOTAL PROJECT BENEFITS AND COSTS:	**(1,180,083)**	**450,479**	**477,629**	**506,501**	**537,201**	
YEARLY NPV:	**(1,145,712)**	**424,620**	**437,098**	**450,019**	**463,395**	**629,421**
CUMULATIVE NPV:	**(1,145,712)**	**(721,091)**	**(283,993)**	**166,026**	**629,421**	
RETURN ON INVESTMENT:	**24.44%** (629,421/2,575,331)					
BREAK-EVEN POINT:	**3.63 years** [break-even occurs in year 4; (450,019 − 166,026)/450,019 = 0.63]					
INTANGIBLE BENEFITS:	This service is currently provided by competitors Improved customer satisfaction					

FIGURE 11-5 Cost–Benefit Analysis

Determining Net Present Value and Return on Investment There are several problems with the cash-flow method: (1) it does not consider the time value of money (i.e., a dollar today is worth *more* than a dollar tomorrow), and (2) it does not show the overall "bang for the buck" that the organization is receiving from its investment. Therefore, some project teams add additional calculations to the spreadsheet to provide the approval committee with a more-accurate picture of the project's worth.

Net present value (NPV) is used to compare the present value of future cash flows with the investment outlay required to implement the project. For example, if you have a friend who owes you a dollar today but instead gives you a dollar three years from now, you've been had! Given a 10 percent increase in value, you'll be receiving the equivalent of 75 cents in today's terms.

NPV can be calculated in many different ways, some of which are extremely complex. Figure 11-6 shows a basic calculation that can be used in your cash flow analysis to get more relevant values. In Figure 11-5, the present value of the costs and benefits are calculated first (i.e., they are shown at a discounted rate). Then, net present value is calculated, and it shows the discounted rate of the combined costs and benefits.

The *return on investment (ROI)* is a calculation listed somewhere on the spreadsheet that measures the amount of money an organization receives in return for the money it spends. A high ROI results when benefits far outweigh costs. ROI is determined by finding the total benefits less the costs of the system and dividing that number by the total costs of the system (see Figure 11-6). ROI can be determined per year or for the entire project over a period of time. One drawback of ROI is that it considers only the end points of the investment, not the cash flow in between, so it should not be used as the sole indicator of a project's worth. The spreadsheet in Figure 11-5 shows an ROI figure.

Determining the Break-Even Point If the project team needs to perform a rigorous cost–benefit analysis, it might need to include information about the length of time before the project will break even, or when the returns will match the amount invested in the project. The greater the time it takes to break even, the riskier the project. The *break-even point* is determined by looking at the cash flow over time and identifying the year in which the benefits are larger than the costs (see Figure 11-5). Then, the difference between the yearly and

Calculation	Definition	Formula
Present Value (PV)	The amount of an investment today compared to that same amount in the future, taking into account inflation and time.	$\dfrac{\text{Amount}}{(1+\text{interest rate})^{n}}$ $n = $ number of years in future
Net Present Value (NPV)	The present value of benefit less the present value of costs.	PV Benefits − PV Costs
Return on Investment (ROI)	The amount of revenues or cost savings results from a given investment.	$\dfrac{\text{Total benefits} - \text{Total costs}}{\text{Total costs}}$
Break-Even Point	The point in time at which the costs of the project equal the value it has delivered.	$\dfrac{\text{Yearly NPV* } - \text{ Cumulative NPV}}{\text{Yearly NPV*}}$

* Use the Yearly NPV amount from the first year in which the project has a positive cash flow.
Add the above amount to the year in which the project has a positive cash flow.

FIGURE 11-6 Financial Calculations Used for Cost–Benefit Analysis

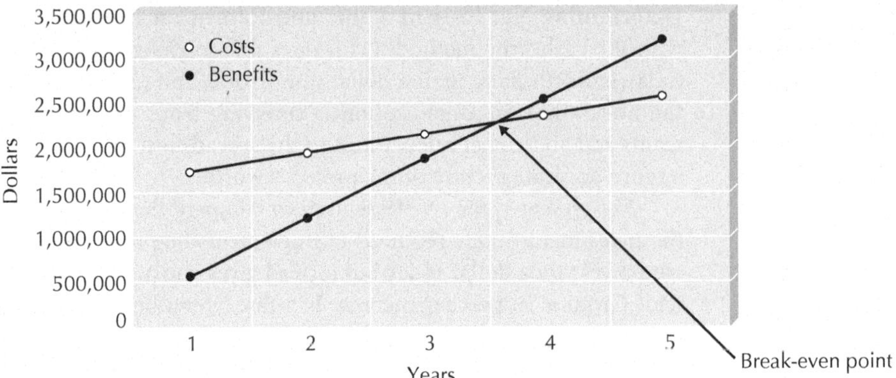

FIGURE 11-7
Break-Even Graph

cumulative NPV for that year is divided by the yearly NPV to determine how far into the year the break-even point will occur. See Figure 11-6 for the break-even calculation. The break-even point also can be depicted graphically, as shown in Figure 11-7. The cumulative present value of the costs and benefits for each year is plotted on a line graph; the point at which the lines cross is the break-even point.

Organizational Feasibility

The final type of feasibility analysis is to assess the *organizational feasibility* of the system, how well the system ultimately will be accepted by its users and incorporated into the ongoing operations of the organization. There are many organizational factors that can influence the project, and seasoned developers know that organizational feasibility can be the most difficult feasibility dimension to assess. In essence, an organizational feasibility analysis attempts to answer the question, If we build it, will they come?

One way to assess the organizational feasibility of the project is to understand how well the goals of the project align with business objectives. *Strategic alignment* is the fit between the project and business strategy—the greater the alignment, the less risky the project will be from an organizational feasibility perspective. For example, if the marketing department has decided to become more customer focused, then a CRM project that produces integrated customer information would have strong strategic alignment with marketing's goal. Many IT projects fail when the IT department initiates them, because there is little or no alignment with business unit or organizational strategies. It's best to partner with business customers for IT projects.

A second way to assess organizational feasibility is to conduct a *stakeholder analysis*.[3] A stakeholder is a person, group, or organization that can affect (or will be affected by) a new system. In general, the most important stakeholders in the introduction of a new system are the project champion, system users, and organizational management (see Figure 11-8), but systems sometimes affect other stakeholders as well. For example, the IS department can be a stakeholder of a system because IS jobs or roles may be changed significantly after its implementation.

The *champion* is a high-level, non–information systems executive who is usually the project sponsor who created the system request. The champion supports the project with time, resources (e.g., money), and political support within the organization by communicating the importance of the system to other organizational decision makers. More than one champion is preferable because if the champion leaves the organization, the support could leave as well.

---

[3] A good book that presents a series of stakeholder analysis techniques is R. O. Mason and I. I. Mittroff, *Challenging Strategic Planning Assumptions: Theory, Cases, and Techniques* (New York: Wiley, 1981).

	Role	Techniques for Improvement
Champion	A champion: • Initiates the project • Promotes the project • Allocates his or her time to project • Provides resources	• Make a presentation about the objectives of the project and the proposed benefits to those executives who will benefit directly from the system. • Create a prototype of the system to demonstrate its potential value.
Organizational Management	Organizational managers: • Know about the project • Budget enough money for the project • Encourage users to accept and use the system	• Make a presentation to management about the objectives of the project and the proposed benefits. • Market the benefits of the system using memos and organizational newsletters. • Encourage the champion to talk about the project with his or her peers.
System Users	Users: • Make decisions that influence the project • Perform hands-on activities for the project • Ultimately determine whether the project is successful by using or not using the system	• Assign users official roles on the project team. • Assign users specific tasks to perform with clear deadlines. • Ask for regular feedback from users (e.g., at weekly meetings).

FIGURE 11-8 Some Important Stakeholders for Organizational Feasibility

Whereas champions provide day-to-day support for the system, *organizational management* support conveys to the rest of the organization the belief that the system will make a valuable contribution and that necessary resources will be made available. Ideally, management should encourage people in the organization to use the system and to accept the many changes that the system will likely create.

A third important group of stakeholders are the *system users* who ultimately use the system once it has been installed in the organization. Too often, the project team meets with users at the beginning of a project and then disappears until after the system is created. In this situation, rarely does the final product meet the expectations and needs of those who are supposed to use it because needs change and users become savvier as the project progresses. User participation should be promoted throughout the development process by getting users involved in the development of the system (e.g., performing tasks, providing feedback, and making decisions). From a DevOps approach (see Chapter 1), IT operations personnel are also an important group of stakeholders.

Finally, the feasibility study helps organizations make wiser investments by forcing project teams to consider technical, economic, and organizational factors that can affect their projects. It protects IT professionals from criticism by keeping the business units educated about decisions and positioned as the leaders in the decision-making process. Remember, the feasibility study **should be revised** several times during the project at points where the project team makes critical decisions about the system (e.g., before each iteration of the development process).

PROJECT SELECTION

Once the feasibility analysis has been completed, it is submitted to the approval committee, along with a revised system request. The committee then decides whether to approve the project, decline the project, or table it until additional information is available. At the project level, the committee considers the value of the project by examining the *business need* (found in the system request; see Chapter 2) and the risks of building the system (presented in the feasibility analysis).

<table>
<tr><td>Size</td><td>What is the size? How many people are needed to work on the project?</td></tr>
<tr><td>Cost</td><td>How much will the project cost the organization?</td></tr>
<tr><td>Purpose</td><td>What is the purpose of the project? Is it meant to improve the technical infrastructure? Support a current business strategy? Improve operations? Demonstrate a new innovation?</td></tr>
<tr><td>Length</td><td>How long will the project take before completion? How much time will go by before value is delivered to the business?</td></tr>
<tr><td>Risk</td><td>How likely is it that the project will succeed or fail?</td></tr>
<tr><td>Scope</td><td>How much of the organization is affected by the system? A department? A division? The entire corporation?</td></tr>
<tr><td>Return on investment</td><td>How much money does the organization expect to receive in return for the amount the project costs?</td></tr>
</table>

FIGURE 11-9
Ways to Classify
Projects

Before approving the project, however, the committee also considers the project from an organizational perspective; it must keep in mind the company's entire portfolio of projects. This way of managing projects is called *portfolio management*. Portfolio management takes into consideration the different kinds of projects that exist in an organization—large and small, high risk and low risk, strategic and tactical. (See Figure 11-9 for the different ways of classifying projects.) A good project portfolio has the most appropriate mix of projects for the organization's needs. The committee acts as portfolio manager with the goal of maximizing the cost–benefit performance and other important factors of the projects in their portfolio. For example, an organization might want to keep high-risk projects to less than 20 percent of its total project portfolio.

The approval committee must be selective about where to allocate resources. This involves *trade-offs* in which the organization must give up something in return for something else to keep its portfolio well balanced. If there are three potentially high-payoff projects, yet all have very high risk, then perhaps only one of the projects will be selected. Also, there are times when a system at the project level makes good business sense, but it does not make sense at the organization level. Thus, a project may show a very strong ROI and support important business needs for a part of the company, but it is not selected. This could happen for many reasons—because there is no money in the budget for another system, the organization is about to go through some kind of change (e.g., a merger), projects that meet the same business requirements already are under way, or the system does not align well with the current or future corporate strategy.

Ethical Considerations[4]

One final organizational consideration that the approval committee must consider today before approving the project is the societal and humanitarian impact of the project. In other words, what is the ethical responsibility of the organization and development team for the deployment of the proposed project? Even though there are many information systems issues that have an ethical component to them, e.g., hacking, whistleblowing, privacy, computer crime, software piracy loss of employment, and viruses, in this section, we only describe a few

[4] For more information see M. David Ermann and Michele S. Shauf, *Computers, Ethics, and Society, Third Edition* (Oxford, UK: Oxford University Press, 2003); Tom Forester and Perry Morrison, *Computer Ethics: Cautionary Tales and Ethical Dilemmas in Computing* (Cambridge, MA: MIT Press, 1990); Enid Mumford, *Systems Design: Ethical Tools for Ethical Change* (London, UK: 1996); George Reynolds, *Ethics in Information Technology, Second Edition* (Boston, MA: Thomson Course Technology, 2007).

issues that are related to the development of a system. These issues include deskilling of the workforce, employee monitoring, technostress, and the health effects of IT.

One of the typical justifications for the development of an information system has always been the potential cost savings and employee productivity improvement. However, from an ethical perspective this implies two things. First, in an economic upturn, the use of IT can make the current employees more productive, hence not requiring the expansion of the workforce. But, in an economic downturn, it implies replacing human employees with IT capital. In other words, potentially firing current employees. Second, it is possible using an IT system to cause the *deskilling of the workforce*. This is especially true with the use of AI-based systems. The upside of this is that the workforce will be less expensive. However, the downside of this is the potential increase of employee stress, boredom, and fatigue which can lead to a decrease in employee job satisfaction and motivation. This can actually cause employee productivity to decrease.

When considering the potential downsides of deskilling and replacing employees, there could be a need to increase *employee monitoring*. Using IT to monitor employees can be both a positive and a negative. Supporters of IT-based monitoring suggest that it can provide a cheap, practical, and accurate set of measures as to employee performance. This is true if the measures being used are actually measuring what they purport to measure. However, in the past, this has not always been the case.[5] Consequently, much care must be taken when developing or implementing monitoring systems. This also include systems that could be used to monitor employees such as Microsoft Teams. In the past, some research has shown that employee monitoring improves productivity. However, recent studies have shown that employee monitoring can increase job stress and decrease trust which can lower in employee job satisfaction, motivation, and productivity. Furthermore, employee monitoring has been shown to decrease the quality of the work product.

The use of IT-based systems can increase so-called *technostress*. Much of technostress is caused by the grown of the expectations that employees must meet. For example, telework has provided benefits to both employees and employers. However, it also has increased the expectation that employees are available 24/7. Research has shown that some employees are disconnecting for downtime would place them at a competitive disadvantage in the workforce. This is especially true in the service industries. Obviously, this type of expectation can increase employee stress which again can decrease employee job satisfaction, motivation, and productivity. Another example includes the expectation of multitasking. Even though cognitively speaking, humans can not actually focus their attention on multiple things at a time, the expectation is there. Consequently, employees are expected to constantly switch their attention among the multiple streams of information that they monitor. This not only includes monitoring multiple "open" windows on a desktop, for example, in a dashboard, but also having to monitor multiple information sources across multiple devices.

Another unforeseen consequence of *IT health effects* on people. Sitting at a desk and staring at a computer screen all day has been shown to cause health problems. Some of the health problems associated with the use of IT includes eye strain, carpal tunnel syndrome, headaches, neck problems, backaches, sleep deprivation, and fatigue. All of these can drive down employee job satisfaction, motivation, and productivity. Obviously, this is the exact opposite of what organizations desire.

---

[5] For example, IT project managers used to count the number of lines of code implemented by a programmer per day and used it as a surrogate for measuring the quality of the programmer. However, any serious programmer realized very quickly that there were a number of ways in which a required function could be implemented. In many cases, the more lines of code written, the less efficient the function would be. Consequently, this productivity type of measure actually encouraged poor code to be written.

Finally, only considering economic, organizational, and technical feasibility issues are no longer sufficient to determine whether an IT project should be approved or not. In today's world, the above ethical considerations also need to be addressed.

Green IT[6] Given all the computing power being deployed to solve today's business problems, Green IT has become an important ethical consideration. This is especially relevant when considering cloud-based solutions (see Chapter 10) and given the amount of energy that many AI applications require.[7] *Green IT* is a broad term that encompasses virtually anything that helps reduce the environmental impact of IT. Some of the topics included are e-waste, greening data centers, and the dream of the paperless office.

First, when it comes to disposing old electronic devices, care must be taken. Old computers contain very toxic material, including lead, PCBs, mercury, and cadmium. One of the major Green IT issues is how to dispose of this *e-waste*. One of the most disturbing trends in dealing with e-waste is the shipping of the e-waste from the developed world to the developing world where environmental standards can be lower. Owing to "backyard recycling" techniques used in these locations, the toxic material contained in the e-waste shows up in the soil, water, and air. Alternatives to simply dumping old computers into the trash include extending the replacement cycles of the machines by converting the machines from Windows-based machines to Linux-based machines. Linux takes less "horsepower" to run than Windows. Therefore, for certain applications, a Linux-based desktop is more than sufficient to implement parts of the application architecture layer.

Second, large data centers use as much electricity in a day as a small city. Consequently, given this level of power consumption, creating *green data centers* in the future will be crucial. There are a whole set of ways to create a green data center. One way is to pay very close attention to where the data center is to be located. Placing the data center in the shade of a mountain or tall building will reduce the cost of energy required. For example, HP placed one of its data centers in northeast England so that it could be cooled by the cold winds that blow onto shore from the North Sea.[8] Looking into alternative energy possibilities is another way to deal with energy consumption. Even more effective is to locate data centers in cold climates. For example, Google has been in the business of buying wind farms to generate the power for its data centers, and HP has shown how a cow manure-based methane power plant could be created to generate the power to run a data center in dairy country.[9]

The third way to consider making your IT infrastructure greener is to consider the cloud (see Chapter 10). With the cloud's virtualization capabilities, the number of high-powered servers and desktops can be reduced. However, you will need to perform some trade-offs between the obstacles of moving to the cloud and the move toward a greener IT. The fourth way to address the power demands for a modern IT infrastructure is by only purchasing Energy Star compliant electronics. The fifth way is to encourage employees to have their machines go to "sleep" to save energy when the machines have been idle for some period of time.

The *paperless office* idea has been around for a very long time. However, up until now, the idea has been more fantasy than reality. Today, with the advent of multiuse tablets, such

[6] Caril Baroudi, Jeffrey Hill, Arnold Reinhold, and Jhana Senxian, *Green IT for Dummies*[TM] (Hoboken, NJ: Wiley, 2009).

[7] James Vincent, "How much electricity does AI consume?" *The Verge* (February 16, 2024) Retrieved March 27, 2024 from www.theverge.com/24066646/ai-electricity-energy-watts-generative-consumption.

[8] Andrew Nusca, "Smart Takes: HP Opens First Wind-Cooled Green Data Center; Most Efficient to Date," *SMARTPLANET* (February 11, 2010). Retrieved August 2014 from www.smartplanet.com/blog/smart-takes/hp-opens-first-wind-cooled-green-data-center-most-efficient-to-date.

[9] Google Data Centers, *Renewable Energy*. Retrieved August 2014 from www.google.com/about/datacenters/renewable.

as Apple's iPad™, the paperless office is becoming a reality. When considering the cloud and the apps available on the iPad™, it is possible not only to create a paperless office but also to have the paperless office effectively be a portable office.

STAFFING THE PROJECT

Staffing the project includes determining how many people should be assigned to the project, matching people's skills with the needs of the project, motivating them to meet the project's objectives, and minimizing the conflict that will occur over time. The deliverables for this part of project management are a staffing plan, which describes the number and kinds of people who will work on the project, the overall reporting structure, and the project charter, which describes the project's objectives and rules.

One of the rules of systems development is that the more developers who are involved in a project, the longer the system will take to build. This is because as the size of the team increases, the need for coordination increases exponentially, and the more coordination required, the less time developers can spend developing the system. The best size is the smallest possible team. When projects are so complex that they require a large team, the best strategy is to try to break the project into a series of smaller parts that can function as independently as possible.[10] However, before describing the development of a staffing plan, we describe Tuckman's stages of small group development, a set of characteristics of jelled teams, how to handle team conflict, motivating factors, and, given a multicultural world of systems development, a set of cultural issues that should be addressed.

Tuckman's Stages of Small Group Development[11]

Agile developers in particular (discussed in Chapter 13) have embraced Tuckman's stages of small group development. The stages include forming, storming, norming, performing, and adjourning. In this section, we describe each of the stages.

As the name implies, the *forming stage* deals with the startup characteristics that a new team possess. These include members getting to know one another by questioning one another, acting very independent, only being self-motivated, and to some degree attempting to focus on identifying the objectives and purpose of the group.

The *storming stage* sees members attempting to "flex their muscles" in an attempt to demonstrate their individual worth to the group. This stage includes lots of potential for resistance among the group members that can increase the conflict that is natural in a new team. However, as they begin to know one another, group members begin developing group norms and expectations.

As the group evolves into the *norming stage*, the characteristics of the group moves much more toward becoming a team. The group members become much more engaged with one another, anxiety of being in a group begins to subside, members begin to support one another, members become much more accepting of other members' behavior, and the group cohesion becomes a real asset for group performance.

[10] One of the best books on managing programming (even though it was first written more than 30 years ago) is that by Frederick P. Brooks, Jr. *The Mythical Man-Month*, 20th Anniversary Edition (Reading, MA: Addison-Wesley, 1995).

[11] The material in the section is based on, Bruce W. Tuckman "Development Sequence in Small Groups," *Psychological Bulletin* 63, no. 6, (1965): 384–99; Bruce W. Tuckman and Mary Ann C. Jensen, "Stages of Small-Group Development Revisited," *Group & Organization Studies,* 2, no. 4 (December 1977): 419–27; Denise A. Bonebright, "40 years of storming: a historical review of Tuckman's model of small group development," *Human Resource Development International* 13, no. 1 (February 2010): 111–20.

The *performing stage* is the stage that the group becomes a team and not simply a loose connection of individuals working together. The idea of an independent contractor mentality is replaced by an interdependence that supports group decision-making, group problem-solving, and group-learning. This stage is most associated with the idea of a "jelled team" (see next section).

The *adjourning stage* is the stage that the team enters once the project has been completed. During this stage a review is typically completed that recognizes both the individual and team effort that was required to complete the project. If the group attained a jelled team status, members of the team will actually be sad that the team is being disbanded.

Characteristics of a Jelled Team[12]

The idea of a jelled team has existed for a long time. Most (if not all) student groups are **not** representative of the idea of a jelled team, and you may have never had the opportunity to appreciate the effectiveness of a true team. In fact, DeMarco and Lister point out that teams are not created; they are grown. Typically, in class projects, students are assigned or asked to form a group, which makes the ability to grow a team very limited. However, growing development teams is crucial in information systems development. The whole set of agile software development approaches hinges on growing jelled teams.

According to DeMarco and Lister,[13] "[a] *jelled team* is a group of people so strongly knit that the whole is greater than the sum of the parts. The production of such a team is greater than that of the same people working in unjelled form." They go on to state that a jelled "team can become almost unstoppable, a juggernaut for success." When is the last time that you worked with a group on a class project that could be described "a juggernaut for success"? Demarco and Lister identify five characteristics of a jelled team.

First, jelled teams have a very low turnover during a project. Typically, members of a jelled team feel a responsibility to the other team members. This responsibility is felt so intensely that for a member to leave the team, the member would feel that they were letting the team down and that they were breaking a bond of trust.

Second, jelled teams have a strong sense of identity. In many classes, when you are part of a group, the group chooses some cute name to identify the group and differentiate it from the other groups. However, in this case, it is not simply the choosing of a name. It is instead evolving every member into something that only exists within the team. This can be seen when members of the team tend to do non–work-related activities together, e.g., do lunch together as a team or form a basketball team composed of only members of the development team.

Third, the strong sense of identity tends to lead the team into feeling a sense of eliteness. The members of a jelled development team almost have a swagger about the way they relate to nonteam employees. Good examples that come to mind that possess this sense of eliteness outside of the scope of information systems development teams are certain sports teams, U.S. Navy Seal teams, or big city police force SWAT teams. In all three examples, each team member is highly competent in his or her specialty area, and each other team member knows (not thinks) that he or she can depend on the team members performing his or her individual jobs with a very high-level of skill.

Fourth, during the development process, jelled teams feel that the team owns the information system being developed and not any one individual member. In many ways, you could almost say that jelled teams are a little communistic in nature. By this we mean that

---

12 The material in the section is based on T. DeMarco and T. Lister, *Peopleware: Productive Projects and Teams*, 2nd Ed. (New York: Dorset House, 1999); P. Lencioni, *The Five Dysfunctions of a Team: A Leadership Fable* (San Francisco: Jossey-Bass, 2002).

13 T. DeMarco and T. Lister, *Peopleware: Productive Projects and Teams*, 2nd Ed., p. 123.

the individual contributions to the effort are not important to a true team. The only thing that matters is the output of the team. However, this is not to imply that a member who does not deliver his or her fair share will not go unpunished. In a jelled team, any member who is not producing is breaking his or her bond of trust with the other team members (see the first characteristic).

The final characteristic of a jelled team is that team members really enjoy (have fun) doing their work. The members actually like to go to work and be with their team members. Much of this can be attributed to the level of challenge they receive. If the project is challenging and the members of the team are going to learn something from completing the project, the members of a jelled team will enjoy tackling the project.

When a team jells, they will avoid the five dysfunctions of a team defined by Lencioni. Lack of trust is the primary cause of a team becoming dysfunctional. Lencioni describes four other causes of a team becoming dysfunctional that can come from the lack of trust. First, dysfunctional teams fear conflict, whereas members of a jelled team never fear conflict.[14] Going to a member of a jelled team and admitting that you do not know how to do something is no big deal. In fact, it provides a method for the team member to help out, which would increase the level of trust between the two members. Second, dysfunctional teams do not have a commitment to the team from the individual members. Instead, they tend to focus on their individual performance instead of the team's performance. This can even be to the detriment of the development team. Obviously, this is not an issue for jelled teams. Third, dysfunctional teams try to avoid accountability. With jelled teams, accountability is not an issue. Members of a jelled team feel a high level of responsibility to the other team members. No team member ever wants to let down the team. Furthermore, owing to the bond that holds jelled teams together, no member has any problem with holding other members accountable for their performance (or lack of performance). Fourth, dysfunctional teams do not pay attention to the team's results. Again, in this case, the cause of this dysfunction is that the individual members only focus on their individual goals. From a team management perspective, the team leader should focus on getting the goals of the team aligned; a jelled team will attain the goals.

Handling Conflict

Before a team is jelled, staffing the project in a manner to minimize conflict among group members is paramount. *Group cohesiveness* (the attraction that members feel to the group and to other members) contributes more to productivity than do project members' individual capabilities or experiences.[15] Clearly defining the roles on the project and holding team members accountable for their tasks are a good way to begin mitigating potential conflict on a project. Some project managers develop a *project charter,* which lists the project's norms and ground rules. For example, the charter may describe when the project team should be at work, when staff meetings will be held, how the group will communicate with each other, and what are the procedures for updating the workplan as tasks are completed. Figure 11-10 lists additional techniques that can be used at the start of a project to keep conflict to a minimum.

Motivation Factors

Assigning people to tasks isn't enough; project managers need to motivate the people to ensure a project's success. *Motivation* has been found to be the number one influence on

---

[14] When conflict occurs, it is necessary to address it in an effective manner.

[15] B. Lakhanpal, "Understanding the Factors Influencing the Performance of Software Development Groups: An Exploratory Group-Level Analysis," *Information and Software Technology* 35, no. 8 (1993): 468–473.

- Clearly define plans for the project.
- Make sure that the team understands how the project is important to the organization.
- Develop detailed operating procedures and communicate these to the team members.
- Develop a project charter.
- Develop schedule commitments ahead of time.
- Forecast other priorities and their possible impact on the project.

Source: H. J. Thamhain and D. L.Wilemon, "Conflict Management in Project Life Cycles," *Sloan Management Review* (Spring 1975).

FIGURE 11-10
Conflict-Avoidance
Strategies

people's performance,[16] but determining how to motivate the team can be quite difficult. You might think that good project managers motivate their staff by rewarding them with money and bonuses, but most project managers agree that this is the last thing that should be done. The more often managers reward team members with money, the more they expect it—and most times monetary motivation won't work. Furthermore, Couger and Zawacki found that information systems developers had a high need to be able to personally grow in their profession which would lead to a high level of internal motivations, a high level of quality performance, and a low level of absenteeism.[17] To attain these goals, Pink[18] has suggested a set of principles to follow to motivate individuals in twenty-first century firms. In this section, we adapt his suggestions to information systems development teams.

Pink suggests considering using some form of the 20 percent time rule to motivate individuals. This rule suggests that 20 percent of an employee's time should be spent on some idea in which he or she believes. The project does not have to be related to the project at hand. On the surface, this sounds like a colossal waste of time, but this idea should not be discarded. Google's Gmail and Google News were developed using the 20 percent time rule. If 20 percent sounds too high, Pink suggests that you consider 10 percent to begin with.

He recommends that firms should be willing to fund small "Now That" awards. These awards are given as small signs of appreciation for doing a great job. However, these awards are not given by a manager to an employee but from an employee to a peer of the employee. The awards are monetary, but they are very small, typically $50. As such, they really are not relevant from a monetary perspective. However, they are very relevant because they are given by one of the employee's colleagues to show that some action that the employee did was appreciated.

Pink endorses the idea of applying Robert Reich's (President's Clinton's Secretary of Labor) pronoun test. If an employee (or team member) refers to the firm (the team) as "they," then there is the real possibility that the employee feels disengaged or possibly alienated. On the other hand, when employees refer to the firm as "we," they obviously feel like they are part of the organization. From a team perspective, this could be an indication that the team has begun to jell.

Pink suggests that management should periodically consider giving each employee a day on which he or she can work on anything he or she wants. In some ways, this is related to the 20 percent rule. It does not necessarily require one day a week (20 percent), but it does require some deliverable. The deliverable can be a new utility program that could be used by lots of

---

[16] Barry W. *Boehm, Software Engineering Economics* (Englewood Cliffs, NJ: Prentice Hall, 1981). One of the best books on managing project teams is that by Tom DeMarco and Timothy Lister, *Peopleware: Productive Projects and Teams* (New York: Dorset House, 1987).

[17] J. Daniel Cougar and Robert A Zawacki, *Motivating and Managing Computer Personnel,* (New York, NY: John Wiley & Sons, 1980).

[18] D. H. Pink, *Drive: The Surprising Truth About What Motivates Us* (New York, NY: Riverhead Books, 2009).

different projects, it could be a new prototype of a new software product, or it could be an improvement for a business process that is used internally. The goal is to provide team members with the ability to focus on interesting and challenging problems that might (or might not) provide results to the firm's bottom line. Regardless, it demonstrates an amount of trust and respect that the firm has for its employees.

He recommends that managers remove the issue of compensation from the motivation equation. By this, he means that all employees should be paid a sufficient amount so that compensation awards are not an issue. Technical employees on project teams are much more motivated by recognition, achievement, the work itself, responsibility, advancement, and the chance to learn new skills.[19] Simplistic financial awards, such as raises that are perceived as being unjust, can actually demotivate the overall team and lower overall performance.

He advocates that twenty-first century bosses (team leaders) need to be willing to give up control. Many of the agile development approaches make similar suggestions. Appelo[20] suggests that an open-door policy that is supported by a team leader actually can be self-defeating. In the case of software development teams, an open-door policy implies that the team leader has a door that can be left open, whereas the poor individual team member does not have an office with a door. In this case, Appelo suggests that the team leader move from the office with a door to the same shared space in which the team resides. One of Pink's other ideas is for the team leader to not use controlling language such as telling the team member that he or she "must" do something. Instead, the team leader should ask the team member to "consider" or "think about" the idea. In some ways, a true team leader should never receive credit for any ideas associated with the team. Instead, a team leader should make suggestions and encourage the team members to consider ideas and, most importantly, let the team member and the team receive the credit.

Pink provides evidence that intrinsic motivation is very important for twenty-first century knowledge workers. Pink suggests that intrinsically motivating individuals requires providing them with a degree of autonomy, supporting them in such a way that they can master their area of expertise, and encouraging them to pursue projects with a purpose. Providing team members with autonomy relates to the jelled team concept of trust. Team leaders need to trust the team members to deliver the software for which they are responsible. Supporting team members so that they can master their area of expertise can be as simple as providing support to attend conferences, seminars, and training sessions that deal with the member's area of expertise. It also could imply providing the team member with a high-end development environment. For example, when building information visualization and virtual reality applications, special hardware and software environments can make it much easier to master the technology to develop the application. Finally, today it is very important for team members to feel that what they are doing can make a difference. A team leader should encourage the team members to tackle problems that can impact people's lives. This can easily be accomplished through the use of the 20 percent rule.

Cultural Issues

One of the major issues facing information systems development organizations is the offshoring of the implementation aspects of information systems development. Conflicts caused by different national and organizational cultures are now becoming a real area of concern. With

---

[19] F. H. Hertzberg, "One More Time: How Do You Motivate Employees?" *Harvard Business Review* (January–February 1968).

[20] J. Appelo, *Management 3.0: Leading Agile Developers, Developing Agile Leaders* (Upper Saddle River, NJ: Addison-Wesley, 2011).

the potential of cloud computing (see Chapter 10) potentially enabling even more outsourcing, the potential of cultural conflict is even greater.

A simple example that can demonstrate cultural differences with regard to student learning is the idea of plagiarism. What exactly does plagiarism really imply? Different cultures have very different views. In some cultures, one of the highest forms of respect is simply to quote an expert. However, in these same cultures, there is no need to reference the expert. The act of quoting the expert itself is the act of respect. In some cases, actually referencing the expert through the use of quotation marks and a footnote may be viewed as an insult to the expert and the reader because it is obvious to the reader that the writer did not expect the reader to recognize the expert's quote. This expectation was caused by either the reader's own ignorance or the expert's lack of reputation. Either way, the writer would be insulting someone through the use of quotation marks and footnotes. These cultures tend to be collectivist in nature (see Chapter 9). Consequently, since the collective owns all ideas, there is no concept of theft of ideas. However, in the United States, the opposite is true. If a writer does not use quotation marks and footnotes to appropriately give credit to the source of the quote (or paraphrase), then the writer is guilty of theft.[21] Even self-plagiarism can be considered inappropriate. Obviously, in today's global world, plagiarism is not a simple issue.

Another simple example of cultural differences, regarding student learning, is the idea of students working together to complete homework assignments. Even though we all know that research has shown that students learn better in groups, in the United States, we view students who turn in the same assignment as cheaters.[22] In other cultures, individual performance is not as important as the performance of the group. Again, these cultures are collectivist in nature. Consequently, helping a fellow student to understand the assignment and to perform better in the class would be the expectation. Furthermore, this attitude extends to test taking. If a fellow student is struggling on a test and if you were from a collectivist culture, it would be your duty to allow your fellow student to copy your answer. Obviously, this is another example of a substantive cultural difference. From a business perspective, these different views of plagiarism and cheating could have serious implications for the protection of intellectual property.

As we stated previously, with offshore outsourcing, information systems development teams can be geographically dispersed and multicultural in their membership. Given the above issues and when we consider the cultural differences Hall and Hofstede identified (see Chapter 9), cultural issues add a new wrinkle in the management of developing a successful information system.[23] From an information systems development perspective, *context* could influence the ability of a team member to see (or not see) potential creative solutions that are out of the box or affect a team member's ability (or inability) to understand the entire problem under consideration. Furthermore, given this dimension, the level of detail in direction could be varied between cultures. Hofstede's *individualism* and *collectivism* dimension partially explains the results regarding plagiarism and cheating described above. Given the importance that intellectual property plays in IT, this potentially could be a real problem when offshoring development to a collectivist culture. Furthermore, Hall's *speed of messages* and context dimensions could also affect the way this could be addressed. Depending on the culture, too

---

[21] A wonderful little book on plagiarism is Richard A Posner, *The Little Book of Plagiarism* (New York: Pantheon Books, 2007).

[22] In this case, the recent work of Roger Schank is very enlightening. For example see, Roger C. Schank, *Making Minds Less Well Educated than Our Own* (Mahwah, NJ: Lawrence Erlbaum Associates, 2004).

[23] See Geert Hofstede, *Culture's Consequences: Comparing Values, Behaviors, Institutions and Organizations across Nations,* 2nd Ed. (Thousand Oaks, CA: Sage, 2001); Geert Hofstede, Gert Jan Hofstede, and Michael Minkov, *Cultures and Organizations: Software of the Mind,* 3rd Ed. (New York, NY: McGraw-Hill, 2010); Edward T. Hall, *Beyond Culture* (New York: Anchor Books, 1981).

much detail could be insulting, but attempting to put this issue into a contextual frame that is culturally sensitive is difficult.

When managing programmers in a multicultural setting, Hall's time dimension must also be considered. In *monochronic time* cultures, deadlines are critical. This is probably why *time-boxing* has been relatively successful as a method to control projects. However, in a *polychronic time* culture, a *deadline* is nothing more than a suggestion. Obviously, when managing programmers, understanding how the culture considers time is very important to have both a successful product delivery and a successful development process.

Hofstede's other previously mentioned dimensions are *power distance*, *uncertainty avoidance*, and *masculinity versus femininity*. Managing programmers in a culture with a high power distance value is different than with a culture with a low power distance. For example, in the United States, programmers see themselves as equals to their managers. In fact, in some firms, the president of the firm can be found "coding" solutions alongside a brand-new hire. This somewhat explains the growing popularity of agile methods (see Chapter 13). In comparison, in a high power distance culture, the president of the firm would never stoop to performing the same tasks as a new hire. It would be insulting to the president and embarrassing to the new hire.

Regarding uncertainty avoidance, the choice of systems development approach could be affected. In a culture that prefers everything to be neat and ordered, a systems development methodology that is very rule-driven would be beneficial. Also, development team member professional certification and team and firm ISO or CMMI certifications would lend credibility to the team, whereas in a culture that willingly takes on risk, certifications might not increase the perceived standing of the development team.

When managing programmers in a masculine culture, it is critical to provide recognition to the top-performing members of the development team and to recognize the top-performing teams. On the other hand, when considering a feminine culture, it is more important to ensure that the workplace is a supportive, noncompetitive, and nurturing environment.

Hofstede has identified a fifth dimension, *long*-versus *short-term orientation*, which deals with how the culture views the past and the future. In a long-term focused culture, team development and a deep relationship with a client is very important, while in a culture that emphasizes the short term, delivering a high-quality product on time is all that really matters.

For years, project managers in the United States have had to bring together individuals from very different backgrounds. Moreover, there was always a common spoken and written language, English, and the melting pot idea that guaranteed some level of commonality among the team members.[24] However, in today's "flat world," there is no longer any common culture or common spoken and written language. From an information systems development perspective, the common languages tend to be UML, Java, SQL, C++, Objective-C, and Visual Basic, not English. However, at this time, there is no common culture. Consequently, understanding cultural issues will be extremely important for the near future to successfully manage international and multicultural development teams.

Staffing Plan

Taking the above into consideration, a project manager must determine the average number of staff needed for the project. To calculate this figure, divide the total person-months of effort by the optimal schedule. So, to complete a forty-person-month project in ten months, a team

---

[24] People who grew up in different areas of the United States (e.g., New York City, Nashville, Minneapolis, Denver, and Los Angeles) are, in a very real sense, culturally different. For an interesting take on this, see Joel Garreau, *The Nine Nations of North America* (New York NY: Avon Books, 1981). However, the prevalence of the Internet and cable TV has created much more of a shared culture in the United States than in many other parts of the world. Obviously, the Internet and cable TV also could affect the world in the long run.

should have an average of four full-time staff members, although the specific staff may change over time as different specialists enter and leave the team (e.g., business analysts, programmers, and technical writers).

Many times, the temptation is to assign more staff to a project to shorten the project's length, but this is not a wise move. Adding staff resources does not translate into increased productivity; staff size and productivity share a disproportionate relationship, mainly because it is more difficult to coordinate a large number of staff members. The more a team grows, the more difficult it becomes to manage. Imagine how easy it is to work on a two-person project team: The team members share a single line of communication. But adding two people increases the number of communication lines to six, and greater increases lead to more dramatic gains in communication complexity. Figure 11-11 illustrates the impact of adding team members to a project team.

One way to reduce efficiency losses on teams is to understand the complexity that is created in numbers and to build a *reporting structure* that tempers its effects. The general rule is to keep team sizes to fewer than eight to ten people; therefore, if more people are

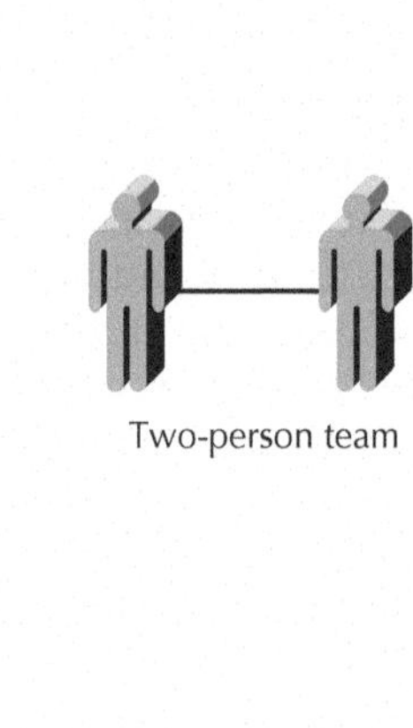

Two-person team

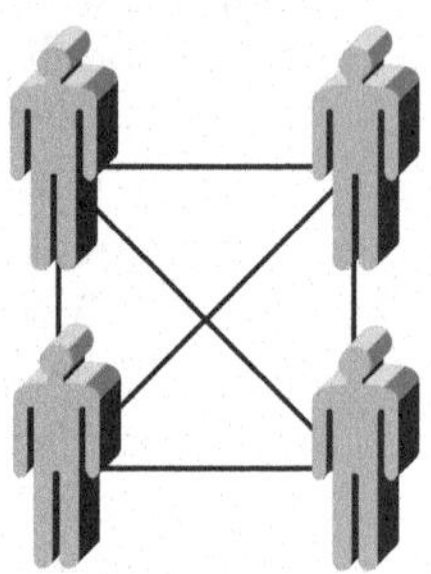

Four-person team

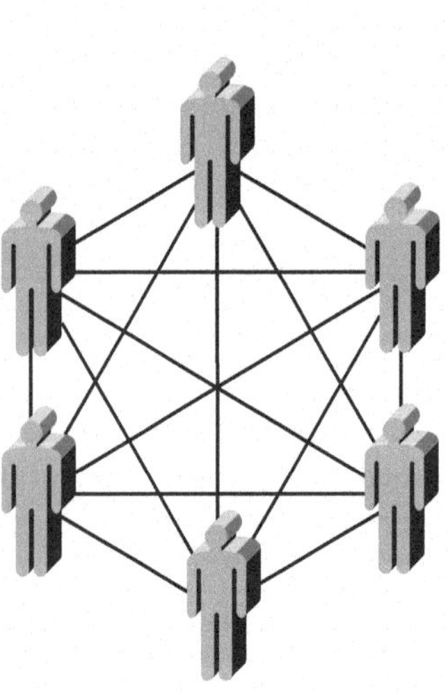

Six-person team

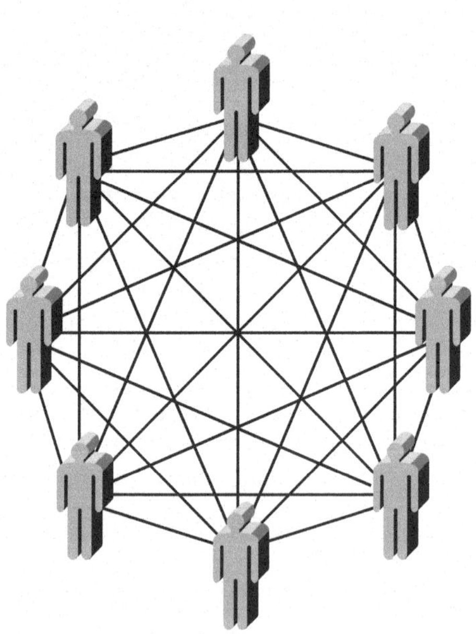

Eight-person team

FIGURE 11-11
Increasing Complexity with Larger Teams

needed, create sub-teams. In this way, the project manager can keep the communication effective within small teams, which, in turn, communicate to a contact at a higher level in the project.

After the project manager understands how many people are needed for the project, he or she creates a *staffing plan* that lists the roles and the proposed reporting structure that are required for the project. Typically, a project has one project manager who oversees the overall progress of the development effort, with the core of the team comprising the various types of analysts described in Chapter 1. A *functional lead* is usually assigned to manage a group of analysts, and a *technical lead* oversees the progress of a group of programmers and more technical staff members.

There are many structures for project teams; Figure 11-12 illustrates one possible configuration of a project team. After the roles are defined and the structure is in place, the project manager needs to think about which people can fill each role. Often, one person fills more than one role on a project team.

When you make assignments, remember that people have *technical skills* and *interpersonal skills*, and both are important a project. Technical skills are useful when working with technical tasks (e.g., programming in Python) and in trying to understand the various roles that technology plays in the particular project (e.g., how a Web server should be configured on the basis of a projected number of hits from customers). Interpersonal skills, on the other hand, include interpersonal and communication abilities that are used when dealing with business users, senior management executives, and other members of the project team. They are particularly critical when performing the requirements-gathering activities and when addressing organizational feasibility issues. Each project requires unique technical and interpersonal skills.

Ideally, project roles are filled with people who have the right skills for the job. However, the people who fit the roles best might not be available; they may be working on other projects, or they might not exist in the company. Therefore, assigning project team members really is a combination of finding people with the appropriate skill sets and finding people who are available. When the skills of the available project team members do not match what is actually required by the project, the project manager has several options to improve the situation. First, people can be pulled off other projects, and resources can be shuffled around. This is the most disruptive approach from the organization's perspective. Another approach is to use outside help—such as a consultant or contractor—to train team members and start

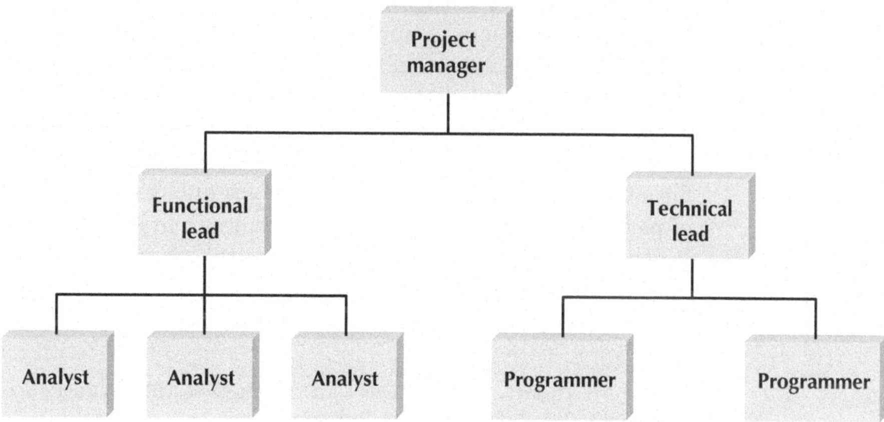

FIGURE 11-12
Possible Reporting Structure

them off on the right foot. Mentoring may also be an option; a project team member can be sent to work on another similar project so that he or she can return with skills to apply to the current job.

MEETING MANAGEMENT[25]

Possibly the most dreaded aspect of any job is the requirement to attend meetings. In general, many participants consider meetings to be a colossal waste of time. In fact, some research suggests that 60% of meeting participants tend to work on other things during meetings and nearly 50% of the participants would rather do any other unpleasant activity to avoid attending the meetings. This is especially true when it comes to information systems development team meetings. However, in other research, only 7% of meeting participants considered meetings to be unproductive. Based on these divergent results and given the amount of time (money) spent in meetings, project managers must be very effective and efficient in managing meetings. Below we provide a set of recommendations for holding successful, productive meetings.

First, meeting leadership must become an organizational priority. This requires taking meeting management seriously by periodically evaluating meeting leaders as to their effectiveness.

Second, meetings should have an agenda. However, the existence of an agenda is not going to guarantee effective meetings. Effective meetings have a purpose and are focused on only a few goals. Each stated goal must be doable in the allotted time. And should be assigned to a participant who is responsible for meeting the goal. One possible meeting agenda/reporting form is portrayed in Figure 11-13.

Third, the length of meetings should be minimized. Even though on the surface it may make sense to have a longer meeting with more goals, longer meetings tend to be less focused and consequently, less effective. Furthermore, do not schedule meetings using a standard amount of time. Only schedule the meeting for the amount of time necessary. For example, if a meeting is only going to have 20 minutes of work to be accomplished, do not schedule it for 30 minutes; schedule it for 20 minutes. Otherwise, the extra 10 minutes will be filled with nonproductive work. This is a waste of resources.

Fourth, only participants that can help reach the goals of the meeting should be invited to participate. Having too many meeting participants can lead to many distractions, free loading, and multitasking. None of which leads to effective meetings.

Fifth, don't be stuck with the traditional meeting location, sitting around a table. In a conference room. A simple way to vary location is simply to randomly assign seating. Sitting arrangements can affect the effectiveness of a meeting. Two other promising approaches to vary location are the standing and walking meetings. A standing meeting is one in which all participants must stand during the entire meeting. Standing tends to speed things along in a meeting. A walking meeting is one in which the participants go for a walk. Obviously, a walking meeting is only going to be effective for a small number of participants. However, a change of scenery can increase the effectiveness of a meeting. When considering how to organize a meeting, always be cognizant of any physical limitations of the participants.

---

[25] Most of this material is adapted from Steven G. Rogelberg, *The Surprising Science of Meetings: How You Can Lead Your Team to Peak Performance* (New York, NY: Oxford University Press, 2019).

Meeting Agenda/Reporting Form

Group Number/Name: _______________________________   **Location:** _______________________________

Date: _____________________   **Start Time:** _______________   **End Time:** _______________

Attendees: (List the persons attending the meeting—not everyone needs to attend every meeting.)

Purpose: (Overview description)

Agenda: (What are you planning to do in this meeting? Keep it short and focused on the topic)
1. Announcements and any results/updates regarding previous meeting
2. **List Major Goals:**
   - **A.**
   - **B.**
   - **C.**
3. Summarize Meeting Accomplishments

Goal A (Do this for each major goal):
- **a. Description:**

- **b. Responsible Member:** _____________________
- **c. Required preparation before meeting:**
   (List any materials and their location that should be reviewed by participants before the meeting)

- **d. Estimated amount of meeting time to be devoted to this goal:** _____________
- **e. Determine action items:**

What	Who	By When

Accomplishments of Meeting: (A paragraph or two that relates what happened at the meeting—may include lists of key points discussed, decisions made, and deliverables or action items worked. Take notes during the meeting, write the description immediately after the meeting.)

Unresolved Issues: (List the problems and issues that hinder your progress.)

FIGURE 11-13   Sample Meeting Agenda/Reporting Form

IS DEVELOPMENT TEAM MANAGEMENT

Once the project team has been staffed, the project manager must actively coordinate the activities of the development team. Coordination can be done through both high-tech and low-tech means. The simplest approach is to have a weekly project meeting to discuss any changes to the system that have arisen during the past week—or any issues that have come up. Regular meetings, even if they are brief, encourage widespread communication and discussion of issues before they become problems.

The Unified Process supports coordination via the supporting workflows (Chapter 1). In addition to the project management workflow, the Unified Process supports coordination on the environment, infrastructure management, and the configuration and change management workflows. We describe these workflows in Chapter 12. Finally, the project manager must manage the schedule, the scope, and the amount and type of risk that the project faces.

Managing the Schedule

The estimates that are produced during inception need to be refined as the project progresses. This does not mean that estimates were poorly done at the start of the project; rather, it is virtually impossible to develop an exact assessment of the project's schedule at the beginning of the development process. When a system is first requested, the project sponsor and manager attempt to predict how long the development process will take, how much it will cost, and what it will ultimately do when it is delivered (i.e., its functionality). However, the estimates are based on very little knowledge of the system. Therefore, the project manager should expect to be satisfied with broad ranges of estimates that become more and more specific as the project's product becomes better defined. That is, as the system moves into elaboration, more information is gathered, the system concept is developed, and the estimates become even more accurate and precise. As the system moves closer to completion, the accuracy and precision increase, until it is delivered. Consequently, it is critical that the time estimates be revised as construction of the system proceeds.

According to one of the leading experts in software development,[26] a well-done project plan (prepared at the end of inception) has a 100 percent margin of error for project cost and a 25 percent margin of error for schedule time. In other words, if a carefully done project plan estimates that a project will cost $100,000 and take twenty weeks, the project will actually cost between $0 and $200,000 and take between fifteen and twenty-five weeks.

A common cause for this problem is the unnoticed day-by-day slippages in the schedule. One package is a day late here; another one is a day late there. Pretty soon these minor delays add up and the project is noticeably behind schedule. Once again, the key to managing the programming effort is to watch these minor slippages carefully and update the schedule accordingly. So, what happens if you overshoot an estimate (e.g., analysis ends up lasting two weeks longer than expected)? There are a number of ways to adjust future estimates. If the project team finishes a step ahead of schedule, most project managers shift the deadlines sooner by the same amount but do not adjust the promised completion date. The challenge, however, occurs when the project team is late in meeting a scheduled date. Three possible responses to missed schedule dates are presented in Figure 11-14. If, early in the project, an estimate proves to be too optimistic, planners should not expect to make up for lost time—very few projects end up doing this. Instead, they should change future estimates to include an increase similar to the one that was experienced. For example, if the first phase was completed 10 percent over schedule, planners should increase the rest of their estimates by 10 percent.

Managing Scope

An analyst may assume that a project will be safe from scheduling problems because he or she carefully estimated and planned the project up front. However, the most common reason for schedule and cost overruns—*scope creep*—occurs after the project is under way. Scope creep happens when new requirements are added to the project after the original project scope was finalized. Scope creep can be very expensive because changes made late in system development

---

[26] Barry W. Boehm et al., "Cost Models for Future Software Life Cycle Processes: COCOMO 2.0," in J. D. Arthur and S. M. Henry (eds.), *Annals of Software Engineering: Special Volume on Software Process and Product Measurement* (Amsterdam: J. C. Baltzer AG Science Publishers, 1995).

Assumptions	Actions	Level of Risk
If you assume the rest of the project is simpler than the part that was late and is also simpler than believed when the original schedule estimates were made, you can make up lost time.	Do not change schedule.	High risk
If you assume the rest of the project is simpler than the part that was late and is no more complex than the original estimate assumed, you can't make up the lost time, but you will not lose time on the rest of the project.	Increase the entire schedule by the total amount of time that you are behind (e.g., if you missed the scheduled date by two weeks, move the rest of the schedule dates to two weeks later). If you included padded time at the end of the project in the original schedule, you might not have to change the promised system delivery date; you'll just use up the padded time.	Moderate risk
If you assume that the rest of the project is as complex as the part that was late (your original estimates were too optimistic), then all the scheduled dates in the future underestimate the real time required by the same percentage as the part that was late.	Increase the entire schedule by the percentage of weeks that you are behind (e.g., if you are two weeks late on part of the project that was supposed to take eight weeks, you need to increase all remaining time estimates by 25 percent). If this moves the new delivery date beyond what is acceptable to the project sponsor, the scope of the project must be reduced.	Low risk

FIGURE 11-14
Possible Actions When a Schedule Date Is Missed

can require much of the completed system design (and even programs already written) to be redone. It can happen for many reasons: Users might suddenly understand the potential of the new system and realize new functionality that would be useful; developers might discover interesting capabilities to which they become very attached; a senior manager might decide to let this system support a new strategy that was developed at a recent board meeting. Regardless, any proposed change during construction must require the approval of the project manager and should only be done after a quick cost–benefit analysis has been done.

Fortunately, using an iterative and incremental development process allows the team to deal with changing requirements in an effective way. However, the more extensive the change becomes, the greater the impact on cost and schedule. The keys are to identify the requirements as well as possible in the beginning of the project and to apply analysis techniques effectively. For example, if needs are fuzzy at the project's onset, a combination of intensive meetings with the users and prototyping would allow users to "experience" the requirements and better visualize how the system could support their needs.

Of course, some requirements may be missed no matter what precautions are taken. However, the project manager should allow only absolutely necessary requirements to be added after the project begins. Even at that point, members of the project team should carefully assess the ramifications of the addition and present the assessment to the users. Any change that is implemented should be carefully tracked so that an audit trail exists to measure the change's impact.

Sometimes changes cannot be incorporated into the present system even though they truly would be beneficial. In this case, these additions should be recorded as future enhancements to the system. The project manager can offer to provide functionality in future releases of the system, thus getting around telling someone "no."

Another approach to scope management is a technique called *timeboxing*. Up until now, we have described task-oriented projects. In other words, we have described projects that have a schedule driven by the tasks that need to be accomplished, so the greater number of tasks and requirements, the longer the project will take. Some companies have little patience for development projects that take a long time, and these companies take a time-oriented approach that places meeting a deadline above delivering functionality.

Think about the use of word processing software. For 80 percent of the time, only 20 percent of the features, such as the spelling checker, boldfacing, and cutting and pasting, are used. Other features, such as document merging and creating mailing labels, may be nice to have, but they might not be a part of day-to-day needs for a large number of users. The same goes for other software applications; most users rely on only a small subset of their capabilities. Ironically, most developers agree that typically 75 percent of a system can be provided relatively quickly, with the remaining 25 percent of the functionality demanding most of the time.

To resolve this incongruency, the technique of timeboxing has become quite popular. This technique sets a fixed deadline for a project and delivers the system by that deadline no matter what, even if functionality needs to be reduced. Timeboxing ensures that project teams don't get hung up on the final finishing touches that can drag out indefinitely, and it satisfies the business by providing a product within a relatively short time frame.

Several steps are involved in implementing timeboxing on a project. First, set the date of delivery for the proposed goals. The deadline should not be impossible to meet, so it is best to let the project team determine a realistic due date. Next, build the core of the system to be delivered; you will find that timeboxing helps create a sense of urgency and helps keep the focus on the most important features. Because the schedule is absolutely fixed, functionality that cannot be completed needs to be postponed. It helps if the team prioritizes a list of features beforehand to keep track of what functionality the users absolutely need. Quality cannot be compromised, regardless of other constraints, so it is important that the time allocated to activities is not shortened unless the requirements are changed (e.g., don't reduce the time allocated to testing without reducing features). At the end of the time period, a high-quality system is delivered, but it is likely that future iterations will be needed to make changes and enhancements. In that case, the timeboxing approach can be used once again.

Managing Risk

One final facet of team management is *risk management*, the process of assessing and addressing the risks that are associated with developing a project. As the construction step moves to a close, the list of risks changes as some items are removed and others surface. The best project managers, however, work hard to keep risks from having an impact on the schedule and costs associated with the project. Many things can cause risks: weak personnel, scope creep, poor design, and overly optimistic estimates. The project team must be aware of potential risks so that problems can be avoided or controlled well ahead of time.

Typically, project teams create a *risk assessment*, or a document that tracks potential risks along with an evaluation of the likelihood of each risk and its potential impact on the project (Figure 11-15). A paragraph or two is also included to explain potential ways that the risk can be addressed. There are many options: The risk could be publicized, avoided, or even eliminated by dealing with its root cause. For example, imagine that a project team plans to use new technology, but its members have identified a risk in the fact that its members do not have the right technical skills. They believe that tasks may take much longer to perform because of a high learning curve. One plan of attack could be to eliminate the root cause of the risk—the lack of technical experience by team members—by finding the time and resources needed to provide proper training to the team.

Most project managers keep abreast of potential risks, even prioritizing them according to their magnitude and importance. Over time, the list of risks will change as some items are removed and others surface. The best project managers, however, work hard to keep risks from having an impact on the schedule and costs associated with the project.

<table>
<tr><td colspan="2" align="center">Risk Assessment</td></tr>
<tr><td>RISK 1:</td><td>The development of this system likely will be slowed considerably because project team members have not programmed in Java prior to this project.</td></tr>
<tr><td>Likelihood of risk:</td><td>High probability of risk.</td></tr>
<tr><td>Potential impact on the project:</td><td>This risk will probably increase the time to complete programming tasks by 50 percent.</td></tr>
<tr><td colspan="2">Ways to address this risk:</td></tr>
<tr><td colspan="2">It is very important that time and resources are allocated to up-front training in Java for the programmers who are used for this project. Adequate training will reduce the initial learning curve for Java when programming begins. Additionally, outside Java expertise should be brought in for at least some part of the early programming tasks. This person should be used to provide experiential knowledge to the project team so that Java-related issues (of which novice Java programmers would be unaware) are overcome.</td></tr>
<tr><td>RISK 2:</td><td align="center">. . .</td></tr>
</table>

FIGURE 11-15
Sample Risk Assessment

PROJECT ASSESSMENT

The goal of *project assessment* is to understand what was successful about the system and the project activities (and, therefore, should be continued in the next system or project) and what needs to be improved. Project assessment is not routine in most organizations, except for military organizations, which are accustomed to preparing *after-action reports*. The purpose of an after-action report is to simply provide an objective, rational description of everything that happened, good and bad, during an operation. Nonetheless, assessment can be an important component in organizational learning because it helps organizations and people understand how to improve their work. It is particularly important for junior staff members because it helps promote faster learning. There are two primary parts to project assessment—project team review and system review.

Project Team Review

A *project team review* focuses on the way the project team carried out its activities. Each project member prepares a short two- to three-page document that reports and analyzes his or her performance. The focus is on performance improvement, not penalties for mistakes made. By explicitly identifying mistakes and understanding their causes, project team members will, it is hoped, be better prepared for the next time they encounter a similar situation—and less likely to repeat the same mistakes. This is especially true when something fails, e.g., the team misses a deadline, the system fails tests, or the system blows up while in production. This type of review has become known as *blameless post-mortems*. Likewise, by identifying excellent performance, team members will be able to understand why their actions worked well and how to repeat them in future projects. By supporting blameless post-mortems, the system development organization supports a *just culture*. A just culture, according to Dekker, is one that supports the idea of *psychological safety* where a team member knows that it is safe to admit to mistakes. In this way, the organization can learn about different mistakes and hopefully be able to avoid them in the future.[27] From a motivation perspective (see Chapter 2),

---

[27] See Sidney Dekker, *Just Culture: Balancing Safety and accountability,* 2nd Ed. (Surrey, UK: Ashgate Publishing, 2012); Sidney Dekker, *The Field Guide to Understanding "Human Error,"* 3rd Ed. (Boca Raton, FL: CRC Press, 2014); Gene Kim, Jez Humble, Patrick Debois, John Willis, *The DevOps Handbook: How to Create World-Class Agility, Reliability, & Security in Technology Organizations* (Portland, OR: IT Revolution Press, 2016).

supporting a just culture where the team members feel safe is critical to the development of "jelled" teams. And, having jelled teams is critical to the overall success of the systems development organization.

The project manager, who meets with the team members to help them understand how to improve their performance, assesses the documents prepared by each team member. The project manager then prepares a summary document that outlines the lessons learned from the project. This summary identifies what actions should be taken in future projects to improve performance but is careful not to identify team members who made mistakes, i.e., a blameless post-mortem. The summary should be circulated as widely as possible to increase the potential for other members of the organization to learn from the team's experience. At the least, the summary should be circulated among all project managers to help them understand how to manage their projects better.

System Review

The focus of the *system review* is to understand the extent to which the proposed costs and benefits from the new system identified during feasibility analysis were actually recognized from the implemented system. Project team review is usually conducted immediately after the system is installed while key events are still fresh in team members' minds, but system review is often undertaken several months after the system is installed because it often takes a while before the system can be properly assessed.

System review starts with the system request and feasibility analysis prepared at the start of the project. The detailed analyses prepared for the expected business value (both tangible and intangible) as well as the economic feasibility analysis are reexamined, and a new analysis is prepared after the system has been installed. The objective is to compare the anticipated business value against the actual realized business value from the system. This helps the organization assess whether the system actually provided the value it was planned to provide. Whether or not the system provides the expected value, future projects can benefit from an improved understanding of the true costs and benefits.

A formal system review also has important behavior implications for *project initiation*. Because everyone involved with the project knows that all statements about business value and the financial estimates prepared during project initiation will be evaluated at the end of the project, they have an incentive to be conservative in their assessments. No one wants to be the project sponsor or project manager for a project that goes radically over budget or fails to deliver promised benefits.

TRADITIONAL PROJECT MANAGEMENT TOOLS

Before we get to creating a workplan that is suitable to manage and control an object-oriented systems development project, we need to introduce a set of project management tools that have been used to successfully manage traditional software development projects (and many other types of projects): a work-breakdown structure, a Gantt chart, and a network diagram. To begin with, we must first understand what a task is. A *task* is a unit of work that will be performed by a member or members of the development team, such as feasibility analysis. Each task is described by information such as its name, start and completion dates, person assigned to complete the task, deliverables, completion status, priority, resources needed, estimated time to complete the task, and the actual time it took to complete the task (see Figure 11-16). The first thing a project manager must do is to identify the tasks that need to be accomplished and determine how long each task will take. Tasks and their identification and documentation are the basis of all three of these tools. Once the tasks have been identified

Workplan Information	Example
Name of the task	Perform economic feasibility
Start date	Jan 05, 2026
Completion date	Jan 19, 2026
Person assigned to the task	Project sponsor: Mary Smith
Deliverable(s)	Cost–benefit analysis
Completion status	Open
Priority	High
Resources that are needed	Spreadsheet software
Estimated time	16 hours
Actual time	14.5 hours

FIGURE 11-16
Task Information

and documented, they are organized within a work breakdown structure that is used to drive the creation of Gantt charts and network diagrams that can be used to graphically portray a traditional workplan. These techniques help a project manager understand and manage the project's progress over time.

Work Breakdown Structures

A project manager can use a structured, top-down approach whereby high-level tasks are first defined and then broken down into subtasks. For example, Figure 11-17 shows a list of high-level tasks needed to implement a new IT training class. Some of the main steps in the process include identifying vendors, creating and administering a survey, and building new classrooms. Each step is then broken down in turn and numbered in a hierarchical fashion. There are eight subtasks (i.e., 7.1–7.8) for creating and administering a survey, and there are three subtasks (7.2.1–7.2.3) that make up the review initial survey task. A list of tasks hierarchically numbered in this way is called a *work breakdown structure (WBS)*. The number of tasks and level of detail depend on the complexity and size of the project. At a minimum, the WBS must include the duration of the task, the current status of the task (i.e., open and complete), and the *task dependencies*, which occur when one task cannot be performed until another task is completed. For example, Figure 11-17 shows that incorporating changes to the survey (task 7.4) takes a week to perform, but it cannot occur until after the survey is reviewed (task 7.2) and pilot tested (task 7.3). Key *milestones*, or important dates, are also identified on the workplan.

There are two basic approaches to organizing a traditional WBS: by development phase or by product. For example, if a firm decided that it needed to develop a website, the firm could create a WBS based on the inception, elaboration, construction, and transition phases of the Unified Process. In this case, a typical task that would take place during inception would be feasibility analysis. This task would be broken down into different types of feasibility analysis: technical, economic, and organizational. Each of these would be further broken down into a set of subtasks. Alternatively, the firm could organize the workplan along the lines of the different products to be developed. For example, in the case of a website, the products could include applets, application servers, database servers, the various sets of Web pages to be designed, a site map, and so on. Then these would be further decomposed into the different

Task Number	Task Name	Duration (in weeks)	Dependency	Status
1	Identify vendors	2		Complete
2	Review training materials	6	1	Complete
3	Compare vendors	2	2	In Progress
4	Negotiate with vendors	3	3	Open
5	Develop communications information	4	1	In Progress
6	Disseminate information	2	5	Open
7	Create and administer survey	4	6	Open
7.1	Create initial survey	1		Open
7.2	Review initial survey	1	7.1	Open
7.2.1	Review by Director of IT Training	1		Open
7.2.2	Review by Project Sponsor	1		Open
7.2.3	Review by Representative Trainee	1		Open
7.3	Pilot test initial survey	1	7.1	Open
7.4	Incorporate survey changes	1	7.2, 7.3	Open
7.5	Create distribution list	0.5		Open
7.6	Send survey to distribution list	0.5	7.4, 7.5	Open
7.7	Send follow-up message	0.5	7.6	Open
7.8	Collect completed surveys	1	7.6	Open
8	Analyze results and choose vendor	2	4, 7	Open
9	Build new classrooms	11	1	In Progress
10	Develop course options	3	8, 9	Open

FIGURE 11-17
Work Breakdown Structure

tasks associated with the phases of the development process. Either way, once the overall structure is determined, tasks are identified and included in the WBS. We return to the topic of WBSs and their use in iterative planning later in this chapter.

Gantt Chart

A *Gantt chart* is a horizontal bar chart that shows the same task information as the project WBS but in a graphical way. Sometimes a picture really is worth a thousand words, and the Gantt chart can communicate the high-level status of a project much faster and easier than the WBS. Creating a Gantt chart is simple and can be done using a spreadsheet package, graphics software, or a project management package.

First, tasks are listed as rows in the chart, and time is listed across the top in increments based on the needs of the projects (see Figure 11-18). A short project may be divided into hours or days, whereas a medium-sized project may be represented using weeks or months. Horizontal bars are drawn to represent the duration of each task; the bar's beginning and end mark exactly when the task will begin and end. As people work on tasks, the appropriate bars

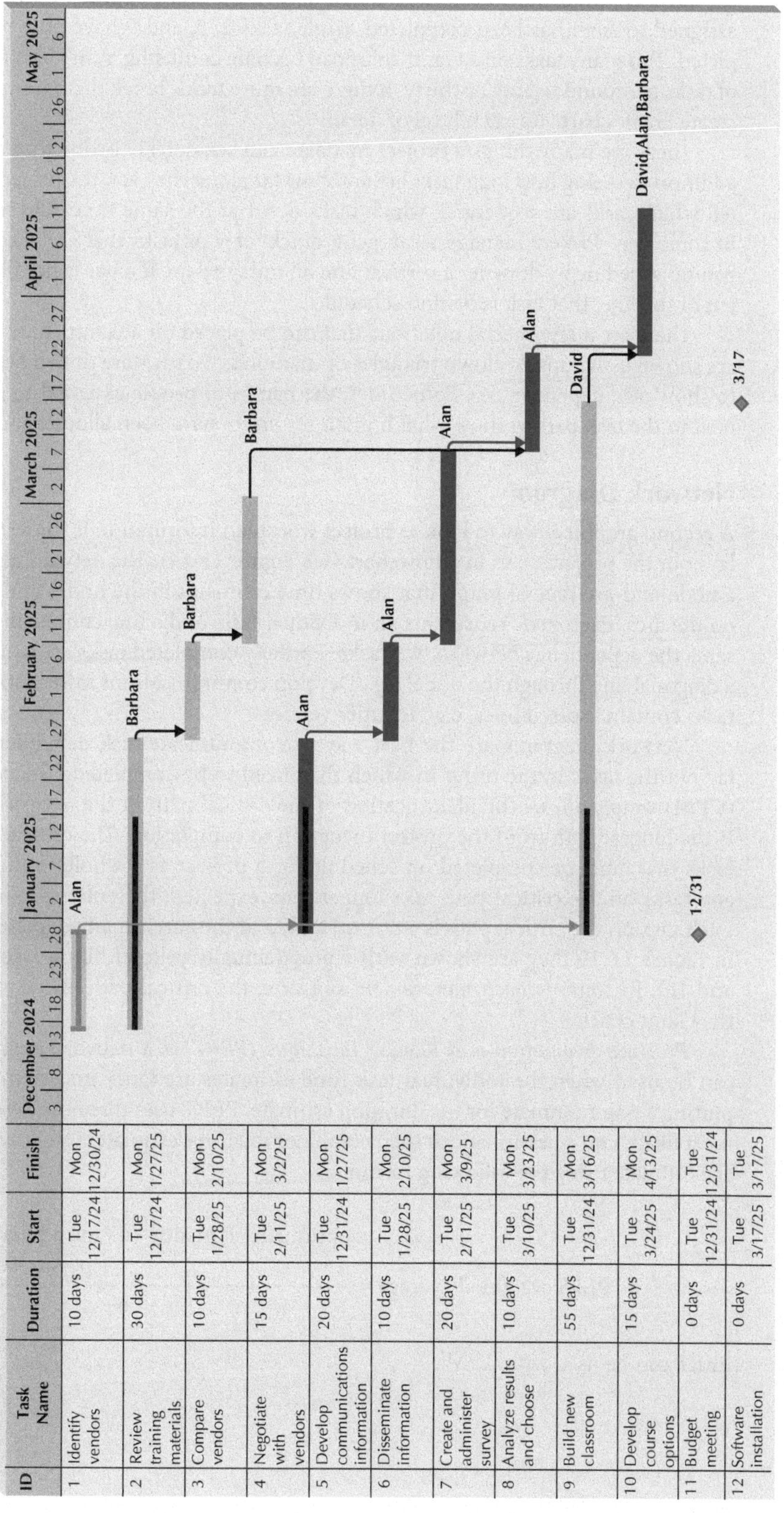

FIGURE 11-18 Gantt Chart

451

are filled in proportionately to how much of the task is finished. For example, task 1 that was assigned to Alan has been completed, while tasks 2, 5, and 9 have only been partially completed. Too many tasks on a Gantt chart can become confusing, so it's best to limit the number of tasks to around twenty or thirty. If there are more tasks, break them down into subtasks and create Gantt charts for each level of detail.

There are many things a project manager can see quickly by looking at a Gantt chart. In addition to seeing how long tasks are and how far along they are, the project manager also can tell which tasks are sequential, which tasks occur at the same time, and which tasks overlap in some way. Project managers can get a quick view of tasks that are ahead of schedule and behind schedule by drawing a vertical line on today's date. If a bar is not filled in and is to the left of the line, that task is behind schedule.

There are a few special notations that can be placed on a Gantt chart. Project milestones are shown using upside-down triangles or diamonds. Arrows are drawn between the task bars to show task dependencies. Sometimes, the names of people assigned to each task are listed next to the task bars to show what human resources have been allocated to the tasks.

Network Diagram

A second graphical way to look at project workplan information is the *network diagram* that lays out the project tasks in a flowchart (see Figure 11-19). The network diagram is drawn as a node-and-arc type of graph that shows time estimates in the nodes and task dependencies on the arcs. Each *node* represents an individual task, and a line connecting two nodes represents the dependency between two tasks. Partially completed tasks are usually displayed with a diagonal line through the node, e.g., Develop communications information, and completed tasks contain crossed lines, e.g., Identify vendors.

Network diagrams are the best way to communicate task dependencies because they lay out the tasks in the order in which they need to be completed. The *critical path method* (CPM) simply allows the identification of the critical path in the network. The critical path is the longest path from the project inception to completion. The critical path shows all the tasks that must be completed on schedule for a project as a whole to finish on schedule. If any tasks on the critical path take longer than expected, the entire project will fall behind. Each task on the critical path is a *critical task*, and they are usually depicted in a unique way; in Figure 11-19 they are shown with a gray (actually yellow) filling (see tasks 1, 5, 6, 7, 8, and 10). In some *project management software*, the critical path also can be highlighted in the Gantt chart.

Program Evaluation and Review Technique (PERT) is a network analysis technique that can be used when the individual task time estimates are fairly uncertain. Instead of simply putting a point estimate for the duration estimate, PERT uses three time estimates: optimistic, most likely, and a pessimistic. It then combines the three estimates into a single weighted average estimate using the following formula:

$$\text{PERT weighted average} = \frac{\text{optimistic estimate} + (4 * \text{most likely estimate}) + \text{pessimistic estimate}}{6}$$

PERT can be used with CPM.

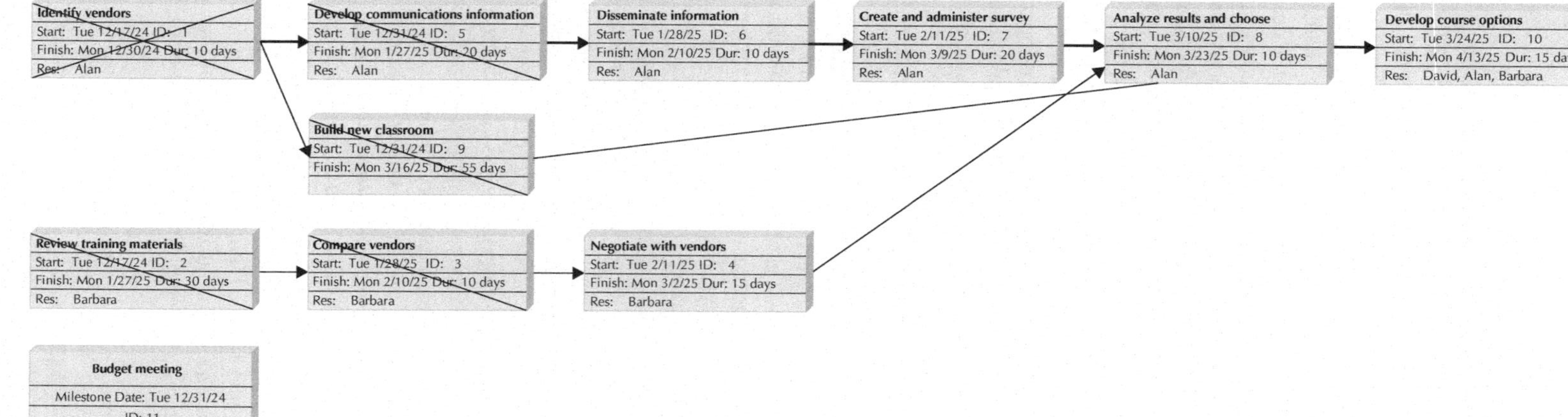

FIGURE 11-19 Network Diagram

PROJECT EFFORT ESTIMATION

The science (or art) of project management is in making *trade-offs* among three important concepts: the functionality of the system, the time to complete the project (when the project will be finished), and the cost of the project. Think of these three things as interdependent levers that the project manager controls throughout the development of the system. Whenever one lever is pulled, the other two levers are affected in some way. For example, if a project manager needs to readjust a deadline to an earlier date, then the only solutions are to decrease the functionality of the system or to increase costs by adding more people or having them work overtime. Often, a project manager has to work with the project sponsor to change the goals of the project, such as developing a system with less functionality or extending the deadline for the final system, so that the project has reasonable goals that can be met. In the beginning of the project, the manager needs to estimate each of these levers and then continuously assess how to roll out the project in a way that meets the organization's needs. *Estimation* is the process of assigning projected values for time and effort. The estimates developed at the start of a project are usually based on a range of possible values and gradually become more specific as the project moves forward. That is, the range of values for the inception phase will be much greater than for the transition phase.

The numbers used to calculate these estimates can be taken from projects with similar tasks and technologies or provided by experienced developers. The numbers should be conservative. A good practice is to keep track of the actual values for time and effort during the development process so that numbers can be refined along the way and the next project can benefit from real data.

There are a variety of ways to estimate the time required to build a system. Because the Unified Process is use-case driven, we use an approach that is based on use cases: use-case points.[28] *Use-case points*, originally developed by Gustav Karner of Objectory AB,[29] are based on unique features of use cases and object orientation. From a practical point of view, to estimate effort using use-case points, the use cases and the use-case diagram must have been created.[30]

Use-case models have two primary constructs: actors and use cases. An *actor* represents a *role* that a user of the system plays, not a specific user. For example, a role could be secretary or manager. Actors can also represent other systems that will interact with the system under development. For use-case point estimation purposes, actors can be classified as simple, average, or complex. *Simple actors* are separate systems with which the current system must communicate through a well-defined *application program interface (API)*. *Average actors* are separate systems that interact with the current system using standard communication protocols, such as TCP/IP, FTP, or HTTP, or an external database that can be accessed using standard SQL. *Complex actors* are typically end users communicating with the system. Once all of the actors have been categorized as being simple, average, or complex, the project manager counts the number of actors in each category and enters the values into the unadjusted actor-weighting table contained in the use-case point–estimation worksheet (see Figure 11-20). The project manager then computes the *Unadjusted Actor Weight Total (UAW)*. This is computed by summing the individual results that were computed by multiplying the weighting factor by the number of actors of each type. For example, if we assume that the use-case diagram has zero simple, zero average, and four complex actors that interact with the system being developed, the UAW will equal 12 (see Figure 11-21).

A *use case* represents a major business process that the system will perform that benefits the actor(s) in some manner. Depending on the number of unique transactions that the use

---

[28] The material in this section is based on descriptions of use-case points contained in Raul R. Reed, Jr., *Developing Applications with Java and UML* (Reading, MA: Addison-Wesley, 2002); Geri Schneider and Jason P. Winters, *Applying Use Cases: A Practical Guide* (Reading, MA: Addison-Wesley, 1998); Kirsten Ribu, "Estimating Object-Oriented Software Projects with Use Cases" (Master's thesis, University of Oslo, 2001).

[29] Objectory AB was acquired by Rational in 1995 and Rational is now part of IBM.

[30] We cover the details of use-case modeling in Chapter 3.

Unadjusted Actor Weighting Table:

Actor Type	Description	Weighting Factor	Number	Result
Simple	External System with well-defined API	1		
Average	External System using a protocol-based interface, e.g., HTTP, TCT/IP, or a database	2		
Complex	Human	3		
		Unadjusted Actor Weight Total (UAW)		

Unadjusted Use-Case Weighting Table:

Use-Case Type	Description	Weighting Factor	Number	Result
Simple	1–3 transactions	5		
Average	4–7 transactions	10		
Complex	>7 transactions	15		
		Unadjusted Use-Case Weight Total (UUCW)		

Unadjusted Use-Case Points (UUCP) = UAW + UUCW

Technical Complexity Factors:

Factor Number	Description	Weight	Assigned Value (0–5)	Weighted Value	Notes
T1	Distributed system	2.0			
T2	Response time or throughput performance objectives	1.0			
T3	End-user online efficiency	1.0			
T4	Complex internal processing	1.0			
T5	Reusability of code	1.0			
T6	Ease of installation	0.5			
T7	Ease of use	0.5			
T8	Portability	2.0			
T9	Ease of change	1.0			
T10	Concurrency	1.0			
T11	Special security objectives included	1.0			
T12	Direct access for third parties	1.0			
T13	Special user training required	1.0			
			Technical Factor Value (TFactor)		

*Technical Complexity Factor (TCF) = 0.6 + (0.01 * TFactor)*

Environmental Factors:

Factor Number	Description	Weight	Assigned Value (0–5)	Weighted Value	Notes
E1	Familiarity with system development process being used	1.5			
E2	Application experience	0.5			
E3	Object-oriented experience	1.0			
E4	Lead analyst capability	0.5			
E5	Motivation	1.0			
E6	Requirements stability	2.0			
E7	Part-time staff	−1.0			
E8	Difficulty of programming language	−1.0			
			Environmental Factor Value (EFactor)		

*Environmental Factor (EF) = 1.4 + (−0.03 * EFactor)*

*Adjusted Use-Case Points (UCP) = UUCP * TCF * ECF*

*Effort in Person Hours = UCP * PHM*

FIGURE 11-20 Use-Case Point–Estimation Worksheet

Unadjusted Actor Weighting Table:

Actor Type	Description	Weighting Factor	Number	Result
Simple	External system with well-defined API	1	0	0
Average	External system using a protocol-based interface, e.g., HTTP, TCT/IP, or a database	2	0	0
Complex	Human	3	4	12
		Unadjusted Actor Weight Total (UAW)		**12**

Unadjusted Use-Case Weighting Table:

Use-Case Type	Description	Weighting Factor	Number	Result
Simple	1–3 transactions	5	3	15
Average	4–7 transactions	10	4	40
Complex	>7 transactions	15	1	15
		Unadjusted Use-Case Weight Total (UUCW)		**70**

Unadjusted Use-Case Points (UUCP) = UAW + UUCW   82 = 12 + 70

Technical Complexity Factors:

Factor Number	Description	Weight	Assigned Value (0–5)	Weighted Value	Notes
T1	Distributed system	2.0	0	0	
T2	Response time or throughput performance objectives	1.0	5	5	
T3	End-user online efficiency	1.0	3	3	
T4	Complex internal processing	1.0	1	1	
T5	Reusability of code	1.0	1	1	
T6	Ease of installation	0.5	2	1	
T7	Ease of use	0.5	4	2	
T8	Portability	2.0	0	0	
T9	Ease of change	1.0	2	2	
T10	Concurrency	1.0	0	0	
T11	Special security objectives included	1.0	0	0	
T12	Direct access for third parties	1.0	0	0	
T13	Special user training required	1.0	0	0	
			Technical Factor Value (TFactor)	**15**	

*Technical Complexity Factor (TCF) = 0.6 + (0.01 * TFactor)   0.75 = 0.6 + (0.01 * 15)*

Environmental Factors:

Factor Number	Description	Weight	Assigned Value (0–5)	Weighted Value	Notes
E1	Familiarity with system development process being used	1.5	4	6	
E2	Application experience	0.5	4	2	
E3	Object-oriented experience	1.0	4	4	
E4	Lead analyst capability	0.5	5	2.5	
E5	Motivation	1.0	5	5	
E6	Requirements stability	2.0	5	10	
E7	Part-time staff	−1.0	0	0	
E8	Difficulty of programming language	−1.0	4	−4.0	
			Environmental Factor Value (EFactor)	**25.5**	

*Environmental Factor (EF) = 1.4 + (−0.03 * EFactor)   0.635 = 1.4 + (−0.03 * 25.5)*
*Adjusted Use-Case Points (UCP) = UUCP * TCF * ECF   33.3375 = 70 * 0.75 * 0.635*
*Effort in person-hours = UCP * PHM   666.75 = 20 * 33.3375*

FIGURE 11-21   Use-Case Point Estimation for the Appointment System

case must address, a use case can be categorized as being simple, average, or complex. A use case is classified as *simple* if it supports one to three transactions, as *average* if it supports four to seven transactions, or as *complex* if it supports more than seven transactions. Once all of the use cases have been successfully categorized, the project manager enters the number of each type of use case into the unadjusted use-case weighting table contained in the use-case point–estimation worksheet (see Figure 11-20). By multiplying by the appropriate weights and summing the results, we get the value for the *unadjusted use-case weight total (UUCW)*. For example, if we assume that we have three simple use cases, four average use cases, and one *complex use case*, the value for the unadjusted use-case weight total is 70 (see Figure 11-21). Next, the project manager computes the value of the *unadjusted use-case points (UUCP)* by simply summing the unadjusted actor weight total and the unadjusted use-case weight total. In this case the value of the UUCP equals 82 (see Figure 11-21).

Use-case point-based estimation also has a set of factors that are used to adjust the use-case point value. In this case, there are two sets of factors: *technical complexity factors (TCFs)* and *environmental factors (EFs)*. There are thirteen separate technical factors and eight separate environmental factors. The purpose of these factors is to allow the project to be evaluated for the complexity of the system being developed and the experience levels of the development staff, respectively. Obviously, these types of factors can affect the effort that a team requires to develop a system. Each of these factors is assigned a value between 0 and 5, 0 indicating that the factor is irrelevant to the system under consideration and 5 indicating that the factor is essential for the system to be successful. The assigned values are then multiplied by their respective weights. These weighted values are then summed up to create a *technical factor value (TFactor)* and an *environmental factor value (EFactor)* (see Figure 11-20).

The technical factors include the following (see Figure 11-20):

- Whether the system is going to be a distributed system
- The importance of response time
- The efficiency level of the end user using the system
- The complexity of the internal processing of the system
- The importance of code reuse
- How easy the installation process has to be
- The importance of the ease of using the system
- How important it is for the system to be able to be ported to another platform
- Whether system maintenance is important
- Whether the system is going to have to handle parallel and concurrent processing
- The level of special security required
- The level of system access by third parties
- Whether special end user training is to be required.

Assuming the values for the technical factors are T1 (0), T2 (5), T3 (3), T4 (1), T5 (1), T6 (2), T7 (4), T8 (0), T9 (2), T10 (0), T11 (0), T12 (0), and T13 (0), respectively, the *technical factor value (TFactor)* is computed as the weighted sum of the individual technical factors. In this case TFactor equals 15 (see Figure 11-21). Plugging this value into the *technical complexity factor (TCF)* equation (0.6 + (.01 * TFactor)) of the use-case point worksheet gives a value of .75 for the TCF of the system (see Figures 11-20 and 11-21).

The environmental factors include the following (see Figure 11-20):

- The level of experience the development staff has with the development process being used
- The application being developed

- The level of object-oriented experience
- The level of capability of the lead analyst
- The level of motivation of the development team to deliver the system
- The stability of the requirements
- Whether part-time staff have to be included as part of the development team
- The difficulty of the programming language being used to implement the system

Assuming the values for the environmental factors were E1 (4), E2 (4), E3 (4), E4 (5), E5 (5), E6 (5), E7 (0), and E8 (4) gives an *environmental factor value (EFactor)* of 25.5 (see Figure 11-20). Like the TFactor, Efactor is simply the sum of the weighted values. Using the *environmental factor (EF)* equation (1.4 + (−0.03 * EFactor)) of the use-case point worksheet produces a value of .635 for the EF of the system (see Figures 11-20 and 11-21). Plugging the TCF and EF values, along with the UUCP value computed earlier, into the adjusted use-case points equation (UUCP * TCF * EF) of the worksheet yields a value of 33.3375 *adjusted use-case points (UCP)* (see Figure 11-21).

Now that we know the estimated size of the system by means of the value of the adjusted use-case points, we are ready to estimate the *effort* required to build the system. In Karner's original work, he suggested simply multiplying the number of use-case points by 20 to estimate the number of person-hours required to build the system. However, based on additional experiences using use-case points, a decision rule to determine the value of the *person-hours multiplier (PHM)* has been created that suggests using either 20 or 28, based on the values assigned to the individual environmental factors. The decision rule is:

If the sum of (number of Efactors E1 through E6 assigned value < 3) and
        (number of Efactors E7 and E8 assigned value > 3)
    ≤ 2
   PHM = 20
Else If the sum of (number of Efactors E1 through E6 assigned value < 3) and
      (number of Efactors E7 and E8 assigned value > 3)
    = 3 or 4
   PHM = 28
Else
   Rethink project; it has too high of a risk for failure

Based on these rules, because none of Efactors E1 through E6 have a value less than 3 and only Efactor E8 has a value greater than 3, the sum of the number EFactors is 1. Thus, the system should use a PHM of 20. Plugging the values for UCP (33.3375) and PHM (20) into the effort equation (UCP * PHM) gives an estimated number of person-hours of 666.75 hours (see Figures 11-20 and 11-21).

CREATING AND MANAGING THE WORKPLAN

Once a project manager has a general idea of the functionality and effort for the project, he or she creates a *workplan*, which is a dynamic schedule that records and keeps track of all the tasks that need to be accomplished over the course of the project. The workplan lists each task, along with important information about it, such as when it needs to be completed, the person assigned to do the work, and any deliverables that will result. The level of detail and the amount of information captured by the workplan depend on the needs of the project, and the detail usually increases as the project progresses.

The overall objectives for the system should be listed on the system request, and it is the project manager's job to identify all the tasks that need to be accomplished to meet those objectives. This sounds like a daunting task. How can someone know everything that needs to be done to build a system that has never been built before?

One approach for identifying tasks is to get a list of tasks that has already been developed and to modify it. There are standard lists of tasks, or methodologies, that are available for use as a starting point. As we stated in Chapter 1, a *methodology* is a formalized approach to implementing a systems development process (i.e., it is a list of steps and deliverables). A project manager can take an existing methodology, select the steps and deliverables that apply to the current project, and add them to the workplan. If an existing methodology is not available within the organization, methodologies can be purchased from consultants or vendors, or books such as this textbook can serve as a guide. Because most organizations have a methodology they use for projects, using an existing methodology is the most popular way to create a workplan. In our case, because we are using a Unified Process-based methodology, we can use the phases, workflows, and iterations as a starting point to create an evolutionary work breakdown structure and an iterative workplan.

Evolutionary Work Breakdown Structures and Iterative Workplans[31]

Because object-oriented systems approach to systems analysis and design support incremental and iterative development, any project planning approach for object-oriented systems development also requires an incremental and iterative process. In the description of the enhanced Unified Process in Chapter 1, the development process was organized around iterations, phases, and workflows. In many ways, a workplan for an incremental and iterative development process is organized in a similar manner. For each iteration, there are different tasks executed on each workflow. This section describes an incremental and iterative process using evolutionary WBSs for project planning that can be used with object-oriented systems development.

Evolutionary WBSs allow the analyst to develop an *iterative workplan*. First, evolutionary WBSs are organized in a standard manner across all projects: by workflows, phases, and then the specific tasks that are accomplished during an individual iteration. Second, evolutionary WBSs are created in an incremental and iterative manner. This encourages a more realistic view of both cost and schedule estimation. Third, because the structure of an evolutionary WBS is not tied to any specific project, evolutionary WBSs enable the comparison of the current project to earlier projects. This supports learning from past successes and failures.

In the case of the enhanced Unified Process, the workflows are the major points listed in the WBS. Next, each workflow is decomposed along the phases of the enhanced Unified Process. After that, each phase is decomposed along the tasks that are to be completed to create the deliverables associated with an individual iteration contained in each phase (see Figure 1-4). The template for the first two levels of an evolutionary WBS for the enhanced Unified Process would look like Figure 11-22.

As each iteration through the development process is completed, additional iterations and tasks are added to the WBS (i.e., the WBS evolves along with the evolving information system).[32] For example, typical activities for the inception phase of the project management

---

[31] This material in this section is based on Walker Royce, *Software Project Management: A Unified Framework* (Reading, MA: Addison-Wesley, 1998).

[32] Good sources that help explain this approach are Phillippe Krutchen, "Planning an Iterative Project," *The Rational Edge* (October 2002); Eric Lopes Cordoza and D. J. de Villiers, "Project Planning Best Practices," *The Rational Edge* (August 2003).

I. Business Modeling
   a. Inception
   b. Elaboration
   c. Construction
   d. Transition
   b. Production

II. Requirements
   a. Inception
   b. Elaboration
   c. Construction
   d. Transition
   e. Production

III. Analysis
   a. Inception
   b. Elaboration
   c. Construction
   d. Transition
   e. Production

IV. Design
   a. Inception
   b. Elaboration
   c. Construction
   d. Transition
   e. Production

V. Implementation
   a. Inception
   b. Elaboration
   c. Construction
   d. Transition
   e. Production

VI. Test
   a. Inception
   b. Elaboration
   c. Construction
   d. Transition
   e. Production

VII. Deployment
   a. Inception
   b. Elaboration
   c. Construction
   d. Transition
   e. Production

VIII. Configuration and Change Management
   a. Inception
   b. Elaboration
   c. Construction
   d. Transition
   e. Production

IX. Project Management
   a. Inception
   b. Elaboration
   c. Construction
   d. Transition
   e. Production

X. Environment
   a. Inception
   b. Elaboration
   c. Construction
   d. Transition
   e. Production

XI. Operations and Support
   a. Inception
   b. Elaboration
   c. Construction
   d. Transition
   e. Production

XII. Infrastructure Management
   a. Inception
   b. Elaboration
   c. Construction
   d. Transition
   e. Production

FIGURE 11-22
Evolutionary WBS Template for the Enhanced Unified Process

workflow would include identifying the project, performing the feasibility analysis, selecting the project, and estimating the effort. The inception phase of the requirements workflow would include determining the requirements gathering and analysis techniques, identifying functional and nonfunctional requirements, interviewing stakeholders, developing a vision document, and developing use cases. Typically no tasks are associated with the inception phase of the operations and support workflow. A sample evolutionary WBS for planning the inception phase of the enhanced Unified Process, based on Figures 1-4 and 11-22, is shown in Figure 11-23. Notice the last two tasks for the project management workflow are "create workplan for first iteration of the elaboration phase" and "assess the inception phase"; the last two things to do are to plan for the next iteration in the development of the evolving system and to assess the current iteration. As the project moves through later phases, each workflow has tasks added to its iterations. For example, the analysis workflow will have the creation of the functional, structural, and behavioral models during the elaboration phase. Finally, when an iteration includes a lot of complex tasks, traditional tools, such as Gantt charts and network diagrams, can be used to detail the workplan for that specific iteration.

	Duration	Dependency
I. Business Modeling		
a. Inception		
1. Understand current business situation	0.50 days	
2. Uncover business process problems	0.25 days	
3. Identify potential projects	0.25 days	
b. Elaboration		
c. Construction		
d. Transition		
e. Production		
II. Requirements		
a. Inception		
1. Identify appropriate requirements analysis technique	0.25 days	
2. Identify appropriate requirements gathering techniques	0.25 days	
3. Identify functional and nonfunctional requirements		II.a.1, II.a.2
A. Schedule Interview and Observation sessions	3 days	
B. Perform document analysis	5 days	II.a.3.A
C. Conduct interviews		II.a.3.A
1. Interview project sponsor	0.5 days	
2. Interview inventory system contact	0.5 days	
3. Interview special order system contact	0.5 days	
4. Interview ISP contact	0.5 days	
5. Interview CD Selection Web contact	0.5 days	
6. Interview other personnel	1 day	
D. Observe retail store processes	0.5 days	II.a.3.A
4. Analyze current systems	4 days	II.a.1, II.a.2
5. Create requirements definition		II.a.3, II.a.4
A. Determine requirements to track	1 day	
B. Compile requirements as they are elicited	5 days	II.a.5.A
C. Review requirements with sponsor	2 days	II.a.5.B
b. Elaboration		
c. Construction		
d. Transition		
e. Production		
III. Analysis		
a. Inception		
1. Identify business processes	3 days	
2. Identify use cases	3 days	III.a.1
b. Elaboration		
c. Construction		
d. Transition		
e. Production		
IV. Design		
a. Inception		
1. Identify potential classes	3 days	III.a
b. Elaboration		
c. Construction		
d. Transition		
e. Production		

FIGURE 11-23
Evolutionary WBS for a Single Iteration-Based Inception Phase

	Duration	Dependency

V. Implementation
  a. Inception
  b. Elaboration
  c. Construction
  d. Transition
  e. Production

VI. Test
  a. Inception
  b. Flaboration
  c. Construction
  d. Transition
  e. Production

VII. Deployment
  a. Inception
  b. Elaboration
  c. Construction
  d. Transition
  e. Production

VIII. Configuration and Change Management
  a. Inception
    1. Identify necessary access controls for developed artifacts. — 0.25 days
    2. Identify version control mechanisms for developed artifacts. — 0.25 days
  b. Elaboration
  c. Construction
  d. Transition
  e. Production

IX. Project Management
  a. Inception
    1. Create workplan for the inception phase. — 1 day
    2. Create system request. — 1 day
    3. Perform feasibility analysis — IX.a.2
      A. Perform technical feasibility analysis — 1 day
      B. Perform economic feasibility analysis — 2 days
      C. Perform organizational feasibility analysis — 2 days
    4. Identify project effort. — 0.50 days — IX.a.3
    5. Identify staffing requirements. — 0.50 days — IX.a.4
    6. Compute cost estimate. — 0.50 days — IX.a.5
    7. Create workplan for first iteration of the elaboration phase. — 1 day — IX.a.1
    8. Assess inception phase. — 1 day — I.a, II.a, III.a IV.a, V.a, VI.a VII.a, VIII.a, IX.a, X.a, XI.a XII.a

  b. Elaboration
  c. Construction
  d. Transition
  e. Production

FIGURE 11-23
Continued

	Duration	Dependency
X. Environment		
a. Inception		
1. Acquire and install CASE tool.	0.25 days	
2. Acquire and install programming environment.	0.25 days	
3. Acquire and install configuration and change management tools.	0.25 days	
4. Acquire and install project management tools.	0.25 days	
b. Elaboration		
c. Construction		
d. Transition		
e. Production		
XI. Operations and Support		
a. Inception		
b. Elaboration		
c. Construction		
d. Transition		
e. Production		
XII. Infrastructure Management		
a. Inception		
1. Identify appropriate standards and enterprise models.	0.25 days	
2. Identify reuse opportunities, such as patterns, frameworks, and libraries.	0.50 days	
3. Identify similar past projects.	0.25 days	
b. Elaboration		
c. Construction		
d. Transition		
e. Production		

FIGURE 11-23
Continued

CHAPTER REVIEW

After reading and studying this chapter, you should be able to:

- ☐ Discuss the purpose of the feasibility study.
- ☐ Describe the issues that are considered when evaluating a project's technical feasibility.
- ☐ Develop an economic feasibility assessment for a project.
- ☐ Understand and evaluate the organizational feasibility of a project.
- ☐ Explain how projects are selected.
- ☐ Describe the Tuckman stages of small group development.
- ☐ Describe the characteristics of a "jelled" team.
- ☐ Describe cultural issues as they are related to intellectual property.
- ☐ Describe how Hall's and Hofstede's cultural dimensions can affect the adoption of an information system.
- ☐ Describe the recommendations for holding effective meetings.

☐ Describe issues relating to motivating software developers.
☐ Describe how iterative and incremental development using timeboxing addresses scope management.
☐ Describe a task.
☐ Create a standard work breakdown structure, a Gantt Chart, and a Network Diagram.
☐ Perform PERT analysis and identify the critical path.
☐ Estimate the system development effort using use-case points.
☐ Create an evolutionary work breakdown structure.

KEY TERMS

Actor
Adjourning stage
Adjusted use-case points (UCP)
After-action report
Application program interface (API)
Approval committee
Average actors
Average use case
Blameless post-mortems
Break-even point
Business need
Business requirement
Business value
Cash-flow method
Champion
Collectivism
Compatibility
Complex actors
Complex use case
Context
Cost–benefit analysis
Critical path method
Critical task
Deskilling of the workforce
Development costs
Economic feasibility
Effort
Emerging technology
Employee monitoring
Environmental factor (EF)
Environmental factor value (EFactor)
Estimation

Evolutionary WBS
Familiarity with the functional area
Familiarity with the technology
Feasibility analysis
Feasibility study
Femininity
First mover
Forming stage
Functional lead
Functionality
Gantt chart
Group cohesiveness
Individualism
Intangible benefits
Intangible costs
Intangible value
Iterative workplan
Institutionalization
Interpersonal skills
IT health effects
Just culture
Long-term orientation
Masculinity
Methodology
Milestone
Monochronic time
Motivation
Net present value (NPV)
Network Diagram
Node
Norming stage
Operational costs
Organizational feasibility

Organizational management
Performing stage
Person-hours multiplier (PHM)
Program evaluation and review technique (PERT)
Polychronic time
Portfolio management
Power distance
Project
Project assessment
Project charter
Project initiation
Project management
Project management software
Project manager
Project size
Project sponsor
Project team review
Psychological safety
Reporting structure
Return on investment (ROI)
Risk assessment
Risk management
Risks
Scope creep
Short-term orientation
Simple actors
Simple use case
Special issues
Speed of messages
Staffing plan
Stakeholder
Stakeholder analysis
Storming stage

Strategic alignment
System request
System review
System users
Tangible benefits
Tangible value
Task
Task dependency
Technical complexity factor (TCF)
Technical factor value (TFactor)
Technical feasibility
Technical lead
Technical risk analysis
Technical skills
Technostress
Timeboxing
Trade-offs
Unadjusted actor weight total (UAW)
Unadjusted use-case points (UUCP)
Unadjusted use-case weight total (UUCW)
Uncertainty avoidance
Use case
Use-case points
Work breakdown structure (WBS)
Workplan

QUESTIONS

1. What is the purpose of an approval committee? Who is usually on this committee?
2. What is the difference between intangible value and tangible value? Give three examples of each.
3. What are the purposes of the feasibility analysis? How is it used in the project selection process?
4. Describe the three techniques for feasibility analysis.
5. Describe a risky project in terms of technical feasibility. Describe a project that would *not* be considered risky.
6. What are the steps for assessing economic feasibility? Describe each step.
7. List two intangible benefits. Describe how these benefits can be quantified.
8. List two tangible benefits and two operational costs for a system. How would you determine the values that should be assigned to each item?
9. Explain the net present value and return on investment for a cost–benefit analysis. Why would these calculations be used?
10. What is the break-even point for the project? How is it calculated?
11. What is stakeholder analysis? Discuss three stakeholders that would be relevant for most projects.
12. Why do many projects end up having unreasonable deadlines? How should a project manager react to unreasonable demands?
13. What are the trade-offs that project managers must manage?
14. Describe Tuckman's five stages of small group development.
15. Define the five characteristics of a jelled team.
16. List three techniques to reduce conflict.
17. How can different national or organizational cultures affect the management of an information systems development project?
18. What are the best ways to motivate a team? What are the worst ways?
19. When offshoring development, how could differences in Hall's context dimension of culture affect the contribution of a team member to the successful development of an information system? What about Hall's time or speed of messages dimensions?
20. What are Hofstede's five dimensions of cultural differences? How could differences in them influence the effectiveness of an information systems development team?
21. Describe the differences between a technical lead and a functional lead. How are they similar?
22. Describe three technical skills and three interpersonal skills that are very important to have on any project.
23. Describe how to make meetings more effective.
24. In The Mythical Man-Month, Frederick Brooks argues that adding more programmers to a late project makes it later. Why?
25. What is scope creep, and how can it be managed?
26. What is timeboxing, and why is it used?
27. Create a list of potential risks that could affect the outcome of a project.
28. Why is project assessment important?
29. How is project team review different from system review?
30. Why is the ideas of psychological safety, blameless post-mortems, and a just culture important when performing a project team review?
31. Compare and contrast the Gantt chart with the network diagram.
32. Some companies hire consulting firms to develop the initial project plans and manage the project but use their own analysts and programmers to develop the system. Why do you think some companies do this?
33. What is a use-case point? For what is it used?
34. What process do we use to estimate systems development based on use cases?
35. Name two ways to identify the tasks that need to be accomplished over the course of a project.
36. What are the problems associated with conventional WBSs?
37. What is an evolutionary WBS? How does it address the problems associated with a conventional WBS?
38. What is an iterative workplan?

EXERCISES

A. Different views of plagiarism and collaborative learning were described as examples of differences among different cultures today. Using the Web, identify other differences that could affect the success of an information systems development team.

B. Besides Hall and Hofstede, both David Victor and Fons Trompenaars have identified a set of cultural dimensions that could be useful in information systems development. Using the Web, identify their dimensions.

C. Locate a news article in an IT trade magazine (e.g., *Computerworld*) about an organization that is implementing a new computer system. Describe the tangible and intangible value that the organization is likely to realize from the new system.

D. Car dealers have realized how profitable it can be to sell automobiles using the Web. Pretend that you work for a local car dealership that is part of a large chain such as CarMax. Create a system request you might use to develop a Web-based sales system. Remember to list special issues that are relevant to the project.

E. Suppose that you are interested in buying a new computer. Create a cost–benefit analysis that illustrates the return on investment that you would receive from making this purchase. Computer-related websites (e.g., Apple, Dell, HP) should have real tangible costs that you can include in your analysis. Project your numbers out to include a three-year period and provide the net present value of the final total.

F. The Amazon.com website originally sold books; then the management of the company decided to extend their Web-based system to include other products. How would you have assessed the feasibility of this venture when the idea first came up? How risky would you have considered the project that implemented this idea? Why?

G. Interview someone who works in a large organization and ask him or her to describe the approval process that exists for approving new development projects. What do they think about the process? What are the problems? What are the benefits?

H. Visit a project management website, such as the Project Management Institute (www.pmi.org). Most have links to project management software products, white papers, and research. Examine some of the links for project management to better understand a variety of Internet sites that contain information related to this chapter.

I. Select a specific project management topic such as CASE, project management software, or timeboxing and search for information on that topic using the Web. Any search engine (e.g., Bing and Google) can provide a starting point for your efforts.

J. Pretend that the career services office at your university wants to develop a system that collects student résumés and makes them available to students and recruiters over the Web. Students should be able to input their résumé information into a standard résumé template. The information then is presented in a résumé format, and it also is placed in a database that can be queried using an online search form. You have been put in charge of the project. Develop a plan for estimating the project. How long do you think it would take for you and three other students to complete the project? Provide support for the schedule that you propose.

K. Refer to the situation in exercise J. You have been told that recruiting season begins a month from today and that the new system must be used. How would you approach this situation? Describe what you can do as the project manager to make sure that your team does not burn out from unreasonable deadlines and commitments.

L. Consider the system described in exercise J. Create a workplan listing the tasks that will need to be completed to meet the project's objectives. Create a Gantt chart and a network diagram in a project management tool (e.g., Microsoft Project) or using a spreadsheet package to graphically show the high-level tasks of the project.

M. Suppose that you are in charge of the project that is described in exercise J and the project will be staffed by members of your class. Do your classmates have all the right skills to implement such a project? If not, how will you go about making sure that the proper skills are available to get the job done?

N. Complete a use-case point worksheet to estimate the effort to build the system described in exercises J, K, L, and M. You will need to make assumptions regarding the actors, the use cases, and the technical complexity and environmental factors.

O. Consider the application that is used at your school to register for classes. Complete a use-case point worksheet to estimate the effort to build such an application.

You will need to make some assumptions about the application's interfaces and the various factors that affect its complexity.

P. Pretend that your instructor has asked you and two friends to create a Web page to describe the course to potential students and provide current class information (e.g., syllabus, assignments, and readings) to current students. You have been assigned the role of leader, so you will need to coordinate your activities and those of your classmates until the project is completed. Describe how you would apply the project management techniques that you have learned in this chapter in this situation. Include descriptions of how you would create a workplan, staff the project, and coordinate all activities—yours and those of your classmates.

Q. Select two project management software packages and research them using the Web or trade magazines. Describe the features of the two packages. If you were a project manager, which one would you use to help support your job? Why?

R. In 1997, Oxford Health Plans had a computer problem that caused the company to overestimate revenue and underestimate medical costs. Problems were caused by the migration of its claims processing system from the Pick operating system to a UNIX-based system that uses Oracle database software and hardware from Pyramid Technology. As a result, Oxford's stock price plummeted, and fixing the system became the number one priority for the company. Suppose that you have been placed in charge of managing the repair of the claims processing system. Obviously, the project team will not be in good spirits. How will you motivate team members to meet the project's objectives?

MINICASES

1. The Amberssen Specialty Company is a chain of twelve retail stores that sell a variety of imported gift items, gourmet chocolates, cheeses, and wines in the Toronto area. Amberssen has an IS staff of three people who have created a simple but effective information system of networked point-of-sale registers at the stores and a centralized accounting system at the company headquarters. Harry Hilman, the head of Amberssens IS group, has just received the following memo from Bill Amberssen, Sales Director (and son of Amberssen's founder).

Harry—it's time Amberssen Specialty launched itself on the Internet. Many of our competitors are already there, selling to customers without the expense of a retail storefront, and we should be there too. I project that we could double or triple our annual revenues by selling our products on the Internet. I'd like to have this ready by Thanksgiving, in time for the prime holiday gift-shopping season. Bill

After pondering this memo for several days, Harry scheduled a meeting with Bill so that he could clarify Bill's vision of this venture. Using the standard content of a system request as your guide, prepare a list of questions that Harry needs to have answered about this project.

2. The Decker Company maintains a fleet of ten service trucks and crews that provide a variety of plumbing, heating, and cooling repair services to residential customers. Currently, it takes on average about six hours before a service team responds to a service request. Each truck and crew averages twelve service calls per week, and the average revenue earned per service call is $150. Each truck is in service fifty weeks per year. Owing to the difficulty in scheduling and routing, there is considerable slack time for each truck and crew during a typical week.

In an effort to more efficiently schedule the trucks and crews and improve their productivity, Decker management is evaluating the purchase of a prewritten routing and scheduling software package. The benefits of the system will include reduced response time to service requests and more productive service teams, but management is having trouble quantifying these benefits.

One approach is to make an estimate of how much service response time will decrease with the new system, which then can be used to project the increase in the number of service calls made each week. For example, if the system permits the average service response time to fall to four hours, management believes that each truck will be able to make sixteen service calls per week on average—an increase of four calls per week. With each truck making four additional calls per week and the average revenue per call at $150, the revenue increase per truck per week is $600 (4 × $150). With ten trucks in service fifty weeks per year, the average annual revenue increase will be $300,000 ($600 × 10 × 50).

Decker Company management is unsure whether the new system will enable response time to fall to four hours on average or if it will be some other number. Therefore, management has developed the following range of outcomes that may be possible outcomes of the new system, along with probability estimates of each outcome's occurring.

New Response Time	# Calls/Truck/ Week	Likelihood
2 hours	20	20%
3 hours	18	30%
4 hours	16	50%

Given these figures, prepare a spreadsheet model that computes the expected value of the annual revenues to be produced by this new system.

3. Emily Pemberton is an IS project manager facing a difficult situation. Emily works for the First Trust Bank, which has recently acquired the City National Bank. Before the acquisition, First Trust and City National were bitter rivals, fiercely competing for market share in the region. Following the acrimonious takeover, numerous staff were laid off in many banking areas, including IS. Key individuals were retained from both banks' IS areas, however, and were assigned to a new consolidated IS department. Emily has been made project manager for the first significant IS project since the takeover, and she faces the task of integrating staffers from both banks on her team. The project they are undertaking will be highly visible within the organization, and the time frame for the project is somewhat demanding. Emily believes that the team can meet the project goals successfully, but success will require that the team become cohesive quickly and that potential conflicts be avoided. What strategies do you suggest that Emily implement in order to help ensure a successfully functioning project team?

4. Tom, Jan, and Julie are IS majors at Great State University. These students have been assigned a class project by one of their professors, requiring them to develop a new Web-based system to collect and update information on the IS program's alumni. This system will be used by the IS graduates to enter job and address information as they graduate and then make changes to that information as they change jobs and/or addresses. Their professor also has a number of queries that she is interested in being able to implement. Based on their preliminary discussions with their professor, the students have determined that the only actor is an IS graduate. They identified one simple use case, four average use cases, and two complex use cases. You need to assign reasonable values to each of the technical complexity and environmental factors. Calculate the effort for this project.

5. In looking for a capstone project for your final MIS course, you found a possible project. The master gardeners in Blint County have created a database of all of the plants in their arboretum. The database is actually a spreadsheet created by one of the volunteers. Along with providing a plant inventory, it is used to print labels of all of the plants that the other master gardeners grow for the annual plant. More than 5,000 plants are supplied each year by 100 gardeners from their home gardens. Because the type and numbers of plants change each year and because the members e-mail the information in varying formats, label printing has become an onerous task. Pam, who prints the labels each year, wants help in making this task manageable. She provided an example of a typical email as well as the type of information she needs.

E-mail
Lilies—labels needed 32–
Lilium lancifolium / lilium tigrinum
Tiger Lily perennial light shade 4'
Ice plant (pink)—labels needed 3
Delosperma cooperi Hardy Ice Plant succulent full sun 2–5"
Information for Labels
Botanical Name
Common Name
Plant Type
Light Requirement
Height and Width

In order to have this accepted as your project, you need to form a team with the necessary skills and to create a systems request. How would you approach this project? What additional information do you need from Pam in order to begin estimating the scope of this project? Assuming that you have received this information, create a systems request. Also create a list of skills needed, the number of team members required, and a project plan.

CHAPTER 12

FINISHING TOUCHES: FINAL UNIFIED PROCESS WORKFLOWS

This chapter examines the final Unified Process workflows that address managerial concerns when developing a new information system. These workflows deal with setting up and maintaining the necessary development environment, addressing the technical aspects of configuration and change management, developing both system and user documentation, focusing on organizational issues in deploying new information systems, and supporting the post-implementation activities of system support and system maintenance.

OBJECTIVES

- Understand how the environment and infrastructure workflows support the development of information systems.
- Understand how the configuration and change management workflow support the management of developing information systems.
- Understand how the implementation workflow not only supports programming, but also supports the development of user documentation.
- Understand how the deployment workflow addresses cultural issues in adopting new information technology, organizational change management, and different approaches to conversion from the old system to the new system.
- Understand how the operations and support workflow addresses system support and maintenance after the system is deployed.

INTRODUCTION

"It must be remembered that there is nothing more difficult to plan, more doubtful of success, nor more dangerous to manage than the creation of a new system. For the initiator has the animosity of all who would profit by the preservation of the old institution and merely lukewarm defenders in those who would gain by the new."

—Niccolò Machiavelli, *The Prince*, 1513

Although written 500 years ago, Machiavelli's comments are still true today. Managing the change to a new system—whether it is computerized or not—is one of the most difficult tasks in any organization. Because of the challenges involved, most organizations begin developing their conversion and change management plans while the programmers are still developing the software. Leaving conversion and change management planning to the last minute is a recipe for failure.

In many ways, using a computer system or set of work processes is much like driving on a dirt road. Over time, with repeated use, the road begins to develop ruts in the most used parts of the road. Although these ruts show where to drive, they make change difficult. As people

469

use a computer system or set of work processes, those systems or work processes begin to become habits or norms; people learn them and become comfortable with them. These systems or work processes then begin to limit people's activities and make it difficult for them to change because they begin to see their jobs in terms of these processes rather than of the final business goal of serving customers.

One of the earliest models for managing organizational change was developed by Kurt Lewin.[1] Lewin argued that change is a three-step process: unfreeze, move, refreeze (Figure 12-1). First, the project team must *unfreeze* the existing habits and norms (the as-is system) so that change is possible. Most of system development to this point has laid the groundwork for unfreezing. Users are aware of the new system being developed, some have participated in an analysis of the current system (and so are aware of its problems), and some have helped design the new system (and so have some sense of the potential benefits of the new system). These activities have helped to unfreeze the current habits and norms.

The second step is to help the organization move to the new system via a *migration plan*. The migration plan has two major elements. One is technical, which includes how the new system will be installed and how data in the as-is system will be moved into the to-be system. The second component is organizational, which includes helping users understand the change and motivating them to adopt it.

The third step is to *refreeze* the new system as the habitual way of performing the work processes—ensuring that the new system successfully becomes the standard way of performing the business function it supports. By providing ongoing support for the new system and immediately beginning to identify improvements for the next version of the system, the organization helps solidify the new system as the new habitual way of doing business.

Change management is the most challenging of the three components because it focuses on people, not technology, and because it is the one aspect of the project that is the least controllable by the project team. Change management means winning the hearts and minds of potential users and convincing them that the new system actually provides value.

Maintenance is the costliest aspect of the installation process, because the cost of maintaining systems usually greatly exceeds the initial development costs. It is not unusual for organizations to spend 60 to 80 percent of their total IS development budget on maintenance. Although this might sound surprising initially, think about the software you use. How many software packages do you use that are the very first version? Most commercial software packages become

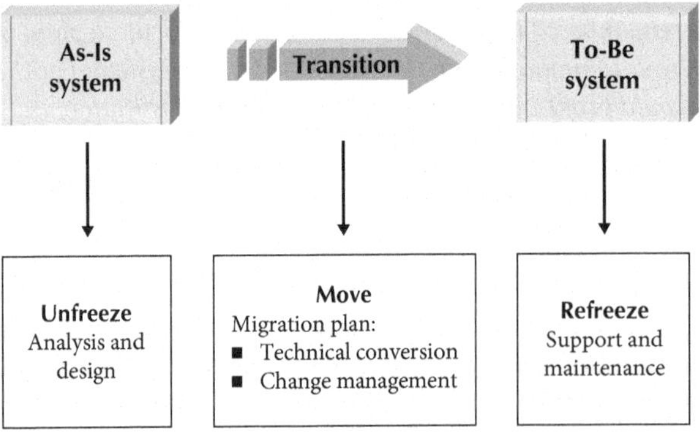

FIGURE 12-1
Implementing Change

---

[1] Kurt Lewin, "Frontiers in Group Dynamics," *Human Relations* 1, no. 5 (1947): 5–41; Kurt Lewin, "Group Decision and Social Change," in E. E. Maccoby, T. M. Newcomb, and E. L. Hartley (eds.), *Readings in Social Psychology* (New York: Holt, Rinehart, & Winston, 1958), pp. 197–211.

truly useful and enter widespread use only in their second or third version. Maintenance and continual improvement of software is ongoing, whether it is a commercially available package or software developed in-house. Would you buy software if you knew that no new versions were going to be produced? Of course, commercial software is somewhat different from custom in-house software used by only one company, but the fundamental issues remain.

Before we get into the details of successfully deploying a new information system in an organization, there are a set of activities associated with different workflows that must be completed. First, we must set up the appropriate environment and infrastructure to support the development of the system. Second, we must carefully manage the process of configuring and changing the evolving system. Third, in addition to programming the software, we must carefully develop the user documentation to make sure that the system will be easily used. Fourth, when we deploy the system, we need to be cognizant of issues related to culture and organizational change, and the different approaches to convert the organization from the old to the new system. Finally, once the system has been successfully deployed, we need to be aware of activities related to supporting and maintaining the new system.

ENVIRONMENT AND INFRASTRUCTURE MANAGEMENT WORKFLOWS

The environment and infrastructure management workflows support the development team throughout the development process. The environment workflow primarily deals with choosing the correct set of tools that will be used throughout the development process and identifying the appropriate set of standards to be followed during the development process. Infrastructure management workflow deals with choosing the appropriate level and type of documentation that will be created during the development process. For example, the project team must put mechanisms in place to keep the development effort well organized. Many project teams set up three areas in which developers can work: a development area, a testing area, and a production area. These areas can be different directories on a server hard disk, different servers, or different physical locations, but the point is that files, data, and programs are separated based on their status of completion. At first, developers access and build files within the development area and then copy them to the testing area when the developers are finished. If a program does not pass a test, it is sent back to development. Once all programs are tested and ready to support the new system, they are copied into the production area—the location where the final system will reside. Other activities associated with the infrastructure management workflow include developing, modifying, and reusing predefined components, frameworks, libraries, and patterns (see Chapters 4 and 7). In this section, we describe three useful things that support the development team: CASE tools, the use of standards, and documentation.

CASE Tools

Computer-aided software engineering (CASE) is a category of software that automates all or part of the development process. Some CASE software packages are used primarily to support the analysis workflow to create integrated diagrams of the system and to store information regarding the system components, whereas others support the design workflow that can be used to generate code for database tables and system functionality. Other CASE tools contain functionality that supports tasks throughout the system-development process. CASE comes in a wide assortment of flavors in terms of complexity and functionality, and many good tools are available in the marketplace to support object-oriented systems development (e.g., IBM's Rational UML and Visual Paradigm).

The benefits of using CASE are numerous. With CASE tools, tasks can be completed and altered faster, development documentation is centralized, and information is illustrated through diagrams, which are typically easier to understand. Potentially, CASE can reduce maintenance costs, improve software quality, and enforce discipline. Some project teams even use CASE to assess the magnitude of changes to the project. Many modern CASE tools that support object-oriented systems development support a development technique known as *round-trip engineering*. Round-trip engineering supports not only code generation but also the reverse engineering of UML diagrams from code. In this way, the system can evolve via diagrams and via code in a round-trip manner.

Of course, like anything else, CASE should not be considered a silver bullet for project development. The advanced CASE tools are complex applications that require significant training and experience to achieve real benefits. Our experience has shown that CASE is a helpful way to support the communication and sharing of project diagrams and technical specifications as long as it is used by trained developers who have applied CASE on past projects. All CASE tools use a *CASE repository* to store diagrams, models, and I/O designs and to ensure consistency across iterations.

CASE tools used during construction can be very helpful for change control because many CASE tools are set up to track the status of programs and help manage programmers as they work. In most cases, maintaining coordination is not conceptually complex. It just requires a lot of discipline and attention to tracking small details.

Standards

Project team members need to work together, and most project management software and CASE tools support them by providing access privileges to everyone working on the system. However, without set procedures, collaboration can result in confusion. To make matters worse, people sometimes are reassigned in the middle of a project. It is important that their project knowledge does not leave with them and that their replacements can get up to speed quickly.

One way to make certain that everyone is performing tasks in the same way and following the same procedures is to create *standards* that the project team must follow. Standards can include formal rules for naming files, forms that must be completed when goals are reached, and programming guidelines. Figure 12-2 shows some examples of the types of standards that a project can create. When a team forms standards and then follows them, the project can be completed faster because task coordination becomes less complex.

Standards work best when they are created at the beginning of each major phase of the project and communicated clearly to the entire project team. As the team moves forward, new standards are added when necessary. Some standards (e.g., file naming conventions and status reporting) are applied during the entire development process, whereas others (e.g., programming guidelines) are appropriate only for certain tasks.

Documentation

Finally, during the inception phase of the infrastructure workflow, project teams establish good *documentation* standards that include detailed information about the tasks of the Unified Process. Typically, the standards for the required documentation are set by the development organization. The development team only needs to ascertain which documentation standards are appropriate for the current systems development project. Often, the documentation is stored in a *project binder(s)* that contains all the deliverables and all the internal communication that takes place—the history of the project. The good news is that Unified Process has a set of standard documentation that is expected. The documentation typically includes the system request, the feasibility analysis, the original and later versions of the effort estimation, the evolving workplan, and the UML diagrams for the functional, structural, and behavioral models.

Types of Standards	Examples
Documentation standards	The date and project name should appear as a header on all documentation. All margins should be set to 1 inch. All deliverables should be added to the project binder and recorded in its table of contents.
Coding standards	All modules of code should include a header that lists the programmer, last date of update, and a short description of the purpose of the code. Indentation should be used to indicate loops, if-then-else statements, and case statements. On average, every program should include one line of comments for every five lines of code.
Procedural standards	Record actual task progress in the workplan every Monday morning by 10 AM. Report to project update meeting on Fridays at 3:30 PM. All changes to a requirements document must be approved by the project manager.
Specification requirement standards	Name of program to be created Description of the program's purpose Special calculations that need to be computed Business rules that must be incorporated into the program Pseudocode Due date
User interface design standards	Labels will appear in boldface text, left-justified, and followed by a colon. The tab order of the screen will move from top left to bottom right. Accelerator keys will be provided for all updatable fields.

FIGURE 12-2
A Sampling of
Project Standards

A poor project management practice is waiting until the last minute to create documentation; this typically leads to an undocumented system that no one understands. Good project teams learn to document a system's history as it evolves while the details are still fresh in their memory. In most CASE tools that support object-oriented systems development, some of the documentation can be automated. For example, if the programming language chosen to implement the system in is Java, then it is possible to automatically create HTML manual pages that will describe the classes being implemented. This is accomplished through the javadoc[2] tool that is part of the Java development environment. Other tools enable the developer to automatically generate HTML documentation for the UML diagrams.[3] Even though virtually all developers hate creating documentation and documentation takes valuable time, it is a good investment that will pay off in the long run.

CONFIGURATION AND CHANGE MANAGEMENT WORKFLOW

This workflow primarily addresses the need of keeping the different parts of the developing system in sync and controlling access to and modification of the different IT artifacts created during the system development process. These artifacts include the workplans and estimations

---

[2] See Oracle, *Javadoc Tool*. Retrieved May 2014 from www.oracle.com. www.oracle.com/technetwork/java/javase/documentation/index-jsp-135444.html.

[3] For example, see Doc. Composer with the Visual Paradigm Case tool.

(Chapter 11), analysis models (Chapters 2–6), design specifications (Chapters 7–10), source code, and test specifications (Chapters 3–10). With the continuous delivery and deployment of system releases of agile and DevOps approaches, this becomes very critical. Otherwise, the system can be broken easily.[4]

Keeping files and programs in different places based on completion status helps manage *change control*, the action of coordinating a system as it changes through construction. Another change control technique is keeping track of which programmer changes which classes and packages by using a *program log*. The log is merely a form on which programmers sign out classes and packages to write and sign in when they are completed. Both the programming areas and program log help the analysts understand exactly who has worked on what and the system's current status. Without these techniques, files can be put into production without the proper testing (e.g., two programmers can start working on the same class or package at the same time).

One of the major approaches used to address configuration and change management uses the idea of an artifact library and version controls. The *artifact library* stores all of the artifacts and the relationships among them. For example, a set of CRC cards (Chapter 4) could have a test that specifies that all related use case scenarios (Chapters 3 and 5) should be role played to ensure the fidelity of the CRC cards to support the use case. In addition to storing the artifacts themselves, the library also would store the relationships among all of the use-case scenarios, the CRC cards, and the role play test specification. These *dependency relationships* allow the project manager to ensure that all of the artifacts are kept in sync and to support the idea of traceability. *Traceability* refers to the notion of knowing who made the changes to what artifact. This supports the idea of *accountability* where each and every developer is accountable for the work that they have performed. Furthermore, by storing all of these relationships, developers can always trace an artifact back to the requirements (Chapters 2 and 3) that it supports.

Version controls support the rolling back of the system, or part of a system, to a previous version. Consequently, if something is deployed, put into production, and it does not work properly, the new version can be removed, the previous version can be deployed, and the new version can be brought back into development. The infrastructure includes the ability to continuously integrate, test, monitor, deliver, and deploy the software in real time. This includes automatically testing, deploying, and sometimes retracting the artifact from production. However, the only way that this can work is if the problem is well understood by the time the deployment is to be executed and the actual software being deployed is sufficiently limited.

Another aspect of configuration and change management is the requirement to control who has access to the artifact and the type of access that is granted to the artifact. Not everyone should have access to the artifacts. This access can be controlled in the same way that access is controlled to software and data of deployed systems. Typical approaches include capability lists, access control lists, and role-based access controls. Furthermore, authentication of the user and encryption of the artifacts should be supported. We describe these topics with the discussion of the non-functional security requirements in Chapter 10.

IMPLEMENTATION WORKFLOW

When you normally think of the activities that take place during the implementation workflow, you think of programming. And you would be correct. Programming is the primary activity that takes place in the implementation workflow. However, in this case, programming

---

[4] See Jez Humble, David Farley, *Continuous Delivery: Reliable Software Releases Through Build, Test, and Deployment Automation* (Boston, MA: Pearson Education, 2011); Gene Kim, Jez Humble, Patrick Debois, John Willis, *The DevOps Handbook: How to Create World-Class Agility, Reliability, & Security in Technology Organizations* (Portland OR: IT Revolution Press, 2016).

doesn't simply mean coding new classes. It includes incorporating pre-existing classes into the overall solution. This includes the integration of libraries, frameworks, and components into the evolving solution (see Chapters 4 and 6). In addition to coding the system, the user documentation needs to be created.

Developing User Documentation

Developing user documentation of the system must be done throughout system development. In many ways, the documentation of a system is a system. Indeed, many large software systems have almost equally large documentation, systems (e.g., support.microsoft.com for Microsoft Office and other products). So, developing documentation can follow a similar, but simpler, approach as software development. In this case, creating use cases and developing the user interfaces to the documentation make sense. Therefore, virtually all topics relevant to designing the human-computer interaction layer (see Chapter 9) are applicable to developing documentation. There are two fundamentally different types of documentation: system documentation and user documentation. *System documentation* (see Environment and Infrastructure Management Workflow section above) is intended to help programmers and systems analysts understand the application software and enable them to build it or maintain it after the system is installed. System documentation is largely a by-product of the systems analysis and design process and is created as the project unfolds. Each step and phase produces documents that are essential in understanding how the system is or is to be built, and these documents are stored in the project binder(s).

User documentation (such as user's manuals, training manuals, and online help systems) is designed to help the user operate the system. Although most project teams expect users to have received training and to have read the user's manuals before operating the system, unfortunately, this is not always the case. It is more common today—especially in the case of commercial software packages—for users to begin using the software without training or reading the user's manuals. In this section, we focus on user documentation.[5]

User documentation is often left until the end of the project, which is a dangerous strategy. Developing good documentation takes longer than many people expect because it requires much more than simply writing a few pages. Producing documentation requires designing the documents (whether on paper or online), writing the text, editing the documents, and testing them. For good-quality documentation, this process usually takes about three hours per page (single-spaced) for paper-based documentation or two hours per screen for online documentation. Thus "simple" documentation, such as a ten-page user's manual and a set of twenty help screens, takes seventy hours. Of course, lower-quality documentation can be produced faster.

The time required to develop and test user documentation should be built into the project plan. Most organizations plan for documentation development to start once the interface design and program specifications are complete. The initial draft of documentation is usually scheduled for completion immediately after the unit tests are complete. This reduces (but doesn't eliminate) the chance that the documentation will need to be changed due to software changes and still leaves enough time for the documentation to be tested and revised before the acceptance tests are started.

Although paper-based manuals are still important, online documentation is more pervasive. There are four key strengths of online documentation. First, since the user can type in a variety of keywords to view information almost instantaneously, searching for informa-

---

[5] For more information on developing documentation, see Thomas T. Barker, *Writing Software Documentation* (Boston: Allyn & Bacon, 1998).

tion is often very simple (provided the help search index is well designed). Second, the same information can be presented several times in many different formats, so that the user can find and read the information in the most informative way. Third, online documentation provides many new ways for the user to interact with documentation that is not possible in static paper documentation. For example, it is possible to use links or "tool tips" (i.e., pop-up text; see Chapter 9) to explain unfamiliar terms, and one can write "show-me" routines that demonstrate on the screen exactly what buttons to click and text to type. Finally, online documentation is significantly less expensive to distribute than paper documentation.

Types of User Documentation There are three fundamentally different types of user documentation: reference documents, procedures manuals, and tutorials. *Reference documents* (also called the help system) are designed to be used when the user needs to learn how to perform a specific function (e.g., updating a field and adding a new record). Often people read reference information when they have tried and failed to perform the function; writing reference documents requires special care because the user is often impatient or frustrated when he or she begins to read them.

Procedures manuals describe how to perform business tasks (e.g., printing a monthly report and taking a customer order). Each item in the procedures manual typically guides the user through a task that requires several functions or steps in the system. Therefore, each entry is typically much longer than an entry in a reference document.

Tutorials—obviously—teach people how to use major components of a system (e.g., an introduction to the basic operations of the system). Each entry in the tutorial is typically longer still than the entries in procedures manuals, and the entries are usually designed to be read in sequence (whereas entries in reference documents and procedures manuals are designed to be read individually).

Regardless of the type of user documentation, the overall process for developing it is similar to the process of developing interfaces (see Chapter 9). The developer first designs the general structure for the documentation and then develops the individual components within it.

Designing Documentation Structure The general structure used in most online documentation, whether reference documents, procedures manuals, or tutorials, is to develop a set of *documentation navigation controls* that lead the user to *documentation topics*. The documentation topics are the material that user wants to read, whereas the navigation controls are the way the user locates and accesses a specific topic. As such, using storyboards, windows navigation diagrams (WND), and wireframe diagrams are useful (see Chapter 9).

Designing the structure of the documentation begins by identifying the different types of topics and navigation controls that need to be included. Figure 12-3 shows a commonly used structure for online reference documents (i.e., the help system). The documentation topics generally come from three sources. The first and most obvious source of topics is the set of commands and menus in the user interface. This set of topics is very useful if the user wants to understand how a particular command or menu is used.

However, the users often don't know what commands to look for or where they are in the system's menu structure. Instead, users have tasks they want to perform, and rather than thinking in terms of commands, they think in terms of their tasks. Therefore, the second and often more useful set of topics focuses on how to perform certain tasks, usually those in the use scenarios, WNDs, and the real use cases from the user interface design (see Chapter 9). These topics walk the user through the set of steps (often involving several keystrokes or mouse clicks) needed to perform some task.

The third topic is definitions of important terms. These terms are usually the use cases and classes in the system, but sometimes they also include commands.

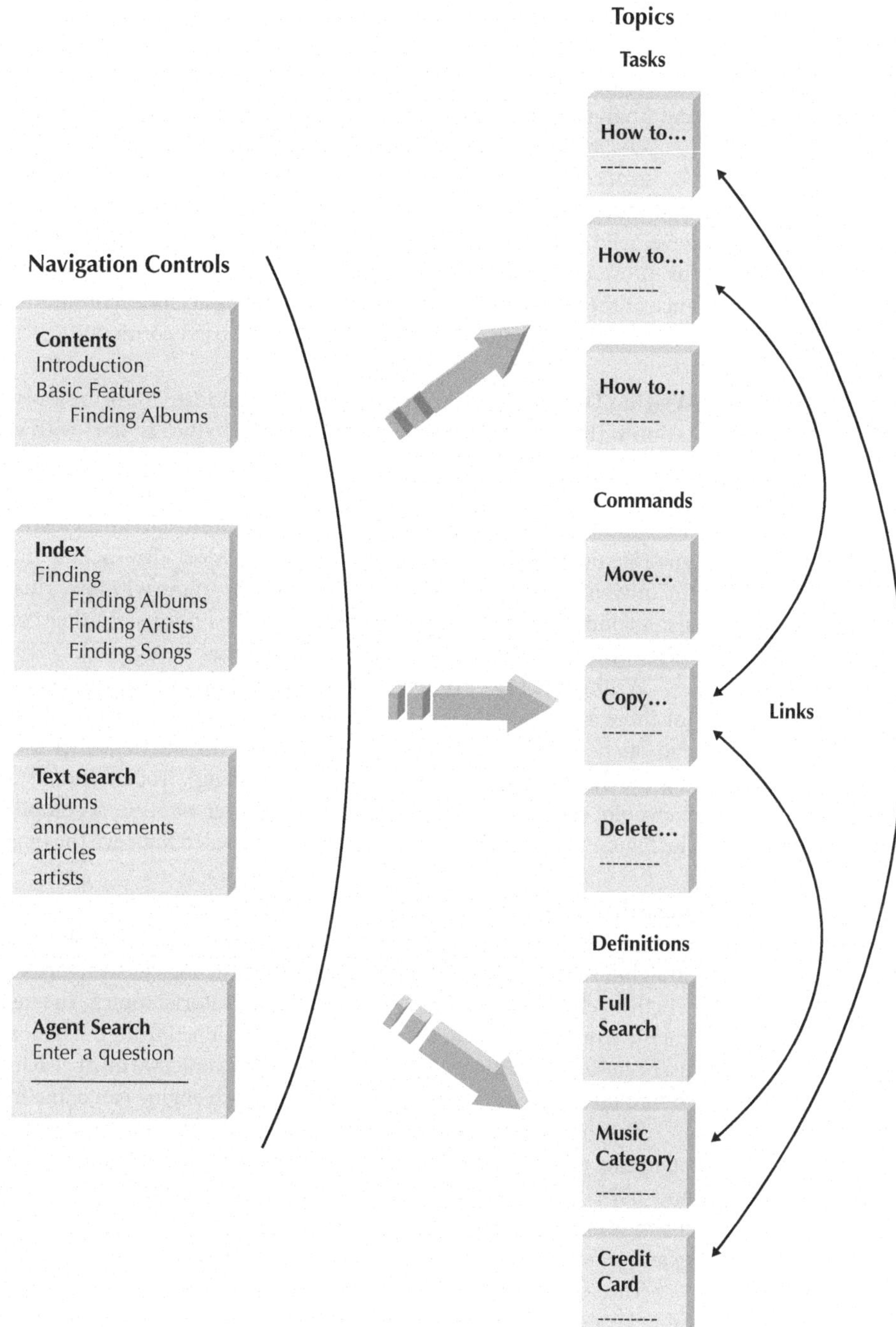

FIGURE 12-3
Organizing Online
Reference Documents

There are five general types of navigation controls for topics, but not all systems use all five types (see Figure 12-3). The first is the table of contents that organizes the information in a logical form, as though the users were to read the reference documentation from start to finish. The index provides access into the topics based on important keywords, in the same way that the index at the back of a book helps us find topics. Text search provides the ability to search through the topics either for any text the user types or for words that match a developer-specified set of words that is much larger than the set of words in the index. Unlike the index, text search typically provides no organization to the words (other than alphabetical). Some systems provide the ability to use an intelligent agent to help in the search. The fifth and final navigation controls to topics are the hyperlinks between topics that enable the user to click and move among topics.

Procedures manuals and tutorials are similar but often simpler in structure. Topics for procedures manuals usually come from the use scenarios, WNDs, and the real use cases developed during interface design and from other basic tasks the users must perform. Topics for tutorials are usually organized around major sections of the system and the level of experience of the user. Most tutorials start with the basic, most commonly used commands and then move into more complex and less commonly used commands.

Writing Documentation Topics The general format for topics is fairly similar across application systems and operating systems. Topics typically start with very clear titles, followed by some introductory text that defines the topic and then by detailed, step-by-step instructions on how to perform what is being described. Many topics include screen images to help the user find items on the screen; some also have tutorials and videos available online that demonstrate the functions of interest to the user. Most also include navigation controls to enable the movement among topics, usually at the top of the window, plus links to other topics. Some also include links to related topics that include options or other commands and tasks the user might want to perform in concert with the topic being read.

Writing the topic content can be challenging. It requires a good understanding of the user (or more accurately the range of users) and a knowledge of what skills the users currently have and can be expected to import from other systems and tools they are using or have used (including the system that the new system is replacing). Topics should always be written from the viewpoint of the user and describe what the user wants to accomplish, not what the system can do. Figure 12-4 provides some general guidelines to improve the quality of documentation text.[6]

Identifying Navigation Terms As we write the documentation topics, we also begin to identify the terms that will be used to help users find topics. The table of contents is usually the most straightforward because it is developed from the logical structure of the documentation topics, whether reference topics, procedure topics, or tutorial topics. The items for the index and search engine require more care because they are developed from the major parts of the system and the users' business functions. Every time we write a topic, we must also list the terms that will be used to find the topic. Terms for the index and search engine can come from four distinct sources.

The first source for index terms is the set of the commands in the user interface, such as open file, modify customer, and print open orders. All commands contain two parts (action and object). It is important to develop the index for both parts because users could search for information using either part. A user looking for more information about saving files, for example, might search by using the term save or the term files.

The second source is the set of major concepts in the system, which are often use cases and classes. In the case of the Appointment system, for example, this might include appointment, symptoms, or patient.

A third source is the set of business tasks the user performs, such as ordering replacement units or making an appointment. Often these are contained in the command set, but sometimes they require several commands and use terms that do not always appear in the system. Good sources for these terms are the use scenarios and real use cases developed during interface design (see Chapter 9).

---

[6] One of the best books to explain the art of writing is William Strunk and E. B. White, *Elements of Style*, 4th Ed. (Needham Heights, MA: Allyn & Bacon, 2000).

Guideline	Before the Guideline	After the Guideline
Use the active voice: The active voice creates more active and readable text by putting the subject at the start of the sentence, the verb in the middle, and the object at the end.	Finding albums is done using the album title, the artist's name, or a song title.	You can find an album by using the album title, the artist's name, or a song title.
Use e-prime style: E-prime style creates more active writing by omitting all forms of the verb to be.	The text you want to copy must be selected before you click on the copy button.	Select the text you want to copy before you click on the copy button.
Use consistent terms: Always use the same term to refer to the same items, rather than switching among synonyms (e.g., change, modify, and update).	Select the text you want to copy. Pressing the copy button will copy the marked text to the new location.	Select the text you want to copy. Pressing the copy button will copy the selected text to the new location.
Use simple language: Always use the simplest language possible to accurately convey the meaning. This does not mean you should "dumb down" the text but that you should avoid artificially inflating its complexity. Avoid separating subjects and verbs and try to use the fewest words possible. (When you encounter a complex piece of text, try eliminating words; you may be surprised at how few words are really needed to convey meaning.)	The Georgia Statewide Academic and Medical System (GSAMS) is a cooperative and collaborative distance learning network in the state of Georgia. The organization in Atlanta that administers and manages the technical and overall operations of the currently more than 300 interactive audio and video teleconferencing classrooms throughout Georgia system is the Department of Administrative Service (DOAS). (56 words)	The Department of Administrative Service (DOAS) in Atlanta manages the Georgia Statewide Academic and Medical System (GSAMS), a distance learning network with more than 300 teleconferencing classrooms throughout Georgia. (29 words)
Use friendly language: Too often, documentation is cold and sterile because it is written in a very formal manner. Remember, you are writing for a person, not a computer.	Blank disks have been provided to you by Operations. It is suggested that you ensure your data are not lost by making backup copies of all essential data.	You should make a backup copy of all data that are important to you. If you need more diskettes, contact Operations.
Use parallel grammatical structures: Parallel grammatical structures indicate the similarity among items in list and help the reader understand content.	Opening files Saving a document How to delete files	Opening a file Saving a file Deleting a file
Use steps correctly: Novices often intersperse action and the results of action when describing a step-by-step process. Steps are always actions.	1. Press the customer button. 2. The customer dialogue box will appear. 3. Type the customer ID and press the submit button and the customer record will appear.	1. Press the customer button. 2. Type the customer ID in the customer dialogue box when it appears. 3. Press the submit button to view the customer record for this customer.
Use short paragraphs: Readers of documentation usually quickly scan text to find the information they need, so the text in the middle of long paragraphs is often overlooked. Use separate paragraphs to help readers find information more quickly.		

Source: Based upon material from T. T. Barker, *Writing Software Documentation* (Boston: Allyn & Bacon, 1998).

Figure 12-4　Guidelines for Crafting Documentation Topics

A fourth, often controversial, source is the set of synonyms for the three sets of preceding items. Users sometimes don't think in terms of the nicely defined terms used by the system. They might try to find information on how to stop or quit rather than exit, or erase rather than delete. Including synonyms in the index increases the complexity and size of the documentation system but can greatly improve the usefulness of the system to the users.

DEPLOYMENT WORKFLOW

The deployment workflow is typically associated with the transition phase of the Unified Process. However, given the existence of legacy systems, deployment may need to start much earlier in the development process to address the conversion of old database systems to the new database system. Also, as we saw in Chapter 10, deploying the new system over the application architecture, which portrayed the deployment of the application over the system's network and hardware, is a primary focus of the deployment workflow. In this section, we describe many of the managerial concerns of deploying new systems that can affect the success of the system. These concerns include issues related to culture and IT adoption, organizational change management, and different approaches to the actual conversion from the old system to the new system.

Cultural Issues and Information Technology Adoption[7]

Cultural issues are one of the things that are typically identified as at least partially to blame when there is a failure in an organization. Cultural issues have been studied at both organizational and national levels. In previous chapters, we discussed the effect that cultural issues can have on designing the human–computer interaction and application architecture layers (see Chapters 9 and 10) and the management of programmers (Chapter 11). The cultural dimensions identified by Hall and Hofstede included speed of messages, context, time, power distance, uncertainty avoidance, individualism versus collectivism, masculinity versus femininity, and long- versus short-term orientation.[8] In this chapter, we describe how these dimensions can affect the successful deployment of an information system that supports a global information supply chain.

Hall's first dimension, *speed of messages*, has implications for the development of documentation and training approaches. In a culture that values "deep" content, so that members of the culture can take their time to thoroughly understand the new system, simply providing an online help system is not going to be sufficient to ensure the successful adoption of the new information system. However, in a culture that prefers "fast" messages, an online help system could be sufficient.

Hall's second dimension, *context*, also affects the adoption and deployment of a new system. In high-context cultures, it is expected that the new information system will be placed into the entire context of the enterprise-wide system. Members of this type of society expect to be able to understand exactly where the system fits into the firm's overall picture. Again, like the speed of messages dimension, this affects the training approach used and the documentation developed.

Hall's third dimension, time, can also affect the adoption and deployment of a new system. In a *polychronic time* culture, the training could need to be spread out over a longer period of time, when compared to a *monochronic* time culture. In a monochromic time culture, interruptions would be considered rude. Consequently, training could be accomplished in a small set of intense sessions. However, with a polychronic time culture, because interruptions may occur frequently, maximum flexibility in setting up the training sessions may be necessary.

Hofstede's first dimension, *power distance*, addresses how power issues are dealt with in the culture. For example, if a superior in an organization has an incorrect belief about an important issue, can a subordinate point out this error? In some cultures, the answer is

---

[7] A good summary of cultural issues and information systems is Dorothy E. Leidner and Timothy Kayworth, "A Review of Culture in Information Systems Research: Toward a Theory of Information Technology Culture Conflict," *MIS Quarterly* 30, no. 2 (2006): 357–399.

[8] See Geert Hofstede, *Culture's Consequences: Comparing Values, Behaviors, Institutions and Organizations across Nations*, 2nd Ed. (Thousand Oaks, CA: Sage, 2001); Geert Hofstede, Gert Jan Hofstede, and Michael Minkov, *Cultures and Organizations: Software of the Mind*, 3rd Ed. (New York: McGraw-Hill, 2010); Edward T. Hall, *Beyond Culture* (New York: Anchor Books, 1981).

a resounding no. Consequently, this dimension could have major ramifications for the successful deployment of an information system. For example, in a culture with a high power distance, the deployment of a new information system is dependent on the impression of the most important stakeholder (see Chapter 11). Therefore, much care must be taken to ensure that this stakeholder is pleased with the system. Otherwise, it might never be used.

Hofstede's second dimension, *uncertainty avoidance*, is based on the degree to which the culture depends on rules for direction, how well individuals in the culture handle stress, and the importance of employment stability. For example, in a high-uncertainty-avoidance culture, the use of detailed procedures manuals and good training can reduce the uncertainty in adopting the new system.

Hofstede's third dimension, *individualism* versus *collectivism*, is based on the level of emphasis the culture places on the individual or the collective. The relationship between the individual and the group is important for the success of an information system. Depending on the culture's orientation, the success of an information system being transitioned into production can depend on whether the focus of the information system will benefit the individual or the group.

Hofstede's fourth dimension, *masculinity* versus *femininity*, addresses how well masculine and feminine characteristics are valued by the culture. Some of the differences that could affect the adoption of an information system include employee motivational issues. In a masculine culture, motivation would be based on advancement, earnings, and training, whereas in a feminine culture, motivations would include friendly atmosphere, physical conditions, and cooperation. Depending on how the culture views this dimension, different motivations might need to be used to increase the likelihood of the information system being successfully deployed.

The fifth dimension, *long-* versus *short-term orientation*, deals with how the culture views the past and the future. In East Asia, long-term thinking is highly respected, whereas in North America and Europe, short-term profits and the current stock price seem to be the only things that matter. Based on this dimension, all the political concerns raised previously in this text become very important. For example, if the local culture views success only in a short-term manner, then any new information system that is deployed to support one department of an organization may give that department a competitive advantage over other departments in the short run. If only short-run measures are used to judge the success of a department, then it would be in the interest of the other departments to fight the successful deployment of the information system. However, if a longer-run perspective is the norm, then the other departments could be convinced to support the new information system because they could have new supportive information systems in the future.

Obviously, when reviewing these dimensions, we can see they interact with each other. The most important thing to remember from an IT perspective is that we must be careful not to view the local user community through our eyes; in a global economy, we must take into consideration the local cultural concerns for the information system to be deployed in a successful manner.

Organization Change Management[9]

In the context of a systems development project, change management is the process of helping people adopt and adapt to the to-be system and its accompanying work processes without undue stress. There are three key roles in any major organizational change. The first is the

---

[9] Many books have been written on change management. Some of our favorites are the following: Patrick Connor and Linda Lake, *Managing Organizational Change*, 2nd Ed. (Westport, CT: Praeger, 1994); Douglas Smith, *Taking Charge of Change* (Reading, MA: Addison-Wesley, 1996); Daryl Conner, *Managing at the Speed of Change* (New York: Villard Books, 1992); Mary Lynn Manns and Linda Rising, *Fearless Change: Patterns for Introducing New Ideas* (Boston: Addison-Wesley, 2005).

sponsor of the change—the person who wants the change. This person is the business sponsor who first initiated the request for the new system (see Chapter 2). Usually, the sponsor is a senior manager of the part of the organization that must adopt and use the new system. It is critical that the sponsor be active in the change management process because a change that is clearly being driven by the sponsor, not by the project team or the IS organization, has greater legitimacy. The sponsor has direct management authority over those who adopt the system.

The second role is that of the *change agent*—the person(s) leading the change effort. The change agent, charged with actually planning and implementing the change, is usually someone outside of the business unit adopting the system and therefore has no direct management authority over the potential adopters. Because the change agent is an outsider, he or she has less credibility than the sponsor and other members of the business unit. After all, once the system has been installed, the change agent usually leaves and thus has no ongoing impact. However, this individual has typically seen changes at dozens of other business units or organizations which can help incorporate best practices that can be tailored to the circumstances of the current change.

The third role is that of *potential adopters*, or targets of the change—the people who actually must change. These are the people for whom the new system is designed and who will ultimately choose to use or not use the system.

In the early days of computing, many project teams simply assumed that their job ended when the old system was converted to the new system at a technical level. The philosophy was "build it and they will come." Unfortunately, that happens only in the movies. Resistance to change is common in most organizations. Therefore, the change management plan is an important part of the overall installation plan that glues together the key steps in the change management process. Successful change requires that people want to adopt the change and are able to adopt the change. The change management plan has four basic steps: revising management policies, assessing the cost and benefit models of potential adopters, motivating adoption, and enabling people to adopt through training. However, before we can discuss the change management plan, we must first understand why people resist change.

Understanding Resistance to Change[10]

People resist change—even change for the better—for very rational reasons. What is good for the organization is not necessarily good for the people who work there. For example, consider an order-processing clerk who used to receive orders to be shipped on paper shipping documents but now uses a computer to receive the same information. Rather than typing shipping labels with a typewriter, the clerk now clicks on the print button on the computer and the label is produced automatically. The clerk can now ship many more orders each day, which is a clear benefit to the organization. The clerk, however, probably doesn't really care how many packages are shipped. His or her pay doesn't change; it's just a question of which the clerk prefers to use, a computer or typewriter. Learning to use the new system and work processes—even if the change is minor—requires more effort than continuing to use the existing, well-understood system and work processes.

So why do people accept change? Simply put, every change has a set of costs and benefits associated with it. If the benefits of accepting the change outweigh the costs of the change, then people change. Sometimes the benefit of change is avoidance of the pain that might be experienced if the change were not adopted (e.g., if you don't change, you are fired, so one of the benefits of adopting the change is that you still have a job).

In general, when people are presented with an opportunity for change, they perform a cost–benefit analysis (sometime consciously, sometimes subconsciously) and decide the

---

[10] This section benefited from conversations with Dr. Robert Briggs.

extent to which they will embrace and adopt the change. They identify the costs of and benefits from the system and decide whether the change is worthwhile. However, it is not that simple, because most costs and benefits are not certain. There is some uncertainty as to whether a certain benefit or cost will actually occur; so both the costs of and benefits from the new system need to be weighted by the degree of certainty associated with them (Figure 12-5). Unfortunately, most humans tend to overestimate the probability of costs and underestimate the probability of benefits.

There are also costs and, sometimes, benefits associated with the actual *transition process* itself. For example, suppose we found a nicer house or apartment than our current one. Even if we liked it better, we might decide not to move simply because the cost of moving outweighed the benefits from the new house or apartment itself. Likewise, adopting a new computer system might require us to learn new skills, which could be seen as a cost to some people or as a benefit to others, if they perceived that those skills would somehow provide other benefits beyond the use of the system itself. Once again, any costs and benefits from the transition process must be weighted by the certainty with which they will occur (see Figure 12-5).

Taken together, these two sets of costs and benefits (and their relative certainties) affect the acceptance of change or resistance to change that project teams encounter when installing new systems in organizations. The first step in change management is to understand the factors that inhibit change—the factors that affect the perception of costs and benefits and certainty that they will be generated by the new system. It is critical to understand that the *real costs* and *real benefits* are far less important than the *perceived costs* and *perceived benefits*. People act on what they believe to be true, not on what is true. Thus, any understanding of how to motivate change must be developed from the viewpoint of the people expected to change, not from the viewpoint of those leading the change.

Revising Management Policies

The first major step in the change management plan is to change the management policies that were designed for the as-is system to new management policies designed to support the to-be system. *Management policies* provide goals, define how work processes should be performed, and determine how organizational members are rewarded. No computer system will be successfully adopted unless management policies support its adoption. Many new computer systems bring changes to business processes; they enable new ways of working. Unless the policies that provide the rules and rewards for those processes are revised to reflect the new opportunities that the system permits, potential adopters cannot easily use it.

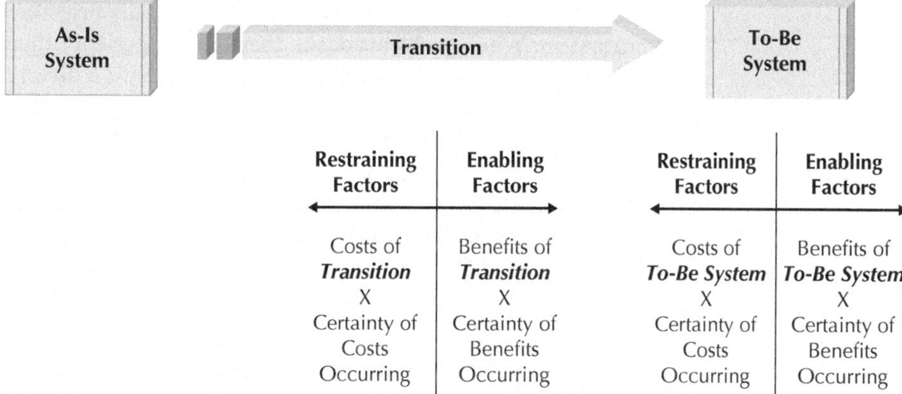

FIGURE 12-5
The Costs and Benefits of Change

Management has three basic tools for structuring work processes in organizations.[11] The first are the *standard operating procedures* (SOPs) that become the habitual routines for how work is performed. The SOPs are both formal and informal. Formal SOPs define proper behavior. Informal SOPs are the norms that have developed over time for how processes are actually performed. Management must ensure that the formal SOPs are revised to match the to-be system. The informal SOPs will then evolve to refine and fill in details absent in the formal SOPs.

The second aspect of management policy is defining how people assign meaning to events. What does it mean to "be successful" or "do good work"? Policies help people understand meaning by defining *measurements* and *rewards*. Measurements explicitly define meaning because they provide clear and concrete evidence about what is important to the organization. Rewards reinforce measurements because "what gets measured gets done" (an overused but accurate saying). Measurements must be carefully designed to motivate desired behavior.

A third aspect of management policy is *resource allocation*. Managers can have clear and immediate impacts on behavior by allocating resources. They can redirect funds and staff from one project to another, create an infrastructure that supports the new system, and invest in training programs. Each of these activities has both a direct and symbolic effect. The direct effect comes from the actual reallocation of resources. The symbolic effect shows that management is serious about its intentions. There is less uncertainty about management's long-term commitment to a new system when potential adopters see resources being committed to support it.

Assessing Costs and Benefits

The next step in developing a change management plan is to develop two clear and concise lists of costs and benefits provided by the new system (and the transition to it) compared with the as-is system. The first list is developed from the perspective of the organization, which should flow easily from the business case developed during the feasibility study and refined over the life of the project (see Chapter 11). This set of organizational costs and benefits should be distributed widely so that everyone expected to adopt the new system should clearly understand why the new system is valuable to the organization.

The second list of costs and benefits is developed from the viewpoints of the different potential adopters expected to change, or stakeholders in the change. For example, one set of potential adopters may be the frontline employees, another may be the first-line supervisors, and yet another might be middle management. Each of these potential adopters, or stakeholders, may have a different set of costs and benefits associated with the change—costs and benefits that can differ widely from those of the organization. In some situations, unions may be key stakeholders that can make or break successful change.

Many systems analysts naturally assume that frontline employees are the ones whose set of costs and benefits are the most likely to diverge from those of the organization and thus are the ones who most resist change. However, they usually bear the brunt of problems with the current system. When problems occur, they often experience them firsthand. Middle managers and first-line supervisors are the most likely to have a divergent set of costs and benefits and, therefore, resist change because new computer systems often change how much power they have. For example, a new computer system may improve the organization's control over a work process (a benefit to the organization) but reduce the decision-making power of middle management (a clear cost to middle managers).

An analysis of the costs and benefits for each set of potential adopters, or stakeholders, will help pinpoint those who will likely support the change and those who might resist the

---

[11] This section builds on the work of Anthony Giddons, *The Constitution of Society: Outline of the Theory of Structure* (Berkeley: University of California Press, 1984). A good summary of Giddons's theory that has been revised and adapted for use in understanding information systems is an article by Wanda Orlikowski and Dan Robey, "Information Technology and the Structuring of Organizations," *Information Systems Research* 2, no. 2 (1991): 143–169.

change. The challenge at this point is to try to change the balance of the costs and benefits for those expected to resist the change so that they support it (or at least do not actively resist it). This analysis could uncover some serious problems that have the potential to block the successful adoption of the system. It may be necessary to reexamine the management policies and make significant changes to ensure that the balance of costs and benefits is such that important potential adopters are motivated to adopt the system.

Figure 12-6 summarizes some of the factors that are important to successful change. The first and most important reason is a compelling personal reason to change. All change

	Factor	Examples	Effects	Actions to Take
Benefits of to-be system	Compelling personal reason(s) for change	Increased pay, fewer unpleasant aspects, opportunity for promotion, most existing skills remain valuable	If the new system provides clear personal benefits to those who must adopt it, they are more likely to embrace the change.	Perform a cost–benefit analysis from the viewpoint of the stakeholders, make changes where needed, and actively promote the benefits.
Certainty of benefits	Compelling organizational reason(s) for change	Risk of bankruptcy, acquisition, government regulation	If adopters do not understand why the organization is implementing the change, they are less certain that the change will occur.	Perform a cost–benefit analysis from the viewpoint of the organization and launch a vigorous information campaign to explain the results to everyone.
	Demonstrated top management support	Active involvement, frequent mentions in speeches	If top management is not seen to actively support the change, there is less certainty that the change will occur.	Encourage top management to participate in the information campaign.
	Committed and involved business sponsor	Active involvement, frequent visits to users and project team, championing	If the business sponsor (the functional manager who initiated the project) is not seen to actively support the change, there is less certainty that the change will occur.	Encourage the business sponsor to participate in the information campaign and play an active role in the change management plan.
	Credible top management and business sponsor	Management and sponsor who do what they say instead of being members of the "management fad of the month" club	If the business sponsor and top management have credibility in the eyes of the adopters, the certainty of the claimed benefits is higher.	Ensure that the business sponsor and/or top management has credibility so that such involvement will help; if there is no credibility, involvement will have little effect.
Costs of transition	Low personal costs of change	Few new skills needed	The cost of the change is not borne equally by all stakeholders; the costs are likely to be higher for some.	Perform a cost–benefit analysis from the viewpoint of the stakeholders, make changes where needed, and actively promote the low costs.
Certainty of costs	Clear plan for change	Clear dates and instructions for change, clear expectations	If there is a clear migration plan, it will likely lower the perceived costs of transition.	Publicize the migration plan.
	Credible change agent	Previous experience with change, does what he/she promises to do	If the change agent has credibility in the eyes of the adopters, the certainty of the claimed costs is higher.	If the change agent is not credible, then change will be difficult.
	Clear mandate for change agent from sponsor	Open support for change agent when disagreements occur	If the change agent has a clear mandate from the business sponsor, the certainty of the claimed costs is higher.	The business sponsor must actively demonstrate support for the change agent.

FIGURE 12-6 Major Factors in Successful Change

is made by individuals, not organizations. If there are compelling reasons for the key groups of individual stakeholders to want the change, then the change is more likely to be successful. Factors such as increased salary, reduced unpleasantness, and—depending on the individuals—opportunities for promotion and personal development can be important motivators. However, if the change makes current skills less valuable, individuals might resist the change because they have invested a lot of time and energy in acquiring those skills, and anything that diminishes those skills may be perceived as diminishing the individual.

There must also be a compelling reason for the organization to need the change; otherwise, individuals become skeptical that the change is important and are less certain it will, in fact, occur. Probably the hardest organization to change is an organization that has been successful because individuals come to believe that what worked in the past will continue to work. By contrast, in an organization that is on the brink of bankruptcy, it is easier to convince individuals that change is needed. Commitment and support from credible business sponsors and top management are also important in increasing the certainty that the change will occur.

The likelihood of successful change is increased when the cost of the transition to individuals who must change is low. The need for significantly different new skills or disruptions in operations and work habits can create resistance. A clear migration plan developed by a credible change agent who has support from the business sponsor is an important factor in increasing the certainty about the costs of the transition process.

Motivating Adoption

The single most important factor in motivating a change is providing clear and convincing evidence of the need for change. Simply put, everyone who is expected to adopt the change must be convinced that the benefits from the to-be system outweigh the costs of changing.

There are two basic strategies to motivate adoption: informational and political. Both strategies are often used simultaneously. With an *informational strategy*, the goal is to convince potential adopters that the change is for the better. This strategy works when the cost–benefit set of the target adopters has more benefits than costs. In other words, there really are clear reasons for the potential adopters to welcome the change.

Using this approach, the project team provides clear and convincing evidence of the costs and benefits of moving to the to-be system. The project team writes memos and develops presentations that outline the costs and benefits of adopting the system from the perspective of the organization and from the perspective of the target group of potential adopters. This information is disseminated widely throughout the target group, much like an advertising or public relations campaign. It must emphasize the benefits and increase the certainty in the minds of potential adopters that these benefits will actually be achieved. In our experience, it is always easier to sell painkillers than vitamins; that is, it is easier to convince potential adopters that a new system will remove a major problem (or other source of pain) than that it will provide new benefits (e.g., increase sales). Therefore, informational campaigns are more likely to be successful if they stress reducing or eliminating problems rather than focusing on providing new opportunities.

The other strategy for motivating change is a *political strategy*. With a political strategy, organizational power, not information, is used to motivate change. This approach is often used when the cost–benefit set of the target adopters has more costs than benefits. In other words, although the change might benefit the organization, there are no reasons for the potential adopters to welcome the change.

The political strategy is usually beyond the control of the project team. It requires someone in the organization who holds legitimate power over the target group to influence the group to adopt the change. This may be done in a coercive manner (e.g., adopt the system or you're fired) or in a negotiated manner, in which the target group gains benefits in other ways that are linked to the adoption of the system (e.g., linking system adoption to increased training opportunities). Management policies can play a key role in a political strategy by linking salary to certain behaviors desired with the new system.

In general, for any change that has true organizational benefits, about 20 to 30 percent of potential adopters will be *ready adopters*. They recognize the benefits, quickly adopt the system, and become proponents of the system. Another 20 to 30 percent are *resistant adopters*. They simply refuse to accept the change and they fight it, either because the new system has more costs than benefits for them personally or because they place such a high cost on the transition process itself that no amount of benefits from the new system can outweigh the change costs. The remaining 40 to 60 percent are *reluctant adopters*. They tend to be apathetic and will go with the flow to either support or resist the system, depending on how the project evolves and how their coworkers react to the system. Figure 12-7 illustrates the actors who are involved in the change management process.

The goal of change management is to actively support and encourage the ready adopters and help them win over the reluctant adopters. There is usually little that can be done about the resistant adopters because their set of costs and benefits may be divergent from those of the organization. Unless there are simple steps that can be taken to rebalance their costs and benefits or the organization chooses to adopt a strongly political strategy, it is often best to ignore this small minority of resistant adopters and focus on the larger majority of ready and reluctant adopters.

Enabling Adoption: Training

Potential adopters might want to adopt the change, but unless they can adopt it, they won't. Careful *training* enables adoption by providing the skills needed to adopt the change. Training is probably the most self-evident part of any change management initiative. How can an organization expect its staff members to adopt a new system if they are not trained? However, we have found that training is one of the most overlooked parts of the process. Many organizations and project managers simply expect potential adopters to find the system easy to learn. Because the system is presumed to be so simple, it is taken for granted that potential adopters should be able to learn with little effort. Unfortunately, this is usually an overly optimistic assumption.

Every new system requires new skills, either because the basic work processes have changed or because the computer system used to support the processes is different. The more radical the changes to the business processes, the more important it is to ensure the organization has the new skills required to operate the new business processes and supporting information systems. In general, there are three ways to get these new skills. One is to hire new employees who have the needed skills that the existing staff does not. Another is to outsource the processes to an organization that has the skills that the existing staff does not. Both these approaches are controversial and are usually considered only when the new skills needed are likely to be the most different from the set of skills of the current staff. In most cases, organizations choose the third alternative: training existing staff in the new business processes and the to-be system. Every training plan must consider what to train and how to deliver the training.

FIGURE 12-7
Actors in the Change
Management Process

Sponsor	Change Agent	Potential Adopters
The sponsor wants the change to occur.	The change agent leads the change effort.	Potential adopters are the people who must change.
		20–30 percent are ready adopters.
		20–30 percent are resistant adopters.
		40–60 percent are reluctant adopters.

What to Train What training should you provide to the system users? It's obvious: how to use the system. The training should cover all the capabilities of the new system so that users understand what each module does, right? Wrong. Training for business systems should focus on helping the users to accomplish their jobs, not on how to use the system. The system is simply a means to an end, not the end in itself. This focus on performing the job (i.e., the business processes), not using the system, has two important implications. First, the training must focus on the activities around the system as well as on the system itself. The training must help the users understand how the computer fits into the bigger picture of their jobs. The use of the system must be put in context of the manual business processes as well as of those that are computerized, and it must also cover the new management policies that were implemented along with the new computer system.

Second, the training should focus on what the user needs to do, not what the system can do. This is a subtle—but very important—distinction. Most systems provide far more capabilities than the users will need to use (e.g., when was the last time you wrote a macro in Microsoft Word?). Rather than attempting to teach the users all the features of the system, training should instead focus on the much smaller set of activities that users perform on a regular basis and ensure that users are truly experts in those. When the focus is on the 20 percent of functions that the users will use 80 percent of the time (instead of attempting to cover all functions), users become confident about their ability to use the system, and can gradually pick up other functions as needed. Training should mention the other little-used functions but only so that users are aware of their existence and know how to learn about them when their use becomes necessary.

One source of guidance for designing training materials is the use cases. The use cases outline the common activities that users perform and thus can be helpful in understanding the business processes and system functions that are likely to be most important to the users.

How to Train There are many ways to deliver training. The most commonly used approach is *classroom training*, in which many users are trained at the same time by the same instructor. This has the advantage of training many users at one time with only one instructor and creates a shared experience among the users.

It is also possible to provide *one-on-one training*, in which one trainer works closely with one user at a time. This is obviously more expensive, but the trainer can design the training program to meet the needs of individual users and can better ensure that the users really do understand the material. This approach is typically used only when the users are very important (they could become system evangelists that train other people) or when there are very few users.

Another approach that is becoming more common is to use some form of *computer-based training (CBT)*, in which the training program is delivered via computer, shared from an internal or external platform. CBT programs can include text slides, audio, video, and animation. Figure 12-8 summarizes four important factors to consider in selecting a training method: cost to develop, cost to deliver, impact, and reach. CBT is typically more expensive to develop than one-on-one or classroom training, but it is less expensive to deliver. One-on-one training has the most impact on the user because it can be customized to the user's precise needs, knowledge, and abilities, whereas CBT has the least impact. However, CBT has the greatest reach—the ability to train the most users over the widest distance in the shortest time—because it is much simpler to distribute than classroom and one-on-one training, simply because no instructors are needed.

Figure 12-8 suggests a clear pattern for most organizations. If there are only a few users to train, one-on-one training is the most effective. If there are many users to train, many organizations turn to CBT. Quite often, large organizations use a combination of all three methods.

	One-on-One Training	Classroom Training	Computer-Based Training
Cost to develop	Low to Medium	Medium	High
Cost to deliver	High	Medium	Low
Impact	High	Medium to High	Low to Medium
Reach	Low	Medium	High

FIGURE 12-8
Selecting a Training Method

Regardless of which approach is used, it is important to leave the users with a set of easily accessible materials that can be referred to long after the training has ended (usually a quick reference guide and a set of manuals).

Conversion

Conversion is the technical process by which a new system replaces an old system. Conversion moves the users from using the as-is business processes and computer programs to the to-be business processes and programs. The migration plan specifies what activities will be performed when and by whom and includes both technical aspects (such as installing hardware and software and converting data from the as-is system to the to-be system) and organizational aspects (such as training and motivating the users to embrace the new system). Conversion refers to the technical aspects of the migration plan.

There are three major steps to the conversion plan before commencement of operations: Install hardware, install software, and convert data (Figure 12-9). Although it may be possible to do some of these steps in parallel, usually they must be done sequentially at any one location.

The first step in the conversion plan is to buy and install any needed hardware. In many cases, no new hardware is needed, but sometimes the project requires new hardware such as servers, client computers, printers, and networking equipment. It is critical to work closely with vendors who are supplying needed hardware and software to ensure that the deliveries are coordinated with the conversion schedule so that the equipment is available when it is needed. Nothing can stop a conversion plan in its tracks as easily as the failure of a vendor to deliver needed equipment.

Once the hardware is installed, tested, and certified as being operational, the second step is to install the software. This includes the to-be system under development and, sometimes, additional software that must be installed to make the system operational. At this point, the system is usually tested again to ensure that it operates as planned.

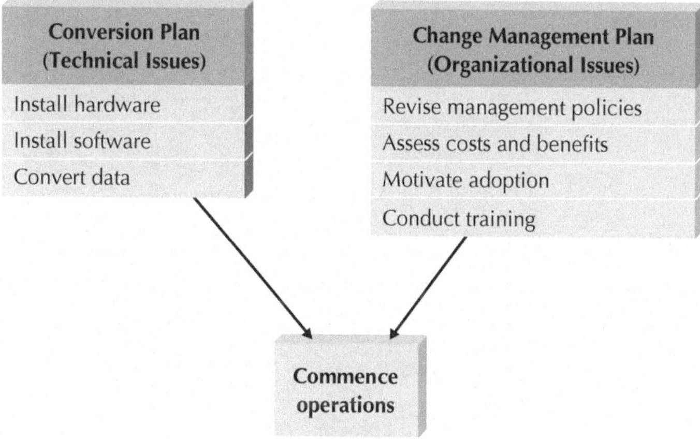

FIGURE 12-9
Elements of a Migration Plan

The third step is to convert the data from the as-is system to the to-be system. Data conversion is usually the most technically complicated step in the migration plan. Often, separate programs must be written to convert the data from the as-is system to the new formats required in the to-be system and store it in the to-be system files and databases. This process is often complicated by the fact that the files and databases in the to-be system do not exactly match the files and databases in the as-is system (e.g., the to-be system may use several tables in a database to store customer data that were contained in one file in the as-is system). Formal test plans are always required for data conversion efforts (see Chapter 7).

Conversion can be thought of along three dimensions: the style in which the conversion is done (*conversion style*), what location or work groups are converted at what time (*conversion location*), and what modules of the system are converted at what time (*conversion modules*). Figure 12-10 shows the potential relationships among these three dimensions.

Conversion Style The conversion style is the way users are switched between the old and new systems. There are two fundamentally different approaches to the style of conversion: direct conversion and parallel conversion.

With *direct conversion* (sometimes called cold turkey, big bang, or abrupt cutover), the new system instantly replaces the old system. The new system is turned on, and the old system is immediately turned off. This is the approach that we are likely to use when we upgrade commercial software (e.g., Internet Explorer to Microsoft Edge) from one version to another; we simply begin using the new version and stop using the old version. Direct conversion is the simplest and most straightforward. However, it is the riskiest because any problems with the new system that have escaped detection during testing can seriously disrupt the organization.

With *parallel conversion*, the new system is operated side by side with the old system; both systems are used simultaneously. For example, if a new accounting system is installed, the organization enters data into both the old system and the new system and then carefully compares the output from both systems to ensure that the new system is performing correctly. After some time period (often one to two months) of parallel operation and intense comparison between the two systems, the old system is turned off and the organization continues using the new system. This approach is more likely to catch any major bugs in the new system and prevent the organization from suffering major problems. If problems are discovered in the new system, the system is simply turned off and fixed and then the conversion process starts again. The problem with this approach is the added expense of operating two systems that perform the same function. It is possible to build an API or some other system that helps

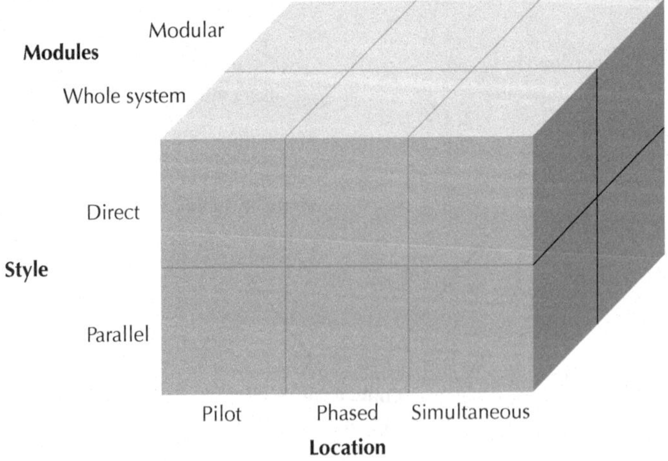

FIGURE 12-10
Conversion
Strategies

replicate entering data into the new/old system to save the users some time and effort. This will allow more emphasis on comparing the outputs from the parallel systems. However, this approach does bring added costs and could introduce errors of its own.

Conversion Location Conversion location refers to the parts of the organization that are converted when the conversion occurs. Often, parts of the organization are physically located in different offices (e.g., Toronto, Tokyo, and Dubai). In other cases, location refers to different organizational units located in different parts of the same office complex (e.g., order entry, shipping, and purchasing). There are at least three fundamentally different approaches to selecting the way different organizational locations are converted: pilot conversion, phased conversion, and simultaneous conversion.

With a *pilot conversion*, one or more locations or units or work groups within a location are selected to be converted first as part of a pilot test. The locations participating in the pilot test are converted (using either direct or parallel conversion). If the system passes the pilot test, then the system is installed at the remaining locations (again using either direct or parallel conversion). Pilot conversion has the advantage of providing an additional level of testing before the system is widely deployed throughout the organization, so that any problems with the system affect only the pilot locations. However, this type of conversion obviously requires more time before the system is installed at all organizational locations. Also, it means that different organizational units are using different versions of the system and business processes, which can make it difficult for them to exchange data.

With *phased conversion*, the system is installed sequentially at different locations. A first set of locations is converted, then a second set, then a third set, and so on, until all locations are converted. Sometimes there is a deliberate delay between the different sets (at least between the first and the second), so that any problems with the system are detected before too much of the organization is affected. In other cases, the sets are converted back-to-back so that as soon as those converting one location have finished, the project team moves to the next and continues the conversion. Phased conversion has the same advantages and disadvantages as pilot conversion. In addition, it means that fewer people are required to perform the actual conversion (and any associated user training) than if all locations were converted at once.

Simultaneous conversion, as the name suggests, means that all locations are converted at the same time. The new system is installed and made ready at all locations; at a preset time, all users begin using the new system. Simultaneous conversion is often used with direct conversion, but it can also be used with parallel conversion. Simultaneous conversion eliminates problems with having different organizational units using different systems and processes. However, it also means that the organization must have sufficient staff to perform the conversion and train the users at all locations simultaneously.

Conversion Modules Although it is natural to assume that systems are usually installed in their entirety, this is not always the case. Practically speaking, there are two approaches: whole system and modular conversion.

A *whole-system conversion*, in which the entire system is installed at one time, is the most common. It is simple and the easiest to understand. However, if the system is large and/or extremely complex (e.g., an enterprise resource-planning system such as SAP), the whole system can prove too difficult for users to learn in one conversion step.

When the *modules*[12] within a system are separate and distinct, organizations sometimes choose to convert to the new system one module at a time—i.e., using *modular conversion*. Modular conversion requires special care in developing the system (and usually adds extra

---

[12] In this case, a module is typically a component or a package, i.e., a set of collaborating classes.

cost). Each module either must be written to work with both the old and new systems or object wrappers (see Chapter 6) must be used to encapsulate the old system from the new. When modules are tightly integrated, this is very challenging and therefore is seldom done. However, when there is only a loose association between modules, module conversion is easier. For example, consider a conversion from an old version of Microsoft Office to a new version. It is relatively simple to convert from the old version of Word to the new version without simultaneously having to change from the old to the new version of Microsoft Excel. Modular conversion reduces the amount of training required to begin using the new system. Users need training only in the new module being implemented. However, modular conversion does take longer and has more steps than does the whole-system process.

Selecting the Appropriate Conversion Strategy Each of the three dimensions in Figure 12-10 is independent, so that a conversion strategy can be developed to fit in any one of the boxes in this figure. Different boxes can also be mixed and matched into one *conversion strategy*. For example, one commonly used approach is to begin with a pilot conversion of the whole system using parallel conversion in a handful of test locations. Once the system has passed the pilot test at these locations, it is then installed in the remaining locations using phased conversion with direct cutover. There are three important factors to consider in selecting a conversion strategy: *risk*, *cost*, and the *time* required (Figure 12-11).

After the system has passed a rigorous battery of unit, system, integration, and acceptance testing, it should be bug free . . . maybe. Because humans make mistakes, nothing built by people is perfect. Even after all these tests, there might still be a few undiscovered bugs. The conversion process provides one last step in which to catch these bugs before the system goes live and the bugs have the chance to cause problems.

Parallel conversion is less risky than direct conversion because it has a greater chance of detecting bugs that have gone undiscovered in testing. Likewise, pilot conversion is less risky than phased conversion or simultaneous conversion because if bugs do occur, they occur in pilot test locations whose staff are aware that they might encounter bugs. Because potential bugs affect fewer users, there is less risk. Likewise, converting a few modules at a time lowers the probability of a bug because there is more likely to be a bug in the whole system than in any given module.

The importance of each risk depends on the system being implemented—the combination of the probability that bugs remain undetected in the system and the potential cost of those undetected bugs. If the system has indeed been subjected to extensive methodical testing, including alpha and beta testing, then the probability of undetected bugs is lower than if the testing was less rigorous. However, there still might have been mistakes made in the analysis process, so that although there might be no software bugs, the software might fail to properly address the business needs.

| | Conversion Style | | Conversion Location | | | Conversion Modules | |
| | Direct | Parallel | Pilot | Phased | Simultaneous | Whole-System | Modular |
Characteristic	Conversion	Conversion	Conversion	Conversion	Conversion	Conversion	Conversion
Risk	High	Low	Low	Medium	High	High	Medium
Cost	Low	High	Medium	Medium	High	Medium	High
Time	Short	Long	Medium	Long	Short	Short	Long

FIGURE 12-11 Characteristics of Conversion Strategies

Assessing the cost of a bug is challenging, but most analysts and senior managers can make a reasonable guess at the relative cost of a bug. For example, the cost of a bug in an automated stock market trading program or a heart–lung machine keeping someone alive is likely to be much greater than a bug in a computer game or word processing program. Therefore, risk is likely to be a very important factor in the conversion process if the system has not been as thoroughly tested as it might have been or if the cost of bugs is high. If the system has been thoroughly tested or the cost of bugs is not that high, then risk becomes less important to the conversion decision.

As might be expected, different conversion strategies have different costs. These costs can include things such as salaries for people who work with the system (e.g., users, trainers, system administrators, external consultants), travel expenses, operation expenses, communication costs, and hardware leases. Parallel conversion is more expensive than direct cutover because it requires that two systems (the old and the new) be operated at the same time. Employees must then perform twice the usual work because they have to enter the same data into both the old and the new systems. Parallel conversion also requires the results of the two systems to be completely crosschecked to make sure there are no differences between the two, which entails additional time and cost.

Pilot conversion and phased conversion have somewhat similar costs. Simultaneous conversion has higher costs because more staff are required to support all the locations as they simultaneously switch from the old to the new system. Modular conversion is more expensive than whole-system conversion because it requires more programming. The old system must be updated to work with selected modules in the new system, and modules in the new system must be programmed to work with selected modules in both the old and new systems.

The final factor is the amount of time required to convert between the old and the new system. Direct conversion is the fastest because it is immediate. Parallel conversion takes longer because the full advantages of the new system do not become available until the old system is turned off. Simultaneous conversion is fastest because all locations are converted at the same time. Phased conversion usually takes longer than pilot conversion because once the pilot test is complete all remaining locations are usually (but not always) converted simultaneously. Phased conversion proceeds in waves, often requiring several months before all locations are converted. Likewise, modular conversion takes longer than whole-system conversion because the models are introduced one after another.

OPERATIONS AND SUPPORT WORKFLOW[13]

The goal of post-implementation activities is the *institutionalization* of the use of the new system—i.e., to make it the normal, accepted, routine way of performing the business processes. *Post-implementation* activities attempt to refreeze the organization after the successful transition to the new system. Although the work of the project team naturally winds down after implementation, the business sponsor and sometimes the project manager are actively involved in refreezing. These two—and, ideally, many other stakeholders—actively promote the new system and monitor its adoption and usage. They usually provide a steady flow of information about the system and encourage users to contact them to discuss issues.

In this section, we examine two key post-implementation activities that take place on the operations and support workflow during the production phase of the Unified Process: *system support* (providing assistance in the use of the system) and *system maintenance* (continuing to refine and improve the system).

---

[13] The material in this section is related to the Enhanced Unified Process's Production Phase (see Figure 1-18).

System Support

Once the project team has installed the system and performed the change management activities, the system is officially turned over to the *operations group*. This group is responsible for operating the system, whereas the project team was responsible for developing the system. Members of the operations group are usually closely involved in the installation activities because they are the ones who must ensure that the system actually works. After the system is installed, the project team leaves but the operations group remains.

Providing system support means helping the users to use the system. Usually, this means providing answers to questions and helping users understand how to perform a certain function; this type of support can be thought of as *on-demand training*. *Online support* is the most common form of on-demand training. This includes the documentation and help screens built into the system, as well as separate websites that provide answers to *frequently asked questions (FAQs)*, which enable users to find answers without contacting a person. Custom-built Artificial Intelligence (AI) chatbots can also help with some of this training. Obviously, the goal of most system support is to provide sufficiently good online support so that the user doesn't need to contact a person, because providing online support is much less expensive than providing a person to answer questions.

Most organizations also provide a *help desk* that provides a place for a user to talk with a person who can answer questions (usually over the phone but sometimes in person). The help desk supports all systems, not just one specific system, so it receives calls about a wide variety of software and hardware. The help desk is operated by *level-1 support* staff who have very broad computer skills and are able to respond to a wide range of requests, from network problems and hardware problems to problems with commercial software and problems with the business application software developed in-house.

The goal of most help desks is to have the level-1 support staff resolve 80 percent of the help requests they receive on the first call. Again, a custom-built AI chatbot can sometimes be useful in this context. If the issue cannot be resolved by level 1 support staff, a *problem report* (Figure 12-12) is completed (often using a special computer system designed to track problem reports) and passed to a *level-2 support* staff member.

The level-2 support staff members are people who know the application system well and can provide expert advice. For a new system, they are usually selected during the

Problem Report:		Date:	Time:
Support Person Name:			
Email Address:		Phone Number:	
Name of Person Reporting Problem:			
Email Address:		Phone Number:	
Software and/or Hardware Causing Problem:			
Location of Problem:			
Description of Problem:			
Action Taken:			
Disposition of Problem:			
☐ Problem Fixed ☐ Problem Forwarded to System Maintenance			

FIGURE 12-12
Elements of a
Problem Report

implementation phase and become familiar with the system as it is being tested. Sometimes the level-2 support staff members participate in training during the change management process to become more knowledgeable about the system, the new business processes, and the users themselves.

The level-2 support staff works with users to resolve problems. Most problems are successfully resolved by the level-2 staff, but there are other levels of support staff that specialize in certain areas of the system (e.g., level-3 network support). However, sometimes, particularly in the first few months after the system is installed, the problem turns out to be a bug in the software that must be fixed. In this case, the problem report becomes a *change request* that is passed to the system maintenance group (see the next section).

System Maintenance

System maintenance is the process of refining the system to make sure it continues to meet business needs. This could also include patching software with the latest updates. More money and effort are devoted to system maintenance than to the initial development of the system, simply because a system continues to change and evolve as it is used. Most beginning systems analysts and programmers work first on maintenance projects, usually only after they have gained some experience, are they assigned to new development projects.

Every system is "owned" by a project manager in the IS group (Figure 12-13). This individual is responsible for coordinating the system's maintenance effort for that system. Whenever a potential change to the system is identified, a change request is prepared and forwarded to the project manager. The change request is a smaller version of the *system request* discussed in Chapter 2. It describes the change requested and explains why the change is important.

Changes can be small or large. Change requests that are likely to require a significant effort are typically handled in the same manner as system requests. Minor changes typically follow a smaller version of this same process. There is an initial assessment of feasibility and of costs and benefits, and the change request is prioritized. Then a systems analyst (or a programmer/analyst) performs the analysis, which might include interviewing users, and prepares an initial design before programming begins. The new (or revised) program is then extensively tested before the system is converted from the old system to the revised one.

Change requests typically come from five sources. The most common source is problem reports from the operations group that identify bugs in the system that must be fixed. These are usually given immediate priority because a bug can cause significant problems. Even a minor bug can cause major problems by upsetting users and reducing their acceptance of and confidence in the system.

The second most common source of change requests is enhancement to the system from users. As users work with the system, they often identify minor changes in the design that can make the system easier to use or identify additional functions that are needed. Such enhancements are important in satisfying the users and are often key in ensuring that the system changes as the business requirements change. Enhancements are often given second priority after bug fixes.

The third source of change requests is other system development projects. For example, if the doctor in the appointment problem decided that he or she would like to have a Web-based appointment system that would allow patients to directly interact with the current appointment system, it is likely that other systems, such as billing, would have to be modified to ensure that the two systems would work together. These changes required by the need to integrate two systems are generally rare but are becoming more common as system integration efforts become more common.

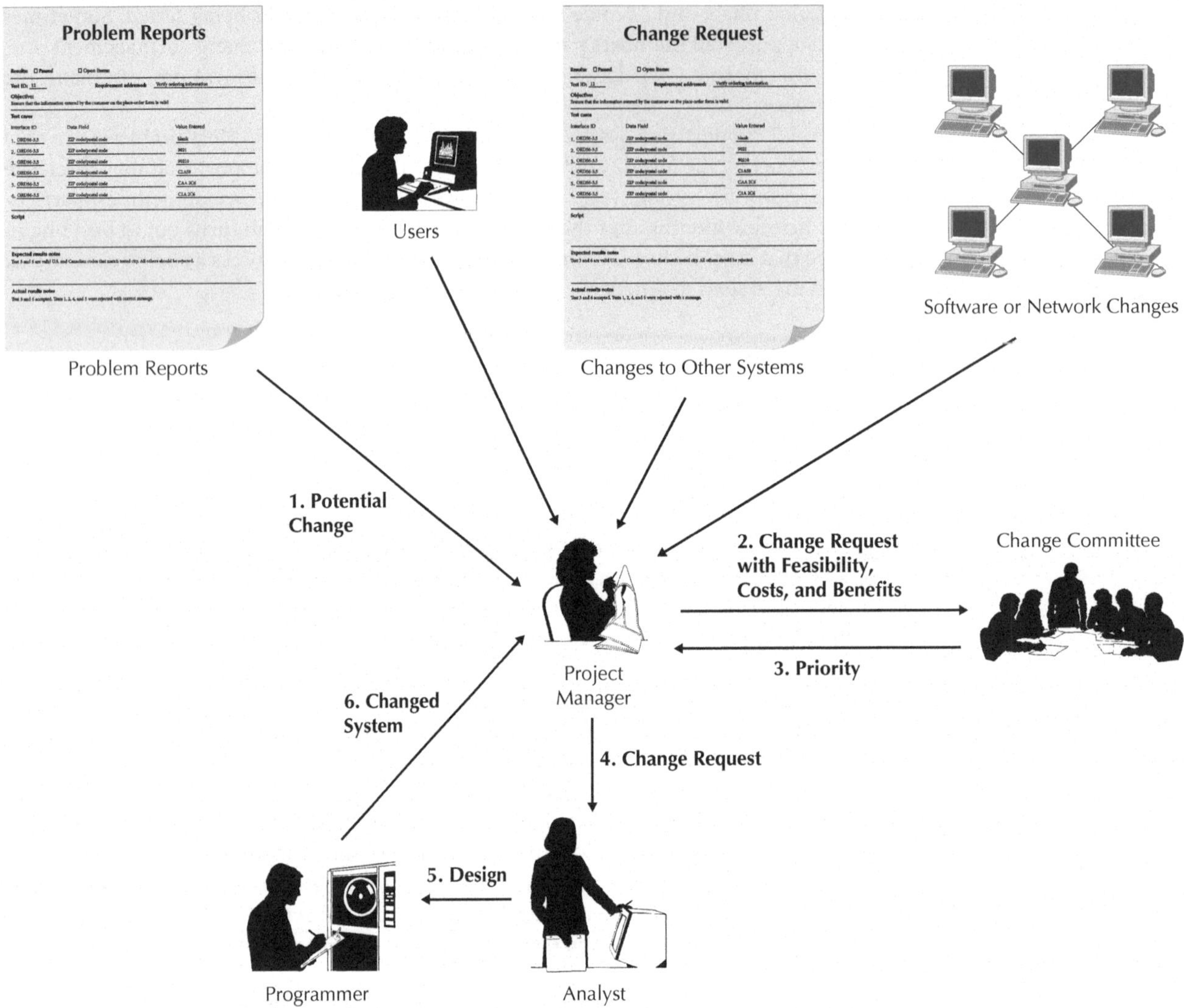

FIGURE 12-13 Processing a Change Request

The fourth source of change requests is those that occur when underlying software or networks change. For example, new versions of Windows often require an application to change the way the system interacts with Windows or enables application systems to take advantage of new features that improve efficiency. This could also include software patches mentioned earlier. Although users might never see these changes (because most changes are inside the system and do not affect its user interface or functionality), in some cases, these changes can be among the most challenging to implement because analysts and programmers must learn about the new system characteristics, understand how application systems use (or can use) those characteristics, and then make the needed programming changes.

The fifth source of change requests is senior management. These change requests are often driven by major changes in the organization's strategy or operations. These significant change requests are typically treated as separate projects, but the project manager responsible for the initial system is often placed in charge of the new project.

CHAPTER REVIEW

After reading and studying this chapter, you should be able to:

- ☐ Describe the importance of CASE Tools, standards, and system documentation in managing information systems development projects.
- ☐ Describe the different types of user documentation with an information system.
- ☐ Describe how to develop the user documentation of an information system.
- ☐ Describe cultural issues as they relate to information technology adoption.
- ☐ Describe how Hall's and Hofstede's cultural dimensions can affect information technology adoption.
- ☐ Discuss why people resist and accept change.
- ☐ Describe the major steps in a change management plan.
- ☐ Discuss the different strategies to motivate adoption of a new system.
- ☐ Discuss why training is crucial to the acceptance of a new system.
- ☐ Describe the technical and managerial issues related to system conversion.
- ☐ Discuss the three dimensions of system conversion.

KEY TERMS

Artifact library
CASE repository
Change agent
Change control
Change management
Change request
Classroom training
Collectivism
Computer-based training (CBT)
Computer-aided software engineering (CASE)
Context
Conversion
Conversion location
Conversion modules
Conversion strategy
Conversion style
Cost
Dependency relationships
Direct conversion
Documentation
Documentation navigation controls

Documentation topics
Femininity
Frequently asked questions (FAQ)
Help desk
Individualism
Informational strategy
Institutionalization
Level 1 support
Level 2 support
Long-term orientation
Masculinity
Management policies
Measurements
Migration plan
Modular conversion
Modules
Monochronic time
On-demand training
One-on-one training
Online support
Operations group
Parallel conversion
Perceived benefits

Perceived costs
Phased conversion
Pilot conversion
Political strategy
Polychronic time
Post-implementation
Potential adopter
Power distance
Problem report
Procedures manuals
Program log
Project binder
Ready adopters
Real benefits
Real costs
Reference documents
Refreeze
Reluctant adopters
Resistant adopters
Resource allocation
Rewards
Risk
Round trip engineering
Short-term orientation

Simultaneous conversion
Speed of messages
Sponsor
Standard operating procedure (SOP)
Standards
System documentation
System maintenance
System request
System support
Time
Traceability
Training
Transition process
Tutorials
Uncertainty avoidance
Unfreeze
User documentation
Version controls
Whole-system conversion

QUESTIONS

1. Describe three types of standards and provide examples of each.
2. What belongs in the project binder? How is the project binder organized?
3. Compare and contrast user documentation and system documentation.
4. Why is online documentation becoming more important?

5. What are the primary disadvantages of online documentation?

6. Compare and contrast reference documents, procedures manuals, and tutorials.

7. What are five types of documentation navigation controls?

8. What are the commonly used sources of documentation topics? Which is the most important? Why?

9. What are the commonly used sources of documentation navigation controls? Which is the most important? Why?

10. When it comes to IT adoption, what are the cultural issues of which developers should be aware?

11. What are the three basic steps in managing organizational change?

12. What are the major components of a migration plan?

13. What are the three key roles in any change management initiative?

14. Why do people resist change? Explain the basic model for understanding why people accept or resist change.

15. What are the three major elements of management policies that must be considered when implementing a new system?

16. Compare and contrast an information change management strategy with a political change management strategy. Is one better than the other?

17. Explain the three categories of adopters you are likely to encounter in any change management initiative.

18. How should you decide what items to include in your training plan?

19. Compare and contrast three basic approaches to training.

20. Compare and contrast direct conversion and parallel conversion.

21. Compare and contrast pilot conversion, phased conversion, and simultaneous conversion.

22. Compare and contrast modular conversion and whole-system conversion.

23. What is the role of the operations group in system development?

24. Compare and contrast two major ways of providing system support.

25. How is a problem report different from a change request?

26. What are the major sources of change requests?

27. What do you think are three common mistakes that novice analysts make in migrating from the as-is to the to-be system?

28. Some experts argue that change management is more important than any other part of system development. Do you agree or not? Explain.

29. In our experience, change management planning often receives less attention than conversion planning. Why do you think this happens?

EXERCISES

A. Suppose you are installing a new accounting package in your small business. What conversion strategy would you use? Develop a conversion plan (i.e., technical aspects only).

B. Suppose you are installing a new room reservation system for your university that tracks which courses are assigned to which rooms. Assume that all the rooms in each building are "owned" by one college or department and only one person in that college or department has permission to assign them. What conversion strategy would you use? Develop a conversion plan (i.e., technical aspects only).

C. Suppose you are installing a new payroll system in a very large multinational corporation. What conversion strategy would you use? Develop a conversion plan (i.e., technical aspects only).

D. Consider a major change you have experienced in your life (e.g., taking a new job, starting a new school).

Prepare a cost–benefit analysis of the change in terms of both the change and the transition to the change.

E. Suppose you are the project manager for a new library system for your university. The system will improve the way students, faculty, and staff can search for books by enabling them to search over the Web, rather than using only the current text-based system available on the computer terminals in the library. Prepare a cost–benefit analysis of the change in terms of both the change and the transition to the change for the major stakeholders.

F. Prepare a plan to motivate the adoption of the system in exercise E.

G. Prepare a training plan that includes both what you would train and how the training would be delivered for the system in exercise E.

H. Suppose you are leading the installation of a new DSS to help admissions officers manage the admissions process at your university. Develop a change management plan (i.e., organizational aspects only).

I. Suppose you are the project leader for the development of a new Web-based course registration system for your university that replaces an old system in which students had to go to the coliseum at certain times and stand in line to get permission slips for each course they wanted to take. Develop a migration plan (including both technical conversion and change management).

J. Suppose you are the project leader for the development of a new airline reservation system that will be used by the airline's in-house reservation agents. The system will replace the current command-driven system designed in the 1970s that uses terminals. The new system uses PCs with a Web-based interface. Develop a migration plan (including both conversion and change management) for your telephone operators.

K. Develop a migration plan (including both conversion and change management) for the independent travel agencies that use the airline reservation system described in exercise J.

MINICASES

1. Nancy is the IS department head at MOTO Inc., a human resources management firm. The IS staff at MOTO Inc. completed work on a new client management software system about a month ago. Nancy was impressed with the performance of her staff on this project because the firm had not previously undertaken a project of this scale in-house. One of Nancy's weekly tasks is to evaluate and prioritize the change requests that have come in for the various applications used by the firm.

Right now, Nancy has five change requests for the client system on her desk. One request is from a system user who would like some formatting changes made to a daily report produced by the system. Another request is from a user who would like the sequence of menu options changed on one of the system menus to more closely reflect the frequency of use for those options. A third request came in from the billing department.

This department performs billing through a billing software package. A major upgrade of this software is being planned, and the interface between the client system and the bill system need to be changed to accommodate the new software's data structures. The fourth request seems to be a system bug that occurs whenever a client cancels a contract (a rare occurrence, fortunately). The last request came from Susan, the company president. This request confirms the rumor that MOTO Inc. is about to acquire another new business. The new business specializes in the temporary placement of skilled professional and scientific employees and represents a new business area for MOTO Inc. The client management software system will need to be modified to incorporate the special client arrangements that are associated with the acquired firm.

How do you recommend that Nancy prioritize these change requests for the client/management system?

2. Sky View Aerial Photography offers a wide range of aerial photographic, video, and infrared imaging services. The company has grown from its early days of snapping pictures of client houses to its current status as a full-service aerial image specialist. Sky View now maintains numerous contracts with various governmental agencies for aerial mapping and surveying work. Sky View has its offices at the airport, where it keeps its fleet of specially equipped aircraft. Sky View contracts with several freelance pilots and photographers for some of its aerial work and also employs several full-time pilots and photographers.

The owners of Sky View Aerial Photography recently contracted with a systems development consulting firm to develop a new information system for the business. As the number of contracts, aircraft, flights, pilots, and photographers increased, the company experienced difficulty keeping accurate records of its business activity and the utilization of its fleet of aircraft. The new system will require all pilots and photographers to swipe an ID badge through a reader at the beginning and conclusion of each photo flight, along with recording information about the aircraft used and the client served on that flight. These records are to be reconciled against the actual aircraft utilization logs maintained and recorded by the hangar personnel.

The office staff was eagerly awaiting the installation of the new system. Their general attitude was that the system would reduce the number of problems and errors that they encountered and would make their work easier. The pilots, photographers, and hangar staff were less enthusiastic, being unaccustomed to having their activities monitored in this way.

a. Discuss the factors that might inhibit the acceptance of this new system by the pilots, photographers, and hangar staff.

b. Discuss how an informational strategy could be used to motivate adoption of the new system at Sky View Aerial Photography.

c. Discuss how a political strategy could be used to motivate adoption of the new system at Sky View Aerial Photography.

PART FOUR

FUTURE DIRECTIONS

The primary future direction of systems analysis and design is in agile development. Whereas the Unified Process is considered to be a heavy weight methodology, agile approaches are very light weight. The emphasis of agile approaches is streamlining the system-development process by eliminating much of the modeling and documentation overhead and the time spent on those tasks.

CHAPTER 13 AGILE METHODOLOGIES AND MODELING FOR INFORMATION SYSTEMS

Agile Foundations: Values and Principles

Common Agile Frameworks

Effective Agile Practices and Tools

Agile Modeling

Limitations of Agile

AGILE METHODOLOGIES AND MODELING FOR INFORMATION SYSTEMS

In the previous chapters you learned how to use the Unified Process methodology to follow the systems development life cycle (SDLC) steps to create and manage information systems. A major alternative to the Unified Process is the *agile methodology*. Today there are several versions of the agile methodology (or agile for short) that align with the values and principles outlined in the Agile Manifesto. Each of these versions are sometimes referred to as an agile framework or approach, as opposed to a methodology because there is a desire to not be seen as rigid and overly prescriptive. An agile approach to creating and managing information systems is gaining steady acceptance and is especially powerful for short-term, non-mission critical projects. In this chapter we provide an overview of agile and describe core values and practices, including the challenging issue of modeling in agile.

OBJECTIVES

- Understand the values, and fundamental principles of agile and how it fits within the systems development life cycle (SDLC).
- Understand the differences of some of the popular frameworks of agile.
- Be familiar with the popular agile modeling approaches.
- Be familiar with some of the popular practices of agile.
- Be familiar with the basic principles of agile modeling.
- Be familiar with alternative approaches to agile modeling.
- Recognize the potential of evolving research in agile modeling.

INTRODUCTION

When we say "agile" in an organizational context, we mean that an organization (business, non-profit organization, government agency, and entire government) can quickly and efficiently adapt to changing circumstances. Most people would agree that this is a desirable characteristic of organizations because it makes them capable of surviving and thriving in the changing economic, political and cultural environment. For example, if customer preferences shift to more environmentally friendly products, an agile business is one that would more easily adapt to these changes and deliver these types of products. Likewise, if most of the public prefers to see increased infrastructure spending, an agile government would be the one able to expediently deliver on these needs. As a result, the public could soon enjoy new airports, railways, roads, and bridges. It is in this same sense of agility that agile systems development was born. Agile development seeks to better address the changing opportunities and challenges of the modern digital world.

The writers of the Agile Manifesto, the creators of agile, felt that too many software development projects focused on the wrong things during software development. It was not necessarily that other methodologies were characteristically bad, instead there was too much focus on gathering all the requirements at one time at the beginning of the project, documenting them, and defining success by how well the project adhered to the requirements. These other methodologies did not allow for flexibility during software development. Today, most businesses want to implement aspects of agile software development, particularly seeking to leverage their iterative and incremental nature.

The rest of this chapter will help you become more familiar with agile software development. We start by defining and describing agile software development. We provide some historical context to give you an opportunity to appreciate the intentions behind its creation. While agile introduced some new ways of thinking about creating and managing IS, it has not been the "silver bullet" to fix all problems with software development methodologies. This will lead us to the next section of this chapter that will provide an overview of some of the different frameworks of agile that are available today. These different frameworks have been created in response to some of the challenges with using agile beyond what was outlined in the Agile Manifesto. We conclude by showing you some modeling approaches that can be helpful while you work using agile.

AGILE FOUNDATIONS: VALUES AND PRINCIPLES

The Inception of Agile

As you have probably recognized by this point, creating and managing information systems (IS) is challenging and involves managing risks. [If you have not yet done so, please go back and read Chapter 1 for an overview.] This is why software development methodologies are incredibly helpful, as they provide a way to manage risk for successful software development. Prior to having formal software development methodologies, systems analysts and other project members had less certainty about whether the work they were doing would provide software that would be valuable to their customers. Formal software development methodologies introduced structure and steps that could be followed while creating IS. With a methodology in hand, systems analysts and other project members could manage software development in the same way that someone in operations management might manage a new product launch. This would decrease the risk for software development projects and increase the chances that software could deliver more efficiency and effectiveness for the business.

However, a group of prominent software developers were unhappy with many of the existing software development methodologies and wrote the Agile Manifesto in 2001[1] to suggest another approach. They were dissatisfied with the alarming and stubbornly high rate of projects failure (recall some numbers from Chapter 1). One of the biggest motivations for the creation of a new approach was that existing methodologies had a long gap of time between when all project requirements were gathered and then implemented. There were many reasons for this delay. For example, it took a lot of time to create all the necessary project management documents and "sign off" agreements, the time it took to develop software then was much slower than it is today (e.g., Generative AI was not available to automatically write code for individuals who provided it a prompt for what they wanted). However, this delay had inherent uncertainty and risk because users might change their mind by the time

---

[1] https://agilemanifesto.org/.

the software was implemented, or there could even be a realization that the requirements the systems analysts and other projects members thought were accurate, turned out not to be accurate because users are not always good at stating or recalling requirements or because their requirements changed due to changing circumstances.[2] The Agile Manifesto directly challenged the overhead of software project management and delays in building software. The tradition of gathering all the requirements up front and building a detailed project plan with all the steps outlined in advance in order to manage the project constraints of time, budget, and scope in a linear and predictable manner was rarely successful. Instead, the Agile Manifesto urged for shorter iterations between gathering requirements and building software. This way, the software can be given to users for evaluation and feedback prior to another iteration of work. In the next sections, we examine Agile Manifesto's values and the practices that have emerged.

Agile Values: The Essence of Agile Approach

The *Agile Manifesto* outlines four core values that form the foundation of the original agile methodology. These values promote face-to-face communication, *working software*, customer collaboration, and adaptability over rigid processes and documentation. They serve as guiding principles for Agile teams, shaping how they approach development and interact among themselves and with their customers. By promoting these values, Agile aims to create a more responsive, efficient, and effective development process that meets the evolving needs of customers. Each of these values introduces a different way of thinking about software development compared to how it was carried out traditionally.

Value 1: Individuals and Interactions Over Processes and Tools *Processes* and *tools* are essential for organizing work and supporting collaboration, but they may also hinder personal *interactions*. Personal interactions are essential for understanding what needs to be done. Agile software development teams focus on building strong relationships and creating an open, communicative environment where team members can share ideas, give and receive feedback, and work together to achieve common goals. Less emphasis should be placed on the specific tools (e.g., programming language) and adhering to a specific process. Each project might be different and there is no reason to be constrained by trying to fit a square peg (i.e., the process and tools) into a round hole (i.e., the solution needed). Most Agile methodologies include short daily meetings to keep everyone on the team in sync with the progress, challenges, and opportunities for the project.

Value 2: Working Software Over Comprehensive Documentation As you can see from the previous chapters, documentation takes time to develop. Documentation is often used to gain buy-in and shared understanding from all individuals involved in the project. Agile shifts the focus to creating systems that can provide value to the stakeholders. The working systems and the value they produce become the evidence of the buy-in and shared understanding as opposed to the documentation. This value encourages teams to produce systems iteratively and incrementally, delivering small, usable increments early and often. The moment code is written, an Agile methodology encourages to think about managing a product as opposed to the project. As the iterations progress, the goal becomes how can the product continue to deliver maximal value for the customers.

---

[2] Browne, G. J., and Ramesh, V. 2002. "Improving Information Requirements Determination: A Cognitive Perspective," *Information & Management* (39:8), pp. 625–645 provides a good overview for challenges and suggestions to improve gathering requirements.

Value 3: Customer Collaboration Over Contract Negotiation Traditional methodologies commonly involve detailed contracts that specify the project's scope, timeline, and deliverables. These contracts can become sources of conflict and rigidity when requirements change, or unforeseen challenges arise. Agile promotes a more flexible and trusting relationship with customers, where ongoing feedback and open communication help shape the system as it evolves. Instead of pointing fingers when the software is not yet delivering its desired value, close collaboration becomes an opportunity to continue to improve the product.

Value 4: Responding to Change Over Following a Plan This last value prioritizes adaptability and responsiveness in the face of constant change. Traditional project management relies on detailed plans that define the project's course from start to finish. These plans can be requirements documentation, data models and other diagrams you saw in the previous chapters. However, development can be unpredictable, with *changing requirements*, technologies, and market conditions. Agile encourages teams to embrace change and adjust their plans as needed to reflect new information and priorities.

Agile Principles: Guiding Practices

In addition to the core values, the Agile Manifesto provides twelve principles that offer more concrete guidance on Agile practices. You will notice some connection and overlap between the guiding practices, but they seek to realize the values described above.

Principle 1: Customer Satisfaction Through Early and Continuous Delivery The principle suggests delivering system features early and often. By releasing functional increments of the product regularly, Agile teams can gather feedback, validate their work, and adjust their work to better meet the evolving and emerging requirements.

Principle 2: Welcome Changing Requirements, Even Late in Development Agile processes seek to harness change for the customer's competitive advantage. This means recognizing that requirements can evolve, and new requirements may emerge as the project progresses. This adaptability ensures that the final product aligns with the latest customer needs and market conditions. The developers (and all other Agile project members) and customers should see themselves on the same team and ultimately working together to make the best decisions for their team.

Principle 3: Deliver Working Software Frequently Frequent delivery of system features ranging from a few weeks to a few months, with a preference for shorter timescales (e.g., two weeks) enables continuous customer feedback, testing and validation. By dividing the development process into smaller, manageable increments (such as Sprints in Scrum, as discussed later), the developer teams can maintain a steady pace and adapt to changes more easily. These frequent releases ensure the system is steadily improving.

Principle 4: Business and Developers Must Work Together Daily This principle emphasizes the importance of ongoing, close physical dialog between developers and stakeholders to ensure that the development remains aligned with the changing requirements. Daily interactions also help bridge the gap between technical and non-technical team members, facilitating open communication, shared understanding, and effective decision making. It allows more opportunities for the voice of the customer to be heard and relationships to be cemented. The less friction there is between the customer and the Agile project team, the better they can work together.

Principle 5: Build Projects Around Motivated Individuals Agile teams should be composed of members who have the skills, motivation, and resources they need to succeed. Trust and autonomy are also key as they enable developers to take ownership of their work and make decisions that drive the project forward. When individuals are motivated to make optimal decisions that benefit the team (see Principle 2) then the project is more likely to be successful.

Principle 6: Face-to-Face Conversation Is the Most Effective Communication Physical face-to-face interaction is the most effective way to convey information, resolve issues, and build relationships among team members and with the customers. In cases where physical interactions are impossible, frequent video calls and site visits are essential.

Principle 7: Working Software Is the Primary Measure of Progress Working, error-free software code that delivers desired value is the only tangible evidence of progress. The ultimate goal of development is to deliver usable systems that meet customer needs and deliver organizational value. Other goals, such as documentation, are important, but are secondary.

Principle 8: Maintain a Sustainable Pace of Work Agile teams should aim for a consistent, manageable workload, avoiding the burnout and fatigue associated with long hours and intense periods of work. By establishing a steady rhythm, teams can maintain high productivity, quality, and motivation over the course of the project. In some sense, this might be "indefinitely" since Agile projects do not have defined end dates. Even if specific individuals move to different assignments, take a job with another organization, etc., there should be specific people to keep the project moving.

Principle 9: Continuous Attention to Technical Excellence and Good Design Over the long run of the project, the teams should not take a lazy or haphazard approach to design and programming. Instead, they should strive to create the best programming code possible, with some understandable tradeoffs that may require more iterations to improve (e.g., if someone is trying to hit a deadline, working software is better than perfection as in Principle 7). This requires the commitment to improving technical practices and maintaining an easy (for others) to understand, clean, and adaptable codebase. This includes using best practices such as pair programming, continuous integration, automated testing, and design patterns.

Principle 10: Simplicity—the Art of Maximizing the Amount of Work Not Done Some see simplicity as key to Agile success. Agile teams should focus on the most important features and avoid unnecessary complexity. The idea of developer "gold plating" (e.g., adding unnecessary features to a product that users did not want) is not welcome. In many ways, documentation is avoided because it is seen as an unwanted burden. This principle encourages teams to prioritize tasks, eliminate waste, and deliver the *minimum viable product* that meets user needs.

Principle 11: Self-Organizing Teams Agile proponents argue that the best designs emerge from self-organizing teams. By empowering teams to take ownership of their processes and solutions, Agile development promotes innovation, collaboration, and accountability. The less hierarchy and managerial mandates given, the more efficiently and effectively the team will work as they figure their own strategies for management and accomplishing the work. Working closely together (Principle 6) supports this principle as well.

Principle 12: Regular Reflection on How to Become More Effective This principle suggests that the teams should periodically reflect on what they did, what challenges they faced, and how to enhance their practices moving forward. This should be done at regular intervals, to ensure the problems are addressed promptly and not repeated in future projects or iterations.

Realizing Agile Values and Principles

The four *Agile values* provide a broad philosophical framework for Agile practices, while the twelve principles offer specific suggestions for how to realize these values and deliver high quality systems. However, these values and principles remain high-level and are relatively vague. For example, how exactly do you maximize the work not done? Much room for interpretation exists, which may result in development practices that do not deliver on their promise.

A major concern about Agile is the possibility of "programmers gone wild" scenario. In this scenario, the values and principles of Agile may be misinterpreted as not following any plan, and doing whatever suits the moment in hopes something good comes out of it. That is rarely a recipe for anything but a disaster. In the age of digital information, ubiquitous computing and mind-blowing artificial intelligence, information systems impact the lives of humans and the broader environment in dramatic, and often unpredictable ways. The development of information systems should never be taken lightly. Practicing Agile responsibly is greatly facilitated by following proven and established Agile frameworks, practices, and tools.

COMMON AGILE FRAMEWORKS

The popular *agile frameworks* were developed by the leading thinkers in the agile community and are generally consistent with the values and principles outlined in the Agile Manifesto (some of these frameworks were created before the Agile Manifesto). These frameworks have been applied in different scenarios and shown to be effective (although, arguably, none is without limitations). Much research is also conducted on evaluating the benefits and limitations of these frameworks so that the developers can make informed decisions about them.

Frameworks provide approaches for implementing Agile practices in systems development, each with its unique processes, roles, and artifacts. These frameworks can be divided into two groups. One group of frameworks was created with smaller, co-located teams in mind. This is closer to the ideal circumstances in the Agile Manifesto. Popular Agile frameworks in this group include Scrum and Extreme Programming (XP), among others. One way to label this group of frameworks is *team agile frameworks*, and this helps recognize that it was meant for a single team. However, sometimes there were larger efforts that needed multiple teams that were not co-located, for example, 50 or more people with at least six teams and in at least two different geographical locations.[3] An agile framework needed to be *scaled* to fit this context, and two popular *scaled agile frameworks* are Scrum@Scale[4] and *Scaling Agile Framework* (SAFe).[5]

By understanding the differences and tradeoffs in these frameworks, you can choose the one that best fits your needs. Each of these frameworks has their own language and terms that they use, and all will need careful implementation and adaptation to work within the organization's specific industry and culture. The goal in describing the frameworks below is not for you to master them, but instead to help you see ways that agile values and principles have been enacted in practice today.

---

[3] S. Beecham, T. Clear, R. Lal, and J. Noll, "Do scaling agile frameworks address global software development risks? An empirical study," *Journal of Systems and Software* 171 (January 2021), https://www.sciencedirect.com/science/article/pii/S0164121220302181.

[4] CAPGemini, "Which Agile-Scalin Fframework Should You Trust For Your Distributed Agile Delivery," (June 29, 2020), https://www.capgemini.com/insights/expert-perspectives/which-agile-scaling-framework-should-you-trust-for-your-distributed-agile-delivery/.

[5] https://scaledagileframework.com/.

Scrum[6]

Scrum is the most widely used team agile framework. It is a framework that focuses on delivering work in fixed-length iterations called *sprints*, typically lasting two to four weeks. At the end of the sprint, a system is delivered to the customer. Scrum is a term that is well known to rugby fans. In rugby, a scrum is used to restart a game. In a nutshell, the creators of the Scrum framework believe that no matter how much you plan, as soon as the software begins to be developed, chaos breaks out and the plans go out the window.[7] The best you can do is to react to where the proverbial rugby ball squirts out. You then sprint with the ball until the next scrum.

The Scrum framework outlines roles, ceremonies, and artifacts (e.g., user stories, tools, and feature lists) that facilitate planning, coding, testing, and delivery of systems. The key roles in Scrum are *Product Owner*, Scrum Master, and Development Team:

- The Product Owner represents the customer, provides, clarifies and verifies the requirements, and prioritizes the work.

- The *Scrum Master* is the guardian of the Scrum methodology. The Scrum Master explains scrum framework, the values and principles of agile to the customer and the development team and ensures the adherence to the framework and agile methodology. Being in this role puts this person in a good position to oversee the entire process and find ways to improve it.

- The Development Team is made of coders, testers, usability experts, researchers and possibly others (e.g., ethics experts and psychologists). The Development team carries out the necessary activities to develop the system that delivers the desired value.

Scrum relies on *ceremonies*—events that facilitate communication, planning, review, and execution of the project. It commonly includes Sprint Planning, Daily Scrum Stand ups, Sprint Reviews, Sprint Retrospectives and Backlog refinement. The ceremonies commonly involve the members of the Development Team.

Scrum meetings are one of the most interesting aspects of the Scrum development process. All team members are expected to attend the meetings, but anyone (e.g., customers) can also attend. However, with very few exceptions, only team members may speak. One prominent exception is customers providing feedback on the business relevance of the work being performed by the specific team. In meetings, all team members typically stand in a circle and report on what they accomplished during the previous day, state what they plan to do today, and describe anything that blocked progress the previous day. To enable continuous progress, any block identified is dealt with within one hour. From a Scrum point of view, it is better to make a "bad" decision about a block at this point in development than to not make a decision. Because the meetings take place each day, a bad decision can easily be undone. Larman[8] suggests that each team member should report any additional requirements that have been uncovered during the sprint and anything that the team member learned that could be useful for other team members to know.

Scrum has a few key practices to provide some direction. Teams are self-organized and self-directed. Unlike other approaches, Scrum teams do not have a designated team leader.

---

[6] For more information, see C. Larman, *Agile & Iterative Development: A Manager's Guide* (Boston: Addison-Wesley, 2004); K. Schwaber and M. Beedle, *Agile Software Development with Scrum* (Upper Saddle River, NJ: Prentice Hall, 2001); R. Wysocki, *Effective Project Management: Traditional, Agile, Extreme,* 5th Ed. (Indianapolis, IN: Wiley Publishing, 2009).

[7] Scrum developers are not the first to question the use of plans. One of President Eisenhower's favorite maxims was, "In preparing for battle I have always found that plans are useless, but planning is indispensable." M. Dobson, *Streetwise Project Management: How to Manage People, Processes, and Time to Achieve the Results You Need* (Avon, MA: F+W Publications, 2003), p. 43.

[8] C. Larman, *Agile & Iterative Development: A Manager's Guide* (Boston: Addison-Wesley, 2004).

Instead, teams organize themselves in a symbiotic manner and set their own goals for each sprint (iteration). Once a sprint has begun, Scrum teams do not consider any additional requirements. Any new requirements that are uncovered are placed on a backlog of requirements that still need to be addressed. At the beginning of every workday, a Scrum meeting takes place. At the end of each sprint, the team demonstrates the software to the client. Based on the results of the sprint, a new plan begins for the next sprint. Artifacts such as the Product Backlog, Sprint Backlog, and Product Increment help the team organize and track their work.

eXtreme Programming

Extreme programming (*XP*) is as controversial as alluring, and in some cases it can be incredibly powerful. As the name suggests, it seeks to take agile practices to the extreme. The idea is not only to embrace change, but to turn change into an inspiration and ally.

XP may not be for every project, but if executed well, and in the right circumstances, eXtreme programming can deliver outsized value, the one hard to match with other approaches.

Extreme Programming (XP) promotes five core values:

- Communication
- Simplicity
- Feedback
- Courage
- Respect

Communication is critical for XP, as it relies on intense contact and continuous dialog between developers, customers and users to ensure everyone is always "on the same page." The developers should be in constant contact with the customers, ideally working side-be-side. Indeed, some consider customers and users to be part of the development team.

Simplicity is the idea to be as lean as possible and avoid any unnecessary effort or deliverables. XP requires developers to follow the *KISS* principle.[9] Being in close proximity to the users should permit early discovery of the top priority features. Communication also allows the developers to explain to the users why certain features may not be as important as they seem.

The developers must provide rapid *feedback* to the end users on a continuous basis. This ensures the development progresses as rapidly and smoothly as possible, with constant oversight by customers and users.

Everyone on the development team should feel responsible for the final product, i.e. should demonstrate *courage*. XP often involves hard decisions on what to prioritize and what to ignore (recall simplicity). It takes courage to stand up and challenge the team or the customers in the shaping of the development priorities. It also takes courage to embrace the great uncertainty and change that comes from such a streamlined approach to development. It takes guts to say to a person who signs your paycheck: "You aren't gonna need it" (YAGNI)! What if you end up being wrong? Can you ever be sure what someone might need in the future? In short, it's not easy to be courageous, but you can make a huge difference if you responsibly practice courage.

To foster the culture of change, openness and understanding, everyone involved needs to have the utmost *respect* for each other. This ensures that everyone's perspective can be considered, and conflicts can be resolved in an amicable and productive way.

These five values provide a foundation that XP developers use to create any system. In addition, XP developers subscribe to a number of practices. Among the key XP practices

---

[9] Keep it simple, stupid.

stemming from the core values are automation, small releases, user stories, continuous testing, adherence to standards, coding performed by pairs of developers (or pair programming), continuous code integration, and close interactions with users to build systems very quickly.

An XP project begins with user stories—types of requirements models—that describe what the system needs to do. XP projects deliver results quickly and they rarely get bogged down in gathering requirements for the system. Sometimes even user stories are skipped, as working with customers and users directly may permit efficient verbal discovery of the requirements (although as you will see later, we still suggest performing modeling, even when you have the ability to talk to customers).

Once what needs to be done is more or less clear, programmers typically create automated tests that the future code should pass should it adhere to the understood requirements. Afterwards, pairs of programmers create small, simple modules and immediately test these to meet those needs. Users are required to be available to clear up questions and issues as they arise. Standards are very important to minimize confusion, so XP teams use a common set of names, descriptions, and coding practices.

Testing and efficient coding practices are the core of XP. Code is tested continuously, multiple times a day, and is placed into an integrative testing environment. If bugs exist, the code is backed out until it is completely free of errors.

XP adherents claim many strengths associated with developing software using XP. A key benefit of XP is the ability to rapidly react to change. The system is developed in an evolutionary and incremental manner, which allows the requirements to evolve as the stakeholders understand the potential that the technology has in providing a solution to their problem. As programmers work closely with the customers, there is a great deal of mutual understanding among everyone. Because programming is done in pairs, a shared responsibility for each software component develops among the programmers. As a result of these practices, the quality of the final product tends to increase during each iteration. *Customer satisfaction* with the final product can be very high.

For small projects with highly motivated, cohesive, stable, and experienced teams, XP should work just fine. However, if the project is not small or the teams aren't jelled,[10] the success of an XP development effort is doubtful. This challenges the whole idea of bringing outside contractors into an existing team environment using XP.[11] Although, this practice is not uncommon. The chance of outsiders jelling with insiders might simply be too optimistic.

XP requires a great deal of discipline, otherwise projects will become unfocused and chaotic. We recommend XP for small groups of developers—no more than ten developers—and it is not recommended for large mission-critical applications. It is also not very effective for situations where requirements are known to be stable. For example, a common task in the industry is converting legacy data storage systems into streamlined formats. For instance, you may be asked to collect several spreadsheets that different accountants have been using to track their customers and develop a unified database to replace them. If the structure of the spreadsheets has been relatively standardized and remained stable for some time, this is a low change and stable requirements project. Adopting an XP approach may not be needed in this case.

Owing to the lack of analysis and design documentation, there is mainly code documentation associated with XP, so maintaining large systems built with XP may be impossible. Auditing XP development processes and the resulting systems can be a major challenge.

---

[10] Recall that a *jelled team* is one that has low turnover, a strong sense of identity, a sense of eliteness, a feeling that they jointly own the product being developed, and enjoyment in working together. For more information regarding jelled teams, see T. DeMarco and T. Lister, *Peopleware: Productive Projects and Teams* (New York: Dorset/House, 1987).

[11] Considering the tendency for offshore outsourcing, this is a major obstacle for XP to overcome. For more information on offshore outsourcing, see P. Thibodeau, "ITAA Panel Debates Outsourcing Pros, Cons," Computerworld Morning Update (September 25, 2003); S. W. Ambler, "Chicken Little Was Right," *Software Development* (October 2003).

Finally, the methodology needs a lot of on-site user input, something to which many organizational units cannot commit. Some organizations may be initially enthusiastic about embracing XP, but this enthusiasm may quickly wean as they discover the time and effort commitment this involves on the part of their functional employees.

At the same time, some of the techniques associated with XP are useful in object-oriented systems development. For example, user stories, pair programming, and continuous testing and integration are invaluable tools from which object-oriented systems development could benefit.[12] Hence, it is valuable to understand the values and practices of XP, even if you don't plan to explicitly follow them.

Scrum@Scale (S@S)

What happens to the Scrum framework when there is a need to scale it beyond one team and to multiple areas of the organization? There are actually a few frameworks that tackle this challenge. One option is Large Scale Scrum (LeSS), another is Enterprise Scrum, and the one we will describe is Scrum@Scale. All are essentially some forms of a scrum of scrum teams with varying levels of prescription.

The *Scrum@Scale*[13] framework was developed by Jeff Sutherland and suggests two cycles that are related to scrum: (1) the *scrum master cycle*; and (2) the *product owner cycle*. Within each cycle is a group of "executives" that are trying to support the multiple teams: an *Executive Action Team* (EAT) supports the scrum master cycle, and the *Executive MetaScrum* (EMS) supports the product owner cycle.

In Scrum@Scale, each team still has a product owner, scrum master, and development team. However, there is now an added layer for all scrum masters and product owners from each team to coordinate with each other. This coordination happens in a *"scrum of scrums"*, and there is a corresponding *Scrum of Scrums Master* (SoSM) and a *Chief Product Owner* (CPO) to handle the sprints and backlogs.

In the scrum master cycle, the SoSM primarily coordinates and communicates across several teams to determine what will be accomplished during a sprint as well as subsequent release plans. The focus is on issues across teams, as opposed to just within one team. They can also work to identify and implement process improvements to ease the coordination in the future. Unfortunately, the SoSM might not be able to remove all obstacles across the entire organization. Instead, an EAT (including one Scrum Master and Product Owner) has the political and financial resources within the entire organization, including working across non-agile parts of the organization, to handle this. The EAT also sets the ideals for the organization with respect to scrum, business agility, and measures the quality of both. The goal is continuous learning and improvement across the organization.

The product owner cycle is led by a CPO and the main focus is setting a common strategic vision for the entire product and coordinating all stakeholder and customer needs through a unified backlog. This unified backlog can also feed into individual team backlogs, but the primary goal is meeting business objectives. This cycle is supported by an Executive MetaScrum (EMS) consisting of chief product owners, executives, and key stakeholders to negotiate priorities, handle budgeting, and ensure teams are aligned to deliver the most value for the organization. The EMS works in a sprint of its own to set customer priorities which then feeds all other product work being done in the organization.

---

[12] Many of the observations on the utility of XP as a development approach were based on conversations with Brian Henderson-Sellers and the experience of one of the textbook's co-authors (R.L.) who practiced a version of XP for many years.

[13] https://www.scrumatscale.com/scrum-at-scale-guide-online/.

Together, the scrum master cycle and the product owner cycle work to run the scrum framework at a much larger scale within an organization. They iterate through activities related to the work described above within each cycle and also overlap at times. This overlap of the cycles includes activities like coordinating the team processes that should be followed by all teams, the product backlog, and ensuring transparency of metrics regarding agility across the entire organization. If there are too many individual teams, coordination can become challenging, so it is possible for teams to be grouped into smaller scrum of scrums and there can be an added coordination layer known as a scrum of scrum of scrums. For example, if there are 21 teams then there could be three scrum of scrums consisting of seven teams each. To help facilitate coordination among the three scrum of scrums, there could be one scrum of scrum of scrums.

The specific agile practices that are implemented will vary slightly based on the specific rules that are created, however organizations can customize a broad agile mindset to work with their given culture and industry. For example, a health care organization has high levels of government compliance that it must follow, so the EAT would need to set more specific guidelines and documentation that can be created from product backlogs and working products. Similarly, in the airline industry, a carrier that is perceived to be more relaxed would probably implement more transparency around metrics and be less hierarchical compared to a carrier that has a more formal office culture.

Scaling Agile Framework (SAFe)[14]

SAFe's was created by Dean Leffingwell and is also based on the scrum framework. SAFe stresses the importance of the goal of making the entire organization agile. As a result of this effort, the individual product owners do not have as much authority and autonomy compared to scrum and other frameworks. Another thing to keep in mind about SAFe is that it need not be about just software development, instead it could be used for making any product or service agile in our digital age, especially as many are enabled by technology. SAFe incorporates other popular approaches such as lean, design thinking, and systems thinking. There are a lot of new terms and concepts that you will see below as SAFe is prescriptive about what is needed in a scaled agile framework for an entire organization.

SAFe is organized around seven core competencies (i.e., knowledge, skills, events, and behaviors) that organizations will need to be agile at scale. These competencies are all wrapped into a business agility value stream as a reminder of the core reason for practicing SAFe; to make the business agile and deliver business value. SAFe can be implemented in an essential, large solution, portfolio, or full configuration. The first four competencies below comprise the essential configuration of SAFe. Competencies 5 and 6 build on the essential configuration to create the large solution configuration, and competency 7 provides the portfolio layer. The large solution configuration provides guidance for large and complex products. The portfolio configuration provides guidance for managing a portfolio of products, including budgeting and governance. When all seven competencies are used, then it is a full SAFe configuration.

Lean Agile Leadership encourages leaders to set a lean mindset (creating value with as few resources and waste as possible) and be an example of it. Leaders must be champions of an agile mindset and encourage their practices by rewarding their success and allowing failures that lead to continuous improvement.

---

[14] For more information, see Richard Knaster and Dean Leffingwell, *Safe Distilled: Applying the Scaled Agile Frameworkâ for Lean Software and Systems Engineering* (Boston, MA: Addison-Wesley, 2017); Dean Leffingwell with Alex Yakyma, Richard Knaster, Drew Jemilo, and Inbar Oren, *SAFeâ Reference Guide: Scaled Agile Frameworkâ for Lean Software and Systems Engineering* (Boston, MA: Addison-Wesley, 2017).

Agile Product Delivery encourages focusing on customers, using design thinking, and implementing in a continuous manner based on customer needs. Focusing on customers means embracing customer needs as the top priority and creating positive experiences for them. Customers should be a high priority with every decision. Design thinking encourages a thorough understanding of a problem and implementing the right (feasible) solution in an iterative manner with agile release trains (ARTs). Solutions should be released when customers need them. Some customers may prefer releases at specific intervals (e.g., every quarter), whereas others might want solutions released as soon as they are available to add value. This continuous implementation is often done through another philosophy of DevOps (Development + Operations).

Team and Technical Agility encourages the use of agile teams in a scrum-like manner and points to the values of the Agile Manifesto. Teams are organized into teams of agile teams because it takes multiple teams to deliver a product solution. This competency encourages each team to follow the quality best practices for their domain (e.g., software, security, etc.).

Continuous Learning Culture encourages the entire enterprise to become learning centered. This happens at the individual level, the team level, and the organizational level. This also encourages the organization to understand how all of their systems connect and provide value as a greater whole, and that everyone be aware of the assumptions and values while working with an open mindset to new solutions. This competency also encourages everyone to relentlessly deliver value and also innovate.

Enterprise Solution Delivery provides ten practices that help an organization apply lean systems engineering, coordinate multiple releases and suppliers, and ensure that all systems continuously evolve.

Organizational Agility encourages organizational thinking that moves from control of processes to creation of value using a lean mindset. The entire operations of the business and even the strategy should be transformed and developed to a lean mindset. Business and technology teams should be agile.

Last, *Lean Portfolio Management* brings together the alignment of an organization's strategy across all its investments. It encourages budgeting that is also lean. Metrics should be established that allow the organization to track its progress toward being lean.

The seven competencies of SAFe are achieved through business agility value stream. This stream is the process by which the competencies are implemented and includes the following steps:

1. Sense the opportunity: There should be ongoing awareness of what's going on in your industry through activities like market research and customer feedback.

2. Fund an MVP (Minimum Viable Product): This should happen quickly when there is ongoing portfolio management. The key is just enough funding to experiment or test some hypotheses for creative value through a solution; think prototype.

3. Organize around value: Build teams and organize or re-organize agile teams to build the MVP.

4. Connect to customer: Creating positive experiences for customers should stay central during solution delivery.

5. Deliver an MVP: There might be several iterations (e.g., scrums) with releases that take place while building value.

6. Pivot or persevere: If the MVP met the need and created value as intended, then further development should take place. Alternatively, other opportunities might be pursued instead. This may also lead to completely new solutions within the same opportunity.

7. Deliver value continuously: This step ensures that releases are ongoing.

8. Learn and adapt: There should always be learning to drive positive change within the organization.

SAFe believes that a venture into a new business opportunity will create an MVP in two to six months instead of the 18 to 24 required for a phased system that moves linearly through each step.

As you can see, SAFe is a mindset and operational (way of working) change for the entire organization. It requires a strong commitment from the leaders of the organization. SAFe also implies that everyone is trained on this agile framework and knows their roles and responsibilities. The culture of the organization must embrace agile thinking to make SAFe work. There are a lot of competencies and steps that are needed to make SAFe work, and the transition to it might take some time for a large organization.

EFFECTIVE AGILE PRACTICES AND TOOLS

Agile methodologies rely on established practices designed to support flexibility, collaboration, and iterative development. These practices help teams be productive, well-organized and maintain focus on delivering maximal value. You have read about some of these practices in our descriptions of agile frameworks above, but we go into a bit more detail below for some of these practices, to give you a better sense of what they are. Some of the common Agile practices include:

- Daily standups
- User stories
- Pair programming
- Continuous integration
- Kanban board
- Retrospectives

Agile also encourages the use of specialized tools to enhance communication and productivity. These include project management platforms like Jira and Trello (https://www.atlassian.com), continuous integration tools, like GitHub (https://github.com), and automated testing systems, such as Tricentis (https://www.tricentis.com). Together, these practices and tools allow agile teams to be effective at engaging with customers, adapting to changing requirements and maintaining high productivity and quality.

Daily Standups

Agile developers favor efficiency and always look for ways to avoid effort and resources. This includes the precious time of the development team. Hence, long meetings are generally avoided. Productive and motivated employees commonly find long meetings frustrating and demoralizing. Instead, brief, concise meetings, best known as *daily standups* are preferred.

Daily standups are short, rather informal, fixed time interval meetings that are held every day and follow structured rules to avoid the temptation to turn these into never-ending discussions. The meetings commonly last from five to fifteen minutes. These meetings are a major part of many agile frameworks, including Scrum (where they are known as Daily Scrum) and eXtreme Programming, to name some.

Daily standups are true to their name as everyone usually stands. This intentionally introduces a bit of physical discomfort, thereby conveying the need to end the meeting within the required short timeframe. The people at the meeting are the entire development team and sometimes customer representatives.

The primary aim of the meetings is to ensure that the team is "on the same page" and any major issues are promptly discovered and solved later. This is typically done by asking the team members a standard set of questions every meeting. These questions can vary from project and agile framework, but some common ones are:

- What did you do yesterday?
- What will you do today?
- What (if anything) is blocking your progress?

The idea is to take turns and answer these questions briefly. If any of these questions require additional discussion, focused followed-up meetings can be set up with the affected members of the team.

The process is often self-organized but may also involve members in a particular Agile role who could launch the process initially or could be responsible for ensuring the process is followed. For example, in the Scrum framework, the Scrum Master often facilitates the daily standups, especially at the early stages of a project or when the team is new to Scrum practices.

The daily standups address many challenges of agile development and seek to realize a number of Agile principles and values. A significant benefit of daily standup meetings is increased team communication, collaboration, and cohesion. By bringing the team together daily, members become more comfortable working together, discover who is working on what component, learn from each other, and appreciate the scope of the entire project. As Agile promotes team self-organization and employee autonomy, these daily meetings instill a collective sense of ownership of the final system, which increases the chances of its success. To gain the most out of the practice of daily standups, we recommend:

- Keep the discussion focused and concise to avoid digressions.
- Respect the time limits but ensure every team member has the opportunity to comfortably express themselves. If this becomes impossible due to the size of the team, or complexity of the project, two options are possible:
  - Increase the length of the meetings from five to fifteen minutes (but generally not more).
  - Reduce the set of questions asked, focusing on the most important ones.
- Hold meetings in the same location, free of distractions but spacious enough so all team members feel comfortable.
- Even when holding such meetings virtually, encourage everyone to stand and have their cameras on.

User Stories

While agile developers shun documentation and rarely develop models like those you saw in the previous chapters, they still need to understand and somehow capture user requirements. User stories (or simply, stories) are a common feature in agile frameworks. They are concise, informal descriptions of system functionality from the perspective of the user (or customer). Unlike traditional models, user stories are brief and written in everyday language. This approach helps ensure that the needs of the users are clearly understood and communicated within the development team. User stories also help prioritize work based on the value delivered to the user. This prioritization is essential in Agile, where the focus is on delivering the most valuable features first. Recall, in this way, user stories act similar to other modeling artifacts (e.g., UML activity diagram) you saw in this textbook.

A *user story* typically includes three ingredients: the user role, the desired action or functionality, and the benefit or value. These components ensure that the story is not just about functionality but also about why that functionality is important. Consider the story "As a manager, I want to rank my sales representatives by revenue they generated so that I can give a bonus to the top performing employee." The user role is "manager," the desired action is "sort the sales representatives by revenue," and the benefit is the ability to "give bonus."

Additionally, user stories often include *acceptance criteria*. These criteria provide clear guidelines for developers and software quality testers to ensure the delivered functionality meets the user's needs. They serve as a communication tool between customers, developers, and testers. By clearly stating what is required, acceptance criteria ensure that everyone has the same understanding of what "done" means for a particular feature.

Returning to the user story of ranking sales representatives, the following are *some* of the acceptance criteria that can be defined:

1. Access to Ranking Feature, given that the manager is logged into the sales management system, allow the manager to navigate to the "Team Performance" or "Sales Ranking" section, and display an option to rank the sales team by revenue.

2. Display of Sales Team List, given that the manager is in the "Sales Ranking" section, display a list of all sales team members along with their respective revenue figures.

3. Sorting Functionality, given that the manager is viewing the sales team list, allow the selection of an option to sort the list by revenue, after which the list should be updated to rank the team members in descending order by their total revenue.

These and other acceptance criteria ensure that the ranking feature meets the manager's needs and provide clear, actionable guidelines for developers and testers. They cover various aspects, including the accessibility of the feature, accuracy of revenue data, ease of use, and the ability to filter and export the rankings. By adhering to these criteria, the development team can ensure that the functionality aligns with the user story's goals and enhances the manager's ability to reward top-performing employees. A detailed example of a user story with acceptance criteria in another (ride sharing app) context is shown in Figure 13-1.

In Agile projects, user stories are used throughout the development process. They are typically stored in a system *backlog*, a prioritized list of features and improvements for the system. During each iteration or sprint, the team selects a set of user stories to work on, aiming to complete them by the end of the cycle. Like traditional models (e.g., UML diagrams), user stories are also used in planning meetings to estimate effort, discuss implementation details, and ensure that everyone understands what is being built and why. This planning process helps to align the team's work with the project's goals and timelines. Before implementing a user story, the developers should discuss it with the customers.

While user stories are a powerful tool for managing requirements in Agile, they can also present challenges. One common issue is writing stories that are too vague or too broad, making them difficult to implement. Another challenge is ensuring that all team members have a shared understanding of the story, which requires regular communication and discussion. To help mitigate these challenges, we recommend:

- Strive to write clear, concise stories that focus on a single piece of functionality.
- Always involve users in the creation and review of stories.
- Continually refine the backlog to keep stories relevant and actionable.

	Sections		Explanations
User Story	Title	Renting a Motorcycle for Daily Commute	
	Description	As a daily commuter in Jakarta, I want to easily rent a motorcycle so that I can navigate the city's traffic efficiently and reduce my travel time.	
Components of the User Story	User Role *Who is the user?*	As a daily commuter in Jakarta, Indonesia	This specifies that the primary user for this story is someone who commutes regularly within Jakarta, a bustling metropolitan area known for its heavy traffic.
	Desired Action *What does the user want to achieve?*	I want to easily rent a motorcycle	The user is looking for a convenient way to access a motorcycle for short-term use, aiming to simplify the rental process and make it quick and efficient.
	Benefit or Value *Why does the user want this?*	So that I can navigate the city's traffic efficiently and reduce my travel time.	The motivation behind the desire is to overcome the challenges posed by Jakarta's notorious traffic jams, ensuring a faster and more flexible mode of transportation.
Additional Details	Acceptance Criteria	1. Search and Locate Motorcycles: Users should be able to search for available motorcycles nearby using their current location or a specified address, with real-time updates on availability. 2. Booking and Payment Options: The app should provide multiple booking options (e.g., by hour, day, or week) and support various payment methods, including local options like e-wallets or bank transfers commonly used in Indonesia. 3. GPS Navigation to Motorcycle: Once a motorcycle is booked, the app should provide step-by-step GPS directions to the exact location of the motorcycle.	To ensure that the user story is implemented correctly, some acceptance criteria can be defined.
	Additional Considerations	Localization and Language Support: Given Indonesia's diverse linguistic landscape, the app should support multiple languages, with Bahasa Indonesia being the primary language. Safety and Compliance: The app should provide safety tips for riders and ensure compliance with local traffic laws and regulations. This could include verifying that users have a valid motorcycle license. Cultural Relevance: Considering cultural preferences, the app might offer features like the ability to choose between different types of motorcycles (e.g., scooters vs. standard motorcycles) and provide options that cater to varying income levels.	By addressing these aspects, the user story not only guides the development of a specific feature but also ensures that the app is tailored to the needs and context of its users in Indonesia.

FIGURE 13-1 Example of a User Story for a Motorcycle Sharing App in Indonesia

- Use support tools like story mapping to visualize and prioritize work.[15]
- For additional guidance and to stay up to date with the developments, follow relevant research.[16]

By adhering to these suggestions, agile teams can maximize the benefits of user stories and ensure they remain aligned with the customer and user needs.

Pair programming

Pair programming is a powerful systems development technique that involves two programmers working side-by-side at one workstation, sharing the same computer and coding responsibilities. Pair programming is common in agile methodologies, including XP and Scrum.

Pair programming aims to improve code quality, enhance problem-solving capabilities, and increase communication and knowledge sharing. In a pair programming setup, one programmer, known as the "driver," writes the code, while the other, called the "navigator," reviews the code as it is written. The roles are frequently swapped, allowing both programmers to contribute actively to the task, and take a break from a given task.

Teams may decide to pair program for the entire day or during specific phases of the development process, such as when tackling complex or high-risk tasks. To implement pair programming effectively, teams need to establish a culture of collaboration and mutual respect, where each programmer feels comfortable sharing their ideas and receiving feedback.

To support pair programming, specialized development tools have been created. Tools that facilitate screen sharing and remote collaboration include Visual Studio Live Share (https://visualstudio.microsoft.com/services/live-share) or Code With Me (https://www .jetbrains.com).

Pair programming offers several major benefits:

- It enhances code quality by ensuring continuous review and feedback. Since the navigator is actively watching and analyzing the code, potential errors and bugs are identified and addressed in real-time, reducing the likelihood of defects making it to the final version of the system.
- It fosters knowledge transfer and skill development. Junior developers can learn from more experienced colleagues, and everyone on the team can become familiar with different parts of the system, reducing the risks associated with knowledge silos.
- It encourages better design decisions. With two minds working on the same problem, solutions are often more robust and well-thought-out, combining different perspectives and ideas.

Despite its benefits, pair programming introduces several challenges. Pair programming requires a trusting relationship between team members. As you know from any of the relationships you have ever had, no relationship is without friction. Many issues may emerge when you put two different human beings together, behind the same desk. These issues run a wide gamut from feeling the pressure from being in proximity to one another, to feeling

---

[15] Some story mapping tools include Miro (https://miro.com) and TheyDo (https://www.theydo.com).

[16] As examples, see Lucassen, G., Robeer, M., Dalpiaz, F. *et al.* Extracting conceptual models from user stories with Visual Narrator. *Requirements Eng* **22**, 339–358 (2017); Gupta, A., Poels, G., Bera, P. (2019). Creation of Multiple Conceptual Models from User Stories – A Natural Language Processing Approach. In: Guizzardi, G., Gailly, F., Suzana Pitangueira Maciel, R. (eds) Advances in Conceptual Modeling. ER 2019. *Lecture Notes in Computer Science*, vol 11787. Springer, Cham; M. Hvalshagen, R. Lukyanenko, B. M. Samuel Empowering Users with Narratives: Examining the Efficacy of Narratives for Understanding Data-Oriented Conceptual Models. *Information Systems Research* 34, no. 3 (2022):890–909.

insecure about the coding, testing or modeling abilities in front of somebody else, to feeling claustrophobic as a result of someone else encroaching upon your personal space, to simply having different mindsets or even different beliefs about life (which inevitably are discovered when people interact closely). To mitigate these issues, agile project leaders should rotate pairs regularly and encourage open communication to find compatible working arrangements.

Another challenge is to ensure pair programming results in net productivity gain. Productivity can be lost because of two different developers taking turns to develop code, instead of developing the code separately. Pair programming is especially powerful for complex projects that require multiple people to constantly reflect on the code they are writing. It may not be worthwhile if the development process is straightforward and follows widely known design patterns. To maximize the effectiveness of pair programming, we recommend:

- Fostering the culture of openness and transparency, to ensure any concerns or apprehensions are fully understood by the project leadership.
- Periodically rotating the teams, to ensure fatigue and conflict does not arise or persist.
- Encouraging the pairs to frequently switch roles between driver and navigator to keep both team members engaged and motivated, while giving them a chance to take breaks from a given activity.
- Staying up to date on the most recent and effective software that facilitates and enables pair programming.
- As peer pressure may deter someone from taking personal breaks, we suggest introducing mandatory breaks, at intervals higher than typical breaks when individuals are working solo.
- Plan fun activities throughout the day inside the office and outside. It could be as simple as sending the team to training together. The key is giving time and space for relationships to form.
- Encourage respect. Everyone is human, after all. Even if there are stark philosophical disagreements, everyone should be adhering to agile practices and rules set by the agile project leader, for example, the Scrum Master.
- Staying up to date on the best practices and research in pair programming, team dynamics, and organizational behavior, as putting people in close proximity to one another carries a host of significant challenges that are often difficult to detect, especially for those agile leaders whose expertise is technical excellence rather than psychological and organizational issues.

By adhering to these practices, teams can effectively harness pair programming as a tool of collaboration, learning, and productivity.

As a final note, did you know that pair programming can be scaled to include the entire team working on the same code, taking turns coding and inspecting? In this case, you have *mob programming*.[17] Mob programming can be especially useful when the problem is so unruly as to desire everyone's undivided attention. Keep this trick in mind should you encounter one of those impossible challenges. It may be just the solution you need.

Continuous Integration

Agile development is fast paced, and commonly occurs in an evolving, grassroots and organic fashion. In many frameworks, such as Scrum, there can be little coordination of the efforts of

---

[17] Pearl, Mark (2018) *Code with the Wisdom of the Crowd: Get Better Together with Mob Programming* (Pragmatic Bookshelf, 2018).

individual developers or sub-teams. As a result, developers working on different components of the system may create solutions that could conflict with one another. This and other challenges are addressed through a key agile practice of *continuous integration.*

Continuous Integration (CI) involves the frequent merging of all developers' individual solutions into a common solution in production (or production simulation), multiple times a day. Imagine an application form for college, as a component of a larger system that is being built. Every time a developer finishes a small part of the system (e.g., code that validates student input on an application page for common typos), instead of waiting until everyone finishes the rest of the code related to the page, the developer sends this code to the automated code building and testing software on the machine that runs the system. The automated code building and testing software merges the new code with the existing code of the system at that point. This way both the original developer and the rest of the team can see how that code fits with the overall system, allowing everyone to make any necessary corrections and adjustments to the new code and the other individual components.

To support CI, developers typically set up a shared code version control system where all team members post their code changes. Tools like GitHub (https://github.com) or Mercurial (https://www.plutora.com) are commonly used as code repositories and version control systems. These tools are key as there needs to be an ability to restore the correctly working product and undo any changes that may be causing problems.

Continuous integration needs to be carefully executed and requires the team's commitment to best practices to ensure the ultimate success. In particular, team members should use their judgment and post new code as frequently as possible, within reason. The aim is to avoid backlogs and posting significant changes, which may create too many bugs to fix efficiently in the grassroots manner. Continuous improvement involves a great deal of automation, particularly for code testing. These tests, however, are only as reliable as their ability to comprehensively evaluate the new code. To maximize the effectiveness of CI, we recommend:

- Fostering the culture of communication, openness and dialog across the entire team, so each team member is aware of the overall progress helping them to judge when to release their code. For example, the practice of daily standups can facilitate this.
- Staying up to date on the most recent and effective software that facilitates CI.
- Agreeing in advance on how to handle significant version conflicts and code errors. This involves deciding what constitutes a conflict that warrants stopping the regular CI routine and stopping the work until a common solution is found and the major issues are resolved.
- Staying up to date on the best practices and research in code sharing, version control, automated testing, forking, and other topics related to CI.

To the extent that the teams can execute on these recommendations, the benefits of continuous improvement can be significant in unlocking the full potential of high-productivity and quality agile development.

Kanban Board

Kanban is another agile framework in its own right[18] that is an adaptation from lean manufacturing. Here, we call attention to the use of one of its workflow practices referred to as a *Kanban board.* Kanban was originally developed as part of the continuous improvement approaches in lean manufacturing. Kanban boards use lots of sticky notes and a large

---

[18] The material in the section is based on David J. Anderson, *Kanban: Successful Evolutionary Change for your Technology Business* (Sequim, WA: Blue Hole Press: 2010); Eric Brechner, *Agile Project Management with Kanban* (Redmond, WA: Microsoft Press, 2015).

whiteboard that has a set of labeled columns. The number of columns depends on the complexity and size of the project. A small project could simply have columns for user stories, to do, in progress, testing, and done displayed together in a board (see Figure 13-2). For each story, a sticky note is created and placed in the story column. Also, a sticky note is created for each and every individual requirement necessary to solve the story. Each requirement should be small enough that a team member would be able to complete it in a short period of time, e.g., a day or a week. These sticky notes are placed in the To Do column in the same row that the story sticky note was placed. Next, a team member chooses one of the requirements from the To Do column on which they plan to work and places it into the In Progress column. The sticky note remains in the In Progress column until it is either completed and placed into the Testing column or the team member discovers that the requirement is too large. In this case, the team member splits the requirement into a set of sub requirements, creates a sticky note for each sub requirement, and replaces the requirement sticky note with the set of sub requirement sticky notes. The sub requirement sticky notes are then placed in the To Do column. Once a sticky note has been placed into the Testing column, the code that represents the solution to the requirement is tested. If the code passes all of the tests, the sticky note is placed into the Done column. Otherwise, the sticky note is returned to the To Do column. This process is repeated over all user stories related to the system until all requirements-based sticky notes are in the Done column.

The Kanban board (see Figure 13-2) has a couple of major advantages as a workflow tool. First, it is very simple to implement. All you need are a set of sticky notes and a whiteboard. Alternatively, digital solutions are offered through software such as Jira (https://www.atlassian.com/software/jira). Second, by simply looking at the board, it is very easy to see the current

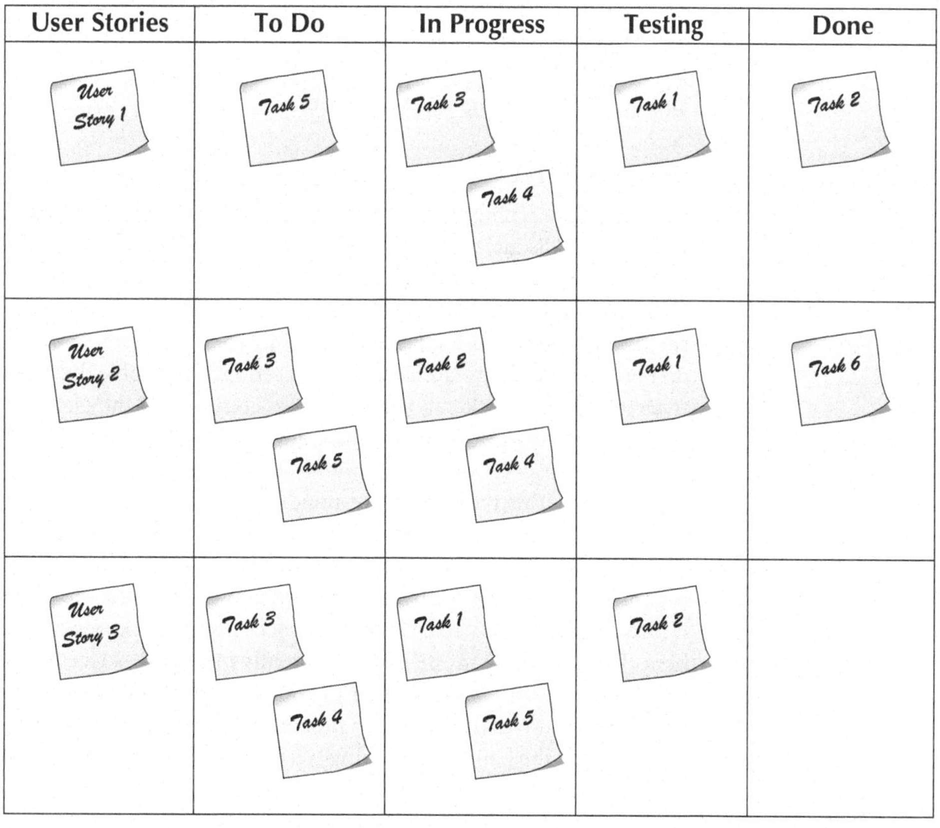

User Stories	To Do	In Progress	Testing	Done
User Story 1	Task 5	Task 3 Task 4	Task 1	Task 2
User Story 2	Task 3 Task 5	Task 2 Task 4	Task 1	Task 6
User Story 3	Task 3 Task 4	Task 1 Task 5	Task 2	

FIGURE 13-2
Simple Kanban Board

status of the project. The example board shown in Figure 13-2 is very simple. For larger, more complex projects, more columns are used. For example, you could have columns for user stories, requirements analysis, design, design review, ready for development, development in progress, development completed, build ready, test ready, unit and integration testing, user acceptance testing, release ready, staging, in production, etc. In other words, larger systems require more management of the development process. To maximize the effectiveness of Kanban boards, we recommend:

- Ensure that each of the tasks for the user stories are clearly articulated as a reasonable unit of work. In general, it is good to keep tasks at the same level of detail.
- Explore the use of different colors or sizes of sticky notes to signify more/less critical stories and tasks, or different colors for different types of stories and tasks.
- There will be some comparisons and pressure to keep up with the rest of the team's progress when workflow is available visually for everyone to see. Be sure to remind and encourage teams that workflow transparency is used to create camaraderie and show progress as part of Agile's goal for transparency, as opposed to judging one team's or individual's apparent faster progress than another. They allow everyone to see where more help might be needed. Some healthy competition may arise, but be sure to manage this, so that it does not cross the line and take a toll on mental health of team members.
- Similar to the prior point, use the workflow tools to limit the amount or scope of work included in any sprint.
- Stay up to date on the best practices and research in workflow transparency, management, and tools.

To the extent that the teams are able to execute on these recommendations, the benefits of Kanban boards and other workflow technologies can be significant to help teams provide transparency with respect to their current tasks and remain focused for better productivity and quality during agile development.

Retrospectives

Continuous learning and improvement are important in many agile frameworks (see Agile Principle 12 discussed earlier). Successful agile teams constantly reflect on their practices and seek ways to improve them. To do so, they hold regular meetings called *retrospectives*. During these meetings, the team looks back at the previous stages in development (e.g., iteration, sprint, the entire project), in order to analyze what went right or wrong, learn from that and do better in the future. Retrospectives commonly involve the entire team, although retrospectives with special task sub teams are also common, if they need is to reflect upon a particular activity within the broader development.

The retrospectives are commonly held regularly, in intervals of several weeks to one to two months. This typically corresponds to the major phases of work under a particular agile framework, such as a Scrum sprint. These intermediate meetings are sometimes called "heartbeat retrospectives." At the end of the entire project, a wrap-up, final retrospective is also organized, to discuss the overall project, and prepare for the next one. The final retrospective is also an opportunity to celebrate the successes and acknowledge the efforts of the team members. To allow the team members to openly talk about successes and failures, it helps to begin retrospectives with an icebreaker to put the team members at ease. Similarly, it is important to hold retrospectives frequently (but without overtaxing the time of the team members), so that they get into the habit of analyzing what went right and wrong, and continuously improve, as the project progresses.

The retrospective should end with the identification of specific and actionable changes that the team can implement in the next iteration to do things better. Commonly, a list of to-dos is created as a way to improve upon the existing process. Ideally, these improvements should directly stem from the issues identified by the team members. This will make the team members feel valued and appreciated. The list should be clear to all team members and is doable within the constraints of the project. To get the most out of retrospectives, we recommend:

- Hold the retrospective meetings regularly, after each major development phase (sprint, iteration). This ensures continuous learning and results in improvements that are manageable for the team.

- Ensure that the efforts of every team member are recognized and thanked.

- Encourage everyone to share their reflections and suggestions for how to improve.

- Always follow up on the suggestions, else those who propose them will be demotivated to make new suggestions in the future.

- Be sure to explain to everyone that the idea is not to point fingers or blame someone, but to be constructive and identify areas for improvement.

Retrospectives are valuable not only for a specific project, but in general, as mechanisms by which teams can become progressively better, across different projects, over time. By considering our recommendations, you can unlock the greater potential of retrospectives as a tool of learning and improvement.

AGILE MODELING

At first glance, it may seem that modeling (e.g., UML) does not align with the values and practices of the agile methodology because it can be seen as a form of documentation that can distract from creating value through working software. As you saw in the previous chapters, modeling is a systematic activity that proceeds with great care and attention through many stages before the implementation of the system can begin. The ethos of modeling appears to be fundamentally misaligned with the values and principles of agile.

Agile developers want to get things done as quickly and efficiently as possible. Each of the four values of agile seems to be in opposition to modeling. Figure 13-3 interprets the values of agile in terms of traditional modeling practices.

Agile Value	Traditional Modeling
Individuals and interactions over processes and tools.	Modeling, at least as traditionally understood, is a structured process of moving from user stories to the diagrams that shape implementation.
Working software over comprehensive documentation.	A comprehensive approach to understanding user requirements produces significant and very detailed documentation.
Customer collaboration over contract negotiation	It is not uncommon to view traditional models as constituting a kind of contract between the development team and the organizational stakeholders; sometimes these models become legal documents. Therefore, it is often critical to get some of the details in the models right and thoroughly verify them with the stakeholders. Once verified and approved, these models can then be referenced in case of post-implementation disagreements about what the final system were to do.
Responding to change over following a plan	The whole point of modeling is to create a blueprint that then can be followed as a roadmap. Models are the structural, behavioral and architectural plans to be followed.

FIGURE 13-3 The Values of Agile in Terms Mapped to Traditional Modeling Practices

Many in the agile community find little use for formal modeling. In the words of Ron Jeffries, a co-author of Agile Manifesto, "software development . . . is best done with as little modeling as possible."[19] Modeling takes time—the time away from building the actual systems. It also assumes requirements do not change drastically after the models are built. This is often not the case, especially in fast-paced environments. Hence, sometimes, modeling is seen as a luxury agile developers cannot afford.

Considering such a seemingly profound rift between the values of Agile and the practices of modeling, a reasonable conclusion could be that modeling is completely irrelevant for agile, and maybe even harmful. We caution that this conclusion is wrong and potentially very dangerous.

Agile methodology was developed as a response to dissatisfaction with insufficient adjustment to changes that comes with extensive planning. However, this should not be misunderstood to mean anything goes. The result can be complete disorder, if not anarchy. Too many agile projects fail to straddle the thin line between being lean and nimble and ensuring important requirements are captured. Indeed, only around 40% of agile projects are successful.[20] Some common causes of agile failure include communication breakdowns and faulty requirements (especially common in large, distributed, online and non-collocated projects). After reading the textbook, you may exclaim: **Modeling is Precisely the Tool to Support Agile!** We agree.

Since the 1970s, modeling has been a proven tool that facilitated the development of information systems. In addition to capturing the requirements for the system, modeling can greatly facilitate communication, enhance mutual understanding, promote problem-solving, and help reconcile different user and development team perspectives. As you saw in numerous examples in the textbook, the very act of modeling helps to gain clarity about the design and ultimately results in a better system.

The problem is not that agile team members do not get value from modeling. Agile developers love to model! Creating user stories is a form of modeling. Sometimes the models are a part of working through a solution, and they never get implemented into the final documentation, but it does not mean that modeling never happened. This is similar to how we "model" in our personal lives. Can you ever make any decision without any planning? Wouldn't you at least make a "pros" and "cons" list? What about trying to foresee how you get to where you want to be in five years? What roadblocks and challenges may await? Last, imagine going on a trip to the wilderness without a map, without the faintest clue where you're going, and not knowing what the end goals are? As a result, you may find yourself stranded amid the echoing howls of wild nature, with no water, shelter or food. Modeling is done to avoid these kinds of predicaments in the context of systems development.

Agile Modeling Methodology—Example of Modeling for Agile Development

Agile developers realize well the power and benefits of modeling. The problem is there are no established modeling approaches that agile practitioners universally embrace. It is not trivial to fit modeling into agile routines. Here, we describe one notable approach pioneered by Scott Ambler called *Agile Modeling* (AM).

---

[19] Ambler, Scott. 2002. *Agile Modeling: Effective Practices for Extreme Programming and the Unified Process.* Hoboken, NJ: John Wiley & Sons, xi.

[20] Johnson, J. 2022. *CHAOS Report: Beyond Infinity*, Centerville: The Standish Group International, Inc.

AM is an agile design philosophy that promotes a set of core principles.[21] These principles must be followed in their totality in order for the benefits of AM to accrue. The AM's core principles are:

- Software is your primary goal
- Enabling the next effort is your secondary goal
- Travel light
- Assume simplicity
- Embrace change
- Incremental change
- Model with a purpose
- Multiple models
- Quality work
- Rapid feedback
- Maximize stakeholder investment

Software is your primary goal The primary objective of systems development is to deliver high-quality software that effectively meets the needs of customers and users. Activities such as creating excessive documentation, producing unnecessary models, or even overly focusing on modeling can give a false sense of progress but do not directly contribute to the actual goal. These tasks may be comforting or superficially productive but often divert attention from the critical work of writing and testing code. Therefore, developers should concentrate on building and refining the software system itself, questioning any activity that does not directly support this goal unless it is clearly justified. This focus ensures that efforts are directed toward producing valuable and functional software for users.

Enabling the next effort is your secondary goal Delivering a working system to users is not enough to guarantee project success; the system must also be robust and adaptable for future developments. To facilitate this, teams should create sufficient documentation to ensure continuity and efficiency for future efforts. This includes transferring knowledge to other developers, retaining and motivating staff, and considering the project's future needs and organizational priorities. Thus, while the immediate focus is on delivering quality software, it is also important to consider long-term sustainability and *effective communication* to support future endeavors.

Travel light "Traveling light" means creating and maintaining only the essential models and documentation needed to complete the project. Every model requires effort, attention, and ongoing maintenance. The more models you create, the more effort you expend with each change, thus reducing your agility. Teams should only maintain a model when it becomes evidently necessary. This approach simplifies development by reducing the effort spent on artifact maintenance, requiring the courage to rely on minimal yet sufficient documentation and models.

Assume simplicity Embracing simplicity is crucial, as the simplest solution is often the most effective and easiest to implement. Overbuilding or over-modeling based on anticipated future needs should be avoided; instead, focus on the current requirements and refine the

---

[21] This material is based on: Ambler, Scott. 2002. *Agile Modeling: Effective Practices for Extreme Programming and the Unified Process.* Hoboken, NJ: John Wiley & Sons.

system as needs evolve. This approach, akin to Occam's Razor, emphasizes minimalism in modeling, ensuring only the minimal facts are modeled. While simplicity might not always be successful, it allows for quick adjustments and reduces the risk of wasting significant effort on complex, possibly unworkable solutions.

Simplicity is perhaps one of the most important principles and requires additional explanation. These also provide more actionable guidance for how to use AM. According to AM, three practices enable simplicity:

- Create simple content. This means that all the requirements, analysis, architecture and design elements that are modeled are kept as simple as possible. For example, a UML class diagram may not show methods, if these do not feature in the considerations of design. Similarly, the visibility of attributes does not need to be shown, unless this is needed explicitly for some purpose.

- Depict models simply. When modeling, choose the simplest notation possible, to promote communication and understanding. This means avoiding crossing lines, curved lines, diagonal lines, different size symbols, too many symbols, unnecessary detail in general.

- Use the simplest tools. According to Ambler, there are many computer-aided software engineering (CASE) tools on the market but "few of them are worth the bother."[22] If a simple tool is sufficient for your needs, then use it. This means that the diagrams are commonly drawn on the whiteboard, on paper and "even on the back of a napkin." And if there is a need to save and share these diagrams, a cell phone camera may be used.

To illustrate simplicity in a concrete modeling scenario, imagine you are part of an Agile development team tasked with creating a ride sharing app in Indonesia. You already saw a user story for this scenario in Figure 13-1. Now, let us create a class diagram consistent with AM. Being responsible for modeling, you follow the simplicity principle and produce a diagram in Figure 13-4. The figure shows a simple UML class diagram that captures the types of data to

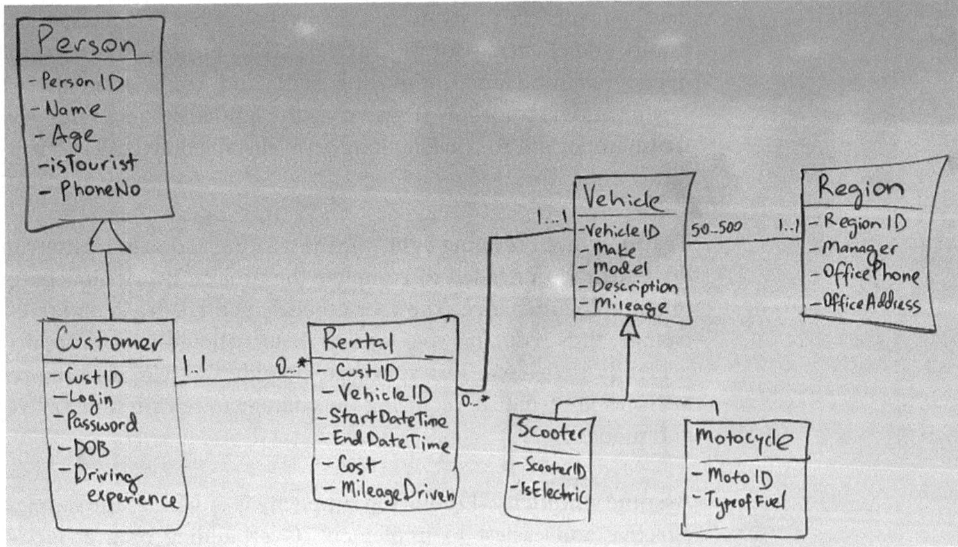

FIGURE 13-4 Agile Modeling-Consistent UML Class Diagram Drawn on a Whiteboard. It captures the types of data to be recorded by a ridesharing app in Indonesia and can support communication among the development team.

[22] From: Ambler (2002:58).

be recorded by the app. You built this diagram after a series of discussions with the client and prospective users. Note the absence of methods, datatypes, and attribute visibility that you are familiar with from Chapter 4. Despite these omissions, the diagram is still very useful. It can be used to quickly visualize the relationship between different types of data to be managed by the app, and hence can be a very effective tool for communicating the requirements for a design iteration. You can have this diagram on the whiteboard in front of the pairs of programmers who are developing the database to store the data for the app. If necessary, a picture could be taken of the diagram and stored in some knowledge management repository. Alternatively, a dedicated sprint for documentation could be added.

Embrace change In software development, change is inevitable and should be embraced as a core aspect of the process. Requirements, stakeholders, and project environments will evolve over time due to various factors, including new insights, personnel changes, and external shifts in the business or technology landscape. Agile methodologies welcome these changes—even late in the development cycle. Agile modelers understand that their initial work is just a starting point and will likely be revised and improved upon as the project progresses. While it's tempting to minimize upfront effort due to anticipated changes, it's crucial to thoroughly understand current requirements and build accordingly, maintaining quality and maximizing stakeholder investment. This balanced approach ensures that the project can adapt to changes without compromising on foundational quality.

Incremental change To embrace change in software development, it is essential to adopt an incremental approach, implementing small, manageable updates rather than attempting a complete overhaul in one large release. The *Agile principles* emphasize delivering functional software frequently, ideally within a few weeks to a couple of months, to maintain flexibility and responsiveness. Agile modeling advocates for creating initial models that are "good enough" rather than striving for perfection from the outset. This means starting with small, focused models or high-level outlines and allowing them to evolve as the project progresses, acknowledging that perfection at the start is neither feasible nor necessary.

Model with a purpose In software development, the purpose and audience of any artifact, such as models, source code, or documents, should be clearly identified before investing time in its creation. Many developers get caught up in the details of making their artifacts sufficiently accurate or detailed without considering the fundamental question of why they are creating them and for whom. Modeling should serve specific, valuable purposes, such as gaining a deeper understanding of the software, communicating with stakeholders, or documenting the system for future maintenance. Invalid reasons for creating models include following a process blindly, fulfilling vague requests, or avoiding direct communication.

Multiple models Each type of model has its own strengths and is suitable for specific situations. For instance, a UML activity diagram is ideal for illustrating process logic, while a class diagram captures the structure of data. By using multiple simple models, developers communicate different facets of a project without overloading themselves or their stakeholders with overly complex representations. It might also be important to show those who are less experienced with modeling how the multiple models connect to each other.[23]

Like a carpenter, a developer should be equipped with a range of techniques and methodologies that they can apply as needed. Having a diverse set of tools and knowing how to use

---

[23] For more on this issue, see Kim, J., Hahn, J., & Hahn, H. (2000). How do we understand a system with (so) many diagrams? Cognitive integration processes in diagrammatic reasoning. *Information Systems Research* 11, no. 3, 284–303.

them enhances effectiveness, ensuring that developers can select the right approach for each task. Just as not every fix-it job at home requires every tool in the toolbox, not every development task requires every technique a developer knows. However, over time, various projects will necessitate the application of different modeling techniques, mirroring the diverse needs encountered in home repair. Do not be afraid to pick up a new tool as needed.

Quality work Agile developers recognize the value of investing time and effort into creating source code to a high standard. Conversely, they prioritize minimal effort for sketches or low-fidelity prototypes, by focusing resources where they will have the greatest impact. This approach is not contradictory but rather reflects a pragmatic balance: if a deliverable is worth keeping, it deserves the investment needed to build it properly; if not, minimal effort suffices to fulfill its temporary purpose without wasting resources.

Rapid Feedback Feedback is vital, with a preference for rapid feedback over delayed feedback whenever possible. This is essential because most errors occur during requirements definition and analysis, and the cost of fixing defects increases exponentially the later they are found. In non-agile projects, late discovery of defects can have significant consequences, as work is performed based on previously completed work, and errors in requirements can invalidate modeling decisions, code, and testing efforts. Rapid feedback of models minimizes the cost and impact of misunderstandings, making it easier and less expensive to address issues early in the development lifecycle.

Maximize Stakeholder Investment In software development, project stakeholders invest significant resources—time, money, and facilities—with the expectation of receiving software that meets their needs. Therefore, it's essential to respect their investment. Stakeholders have the right to determine how their resources are allocated, as they bear the risks and rewards of these decisions. Recognizing this, it is crucial to understand that decisions regarding system documentation are business decisions, not purely technical ones. Ultimately, it is the stakeholders' right to decide whether to keep the suggested model or documentation.

Other Agile Modeling Approaches and Outlook into the Future

While AM is promising, it is not without challenges. For example, AM can struggle with balancing modeling effort against actual development and may encounter challenges and variability in modeling quality, particularly in highly regulated industries. As AM relies on modeling skills of the agile team, it requires the developers to divert their attention from code and underutilizes the opportunity for customers and users to be more involved in modeling. Finally, AM prioritizes communication and understanding, rather than requirements representation and documentation. Yet, it can be very valuable to model requirements as well, especially to ensure that some of the requirements related to health, safety, legal, ethical, and other user concerns are captured completely and accurately, and from the very start. But how can we fully realize the benefits of modeling without slowing down agile development?

First, there are areas of agile development where more formal modeling, like the ones you learned in the previous chapters, is increasingly being accepted. One such area is *model-driven engineering*. Model-driven engineering (MDE) is an approach to software development that uses models as primary artifacts throughout the development process. One of the primary goals of MDE is to automate the generation of executable code from high-level models. Code generation transforms models into source code in a target programming language, allowing developers to focus on the system's abstract representation rather than low-level implementation details. This automation improves productivity, consistency, and maintainability. In MDE projects, therefore, you can approach modeling in a manner very similar to that shown throughout the textbook.

Additionally, on-going research is working to develop new modeling techniques that are sensitive to highly interactive, customer-centric and lean agile development settings. For example, to ensure alignment with agile values and practices, new modeling philosophies such as Universal Conceptual Modeling[24] promote modeling that insists on few rules and embrace trial-and error. The idea is to develop modeling techniques that are even more informal and easier to use than AM, allowing non-technical stakeholders to directly engage in modeling. This can greatly assist agile developers so that they can focus more on code production and testing.

Another hope is the increased automation of modeling. With the growing powers of artificial intelligence (AI), it is becoming possible to create and manage models using AI. This can alleviate the biggest burden of using models in agile settings: the need to create and manage these models, which takes away the time from writing actual software. AI can generate models from user stories and other available documentation. With the help of AI, it may become possible to engage stakeholders in model verification, as well as to ensure these models evolve as requirements change. An AI modeling tool may work "side-by-side" with human agile developers and creating programming code and other software components. That way, rather than diverting time and attention of the developers, AI modeling tools could make agile development even more effective, and together with humans, develop better systems.

With agile now being practiced even in settings traditionally seen as inappropriate for agile (such as mission-critical, highly regulated environments), the challenge of using modeling effectively in these settings continues to grow. Below are our recommendations about the use of modeling in agile development. We first suggest the reasons why you should engage in modeling during agile development. Here are five reasons to model by creating analysis and design diagrams:

1. **Model to slow yourself down.** This may sound ironic, as agile prioritizes speed and efficiency. But with speed come errors. Modeling may take some time away from code, but it never endangers lives or undermines reputations. At the end of the day, modeling is just pretty (or ugly) pictures. Models rarely hurt feelings. Contrast this with code in a live system: code that is oblivious to health, safety, legal, ethical, cultural, environmental, and other issues, can lead to catastrophic consequences. At the bare minimum, modeling forces you to stop and think before you act.

2. **Model to understand the problem at hand and develop better solutions.** Modeling helps you think, as it forces you to externalize your thoughts. If you are not entirely sure whether a particular solution is the right one, before implementing and deploying it, go to the drawing board, alone, with another developer, or together with the relevant stakeholders. Then speak out loud, draw, brainstorm, write short stories. Use a modeling technique that feels right (and if in doubt, reference our previous chapters) to gain clarity of the problem. By externalizing your thoughts, you are likely to discover something you have not considered before or find flaws in your ideas. In addition, when you externalize your thoughts, someone else can now look at them and provide feedback on them.

3. **Model to capture requirements, especially the most critical and important ones.** A key function of modeling is in systematically capturing the requirements for the system you are developing. While some of the requirements gathering may be done informally (recall the XP practice of direct developer-user dialogs), informal techniques offer few assurances that these requirements are accurate and complete.

---

[24] To learn more about Universal Conceptual Modeling, see: Lukyanenko, R., Samuel, B. M., Parsons, J., Storey, V. C., Pastor, O., & Jabbari, A. (2024). Universal conceptual modeling: principles, benefits, and an agenda for conceptual modeling research. *Software and Systems Modeling*, 1–24.

While the point of agile is to embrace change, as IT begins to touch every aspect of human life, it is especially important to get certain "critical" requirements right. Even if it means to "relax" some of the agile values. Anything related to health, safety, legal, ethical, reputational, and other concerns (e.g., impact on the environment), must be captured systematically. Ideally, these requirements should be presented in a rigorous visual manner, so these can be inspected, agreed upon, verified and clearly documented.

4. Model to communicate with others. A model is worth a thousand words. Sometimes it may be difficult to express information technology ideas in natural human language. This is why natural human language is not the language of computing instructions (at the basic level it is binary and assembly). Use the specialized vocabulary of modeling to structure your ideas and share them with others. As a physical object, a model can be printed, shared, attached to a wall, or live on the whiteboard, permitting efficient and scalable communication of ideas.

5. Model to reduce complexity. William James, a famous psychologist and leading thinker of his time, described the world as "blooming and buzzing confusion." Any object you encounter, even a humble pencil, can be described in a myriad (some say, infinite) different ways. A pencil can be short, inexpensive, dull, but also weighing less than 50g, oriented to the north, cold to touch, yellow, not very nutritious, not impressive as a gift, is of little interest to your dog, etc. Imagine how endless a list might be when we deal with more complex objects, such as customer, student, university, stock exchange. Without modeling you will always be stuck in the "blooming and buzzing confusion." Only by modeling can you hope to reduce this complexity to manageable levels, driven by purpose and desire to deliver customer value. Modeling techniques, such as those covered in the previous chapters, have been specifically engineered to help you achieve this complexity reduction in a systematic and effective way. This is why even those who claim they do not model, in reality do so all the time, in their case, they only do it in their minds. However, this is not as effective as doing it explicitly, so you can better visualize your thoughts, and share them with others.[25]

In addition, it helps to think about the System Development Life Cycle (SDLC), even if you do agile development. In SDLC you have to do modeling in a prescribed and systematic way. In Agile, you have much more flexibility. But it is easy to get lost when you don't follow a plan. Here is a simple trick. When you do agile development, always keep SDLC modeling techniques in mind, even if you don't implement them into physical models. Can you imagine developing UML Class diagrams to structure your data, or fill in Class Responsibility Collaborator cards to understand how to accomplish a task? Do you have enough information and understanding to ensure these diagrams are sound? Always ask yourself: does your solution adequately address the process, functional and structural and behavioral and nonfunctional requirements before moving it into production. And if your answer is "no", you know what to do (hint: it may involve some talking to others and perhaps, modeling!)

If you love modeling, but suspect others don't, be respectful to your colleagues who may not share your enthusiasm for modeling. Feel free to explain the modeling benefits to them, without being overly pushy. Worst case, rely on those modeling techniques that are more widely accepted by the agile community, such as user stories.

---

[25] There are other benefits of using models during development. In fact, a whole new discipline is emerging called **Modelology**. **Modelology** seeks to better understand the benefits and uses of models; see: Thalheim, B. (2024). Modelology—The New Science, Life and Practice Discipline. In Information Modelling and Knowledge Bases XXXV (pp. 1–19). IOS Press.

If you are still uncertain, you are not alone, and the good news is, the community continues to search for better ways to integrate modeling into agile settings. Follow the latest developments in agile modeling, as it continuously progresses. Most importantly, never stop learning.

LIMITATIONS OF AGILE

While the idea of being agile is attractive to many organizations and is gaining popularity, the agile methodology is not without limitations. One of the major criticisms deals with today's business environment, where much of the actual information systems development is off-shored, outsourced, and/or subcontracted. Given agile development methodologies requiring co-location of the development team, this seems to be a very unrealistic assumption. As you can see from the practices, such as standups, Kanban boards, retrospectives, continuous integration, all these are incredibly difficult to implement successfully when the teams are not in close proximity to one another.

A second major criticism is that if agile development is not carefully managed, and by definition it is not, the development process can devolve into a "programmers gone wild" environment where programmers attempt to hack together solutions. This is why we highly recommend when practicing agile to remain cognizant of the proven development techniques that we covered in the previous chapters. It is critical not to neglect modeling, even when under extreme time pressure. We believe that to be a successful agile developer requires a thorough knowledge of traditional development approaches, such as Unified Process, even if these are only kept at the back of one's mind.

A third major criticism is that the lack of actual documentation created during the development of the software, raises issues regarding the auditability of the systems being created. Without sufficient documentation, neither the system nor the systems-development process can be assured.

A fourth major criticism is based on whether agile approaches can deliver large mission-critical systems. Just like no one should think to create a nuclear power plant without extensive analysis, planning, and documentation, no one should attempt to write the software code to manage this power plant by brushing aside the need to carefully analyze and design this system. The same goes for airline control, medical diagnosis, military operations, electronic banking, employee payroll, and many other facets of daily life.

We live in the age of digital information, ubiquitous computing, and mind-blowing artificial intelligence. In a world that is critically dependent on information systems, information systems development must be treated with the great care it deserves.

CHAPTER REVIEW

After reading and studying this chapter, you should be able to:

- ☐ Explain the importance of being agile in organizational settings.
- ☐ Describe how and why Agile systems development was created.
- ☐ Appreciate the values and principles laid out in Agile manifesto.
- ☐ Be able to understand the differences between some of the popular agile frameworks.
- ☐ Specify the components of user stories.
- ☐ Understand the power and challenges in common agile practices, such as standups and retrospectives.
- ☐ Understand the challenges of agile modeling.
- ☐ Develop simple diagrams that follow the principles of Agile modeling methodology.
- ☐ Recognize the potential of evolving research in agile modeling and some of the directions it is taking.

KEY TERMS

Agile frameworks
Agile manifesto
Agile modeling
Agile principles
Agile product delivery
Agile values
Changing requirements
Chief product owner
Communication
Comprehensive
  documentation
Continuous delivery
Continuous integration
Continuous learning culture
Contract negotiation
Courage
Customer collaboration

Customer satisfaction
Daily standups
Effective communication
Enterprise solution delivery
Executive action team
Executive metaScrum
eXtreme programming
Feedback
Individuals
Interactions
Kanban board
KISS
Lean agile leadership
Lean portfolio management
Limitations of agile
Measure of progress
Methodology

Minimum viable
  product
Mob programming
Organizational agility
Pair programming
Processes
Product owner
Product owner cycle
Reflection
Respect
Retrospective
SAFe business agility
  value stream
SAFe core competencies
Scaled agile framework
Scaling agile framework
  (SAFe)

Scrum
Scrum ceremonies
Scrum development team
Scrum master
Scrum master cycle
Scrum meetings
Scrum of scrums
Scrum of scrums master
Scrum@Scale
Self-organizing teams
Simplicity
Team agile framework
Team and technical
  agility
Tools
User story
Working software

QUESTIONS

1. Discuss the Agile value of "Responding to change over following a plan" and how it can apply to dealing with conflicts between the team and the customer.

2. Suggest concrete steps you would take to realize the Agile principle of business people and developers must work together daily throughout the project.

3. What is Scrum and why is it considered the most widely used team agile framework?

4. Explain the roles of the Product Owner, Scrum Master, and Development Team in the Scrum framework.

5. What are the ceremonies in Scrum and why are they important?

6. How does Scrum handle new requirements that are uncovered during a sprint?

7. What are the four core values of Extreme Programming (XP) and why are they important?

8. How does XP approach testing and coding practices?

9. What is the role of user stories in an XP project?

10. What are the strengths associated with developing software using XP?

11. What are the limitations or challenges of using XP as a development approach?

12. What is Scrum@Scale (S@S) and how does it differ from Scrum?

13. Explain the roles of the Executive Action Team (EAT) and the Executive MetaScrum (EMS) in Scrum@Scale.

14. What are the seven core competencies of the Scaling Agile Framework (SAFe)?

15. How does SAFe approach the management of a portfolio of products?

16. What are the steps in the business agility value stream in SAFe?

17. Discuss the potential challenges an organization might face when implementing SAFe.

18. Contrast the traditional view of modeling with Agile's perspective on the value of documentation. How does each approach view the role and importance of documentation in software development?

19. How would you ensure that your team exhibits continuous attention to technical excellence and good design.

20. What is the "programmers gone wild" scenario? Why does it happen? How can it be avoided?

21. Explain the components of the user story, acceptance criteria and any additional considerations.

22. Describe best practices in pair programming and explain how they can foster good quality and productivity.

23. Explain the steps of continuous integration and suggest how software systems can support these steps.

24. Explain how the principle of "Travel Light" in Agile Modeling helps maintain agility.

25. Provide examples of how excessive modeling might hinder agility in a software project.

26. Discuss the significance of the Agile Modeling principle "Model with a Purpose."

27. Identify and describe three ways in which modeling can enhance communication and mutual understanding among stakeholders in an Agile project.
28. How does Agile Modeling address the challenge of change in software development?
29. Discuss the principles that support adaptability and responsiveness in Agile Modeling.
30. Why is obtaining "Rapid Feedback" in Agile Modeling essential, and how does it impact the development process?
31. Describe the benefits of using multiple types of models in Agile development.
32. Explain how artificial intelligence could potentially change the future of agile modeling.
33. Describe model driven development and explain how it may change the traditional view of agile community toward modeling?
34. If an agile developer comes to you and says that their team uses absolutely no modeling, would you agree that this is indeed the case? Why or why not.

EXERCISES

A. Imagine you are part of a Scrum development team working on a mobile app that tracks personal fitness. Your team needs to understand how a married couple will use the app during their backpacking vacation in the Andes Mountains (Argentina, Bolivia, Chile, Colombia, Ecuador, Peru, and Venezuela). Practice creating models that serve a clear purpose and align with the Agile principle of "Model with a Purpose." After creating the diagram, explain how this model will help the team and what decisions it will inform.

B. There is a fine line between doing something flexibly, and efficiently, and descending into anarchy. In the context of software development, suggest what you might do in order to ensure agile software development does not descend into anarchy.

C. Explain how the Scrum framework adheres to the values and principles in Agile manifesto.

D. Explain how the SAFe framework adheres to the values and principles in the Agile manifesto.

E. Write a realistic user story for a facial recognition feature that lets passengers pass airport security in Dubai, UAE. Identify the components of the user story, acceptance criteria and any additional considerations.

F. Write a realistic user story for a website that sells electronic passes to the attractions in Istanbul, Turkey. Identify the components of the user story, acceptance criteria and any additional considerations.

G. Imagine you just finished a project where you were a member of several pair programming teams. Identify the biggest challenge you faced when you practiced pair programming.

H. Describe how you might train an organization that is moving from the team version of scrum to the scaled version of scrum (Scrum@Scale)?

I. In addition to the content in this chapter, take some time to visit and review the Scrum@Scale (www.scrumatscale.com) and SAFe (scaledagileframework.com) websites to learn more. In which circumstances does it make sense to use SAFe or Scrum@Scale? How would you choose between those two scaled agile frameworks?

J. Find another popular *team* level agile framework not described in this chapter. Describe which (and how) Agile Manifesto values and principles are implemented in the framework you identified.

K. Find another popular *scaled* agile framework not described in this chapter. Describe how the scaled agile framework you identified differs from the scaled frameworks discussed in this chapter. Why (which contexts) do you think that an organization might choose to use your identified framework as opposed to the scaled one described in this chapter?

MINICASES

1. You are part of a development team at **Ed System Learning Solutions (EDLS)**, a company specializing in software for educational institutions. Your current project involves developing a new Online **Learning System** called **CourseConnect**. It is a platform for delivering online courses taught by **Advanced Tech University (ATU)**, EDLS' highly valued client. ATU has a long-term arrangement with EDLS geared toward agile development, as ATU greatly values agility and speed-to-market. It bases compensation on pay per hour per developer and a bonus for successful completion of projects. The contract also has a clause

that ATU may terminate the contract at any time, at its discretion. While these terms are stringent, the pay is very generous, and EDLS greatly values its prized customer.

The project is divided into multiple sprints, and the team is following Scrum to ensure quick delivery and flexibility in response to stakeholder feedback. **Sprint 1** focused on setting up the basic infrastructure, including user authentication and a simple course selection dashboard. **Sprint 2** is about to begin, with the primary goal of implementing a feature-rich **Course Management Module** that allows the students to enroll and take courses. The team anticipates two additional sprints, one focusing on the course management by the instructors, and the other, on the handling of final grades. Each Sprint lasts approximately two months.

As you assemble to start your daily standup, a very stressed-looking Dr. Aniket Kasliwal, the principal of ATU, charges into the room and interrupts the meeting. He informs everyone that the competitor, Big Tech Academy, just launched several courses on Generative AI and if ATU doesn't do the same within the next two months, they will lose a lot of potential customers. The good news is, all the ATU professors are ready, and the course materials are prepared. The only missing component is the CourseConnect system. To help with the task, Dr. Kasliwal announced that he was doubling the hourly pay rate for all the developers, allowed EDLS to bring in 10 additional team members and promised an extra bonus for the completed system.

As he walks out of the room, the team begins to digest what had just happened. Suddenly, the discussion zeroes-in on the question of modeling. Everyone looks at you. You just completed training on Agile Modeling and are considered an expert in modeling during agile development.

Questions for discussion:

1. How would you approach modeling for the remaining modules given the extreme urgency of the task? Would you do any modeling at all?

2. If yes, describe the specific models you would create. Who would you consult in developing these models? What would be the purpose of these models and how will they assist in the challenge of delivering the CourseConnect within such a tight deadline? If you miss the deadline of Dr. Kasliwal, would you think that the team would see you as the person responsible for that critical delay?

3. If choose not to model, why? How would you justify decision this to the team? Do you believe the team may later hold you responsible should something go wrong with the project?

2. **Impa Soft**, a systems development company, has recently completed a project for **Teba**, a major car manufacturer in Japan. The project was to develop an app to track car locations in case of theft. The project followed the Scrum framework, which involved conducting regular retrospectives after each sprint. These meetings have been instrumental in identifying areas for improvement, fostering open communication, and celebrating team successes.

As the final wrap-up retrospective for the project approaches, Tsumugi, the project manager, had a meeting with several members of the team who privately expressed discomfort with how Akira, a senior developer, has been managing his part of the project: the user interface of the app. The project sponsor loved the sleek and easy to use interface Akira's team designed. There is no doubt: Akira is highly skilled and has contributed significantly to the project's success. At the same time some team members feel that he often dismisses their ideas and dominates discussions, leading to a stifling of creative solutions and a decrease in morale.

Tsumugi is deliberating what to do. Should she address this issue openly in the upcoming retrospective, knowing that it could lead to a tense confrontation and potentially hurt Akira's feelings or reputation? Or should she handle the issue privately with Akira to avoid possible conflict during the retrospective, despite the Agile principle of fostering open and honest communication?

Questions for discussion:

1. What are the ethical considerations Tsumugi should weigh in deciding whether to address the issue privately or publicly?

2. How can Tsumugi balance the need for open communication with the need to respect individual team members' feelings and contributions?

3. What steps can Tsumugi take to foster a constructive discussion in the retrospective if she decides to bring up the issue with the whole team?

4. If Tsumugi addresses the issue privately and it doesn't resolve the underlying problems, what would be her next steps?

5. How might the decision impact the team's trust in the retrospective process and their willingness to share openly in the future?

It is clear: whatever Tsumugi does, her decision will significantly shape Impa's approach to handling feedback and conflict, setting a precedent for future retrospectives and team interactions.

3. **Kookaburra Tech (KT)** has been approached by the local government in Brisbane, Queensland, Australia to help it implement a smart city solution. A smart city uses information systems and other technologies to enhance the quality of life of its citizens by providing them with improved services while ensuring responsible use of the available resources. A smart city aims to make cities safe, sustainable, inclusive, and citizen-friendly through successfully coordinating technology, people, and the environment.

   A smart city hopes to solve many specific challenges including traffic flow of vehicles, waste management, energy consumption, privacy, safety, and security. It does this by making effective use of its resources and ideally *improving* the quality of life of its citizens. There are several groups that should participate in smart cities: governments, multinational companies, small- and medium-sized enterprises, universities, and research centers.

   You have been assigned as a consultant on this project. This is a new line of work for KT as they have mostly focused on software development in the past. Given the potential scope of impact, you realize that this is going to be a challenging but rewarding project. You have always wanted to do meaningful work that makes a positive impact in the lives of many. Fortunately, you have just completed a course on systems analysis and design. Your supervisor turns to you and asks you to take the lead on choosing the appropriate software development methodology or framework.

Questions for discussion:

1. What software development methodology might be appropriate for this project? If you decide to go with an agile framework—which one makes the most sense?

   a. Why do you think that?

   b. What are the tradeoffs of your methodology choice vs. another one?

2. What considerations do you need to keep in mind given the scale of this project? How might you handle some of those challenges? [Hint: Think about the prior chapters of this textbook too.]

3. What considerations do you need to keep in mind since this is a new line of work for **Kookaburra Tech**? What are some ideas that you have in order to support the considerations? [Hint: Again, think about the prior chapters of this textbook too.]

NOTE: *Italic* page numbers indicates figures.

B